DATE DUE

			PRINTED IN U.S.A.

Romanticism

GREAT ARTISTS OF THE WESTERN WORLD

Romanticism

Francisco de Goya

William Blake

Caspar David Friedrich

Eugène Delacroix

MARSHALL CAVENDISH · LONDON · NEW YORK · SYDNEY

Staff Credits

Editors	Clive Gregory LLB Sue Lyon BA (Honours)	**Picture Researchers**	Vanessa Fletcher BA (Honours) Flavia Howard BA (Honours) Jessica Johnson BA
Art Editors	Chris Legee BFA Kate Sprawson BA (Honours) Keith Vollans LSIAD	**Production Controllers**	Tom Helsby Alan Stewart BSc
Deputy Editor	John Kirkwood BSc (Honours)	**Secretary**	Lynn Smail
Sub-editors	Caroline Bugler BA (Honours), MA Sue Churchill BA (Honours) Alison Cole BA, MPhil Jenny Mohammadi Nigel Rodgers BA (Honours), MA Penny Smith Will Steeds BA (Honours), MA	**Editorial Director** **Publishing Manager** **Managing Editor** **Consultant and Authenticator**	Maggi McCormick Robert Paulley BSc Alan Ross BA (Honours) Sharon Fermor BA (Honours) Lecturer in the Extra-Mural Department of London University and Lecturer in Art History at Sussex University
Designers	Stuart John Julie Stanniland		

Reference Edition Published 1988

Published by Marshall Cavendish Corporation
147 West Merrick Road
Freeport, Long Island
N.Y. 11520

Typeset by Litho Link Ltd., Welshpool
Printed and Bound by Dai Nippon
Printing Co., Hong Kong Ltd.

Library of Congress Cataloging-in-Publication Data

Main entry under title:

Great Artists of the Western World II.

    Includes index.
    1. Artists – Biography. I. Marshall Cavendish
Corporation.
N40.G774 1988   709'.2'2 [B]   88–4317
ISBN 0–86307–900–8 (set)

ISBN 0–86307–900–8 (set)
    0–86307–757–9 (vol)

Preface

Looking at pictures can be one of the greatest pleasures that life has to offer. Note, however, those two words 'can be'; all too many of us remember all too clearly those grim afternoons of childhood when we were dragged, bored to tears and complaining bitterly, through room after room of Italian primitives by well-meaning relations or tight-lipped teachers. It was enough to put one off pictures for life – which, for some of us, was exactly what it did.

For if gallery-going is to be the fun it should be, certain conditions must be fulfilled. First, the pictures we are to see must be good pictures. Not necessarily great pictures – even a few of these can be daunting, while too many at a time may prove dangerously indigestible. But they must be well-painted, by good artists who know precisely both the effect they want to achieve and how best to achieve it. Second, we must limit ourselves as to quantity. Three rooms – four at the most – of the average gallery are more than enough for one day, and for best results we should always leave while we are still fresh, well before satiety sets in. Now I am well aware that this is a counsel of perfection: sometimes, in the case of a visiting exhibition or, perhaps, when we are in a foreign city with only a day to spare, we shall have no choice but to grit our teeth and stagger on to the end. But we shall not enjoy ourselves quite so much, nor will the pictures remain so long or so clearly in our memory.

The third condition is all-important: we must know something about the painters whose work we are looking at. And this is where this magnificent series of volumes – one of which you now hold in your hands – can make all the difference. No painting is an island: it must, if it is to be worth a moment's attention, express something of the personality of its painter. And that painter, however individual a genius, cannot but reflect the country, style and period, together with the views and attitudes of the people among whom he or she was born and bred. Even a superficial understanding of these things will illuminate a painting for us far better than any number of spotlights, and if in addition we have learnt something about the artist as a person – life and loves, character and beliefs, friends and patrons, and the places to which he or she travelled – the interest and pleasure that the work will give us will be multiplied a hundredfold.

Great Artists of the Western World will provide you with just such an insight into the life and work of some of the outstanding painters of Europe and America. The text is informative without ever becoming dry or academic, not limiting itself to the usual potted biographies but forever branching out into the contemporary world outside and beyond workshop or studio. The illustrations, in colour throughout, have been dispensed in almost reckless profusion. For those who, like me, revel in playing the Attribution Game – the object of which is to guess the painter of each picture before allowing one's eye to drop to the label – the little sections on 'Trademarks' are a particularly happy feature; but every aficionado will have particular preferences, and I doubt whether there is an art historian alive, however distinguished, who would not find some fascinating nugget of previously unknown information among the pages that follow.

This series, however, is not intended for art historians. It is designed for ordinary people like you and me – and for our older children – who are fully aware that the art galleries of the world constitute a virtually bottomless mine of potential enjoyment, and who are determined to extract as much benefit and advantage from it as they possibly can. All the volumes in this collection will enable us to do just that, expanding our knowledge not only of art itself but also of history, religion, mythology, philosophy, fashion, interior decoration, social customs and a thousand other subjects as well. So let us not simply leave them around, flipping idly through a few of their pages once in a while. Let us read them as they deserve to be read – and welcome a new dimension in our lives.

John Julius Norwich is a writer and broadcaster who has written histories of Venice and of Norman Sicily as well as several works on history, art and architecture. He has also made over twenty documentary films for television, including the recent Treasure Houses of Britain series which was widely acclaimed after repeated showings in the United States.

Lord Norwich is Chairman of the Venice in Peril Fund, and member of the Executive Committee of the British National Trust, an independently funded body established for the protection of places of historic interest and natural beauty.

John Julius Norwich

Contents

Introduction

The eternal struggle *(above) In* The Good and Evil Angels *(c.1795), William Blake symbolically depicts the battle of opposing moral forces for the innocent soul of the child.*

The Romantic movement developed during the dying years of the 18th century and blossomed in the first few decades of the 19th century. Beyond this bald, chronological fact, it remains an artistic phenomenon that defies close analysis. In part, this is due to other, misleading connotations that the word 'romantic' has acquired in our own time and, in part, it is because the movement itself was so bewilderingly disparate.

Romanticism had no manifesto or creed. It varied radically in the different countries where it took root. There were no presiding Schools, no common set of ideals, no stylistic conformity. One only has to compare a Friedrich landscape with one by Turner, or a history painting by Fuseli with

an example by Delacroix, to appreciate the enormous scope and variety of the movement.

The Dark Side of Humanity
In addition, many artists had Romantic tendencies rather than a full-blooded commitment to the style. Certainly, this was true in the case of Goya. The first part of his career was taken up with decorative painting in the late Rococo manner such as in The Straw Manikin (p.19), where he followed in the wake of Tiepolo, and, in his uncompromising portraits, he maintained a tradition that stemmed from Velázquez and Rembrandt. Goya's reputation as a Romantic derives mainly from his prints and from the so-called black paintings of his old age.

The linking factor between these works was the artist's willingness to explore the darker side of human nature. In the Caprichos (1799) and the Proverbios (c.1820), Goya portrayed the vein of superstition, greed and cruelty that lurked beneath the veneer of civilization. There were precedents for such themes: Hogarth's engravings had recently satirized contemporary society, and Goya would certainly have been familiar with the horrifying fantasies of Bosch and Bruegel. However, in Goya's case, there was no comforting suggestion that these ills could be redressed by means of a stricter religious faith or by social reform.

This pessimism was underlined in the fourteen black paintings which Goya executed on the walls of his own house. The mood here was dominated by an air of inescapable brutality and self-destruction. Saturn's distorted features appeared to reflect his own revulsion at his terrible act of cannibalism (p.33) and, in one of the most haunting scenes, Goya depicted two men, already sinking in a mire, beating each other senselessly with clubs.

Many of the Spaniard's pictures cannot be precisely explained. Often the source was literary but, in the case of his graphic work where the captions were usually added as an afterthought, it seems probable that Goya's images preceded his ideas and, accordingly, the Surrealists were later to hail him as a pioneer in the study of the mysteries of the subconscious mind.

Significantly, these works were not geared towards any commercial market. The black paintings remained in Goya's family for years and were not exhibited until 1878. Similarly, neither the Disasters of War nor the Proverbios were published during his lifetime, the latter only appearing in its complete form in 1877.

The Romantic Visionary

This dichotomy of the public and private artist did not apply to William Blake. His attempts to make money were invariably disastrous – his independent exhibition of 1809-10 met only with apathy and his relations with publishers were frequently troubled. However, the indulgent support of his two principal patrons, Thomas Butts and the young artist John Linnell, did enable him to work as he wished.

Blake, like Goya, was a visionary who probed beneath the surface to depict men's souls. Unlike his Spanish counterpart, however, he believed in the essential sanctity of humanity. For Blake, a child

arrived in the world spiritually intact and it was only the corrupting influences of civilization that degraded him. It was the artist's function to recapture this childlike vision and demonstrate to the spectator the means of restoring an innocent 'state of nature'.

In Blake's eyes, the barriers to personal liberation were both external and internal. From outside came the political oppression of governments and the social oppression of the owners of the 'dark satanic mills'. From inside came the philosophical oppression that was fuelled by Christian morality and by Reason.

The latter, in particular, was a target for criticism in Blake's paintings. Where Goya had called for a blend of reason and imagination – the subtitle of the Sleep of Reason Produces Monsters (p.17) reads 'Imagination abandoned by reason produces impossible monsters; united with her, she is the mother of the arts' – Blake declared the supremacy of the imagination. His depictions of both God the Creator (p.56) and Newton (p.58) were negative images, the inclusion of the dividers showing that both were guilty of seeking to impose limits and rules upon the infinity of the universe. These restraints were anathema to Blake, who commented succinctly that 'the road of excess leads to the palace of wisdom'.

Blake channelled his exuberance into the revival

The artists
(top to bottom) A self-portrait of Delacroix in his mid-thirties; Friedrich in a portrait by Caroline Bardua; Goya in a self-portrait of c.1815; Blake at the age of 50 by Thomas Phillips.

of past art forms. His own style was based firmly on that of Michelangelo, but his greatest love was for the art of the Middle Ages. With his illustrated books, he sought to emulate the illuminated manuscripts of the days before printing, and Blake also experimented with tempera painting, the medium which preceded oils, as in The Canterbury Pilgrims (pp.48-9).

Landscapes of the Mind

The taste for medieval art was a common feature of Romanticism – and, indeed, the movement took its name from the romances of the early troubadors. Unlike Classical artists, who sought to recapture the harmonious spirit of antiquity, the Romantics preferred the naive charm and primitive feel of paintings and literature that had fallen from favour during the Renaissance.

In Germany this nostalgia for a lost age took on a special significance, as the Romantics used it to try to identify a spirit of German nationalism with which to counter the French invaders (see p.80). Caspar David Friedrich allied himself to this movement during the French occupation although his main concern was with landscape.

It is in landscape painting, perhaps, that the true diversity of Romanticism is most apparent. In all its exponents, there was a reaction against the 18th-century taste for ordered and descriptive views and, in most, there was a tendency to invest nature with emotional or divine qualities. Blake's claim 'To see a World in a Grain of Sand and a Heaven in a Wild Flower . . .' was echoed by Friedrich's comment that 'the Divine is everywhere, even in a grain of sand' (p.82). In practice, however, these beliefs inspired a dazzling variety of responses, from the apocalyptic visions of John Martin to the rhapsodic sweep of Turner and the gilded lyricism of Corot.

In Friedrich's case the emphasis was on piety. His landscapes have been described as 'visual prayers' in which the Christian message was sometimes obvious (p.78), but was more frequently put across through the use of a low-key symbolism. Thus, in Moonrise over the Sea (p.93), for example, the rocks denote faith and the ships coming into harbour represent Christian solace.

However, Friedrich's religious intentions were largely undercut by the melancholy atmosphere that pervaded his work. He invariably chose to depict the most changeable aspects of nature –

mists, storms, twilights – as a parallel to Man's own transient state. Alongside this air of mortality which he infused into his paintings, Friedrich also stressed the insignificance of human fate. In his Arctic Shipwreck (p.94), the foundering of the vessel called Hope seems almost trivial beside the massive upheavals in the icy landscape.

The Power of Colour

If Friedrich's art portrays one aspect of the Romantic hero – bewilderment when confronted with the scale of the universe – then Delacroix's art illustrates a very different side to his nature: one of confidence, passion and a revelling in the senses. Delacroix was thrown into the forefront of French art at a young age, following the premature death of Géricault, and the stir created by his large canvases of the 1820s (pp.120-25) epitomized the Romantic struggle in France.

There, the confrontation in the Salons between Ingres and Delacroix was hailed as the battle between Classicism and Romanticism. In fact, however, it only marked a re-opening of the old Poussin/Rubens dispute that had raged more than a century before. In this, the advocates of the supremacy of draughtsmanship in art (championed by the linear style of Poussin and Ingres) were challenged by the colourists (Rubens and Delacroix), who emphasized the importance of painterly qualities. There was added venom in this dispute because, owing to the dominance in recent French art of the linear, Neo-Classical style, Ingres was seen as the defender of authority, while Delacroix was viewed as a renegade and a usurper.

In reality, however, the dividing line between the two styles was very thin. The exoticism of Ingres' Turkish bath scenes was far more Romantic than the sober beauty of Delacroix's Arab pictures while, even in his earliest years, the latter nurtured ambitions of becoming a traditional mural painter. This Delacroix eventually achieved in the 1830s, producing a series of semi-classical decorative schemes for the French government.

The ramifications of the Romantic movement were enormous. In England, the revivalist trend was continued by the Pre-Raphaelites, who are sometimes described as late Romantics. Elsewhere, the Romantic concern with depicting the spiritual and emotional aspects of human nature played an important role in the development of the Surrealist and Symbolist movements.

Goya: Self-portrait c. 1815/Prado, Madrid

1746-1828

Francisco de Goya was the greatest painter of 18th century Spain. Born in an isolated village, he went to Madrid at 18 to work in the studio of Francisco Bayeu, whose sister he later married. Madrid was the centre of Spanish culture and society, but Goya was slow to make his name, becoming a royal painter only when he was 43. From then on his future was assured, and he quickly rose to even higher eminence.

Goya first earned his reputation painting cartoons for tapestries, and further success came from portraits. But his most remarkable works were produced after a serious illness left him permanently deaf. Paintings and etchings of his bizarre, fantastic 'imaginings' were followed by satires on high society and ghastly visions of the horrors of war. His late 'black paintings' were more dramatic still, with immense, if gloomy, impact.

11

The 'Deaf Man' of Madrid

At the age of 47 – four years after his appointment as painter to the Spanish king – Goya was struck by deafness. He watched in silence the downfall of the monarchy and the disasters of war.

Francisco de Goya y Lucientes, the son of a gilder, was born on 30 March 1746 in the desolate village of Fuendetodos in western Spain. When he was 14, the family moved to Saragossa, the capital of his native region of Aragon, and Francisco was apprenticed to the painter José Luzán – at that time the leading artist of Saragossa. (One of his specialities was adding drapery to nude figures in religious pictures, for which he was given the official title of 'Reviser of Indecent Paintings'.) In Saragossa, Goya also met the painter Francisco Bayeu, who was 12 years older than him and enjoying the rapidly growing success that in 1763 led him to the court of Madrid. Goya moved to Madrid soon after Bayeu and worked in his studio.

MADRID, CENTRE OF THE ARTS

To be established at Madrid was, at this time, virtually the only way in which a provincial Spanish artist could gain more than mere local recognition. The great wealth of the Spanish monarchy and its lavish patronage of the arts also attracted some of the major painters from elsewhere in Europe. In the 1760s and 1770s the two most important painters at the court were the Venetian Giambattista Tiepolo and the German Anton Raffael Mengs, both of whom had a major influence on Goya's evolution as an artist.

In 1763 and 1766 Goya made unsuccessful attempts to enter the recently founded Madrid Academy of Art and then, probably in 1770, he did what was customary for ambitious young artists: he went to Italy. Here he enjoyed his first minor success, getting an honourable mention in a

Key Dates

1746 born 30 March in Fuendetodos, Spain
1764 moves to Madrid
1770 visits Rome
1773 marries Josefa Bayeu in Madrid
1774 first cartoon for royal tapestries
1784 birth of Goya's only surviving heir, his son Javier
1789 appointed royal painter by Charles IV
1793 serious illness leaves him deaf
1796 stays at Duchess of Alba's estate
1808 French seize Madrid
1812 death of Josefa
1814 Spanish monarchy restored; Goya paints *The Third of May 1808*
1819 buys 'House of the Deaf Man' outside Madrid; suffers serious illness
1824 settles in Bordeaux
1828 dies in Bordeaux

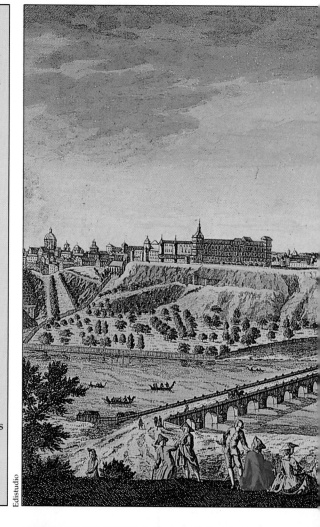

Edistudio

Arxiu Mas

Goya/Josefa Bayeu/detail/Prado, Madrid

Josefa Bayeu
In 1773, Goya married Josefa Bayeu, the sister of his teacher. She bore him several children, but only his son Javier reached maturity. Josefa, painted here by Goya, died in 1812 at Madrid.

The family home
Goya grew up in the rocky, arid region of Aragon. His birthplace, a two-storey stone house in the village of Fuendetodos, has been preserved as a memorial to him.

Arxiu Mas

The Spanish capital
When Goya moved to Madrid in 1764, to work with his future brother-in-law, Francisco Bayeu, he entered one of Europe's most modern cities. This view across the River Manzanares shows a panorama stretching from the Royal Palace on the left to the magnificent Church of S. Francisco el Grande on the right. Madrid was to be Goya's home for the next 55, very productive years.

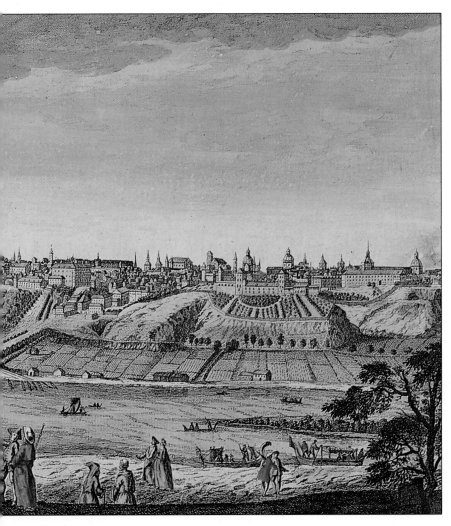

painting competition organized by the Art Academy of Parma. In 1771 he returned to Spain, and two years later married Bayeu's sister, Josefa. The following year he was summoned to work, first under Mengs and then Bayeu, on cartoons for tapestries to be woven at the Royal Factory of Santa Barbara in Madrid. This task was to occupy him sporadically until 1792.

Goya's beginnings as an artist were slow and unremarkable. It was not until the 1780s, when he was already in his mid-30s, that important official recognition came his way. In 1780 he was elected a member of the Madrid Academy and five years later he was made Deputy Director of Painting there. After Charles IV was crowned in 1789, Goya achieved his ambition of becoming one of the royal painters, a promotion which he celebrated by adding the aristocratic 'de' to his name.

In the 1790s, with the tapestry designs completed, Goya devoted himself principally to the types of work by which he is best known today – portraits and imaginative compositions. Towards the end of 1792 a traumatic change occurred in his life when he developed a mysterious illness – variously and unconvincingly interpreted as syphilis, lead poisoning from the use of white paint, and even a particularly severe nervous breakdown. At any rate, it caused him temporary paralysis and partial blindness, and left him permanently deaf. The illness had a significant effect on the development of Goya's art. While convalescing in 1793 he painted a series of small oil paintings of bizarre subjects of 'fantasy and invention', as Goya himself described them, telling the Academy later that he had produced them 'In order to occupy an imagination mortified by the contemplation of my sufferings'.

Goya's increasingly introverted and morbidly imaginative tendencies as an artist were not greatly appreciated by his contemporaries. But they did not in any way impede his rising eminence in the Madrid art world. In 1795, on the death of Bayeu, he was promoted to Director of Painting at the

A tapestry for the King
Goya's first important commission in Madrid was to design tapestries for King Charles III. The Swing was woven by the Royal Tapestry Manufactory from a painting by Goya in 1779.

AISA

AISA

The Royal Family
(left) Goya painted The Family of Charles IV *in 1800. His avoidance of flattery led one critic to comment that the King and Queen looked like 'the corner baker and his wife after they have won the lottery'. Prince Ferdinand is in blue on the left; his bride-to-be has her face averted, as their engagement had not been officially announced. Goya himself is in the background at his easel.*

The Escorial Palace
(right) As court painter, Goya often visited this royal residence in the Guadarrama mountains outside Madrid. This palace-monastery, built in 1563 as a retreat, is where the Spanish monarchs are buried.

Academy, and in 1798 received the prestigious commission to decorate the Madrid church of S. Antonio de la Florida. The following year he was appointed First Painter to the King. By now he could count among his friends and patrons many leading intellectuals and aristocrats in Madrid.

THE NAKED MAJA

Goya was on particularly close terms with the widowed Duchess of Alba – a beautiful, intelligent and powerful woman. Their relationship was the source of much gossip, especially after Goya spent the summer of 1796 on her estate in Andalusia, where the Duchess had moved after the death of her husband. One of the most popular legends in the history of art holds that she was the model for Goya's famous pair of paintings, *The Naked Maja* (opposite) and *The Clothed Maja* (pp.24-5).

Such speculation has often been used to flesh out the rather meagre information we have concerning the less public aspects of Goya's personality. He has been depicted variously as a relentless womanizer, a manic-depressive, a revolutionary, and a sort of Hamlet-like figure viewing society with growing scepticism and pessimism and ultimately achieving an almost other-worldly detachment from it. However, the evidence for all this is scanty. The known facts of Goya's life reveal little more than a great concern with his social standing, financial shrewdness, a love of pigeon-shooting, and an unwillingness to allow political or other forms of idealism get in the way of the practical considerations of living.

The first half of Goya's life was a time of political stability in Spain. But the reign of Charles IV (1789-1808) saw mounting unrest, made even worse by the international repercussions of the French Revolution. Charles was a weak and lazy ruler, greatly influenced by his strong-minded wife, Maria Luisa, who in turn was led by the upstart favourite, Manuel de Godoy. The rule of this 'trinity on earth', as the queen described it, was highly unpopular with both nobility and public alike. Eventually, in 1808, mass disturbances caused the downfall of Godoy and forced Charles IV to resign in favour of his son Ferdinand VII.

Ferdinand, in league with the French, at first welcomed Napoleon's armies into Spain. But almost immediately he was forced to hand over his throne to Napoleon's brother, Joseph. The French occupation provoked serious rioting in Madrid and led to a bloody civil war. Goya's own allegiances are not clear, but he was appalled by the brutality of the fighting, and in his horrific series of etchings, the *Disasters of War*, he portrayed atrocities committed by both sides.

HONOURED BY THE ENEMY

Whatever Goya's political views, he also had to make a living, and it was therefore prudent of him, if not especially principled, to swear allegiance to the French king and accept from him in 1811 the Royal Order of Spain. This caused him trouble later when Ferdinand VII was restored to the throne in 1814, following the intervention of British troops under the Duke of Wellington (whom Goya

The British blockade Cadiz
At the turn of the century, the Spanish monarchy was shaken by the upheavals of the Napoleonic wars, in which they were at first reluctant allies of the French. In 1796, the two countries planned a joint attack on the English coast, but their navies were foiled by Jervis at the Battle of Cape St Vincent in February 1797. Cadiz was then blockaded for a year.

The Beautiful Duchess

In 1796, Goya's relationship with the widowed Duchess of Alba caused scandal in Madrid. At 34, this high-born lady was nearly 16 years younger than Goya, and famous for her capricious nature. She and her husband had been Goya's patrons, and when the Duke died that summer, she retired with the artist to her country estate at Sanlucar. Here it has been supposed they became lovers. Certainly his notebook reveals an idyllic atmosphere, and some of his sketches depict women in erotic poses, for which the Duchess may have modelled.

The Duchess in love
Goya's portrait of the Duchess, dated 1797, suggests a close relationship between them. The names inscribed on her two rings are 'Alba' and 'Goya' and she points to the words 'Solo (only) Goya', written in the sand.

The Naked Maja (c.1800)
Legend has it that the Duchess of Alba posed for this erotic painting, which later led Goya into the hands of the Inquisition.

Prado, Madrid

Hispanic Society of America, New York

was also quite happy to portray). But Goya escaped the punishment meted out to some of his liberal friends by claiming that he had never worn the medal awarded to him by the French. In addition he offered to paint for the king his two famous scenes of the Madrid rioting that had led to the war: *The Second of May, 1808* (pp.18-19) and *The Third of May, 1808* (pp. 30-31).

The gloom of Goya's later paintings reflects the morbidly repressive atmosphere in Spain following the restoration of Ferdinand VII. Universities and theatres were closed down, press censorship was introduced, and the dreadful religious tribunal, the Inquisition, was re-established. No sooner had Goya been exonerated from the charge of having 'accepted employment from the usurper' than he found himself summoned in front of the Inquisition to explain why and for whom he had painted the allegedly obscene *Naked Maja* and its companion piece. The artist had other problems to contend with. His wife had died in 1812, and he was now embarked on an affair with a married woman, Leocadia Weiss, which put him at the centre of malicious gossip.

WITHDRAWAL FROM PUBLIC LIFE

Ferdinand VII took hardly any interest in Goya, but kept him on as his First Painter. And when Goya eventually retired from the post, Ferdinand awarded him a generous pension, which enabled him to live comfortably until his death. He virtually withdrew from public life after 1815, and worked almost exclusively for himself and for his close circle of friends.

Napoleon enters Madrid
Six months after deposing the Spanish monarchy, Napoleon himself entered Madrid on 4 December 1808. He stayed only briefly, to direct operations against the Spanish resistance and the advancing British forces.

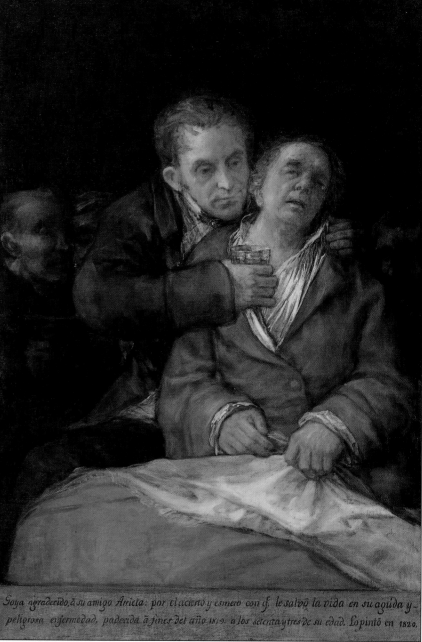

Minneapolis Institute of Arts/Ethel Morrison van Derlip Fund

Jean-Loup Charmet

In 1819, serious illness struck Goya again, and he recovered only thanks to the intervention of the fashionable Madrid doctor, Eugenio Garcia Arrieta. In gratitude, Goya painted an extraordinary double portrait, showing himself half-dying in bed being supported by Arrieta, who is offering him a draught of medicine; in the background is a group of dark and sinister figures. Similar reflections on death and old age are to be found in the 'black paintings' that he executed between 1820 and 1823 on the walls of his newly acquired house (the 'Quinta del Sordo' or 'House of the Deaf Man') in the country outside Madrid.

The three years during which the artist was engaged on these works, perhaps the most terrifying and technically astonishing in his career, saw a brief moment of liberalization in Ferdinand's regime. However, by the end of 1823, reaction had set in again, and many of Goya's liberal friends sought refuge in France. A number of them went to Bordeaux, including Leocadia Weiss, who took the two children she had supposedly had by Goya.

Arxiu Mas

Francisco de Goya

The Sleep of Reason Produces Monsters
Designed originally as the frontispiece to his Caprichos *series, this etching, dated 1797-8, sums up Goya's view of humanity. When reason is allowed to sleep, monsters of the irrational world take over.*

The Fotomas Index

Prado, Madrid

British Museum, London

Self-portrait with Dr Arrieta (1820)
(left) As the inscription beneath the picture explains, Goya painted this moving portrait of himself and his doctor after recovering from 'an acute and dangerous illness suffered at the end of 1819, at the age of 73.'

House of the Deaf Man
(below) In February 1819, Goya bought a country property of 25 acres on the right bank of the River Manzanares, with the single-storey Quinta del Sordo (House of the Deaf Man). After his illness, Goya decorated the walls with 14 'black paintings'.

La Manola (1820)
(above) This portrait is thought to be of Leocadia Weiss, who lived with Goya until his death. Although one of the 'black paintings' decorating the walls of the Quinta del Sordo, it has none of the nightmarish quality of the others.

Arxiu Mas

He joined her there soon afterwards, having been granted temporary leave of absence by the king on the pretext that he needed to take the waters at Plombières for his health.

Goya was found by his friends now to be 'deaf, old, slow and feeble'. But his enthusiasm for life was apparently as strong as ever, and his artistic powers were undimmed. He still had enough strength to make an extended sight-seeing trip to Paris, and even began experimenting with the new medium of lithography in his series the *Bulls of Bordeaux*. To the surprise of his fellow exiles, he made two brief return trips to Spain, on the first of which (in 1826) he officially handed in his resignation as court painter.

In the spring of 1828, he was visited in Bordeaux by his daughter-in-law and grandchildren. The excitement caused by their visit made him, in his own words, a 'little indisposed'. He died on 16 April following a paralytic stroke, aged 82. His mortal remains were returned to Spain in 1900 and interred in the cemetery of San Isidro in Madrid.

The Dark Side of Humanity

Goya began his career designing colourful tapestries for royal palaces. But his own traumatic illness and the dreadful events of the war against France led him to depict scenes of horrific violence.

Goya is almost universally regarded as the greatest European painter of his period. The originality, emotional range and technical freedom of his work set him apart from other artists. Indeed, among his contemporaries we have to look to Beethoven to find his equal in grandeur of imagination and power of expression.

Although Goya produced a huge amount of work as a painter and a graphic artist, he was slow to develop, and it was not until he was well over 30 that he produced work that was especially remarkable or original. His early career was taken up mainly with the repetitive task of designing tapestries to be executed at the Royal Factory of Santa Barbara in Madrid.

A TRAUMATIC ILLNESS

Goya was employed on the tapestry designs until 1792, but by that time the direction of his art had changed radically. In the 1780s he had some success as a religious painter, and in 1789 he was appointed one of the painters to the king, which meant that painting portraits would be one of his major tasks. But the most significant change in his approach to art came with the severe but mysterious illness which he suffered in 1792-3.

The traumatic effect this had on him deepened his awareness of the pain and suffering in human life, and he turned increasingly to sombre or sinister subjects.

In the two fields for which he is best known – portraiture and imaginative subjects – Goya showed both his links with the great masters of the past and his startling originality. He is reputed to have said that his only masters were 'Velázquez, Rembrandt and Nature'. These two painters (the leading artists of Spain and Holland in the 17th century) were among the greatest portraitists who ever lived, and Goya followed them in their penetrating depiction of character. Goya also shared with them a virtuosity in the handling of paint that distinguishes him from most contemporary artists, who favoured a smooth,

The Second of May, 1808 (1814)
(right) Goya commemorated the uprising of the people of Madrid against Napoleon's cavalry in one of the most terrifying and convincing battle scenes in the history of art. There is no sense of good triumphing over evil; instead Goya shows ghastly and bloody confusion. His theme is not patriotism, but horror at man's inhumanity.

An unorthodox painter
(left) This is a detail from a self-portrait Goya painted in about 1790. His lack of orthodoxy is seen not only in his odd appearance, but also in the vigorous sketching technique and the way in which Goya has boldly silhouetted himself against the golden light.

Arxiu Mas

Collection Villagonzalo, Madrid

Edistudio

The Straw Manikin (1792)
(*left*) *Between 1775 and 1792 Goya made 63 full-size cartoons for the royal tapestry works. The designs had to be bold and colourful to make suitable wall-hangings. Some of them are huge, the largest being more than 20 feet wide; this one is 8'9" by 5'3".*

The master engraver
(*below*) *Goya made almost 300 engravings in his career, but was over 50 when he published the first of his great series, the* Caprichos, *in 1799. Three other major series followed: the* Disasters of War (*begun 1810*), Tauromaquia (*begun 1815*) *and the* Proverbios (*begun 1816*).

Etching from the Proverbios/British Museum, London

Etching from the Tauromaquia/Biblioteca Nacional, Madrid

Etching from the Disasters of War/British Museum, London

19

COMPARISONS

Bizarre Fantasies

Goya's imaginative scenes are deeply personal works, but they also form part of a long tradition of elaborate and bizarre fantasy. Hieronymus Bosch was a Flemish artist, whose paintings were particularly popular in Spain – the royal family owned the finest collection in the world. In the 20th century the Spanish painter Salvador Dali is the most famous representative of Surrealism – a movement that explored the subconscious in disturbing, irrational scenes.

Salvador Dali
(b.1904)
Premonition of Civil War
(below) Dali depicts a world of neurotic fantasies rendered horribly believable by his smooth technique.

Hieronymus Bosch
(c.1450-1516)
The Temptation of St Anthony (detail)
(below) Bosch's wierd and colourful paintings draw on folk legends as well as religious symbolism. Although he has become immensely popular in the 20th century and has been intensively studied, much about his work is still baffling to scholars.

detailed finish. 'Where does one see lines in nature?' he asked. 'I see no lines or details, I don't count each hair on the head of a passer-by, or the buttons on his coat. There is no reason why my brush should see more than I do.'

In his imaginative scenes Goya also drew on a rich tradition, for Spain was a country of religious fervour and the agonies and ecstasies of the saints had been celebrated in art for centuries, often with a grisly concentration on the suffering of martyrs. Two centuries before Goya, the Spanish king Philip II had avidly collected the bizarre works of the Flemish painter Hieronymus Bosch, and Goya would have seen the work of his great spiritual predecessor in the royal collection.

THE BLACK PAINTINGS

Goya's probing of the darker side of human nature began to emerge in his series of etchings the *Caprichos*, in which he combined caricatures of contemporary life with gruesome fantasy. The ultimate development of this kind of theme came in his so-called 'black paintings', which he painted on the walls of his own house soon after recovering from his near fatal illness of 1819. In these virtually colourless works depicting morbid and terrifying scenes, Goya handled paint with a freedom that

could almost be called ferocious. Here Goya was painting purely for himself – a startling notion at this time, when the concept of artistic self-expression was in its infancy.

Goya's technical virtuosity and resourcefulness are as apparent in his graphic work as in his painting. He drew in pencil, in ink and in brush wash, among other media, and as a printmaker he excelled in aquatint, etching and lithography. Aquatint and etching both use acid to 'bite' into a metal printing plate a design that the artist has brushed or drawn on it; lithography involves drawing on stone with a wax crayon and then printing from it using an oil-based ink that adheres only to the parts that have been touched by the wax. Lithography was invented in 1798 and Goya was the first great master of the technique.

SERIES OF ENGRAVINGS

As well as the *Caprichos*, Goya produced three other great series of engravings: the *Disasters of War*, which records the appalling events following the French invasion of 1808; the *Tauromaquia*, a series on bullfighting; and the *Proverbios*, an enigmatic series showing various aspects of human folly. Of these, the *Disasters of War* are perhaps the most devastating. There are no heroes in Goya's war, and no glory – only death and mutilation, pain and degradation. His prints still have a shocking impact today, even though we have become accustomed to seeing such brutalities recorded in photographs and films. They stand as timeless portrayals of the conflicting forces of good and evil, life and death, light and darkness.

Academia de San Fernando, Madrid

TRADEMARKS

Anguished Faces

Goya often exaggerates facial contortions, but they always look appropriate in the context of his paintings. He endured a great deal of suffering during his own illnesses and painted both physical and mental agony with a conviction few artists have matched.

The Madhouse (c.1800) *(above and right) Goya was not the first artist to depict madhouse scenes but no-one before him had evoked such pain and pity. There was a tradition of including lunatics who crown themselves as monarchs or popes, as shown in the detail. Goya's madmen, however, are not stock characters but disquieting portrayals of individuals in genuine mental torment.*

The Third of May, 1808

In 1814 Goya painted two large and powerful canvases to commemorate the uprising in 1808 of the citizens of Madrid against the French army of occupation. The first (pp. 18-19) shows street fighting on 2 May, and the second shows the reprisals taken by the French the next day. Dozens of rioters were executed alongside numerous other captives, who had been arrested without any proof of their involvement in the revolt. Goya offered to paint the pictures when Ferdinand VII was restored to the Spanish throne 'to perpetuate by means of the brush the most notable and heroic actions and scenes of our glorious insurrection against the tyrant.'

The execution site
The shootings took place at the Montaña del Principe Pío on the outskirts of Madrid, near the Royal Palace. The executions lasted all day long.

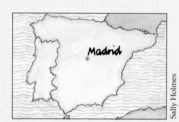

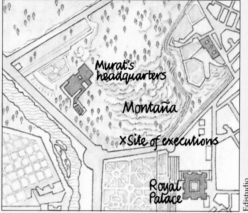

Murat's headquarters

Montaña

✗ Site of executions

Royal Palace

Sally Holmes

Edistudio

AISA

Buildings in the background
Although Goya made no attempt at topographical accuracy, the buildings in The Third of May *may have been suggested by the nearby Royal Palace.*

The Second of May

The riot on 2 May, shown below in a contemporary engraving, was put down by Joachim Murat (right), Napoleon's brother-in-law and a dashing cavalry commander. He had hundreds of Spaniards executed.

Edistudio

The firing squad
*(below) In grim contrast
to the terrified victims,
the French executioners
are shown as ruthless –
and faceless – automatons.
Their uniforms are
sombre, their gestures
mechanical.*

'Light and shade play upon atrocious horrors'

Charles Baudelaire

Prado, Madrid

Salmer

Biblioteca Nacional, Madrid

The victims
*Goya shows a whole
gallery of expressions of
terror and despair. The
unforgettable central
figure, arms outstretched,
stares with impotent
defiance.*

A common sight
*Goya did not himself
witness the executions,
but he had seen similar
events in the war. This
etching is from his*
Disasters of War,
begun in 1810.

Gallery

By 1800, despite the crippling illness that left him deaf, Goya was one of Spain's most successful painters. He moved freely among royalty and the aristocracy, and painted numerous portraits of the court.

The Clothed Maja, which may be a portrait of the Duchess of Alba, was owned by the royal favourite, Manuel de Godoy.

The Clothed Maja *c.1800-05* 37¼" × 74½" Prado Museum, Madrid

The Clothed Maja *was painted as a companion to* The Naked Maja *(p.15) and is, perhaps surprisingly, the more seductive of the two images. The model is shown in the same provocative pose, propped up on plump silk cushions. But here she is dressed in a flimsy pyjama costume which clings to the generous contours of her form. The brushstrokes are bolder and the colours more brazen, stressing the redness of the lips and pink glow on the cheeks. Goya's striking model has often been thought to be the Duchess of Alba, one of the greatest beauties of her day.*

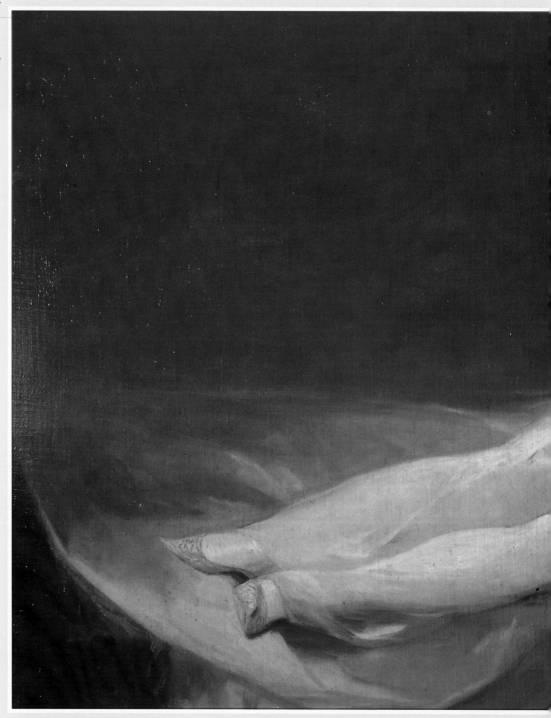

Like the portraits of Doña Isabel de Porcel and the Two Majas on a Balcony, it reveals Goya's interest in costume as well as the subtleties of character.

During the Napoleonic Wars, Goya painted a formal portrait of Wellington, whose army was advancing across Spain. He soon became obsessed with the cruelty and utter futility of the fighting. The Colossus and the famous Third of May, 1808, are both powerful evocations of the catastrophes of warfare.

Towards the end of his life, Goya's works acquired a nightmarish intensity: the gory Saturn Devouring One of His Sons is his most savage and disturbing vision.

Doña Isabel de Porcel *c.1804-5*
32¼″ × 21¼″ National Gallery, London

*Goya painted this splendid portrait of Isabel de Porcel in return for
the hospitality he had received when he stayed with her and her
husband in Granada. She is dressed in the coquettish costume of the
'majas' – then all the rage among the aristocracy – resplendent in a
pink satin gown and black lace mantilla.*

Two Majas on a Balcony *c.1811*
76½″ × 49½″ Metropolitan Museum of Art, New York

The 'majas' were girls from the lower social classes who were renowned for their beauty, their alluring costumes and their flighty lifestyles. Goya shows these two seated on a balcony with their protectors, the 'majos', lurking in the shadows behind. Majas and majos were notorious for their stormy and often violent love affairs.

AISA

The Duke of Wellington *1812*
23″ × 20″ National Gallery, London

Goya painted Arthur Wellesley, then Earl of Wellington, when he was general of the British forces in Spain. It was one of the artist's most frustrating commissions. In the two years after the portrait was finished, Wellington was showered with military honours and insisted that his new decorations should be painted on to the uniform.

Scala

The Colossus *c.1808-12*
45½″ × 41¼″ Prado Museum, Madrid

*In the midst of war, a grim giant looms over fleeing crowds. Goya's
terrifying vision was probably inspired by some lines written by a
Spanish poet about the Napoleonic wars: 'On a height above yonder
cavernous amphitheatre, a pale Colossus rises, caught by the fiery
light of the setting sun.'*

The Third of May, 1808 *1814*
104¾″ × 135¾″ Prado Museum, Madrid

By the eerie light of a large, square lantern, a group of Spanish insurgents are executed by the French forces occupying Madrid. A row of faceless soldiers, all in the same brutal attitude, take aim beneath the night sky. In the face of death, the condemned men react with a mixture of terror, defiance and despair. One covers his face, another clenches his fist, while a priest clasps his hands in prayer.
Goya focuses our attention on the man in their midst, who throws out his arms in a Christ-like gesture of martyrdom. The brilliant white of his shirt, caught by the rays of the lantern, is as arresting as a flash of lightning. To heighten the emotional impact, Goya has painted him much larger than the figures around him: he is kneeling, but if he stood up he would dwarf the firing squad.

The Burial of the Sardine *c.1815-20*
32¾″ × 24½″ Academia de San Fernando, Madrid

Throughout his career, Goya was fascinated by Spain's religious festivals. This strange carnival, which marked the beginning of Lent, climaxed in the ritual burial of a sardine. The revellers donned grotesque masks and carried crudely painted banners, introducing a sinister element to the light-hearted festivities.

AISA

Saturn Devouring One of His Sons *1820-23*
57½″ × 32¾″ Prado Museum, Madrid

*This gruesome image is one of the famous 'black paintings' that
decorated Goya's house, the Quinta del Sordo – it hung in his dining
room. The god Saturn ate his sons because he was afraid that they
might grow up to usurp him. The cruelty of the myth appealed to
Goya, who loathed the irrationality of old age.*

The Spanish Inquisition

For 350 years Spain lay in the grip of a murderous orthodoxy. By Goya's time, thousands had suffered torture and slow death in the cause of Catholic purity, as the Inquisitors rooted out heresy.

From its foundation in the 15th century, the dark shadow of the Inquisition – righteous, militant and implacable – hung over Spain for more than 350 years. Goya himself was summoned before it in 1815, when his painting *The Naked Maja* was judged both 'obscene' and 'immoral'. And, even today, the name generates shudders, carrying with it the whiff of burning flesh and the creaking of the rack.

The Holy Office of the Inquisition – technically an arm of the Church under royal supervision, charged with the rooting out of heresy – was formally established in 1478 and hard at work by 1480. Since it accompanied the unification of the country under Ferdinand and Isabella in the late 15th century, it could rightly claim to be Spain's first truly national institution. It was set up to deal with a special problem: Jews, or more precisely, converted Jews, whose new Catholic faith was suspected of being less than sincere.

These *conversos*, as they were officially known (*marranos*, meaning swine, was the contemptuous nickname given them by Spanish Catholics) dated back to the previous century and the reign of Henry II, who had brought great pressure on his numerous Jewish subjects, enforcing Christianity at sword-

AISA

Hispano-Flemish School/The Virgin of Catholic Monarchs/Prado, Madrid

The King's Inquisitor
(left) An instrument of both Church and state, the Inquisition was established in 1478, during the reign of Ferdinand and Isabella. In this painting Ferdinand kneels at the left in front of his Grand Inquisitor, the Dominican friar Tomás de Torquemada, whose name became a byword for cruelty and persecution.

The Court of the Inquisition
Goya's sombre painting depicts a judiciary session of the Inquisition. The defendants wear tall conical hats and robes painted with flames. Goya himself had to answer to the Inquisition in 1815 over his painting The Naked Maja.

Robert Harding Picture Library

point. Freed as a result from the crippling restrictions under which practising Jews had to live, the *conversos* used their race's traditional energy and resilience to catapult themselves to positions of wealth and power in Spanish society. But many of them clung in secret to the rites of Judaism, which the new persecutors were pledged to stamp out.

PAGEANT OF DEATH

Rapidly, the Inquisition took on the murderous ceremonial that it retained almost to the end of its existence. Tribunals were set up in all the important towns of the Iberian Peninsula. First, an Edict of Faith was proclaimed: heretics were invited to present themselves to the Inquisitors in repentance, and were asked to denounce their unrepentant fellows in exchange for lenient treatment. Next, armed with these denunciations and the reports of their own agents, the Inquisitors made their arrests, and the accused disappeared into the secret silence of an Inquisition prison. The subsequent stage – the interrogation – could last for years, although many of its victims failed to survive the experience.

At last, judgement was given. The accused might be acquitted, although this was rare. If they were found guilty, they could still be 'reconciled' to the Church if they admitted their heresy and professed repentance. Reconciliation could bring with it heavy penalties, including life imprisonment and the complete confiscation of worldly goods to swell the Inquisition's coffers, but at least the lives of the 'reconciled' were spared.

The ultimate penalty, expressed in a chilling euphemism, was 'relaxation'. The impenitent heretic was 'relaxed' into the hands of the civil

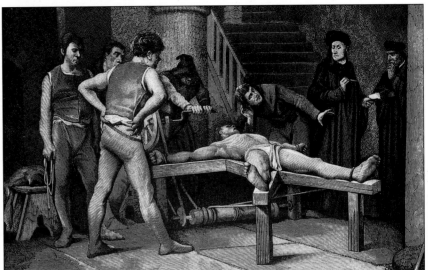

Archiv für Kunst und Geschichte

Trial by torture
(above) If interrogation failed to extract a confession of heresy, both men and women were subjected to torture, and no exceptions were made for youth or old age. Suspects could be arrested on the most trivial evidence, such as changing their linen on Saturdays, or not eating pork.

Goya/The Court of the Inquisition/c.1815/Academia de Bellas Artes San Fernando, Madrid

authorities on the understanding that, on grounds of Christian principle, his blood was not to be shed. The victim – man, woman or child – was ceremoniously burned at the stake.

RITUAL MASS EXECUTION

Executions took place at the greatest of all the Inquisition's ceremonials – the *auto da fé*, the act of faith. Some involved hundreds of penitents, and would generally last all day, or even longer: an *auto* at Seville in 1660, for example, took three days to complete and attracted 100,000 spectators. (The burning ground later became Seville's bullring.) The festivities began with a solemn procession through the town. The penitents wore yellow robes and high dunce's hats, decorated in the case of the relaxees with luridly depicted flames. In the main square, a huge audience listened as clerics preached 'hell-fire' sermons to the unfortunate penitents, who then renounced their 'sins'.

According to their sentence, they might then be stripped half-naked, scourged, and paraded in the streets. Finally, the State took over, and the whole assembly marched off to the place of burning. There, a last minute display of repentance often secured for a heretic the crowning mercy of the garotte (a form of strangulation) – only the most recalcitrant were burnt alive.

The bodies of heretics who had died in prison were also burned. In some cases, the corpses of those who had died years before they had even been denounced were exhumed for the purpose, and any of those who had been lucky enough to flee the country were burned in effigy. The purpose of this last ritual was by no means mere spite. Although the spectacle was much less

Biblioteca Columbina, Seville

The Grand Inquisitor
Diego Deza succeeded Torquemada as Inquisitor General in 1504. This was an office of enormous power which allowed its holder to draw up his own rules, with few restraints from either Pope or King.

A Dutch victim
(below) The long arm of the Inquisition reached distant outposts of the Spanish Empire. This female victim was burnt at the stake in the Netherlands – a Spanish possession until the 17th century.

Public spectacles
Mass trials and executions known as autos da fé, or 'acts of faith' were spectacular public events. Unrepentant heretics wore garments painted with flames and devils.

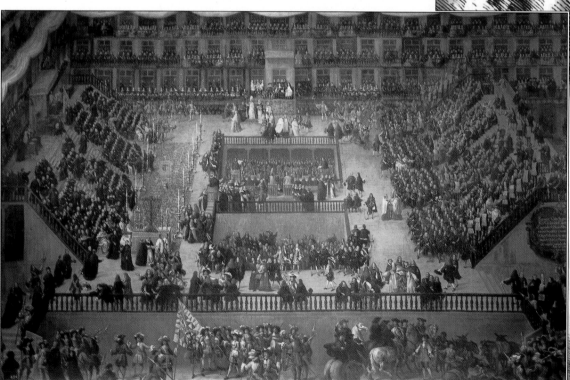

Francisco Rizi/Auto de Fe at Plaza Mayor, Madrid/Prado, Madrid

edifying to onlookers than the real thing, it nevertheless entitled the Inquisition to confiscate the possessions of the deceased.

The Inquisition, in fact, was a very profitable enterprise – one reason for its remarkable staying power. Another reason for its longevity was its total support for the unrestricted power of the monarchy: the Inquisitors were appointed by the king, and the line between enemies of the State and the enemies of the Church could be very fine indeed. Certainly, most of its original victims – the wretched *marranos* – were either eliminated or terrorized into utter submission quite early in the Inquisition's history. Next in line was another class of forced converts, the Moors; and when they were exhausted, the protestant Reformation provided a whole new class of heretics.

The Reformation also saw the beginning of the Inquisition's long bad press abroad. No-one in Europe had cared much about the fate of the Jews, and even less for the Moors, but God-fearing

Francisco de Goya

A legacy of ashes
The Inquisitors goal of 'One God, one Faith, one Baptism' was achieved at grave cost to Spain's cultural life. All books were scrutinized by fanatical censors, who ordered the destruction of suspicious works. Many of the intelligentsia fled, and others were silenced by fear of the Inquisitions.

Museo de Bellas Artes, Valencia

Protestants were a different matter. Yet when north European writers attacked the Inquisition, most Spaniards were outraged by their hypocrisy. In England and Germany, after all, Protestants oppressed Catholics, and by this time everyone was burning alleged witches. In contrast, the Inquisition reports on witchcraft are models of rationality and common sense.

THE END OF BURNING

Elsewhere, though, the craze for burning social deviants gradually died out; in Spain, the social deviants themselves died out first, and the very effectiveness of the Inquisition laid upon the nation a dead hand of orthodoxy. The spirit of free enquiry that transformed most of the rest of Europe in the 18th century never got under way, for the Inquisition gradually assumed total powers of censorship. Universities dwindled, literature paled, and politics remained fossilized in the Middle Ages, even as Spain's Empire crumbled. The Inquisition dealt with the new ideas that flooded in from revolutionary France just as it had with any other unorthodoxy. Though Napoleon's troops swept this abomination away in 1809, it was rapidly re-instituted by the restored King Ferdinand in 1814.

But the revived Inquisition was not what it had been: its time was over and most Spaniards realized it. But it was still a force to be reckoned with. In 1826 a wretched country schoolmaster was charged with the dreadful crime of Deism and put to death. In a hideous parody of the ancient penalty of burning he was garotted and placed in a barrel painted with flames.

As if this were any consolation, he was the Inquisition's last victim. On 15 July 1834, after 356 years, tens of thousands of deaths and untold suffering, the new Queen Regent signed the final edict: 'It is declared that the Tribunal of the Inquisition is definitely suppressed.'

Archiv für Kunst und Geschichte

A Year in the Life 1808

It was a cruel year for Spain, the latest victim of Napoleon's drive for total mastery of Europe. With French troops occupying the nation's key fortresses, King Charles IV was forced to abdicate in favour of his son Ferdinand. Then both were deposed, as the Emperor declared his brother Joseph the new King of Spain. And within weeks the entire country was engulfed in savage guerilla warfare.

Edistudio

38

'In the history of the year 1808', commented the London *Annual Register*, 'the great object of attention is Spain. Spain is the centre around which we arrange all other countries in Europe, and we take more or less interest in them, according to the relation in which they stand to this theatre on which the contest between liberty and tyranny is to be determined.'

When the year opened, however, it was not yet clear that the contest was really between liberty and tyranny or that the stage was to be provided by the Spaniards. Napoleon Bonaparte, the man who had tamed the revolutionary violence of the French and crowned himself their Emperor, was now at the height of his power. Right across Europe, from the borders of Russia to the English Channel, he was acclaimed as the bringer of order and stability, the one ruler strong enough to reconcile the old régime and the aspirations of the revolutionary era.

Whether that acclaim was sincere and unforced, remained to be tested. The British, of course, insisted that it was not. They alone still opposed Napoleon, using their undisputed command of the sea to fight for their share of Europe's trade, and to pose as defenders of Europe's liberties.

FRENCH 'OPPRESSION'

When the Emperor made his tributary states in Germany and Italy close their ports to British ships, the newspapers in London carried stories of the oppressions and indignities to which the people of these places were subjected. In Hamburg, it seemed, ladies could not go for walks in the country without

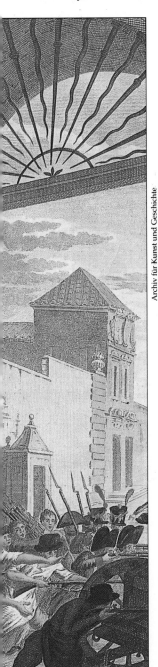

American slavers
(left) From 1 January 1808, it was illegal for any American citizen to import slaves into the United States. Involvement in the trade to foreign countries had been outlawed in 1794.

The end of the pigtail
In the early 19th century, pigtails were fashionable among the Jack Tars of the navy and with military men. They were also worn by the gentry throughout the 18th century, but by 1808 had been abandoned in favour of shorter hairstyles.

The French in Madrid
(left) French troops first entered Spain in 1807, en route for Portugal, which they quickly occupied. Soon Napoleon decided to add Spain itself to his empire, and an army under Marshal Murat seized Madrid in April 1808, savagely repressing a popular uprising on 2 May.

Joseph Bonaparte
(right) After the May riots in Madrid, Napoleon put his eldest brother Joseph on the Spanish throne. Joseph had been a successful King of Naples, instituting many reforms, but soon found that the situation in Spain was desperate. On 1 August he was forced to abandon the capital.

Château de Versailles

being 'searched in a manner that betrayed a complete contempt for common decency'. From this and other examples it was concluded that 'Bonaparte seems determined upon the total destruction of that city'.

The British tended to see all soldiers, especially those of the Emperor Napoleon, as cowards and slaves, fit only to make slaves of others. Sailors, on the other hand, were Jolly Jack Tars, free men themselves and sturdy defenders of the freedom of others. Anything that suggested otherwise was quietly ignored. In Hull, in the spring of 1808, the relatives of a girl who had fallen in love with a merchant seaman decided that the best way to end the affair was to get him press-ganged into the navy. This they did, only to find that she insisted on marrying him all the same. 'He was accordingly brought on shore and escorted

by the press gang to the church, from whence, after the marriage, he was again conveyed to the ship.' The incident was reported in the national press, but not as a case of wrongful use of the press gang. Instead it featured as 'a striking display of the omnipotence of love'.

BRITAIN'S POWERFUL NAVY

British naval strength in 1808 stood at more than 1,000 ships, augmented by over 200 foreign vessels taken as prizes, 'a navy of itself equal to cope with the united navies of France and her vassal allies'. When Portugal was occupied by the French at the end of 1807, the British navy had helped the royal family to escape to their colonies in South America, with which Britain

India's holy river
(left) The River Ganges, which flows across the vast north Indian plains, was traced to its source high up in the Himalayas in 1808. The Ganges is the holy river of the Hindus, and each year millions of pilgrims visit Varanasi – shown here – to cleanse themselves in its waters.

Beethoven's 'Sixth'
(below) Ludwig van Beethoven (1770-1827) completed his famous Sixth Symphony in 1808. 'The Pastoral', as it is known, with its wonderful evocation of nature, was the last symphony Beethoven composed before deafness overcame him in 1810.

was able to maintain a lucrative trade. It was assumed that the same would happen with Spain, where Napoleon had more than 50,000 troops. With these instruments of tyranny over-running their land, and with Jolly Jack Tars waiting at sea to help them, how could the Spaniards fail to struggle for liberty?

In fact, rather to the disappointment of the British, the Spaniards did nothing for several months. Most of them cordially detested their senile King Charles IV, together with his minister Manuel de Godoy. They hoped that the French might be persuaded to turn them out and replace them with the enormously popular heir to the throne, Prince Ferdinand. Although Ferdinand had at one time intrigued with the British, he had recently opened negotiations with Napoleon and had even talked of taking a Bonaparte princess as his consort. The

supporters of Prince Ferdinand, who were in the majority in most areas, welcomed French soldiers and Napoleon occupied many of the key fortresses in Spain without opposition.

CHARLES FORCED TO ABDICATE

In March, an attempt by both Charles and Godoy to seize Ferdinand failed and riots broke out which forced Charles to abdicate in favour of his son. The newly proclaimed King Ferdinand VII entered Madrid in triumph and within a matter of days the Academy had commissioned Goya to paint a ceremonial portrait of him on horseback.

After two short sittings, however, Ferdinand had to leave his capital and the portrait was completed from memory. The

Goethe's Faust
The first part of Faust, *the masterpiece of Germany's greatest playwright and poet, Johann von Goethe (1799-1830), was published in 1808. It tells the legend of a scholar who sells his soul to the devil. Here Mephisto tears Faust away from his lover, the beautiful, innocent Gretchen.*

Archiv für Kunst und Geschichte

Excavations at Pompeii
(left) In the 1st century AD, Pompeii, near Naples, was a flourishing city where wealthy nobles built their villas. Many were decorated with frescoes such as this, from the Villa of the Mysteries. But in AD 79, Mount Vesuvius erupted, and Pompeii was buried under 18ft of volcanic ash. Systematic excavations began in 1808, under Napoleonic rule, but were abandoned seven years later. They were restarted by the Italian government in 1861.

Naples Museum/Bridgeman Art Library

41

reason for his hurried departure was a summons to meet Napoleon at Bayonne in southern France. There the Emperor, by a mixture of trickery and intimidation, got both Charles and Ferdinand to give up their claims to the Spanish crown, which he then bestowed on his brother Joseph Bonaparte.

Meanwhile the people of Madrid had realized that the French were the kidnappers rather than the protectors of their popular young king. On 2 May riots outside the royal palace were put down savagely by French cavalry and early the next day rioters caught with weapons were shot. These events were a signal for widespread uprisings throughout Spain.

Aided and encouraged by Catholic priests and monks, the Spaniards waged ferocious and unrelenting guerilla war against the French. On 19 July a French army of 20,000 men surrendered to the guerillas and in August the ancient city of Saragossa repelled a force of 15,000 that had been besieging it for more than a month. King Joseph managed to make an entry into Madrid but had to leave again after a week because of the advance of the guerillas.

The British government lost no time in signing an alliance with the Spaniards. Its view of the struggle against Napoleon as a defence of liberty was vindicated at last. When at last the French were driven from Spain, after six years of brutal and bitter conflict, Goya painted two unforgettable pictures of the events of May 1808, his personal indictment of French savagery and tyranny. But before long he found himself producing even fiercer indictments of the cruelties practised by the government of the restored King Ferdinand VII.

Napoleon and the Tsar
In September 1808, Napoleon summoned his ally, Tsar Alexander of Russia, to a conference at Erfurt in Germany. The bargaining was tough, and Napoleon found the Tsar 'unspeakably obstinate'. But he finally agreed to defend France's eastern borders, while French troops crossed the Pyrenees for a new assault on Spain.

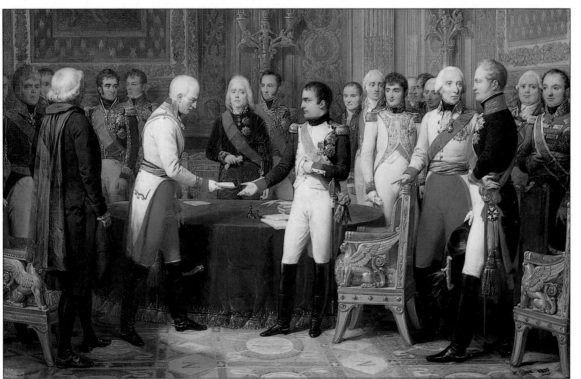

Lauros-Giraudon

Château de Versailles

Student of the air
The French scientist J.L. Gay-Lussac (1778-1850) used a balloon to collect samples of the air at different altitudes. His most important paper – on how gases combine – was written in 1808.

Catch-me-who-can
Richard Trevithick (1771-1833), known as 'the father of the locomotive', built the steam locomotive 'Catch-me-who-can' In 1808, he drove it at 12 mph on a circular railway at Euston, London.

Archiv für Kunst und Geschichte

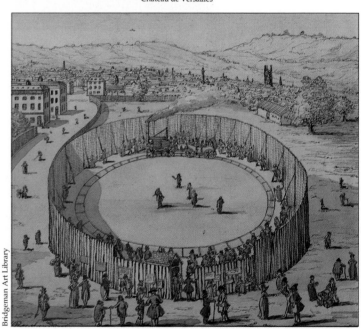

Bridgeman Art Library

Science Museum, London

WILLIAM BLAKE

1757-1827

One of the most distinctive of all English artists, William Blake was a brilliant poet as well as a great painter. A fiercely independent man, he started his career as a commercial engraver, but in his thirties began illustrating his own poems. He soon created a completely personal style and an original technique that perfectly expressed the full intensity of his visionary experiences.

Blake is now recognized as one of the giants of the Romantic period, but in his lifetime his genius was appreciated by only a small circle of admirers. He had few patrons and much of his life was spent in poverty. But lack of material success was of little consequence to Blake – he was completely dedicated to his work and lived in the world of the imagination and the spirit, rather than the world of the flesh.

43

The Visionary Engraver

Blake spent most of his life working as an engraver in London. He was always poor, but derived strength from a happy marriage, deep political convictions and an exceptionally rich spiritual existence.

William Blake was born on 28 November 1757 at 28 Broad Street, in the Soho district of London. He was the second child of a fairly prosperous hosier, and the family occupied a spacious old house in a district made up of private houses and respectable shops. Blake's father positively encouraged his son's artistic leanings. He bought him a few plaster casts, gave him money to buy his own prints, and sent him, at the age of ten, to Henry Pars' drawing school in the Strand, then the best and most fashionable preparatory school for young artists. Here he learnt to draw by copying plaster casts of classical statues.

When the time came for Blake to be apprenticed, his father was unable to afford the cost of his entrance to a painter's studio, and anyway he wanted his son to have the security of a craft. And so, for a premium of 50 guineas, he arranged for Blake to join the workshop of James Basire, master-engraver to the Society of Antiquaries, in Lincoln's Inn Fields.

THE MASTER ENGRAVER

Blake worked under Basire for seven years, becoming himself a master of all the techniques of engraving, etching, stippling and copying. He helped Basire with his engravings for books,

among them Jacob Bryant's famous *New System of Mythology*, which introduced him to the world of ancient religions and legends. Another profound influence was the study he made, at Basire's suggestion, of Gothic architecture and sculpture in Westminster Abbey and other old churches in London. Blake's lifelong love of Gothic art dates from these visits to the Abbey.

After his seven-year apprenticeship, Blake set out to earn his living as an engraver. He continued to live in his father's house and worked on commissions for such publications as the *Ladies' Magazine*. He enrolled as a student at the newly-founded Royal Academy, but could not tolerate the life drawing he was required to do there. According to him, 'copying nature' deadened the vigour of his imagination.

In 1782, at the age of 25, Blake married. His wife, Catherine Boucher, was the illiterate daughter of a Battersea market gardener, and this choice of partner did not please his father. The couple moved to a house in nearby Green Street, but two years later Blake's father died and William

Westminster Abbey
(right) During his seven year apprenticeship to the engraver James Basire, Blake often made drawings in Westminster Abbey.

A Londonder, born and bred
(right) Blake was born in this spacious cornerhouse in Soho, where he lived until he was 25. Two years later he set up a small print-selling shop next door to his old home.

The Abbey monuments
(left) This coloured drawing is one of a series Blake made in 1775; they were used as the basis for engravings illustrating the Abbey's monuments, published in 1780.

The Society of Antiquaries of London

W. Blake/King Sebert

Barnabys

and Catherine returned to Broad Street, living at No. 27, next door to his old home. They were joined by Blake's younger brother, Robert, who became a pupil as well as a member of the household.

For two and a half happy, though not financially successful years, this much-loved brother was Blake's professional and intellectual companion. Then, tragically, Robert fell ill and died, leaving Blake broken-hearted. He nursed him so selflessly that he is said to have gone without sleep for a fortnight. At the moment of his death Blake claimed he had seen 'the released spirit ascend heavenward, clapping its hands for joy'. He said that he continued to communicate with his brother's spirit throughout the rest of his life, deriving much comfort from their conversations. Blake also claimed to communicate freely with angels and other Biblical figures.

After Robert's death, Blake moved to a house in

Blake by his wife
Catherine Blake made this pencil drawing of her husband shortly before his death. It shows Blake as she remembered him 'in his fiery youth'.

Fitzwilliam Museum, Cambridge

Image Bank

J. Bertaux/Taking the Tuileries Palace/Museum de Versailles

The French Revolution, 1789

As a young man, Blake welcomed the French Revolution, and even wrote a poem celebrating it. He maintained his hatred of the monarchy throughout his life.

Poland Street, Soho, where he struggled to fulfil the few commissions that came his way. He was too unworldly in his commercial dealings and too proud in his relations with clients to make himself rich. In his politics he was then extremely radical and took to wearing a red bonnet when the French Revolution broke out. As both a man and an artist, he was a visionary whose imaginative world was far more splendid and inspiring than anything he discovered in the real world. Above all, he was a deeply religious man, for whom everything possessed its own spiritual essence and life.

In 1788 Blake made his first experiments with 'illuminated printing', that is combining words and images together on a single copper plate. For some time he was unable to hit on a technique that was both cheap and suitable, and it worried him badly. Then, one day his dead brother appeared to him in a vision and gave him explicit directions, which he promptly put into action. They proved to

Blake's Soho

Blake lived most of his life in the district of Soho, in the West End of London. Built in the 18th century, this has consistently been a home for craftsmen, artists and writers – among them Canaletto and Shelley as well as Karl Marx and the critic William Hazlitt.

Today Soho is best-known as a red-light district and the centre of London's Chinatown, but in Blake's time it was a typical urban mixture of grand houses – in the squares – and terraces for artisans' families. There was also a workhouse in the district.

Soho Square

(right) In Blake's day, Soho Square was an elegant residential area not far from open fields. Blake lived nearby, first in the family home in Broad Street (now Broadwick Street), then with his wife in Green Street and later in Poland Street.

be perfect for his needs. Using this method, he printed copies of *Songs of Innocence* the following year and taught Mrs Blake how to bind them.

In 1794 he wrote and illustrated his *Songs of Experience*, which betray a much bleaker and more pessimistic outlook. It is believed that he never issued them separately, but always combined them with *Songs of Innocence* in order to show 'the two Contrary States of the Human Soul,' as he put it on the title-page. Helped by his wife, he continued to make and colour sets of the prints as they were commissioned by his customers until the time of his death.

'PARADISE' IN LAMBETH

Shortly before the death of his mother in 1792, the Blakes had left Poland Street and moved to 13 Hercules Buildings in Lambeth. This was evidently a pretty terrace house with a strip of garden behind, in which Blake allowed a wandering vine to grow unpruned and form little arbour Here, according to legend, a friend once discovered Mr and Mrs Blake wearing nothing but helmets and reading aloud from *Paradise Lost*. In any case, the seven years they spent in Lambeth were happy and productive. It was in this house, in 1795, that Blake designed the magnificent series of colour prints, includng *God Judging Adam* (p.57), which are generally thought to mark the high water of his genius as a print-maker.

By and large Blake was not lucky in his patrons, but there was one man who never failed him – Thomas Butts, a civil servant and art collector. Blake referred to him as 'my employer', but in fact he seems to have left Blake free to follow his creative impulse. He simply placed a standing order, as it were, asking for 50 small pictures at a

Tate Gallery, London

Visionary powers
(above) Blake claimed that he was frequently visited by spirits and angels. The Ghost of a Flea (c.1819) is a blood-curdling record of one of his most bizarre visionary experiences. According to his friend John Varley, this extraordinary monster visited Blake twice.

Barnabys

A country interlude
(left) Blake and his wife moved to this idyllic cottage in Felpham, Sussex in 1800. They rented it for three years at £20 per annum, until a fracas with a uniformed soldier sent them hurrying back to London.

Fotomas

guinea each. Blake was able to confide in Butts and was a frequent visitor to his house, which by the end of Blake's life overflowed with his pictures.

William Hayley, a country gentleman and minor poet, was another of Blake's patrons. He commissioned Blake to engrave plates for his proposed life of the poet William Cowper and invited the Blakes to move to Felpham in Sussex to be near his own residence. In 1800 Blake left London for the first time to begin what he later called his 'three years' slumber on the banks of the ocean'. At first Blake thought his new cottage a little paradise, and both he and Catherine loved to go for walks, exploring the countryside.

THE DAUGHTERS OF INSPIRATION

Blake was overwhelmed by the beauty of nature, but he did not take up landscape painting, nor did he ever see nature in anything other than visionary terms. 'Everything is human! Mighty! Sublime!' he wrote. During this period he not only communed with his 'daughters of inspiration', who descended from the tops of trees to talk with him, but he also discovered that the vegetable world was inhabited by fairies. 'Did you ever see a fairy's funeral, madam?' he asked an astounded lady at a party, and proceeded to describe one he had witnessed the previous night.

Meanwhile, his relationship with Hayley was not proving easy. He worked loyally at the jobs he was given, but found them imaginatively unrewarding. By 1802 he was getting restive and would probably have fallen out with Hayley if events had not intervened. In the summer of 1803 Blake had a fight with a soldier who had been sent to cut the grass in his garden. Blake, who was opposed to the war against France, was reported as saying, 'Damn the King, and damn all his

Robert Harding

C.R. Stanley/View of the Strand/London Museum

The Patron's Reward

In 1809 Blake held an exhibition at his brother's shop in Soho, showing his new painting, the *Canterbury Pilgrims*, together with 15 other pictures. Subscribers were invited to order engravings, but not one order was taken. His ever-faithful patron Thomas Butts bought the *Canterbury Pilgrims* – one of Blake's masterpieces – for just £10.

British Museum

The loyal patron
(left) The minor civil servant Thomas Butts filled his house with Blake's pictures.

Canterbury Pilgrims
(right) Blake's painting shows a scene from Chaucer's Canterbury Tales. *The procession presents a picture of 'universal human life'.*

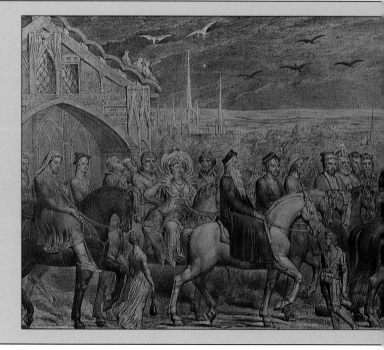

F.J. Fields/Manchester City Art Gallery

The Spirits of Fountain Court
(above) From 1821 until his death in August 1827, Blake lived at No. 3 Fountain Court. This atmospheric picture shows the sparse furnishings of his bedroom – and, hovering over the bed, Blake's spirit visitors.

The Strand
(left) Fountain Court was just off the Strand – an area Blake knew from his drawing school days.

Glasgow Museums and Art Galleries, Stirling Maxwell Collection, Pollok House

water-colours to Butts. However, in the summer of 1818 his life was radically changed by meeting John Linnell, a young portrait and landscape painter, who began to pay him regular sums of money in exchange for a large part of his output. Linnell also introduced him to a group of young admirers, including Samuel Palmer, the painter who came closest to inheriting Blake's visionary inspiration, and John Varley, a landscape painter who was fascinated by astrology and readily swallowed Blake's accounts of his visionary experiences.

POOR BUT HAPPY

In 1821 the Blakes moved to no. 3 Fountain Court, off the Strand, a house owned by his brother-in-law. Although they still lived in very poor circumstances, he seems to have been much happier here. He continued to be an object of veneration to his younger friends. Samuel Palmer went so far as to kiss the threshold whenever he

British Tourist Authority

The final resting place
Blake died in poverty, aged 69, and was buried in an unmarked grave in Bunhill Fields. Not until 100 years later was this tombstone erected in his memory.

called. And Linnell commissioned Blake, at the age of 65, to make 22 magnificent engravings illustrating *The Book of Job*, paying him £5 per plate. Linnell also proposed the second masterpiece of Blake's last years, his illustrations for Dante's *Divine Comedy*. He worked on these until his death, completing over 100 large designs, but engraving only seven plates.

A friend who visited him during his last days recorded that, after finishing a piece of work, 'his glance fell on his loving Kate, no longer young or beautiful, but who had lived with him in these and like humble rooms, in hourly companionship, ever ready helpfulness, and reverent sympathy, for now 45 years. "Stay!" he cried. "Keep as you are! You have ever been an angel to me: I will draw you!"' This was his last work and, sadly, it has been lost. Blake died at Fountain Court on 12 August 1827. To the last he sang songs of praise and joy.

soldiers, they are all slaves.' He was tried for assault and sedition. Hayley managed to get him acquitted, but Blake had to leave Felpham.

He was now 45. On his return to London he chose to live in South Molton Street, but could only afford to rent one floor of a house. Here he lived for the next 17 years, mostly in poverty. He brought back from Felpham his long poem, *Milton*, which he claimed had been dictated to him by his angels, with some assistance from Milton himself. He set about etching plates for this book, and also began work on his engravings for *Jerusalem*, a book which he continued to enlarge until as late as 1820. In the end, he illuminated only one copy.

For the next ten years Blake's life is difficult to trace. He lived in obscurity, continuing to write and paint, but selling very little except his

The Power of the Imagination

An engraver by trade, Blake developed original techniques to illustrate his own poems – and those of Shakespeare, Milton and Dante – with images of strange and unusual power.

Library of Congress, Washington DC

Library of Congress, Washington DC

The art of illumination
These 'illuminated' pages come from Blake's Songs of Innocence *(far left), published in 1789, and its sequel,* Songs of Experience *(left), which appeared in 1794. They combine words and images in a way that recalls medieval manuscripts, but Blake's intensity of vision is completely personal. He finished each copy of the book by hand, so no two copies are identical.*

Tate Gallery, London

William Blake was unique in being almost as great a poet as he was a painter, and it is not absurd to say that for a while he painted his poems and wrote his pictures. From the start, he was intent on developing his own personal symbolism, both in words and pictures, but by the end of his life his poetic world had become highly complicated and difficult to interpret. For this reason, his later poetry is not much read today. His art, however, retained a brilliant clarity and simplicity, though his mystical references are sometimes obscure.

Blake's apprenticeship to James Basire gave him the chance to study engravings of Old Masters, most notably Michelangelo and Raphael. Their influence, spiced with a fashionable interest in the horrific, is to be seen in his earliest engravings. But it was his taste for medieval art, stimulated by his visits to Westminster Abbey, which showed most strongly in *Songs of Innocence* (1789), his first truly

original work, not only as painter and poet, but also as printer.

The printing method Blake used – which he believed had been revealed to him by his dead brother – had the advantage of being cheap, although it called for an exceptional degree of skill and patience. First, he laboriously transferred the text of his poem, in reverse of course, on to a prepared copper plate. Then he added his design and marginal decorations. When these images had been 'etched' into the plate by the use of acid, he made a print, using one or sometimes two tinted inks. Finally, he added his water-colour 'illumination' to the page, with pen or paintbrush.

This extraordinary method turned each copy of *Songs of Innocence* into a separate work of art, for Blake was able to vary the colour range from volume to volume. Early copies have the translucent delicacy of a rainbow, while some later

Satan, Sin and Death (1808)
(right) The power and imaginative grandeur of Milton's Paradise Lost *made a strong appeal to Blake. This water-colour illustration shows Satan about to fight with Death when Sin intervenes, telling him Death is their son.*

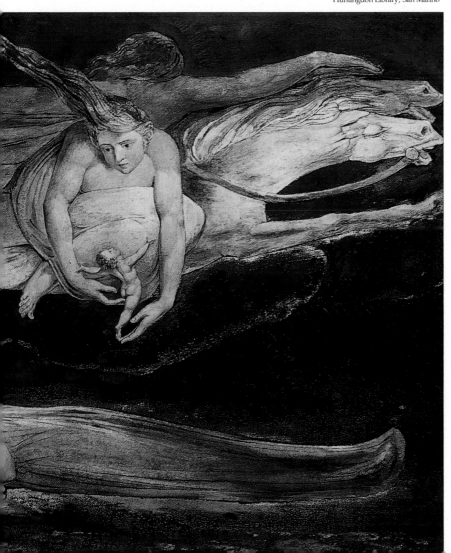

Tate Gallery, London

Jerusalem
The title-page to Blake's most famous poem is dated 1804, but he worked on the illustrations until about 1820.

Canute
(right) One of a series of 'visionary heads' Blake drew in 1819-20 for the painter John Varley, who was keenly interested in astrology and the supernatural.

Huntingdon Library, San Marino

Huntingdon Library, San Marino

copies are more jewelled and glow with gold paint. In 1794, using the same technique, he added *Songs of Experience* and thereafter always printed the two sets of *Songs* as a single book. The designs for *Experience* are noticeably more severe and dark, matching the grimmer character of these poems.

A SECRET TECHNIQUE

Meanwhile, Blake had been experimenting with a new method of print-making, using thick pigments of his own invention based on carpenter's glue. He claimed that this secret had been revealed to him by Joseph, the carpenter father of Jesus. And in 1795 he composed a series of 12 large colour prints, which were not associated with any text. Their bold images, clear-cut forms and rich texture put them among his finest works.

These prints of 1795 draw their subject matter from a bewilderingly wide range of sources, including the Old and the New Testaments, Shakespeare and Milton. Nevertheless, Blake evidently conceived the series as a whole. The clue to their precise meaning still lies buried in his writings, though it is generally thought that each print represents a stage in the Fall of Man, as Blake saw it. Thus, *Newton* (p.58) shows man as a slave

Pity (c.1795)
(left) This print, which Blake finished in water-colour, was inspired by a line from Shakespeare's Macbeth – *'Pity, like a naked newborn babe'.*

51

to pure reason, unenlightened by the imagination, a state of mind hated by Blake. By contrast, the crawling, bestial figure in *Nebuchadnezzar* (p.59) shows man as a slave to the senses.

FREEING THE SPIRIT

All his life Blake fought against oppression, whether it took a political, intellectual or religious form. What he valued above all was imagination and its power to liberate the human spirit from its earthly confinement. Throughout his work, humanity under many different guises struggles to escape from the tyranny of Urizen, who is always depicted as a ferocious, bearded old man, symbol of both the authoritarian father and God, the unfeeling creator of systems and laws. Opposed to him is 'Jesus, the Imagination', otherwise called 'the God within', who reigns in every human soul.

Blake set himself the impossible task of creating a visual symbolism with which to express his spiritual visions, which owed nothing to ordinary existence. It is perhaps for this reason that some of the finest work he did towards the end of his life

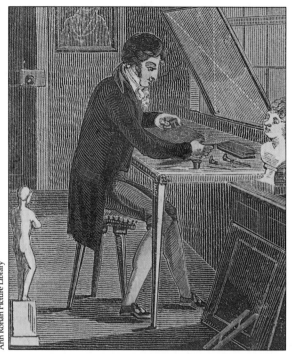

Engraver at work
Blake used various methods of engraving, but they all involved cutting a design into a plate of metal or block of wood, rolling ink over it and taking an impression. Before the development of photography this was not just an art form, but the chief means of reproducing an image on paper.

Ann Ronan Picture Library

The Painter Poets

Many artists have excelled in more than one field, but few have matched Blake's eminence as both a painter and a poet. Michelangelo was so supremely great as a painter, sculptor and architect that his literary work tends to be overshadowed, but he was one of the finest Italian poets of the 16th century. Rossetti, whose father was Italian, made translations of Dante, as well as writing his own poems, the most famous of which is *The Blessed Damozel*.

Michelangelo (1475-1564) **The Creator**
(below) Blake made several copies of such figures – from the Sistine Chapel of the Vatican in Rome – which influenced his own portrayal of the human body.

Manchester City Art Gallery

D.G. Rossetti (1828-82) **Astarte Syriaca**
(above) Rossetti greatly admired Blake and when still a student bought one of his manuscripts. His mysterious symbolism reflects Blake's influence.

Scala/Vision International

Bridgeman Art Library

Tate Gallery, London

TRADEMARKS
Twisted Hair

A distinctive feature of Blake's work is his treatment of long hair. He gives it almost a life of its own, twisting the thick folds into vigorous cascades, which sometimes stand out from the head as if floating on air.

was inspired by visions other than his own – especially those of the Bible writers and of Dante. His engravings for *The Book of Job* amount to a new interpretation of Job's character: he created some unforgettable images for this series, especially the fearsome *Satan Smiting Job with Sore Boils*. And, as the critic John Ruskin noted, Blake was able to surpass even Rembrandt in rendering the effects of glaring, flickering light.

Blake's last years were occupied by his illustrations to Dante's *Divine Comedy*. This series was to have been engraved too, but he died having finished only seven plates. However, he did draw over 100 large designs, some of them painted in glowing water-colours. These beautifully delicate paintings display a new sensuousness and variety of mood; they provide a fitting climax to a career of ceaseless and fiercely independent creativity.

To sum up Blake's work, one cannot do better than quote his own words: 'The imagination is not a State: it is the Human existence itself.'

Satan Smiting Job with Sore Boils (c.1826)
(above and right) Blake simplifies the forms of the human body and creates bold contrasts between different shapes and textures. The detail shows mounds of thick, twisted hair set against Job's sinewy flesh. Blake often returned to the same theme, and this is the final and most powerful version of a subject he had treated twice before.

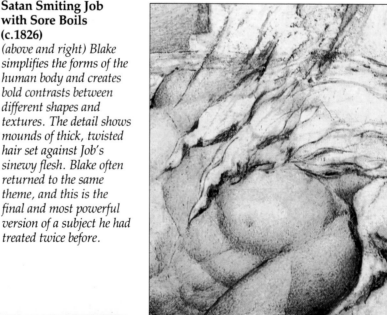

Blake's last design
The final engraving Blake completed, in 1827, was a visiting card for his friend George Cumberland. Although tiny (only three inches long) it is full of vitality.

Fitzwilliam Museum, Cambridge

THE MAKING OF A MASTERPIECE

The Body of Abel Found by Adam and Eve

In one of his finest paintings, Blake shows the murderer Cain running in horror from the scene of his crime, while his father and mother look on in anguish. The exact scene is not described in the Bible – Genesis tells us only that God saw what Cain had done and condemned him to the life of an outcast. Blake was struck by the story's emotional force and had made sketches and a water-colour version 20 years earlier. The final painting (1826) is on a mahogany panel covered with layers of priming, on which he has drawn in ink. This shows through the surface paintwork of delicate tempera – water-colour mixed with diluted glue.

Pencil sketch
This drawing is a study for Blake's water-colour, shown on the opposite page. The main elements of Cain's pose are rendered with brisk strokes of the pencil.

British Museum

The Story of Cain and Abel

And Adam knew Eve his wife; and she conceived and bare Cain, and said, I have gotten a man from the Lord.

And she again bare his brother Abel. And Abel was a keeper of sheep, but Cain was a tiller of the ground.
. . .
And Cain talked with Abel his brother: and it came to pass, when they were in the field, that Cain rose up against Abel his brother, and slew him.

And the Lord said unto Cain, Where is Abel thy brother? And he said, I know not: Am I my brother's keeper?

And he said, What hast thou done? The voice of thy brother's blood crieth unto me from the ground.

And now art thou cursed from the earth, which hath opened her mouth to receive thy brother's blood from thy hand.
. . .
And Cain went out from the presence of the Lord, and dwelt in the land of Nod, on the east of Eden.

Genesis, Chapter 4

(right) A 14th-century manuscript illumination emphasizes the bloodiness of Cain's deed. Like Blake, the artist chooses a spade for the murder weapon, for Cain was 'a tiller of the ground'.

Bodleian Library film strip

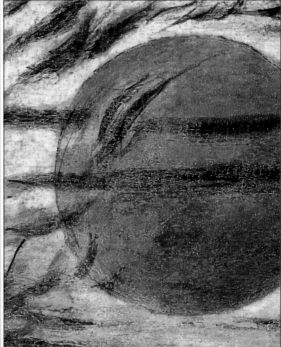

The setting sun
Blake applied powdered gold as well as paint to the mahogany panel. Here it suggests the fiery glow of the sun. The technique may have been suggested to Blake by medieval manuscripts.

> 'I am under the direction of messengers from heaven.'
>
> William Blake

Tate Gallery, London

A water-colour version
Blake painted this water-colour in about 1805. Although the composition is almost identical to the later tempera version, the colour schemes are noticeably different.

Adam's anguish
The head of Adam is drawn in much less detail than that of his murderous son, but powerfully conveys the father's numb horror and confusion.

Fogg Art Museum, University of Harvard

55

Gallery

Blake's output as a painter, engraver and draughtsman was enormous. He often worked on projects over a number of years, gradually bringing them to fruition, and he frequently returned to favourite subjects. Sometimes he would colour a print that he had engraved many years earlier, as with The Ancient of Days.

The Ancient of Days *1794*
9¼″ × 6½″ Whitworth Art Gallery, Manchester

Blake used this design as an illustration to his poem Europe, *and it proved one of his most popular prints – he handcoloured this particular impression for a customer 30 years later. The image was inspired 'by a vision which he declared hovered over his head at the top of the staircase'.*

The Bible was Blake's most frequent source of inspiration, and he recreated its awesome stories – God Judging Adam, Nebuchadnezzar, Cain and Abel – with an intensity few artists have matched. Just as impressive are the products of his own imagination, such as Newton and Glad Day. No other artist has created such a rich personal mythology, or made spiritual beings seem so real.

As a poet, Blake was drawn to other writers who had handled lofty themes in a heroic manner. Towards the end of his life he began illustrating the work of the great Italian poet, Dante, whose imagination matched his own in fervour.

God Judging Adam *1795*
17″ × 21″ Tate Gallery, London

This print was known for many years as Elijah in the Fiery Chariot, *but a faint pencil inscription discovered in 1965 revealed its true subject. Blake may have adapted an earlier design on the subject of Elijah, transforming the prophet's fiery chariot into God's blazing throne.*

Newton 1795
18″ × 22½″ Tate Gallery, London

For Blake, Isaac Newton symbolized the dangers of rationalism. Obsessively absorbed in his diagram, Newton thinks the whole of life can be measured with dividers.

Nebuchadnezzar 1795
17½" × 24¾" Tate Gallery, London

This print forms a pair with Newton, symbolizing the bestial aspects of Man. In the Bible, the Babylonian king Nebuchadnezzar 'was driven from men, and did eat grass as oxen'.

Bridgeman Art Library

Glad Day *c.1795*
10¾″ × 8″ British Museum, London

*The inspiration for this work is uncertain. Blake may have had in
mind a passage in Shakespeare's* Romeo and Juliet *in which 'jocund
day stands tiptoe on the misty mountain tops'. But the print is also
known as* The Dawn of Albion, *a symbolic figure embodying the
personality of England.*

**Dante's Divine Comedy:
The Simoniac Pope** *1824-7*
20¾″ × 14½″ Tate Gallery, London

*In Dante's great poem Blake found flights of fancy to match his own
astonishing imagination. Dante portrayed Pope Nicholas III as being
suspended head downwards in a fiery well as his punishment for
simony — the sin of selling posts in the church.*

The Body of Abel
Found by Adam and Eve *c.1826*
12¾" × 17"
Tate Gallery, London

Blake shows Cain fleeing, as the body of the brother he has just murdered is discovered by his parents Adam and Eve. He has abandoned the grave in which he had intended burying the corpse. The dramatic potential of the subject obviously appealed to Blake, for apart from making other pictures of the subject, he also wrote a short play in 1822, which was called The Ghost of Abel.

**Dante's Divine Comedy:
Beatrice Addressing Dante** *1824-7*
14½″ × 20¾″ Tate Gallery, London

The symbolism of this scene follows that of Dante's poem, in which, the griffin and Beatrice – wearing the crown – represented Christ and the Church. The three girls are Faith, Hope and Charity, and the heads flanking Beatrice are those of the Four Evangelists. Blake shows Dante in the centre, with his book.

Dante's Divine Comedy:
The Inscription over Hell Gate *1824-7*
20¾″ × 14¾″ Tate Gallery, London

This scene shows Dante, in red, guided by the Roman poet Virgil, in
blue, about to pass through the gates of Hell. The inscription is one of
the most famous lines in Dante's poem, which Blake has translated
literally, 'Leave every hope you who in enter'

Dreaming of Jerusalem

Blake's 'fiery youth' was a time of hope for believers in Utopia. Revolutions in America and France gave grounds for optimism that liberty, equality and fraternity could exist in Britain too.

The revolutionary message of Blake's *Jerusalem* – one of the most famous poems in the English language – is easily missed now that it has become a church hymn, almost a patriotic anthem, with its moving evocation of 'England's green and pleasant land'. But in the 1780s, the image of Jerusalem as a city of innocence which could be reclaimed from the hell of industrial Britain's 'dark, satanic mills' was common currency among London's radicals.

Since the Gordon Riots of 1780, when Blake saw the mob march through the streets of Soho and the City to sack Newgate Prison, the government under William Pitt the Younger had taken stern measures to hold down discontent. But when the decade closed with the French Revolution of 1789 – signalled by another mob storming another prison, the Bastille in Paris – the news inspired hopes in London that justice could return to England too. In a land equally oppressed by its king and by the wealthy, swords could be beaten back to ploughshares, the wolf lie down with the lamb, and all men and women enjoy the fruits of their work in harmony with their neighbours.

TOM PAINE, THE REVOLUTIONARY

A well-known 'Liberty Boy' himself, Blake was involved that year with a group of radical authors and pamphleteers who met regularly in the home of Joseph Johnson, at 72 St Paul's Churchyard. Johnson was a publisher and printer who gave weekly dinners for his friends in a cramped upstairs room, and it was here the Blake met some of the most notorious activists of his era, including the revolutionary journalist Thomas Paine, the political philosopher William Godwin, and one of the earliest feminist writers, Mary Wollstonecraft.

Of the three, Paine was already by far the most influential. The son of a Norfolk tradesman who made women's corsets, he had worked as a customs man in Sussex – and organized a claim for better wages – before trying his luck in America. He arrived in Philadelphia in November 1774, a few months before the first shots were fired in the Revolution, and made his name a year later with a pamphlet named *Common Sense*, which

Tom Paine
(right) Author of the famous treatise The Rights of Man, *Tom Paine was born in England but made his name as a journalist in America. His pamphlets urging the colonists to rebel against Britain were highly successful.*

Land of the free
(below) The American Revolution which broke out in 1775, was an inspiration to Europe's radicals. After eight years of bitter fighting, George Washington's citizen army won victory against overwhelming odds. Washington himself, shown here crossing the frozen Delaware River, became the first president of the new republic of the United States.

A. Milliere/National Portrait Gallery, London

Peter Newark's Western Americana

E. Leutze/Washington Crossing the Delaware/Metropolitan Museum, New York

And did those feet in ancient time,
Walk upon England's mountains green:
And was the holy Lamb of God
On England's pleasant pastures seen!

And did the Countenance Divine,
Shine forth upon our clouded hills?
And was Jerusalem builded here
Among these dark Satanic Mills?

Bring me my Bow of burning gold:
Bring me my Arrows of desire:
Bring me my Spear: O clouds unfold:
Bring me my Chariot of fire:

I will not cease from Mental Fight:
Nor shall my Sword sleep in my hand:
Till we have built Jerusalem,
In England's green & pleasant Land.

P.J. de Loutherbourg/Coalbrookdale by Night/Science Museum, London

Dark satanic mills

Blake's rousing poem, written in 1804, expresses his passionate belief that social justice could exist on earth, not just in heaven. Attacking the ugliness and misery of the Industrial Revolution, he summons up a vision of Jerusalem – a city of beauty and freedom that could be built in Britain.

called on Americans everywhere to rise against the British and fight for liberty. The pamphlet sold more than 150,000 copies; it was read by every rank of the new American army, and brought Paine to the attention of Washington himself. In another pamphlet issued soon afterwards, he even coined the name for the new republic: the United States.

Paine returned to Europe in the 1780s, preoccupied with plans for his own invention, a wide-spanned iron bridge. But he was in Paris to witness the first, relatively orderly stages of the Revolution, and left the city with the key to the Bastille, to forward to George Washington as a comradely gift. When Paine reached London, he found the government vehemently attacking the 'savagery' of the Paris mob. In defence of their actions, he wrote his most famous pamphlet, *The Rights of Man*, which Johnson published in 1791.

Here he set out his vision of a just society, with the stirring declaration that 'All men are born equal.'

Among Paine's strongest supporters was Mary Wollstonecraft, a vigorous campaigner for women's rights. They met in 1791 at Johnson's house in St Paul's Churchyard; William Godwin was also present, and was dismayed when Mary talked Paine into silence, but her forceful arguments – published the following year in her *Vindication of the Rights of Woman* – forced both men to adjust their own notions of equality. She condemned marriage, which at that time deprived women of all economic freedom, and insisted on women's right to participate in politics, while calling for sex education, state schools and better job prospects for women.

Outside radical circles, Wollstonecraft's pleas fell on deaf ears, but Paine's pamphlet shook the

Storming the Bastille
When the people of Paris destroyed the hated Bastille prison on 14 July 1789, radicals throughout Europe believed that freedom was at hand. But their hopes were soon dashed: horrific stories of the Reign of Terror drowned revolutionary ardour in a tide of blood.

The struggle for Reform
Alarmed by the French Revolution, the British government crushed all known radicals without mercy. But a campaign for parliamentary reform, led by Henry 'Orator' Hunt, won massive support – despite events such as the brutal 'Peterloo Massacre' of 1819.

Lauros Giraudon

Mary Evans Picture Library

68

government. Alarmed by the success of *The Rights of Man*, which sold thousands of copies throughout Britain and Ireland, Pitt urged George III to action. On 21 May 1792 a royal proclamation banned 'wicked and seditious writings' and Pitt issued a writ against Paine for blasphemous libel – a charge carrying a long prison sentence.

According to one contemporary, Blake himself warned Paine to flee. Paine was at Johnson's house, delivering a rousing speech on liberty, when Blake put his hands on his shoulders and said 'You must not go home, or you are a dead man.' Paine fled that night to Dover, tracked all the way by Pitt's spies, and crossed to France.

A MASSACRE IN PARIS

That September, news reached London of a massacre of royalist prisoners and the start of the Reign of Terror. Lurid reports of a blood-soaked Paris soon dimmed the enthusiasm of numerous English radicals, including the Lake Poets, Wordsworth and Coleridge. Blake himself, who had once worn the red revolutionary bonnet on the streets of London, put his cap away forever. Government repression made such overt shows of support extremely dangerous, especially after 1793, when England joined an alliance of foreign powers pledged to destroy the new French state.

Pitt moved swiftly to silence the radical writers and their publishers. Johnson refused to publish the second edition of *The Rights of Man* for fear of prosecution, and Blake laid aside his own work on *The French Revolution* at the proof stage. William

Godwin's *Political Justice*, published in 1793, escaped solely because of its high price – at three guineas a copy it was unlikely to inflame the poor.

Yet while the flame of protest seemed to be dying, a new generation was being born to take up the radical torch. The poet Percy Bysshe Shelley was born in 1792, the same year *The Rights of Man* appeared; as a schoolboy at Eton he was entranced by Godwin's vision of *Political Justice*, and in 1814 he fell in love with a precocious 16-year-old – the daughter of Godwin and Mary Wollstonecraft, who had reluctantly overcome her own objections to marriage, only to die giving birth to her child.

Shelley's brief life overlapped with the later years of Blake, who had retreated into political silence. The younger poet was protected by his high birth and the prospect of an inheritance; he could speak out far more safely. In 1812 he wrote his own *Declaration of Rights* in support of the Irish, then launched into a fierce defence of the printer Daniel Eaton, who had been sentenced to 18 months' imprisonment – and a spell in the pillory each month – for publishing Paine's last great work, *The Age of Reason*.

SHELLEY'S CALL TO ARMS

Two years later, Shelley met Mary Godwin, and declared his love beside her mother's grave in Old St Pancras Churchyard. Throughout his own short life, he remained true to his radical heritage, despite leaving England for good in 1818. The Peterloo Massacre of the following year stirred him to insurrectionary fury, and in *The Mask of Anarchy* he called on the people of England to : 'Rise like lions after slumber/ In unvanquishable number,/ Shake your chains to earth like dew/ Which in sleep had fallen on you/ Ye are many – they are few.' Shelley died in 1822, when his boat sank in the Bay of Leghorn in Italy, five years before Blake's own death.

A radical alliance
(above) The marriage in 1797 of William Godwin and Mary Wollstonecraft united the leading theorist of the radical movement with one of Britain's first feminists. Mary Wollstonecraft died the same year, giving birth to their daughter – the future Mary Shelley, author of Frankenstein.

Shelley in Italy
The Romantic poet Percy Bysshe Shelley (1792-1822) was inspired by the writings of Godwin and Wollstonecraft, and even married their daughter Mary. A fervent supporter of radical causes, he moved to Italy in 1818, but continued to attack the government. After the Peterloo Massacre he called for revolution in Britain in his poem The Mask of Anarchy.

J. Severn/Shelley amidst the Ruins of the Baths of Caracalla

A Year in the Life 1819

In a year of industrial unrest and demands for political reform, workers demonstrated throughout the north of England. In Manchester, a peaceful crowd was charged by cavalry at the 'Massacre of Peterloo'. But there were technical achievements too: while the first steamship to cross the Atlantic was completing her voyage, gas pipes were being laid for street lighting in London.

Ann Ronan Picture Library

Fotomas

Child labour in the mills
Children as young as six were employed in the cotton mills, minding dangerous machines for up to 16 hours a day. Several Factory Acts, including one in 1819, were passed to improve children's conditions. But it was only in the 1830s that they were properly enforced.

Walker Art Gallery, Liverpool

New mining machinery
This painting, executed around 1819, shows a pit-head using steam-winding gear to raise the coal. The Industrial Revolution was accelerated by technical innovations such as this.

The year was less than a fortnight old when the City of London was invaded by the devotees of King Shiloh, who was said to have been sent by God to set up the new Jerusalem in England and reign for 1,000 years. They marched in their hundreds under the arch of Temple Bar, carrying silken flags and a brazen trumpet, and when they reached the centre of the City, they proclaimed to an immense crowd the end of the kingdom of King George III and the beginning of that of King Shiloh. They were then attacked by the crowd and the result was the first of 1819's many riots.

The disciples of Shiloh, like Blake himself, hated the mercenary world of capitalism and industrialism which was taking over the country. Like him, they saw the new factories as dark satanic mills which would have to be swept away when the time came to build the new Jerusalem in England's green and pleasant land. Many of them had already thrown away their money, convinced that the squalid days of gold and silver were numbered, and they shared Blake's enthusiasm for the world of imagination.

THE NEW INDUSTRIAL AGE

In this they attracted very few followers. For most people, the world of work and wages was all too real. The only trouble about the dark satanic mills, in the eyes of labouring men and women, was that there were not enough of them – or not enough that were actually working. Unemployment, not ungodliness, was the spectre that stalked the land.

The Peterloo Massacre
On 16 August, workers demonstrated at St Peter's Fields, Manchester. Despite their peaceful behaviour, the militia were ordered to seize the speakers, but attacked the crowd, killing 11 and wounding 500.

Raffles of Singapore
To counter Dutch expansion in the East, Sir Thomas Stamford Raffles (1781-1826), was sent from Sumatra to establish a settlement on the southern tip of Malaya. In 1819, he raised the British flag on Singapore Island, and turned it into a flourishing free-trade port.

The technological achievements that so depressed the devout and the imaginative were a source of pride, as well as employment for the great majority of the population. In June, while labourers in London were laying the pipes for the world's first system of urban gas lighting, the steamship *Savannah* arrived in Liverpool from America, the first ship of its kind to cross the Atlantic. Immediately the newspapers were full of accounts of this marvel and of the enormous expansion of commercial prosperity it would make possible. But a similar ship burst its boiler a few weeks later, injuring several people.

From Paris came an even more alarming reminder of the hazards of the new technology. Madame Blanchard, an intrepid lady who had undertaken to let off fireworks from a balloon over the city, was killed when the balloon caught fire.

The birth of Victoria and Albert

Queen Victoria and her German Consort were in fact first cousins, born in the same year – 1819. They met in 1836, when Albert visited England, and Victoria proposed three years later. Albert realized his future was 'high and brilliant, but also plentifully strewn with thorns'. They married on 10 February 1840.

'A frightful brilliancy instantly struck terror into all the spectators, leaving no doubt of the deplorable fate of the aeronaut.'

WORKER'S UNREST

Meanwhile the textile industries of the midland and northern counties were hit by a severe slump and employers began to lay off workers and reduce wages. Thousands of weavers gathered on the sands at Carlisle, determined to resist the cuts, and the authorities responded by stationing a detachment of cavalry in the town. The press agreed that this decision was 'very proper', even though the weavers had done nothing unlawful. In the event, the soldiers were not needed because the employers

The Steamship 'Savannah'

In 1819 the American ship Savannah crossed the Atlantic from New York to Liverpool and the journey was claimed as the first steam-powered crossing. But the Savannah was really a sailing ship with an auxiliary engine – during the 25-day trip, she was under steam for only 80 hours.

gave in and restored wage levels. There was a strike of framework knitters in Leicestershire, with thousands of workers taking to the streets, and in Yorkshire the trades engaged in making blankets held mass demonstrations.

As this discontent became more widespread the official explanation, that it was all due to economic causes, became less and less convincing. It was absurd to pretend, the *Manchester Mercury* wrote angrily, that the trouble was simply the result of 'bad markets, want of trade with foreigners and such like'. It went much deeper: 'we are unsound in the vitals – there's the seat of the mischief – the constitution's become rotten to the core'. The answer was 'radical complete constitutional reform'.

A week later, on 16 August, an enormous crowd of 50-60,000 people gathered at St Peter's Fields in Manchester to hear the

celebrated radical speaker Henry Hunt demand just such a reform. The magistrates, terrified that the meeting might get out of hand, ordered the local constables and yeomanry to keep open a passage through the crowd to the platform where Hunt was speaking. When this unfortunately proved to be impossible, they then ordered the cavalry, which they had been holding in reserve, to charge the crowd.

THE MASSACRE OF PETERLOO

The result was appalling. Men, women and children were cut down, ridden over, crushed and mutilated. Eleven people were killed and many hundreds seriously wounded. As well as being tragic, the 'Massacre of Peterloo', as it became known, was also

Cleopatra's Needle
London's famous landmark was presented to Britain in 1819 by Egypt's Mohammed Ali, but only reached the capital in 1878, when it was erected on the Thames Embankment. The obelisk was originally made for the Pharaoh Thutmosis III at Heliopolis, around 1475 BC.

The first allotments
The Allotments Act of 1819 was designed to help poor villagers, deprived of access to the old common lands by the expansion of agriculture in England. Local councils were required to provide plots of ground where vegetables could be grown – and the idea was later applied in towns, for people without gardens.

National Maritime Museum, Greenwich

deeply divisive in its effects. Not only radical reformers but also many moderate men were deeply shocked. Conservatives, on the other hand, were delighted when the government congratulated the Manchester magistrates on their 'prompt, decisive and efficient measures'.

TROUBLE ON TYNESIDE

There was trouble on Tyneside in October when marines fired on strikers without the Riot Act having been read. There were cries of 'Manchester over again!' and 'Blood for blood!' Soldiers were marched into the north and field guns set up in Leeds and Newcastle. Urged on by lurid reports from their spies, the authorities convinced themselves that the mass demon-strations aimed not at reform but revolt. Ever since the French Revolution of 1789, successive governments had feared the spread of its contagion. Now fears reached fever pitch.

In fact the supposed revolutionaries were a good deal less feverish than the authorities. In London there was indeed a secret directory of 13 men planning to kill the members of the cabinet and take over the capital; but in the country as a whole there was no real danger of armed insurrection. A total of nine convictions in Lancashire for illegal manufacture of pikes constituted the only conceivable evidence of revolutionary intentions. For the most part the aspirations of the radicals were as idealistic as those of the visionaries. There was as much chance of the new Jerusalem being built in England as there was of the guillotine being set up there.

F.W. Burton/National Portrait Gallery, London

George Eliot (1819-80)
Despite her male pen-name, this great English novelist of the Victorian age was actually a woman – Mary Anne Evans. She held very liberal views and for 24 years lived openly with the journalist George Lewes, who was estranged from his wife. Her most famous novels were The Mill on the Floss *(1860),* Silas Marner *(1861) and* Middlemarch *(1872). After Lewes' death, she married a banker in 1880, but died the same year.*

The Mansell Collection

Madame Blanchard's balloon
Madame Blanchard, the wife of an early pioneer of ballooning and parachuting, was a keen balloonist herself. In 1819 she made her last, fatal ascent over the city of Paris – setting light to a firework while airborne, she unfortunately set her balloon on fire.

Caroline Bardua: Caspar David Friedrich (1811)/Staatliche Kunstsammlungen, Dessau

1774-1840

The greatest of the German Romantic artists, Caspar David Friedrich devoted his life to landscape painting, creating mysterious and compelling images of remarkable spiritual intensity. A serious, melancholy figure, whose forbidding appearance was softened by a childlike simplicity, he was only truly content when contemplating the rugged landscapes of his Pomeranian homeland or the stunning German countryside.

Friedrich spent most of his life in Dresden, where he supported the German patriotic movement in the Wars of Liberation. He enjoyed moderate success as an artist, attracting the patronage of the Prussian and the Russian royal families, and made a successful marriage in his mid-forties. But after a major stroke in 1835 he was forced virtually to abandon oil painting. He died in 1840, a sad and broken man.

The Melancholy Romantic

A devout, introspective man, Friedrich spent much of his time alone in the countryside of his beloved Germany. But marriage at 44 to a young, gentle wife brought him unexpected domestic happiness.

Caspar David Friedrich was born on 5 September 1774 in the small town of Greifswald on the Baltic coast, the son of a candle-maker and soap-boiler. Friedrich's father, Adolf Gottlieb, was a fairly successful businessman, but more importantly he was a devout Protestant. And like many middle-class children in northern Germany at the time, Caspar David and his nine brothers and sisters experienced a strict, and almost spartan upbringing. This way of life had a lasting influence on the artist: years later, visitors would comment on the frugality of his home and studio.

It seems that Friedrich always had a natural tendency towards introspection and melancholia. This was intensified by a tragic series of deaths in his childhood: he lost his mother in 1781, when he was just seven years old, and two sisters – one in 1782 and another in 1791. But the most traumatic event was the death of his brother, who drowned while trying to save Friedrich himself in a skating accident. This seems to have added a sense of guilt to his grief, making the contemplation of death almost a duty for him. As he later put it: 'To live

Friedrich/Mutter Heiden/Private Collection

'Mother Heide'
Caspar David's mother died when he was seven years old. After her death, the kindly 'Mother Heide' was employed to keep house and look after the children.

A.G. Friedrich/Oskar Reinhart Foundation, Winterthur

The artist's father
Friedrich drew his father, wrapped up in winter clothes, during a visit home in 1801-2. Adolf's devout, frugal way of life had a lasting influence on him.

Ralph Kleinhempel

Kunsthalle, Hamburg

Friedrich at 27
(left) A sepia self-portrait shows the artist at the time he specialized in this technique. He portrays himself with the trappings of his trade: an eyeshade and a bottle of brown ink or water attached to the buttonhole of his coat.

Memories of home
(right) Friedrich based this imaginary view of a harbour in moonlight on his childhood home of Greifswald. The image of silhouetted ships on still water held a lifelong fascination for him.

Medieval ruins
The ruined Cistercian abbey of Eldena just outside Greifswald provided Friedrich with a picturesque motif which he used again and again in his paintings.

one day eternally, one must give oneself over to death many times.'

The fact that Friedrich's preoccupation with religion and death led him to devote his life to landscape painting makes him very much a child of his time. Possibly the works of a local poet, L.T. Kosegarten, first turned his thoughts in this particular direction. For Kosegarten, who was an admirer of such English nature poets as Thomas Gray, was a pastor as well as a poet, and found religious inspiration in the contemplation of nature, which he referred to as 'Christ's bible'.

PICTURESQUE LANDSCAPES

Caspar David's first art teacher, Johann Gottfried Quistorp, was a friend of Kosegarten. He seems to have nurtured his young pupil's poetic sentiments, but may also have had a more practical purpose in mind when he encouraged Friedrich's specialization in landscape painting. For the vogue for nature poetry had stimulated the public taste for paintings of the countryside – in particular for picturesque views with primeval or medieval associations. And such views were in rich supply for the young painter: indeed, he was surrounded by them in the remote north German province of Pomerania where he lived. There were many signs of pre-historic settlements in the area, particularly

the huge dolmens known as 'Giant's Graves' on the island of Rügen, just off the Baltic coast. The ruined medieval abbey of Eldena a few miles from Greifswald also inspired him.

When he was 20, Friedrich left his home town and travelled to the Danish capital, Copenhagen, to study art. The academy there was the most celebrated in northern Europe, and Friedrich came into contact with the severe Neo-Classical style prevalent at that time. Like all other students, he set about studying the human figure, but was also strongly influenced by the work of one of his teachers, Jens Juel, who often painted local views full of mood and with sentimental associations. Friedrich felt at odds with the strict, academic

Bildarchiv Jürgens/Ost + Europa-Photo

Key Dates

1774 born in Greifswald, on north German coast

1781 mother dies

1787 brother drowns while trying to save Friedrich's life

1794-8 studies art at Copenhagen Academy

1798 settles in Dresden

1803 possible suicide attempt

1805 awarded joint first prize by Goethe for two sepias at Weimar exhibition

1808 exhibits *Cross in the Mountains*

1810 *Abbey in the Oakwoods* bought by Crown Prince of Prussia. Elected member of Berlin Academy

1818 marries Caroline Bommer; visits Greifswald and Rügen

1825 suffers stroke

1835 suffers further severe stroke

1840 dies in Dresden

The cliffs of Rügen
Friedrich made several visits to this starkly beautiful island off the Pomeranian coast, and was inspired by its sheer, chalk cliffs and rocky shoreline.

Bildarchiv Jürgens/Ost + Europa-Photo

approach to art which he encountered at Copenhagen, and later wrote: 'All the teaching and instructing kill man's spiritual nature.'

In 1798, after a brief stay in Berlin, Friedrich went to live in Dresden, which was to remain his base for the rest of his life. The Saxon capital was one of the main art centres of Germany, with a fine collection of Old Masters and a flourishing community of artists and intellectuals. He only ever left the city to visit his relatives back in his native Pomerania, and to make journeys in northern and central Germany to gather material for his landscapes.

At first Friedrich's existence was harsh, but although he lived a somewhat secluded life, the letters written during his first years in Dresden indicate that this was a relatively happy time. Until his name became known in the city, he made his living in various ways: he was employed as a drawing master and even resorted to acting as a guide for tourists. Gradually, he built up a reputation for views of the wild areas of his homeland.

Archiv für Kunst und Geschichte

Staring eyes
(left) Friedrich created this disturbing self-portrait when he was 37. Its most distinctive features are his staring eyes and the long side-burns, which he may have grown to hide the scar resulting from a suicide attempt in 1803.

The poet Goethe
(right) In 1805, Germany's leading poet Johann von Goethe gave Friedrich first prize in the Weimar art exhibition. Though he admired Friedrich's skill, Goethe did not approve of his subject matter.

Nationalgalerie, West Berlin

The move to Dresden was critical to Friedrich, for he arrived around the time when the city was becoming the centre of an influential group of writers and critics known as the 'Dresden Romantics'. Rejecting the dry rationality of the Classical age, they turned instead to an exploration of the exotic, irrational and mystical aspects of experience. One of the major figures of the group, the critic Friedrich Schlegel, was the first to use the word Romantic to describe the dynamic spirituality of the 'modern age'. And though Friedrich had little contact with the leading members of the group, he had friends among their circle, and quickly absorbed their ideas.

ATTEMPTED SUICIDE

It was around 1800 that the artist first began to introduce the mystical and dramatic themes expounded by the Dresden Romantics into his pictures. But there may have also been personal reasons behind this change in his art. Around 1803 he went through an acute period of introspection and depression, and is reported to have tried to kill himself by cutting his throat. There is even a tradition that he grew his beard in order to hide the resulting scar. It is certainly true that Friedrich cultivated a monk-like appearance after this date, acquiring a reputation as an isolated eccentric.

Despite this traumatic incident, the period

Deutsche Fototek

Staatliche Kunstsammlungen, Dresden

The Cross in the Mountains (1808)
This stunning altarpiece stirred up a great controversy when Friedrich exhibited it in 1808. The idea of a devotional landscape painting was an anathema to many of his contemporaries, and arguments between supporters and opponents of the painting raged in the newspapers for over two years. Friedrich's most vehement critic, Freiherr von Ramdohr, thought it a 'veritable presumption, if landscape painting were to sneak into the church and creep on to the altar'.

marks the beginning of his success as an artist. Over the next 10 years Friedrich was to become celebrated throughout Germany, and was patronized by such influential leaders as the Prussian Royal Family and the Duke of Weimar.

An important moment came in 1805 when he shared first prize for the sepias (paintings in a monochrome brown wash) that he sent to the annual exhibition in Weimar. The prize was awarded by the Weimar Friends of Art – in effect, the poet Johann Wolfgang von Goethe and his friend the painter Heinrich Meyer. Goethe was the most celebrated poet and leading cultural figure in Germany at that time and had established an annual art competition in Weimar in the hope of raising pictorial standards. Since his own artistic tastes were classical, it was a rare departure to award a prize for landscape paintings.

Friedrich's growing reputation seems to have encouraged him to move from sepia to the more challenging technique of oil painting. The results of this change can be seen most dramatically in his

J.H.W. Tischbein/Goethe in the Roman Campagna/Städelsches Kunstinstitut, Frankfurt-am-Main

Bildarchiv Preussische Kulturbesitz

Travels in the Mountains

Friedrich made many trips into the remote countryside of Germany, to commune with nature and collect motifs for his paintings. He restricted himself deliberately to his own homeland, and never left Germany after 1798.

Although he preferred to be alone on his travels, Friedrich occasionally made trips with fellow artists. In July 1810, he went on a sketching tour of the Riesengebirge – the 'Giant Mountains' to the south-east of Dresden – with his friend Georg Friedrich Kersting. The dramatic scenery impressed him greatly, and the journey provided him with images which he used in paintings up to 25 years later.

Bildagentur Jürgens/Ost + Europa-Photo

Archiv für Kunst und Geschichte

The travelling artist
This water-colour by Kersting shows Friedrich – his pack on his back – during their sketching tour of the mountains.

Spectacular scenery
The vast panoramic views of the Riesengebirge had a powerful impact on Friedrich's imagination.

The Struggle against Napoleon

Friedrich was an ardent patriot, and when Germany came under the domination of Napoleon in 1806, he was a firm supporter of the German struggle to expel the French from his fatherland. Even before the outbreak of the Wars of Liberation in 1813, he belonged to a group of nationalist writers, philosophers and painters, which included his friend Georg Friedrich Kersting. Unlike Kersting, he took no active role in the fighting, but allied himself to the Freedom Fighters and celebrated their victory against Napoleon in the Battle of Leipzig with a symbolic painting of a French cavalryman about to be swallowed up by a German pine forest.

Photo: Jörg P. Anders

G.F. Kersting/Soldiers on Sentry Duty/Nationalgalerie, West Berlin

Bulloz

The Battle of Dresden
(left) The Battle of Dresden in August 1813 was the last of Napoleon's victories in Germany. Two months later, he was defeated at Leipzig.

Freedom fighters
(above) Three nationalists pose in their resistance uniforms. Friedrich expressed his allegiance to the cause by wearing such a costume.

Photo: Jörg P. Anders

Nationalgalerie, West Berlin

highly controversial picture, *The Cross in the Mountains* (p.78). Completed in 1808, it shows a silhouette of a mountain top with a cross on it. Contemporaries were astounded that the artist had chosen a 'view' to function as an altarpiece, but Friedrich even designed a special frame for it, with religious symbols to emphasize the point.

Although he was harshly criticized for this work, the notoriety it brought him appears to have done Friedrich more good than harm. In 1810, he enhanced his reputation further when he exhibited *Abbey in the Oakwoods* (pp.88-9), and its companion picture *Monk by the Sea*. The pictures were acquired by the Prussian Crown Prince, and Friedrich was made a member of the Berlin Academy.

Friedrich's success as a strange and extreme artist was closely related to the current vogue for the Romantics. Since 1806 Germany had been overrun by Napoleon, and Romanticism became a cultural rallying point, a patriotic means of emphasizing 'Germanness'. Its pure spirituality, naturalism and vigour were in stark contrast to the

Woman at the Window (1822)
Four years after his wedding, Friedrich painted this tender picture of his young wife Caroline at the window of their house in Dresden, overlooking the River Elbe.

Bildagentur Jürgens/Ost + Europa-Photo

'artificial posturings' of French art, and Friedrich – the wild man from the north – was an appropriate symbol for such a movement.

But the movement that enhanced Friedrich's reputation also helped bring about its decline. At a time when Germany was divided into a number of small states, Friedrich was among those patriots who sought unification of the country, as a means of bringing about a democratic society and ending the archaic rule of kings and dukes. But after the Napoleonic Wars, the traditional rulers were very much back in power, seeking to eradicate such radicalism. Friedrich became an increasingly isolated figure, regarded as out of date both for his ideas and for the eccentricity of his art.

A HAPPY MARRIAGE

However, this decline was a slow and gradual one. At first he made a good living from his art, and in 1816 was made a member of the Dresden Academy – a position that carried a small stipend. He felt sure enough of his position to get married in 1818.

Many friends remarked that Friedrich's life-style was little altered by the acquisition of a quiet and unassuming partner. He was 44, and his wife Caroline was less than half his age. But there is a new tone of happiness in his letters: 'It is indeed a droll thing having a wife,' he wrote. 'There is more eating, more drinking, more sleeping, more laughing, more bantering, more fooling around.' Deeply fond of children, Friedrich welcomed the arrival of his own two daughters and a son. And from this time, too, his art shows a greater interest in domestic scenes and daily events.

A royal patron
(left) Tsar Nicholas I of Russia bought many of Friedrich's paintings, largely through the encouragement of the artist's faithful friend, the Russian poet Vasili Zhukovsky. Royal patronage was particularly important at the end of Friedrich's life, when he was ill and in dire financial straits.

Bildarchiv Preussischer Kulturbesitz

The city of Dresden
Friedrich made the Saxon capital of Dresden his home from 1798 until his death in 1840. He delighted in its fine art treasures, beautiful architecture and surrounding countryside, describing the city as 'the German Florence'.

Around this time, Friedrich was making new contacts among a younger generation of artists. His most enduring friendship was with the Norwegian artist Johann Christian Dahl, who arrived in Dresden in 1818. From 1823, Friedrich and Dahl lived in the same house, on the banks of the River Elbe.

For the younger generation, Dahl was the leader, and in 1824 it was Dahl, rather than Friedrich, who was appointed to the teaching post of Professor of Landscape at the Academy. Despite this, they remained friends – though there was a dark period when Friedrich suspected his wife of having an affair with his friend. The suspicions were without foundation, and are probably best explained as a consequence of the growing ill health that he endured in his last years.

In 1825 Friedrich suffered a stroke. This was followed by other attacks, the most severe being that of 1835, which left him greatly incapacitated. Yet this period was one of great artistic achievement. He developed a new sensitivity to colour and many of his finest and most poignant works – including *The Large Enclosure* and *The Stages of Life* (pp.96-7) come from this time.

This was also the period in which he wrote down most of his ideas on art. Though these mainly consisted of attacks upon the empty naturalism and vainglorious classicism of his contemporaries, there are also positive statements of his spiritual approach to art, including his most quoted remark: 'Close your bodily eye, so that you may see your picture first with the spiritual eye. Then bring to the light of day that which you have seen in the darkness so that it may react on others from the outside inwards.'

When Friedrich died in 1840 he was almost a forgotten figure. Not until the end of the 19th century – when symbolism came back into fashion – did his reputation begin to rise once more.

Landscapes of the Spirit

Friedrich transformed the landscape of his native Pomerania into a mystical world, infused with religious feeling. From precise studies of natural objects, he created strange, otherworldly images.

Caspar David Friedrich was the most important German painter of the Romantic era. He lived at a time when landscape painting took on a new significance, to become a means of celebrating the natural world and the divine power that created it. 'The Divine is everywhere', wrote Freidrich, 'even in a grain of sand.' And for him, the mystical experience of nature was such a central concern that he even painted a landscape for an altarpiece.

ART FROM THE INNER DARKNESS

Before beginning a picture, Friedrich advised an artist to 'close his bodily eye' and then bring to light what he saw in the inner darkness. Accounts of the artist in his studio suggest that he did, to some extent, put this into practice. As the painting by Georg Kersting shows (below), he had nothing but the barest essentials around him so that he would not be distracted from his contemplation. His friend Carus records that Friedrich would stand silently before his canvas until the image of a picture stood 'lifelike before his soul'. Then he would sketch it on to the blank canvas in thin outlines and proceed directly to the painting.

The idea that Friedrich worked entirely from the imagination is slightly exaggerated. It is evident

Artothek/Joachim Blauel

Staatliche Graphische Sammlungen, Munich

A grounding in sepia
(left) Before he began to paint in oils, Friedrich worked mainly in sepia ink. He produced small-scale works like the Wanderer at a Milestone *(1802), as well as ambitious landscape views.*

Spiritual imagery
(right) Friedrich often used natural elements as religious symbols. In Oak Tree in the Snow *(1829), the leafless tree is a symbol of death, but also of the hope of resurrection. The dead branch on the ground resembles the crucified Christ.*

Photo: Jörg P. Anders

Friedrich's studio
(left) Georg Kersting's picture of Friedrich in his Studio *(1812) shows the artist standing quietly before a canvas in his bare room. Friedrich felt that ornaments would distract him from his contemplation.*

Morning in the Riesengebirge (1810-11)
Friedrich painted this religious landscape on his return from a walking tour of the Riesengebirge mountains. He built up the composition from sketches he had made on the trip, as well as drawings he had made up to 10 years earlier.

that he consistently used sketches he had made for such individual features as rocks and trees in his pictures. However, he does seem to have used the contemplative method to arrive at his compositions. Despite the fact that his drawings have survived in great number, there are virtually no compositional sketches among them.

This reliance on the mental image emphasizes the visionary nature of Friedrich's work. However, he was not unique – the method was standard among painters of 'ideal' landscapes. What was unusual about Friedrich was that he used the process to arrive at images with powerful, almost hypnotic, impact – memorable images that would stick in the mind.

Early in his career he began to use contrast as a feature of his designs. A central image, like a tree, would be silhouetted against an indefinite background. And Friedrich chose evocative subjects: 'moonlight, sunset glow, the ocean, the

beach, snowy landscapes, churchyards, bleak moors, forest torrents, rocky valleys and the like.' Contemporaries were struck by the haunting, enigmatic quality of his work and searched his paintings for hidden meanings.

RELIGIOUS SYMBOLS

Friedrich often used his landscapes to convey religious ideas. In his description of the *Cross in the Mountains* altarpiece (p.78), for example, he wrote that the rock was a symbol of unshakeable faith, while the evergreen fir trees symbolized the eternal hope of mankind. But he also recognized that his paintings could be interpreted on another, naturalistic level. Describing one of his landscapes, he wrote: 'On a bare stony seashore there stands, raised on high, a cross – to those who see it as such, a consolation, to those who do not, simply a cross.'

For the detailed forms in his pictures, Friedrich

Charlottenburg Castle, West Berlin

Times of Day (1820/21)

(right) These evocations of Morning *and* Evening *are part of a four-picture series showing the 'Times of Day', which – like the four seasons – were traditionally seen as allegories of the stages of life. In* Morning, *a fisherman pushes his boat out through the mists into the deep waters of life. In* Evening, *the setting sun shines through the trees as a promise of eternity.*

Photo: Jörg P. Anders

Niedersächsisches Landesmuseum, Hanover

Niedersächsisches Landesmuseum, Hanover

Nationalgalerie, West Berlin

Man and Woman Gazing at the Moon (1830/35)
(right and below) In this intimate work, the dark moonlit landscape becomes the natural setting for spiritual contemplation. The couple stand together, by the rock of faith, looking at the waxing moon – a symbol of Christ. The ridge of evergreens beyond the dead tree symbolizes mankind's eternal hope of salvation.

Photo: Jörg P. Anders

drew freely on the sketches that he made on his many journeys through northern and central Germany. By and large it seems that these studies were made because the objects interested him, rather than because he had a particular composition in mind. For the most part they were of single objects or small groups – overall views are much rarer. Nor was he concerned about the original location of the forms he combined in his paintings. Rocks and fir trees from northern Bohemia would be incorporated with dolmens and oak trees from Pomerania, apparently without any qualms. It seems that his main concern was to achieve the most striking effect.

A PROBLEM WITH PEOPLE

When it came to putting people in his landscapes, Friedrich was never very happy painting the figures. In his early works, his friend Kersting sometimes drew the figures for him. Later, Friedrich almost invariably chose to show his figures in back view.

Friedrich only began to paint in oils after 10 years of working in water-colour and sepia. From the first he had thought of these media as the means of colouring or tinting drawings, and this habit affected his method of using oils. He painted very thinly, using small brushes. When painting in

Archiv für Kunst und Geschichte

Museum Folkwang, Essen

Woman in the Setting Sun (c.1818)
(above) In some of his more visionary works, Friedrich used a balanced, symmetrical composition. Here, a woman stands transfixed before the sinking sun, an image of God the Father. Like most of Friedrich's figures, she is shown with her back towards us.

Moonlit Landscapes

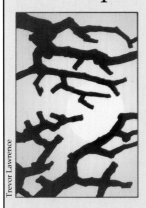

Trevor Lawrence

Friedrich often bathed his landscapes in bright moonlight, silhouetting natural forms, like a dying tree, against the pale sky. In the enigmatic evening light, these forms become charged with a deeper meaning.

Nationalgalerie, West Berlin

Devotional Paintings

When Friedrich designed the *Cross in the Mountains* (p.78) as an altarpiece, he was breaking one of art's most sacred conventions. Traditionally, a religious story or allegory had been told exclusively through the human drama. The figures were immediately recognizable by their attributes – from a simple halo to a palm branch – and the biblical narrative was made explicit through rhetorical gesture and expression. Even in Friedrich's time, it was felt that the imagery of landscape painting was too unfamiliar and obscure for devotional purposes.

Archiv für Kunst und Geschichte

Albrecht Dürer (1471-1528) The Adoration of the Trinity
(left) This altarpiece was commissioned by a Nuremberg merchant for the chapel of an almshouse. It shows the Holy Trinity surrounded by adoring saints and Old Testament prophets, with members of the laity and clergy below. The naturalistic landscape beneath them plays a very minor role in the composition.

Kunsthistorisches Museum, Vienna

Mathis Grünewald (1470/80-1528) The Resurrection
(right) In this panel from Grünewald's Isenheim Altarpiece *(1515) the biblical story is conveyed through a straight-forward, if bizarre, image. The resurrected Christ hovers above his tomb, displaying his wounds and the moon forms a radiant halo around his head. The simplified nocturnal landscape serves merely as a background setting for the supernatural drama.*

Giraudon

Musée d'Unterlinden, Colmar

sepia he had been in the habit of 'stippling' areas – covering them with minute dots, to give a sense of texture and vibrancy. In his early oils he used a similar method to convey the brilliance of sunlight or the shimmer of moonlight.

Over the years Friedrich gradually extended his range of colours and the breadth of his brush strokes. In the 1820s, he came under the influence of his friend J. C. Dahl, the Norwegian painter. Dahl was in the habit of using oil to make direct studies from nature and Friedrich followed suit on a number of occasions. His enchanting picture of his wife looking out of the window of his studio (p.80) was painted in this manner.

Friedrich appears to have abandoned this practice after 1824, but did not forget the lessons he had learnt. His last oil paintings are executed in a richer, thicker manner, and show an enhanced sense of colour. This is particularly true of works like *The Large Enclosure* and *The Stages of Life* (pp.96-7). In these, the purples, yellows and deep blues of the evening sky are conveyed by means of broad, smooth areas of paint.

Friedrich also continued to paint in water-colour and sepia throughout his life, but he tended to use these media more for topographical than for imaginative work. Only after his stroke in 1835 did he return to using sepia predominantly, painting images which are often meditations on death.

The Stages of Life

Friedrich probably painted *The Stages of Life* in 1835, shortly before his second major stroke. It shows the popular promenading point of Utkiek in Wieck, where the people of Greifswald often went to watch the ships as they approached Greifswald harbour. The five figures on the shore have been identified as Friedrich himself and members of his family. They are mirrored by five ships on the sea, sailing quietly towards the bay. Their mysterious silhouettes and the strange gestures of the figures suggest that this is more than just a memento of a family excursion. The picture has been interpreted as a metaphorical voyage through life, ending in death – 'the eternal resting place'.

Bridgeman Art Library

Fishing tackle
(above) Friedrich based this section of the painting on a sketch he had made in Greifswald, 17 years earlier. The long poles with red flags were used to mark the nets lying on the shore. It has been suggested that the hauled-in nets, like the overturned boat further along the beach, are symbols of mortality and death.

Archiv für Kunst und Geschichte

Russell Barnet

Greifswald Harbour
(left) Friedrich painted the harbour of his native town repeatedly, always using the same evocative imagery. He saw the harbour as a place of death, where skeletal ships found peace after their arduous voyages.

A Swedish birthplace
(above) The two small children in the picture are waving the Swedish flag, for Friedrich's Greifswald was originally part of Swedish Pomerania. In 1815, however, Swedish Pomerania was absorbed into Prussia.

A vivid sunset
(right) The ships are silhouetted against a poetic evening sky, streaked with violet and yellow, and with a glimpse of the sickle moon.

Early pencil sketches
(below) The studies of ships that Friedrich used for the painting date back to 1818. Years later, he has emphasized the mast's crucifix form.

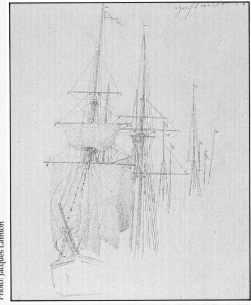

Museum der Bildenden Kunst, Leipzig

Photo: Jacques Lathion

Nasjonalgalleriet, Oslo

'The beauty of nature reminds our soul of life and of what is beyond it.'
Vasili Zhukovsky

The Four Stages of Life

Nick bantock

The figures in the picture represent the four stages of life – childhood, youth, maturity and old age. Friedrich's young children, Gustav Adolf and Agnes, play with a flag, watched by his eldest daughter, Emma. The man facing us is probably a nephew; the elderly man is Friedrich himself.

Gallery

Friedrich's landscapes are distinguished by their powerful mood and atmosphere, which give them a brooding significance. The early Abbey in the Oakwoods is a striking image of death, filled with religious allusions. Together with paintings like The Wanderer, it confirmed Friedrich's reputation for romantic, melancholy scenes.

Following his marriage, however, Friedrich's work acquired a new tenderness. Chalk Cliffs on Rügen is one of his happier pictures, and in the 1820s he became increasingly interested in a more direct and naturalistic approach to landscape. The Village Landscape in Morning Light and Moonrise over the Sea are quiet, contemplative images, while The Watzmann and The Arctic Shipwreck have a more impersonal grandeur.

In his later works, Friedrich's style became richer and more atmospheric. The Stages of Life – one of his most mysterious images – reveals a lasting preoccupation with the theme of mortality.

Abbey in the Oakwoods *1810*
43″ × 67½″ Schloss Charlottenburg, West Berlin

Throughout his life, Friedrich was obsessed with 'death, transience and the grave', as he put it. In this chill, sombre work, he shows a procession of monks carrying a coffin towards a desolate Gothic ruin, surrounded by barren oak trees. For Friedrich, the ruined structure symbolized the incompleteness of earthly existence, while the portal stood as a gateway to the spiritual life beyond.

Ralph Kleinhempel

Wanderer Looking over a Sea of Fog *c.1815*
38¾″ × 29½″ Kunsthalle, Hamburg

*Standing on a rocky cliff, Friedrich's 'wanderer' looks out over a
landscape shrouded in thick mists. Absorbed in thought, he
personifies Friedrich's overwhelming desire for solitude: 'I have to
stay alone in order to fully contemplate and feel nature', he wrote.*

Chalk Cliffs on Rügen *c.1819*
35¾" × 28¼" Oskar Reinhart Foundation, Winterthur

*In 1818, shortly after his marriage, Friedrich took his young wife on a
tour of his homeland and together with his favourite brother,
Christian, they visited the spectacular white cliffs of Rügen. Friedrich
painted this picture later, probably as a honeymoon memento.*

Village Landscape in Morning Light 1822
21³/₄″ × 28″ Nationalgalerie, West Berlin

This pastoral landscape was painted as a companion to Moonrise over the Sea (below). A shepherd rests against the trunk of a leafy oak while his flock graze peacefully in the fertile plains.

Photo: Jörg P. Anders

Moonrise over the Sea 1822
21¾″ × 28″ Nationalgalerie, West Berlin

In contrast to the 'worldly' Village Landscape, this haunting evening scene reveals the promise of a future spiritual existence. The moon is a symbol of mankind's consolation in Christ.

The Arctic Shipwreck 1824
38½″ × 51″ Kunsthalle, Hamburg

Friedrich's monumental vision of a ship being crushed by an iceberg may have been influenced by accounts of William Parry's polar expedition of 1819-20 in search of the Northwest Passage.

Photo: Jörg P. Anders

The Watzmann 1824-25
32¼" × 67" Nationalgalerie, West Berlin

Friedrich had never been to the Alps, so he based his painting of the Watzmann mountain on a water-colour by one of his pupils. A contemporary critic likened the effect to 'sublime church music'.

The Stages of Life *c.1835*
28½″ × 37″ Museum der bildenden
Künste, Leipzig

*This mysterious painting has been interpreted
as a premonition of death, for Friedrich
suffered a severe stroke in June 1835 and was
scarcely able to paint for the last five years of
his life. The artist appears in the painting
wearing a long, fur-trimmed cloak and
walking slowly and deliberately towards the
seashore. His dignified figure is echoed by a
ghostly ship, which has almost reached the
bay. Now nearing the end of its voyage, the
ship is a poignant symbol of man's passage
from birth to death.*

97

The Thrill of the Gothic

During Friedrich's lifetime, Gothic architecture was revived after centuries of neglect. With it came a new literary movement, exploring the imaginary Gothic world in tales of horror and suspense.

Friedrich's use of Gothic buildings in his paintings, to create a mood of elevated spirituality, is a striking feature of his art. The soaring arches and delicate tracery of Gothic architecture (the style that dominated most of Europe from the late 12th to the early 16th century) suggest the otherwordly aspirations of the Middle Ages. And the great medieval cathedrals still evoke awe as masterpieces of design, engineering and craftsmanship.

Such buildings, however, were not always thought of as the supreme works they are acknowledged to be today. During the 16th century, the architectural style of the Italian Renaissance – based on the buildings of ancient Rome – spread all over Europe, and the Gothic style went out of favour. Indeed the word 'Gothic' was originally coined as a term of abuse, implying – quite wrongly – that the style had something to do with the barbarian Goths of the Dark Ages. But in the mid-18th century the Gothic came back into fashion, not only in Germany, but all over Europe.

J.G. Eccardt/Sir Horace Walpole/National Portrait Gallery

Noble inspiration
(above) Horace Walpole, 4th Earl of Orford (1717-97), inspired the Gothic Revival in England. A pioneering figure in both architecture and literature, he was the son of Prime Minister Robert Walpole.

Piranesi's prisons
(right) The engravings of Giambattista Piranesi were eagerly bought by English visitors to Rome in the mid-18th century. His macabre views of 'imaginary prisons' have influenced the Gothic vision into the 20th century – inspiring sets for horror movies.

British Museum, London

The romance of ruins
(above) Friedrich was one of the first painters to appreciate the emotional and symbolic power of ruined buildings. He used crumbling Gothic abbeys to evoke feelings of mystery and melancholy, inspiring a mood of religious contemplation.

Caspar David Friedrich

Gothic grotesquery
The gargoyles and grotesque carvings that leer from the parapets of medieval churches sum up the cruder aspects of the Gothic spirit – in marked contrast to the sublimity of soaring arches and delicate tracery.

Strawberry Hill
(below) Horace Walpole's famous country house was built for show, with many plaster and papier-mâché adornments inspired by decorations in medieval churches. Atmosphere rather than authenticity was Walpole's aim, and he succeeded so triumphantly that a visiting French aristocrat removed his hat in one of the rooms, mistakenly assuming he was in a chapel.

C.D. Friedrich/Ruin at Eldena/Nationalgalerie, Staatliche Museen Preussischer Kulturbesitz, Berlin

In the early days of the 'Gothic Revival', literature played just as important a role as architecture, for the taste for the Gothic embraced not only the grandeur of medieval buildings, but also the sense of mystery they evoked. In Thomas Gray's *Elegy Written in a Country Churchyard* (1751), the poet ruminated on death with all the panoply of 'ivy-mantled tower' and 'mopeing owl'. This first Gothic poem touched a responsive nerve, a romantic yearning for sensation, which proved a fertile legacy for his successors.

It was appropriate that the Gothic Revival should originate in England, for there Gothic architecture had never entirely died out. Sir Christopher Wren, England's most famous architect, designed several buildings in the Gothic style. However, this Gothic survival was very different in spirit from Gothic Revival, which had new and diverse influences.

GHASTLY PRISONS

One of the most important came, somewhat surprisingly, from Italy, where the original Gothic had never taken root. The pioneer there of the Gothic vision was Giambattista Piranesi, whose engravings were immensely popular with English tourists. He was famous for his views of Roman remains, but also made an extraordinarily original series of engravings called *Carceri d'Invenzione* (Imaginary Prisons), depicting huge ghastly interiors in which tiny figures toil up endless staircases towards dark caverns suggestive of torture and unnamed horrors. Piranesi directly inspired two of the leading figures of the Gothic

Charles Wild/Fonthill Abbey/Victoria and Albert Museum

Henry Wallis/Chatterton/The Tate Gallery, London

Chris Barker

Fonthill Abbey
The English eccentric William Beckford built this strange Gothic country house, at great speed. The gigantic tower, 280 feet high, collapsed one night in 1825.

Revival in England: Horace Walpole, a writer, connoisseur and amateur architect; and William Beckford, a collector and eccentric man of letters.

In 1750, Walpole began alterations to his 'cottage', Strawberry Hill in Twickenham. The alterations turned into a major building project that took 20 years to complete – the first great monument of the Gothic Revival. The house still exists today, with its long, delicately-vaulted corridors, a monastic hall with tall, pointed windows and statues of saints lining the walls, and a baronial staircase peopled with suits of armour.

THE FIRST GOTHIC NOVEL

As well as being a landmark in architectural history, Strawberry Hill inspired a new literary genre – the 'Gothic novel', in which mystery and horror were essential ingredients. Walpole himself wrote the first Gothic novel, *The Castle of Otranto* (1764), as a result of a nightmare in which 'I thought myself in an ancient castle . . . and that on the uppermost bannister of a great staircase I saw a gigantic hand in armour'. The hand becomes that of an avenging angel known as the Knight of the Gigantic Sabre, and the story is as labyrinthine as the castle it describes.

Some 20 years after *Otranto*, William Beckford published *Vathek: An Arabian Tale* (1786), which like

François Gérard/Ossian/Musée du Château, Rueil-Malmaison

its predecessor owed a debt to Piranesi. 'I drew chasms, and subterranean hollows, the domain of fear and torture, with chains, racks, wheels, and dreadful engines in the style of Piranesi,' Beckford related. Vathek is a sadistic young caliph who sells his soul to Eblis, the devil, for illusory powers. It marks the beginning, in literary terms, of the Gothic of gargoyles – exotic, rather than medieval – a tradition culminating in Mary Shelley's *Frankenstein* (1818).

Beckford's architectural taste was equally bizarre. For his own private delectation, he had built one of the great architectural extravaganzas of the age – Fonthill Abbey in Wiltshire, a huge country house done up in ecclesiastical garb. At Beckford's insistence the vast structure was completed at insane speed, with up to 600 workmen toiling day and night by the light of huge bonfires, no matter how inclement the weather. But the great endeavour was doomed. On his deathbed the clerk of works confessed to Beckford that the specified foundations to the tower had not been provided, and one night in 1825 the tower collapsed. Beckford, who was informed of this in his London club, simply regretted that he had not been a witness to this spectacular event.

Among the other bizarre products of the Gothic Revival in England were two famous literary forgeries. Thomas Chatterton was a child genius

The Mysteries of Udolpho
Ann Radcliffe's novel (1794) was an early Gothic tale, with handsome villains and ghosts in armour.

The death of Chatterton
(above) Thomas Chatterton, a leading poet of the Gothic movement, poisoned himself in 1770, aged 17. This picture was painted in the attic where he died and shows some of his forgeries of medieval poems – torn into shreds.

Frankenstein
(right) Mary Shelley's novel (1818) was an archetypal Gothic horror story. It was the outcome of a friendly competition in which she and several friends – including Byron – each agreed to write a supernatural tale.

The songs of Ossian
(left) A series of poems allegedly written by a Gaelic bard named Ossian – but actually forged by James MacPherson – were acclaimed throughout Europe. This painting of the dreaming bard is a variant of one commissioned by Napoleon Bonaparte.

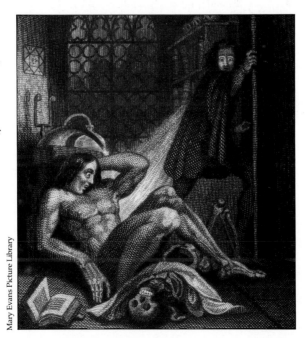

who fabricated medieval poetry under the pseudonym of Thomas Rowley, a 15th century monk from Bristol. In 1768 he began publishing his forged documents, but poverty and lack of recognition drove him to suicide two years later.

And while Chatterton was living his tragically short life, a young Scottish writer called James Macpherson had published several volumes purporting to be translations from a 3rd century Gaelic bard called Ossian. The authenticity of the poems was challenged in Macpherson's lifetime

and convincingly refuted after his death, but the fictitious Ossian nevertheless became a European cult figure, a kind of Homer of the North, and Macpherson's 'translations' were praised by figures as diverse as the Emperor Napoleon and Friedrich's own friend and admirer, Johann Wolfgang von Goethe.

THE GRAVEYARD PAINTER

Germany's most famous poet and playwright, Goethe was also a scientist and a talented amateur artist. His astonishingly broad interests and talents embraced architecture too, and in 1772 he wrote one of the most important books of the Gothic Revival, *Von Deutscher Baukunst* ('Concerning German Architecture'), in which he passionately extolled Strasbourg Cathedral. He even claimed that Gothic was German in origin (in fact it was French) and wrote of 'the deepest sense of truth and beauty in its proportion, growing out of the powerful, rugged German spirit'.

Friedrich himself was less concerned with nationalistic claims than with reviving the spiritual associations of Gothic. Although many of the literary and architectural expressions of the Gothic Revival were thoroughly secular, Friedrich realized that the original Gothic was the greatest visible expression of an age of faith. His paintings capture the sense of sublimity that fired his imagination and Gothic ruins become an exquisite metaphor for the transience of human life. If Gray is the great graveyard poet, Friedrich is the great graveyard painter.

A Year in the Life 1815

With Napoleon in exile on the island of Elba, 1815 promised to be a year of reconciliation. But while the victorious nations squabbled over the spoils at the international Congress of Vienna, the Emperor escaped, rallied his troops, and prepared for a new assault against the allies. The future of Europe would finally be decided on the bloody battlefield of Waterloo.

Escape from Elba

(above) On 27 February 1815, Napoleon set sail from Elba with 1,000 men to regain sovereignty of France. After landing near Cannes on 1 March, he marched towards Paris, taking a difficult route through the Rhone valley to avoid a confrontation with his enemies. His army swelled as soldiers sent to oppose him joined his ranks, and he entered Paris on 20 March to a rapturous welcome.

John Loudon Macadam

(right) The Scottish engineer John Macadam (1756-1836) developed the system of roadmaking known as 'macadamization'. Experiments in his own district of Ayrshire convinced him that roads should be built from crushed stone. In 1815, as surveyor general of Bristol roads, he began a well-organized overhaul of the highways, putting his theories into practice.

The nations of Europe looked forward to 1815 as a year of peace and reconstruction, an opportunity to heal the wounds left by nearly a quarter of a century of war. Napoleon Bonaparte, the French Emperor who had towered over the whole continent like a colossus, was in exile on the island of Elba.

THE CONGRESS OF VIENNA

The kings and princes who had defeated Napoleon, with their ministers and their marshals and their plenipotentiaries, were now gathered in a great international Congress in the Austrian capital of Vienna. They pledged to rebuild the old Europe, which had been shattered by the victories of the French.

But when the year opened, the Congress of Vienna was already deep in disarray as the rulers of Europe quarrelled among themselves. The kings and princes of Germany were especially divided and embittered, because the crucial final campaign against Napoleon had been fought across their lands and they had been forced into and out of alliance with the French. Now those who had been fortunate enough to leave the French side early sought their reward by laying claim to the territories of those who had left late.

One of the greediest of these claims, the Prussian demand for half of the kingdom of Saxony, affected Friedrich directly. Both his parents had come from Prussia and he had been born and brought up in Greifswald on the Baltic coast, previously Swedish but now also claimed by Prussia. But he had made Saxony his adopted home and he had worked tirelessly for her

The Corn Laws
(above) The Corn Laws were introduced in 1815, when renewed trade at the end of the Napoleonic wars brought unwelcome competition for British farmers. These laws, which forbade the import of wheat and other grain when the home price fell below 80 shillings a quarter, were aimed at maintaining high prices and protecting the landed interest, rather than ensuring steady prices or providing cheap bread. They deepened the divide between the rich and the poor.

The Battle of Waterloo
(above) On 18 June 1815, Napoleon launched his final, disastrous attack on Wellington's carefully chosen position near the hamlet of Waterloo. The battle lasted all day, as the French army made a series of unsuccessful attacks on the British lines. The desperate fighting finally ended towards evening: when the French retreated, pursued by cavalry, they left a bloody battleground with 45,000 killed and wounded.

liberation from the French. Now, like countless other German patriots, he found that liberation brought with it the pain of divided loyalty. Instead of giving Saxony freedom he had merely given her a new, Prussian, master.

THE EMPEROR ESCAPES

By the beginning of March the Congress was on the point of breakdown. Then, on 7 March, news reached Vienna of Napoleon Bonaparte's escape from Elba and landing in France. Within a matter of weeks the members of the Congress had patched up their quarrels and had decided on a new war against the usurper.

The King of Saxony, determined not to be caught out again,

issued a proclamation ordering the immediate arrest of anyone in his kingdom who showed any attachment to 'the usurper Bonaparte'. It did him little good. A month later he had to put out another proclamation, bidding farewell to nearly half of his subjects, whom the great powers had finally decided to transfer to Prussian rule.

Meanwhile, in Belgium, where German and British forces were gathering to do battle against Napoleon, there was serious trouble among Saxon troops. Those who came from the areas to be ceded to Prussia mutinied and marched angrily on the headquarters of Blücher, the Prussian commander. His sentries managed to prevent them from breaking into his room, but they continued to protest until at last they were put down by sheer force of numbers and their leaders shot.

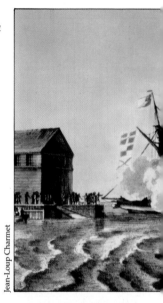

An opera for peace
(left) In 1815 the Prussian architect and painter Karl Friedrich Schinkel (1781-1841) was employed as a set designer by the Berlin Royal Theatre. In his first year he conceived a series of outstanding designs for Mozart's opera The Magic Flute, which was performed on 16 January 1816 to celebrate the restoration of peace.

Archiv für Kunst und Geschichte

Jean-Loup Charmet

Brighton Pavilion
(right) In 1815 the Royal Pavilion at Brighton in Sussex was being rebuilt in extravagant pseudo-oriental style by John Nash (1752-1835), the Prince Regent's Surveyor General. Onion-shaped domes, tent-like roofs and numerous pinnacles and small minarets were added to the original classical structure. The interior was finished with equally exotic Chinese decorations, considered scandalous by the country because of the enormous expense.

Adam Woolfitt/British Tourist Authority

The Duke of Wellington, the British commander, faced similar divisions within his army. On the very morning of the Battle of Waterloo, when he tried to stop some of the Nassau contingent from running away, they shot at him. If they had aimed better, he later observed drily, the history of Europe might have been different.

PATCHWORK ARMIES

The great powers of Europe claimed they were opposing Napoleon in the name of patriotism and nationalism – they had dubbed their earlier victory over him 'the Battle of the Nations'. But the truth was that their forces were made up of a patchwork of nationalities, in which men were ranged against one another, often against their own commanders, because of the squalid haggling that went on between their rulers.

By the beginning of June, Napoleon had consolidated his position as the ruler of France and commander of her armies. He was determined to give Wellington and Blücher the impression that he intended to remain on the defensive, awaiting their invasion of France. Having lulled them with deliberately planted false intelligence, he crossed into Belgium on the morning of 15 June with 125,000 men and took Charleroi, some 30 miles to the south of Brussels.

Next day he attacked Wellington at Quatre Bras and Blücher at Ligny. Wellington held out, but the Prussians were defeated with heavy losses, Blücher himself being unhorsed and almost captured. Napoleon was convinced that he had now driven a

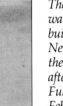

A steam warship
The first steam-powered warship – a floating fort built for the defence of New York harbour – was the USS Fulton, *named after the engineer Robert Fulton, who died on 24 February 1815, just two months after the ship was launched. With 30 cannons and a wooden hull 4½ feet thick it was the most advanced vessel of its time.*

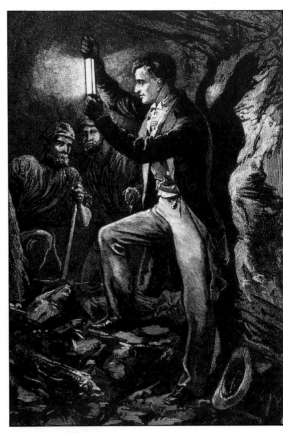

The miner's lamp
(above) Sir Humphry Davy (1778-1829) invented his safety lamp in 1815. Until this time mines were lit with naked flames and explosions were frequent, since the air often contained fire-damp – an inflammable natural gas which leaks from coal seams. Davy enclosed the flames of his oil lamp in a cylinder of fine wire gauze, which absorbed the heat of the flame before it could come into contact with the gas.

Lamarck's theory of evolution
(right) In 1815 the French biologist Jean Baptiste Lamarck (1744-1829) published the first volume of Histoire Naturelle des Animaux . . . *containing his theory of 'transformism'. He argued that animals developed new characteristics to meet their changing needs – and claimed, for example, that the giraffe had developed its long neck through constantly stretching to find food.*

Ann Ronan Picture Library

Ann Ronan Picture Library

wedge between his enemies, for he thought Blücher was fleeing eastwards away from Wellington. He therefore sent 33,000 men to chase Blücher while he dealt with Wellington.

It was a disastrous mistake. The Prussians were in fact falling back in good order, not eastwards but northwards, and they regrouped only 10 miles from Wellington's carefully chosen position near the hamlet of Waterloo. At 11.30 on the morning of Sunday 18 June, Napoleon, supremely confident of victory, launched his attack on that position.

Five hours later it was still intact and the Prussians were falling on his right flank. He decided to use his crack troops, the picked battalions of the Imperial Guard, not against Wellington's centre but against the Prussians. When he finally brought them back and threw them against Wellington it was too late. They broke, the British advanced on a broad front and carried all before them. It was the victory, the *Times* asserted, of 'the ancient order of society' over 'a system of rebellion'.

EXILE ON ST HELENA

Napoleon had already been branded as an outlaw by the Congress of Vienna, but he saw himself as a legitimate sovereign honourably defeated and he surrendered to the British, expecting to be given asylum. Instead he was taken to the lonely island of St Helena in the Atlantic, where he died six years later. Meanwhile, the victorious powers moved their troops into the territories they had awarded themselves. In the autumn Friedrich visited his birthplace, now part of Prussia.

Brazil's royal status
(left) A decree of 16 December 1815 gave the colony of Brazil equal status with Portugal within the United Kingdom of Portugal, Brazil and the Algarves. The Portuguese royal family had lived in Brazil since 1808, when they fled Napoleon's armies; this engraving commemorates the accession of King John VI and the marriage of the Prince Regent, Dom Pedro.

Jean-Loup Charmet

Napoleon's last journey
(right) Forced to abdicate on 22 June, Napoleon made his way to Rochefort, near Bordeaux, hoping to take a ship to America. There, finding his escape route barred by a British blockade, he surrendered to Captain Maitland of HMS Bellerophon. The British Government ordered his transfer to HMS Northumberland and exiled the Emperor to the lonely island of St Helena in the South Atlantic, where he died on 5 May 1821.

Peter Newark's Western Americana

Delacroix: Self-portrait/Louvre, Paris

Eug. Delacroix

1798-1863

Eugène Delacroix was the supreme artist of the French Romantic movement. According to popular rumour, he was the illegitimate son of the famous statesman Talleyrand, and as a young painter he received remarkable help from the State – almost as if someone powerful was secretly pulling strings. He moved in fashionable circles where he was in great demand, despite the fiery nature which smouldered beneath his charm.

For most of his distinguished career, Delacroix painted vast canvases for exhibition at the annual Salon. Their uncompromising subject matter often shocked the critics, but several of his paintings were purchased by the government. For the last three decades of his life, he devoted his energies to painting giant murals for ceremonial and religious buildings. He died at the age of 65, in self-imposed isolation.

107

A Tiger in the Salon

Eugène Delacroix had a dual personality: behind his charming exterior lurked an inner violence, revealed only in his paintings. Friends likened him – in his elegance and ferocity – to a tiger.

Ferdinand Victor Eugène Delacroix was born in the Parisian suburb of Charenton-Saint-Maurice on 26 April 1798. His mother, Victoire, came from an illustrious family of royal cabinet-makers, and her husband, Charles Delacroix, was a member of the revolutionary government, who had voted for the execution of Louis XVI in 1793. Charles had also been Minister of Foreign Affairs, but in 1797 he was demoted to become Ambassador of the French Republic in Holland. He was abroad when Eugène was born, and modern research has revealed doubts about the boy's true parentage.

Although Delacroix seems never to have been aware of them himself, rumours circulated that his real father was a far more powerful figure. For Charles had been replaced as Foreign Minister by Talleyrand, a friend of the family and one of the most brilliant statesmen of his time. And the great Talleyrand, it seems, not only took Charles

Key Dates

1798 born in Charenton-Saint-Maurice, Paris

1805 death of father

1814 death of mother

1816 enrols at Ecole des Beaux-Arts – is impressed by the work of Théodore Géricault

1822 *The Barque of Dante* causes sensation at the Salon. Begins keeping his journal

1824 *Massacre of Chios* exhibited at Salon

1825 visits England

1832 visits North Africa for six months

1833 begins first big state commission

1844 rents house near Fontainebleau; commutes to Paris

1857 elected to Académie des Beaux-Arts

1861 completes decorative scheme of chapel at St Sulpice

1863 dies in Paris

The artist at 20
Delacroix was uneasy about this revealing portrait which Théodore Géricault made of him in 1818: 'The wickedness of my expression almost frightens me', he said. The artist always sought to suppress his wild side.

Réunion des musées nationaux

J.L. David/Coronation of Napoleon/Louvre, Paris

Lauros-Giraudon

Musée des Beaux-Arts, Rouen

Delacroix's job, but also – for a while – his wife.

After his return from Holland, Charles was appointed Prefect of the Gironde region, and the family moved to Bordeaux. The provincial city was quiet compared with Paris, but Eugène's childhood was not uneventful. 'By the age of three', according to his novelist friend Alexandre Dumas, 'he had been hanged, burned, drowned, poisoned and choked.' Hanged when he caught his head in a horse's forage bag, burned when the mosquito net over his bed caught fire, drowned when the servant accidentally dropped him in the harbour of Bordeaux, poisoned when he ate some verdigris and choked when he swallowed a grape.

School-life in Bordeaux was rather less exciting. Delacroix had shown an aptitude for music and the town organist, who had known Mozart, encouraged him to become a violinist. But in 1805, when Eugène was seven years old, his father died, and a few months later the family moved back to Paris. Eugène entered the Lycée Impérial, where he did well without shining, and showed an enthusiasm for literature. Holidays were spent in

Bulloz

Delacroix/Elisabeth Salter/Private Collection

A powerful father
(above and left) Delacroix was born during Napoleon's rise to power, nominally the son of Charles Delacroix, a member of France's revolutionary government. But rumours suggested that his real father was a family friend – the brilliant statesman Charles Talleyrand, who was present at Napoleón's coronation in 1804. A detail from the commemorative painting shows the similarity of their features.

and Roman sculpture, and life drawing from the nude model. Careful drawing and morally uplifting subjects from ancient history or mythology were the order of the day.

But one of the students was a young man called Théodore Géricault, who was interested in a completely individual form of artistic expression. In 1818 Delacroix watched Géricault working on his huge, dramatic painting of a contemporary shipwreck, *The Raft of the Medusa* (p.116). He was so excited, he later recalled, that when he left Géricault's studio he 'started running like a madman', not stopping until he reached his room.

The results of this encounter were seen in 1822, when Delacroix completed his first major painting and offered it to the official Salon. At that time, success at the annual public art show was crucial to a young artist's career, and Delacroix went for broke, producing a very large painting of an

Teenage passion
In his teens, Delacroix became infatuated with his sister's English maid Elisabeth Salter, but his love-letters – in appalling English: 'O my lips are arid since had been cooled so deliciously' – failed to impress her.

Visits to the zoo
Delacroix often visited the Paris zoo, and wrote about its 'extraordinary animals' in his journal. The exotic beasts were a major source of inspiration for his paintings.

Normandy at an old Gothic abbey owned by a cousin, where the picturesque ruins made a powerful impression on him. He took up sketching and was encouraged by his uncle Henri Riesener, who was himself a talented painter. Together, they made occasional visits to the studio of Pierre-Narcisse Guérin, a leading academic painter and teacher.

In 1814, Delacroix's mother died, leaving him inconsolable. He immediately moved in with his sister, Henriette, but his problems increased when she embroiled the family in disastrously expensive legal proceedings, which impoverished them all. A year later, showing the determination that proved one of his most striking characteristics, he enrolled as an art student at Guérin's studio.

A CLASSICAL TRAINING

In 1816, Delacroix moved to the Ecole des Beaux-Arts, then dominated by Neo-Classicist painters, who encouraged a rigidly formal teaching programme of study from plaster-casts of Greek

Jean-Loup Charmet

unconventional subject, *The Barque of Dante* (pp.120-21), drawn from Dante's *Inferno* rather than the conventional myths of Greek heroes. It caused a sensation. Baron Gros, one of Napoleon's favourite painters, had it framed at his own expense and the picture was bought by the state and hung in the Luxembourg Palace galleries.

Delacroix left the Ecole des Beaux-Arts in triumph: 24 years old, bursting with ambition and confident in his own ability. He began to keep a journal, self-consciously forcing himself to examine his motives, experiences and ideas. He was now involved with the burning artistic debates of the day and was drawn towards the circle of 'Romantic' writers, who turned aside from academic tradition and correctness and sought truth in their personal emotional response to the world and human experience. Delacroix's second major Salon painting, *The Massacre of Chios* (p.122), reflected these new concerns, for it showed a bloody incident which had recently occurred in the Greek War of Independence. Gros now turned against his protégé and called his work 'the massacre of painting'. But Delacroix had his supporters too, and his importance among the younger generation of painters was now inescapable.

For the next few years Romanticism was in full flower and Delacroix was recognized as the movement's leading painter, although he consistently refused to accept that he was in any way the leader of a school. Nevertheless, for a time he threw himself into the social and artistic whirl,

Giraudon

The July Uprising
In July 1830, Parisians took to the streets in revolt against their monarch, Charles X, forcing his abdication. Delacroix watched the fighting, but took no active role.

Faithful servant
(right) For the last 30 years of his life, Delacroix was cared for, cosseted and controlled by his devoted housekeeper Jenny le Guillou. Fiercely possessive, she encouraged his increasing isolation from society.

Réunion des musées nationaux

Delacroix/Jenny Le Guillou/Louvre, Paris

The Moroccan Adventur

On New Year's Day 1832, Delacroix left Paris on the journey of a lifetime. A young diplomat, Count Charles de Mornay, was going on an ambassadorial visit to the Sultan of Morocco, and had invited him along to record the trip. The artist was overwhelmed by what he saw – his Oriental imaginings made real.

Six weeks in Tangier were followed by a 200-mile trek to the Sultan's Palace at Meknes, where the French party was given exotic gifts: a lion, a tiger, Arab stallions and gazelles. Delacroix later enjoyed the delights of the 'lovely human gazelles' in a harem in Algiers. The experiences of this six-month trip inspired him for the next 30 years.

ZEFA

The light of Tangier
(above) The bustling streets of Tangier were exhausting as well as exciting. Delacroix wrote that the blazing sun's reflections from the whitewashed walls 'tire me excessively'.

The Sultan's city
(right) Delacroix made numerous sketches during his trip. He filled seven notebooks with drawings and water-colours like these studies made around the walls at Meknes.

reading Byron's poems and applauding the performances of Shakespeare's *Hamlet* that thrilled Paris in 1827. In the audience with him, like as not, were the composer, Hector Berlioz, and the novelist Victor Hugo. Delacroix was friendly with Hugo for a while, producing the costume designs for his play *Amy Robsart*, but their friendship cooled within a few years. Hugo described Delacroix as 'a revolutionary in his studio' but 'a conservative in the drawing-rooms'.

Indeed, according to many contemporaries, Delacroix had a disturbingly dual nature. In the brilliant society in which he moved he was generally regarded as elegant, highly cultivated, witty, yet aloof. One writer reported that 'He was easy, velvety and winning, like one of those tigers

Romantic ruins
Delacroix spent many summers at Valmont, a magnificent estate belonging to his cousins in Normandy. Their manor house was attached to a ruined abbey, and it was in this picturesque setting that he began a love-affair with his cousin Joséphine which spanned three decades.

Jean-Loup Charmet

whose supple, formidable grace he excelled at rendering, and in the drawing rooms everybody used to say: "What a pity so charming a man should paint such pictures".' Yet behind the impeccable facade, 'the tiger' had a violent, passionate nature and a streak of savagery. The poet Charles Baudelaire described him as 'a volcanic crater artistically concealed beneath bouquets of flowers'.

Among Delacroix's acquaintances was the English painter Richard Parkes Bonington, whose use of clear, brilliant colour for depicting episodes from medieval history he greatly admired. Sir Walter Scott was one of his favourite authors: the British influence in general was strong. In 1825 Delacroix had spent a few months in England, visiting painters such as Sir Thomas Lawrence and David Wilkie. His journal describes an ecstatic boat trip on the Thames, drifting through the lush English countryside. The works of John Constable impressed him deeply, although not sufficiently for him to turn often to landscape as a subject.

THE SPIRIT OF ROMANTICISM

In 1827 Delacroix exhibited his third important Salon picture, which more than any other conveys the spirit of the Romantic movement in Paris. The idea for *The Death of Sardanapalus* (pp.124-5) came from one of Byron's poems, but the violence and voluptuous eroticism are all Delacroix's own. The critics were horrified and urged the young painter to take a grip on his talent and not squander it on such excesses. Even Delacroix was shocked by what the painting revealed of his own suppressed sensuality. He had always been appalled by any lack of restraint or control.

Perhaps Delacroix had become obsessed with his own sensual experiences. In his youth he had had a number of love affairs, notably with Elisabeth Salter, an English girl who was his sister's maid, and with his cousin Joséphine de Forget (an attachment which lasted nearly 30 years). But as he grew older, his relationships with women were more often earnest friendships, devoid of sex. Slowly, he became more solitary, more preoccupied with work. His health became a

Réunion des musées nationaux

tombeau de saint en descendant
Creneaux dentelés.

orange
mulatre

Louvre, Paris

A Lasting Friendship

When he was in his mid-40s, the normally solitary Delacroix developed a close friendship with one of the most illustrious couples in France – the composer Frédéric Chopin, and his mistress, the novelist George Sand. Chopin was unimpressed by Delacroix's painting, but the artist adored his music and had a piano installed in his Paris studio, so that Chopin could play whenever he dropped by.

Delacroix spent three summers with the couple at Sand's country home, amid a happy family atmosphere. He was particularly devoted to the composer and treated him as a younger brother – when Chopin died in 1849, Delacroix was devastated.

Delacroix/Frédéric Chopin/Louvre, Paris

Jean-Loup Charmet

Delacroix the dandy
Elegantly dressed, witty and charming, Delacroix was a popular figure in society drawing-rooms.

The artist's studio
Delacroix lived at this studio in Paris' Right Bank district for 12 years from 1845.

major problem. From as early as 1820 he had been subject to fevers that could lay him low for days, and throughout his life he suffered from bouts of laryngitis that could become quite serious and leave him weak and listless. For such an energetic man, he was small and frail, and bursts of hard work often had to be followed by periods of rest.

At the 1831 Salon he exhibited *Liberty Leading the People* (p.126), now his best-known picture, at least in France. He had painted it enthusiastically to glorify and commemorate the revolution of the previous year, which swept 'the citizen king' Louis Philippe to power. It was a huge success, and confirmed his pre-eminence among painters opposed to the insipid productions of the Ecole des Beaux-Arts and the severe classicism advocated by his rival Jean-Auguste-Dominique Ingres, the one truly great exponent of 'official' painting.

At this juncture, an extraordinary stroke of luck came Delacroix's way, one that was to transform

his art. Thanks to the influence of friends, he was chosen to accompany Count Charles de Mornay on an official visit to the Sultan of Morocco. In January 1832, the party set off for Tangier and Meknes, also visiting Spain and Algiers.

After years of sharing the Romantic love of all things oriental, Delacroix was bowled over. The brilliant light and rich colours of North Africa swept him away. He witnessed in person scenes that the Romantics had been conjuring up from their imaginations – fighting horses, fierce and noble warriors from the desert, women secluded in the harem, Dervishes whirling in the streets. He was struck even more forcibly by the simple dignity he found in Islam, which he compared to the heroism of the Greeks. 'In this short time,' he wrote, 'I have lived through 20 times as much as in months spent in Paris.' His vivid memories and his hundreds of notes and sketches were to provide inspiration for the rest of his career.

GOVERNMENT COMMISSIONS

On his return, the government began to shower Delacroix with monumental commissions. While he continued to paint smaller easel pictures with increasing facility and freedom, these major decorative schemes took up the greater part of his energies for the rest of his life. First he decorated the Salon du Roi in the Bourbon Palace, from 1833 to 1837. Then came nine years on the Library of the Bourbon Palace (1838-47) and seven years on the Library of the Luxembourg Palace (1840-7). From 1850 to 1851 he worked on the Galerie d'Apollon in the Louvre. Then came the Salon de la Paix in the Hôtel de Ville (Delacroix's murals were destroyed during the riots of the Commune in 1871) and lastly, from 1849 to 1861, the Chapelle des Saintes-Anges at the great church of Saint-Sulpice.

It would be hard to exaggerate the magnitude of the tasks he set himself, working for months at a stretch to cover huge areas of wall and ceiling, working on preparatory designs, doing endless sketches, and marshalling assistants. A friend

Jean-Loup Charmet

Chopin and Sand
(left and right) Delacroix met Chopin through his mistress George Sand, a prolific, unconventional novelist with a legendary penchant for smoking cigars and wearing men's clothing. Chopin and Sand's affair lasted nine years: as the composer grew weaker with tuberculosis, Sand grew tired of him. The couple parted in 1847, two years before Chopin's death.

Delacroix/George Sand

wrote: 'To conceive of what such labour was like, you had to have seen him at the end of the day . . . pale, tired out, hardly able to talk, dragging himself along as if he'd just escaped from torture.' And while this was going on, he was patiently writing his journal, contributing numerous articles to papers and magazines, working on an unpublished dictionary of the arts, and painting literally hundreds of smaller pictures largely drawn from his North African travels.

As a distraction, Delacroix would attend the private salons of rich patrons of the arts in the mornings, where his wit and intelligence were in great demand. It was said that he had 20 different intonations for a simple polite greeting, ranging from the genuinely cordial to the openly contemptuous. He had only a handful of real friends – among them the formidable woman novelist George Sand and her lover, the composer Chopin – but his enemies kept clear.

A JEALOUS GUARDIAN

As he reached middle age, Delacroix was seen less and less in society. His work demanded too much time. His trusted housekeeper, a Breton peasant woman called Jenny le Guillou, guarded him jealously in increasing seclusion. And from 1844 he rented a house at Champrosay in the forest near Fontainebleau, to recover from the illness and exhaustion that resulted from his labours. From here he commuted to his Paris studio in the Rue Notre-Dame-de-Lorette.

In 1855, when the artist was well into his fifties, a major retrospective exhibition of his paintings won considerable acclaim. Delacroix was awarded the Grande Médaille d'Honneur and created Commander of the Légion d'Honneur. In 1857 he was elected a member of the Académie des Beaux-Arts, a major honour. Then, in 1859, he sent his last pictures to the Salon. They were foolishly attacked by critics and Delacroix resolved to have no more to do with the public exhibition that had been the stage for so much of his early output.

Delacroix now moved to an apartment in Paris, though he still spent a good deal of his time in the country. Hardly anyone seemed to notice when, after a few rare months of good health, he completed the paintings in Saint-Sulpice. He retired to Champrosay bitterly disappointed, his life almost over. Death came on 13 August 1863, in his Paris apartment, after a final bout of the recurring throat complaint.

Murals for a church
(left) Delacroix devoted the second half of his life to painting monumental decorative schemes in the churches and government buildings of Paris. The dramatic murals at Saint-Sulpice were his crowning achievement.

The Expulsion of Heliodorus from the Temple

Boldness and Colour

A true Romantic, Delacroix favoured themes of violence, passion and bloodshed. He approached his subjects with startling boldness, electrifying them with the brilliance of his colours.

In his will, Delacroix left a few paintings to relatives and friends, but asked for the great majority of his works to be sold. When the executors arrived, they made a staggering discovery: the artist's studio contained no fewer than 9,140 separate items. There were 853 paintings, 1,525 pastels, 6,629 drawings and an assortment of engravings, lithographs and sketchbooks. This demonstrates not only what an energetic and productive man Delacroix was, but also how important drawing was to his working method. For every full-scale picture, there might be hundreds of preparatory studies.

Delacroix learned to work this way at the Ecole des Beaux-Arts, where he was trained in the academic method. In part, his teaching consisted of close study of Greek and Roman art, together with the paintings of the Old Masters, particularly Michelangelo and Raphael from the High Renaissance and Poussin and Rubens from the 17th century. By the time he came to work on his

Réunion des musées nationaux

Louvre, Paris

The Giaour and the Pasha (1827)
(below) Some of Delacroix's most exciting works were inspired by the writings of Byron. His favourite was The Giaour – *a dashing tale about a Venetian warrior and his love for the Pasha's concubine.*

Pastel sketches
(above) The exquisite sketches for The Death of Sardanapalus *(pp.124-5) show how important preliminary studies were to Delacroix's working method. He made many drawings for this painting.*

Art Institute of Chicago

Delacroix/The Lion Hunt/Musée des Beaux-Arts, Bordeaux

own large-scale pictures, he had a thorough knowledge of what had gone before, so that he could both draw on the art of the past and also emulate its grandest achievements. Essentially, Delacroix was trained to be a studio painter. While he might keenly observe what he saw in the countryside or city streets, a painting was something to be constructed from the imagination in a studio. Outdoor landscapes, for example, played almost no part in his working method.

WORK IN PROGRESS

When working on one of his Salon pictures, he would first sketch the general composition as it appeared in the mind's eye, perhaps varying the viewpoint or the positions of particular figures. When satisfied with his overall scheme, he would hire professional models and sketch them in the poses of his figures. Then he would concentrate on details, drawing a foot, a sword-hilt or a horse's head. His sketches were put down on paper very quickly – late in his life, he wrote: 'If you are not skilful enough to sketch a man falling out of a window during the time it takes him to get from the fifth storey to the ground, then you will never be able to produce monumental work.'

As colour came to be of prime importance in Delacroix's art, he would use pastels for some of the more developed drawings. Oil sketches would follow, perhaps a rough tone and colour scheme

Réunion des musées nationaux

Louvre, Paris

Dramatic water-colours
(above) Delacroix's early water-colours demonstrate his mastery of tonal effects. In Horse Attacked by a Tiger *(1825), the violence of the conflict is intensified by the skilful modulation of light and shade across the muscular bodies of the animals.*

Lion Hunt (1855)
(detail left) Following the example of the great Flemish master Rubens, Delacroix painted several pictures of lion hunts. In these, he transformed the studies of caged animals he had made in the zoo into fantastic compositions of wild lions engaged in ferocious combat. 'I have no love of reasonable painting', he once wrote. 'There is in me some black depth which must be appeased.'

The Triumph of Apollo/Musées Royaux des Beaux-Arts de Belgique, Brussels

Grand designs
(above) Delacroix devoted much of his career to painting large decorative schemes. This is a working sketch for the ceiling of the Galerie d'Apollon (1850-1).

115

Moments of Drama

The dramatic canvases of Rubens and Géricault, which focus on moments of extreme tension, produced in Delacroix the thrill he demanded from great painting. The wild disorder of Rubens' animal hunts stimulated his imagination: 'He overpowers you with all his liberty and boldness', he wrote. Géricault's *Raft of the Medusa* showed that the same intensity could be wrung from contemporary events: in this case, a shipwreck provided the sensational subject matter.

Artothek

Alte Pinakothek, Munich

Giraudon

Peter Paul Rubens (1577-1640)
The Hippopotamus Hunt
Rubens has decided to show the climax of the hunt, when the horsemen, with their spears raised, are about to kill the hippopotamus.

Théodore Géricault (1791-1824)
The Raft of the Medusa
Géricault painted the survivors at a moment of cruel, false hope. In fact, the ship they had sighted failed to notice them.

for the whole composition, perhaps more finished studies of particular figures. Throughout the months of work, he would go off to the galleries to discover solutions to the particular problems of the moment. The drops of water on the monsters in *The Barque of Dante* (pp.120-21), for example, troubled him and he found the solution by looking at Rubens' painting and splitting the drops into tiny dabs of yellow, white, red and green.

While the careful construction of his compositions reflected the training he had received, Delacroix completely rejected the Neo-Classical style favoured by less adventurous contemporaries. Although he resisted the labels of the critics, he was a Romantic, seeking truth to nature in the free play of his imagination and emotions. He believed that painting should convey not just the nobility, heroism and grand tragedy of Classical mythology, but also express fear, melancholy, passion and eroticism – every facet of heightened emotional experience.

Accordingly, Delacroix turned to the new subject matter of the Romantic movement. Orientalism was one aspect, and he sketched eastern costumes and weapons in a friend's collection. Music and poetry also inspired him. He made friends with Chopin and arranged for the composer to play for him in his studio, while in his

Réunion des musées nationaux

Louvre, Paris

Louvre, Paris

Intense Colours

Delacroix increased the intensity of his paintings by placing primary colours side by side with their 'complementaries'. Each of the three primary colours – red, blue and yellow – has a complementary colour, created by a mixture of the other two. So, for example, green (formed by a mixture of blue and yellow) is the complementary of red, and reveals its true vibrancy.

As Delacroix's colour triangle shows, the complementaries of red, blue and yellow are green, orange and violet.

Women of Algiers (1834)

(left and below) In this beautiful harem scene, Delacroix used primary and complementary colours to create a vibrant colour harmony. In the turban of the negro woman, for example, a brilliant strand of green brings out the intensity of the red in the material. Even in small details like her necklace, red and green beads alternate.

shadows to make the highlights of his flesh tones stand forward. His experience of the light and colour of Morocco encouraged him in this direction, and at about the same time he came across the theoretical writings of the chemist Eugène Chevreul, who observed that pure colours actually create in the eye an illusion that they are surrounded by their complementary – yellow by violet, blue by orange, red by green.

Delacroix's writings show him to have been deeply thoughtful about the theories of art, searching for intellectual solutions that would reveal his vision on canvas. But his approach is best summed up by a more personal dictum: 'One must be bold to extremity; without daring, and even extreme daring, there is no beauty.'

journal he wrote: 'To fire your imagination always remember certain passages from Byron.' The zoo also provided him with ideas and he often went there to study the wild animals. In short, when Delacroix needed the emotional charge that inspired him, he would go out and seek it.

THE POWER OF COLOUR

Colour was his single greatest obsession. For Delacroix it held far greater possibilities than the accurate draughtsmanship taught by the academies, and was the means through which he expressed the full magnificence of his vision. He first discovered the power of colour relationships while working on *The Execution of Doge Marino Faliero* (p.123). Frustrated because the gold cloaks would not glimmer warmly, he resolved to go to the Louvre to examine Rubens, just as he had done earlier when working on *The Barque of Dante*. Getting into a cab, Delacroix saw a shaft of sunlight lighting up the gravel underfoot, casting violet shadows. Suddenly the yellow of the cab glowed with greater intensity. At once he realised that by juxtaposing complementary colours, their richness would be intensified.

Increasingly, Delacroix left black out of his palette, relying on reflected violet and green in the

THE MAKING OF A MASTERPIECE

The Massacre of Chios

In April and May 1822, during the Greek War of Independence, 20,000 Greeks were butchered by the Turks on the small island of Chios. The following year, Delacroix decided to paint a picture of the atrocity, sensing a chance 'to distinguish oneself'.

With characteristic energy, he began by questioning an eye-witness, sketching oriental costumes and making numerous preliminary studies. He even had a friend send him some water-colours from Naples so that he could capture the brilliance of the Mediterranean light. In 1824, the painting was ready for the Salon. But after seeing some works by the English artist John Constable, Delacroix completely repainted the background, adding sparkles of pure colour to the landscape. The finished picture had a mixed reception at the Salon, but was bought by the French government for 6,000 francs.

Louvre, Paris

Greek models
(below) Delacroix made a number of detailed oil studies for the figures in the painting, including this fine portrait of an orphan girl in a cemetery. He hired native Greek models, who were then in great demand in the Paris studios.

Persian influence
(above right) This water-colour sketch for the overall composition was influenced by the decorative shapes and delicate colouring of Persian miniatures. Delacroix copied several examples in his sketch-books, so that he could easily refer to them.

Delacroix/Orphan in a Cemetery/Louvre, Paris

Louvre, Paris

Turkish costumes
(left) Before he painted this magnificent Turkish horseman, Delacroix studied and sketched Turkish costumes and weaponry. A painter friend, Jules Robert Auguste, who had amassed a collection of eastern clothing and artifacts in his Paris house, allowed Delacroix to borrow any items he needed.

Passive victims
(right) Contemporary critics were disturbed by the exhaustion and lethargy of the defeated Greeks in the painting. The novelist Stendhal thought Delacroix had made the massacre seem more like a plague.

Reports abroad
(right) European papers widely reported the atrocities at Chios (then known as Scio) and condemned the 'brutal cruelty' of the Turks.

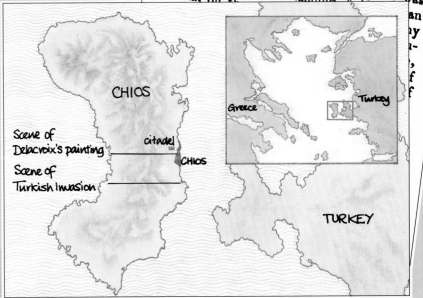

TURKEY.

The Turkish Government, availing itself of its naval superiority, has commenced the reduction of the Greek Islands in a spirit of brutal cruelty which rivals any thing to be found in the detestable records of that barbarous empire. The work of slaughter was begun at Scio, by the landing of Pacha, on th...

The scene of the massacre
(above and right) Chios lies much closer to Turkey than the Greek mainland, and before the War of Independence, the islanders enjoyed special privileges within the Turkish Empire. In 1822, the Chiotes had even refused to rise against their Turkish rulers, but when Greek nationalist forces invaded the island, the unfortunate Chiotes were declared rebels. Bands of Turkish volunteers poured across the narrow straits in small boats, to exact their terrible revenge. Delacroix shows the harbour where they landed and, in the detail above, the town of Chios with its surrounding plains.

Russell Barnet

> 'A terrifying hymn in honour of doom and irremediable suffering'
>
> Charles Baudelaire

Gallery

Delacroix's bold approach to painting was a constant challenge to establishment critics. The Barque of Dante, his first major work, won great acclaim at the 1822 Salon, when Baron Gros hailed it as 'a subdued Rubens'. Two years later, Gros denounced the topical Massacre of Chios as 'The Massacre of Painting'. But for Delacroix this picture marked an exciting new departure. By the time he produced The Execution of Doge Marino Faliero, he was using rich glazes in bold colour patterns. This picture always remained one of his personal favourites.

In 1828, the tumultuous Death of Sardanapalus was greeted by the critics with howls of derision. Delacroix was warned that if he carried on painting in this fashion he could expect no more official commissions. But the rift was repaired when Liberty Leading the People – a rousing scene on the barricades – was bought by the new government of Louis Philippe.

In 1832, Delacroix visited Morocco and his vivid memories of the trip, backed up by copious notes and sketches, provided him with inspiration throughout the rest of his career. For the 1841 Salon, he painted a Jewish wedding he had seen in Tangier, and he returned to North African themes again and again towards the end of his life.

The Barque of Dante *1822*
74½" × 97" Louvre, Paris

For his debut at the Salon, Delacroix painted a scene from Dante's Inferno. Here the poets Dante (in the red cap) and Virgil (in the cloak) are being ferried across the murky lake surrounding the infernal city of Dis. Condemned souls writhe in the waters beneath the boat, and in the distance the fiery city glows red against the dark sky. The muscular poses of the figures are taken from Michelangelo, Rubens and classical sculpture, but the direct inspiration for this sombre masterpiece came from Géricault's painting The Raft of the Medusa *(p.116).*

Lauros-Giraudon

The Massacre of Chios 1824
164″ × 139″ Louvre, Paris

*In September 1821, Delacroix told a friend that he wanted to paint a
subject from 'the recent war between the Turks and the Greeks'. Two
years later, he decided to show one of its most horrifying episodes. The
Greek victims are ranged starkly across the front of the picture, almost
as if they have been superimposed on the landscape.*

The Execution of Doge Marino Faliero *1826*
57″ × 45″ Wallace Collection, London

The elderly Doge Marino Faliero was executed on the giant staircase of the Ducal Palace, Venice for his part in a conspiracy to overthrow the republic. Delacroix knew the story from one of Byron's plays. He was fascinated by the medieval setting and the opulence of the Venetian costumes.

The Death of Sardanapalus *1827*
145″ × 195″ Louvre, Paris

*Delacroix's sumptuous painting is loosely based on
Byron's play,* Sardanapalus, *published in 1821. In
the play, the noble Assyrian king, besieged in his
palace, decides to die on his own funeral pyre and is
joined in the flames by his most devoted concubine. But
in Delacroix's version, Sardanapalus orders his officers
and eunuchs to slaughter all the women of his harem,
together with his pages and even his favourite horses.*

*'None of the objects that have contributed to his
pleasure must survive him', wrote Delacroix in the
Salon catalogue. In place of the king's heroic suicide, he
presents us with an orgy of violence and eroticism. As
the smoke rises, the king reclines on his death-bed,
strangely indifferent to the chaos and bloodshed.*

Réunion des Musées Nationaux

Liberty Leading the People 1830
102″ × 128″ Louvre, Paris

This picture was inspired by the July Revolution of 1830. Delacroix had not taken part in the fighting and felt that the least he could do was 'paint for his country'. The red, white and blue of the French national flag dominate the composition.

The Jewish Wedding 1837–41
41¼" × 55¼" Louvre, Paris

In 1832, when he was staying in Tangier, Delacroix attended a Jewish wedding. His host allowed him to make water-colour sketches of everything he saw, and several years later Delacroix painted the dancing bride, the cool courtyard, the guests and the musicians.

The Taking of Constantinople 1840
161¼″ × 196″ Louvre, Paris

Delacroix painted this large picture of the invading Crusaders for the Palace of Versailles. The elaborate architectural setting was sketched in by the theatrical scene-painter, Ciceri, and his assistants.

Horses Emerging from the Sea 1860
20″ × 24″ Phillips Collection, Washington

This small painting was commissioned by an art dealer and completed just three years before Delacroix's death. The artist described it as 'a view of Dieppe', but it is more reminiscent of his trip to North Africa.

The Death of Byron

When Greece began its fight for independence in 1821, Delacroix's
hero Lord Byron hoped to win glory on the battlefield. But the reality
the poet found there was far from his romantic dreams.

Delacroix/Greece Expiring on the Ruins of Missolonghi/Musée des Beaux-Arts, Bordeaux

Resplendent in a scarlet, gold-trimmed uniform, George Gordon, Lord Byron, stepped ashore from a gun-boat at Missolonghi on the west coast of Greece on 5 January 1824. The dismal, featureless town lay at the edge of a dank lagoon that was little more than a swamp, its stagnant waters the breeding ground for swarms of mosquitoes. Yet this unhealthy spot was a headquarters for Greek nationalist forces striving to free their country from the Turkish Ottoman Empire.

The Greeks welcomed Byron like a delivering angel, with tumultuous applause. A 21-gun salute echoed across the water and all day there was 'feasting and gaiety, amidst the noise of bands and the continuous discharge of muskets'.

The man at the centre of this extraordinary attention was a legend in his own lifetime. Famed throughout Europe for the brilliance of his poetry, he was a restless, volatile figure whose ready wit could be turned with equal facility to either charm or scorn. Amoral, bisexual, almost certainly incestuous, Byron revelled in the satanic reputation that had grown up around him.

CHAMPION OF LIBERTY

Championing the Greeks in their bitter struggle against the Turks was to some extent mere posturing by Byron, but behind his flamboyant gesture lay a genuine compassion for their plight. Visiting Greece a decade earlier, in 1809-10, he had been forcibly struck by the misery of life under

The sufferings of Greece
(left) The cause of freedom – and the terrible suffering of the Greeks during the War of Independence – won the sympathy of artists and intellectuals all over Europe. Delacroix expressed his own outrage in this allegorical picture painted in 1827.

Giraudon

Turkish rule and the Greeks' longing to be free.

When a series of Greek uprisings led to a full-blooded War of Independence in 1821, Byron was eager to demonstrate his allegiance. Nor was he alone in supporting the Greek cause. Educated Europeans had given their backing almost unanimously, although few had ever met a Greek – they saw themselves as defending the civilized principles and values of the Ancient Greek world, on which their own societies were based. The Turks, by contrast, had all the weight of prejudice against them: they were seen as cruel barbarians.

The war began with the wholesale massacre of Turks by Greek guerillas and continued in the same bloody way, with atrocities committed by

Eugène Delacroix

Foreign admirers
(left) Travellers from northern Europe, shown here being guided through dangerous mountain terrain, had been drawn to Greece since the 18th century. They were attracted mainly by the remains of classical civilization, but also by the natural wonders of the landscape.

T. Phillips/Byron/National Portrait Gallery, London

The saviour of the people
(above) Byron had been devoted to Greece since visiting the country in 1809-10, and showed his allegiance to its cause by risking both his fortune and his own person. With his strikingly good looks – brown curly hair, pale complexion and candid blue eyes – he was a figure who inspired hero-worship, and the Greeks welcomed him as a saviour.

Newstead Abbey, Nottingham Museums

The poet's oath
(above) Soon after his arrival in the country, Byron swore his allegiance to the Greek cause over the tomb of Marco Botsaris, a hero of the war against the Turks.

both sides. But the reports of the fighting which reached the cities of northern Europe were written by the organizers of the revolt, and frankly biased in favour of the Greeks. Greek societies were founded in London, Paris and Berlin, and public sympathy reached its height in 1822, when news arrived of the massacre by the Turks of thousands of innocent Greeks on the island of Chios.

AGENT FOR THE CAUSE

Byron at this time was residing in Italy with his mistress, Teresa Guiccioli. But early in 1823, two members of the Greek Committee in London visited Italy to enlist his active help as an agent for the cause. Byron agreed readily, and it quickly became his 'first wish' to be directly involved in the action. By May he was mustering all his financial resources in readiness to sail for Greece.

Byron's preparations were on a typically magnificent scale. He ordered supplies, hired a doctor and chartered his own ship, grandly named the *Hercules*. For himself and his companions he commissioned ostentatious uniforms as well as

Missolonghi
(left) The town where Byron landed and later died was the headquarters of Greek resistance, dominating the strategic Gulf of Corinth. Its swampy situation made it a breeding ground for malaria-carrying mosquitoes.

Greek cavalry
The Greeks were formidable fighters, but they lacked proper funds and organization and their military operations depended mainly on the efforts of local chieftains. Rivalries between different groups meant that the Greeks often spent more energy on squabbling amongst themselves than on fighting the Turks.

Jean-Loup Charmet

elaborate helmets, his own modelled on classical lines, bearing a great plume and his family motto *Crede Byron*, 'have faith in Byron'.

The *Hercules* set sail on 13 July 1823, with a strange crew on board. Apart from Byron and his companions (including Teresa's brother) there were five servants – one of them a huge ex-gondolier named Tita – five horses, Byron's bulldog Moretto and his large Newfoundland dog Lyon. Byron spent the journey fencing, boxing, shooting at empty bottles or at live ducks (to provide dinners for the crew) and swimming every day to keep fit.

DISILLUSIONMENT AND BETRAYAL

On 2 August they sailed into Argostoli, on the island of Cephalonia, whose governor was sympathetic to the cause. But the reception Byron encountered from the nationalist leaders was quite different from the meeting of united comrades he had imagined. He was besieged by requests for aid from every conceivable faction, each at loggerheads with the others, and each demanding Byron's money or his allegiance. He was soon deeply disillusioned. 'The Greeks appear in more danger from their own divisions than from the attacks of the enemy,' he observed, and in his journal – which he soon gave up writing because he could not resist 'abusing the Greeks' in it – he noted angrily 'they are such damned liars'.

At last Byron received an invitation from an important Greek leader, Prince Mavrocordato, to come to Missolonghi. The Prince hoped to launch naval attacks across the Gulf of Corinth against the Turkish strongholds of Patras and Lepanto. Thus it

was that, on that fatal January day in 1824, Byron landed at Missolonghi with high hopes of action.

The first priority was the assault on Lepanto, and Prince Mavrocordato offered Byron a 500-strong troop of Suliote soldiers from the Albanian mountains, whom Byron agreed to finance from his own pocket. A further 100 soldiers were added at the expense of the Greeks and Byron then set about making plans and drilling his private army. But in their cramped quarters, the Suliotes became quarrelsome, and soon threatened mutiny. Byron was incensed, and felt betrayed – he was not only financing the soldiers, but also their dependants, who totalled almost 700 more.

A private matter made his unhappiness even

The fall of Missolonghi
The Turks made sustained attacks on Missolonghi in 1822-3, shortly before Byron's arrival, and renewed them in 1825, the year after his death. The town eventually fell in 1826 and was sacked.

Lauros-Giraudon

A treacherous Greek
(left) The bandit known as Odysseus was one of the most colourful of the Greek freedom fighters. Like Byron, he was handsome and a brilliant athlete, but Byron mistrusted him. He had good reason, for Odysseus murdered all his opponents, whether they were Turks or Greeks.

A tyrannical Turk
(right) Ali Pasha was a Turkish brigand who gained control of much of Albania and Greece. Although he had a splendid court, he was ruthless and devious and was hated by the Greeks as a symbol of Turkish oppression. Byron had met him in 1809 during his first visit to Greece.

more acute. Byron had taken into his service the son of a Greek family he had saved from penury, and his liking for the boy, Loukas, had developed into an aching love – of which the 15-year-old was utterly disdainful. Deeply depressed, and now suffering recurrent bouts of fever because of the damp climate, Byron suddenly experienced a violent fit, which brought him close to death.

Weeks of appalling weather, along with financial difficulties and seething discontent among the troops, did nothing to alleviate either Byron's depression or his ill-health. Then on 9 April he insisted on going riding in torrential rain and, despite the rheumatic pains and fever which broke out that night, he rode out again the next day. His fever was soon compounded by a chill.

The next few days saw his condition weaken. Rallying at times, but often racked by pains and violent coughing, Byron refused his doctors' requests to bleed him. But on 16 April he gave in. Calling the doctors 'a damned set of butchers' he allowed the leeches to be applied, and was bled severely four times in two days. By 18 April, death was inevitable.

Only in his last delirium did Byron achieve the action he had dreamed of. In his imagination he was on the ramparts of Lepanto, shouting 'Forward! Forward! Courage!' But in reality a hero's death escaped him. Without regaining consciousness, he died on 19 April, aged 36.

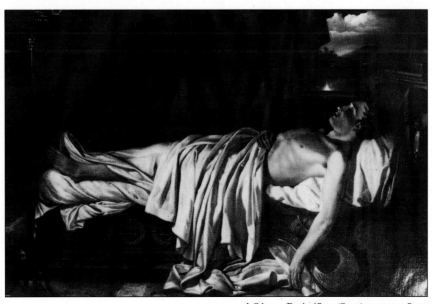

A hero's death
Byron died of fever at Missolonghi on 19 April 1824. This romantic image of the poet on his deathbed shows him with a serene expression and covered in the kind of majestic draperies seen on classical statues. But the unpleasant reality must have been very different.

J. Odevaere/Death of Byron/Groeningemuseum, Bruges

A Year in the Life 1824

As Greece fought for freedom from her Turkish masters – and Byron died of fever at Missolonghi – the Great Powers of Europe stood aloof. But Britain and the United States applauded when Spain's South American colonies declared their independence. It was a mixed year for royalty, with a glittering coronation in Paris, an imposter in Washington and an exotic funeral in London.

Jean-Loup Charmet

The Greek War of Independence
(right) In 1824, Greek nationalist forces defeated a Turkish army at Mitylene – but the same year Turkey's Egyptian allies under Mohammed Ali slaughtered thousands of Greeks on the islands of Kasos and Psara. The bitter fighting had eight more years to run before Turkey finally renounced her suzerainty in 1832, after four centuries of imperial rule.

Sir Walter Scott
(right) Scotland's most famous novelist (1771-1832) published Redgauntlet in 1824, the story of an unsuccessful attempt to put the Young Pretender Bonnie Prince Charlie on the British throne. This portrait by Sir Edwin Landseer was completed the same year.

In January, two Greek deputies, Orlandos and Louriotis, arrived in England to seek financial support for their cause from the London Greek Committee. They were banqueted at the Mansion House in the unexpected presence of the Foreign Secretary, George Canning, and a loan of £80,000 was eventually offered. It was Lord Byron himself, recruited in Italy, who went out to Greece as a commissioner for the Committee to arrange the most effective use of the loan. Yet ironically the first instalment of £40,000 arrived in the *Florida* just two days after his death. On its return journey, the ship carried the mournful cargo of Byron's remains, effects and papers back to England.

The Greek Committees had originally been established to oppose the policies of the European governments, which seemed reactionary and callous. Under the 'Congress System'

the great powers had adopted at Vienna in 1815, England, France, Austria and Russia promised to act together to suppress any nationalist movement which threatened the balance of power. Now the main consideration was whether Russia would intervene on behalf of the Greek rebels.

AUSTRIA AGAINST GREECE

Prince Metternich of Austria, the architect of the Congress System, worked ceaselessly to persuade the Tsar that the Greek revolt should be left 'to burn itself out beyond the pale of civilization'. And despite the pressure of public opinion – inflamed in Paris by Delacroix's *Massacre of Chios* – it was not until 1827 that France, Britain and Russia finally broke with

Workers' rights
(left) The repeal of the Combination Acts in 1824 freed workers from legal constraints that had been in operation for 25 years. These repressive laws, set up in the aftermath of the French Revolution, had declared trade unions to be criminal conspiracies.

St Katharine's Dock
(below) The Scottish engineer Thomas Telford (1757-1834) designed this imposing group of warehouses for the St Katharine Dock Company in London. They were erected in 1824 and used originally to store tea, rubber, marble – and live turtles.

WE ASSIST EACH OTHER IN TIME OF NEED.

Austria and came together to seek mediation for Greece.

Britain's foreign secretary was a forceful critic of Metternich's policy. But his first real break with the Congress System came not over Greece, but with his policy towards South America, when the Spanish colonies, with which Britain had built up a profitable trade, asserted their independence one by one.

THE MONROE DOCTRINE

The danger that Spain might try to win back control by force led Canning to support the doctrine proclaimed in December 1823 by President Monroe of the United States, that the American continents were 'not to be considered as subjects for future colonization by any European power'. Indeed, Canning even floated the idea of a joint Anglo-American initiative in support of the new states.

Within the year, however, Canning came to realise that if the South American republics were not recognized as independent states, they would be forced into even closer reliance on United States protection – with equally bad results for Britain's trade. So in December 1824, Britain took a firm stand and gave recognition to the new republics of Colombia, Mexico and Buenos Aires. King George IV so loathed the idea of this formal support for upstart republics that he refused to read his speech to Parliament, claiming that he had gout and had lost his false teeth. Lord Eldon, the Lord High Chancellor, read it instead.

If 1824 seemed to augur a more liberal age for Britain, the reverse was true for France. Louis XVIII, the Bourbon king who

Roger-Viollet

Mansell Collection

Conception explained
(above) The French chemist Jean-Baptiste Dumas (1800-84) was only 20 when he proved – in collaboration with J.L. Prévost – that sperm was essential to fertilization. He later made crucial advances in organic chemistry, before entering politics to become a senator and master of the French mint.

War in Burma
(right) In 1824, the British armies in India reacted to the growing might of Burma, which had invaded Siam (now Thailand) and was even threatening Calcutta. On 5 August, an invasion force of soldiers and sailors stormed the fort at Syriam on the Irrawaddy River opposite Rangoon. And the First Burmese War (1824-26) left Britain in control of much of Burma's coastline.

Bridgeman Art Library

had been restored to the throne 'in the baggage train of the allies' after Napoleon's defeat at Waterloo, died on 16 September. His 10-year reign had been a political balancing act, for the French Chamber contained all shades of the political spectrum, from out-and-out Republicans to the Ultra-Royalists, who wanted to put the clock back to the time of absolute monarchy before the Revolution.

The Ultras had disliked Louis and the gradual liberalization of his reign, which had made it possible for progressive newspapers such as the liberal *Le Globe* to appear in 1824. Ultra support went to Louis' brother, the Comte d'Artois, who succeeded him on the throne as Charles X. His coronation was a splendid affair, designed to obliterate the memories of Louis' somewhat ignominious accession as well as the coronation of

Napoleon Bonaparte as Emperor of France, held in 1804 at the cathedral of Notre Dame in Paris.

SACRED CEREMONY

Reverting to old French tradition, Charles was crowned at Reims in a five-hour ceremony, which included his anointment with the sacred oil of St Remy: traditionally the most important moment in the coronation of French monarchs. The phial of oil had been thought to have been destroyed during the Revolution, so the discovery of a few precious drops seemed a good omen indeed for the new reign, as did the fact that the young poet Victor Hugo wrote a celebratory poem.

It was a year for royal curiosities too. In May a man claiming

Art for the people
(left) Britain's National Gallery was founded in 1824, following donations of paintings by three collectors, and a gift of £70,000 for their preservation and exhibition. This spurred the House of Commons to contribute a further £70,000. William Wilkins (1778-1839) designed the Gallery which stands imposingly in Trafalgar Square, and was completed in 1838.

Lauros-Giraudon

Coronation of Charles X
The Comte d'Artois succeeded to the throne of France in September 1824, on the death of his brother Louis XVIII. The coronation was rich in pageantry and ancient ritual, but after ruling for only six years Charles was deposed on account of his extreme reactionary stance. He was succeeded by Louis Philippe, the 'Citizen King'.

to be Louis XVII of France – the son of the king guillotined by the revolutionaries in 1793 – turned up in Washington. He declared that he had been carried off in great secrecy from a place of imprisonment and brought up in Austria, from whence he was taken to Cuba and trained as a carpenter. Many who met him were struck by his close resemblance to the classic Bourbon features, and impressed by the 'distinguishing mark' which his 'royal' mother had made on the side of his head – and that of his sister, the Duchess of Angoulême. But the imposter was soon revealed to be a French soldier, whose severe head wounds received during Napoleon's retreat from Moscow had caused 'great derangement of mind'.

The same month, the King and Queen of Hawaii – known in England as the Sandwich Islands – arrived in London to stay at Osborn's Hotel in the Adelphi. They made a striking couple: both were over six feet tall and very fat. But within a few weeks the exotic royal visitors were both dead.

A FATAL SHOCK

Struck down by measles, the Queen expired first on 8 July at the age of 24, despite the ministrations of King George's physician and the Duke of York's surgeon. And the King himself, 'much agitated by the fatal shock', passed on a few days later. The bodies were embalmed 'according to the customs of the Sandwich Islands' and lay in state, draped in war cloaks of brilliant coloured feathers, until their departure for burial at 'Owyhee' in the heart of the Pacific Ocean.

Jean-Loup Charmet

BBC Hulton Picture Library

The 'Liberator'
Simon Bolivar (1783-1830), who gave his name to the republic of Bolivia, freed several Latin-American countries from Spanish rule. In 1824 he completed the liberation of Peru, following that of Venezuela, Ecuador and Colombia.

The Murray River
(right) Discovered in 1824 by the Australian bushman and explorer Hamilton Hume, the Murray flows across south-east Australia from the Snowy Mountains to Adelaide. The river was named after Colonial Secretary Sir George Murray.

Picturepoint

The King of Hawaii
Kamehameha II and his wife Keopuolani visited Britain in 1824 at a time of great change for their island kingdom. The first missionaries had reached Hawaii four years earlier and introduced western knowledge as well as Christianity. Tragically, the royal couple died in London, and the bodies were carried back to Hawaii on a ship commanded by Lord Byron, cousin of the poet.

GALLERY GUIDE

Goya

The Prado, Madrid, contains the vast majority of Goya's early works, such as *The Parasol* and *The Straw Manikin*. It also possesses the masterpieces of his maturity, the so-called black paintings, and his finest royal portraits (p.14), both the clothed and unclothed versions of *The Maja* (pp.15 and 24-5) and his two great pictures commemorating the Spanish uprising in Madrid (pp.18-19 and 30-31). Also in Madrid, the Academy of San Fernando houses excellent examples of his bullfighting and madhouse scenes. Outside Spain, Goya's portrait style is best represented in London, Forth Worth and New York. One of his paintings of labourers – *The Forge* – is at the Frick Collection, New York, while the Meadowes Museum in Dallas has one of his madhouse pictures. Goya's graphic works can be seen in Madrid, London and New York (Hispanic Society).

Blake

The appreciation of Blake's talent has mainly been confined to the English-speaking world and, accordingly, the best selections of his art are to be found in Britain and the United States. The premier collection is in the Tate Gallery, London, but copies of his large colour print of *God Judging Adam* (p.57) can be found in the Metropolitan Museum of Art, New York, and in the Philadelphia Museum of Art. Blake frequently reworked his most potent images so that, for example, the Tate's *Satan Smiting Job with Sore Boils* recurs, in a comparable format, in the Pierpoint Morgan Library, New York. Other major holdings in America include those at the Library of Congress, the Metropolitan Museum of Art and the Museum of Fine Arts in Boston.

Friedrich

Berlin probably owns the largest number of Friedrich's major works. The Nationalgalerie contains several of the most atmospheric moonlight scenes, while the Schloss Charlottenburg possesses two of his gloomiest masterpieces in the *Abbey in the Oakwoods* and the *Monk by the Seashore*. There are fine, misty landscapes in Hanover (p.83), and notable mountain views in Stuttgart and Munich, while the Folkwang Museum in Essen has his spectacular *Mountain Landscape with Rainbow*. Friedrich lived in present-day East Germany, and here his work is best represented at Dresden (p.78) and Leipzig (p.97).

Delacroix

The main concentration of Delacroix's art is in Paris. The Louvre possesses all the major works from the height of his career as a Romantic; in addition, most of the monumental paintings from his later years are still in situ. The finest of these are the superb murals at St Sulpice (p.113), but further examples can be found in the Palais-Bourbon, the Palais du Luxembourg and the Hôtel de Ville. Outside Paris, the Musée des Beaux-Arts, in Bordeaux, has the strongest holding (including the *Lion Hunt*, pp. 114-15), but the sensual aspects of Delacroix's style can be sampled in Lyons and in Lille, while records of his travels can be found in Nantes and Toulouse. Outside France, the Wallace Collection in London features two fine examples of Delacroix's literary painting (p.123), and there are stunning arab pictures in Buffalo, such as *A Street in Meknes*, (Albright Knox Art Gallery) and in New York, such as *The Fanatics of Tangier* (Jerome Hill Collection).

BIBLIOGRAPHY

A. Blunt, *The Art of William Blake*, Columbia University Press, New York, 1959
H. Börsch-Supan, *Caspar David Friedrich*, Braziller, New York, 1974
L. Ettlinger, *Friedrich*, The Masters, Knowledge Industry Publications, White Plains, 1967
V. Florea, *Goya*, Abbey Library, London, 1975
W. Friedlaender, *David to Delacroix*, Schocken Paperbacks, New York, 1968
L. R. Furst, *European Romanticism*, Methuen, New York, 1980
E. Harris, *Goya*, Phaidon, London, 1969

L. Norton (translator), *The Journals of Eugene Delacroix*, Cornell University Press, Ithaca, 1980
M. Paley, *William Blake*, Phaidon, London, 1978
P. Pool, *Delacroix*, Paul Hamlyn, London, 1969
K. Raine, *William Blake*, Thames and Hudson, New York, 1985
R. Schickel, *The World of Goya*, Time-Life Books, Alexandria, 1968
R. Taylor (ed.), *The Romantic Tradition in Germany*, Methuen Inc., New York, 1970
J. Wilson, *Goya's Prints*, British Museum Publications, London, 1981

Leonardo Alenza (1807-45)
Spanish Romantic painter, the principal follower of Goya. No artist in Spain matched the power or originality of the latter's vision, although several drew on his macabre subject-matter. Like Goya, Alenza depicted scenes of madness, sorcery and violence. His best-known works are The Romantics (versions in Madrid and Barcelona).

Richard Parkes Bonington (1802-28)
English painter and watercolourist, active mainly in France. Bonington came from Nottingham but settled in France in 1820, when he entered the studio of Gros. Despite his French training, he was considered a British painter and made his name at the 'English' Salon of 1824, when his work was hung alongside that of Constable. Certainly, his most lasting influence was as a landscapist, but Bonington was also drawn to the more exotic themes of Romanticism. Towards the end of his life, he shared a studio with Delacroix and the two men vied with each other in depicting subjects from Goethe and Byron. Bonington's illustrations to Goethe's Faust appeared in 1828, the year he died.

Edward Calvert (1799-1883)
English painter and engraver, a leading member of the Ancients (cf Samuel Palmer). Calvert's youth was spent in the Navy, but he turned to painting after meeting Fuseli, and was profoundly influenced by the visionary work of Blake and Palmer. Calvert joined the latter at Shoreham and, like him, strove to create scenes of Arcadian beauty. His finest achievement in this respect was The Primitive City (1822, British Museum, London), a superb watercolour into which he introduced a sensual element that was absent in Palmer's work. Calvert followed Blake in his use of woodcuts and copper engravings and, in his so-called Early Engravings (1825-31), he attained a mood of spiritual innocence that came very close to that of the master.

Karl Gustav Carus (1789-1869)
German painter and philosopher. Carus trained as a doctor and lectured in comparative anatomy. However, after meeting Friedrich in 1817, he turned increasingly to painting, accompanying his mentor on sketching trips to Saxony and Bohemia. Carus shared Friedrich's taste for remote hills and desolate mountain valleys, frequently infuzing them with misty, symbolic figures, as in his Monument to the Memory of Goethe (1832, Kunsthalle, Hamburg). He knew the poet, and both Goethe's and Friedrich's ideas helped shape his most famous book, Nine Letters on the Painting of Landscapes (1815-24).

Théodore Chassériau (1819-56)
French painter who successfully blended Romantic and Classical features. Chassériau studied under Ingres, acquiring his gift for firm draughtsmanship, but his admiration for Delacroix and Byron soon led him to tackle more exotic subjects. Like Delacroix, he visited North Africa, producing Moorish scenes that sparkled with the same rich colours as those of his fellow countryman. Chassériau's art carried in it the seeds of the Symbolist movement, which were eventually to blossom in the work of his pupil, Gustave Moreau.

Henry Fuseli (Johann Heinrich Füssli) (1741-1825)
Swiss-born painter, mainly active in England. Fuseli trained as a priest, but left his native Zurich in 1762 and settled in London two years later. There, he worked initially as a translator until Joshua Reynolds persuaded him to take up painting. From 1770 to 1778 he studied in Rome, where he was deeply impressed by the art of

Captive nightmares
(below) Horace Walpole described Piranesi's views of Rome as 'sublime dreams', but his series of fantasy prisons was more influential on Romantic artists.

Bulloz

Michelangelo. On his return to London, Fuseli specialized in literary painting, contributing nine canvases to Boydell's Shakespeare Gallery series (1786-9) and 47 pictures to his own, financially disastrous Milton Gallery project (1790-99). He also painted dream subjects, of which the most notorious was his Nightmare (1781, Institute of Arts, Detroit), epitomizing the Romantics' preoccupation with horror. Fuseli's stiff and unreal figures often carried overtones of cruelty or eroticism, but this did not deprive him of conventional success for, in 1799, he was made Professor of Painting at the Academy, a post he held until his death.

Théodore Géricault (1791-1824)

Seminal figure in the development of French Romanticism. Géricault studied under Vernet and Guérin, although his stirring equestrian portraits of Napoleonic officers owed more to the example of Baron Gros. In 1816, his tour of Italy awakened an admiration for Baroque painting which was reflected in his turbulent shipwreck scene, The Raft of the Medusa (1819, p. 116), one of the greatest masterpieces of the Romantic movement. Géricault's art was tainted by a fascination with cruelty and the macabre. His studies of executed criminals and severed limbs were ghoulish, although his portraits of the inmates of the Salpetrière lunatic asylum were, and still are, disturbingly moving. His lifelong passion for horses also led him to produce superb animal paintings, particularly during his stay in England (1820-22). However, this interest was to prove fatal, since Géricault's premature death was caused by a riding accident.

Paul Huet (1803-69)

French landscape painter. Huet trained under Gros and Guérin, but was more influenced by his friends, Delacroix and Bonington. His taste for depicting scenes of lonely wanderers travelling through stormy landscapes led the poet Théophile Gautier to describe his work as 'Shakespearean'. The Lake (1840, Musée Crozatier, Le Puy-en-Velay) is a typical example.

John Martin (1789-1854)

English Romantic painter and mezzotint engraver. Martin was born near Newcastle and started his career as a decorator of porcelain. Turning to oil painting, he soon made his name at the Royal Academy with Sadak in Search of the Waters of Oblivion (1812, Southampton Art Gallery). Here, as in his other works, he created an apocalyptic vision, with tiny human figures pitted against the vastness of the elements. Martin's dramatic style was hugely popular, due in part to the engravings. His superb illustrations to Milton's Paradise Lost (1827), for example, were also issued independently of the text. Martin's reputation is currently enjoying a revival.

Charles Meryon (1821-68)

French draughtsman and etcher, best-known for his mysterious scenes of Paris. Meryon worked as a naval officer before turning to art in the late 1840s. Colour-blindness precluded a painting career, but the eerie brilliance of his engravings won the admiration of both Victor Hugo and Charles Baudelaire. In his Etchings of Paris (1850-54), Meryon translated the architectural fantasies of Piranesi into a French context while, in later works, he introduced strange flying creatures into the Parisian sky. Meryon suffered attacks of dementia and ended his life in an asylum.

The Nazarenes

Important group of German primitive painters working principally in Italy. The founders, Franz Pforr (1788-1812) and Friedrich Overbeck (1789-1869), set up the 'Brotherhood of St Luke' in Vienna, in 1809. Their aim was to revive the glories of earlier religious painting through the medium of a medieval workshop system. In 1810, they moved to Rome and settled in the deserted monastery of S. Isidoro, where they adopted the dress and lifestyle of monks. Although features like this were patently absurd – and led to the term 'Nazarene' being coined by mocking critics – the group did produce an influential style; its linear simplicity and archaisms being mimicked in both France and England.

Samuel Palmer (1805-81)

English landscape painter, the most important heir to Blake's poetic vision. Palmer was precociously gifted, exhibiting at the Academy from the age of 14. He met Blake in 1824 and was profoundly influenced by his woodcut illustrations to the Pastorals of Virgil (1821), which appeared to him like visions of an earthly paradise. Seeking to recapture this spirit, Palmer settled in the Kent village of Shoreham and began producing his beautiful watercolour landscapes, combining lyrical intensity with a childlike innocence. During his Shoreham period (1827-33), he gathered about him a group of like-minded artists known as 'the Ancients' who included Edward Calvert and George Richmond.

Giovanni Battista Piranesi (1720-78)

Italian architect and engraver, an important forerunner of Romanticism. Piranesi was born in Venice but made his name in Rome with his remarkable views of the city's antiquities. After his death, however, he became better known for his Carceri d'Invenzione (Imaginary Prisons), a series of threatening and claustrophobic architectural fantasies, which stamped their mark on the Romantic imagination.

Philipp Otto Runge (1777-1810)

Along with Friedrich, the most original of the German Romantic painters. After his studies in Copenhagen, Runge moved to Dresden, where he came into contact with Friedrich and the Romantic circle, before finally settling in Hamburg. Early in his career, he began to devise a cycle of paintings representing the Times of the Day. In this highly ambitious project, he intended to fuze classical and Christian motifs into an expression of the cosmic rhythms inherent in Nature. In typical Romantic fashion, he also wished for these paintings to be experienced as part of a gesamtkunstwerk (total work of art), in which suitable recitations of poetry and music would also be featured. Runge's premature death prevented the realization of this grand design. In his finished pictures, however, he exhibited a poetic force that blended well with his naïve, linear style.

Essentials of Production and Operations Management

EHUD MENIPAZ

B.Sc.Eng., M.Sc.Eng., M.B.A., Ph.D., P.E.
Professor
Carleton University

Prentice-Hall, Inc., Englewood Cliffs, New Jersey   07632

Library of Congress Cataloging in Publication Data

MENIPAZ, EHUD.
   Essentials of production and operations management.

   Includes bibliographies and index.
   1. Production management. I. Title.
TS155.M358 1984   658.5   83-22891
ISBN 0-13-286641-2

Editorial/production supervision and interior design: Kim Gueterman
Cover design: Diane Saxe
Manufacturing buyer: Ed O'Dougherty

To Esther, Amit, Liat, and Ronen

Printed in the United States of America

10 9 8 7 6 5 4 3 2 1

ISBN 0-13-286641-2

PRENTICE-HALL INTERNATIONAL, INC., *London*
PRENTICE-HALL OF AUSTRALIA PTY. LIMITED, *Sydney*
EDITORA PRENTICE-HALL DO BRASIL, LTDA., *Rio de Janeiro*
PRENTICE-HALL CANADA INC., *Toronto*
PRENTICE-HALL OF INDIA PRIVATE LIMITED, *New Delhi*
PRENTICE-HALL OF JAPAN, INC., *Tokyo*
PRENTICE-HALL OF SOUTHEAST ASIA PTE. LTD., *Singapore*
WHITEHALL BOOKS LIMITED, *Wellington, New Zealand*

Contents

Part Two: Design

2   PRODUCT AND PROCESS DECISION AND DESIGN   34

3   FACILITY LOCATION   81

8   OPERATIONS SCHEDULING   341

Part Four: Organizing Work Systems

9   JOB DESIGN AND ANALYSIS   407

Part Six: Summary

15   ENHANCING PRODUCTIVITY: PUTTING THE ESSENTIALS TO WORK   671

Preface

This book is intended for use in courses of Production and Operations Management offered by business and engineering schools. The American Association of Collegiate Schools of Business (AACSB) requires that all schools accredited by this body include operations management in their undergraduate curriculum core. This text meets the AACSB production and operations management requirements and may be used at both the undergraduate and graduate levels.

The book has several features that set it apart from others in the operations management field. First, the presentation reflects the underlying principles of Operations Management that can be applied in *both the manufacturing and the service sectors*. Thus, for example, operation control, cost control, quality control, human resources organizing, and the like are discussed in both contexts.

Second, the material does not require preparation in quantitative methods, behavioral sciences, economics, or statistics. Chapter supplements called "Technical Notes" are used extensively to introduce more advanced quantitative techniques, while the basic techniques are presented in the body of each chapter. This allows the reader and the instructor the flexibility to use the book in an introductory-level operations management course or in a more advanced course. In addition to the usual techniques handled in elementary texts, I have included ideas that are quite sophisticated, but that do not require sophisticated mathematical techniques. For example, the chapter on forecasting includes all the standard techniques, but also goes beyond that material and deals with causal models, error sources and measurement. The scheduling, maintenance, project management, and quality control chapters also give an exhaustive descriptive treatment with a more comprehensive quantitative coverage than is provided by the introductory texts now available.

Third, most of the chapters deal with computer aides to operational decisions. Several chapters present computerized policies that are accessible through terminals on a conversational (interactive-mode), real-time, basis. (Alternatively, they can be executed by using micro-computers.) The chapters include the qualitative presentation of conversational computer programs, input requirements, and output samples. The programs are available from the author upon request.

Fourth, a series of problems and solutions is provided at the end of each chapter. These are solved problems that the student may consult before proceeding with the solution of the end-of-chapter problems and the readings or cases provided in the text.

Fifth, a unifying, systems approach, has been used in the presentation of the material. The material follows the classical process school of management approach: design, planning, organizing, and control. Within this process framework, I have integrated a systems approach that stresses the resource conversion process and the interrelationships among the various operations management subsystems. Each chapter is devoted to one or more critical decision topics, while the systems and process approaches provide the overall framework that supports the decision-making.

Sixth, the book is based on a great deal of research and it provides a "state of the art" presentation. It may serve as both a text for operations management courses and a reference on topics that instructors are unable to include in the course because of time limits.

Seventh, an expanded and up-to-date bibliography is provided in each chapter to help the interested student with further reading.

Eighth, several "real-world" examples and appropriate readings are introduced to explain the nature of operations management.

Ninth, each chapter includes discussion questions, a set of solved problems, chapter review problems, and readings with follow-up questions.

The objectives of the book are:

1. To present a conceptual framework of Operations Management that is applicable to both manufacturing and service industries.
2. To provide an Operations Management book that can be used in undergraduate and core graduate survey courses.
3. To provide a modular Operations Management book for which the quantitative skills needed vary according to the particular course outline and selective use of supplements.
4. To provide an understanding of operations management as a major functional area of management.

Part One introduces the reader to a short chronology of operations management and its relationship with other areas of managerial activity. It presents the essentials of operations systems and describes the scope of operations management.

Part Two covers the essentials of the design of operations systems. This strategic overview of operations management includes product and process decision and design, facility location, and project management and control. This part includes supplements on capital budgeting and financial investment analysis, and the distribution model of linear programming.

Part Three covers the planning of operations systems, including forecasting for operations, aggregate planning, layout planning, and operations scheduling. It also includes supplements containing quantitative material that relates to the appropriate subject matter, including linear programming and simulation.

Operations managers deal with a variety of skills and wants. They try to satisfy workers expectations while maintaining a proper level of performance on the job. The task of organizing work systems and, in particular, of employing human resources to achieve a common goal is the subject of Part Four. Job analysis, job design, work measurement, compensation, and motivation topics are studied therein.

Part Five deals with operations control—in particular, inventory management and control, materials requirement planning (MRP), quality control, and maintenance control.

In Section Six, we deal with essentials of productivity and integrate the concepts presented earlier in the book.

Many people have helped in the preparation of this book. I would like to express my appreciation to the reviewers. Among them are: Martin K. Starr of Columbia University, Samuel Mantel, Jr., of the University of Cincinnati, Gabriel Bitran, and Steve Graves of MIT, Seymour J. Fader of Ramapo College, Richard Discenza of the University of Colorado at Colorado Springs, John I. S. Hsu of Villanova University, and various editors at Prentice-Hall, Inc. especially Dennis Hogan and Kim Gueterman. All these individuals read the manuscript or parts of it at various stages of its development and helped to improve and refine the material presented.

I also want to acknowledge the contribution of many colleagues and professional associates in plants and other organizations throughout the world. The knowledge and experiences that they have shared with me throughout the years are reflected in this book.

A book of this scope is based on a wide variety of sources. Some of the material included presents my original contributions to the analysis, application, and conceptual framework of production and operations management. The balance of the material comes from original work by numerous colleagues throughout the world. The sources of these materials are cited where the materials are discussed.

I would also like to thank my students for their help. Among them are David Hopkins and Ingrid Lorenzen.

Finally, I wish to thank my family for their patience, support, interest, and perseverance during the two years of text development and editing.

Ehud Menipaz

1

Operations Systems and Decision Processes

A Frenchman, a Japanese and an American face a firing squad in a joke making the rounds lately. Offered a last wish, the Frenchman asks to hear the "Marseillaise." The Japanese asks to give one more lecture on Japanese management. The American asks to be shot first. "I can't stand one more lecture on Japanese management," he says.

The joke exaggerates, of course. But it's no exaggeration to say that much of the lecturing and writing about Japan of late has been concentrated on the subject of management. Educated, affluent, and concerned societies elsewhere in the world are placing enormous pressure on a discipline that up to not long ago was taken for granted—*the management discipline*.

The complexities of modern society have increased our dependency on organizations and the professionals who manage them. The increased demands on both the private and the public sectors require managers to be more accountable for quality and quantity of products and services than ever before. The quest for maintaining competitiveness has prompted managers to look for new and better methods. This is the reason why we reflect on success stories in other parts of the world, such as Japan and Europe. Operations management, of which many successful Japanese examples have been studied, is one of the more critical aspects of management today.

Generally speaking, business organizations divide management activities into six categories:

Operations management
Financial management

Marketing management
Engineering management
Personnel management
General management

Financial management is concerned with activities that are related to acquiring and controlling capital. Marketing management is concerned with activities necessary to select and sell products and services. Engineering management is concerned with the design of products and processes. Personnel management (human resources management) is concerned with recruiting, training, and job design. General management coordinates the activities of the operations, financial, marketing, personnel, and engineering managers. Operations management deals with the activities required in the process of the production of products and delivery of services.

The term "operations management" is seldom used to label the operations management function. Instead this function is often indicated by describing the operation process with which the organization is involved.

For example, a hospital has a maternity ward director who oversees the operations of this ward. He or she is the maternity ward's "operations manager." A car manufacturer has a production department manager who oversees the assembly of cars. He or she is the assembly department's "operations manager." A wholesale furniture organization has a distribution manager who oversees the operation of delivering the furniture goods. Although the title might be "distribution manager," he or she is, in reality, an "operations manager."

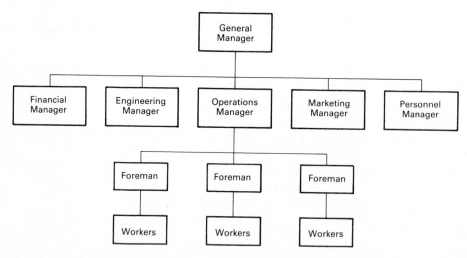

Figure 1.1 An Organization Chart

PRODUCTION PLANNER AND MATERIAL CONTROLLER

—Minimum five years experience in production inventory control and material management. Familiar with electronic techniques and methods. Converts marketing forecasts into detailed plant and procurement schedules. Post secondary electronic education desirable.

Lynes United Services Ltd. is a Calgary-based company, a leader in Drill Stem Testing (DST), and a pioneer in instrumentation manufacturing and design. A comprehensive benefit program and relocation expenses are available. Above-average salary levels are commensurate with experience and abilities.

Qualified applicants, please send your resume to:

Claire D. Bourret
Personnel Coordinator
LYNES UNITED SERVICES LTD.

Operations Manager

A Vancouver company specializing in imported quality furniture from the Orient is commencing wholesale operations out of Toronto.

A responsible person is required to take charge. The successful applicant will be expected to have excellent communication skills and business experience. Exposure to and familiarity with the Eastern Canadian or U.S. furniture market is essential.

This is a challenging position that offers other development possibilities within a growth-oriented company.

Starting salary $18,000. Additional commission negotiable.

Please send complete resume with recent photograph to Box #Box 994.

The Financial Post, 481 University Ave., Toronto M5W 1A7.

OPERATIONS MANAGEMENT OPPORTUNITY

We are looking for an experienced "hands-on" Operations Professional to assume complete responsibility for a large distribution facility.

To achieve your dual objectives of customer satisfaction and operating cost effectiveness you will have demonstrated abilities and knowledge regarding warehousing and delivery, inventory control and order administration.

In addition you are capable of recruiting and developing a strong support staff to ensure that your objectives are met.

To the successful candidate we offer an attractive compensation and fringe benefit package plus plenty of challenge and opportunity.

If you feel you qualify for this challenging assignment we invite you to forward your resume in confidence highlighting your experience and personal achievements to:

Personnel Director
Box 1503, this paper.

Figure 1.2 A Sample of Placement Advertisements in the Area of Production and Operations Management

A SHORT CHRONOLOGY

Operations management (OM) emerged as a distinct function of management as a result of the Industrial Revolution and the accompanying need for training people who could plan, organize, and direct the operations of large, complex systems. The need to increase the efficiency, effectiveness, and productivity of manufacturing operations was the original stimulus for the study of operations management. Since then, many developments have been initiated and applied in the context of service organizations. Figure 1.3 summarizes some of the major contributions to operations management. Most of the terms in Figure 1.3 will be defined and dealt with throughout the book, and the reader is encouraged to consult the figure frequently.

OPERATIONS MANAGEMENT

Operations management deals with the *design, planning, organizing, and controlling of resources to provide goods and services so as to meet customer wants and organizational goals.*

Operations management deals with the *operations system* of the organization, whether it is a manufacturing or service organization. The operations system can be thought of as having three major parts: inputs, processes, and outputs.

The *inputs* to the operations system are: people, materials, equipment, information, money, and energy. These ingredients are necessary for operations to take place. The *processes* are the essence of the operations system. They deal with the transformation of inputs into outputs. The *outputs* of the operations system result from the transformation of the inputs by the processes and can be either goods or services. Let us describe each one of the system parts and use them to classify operations systems.

Inputs

The inputs to the operations system are either tangible (people, material, equipment) or intangible (information, time). Frequently, inputs to the system are outputs from another system.

Outputs

The outputs from an operations system are either intangible or tangible. Examples of intangible outputs are: outgoing patients (hospital), convicted or acquitted persons (justice system), rested guests (hotel), delivered message (advertising company), change of location of people and articles (transportation company), and entertained customers (entertainment organization). Examples

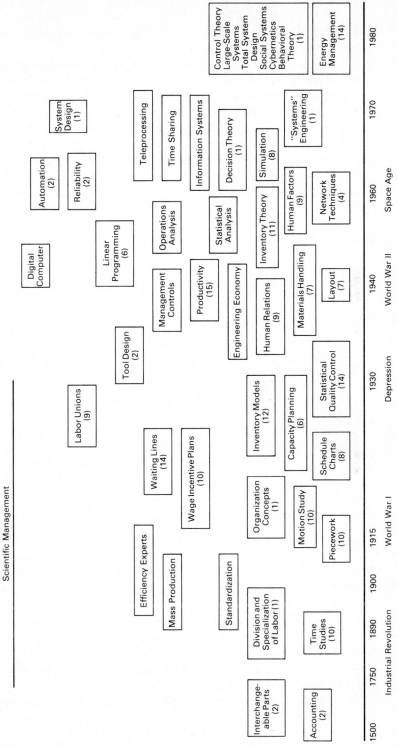

Figure 1.3 A Chronology of Significant Events and Developments in the Evolution of Operations Management (Note: numbers in brackets indicate the chapter in which the term is discussed.)

5

of tangible outputs are metals, heat, electricity, clothing, buildings, meals, fabrics, and electrical appliances.

Tangible outputs comprise items that might themselves constitute inputs for the creation of other such items. Examples are fabrics for clothing and metals that will be transformed into electrical appliances. Such outputs cannot satisfy customer wants until they are in the possession of the customers. Thus, goods may require a service—e.g., transportation to reach the customer.

Two points are evident from the above. First, few organizations will provide only goods or only services. Most will provide both. A company that manufactures home appliances (for example, food processors) uses inputs for the creation of goods for the satisfaction of customer wants. The same customers require a service as well, such as field maintenance or after-sale service.

Second, within an organization resources will be utilized for the creation of goods as well as services. For example, a university registration system, involving secretaries, faculty advisors, desks, and computers, is producing both a service (registration of students into the various programs) and products (the completed registration form, an I.D., and a computer record).

Processes

Thus far we have discussed inputs and outputs. Let us now classify operations systems by looking at processes. This classification is used throughout the book.

The following are examples of organizations that include operations systems: taxi service, ambulance service, coal mine, warehouse, clothing manufacturer, dentist, moving company, fire department, solid waste collection service, gas station, hospital's emergency room, Chinese food "take-out" shop, coin-operated laundry, hotel, food canner, construction company, department store. This list is by no means comprehensive; however, it presents several organizations that include operations systems with service as an output, and others that have goods as an output. Let us classify the nature of the processes for these operations systems.

Production is an obvious process. Physical goods are created from raw material. The clothing manufacturer takes a yarn and transforms it into slacks or dresses. A similar kind of transformation takes place at the coal mine, the Chinese food take-out shop, the food canner, and the construction company. These organizations constitute a fairly homogeneous group, whose processes have one predominant common characteristic: the creation of physical products. The take-out shop may be considered to operate in the manner of a restaurant; however, its predominant characteristic is production—i.e., the production of take-out meals.

Transport is another obvious process. The taxi service, ambulance service, moving company, and solid waste collection service are all engaged in transportation. Here again, the examples have an obvious similarity in that the operations system exists for the purpose of moving something or somebody from place to place.

Of the remaining examples, the department store and the gas station have an obvious similarity in that their processes are concerned with the *supply* of existing items to customers.

This leaves the dentist, the fire department, the hospital emergency room, the coin-operated laundry, and the hotel—a seemingly heterogeneous group. In fact, however, all five examples have at least one important characteristic in common. Their processes treat their customers, whether these be persons (hospital emergency room, hotel, dentist) or items (fire department, coin-operated laundry). We shall refer to this sort of case as *service,* despite the fact that, traditionally, the term "service" or "service sector" might imply a somewhat broader category.

The last class of process is the *storage* category. This category includes all the operations systems in which items are stationed to be used at a later period—for example, a warehouse.

This rough classification of operations systems according to process function therefore yields the following five classes:

1. *Production,* in which the principal characteristic is that something is physically created; i.e., the output consists of goods that differ physically (in form, content, etc.) from those materials that are inputs to the operations system. Production therefore results in some physical transformation, or a change in the *form* of resources.

2. *Transport,* in which the principal characteristic is that someone or something is moved from place to place; i.e., the location of someone or something is changed. The transport operations system utilizes its resources primarily to this end, and such resources are not substantially changed physically. There is no major change in the form of the required resources, and the operations system provides primarily for a change in *place.*

3. *Supply,* in which the principal characteristic is that the ownership or possession of existing goods is changed. Unlike the case with production, the output from this operations system is physically the same as the input. There is no physical transformation, and the operations system provides primarily a change in the *possession* of a resource.

4. *Service,* in which the major characteristic is the treatment or accommodation of something or someone. There is primarily a change in the *state* of the resource (for example, a sick patient becomes healthier). Unlike the case with supply operations systems, the state or condition of the physical outputs differs from that of the inputs by virtue of having been treated in some way.

5. *Storage,* in which the major characteristic is the warehousing or accommodation of something or someone. There is primarily a change in the *availability* of the resource. For example, a bonded storage of spirits will make them available as the duties are paid for them.

Figure 1.4 summarizes this discussion.

No such classification of operations systems can be perfect, and there is some overlap. For example, there is some similarity between *transport* and *service,* in that transport serves or "treats" customers by providing movement. Service (e.g., provided by a dentist) may "treat" customers to such an extent as to physically convert or perhaps create parts. A more detailed subdivision might eliminate such overlap. However, for our largely descriptive purposes, the above classification will suffice.

We can now modify our definition of an operations system to include this classification. An operations system is a configuration of resources combined for the purpose of production, transport, supply, service, or storage. Thus, we may note that *operations management is concerned with the design, planning, organizing, and controlling of systems for production, transport, supply, service, or storage.*

We may employ these definitions in describing either organizations as a whole or parts of those organizations. For example, a hotel (and the parts

FIGURE 1.4   VARIOUS OPERATIONS SYSTEMS AND THEIR PRINCIPAL CHARACTERISTICS

TYPE OF OPERATIONS SYSTEM	PRINCIPAL CHARACTERISTICS	EXAMPLES
Production	Physical creation (i.e., change in the *form* of resources)	Coal mine Clothing manufacturer Chinese take-out shop Food canner Construction company
Transport	Change in location (i.e., change in the *place* of resources)	Taxi service Ambulance service Moving company Solid waste collection service
Supply	Change in ownership or possession (i.e., change in the *possession* of resources)	Department store Fire department
Service	Treatment of something or someone (i.e., change in the *state* of resources)	Dentist Fire department Coin-operated laundry Hospital emergency room Hotel
Storage	Warehousing of a given item (i.e., change in the *availability* of resources)	Warehouse Bonded storage

thereof) has been classified as a service system—i.e., a system utilizing resources for the treatment of customers. However, within this system, the front desk operates as a *service* operations system, whereas the parking lot operates as a *storage* operations system.

OBJECTIVES OF OPERATIONS SYSTEMS

Certain organizations must, out of necessity, make a profit—i.e., total revenues generated must exceed total costs. The concept of profit provides a sufficient basis for establishing objectives for the operations system. However, some operations systems cannot easily be judged against this objective. For example, the hospital, fire department, unemployment office, and other services are not judged primarily on the basis of profit. In such organizations, other objectives have to be established. Even in profit-oriented organizations, some more immediate objectives of operations systems are desirable.

Customer Satisfaction

Operations management has been defined as the process of obtaining and utilizing resources to provide goods and services so as to meet customer wants and organizational goals. Thus, one objective of an operations system is customer satisfaction. The type of the operations system depends upon the details of customer wants.

Figure 1.5 identifies the main factors of customer satisfaction for each type of operations system. The primary factor is the nature of the goods or services provided. Secondary factors are costs and schedules. Thus, the objective of providing customer satisfaction means providing the goods or service at a competitive cost within a reasonable schedule.

Resource Productivity

Given infinite resources, any operations system, however badly managed, might perform adequately with respect to customer satisfaction. Numerous organizations have gone bankrupt despite having loyal and satisfied customers. Customer satisfaction must be provided simultaneously with the achievement of effective or efficient operation (i.e., effective or efficient utilization of resources). *Either* inefficient use of resources *or* inadequate customer service is sufficient to cause the failure of an operations system and, in turn, the failure of the whole organization.

Efficiency is conventionally defined in physical terms: e.g., as the ratio of useful work performed to the total energy expended, or as the ratio of useful output to input. Such definitions assign to efficiency a numerical value between zero and one. It has been pointed out that although this concept might be of

FIGURE 1.5   FACTORS IN CUSTOMER SATISFACTION

OPERATIONS SYSTEM TYPE	FACTORS IN CUSTOMER SATISFACTION	
	Primary Factors	*Secondary Factors*
Production	*Goods* of a given requested or acceptable specification	Cost (i.e., purchase price or cost of obtaining goods) Schedule (i.e., delivery delay from order schedule to request to receipt of goods)
Transport	*Movement* of a given requested or acceptable specification	Cost (i.e., cost of movement) Schedule (i.e., 1. duration, or time to schedule move 2. wait, or delay from transport request to its commencement)
Supply	*Goods* of a given requested or acceptable specification	Cost (i.e., purchase price or cost of obtaining goods) Schedule (i.e., scheduled delivery delay from time of order or request to supply, to receipt of goods)
Service	*Treatment* of a given requested or acceptable specification	Cost (i.e., cost of treatment) Schedule (i.e., 1. scheduled duration or time required for treatment 2. wait, or delay from request for treatment to its commencement)
Storage	*Warehousing* of a given requested or acceptable specification	Cost (i.e., cost of warehousing) Schedule (i.e., duration or time required for treatment)

relevance in essentially physical activities (e.g. the operation of a car engine), it is inappropriate with respect to organizations as a whole. In most cases, organizations should produce an output that is greater than the input; this is the concept of profit or "value added." For this reason the term *effectiveness* might be preferred since it has a broader connotation, suggesting the extent or degree of success in achieving given ends. Since operations management is concerned essentially with the utilization of resources, an objective must be the maximum utilization of such resources—i.e., obtaining maximum effect from such resources or minimizing their loss, underutilization, or waste. The extent of utilization of the potential of resources can be expressed in terms of the proportion of available time used or occupied, space utilization, levels of activity, etc. In each case, it indicates the extent to which the potential or capacity of such resources is utilized. We can refer to this as the objective of *resource productivity*.

Operations management is concerned with providing both satisfactory customer service and resource productivity. Operations management is responsible for a large portion of total resources, and for this reason it has to attempt to balance the two objectives. Certainly, it will be judged according to both of them. One objective must be balanced against the other, since an improvement in one often gives rise to a deterioration in the other; they cannot be optimized individually, and satisfactory performance must be achieved for both combined. All the activities of operations management—i.e., the design, planning, operation, and control of operations systems—must be developed with these twin objectives in mind.

Some ideas employed in developing the classification of operations systems earlier in this chapter are exemplified in Figure 1.6. The nature of the physical resources employed in the particular operations system constituted by a hotel and the customers for that system are indicated. The specific nature of the twin objectives of operations management is also given, together with a brief list of the activities through which such objectives must be satisfied.

Type of Operations System: Hotel

Objectives   Activities to achieve objectives

Resource Productivity

Physical Resources: Relating for example to: Design and Planning:
  Bedrooms   Room occupancy   a. Location of facilities
  Amenities and common   Staff utilization   b. Layout
    facilities, e.g., dining   Inventory levels   c. Specification of
    room, lounges, etc.   Utilization of other   range of facilities
  Service facilities and   facilities   • Number of bedrooms,
    equipment   Energy efficiency   size
  Parking lot   • Number of staff
  Reception staff   • Capacity of other
  Domestic and auxiliary staff   facilities
                                                                            • Operation hours and
                                                                               periods

                          AND

              Customer service

Customers: Relating for example to: Operation and Control:
  The General Public   Cost   a. Security
  (individually or in groups)   Room availability   b. Service, maintenance
                                           and choice   and replacement
                                         Facilities available   of facilities
                                                                            c. Inventory control

Figure 1.6 A Hotel As an Operations System

THE IMPACT OF OPERATIONS RESEARCH

The development of operations management has been greatly influenced by the impact of an analytical approach to problem-solving called *operations research*. This approach originated in England and the U.S. during World War II and was aimed at solving difficult war-related problems through the use of science, mathematics, behavioral science, probability theory, and statistics. The approach enjoyed a considerable amount of success.

Following World War II, the concepts of operations research (OR) were extended to problems in industry, trade, and commerce. A large number of mathematicians began devoting attention to mathematical formulation of a wide variety of operational problems. This mathematical approach to problem-solving had a dramatic impact on operations management education and practice.

As originally conceived, the operations research approach was as follows: a specific problem was identified; specialists from appropriate fields were formed into an interdisciplinary task force to develop a solution; appropriate mathematical relationships were brought to bear on the problem; consideration was given to the interaction of the various components of the operations system being studied; the "best" solution was decided upon and presented to management; and, finally, once the work of the task force was completed, the task force was disbanded.

As currently used, the term "operations research" (sometimes called management science) connotes a set of quantitative methods that are applicable

FIGURE 1.7 OPERATIONAL PROBLEMS

OPERATIONAL PROBLEMS	RELATIVE FREQUENCY (PERCENT)
Labor/industrial relations	7.0
Cost control within production area only	6.7
Production control	6.6
Quality control	6.6
Production process design	6.3
Production planning	6.0
Production scheduling	5.9
Personnel	5.7
Maintenance	5.4
Purchasing	5.4
Inventory control	5.2
Forecasting	3.9
Budgeting	3.6
Safety	3.5
Job shop design	3.2
Long-range planning	3.2
Product design	2.9
Accounting/control	2.0
Standards	1.9
Production selection	1.8
Plant location	1.8
Marketing	1.6
Cost/price estimates	1.3
Delivery	1.1
Finance	0.9

Source: R. R. Britney, "Continuing Education in Production/Operations Management," 34th Annual Meeting, Academy of Management, Seattle, 1974.

to a wide range of managerial and operational problems. This book will present quantitative methods that have been conceived under the operations research (or management science) umbrella, and that have been used extensively by production and operations management personnel in the Fortune 500 companies. Among these techniques one can find: inventory models, linear programming, statistical sampling, forecasting, network analysis, regression and correlation, simulation, and waiting line analysis. These techniques can help the operations manager in identifying, in a numerical way, solutions to operational problems such as: the location of facilities, layout of facilities, determination of capacity requirements, job design, work standards, activities scheduling, inventory control, maintenance control, quality control, and facilities replacement. The relative importance of such operational problems is indicated in Figure 1.7.

THE SYSTEMS APPROACH

This book is a systems approach to operations management. In the systems approach, the organization is viewed as an operations system. *A system is a collection of people, resources, and information that is intended to perform a specific function, or reach a predetermined objective.* The proper identification of the function or objective is critical in understanding the nature of the system. For example, the objective of the quality control department is not only to find defectives, but also to ensure a product of specified quality. The goal of a customer service department is not only to deal with deliveries or unpaid bills, but also to ensure customer satisfaction.

Every system is a subsystem of some larger system. The number of levels, or the hierarchical order, of systems is almost unlimited. For example, a department store, viewed as a system, consists of the following subsystems: purchasing, customer service, display, storage, and store operations. In addition, the department store may be a subsidiary of a chain of stores, such as K-Mart or Saks Fifth Avenue, which are subsystems of all merchandising systems, which are a part of the system of the U.S. economy, and so on. Thus, the operations system is a subsystem of the organization system.

The concept of systems approach to operations management has been developed along with the use of various analytical tools. Thus, this book deals with systems and with some selected analytical tools that are used in the design, planning, organizing, and controlling of operations systems.

Systems Structure and Environment

A system consists of three major components: inputs, processes, and outputs. These components are shown in Figure 1.8.

In viewing the organization as a system, we recognize as well the concept of *control*. Control involves the measurement of outputs, the comparison of the actual outputs to the desired or expected outputs, and the adjustment of inputs

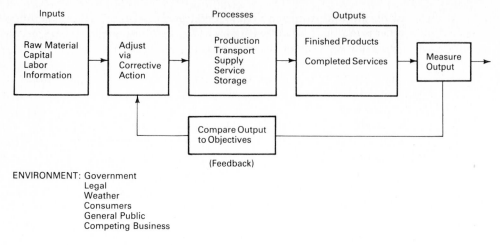

Figure 1.8 System's Components

and processes. The management of the business organization acts as a decision-maker when it is notified of the comparison results and decides whether or not adjustments in the organizational activities are required.

The concept of control, or a feedback mechanism, is an important element of the systems view of business organizations. The feedback mechanism includes the measurement of output, the comparison of the output to the objectives, and an adjustment component. The management constitutes the basic control element of the organization. Thus, given a certain output objective or expected output (perhaps a profit increment), the manager may measure (compare) actual output against expected output. If a difference exists, then a problem is indicated. This formation is used by the management group to formulate a solution that becomes an additional input to the organization as a process (this is the feedback). The purpose of the solution is to modify the operation of the system so as to eliminate the difference between actual and desired (expected) outputs.

The control, or feedback mechanism, adds an adaptive capability to the system. The mechanism includes several elements:

1. A *display device* or *identifier*, which indicates the measured output of the organization or any of the subsystems at any time. *Example:* For a manufacturing plant, the identifier may indicate its production capacity, current running capacity, order backlog, inventory status, orders in process, production lines in operation, and machine breakdowns.

2. An *adjustment unit*, the element that actually causes a change in the input before it enters the system or the process.

3. An *adjustment signal*, which activates the adjustment unit and which is sent after a comparison of output to objectives. *Example:* For a manufacturing

plant, the adjustment unit is the production manager. If a particular large order is received, this manager may order, over time, the use of subcontractors or the expansion of current capacity.

Because the *adjustment signal* and the *adjustment unit* are frequently confused, the difference between the two should be noted. A usual illustrative example concerns an automobile. If one wants to stop an automobile, one presses on the brake pedal. This transmits information (in the form of hydraulic pressure) to the brakes of the car. This information is the adjustment signal. Thus, it is not the brake pedal that stops the car, but the brakes, which are the adjustment unit.

Inputs, outputs, processes, and control elements as shown in Figure 1.8, together constitute a system. There are, in addition, elements that are not a part of the system. They are not inputs, outputs, or processes, but they do affect the system's operations. These elements constitute the system's environment. One can determine whether or not an element is environmental by answering two questions about the element:

1. Is it possible to manipulate the element?
2. Does the element matter relative to the system's goals?

If the answer to the first question is no, but to the second, yes, then the element is an environmental element. Environmental elements may be economic, social, political, physical, or legal. For a fast-food outlet, the economy, the community, and the weather represent environmental elements.

As all systems are subsystems of other systems, it is necessary to limit the analysis of a particular system and its operation to a well-defined area. This limiting procedure is termed "closing the system" or "boundary setting."

THE OPERATIONS SYSTEM

Operations management deals with the operations system of the organization, whether production or service. The operations system is a subsystem, or part, of the organization (which is also a system). Its prime goal is to generate goods or services. In either case, the operations system includes a *conversion process*, and *inputs* and *outputs*, as well as elements of control.

A restaurant, a department store, a construction company, and a hospital each includes the elements of an operations system. Figure 1.9 presents the operations system of a construction company and a department store.

The environment affects the operations system in as much as it imposes unplanned and largely uncontrollable random fluctuations on the various inputs. This causes actual outputs to differ from planned outputs.

The conversion of inputs into outputs varies considerably, depending on the technology involved. *Technology* means the set of conversion activities that

Construction Company

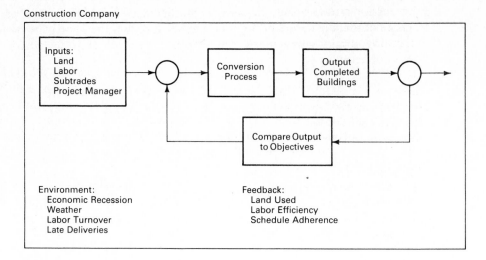

Department Store

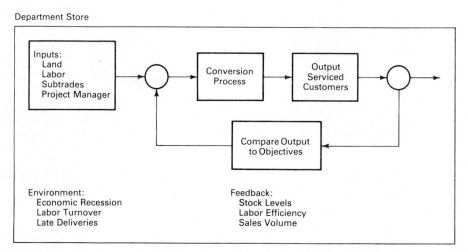

Figure 1.9   The Operations System for a Construction Company and a Department Store

take place throughout the process, using equipment and skills to produce certain outputs. The level of sophistication of the technology involved varies considerably and affects the quality, cost and schedule of the delivery of services and goods.

THE MANAGEMENT OF OPERATIONS SYSTEM

In the last section, we described the operations system. This system should be managed effectively and efficiently. The operations manager has the responsibility to create and operate the operations system and to be in charge of the conversion process that transforms inputs into outputs. The classical process school of management endorses four areas of activities for the manager: design, planning, organizing, and control. The various parts of this book adhere to these areas of activities.

Design   This activity has to do with the overall strategy of operations. The operations manager designs the operations system and the conversion processes. This activity includes strategic decision areas, such as product and process decision and design, as well as facility location. (Part two of the book)

Planning   The operations manager selects the objectives for the operations system of the organization and the policies and procedures that are required to achieve these objectives. This activity includes aggregate planning aided by accurate forecasting, layout planning, and operations scheduling. (Part three of the book)

Organizing   The operations manager identifies the various jobs within the operations system and defines authority and responsibility for each. This activity includes personnel assignment, job design and analysis, work measurement, compensation, and motivation. (Part four of the book)

Control   The operations manager assures that the objectives of the operations system are achieved by monitoring the performance of the system. The control activity is highly affected by the design, planning, and organizing activities. The control activity involves control of quality, maintenance, inventory, and material requirements planning. (Part five of the book)

In operations management, a decision made in regard to one activity may have a significant effect not only on that particular operation, but on other activities as well. For example, a decision to schedule overtime for production people will not only increase the wage bill but will also increase the incoming, in process, and finished goods inventory levels.

MODELING AND MANAGERIAL DECISION PROCESS

Operations managers are aided in decision-making by well-proven quantitative models. Design making through systems analysis involves more than the use of quantitative models. However, models are such a key characteristic of this type of analysis that they merit further discussion. For example, a quantitative model may present the relationship between sales volume (Q, expressed in units), price per unit (p, expressed in dollars) and revenue (R, expressed in dollars):

$$R = pQ$$

Most quantitative models are equations or systems of equations.

There are four necessary steps in the use of quantitative models in managerial decision-making:

1. Construct a quantitative model that satisfies the conditions of the tool to be used and that, at the same time, describes the important factors in the management situation to be analyzed.
2. Define the criteria, the measures that are to be used for comparing the relative merits of various possible courses of action or decisions.
3. Determine the value of the parameters in the analytical model, based on historical data.
4. Use the quantitative model to find the decision that, for the specified parameter values, optimizes the criteria function.

The construction of such a model goes beyond the simply *descriptive* role of traditional physical science models, and introduces the *prescriptive* role of modern systems analysis through the criteria (or *objective*) function. The model formulated should be one that can be solved, although insoluble models have occasionally provoked the development of new solution techniques.

Table 1.1 presents a classification of models, along with some examples. In the analysis of a particular operations management system, any of the types of models shown in Table 1.1 may be useful. However, as the analysis progresses, the models tend less to be of the iconic and analog model types and tend more to be symbolic.

TABLE 1.1   CLASSIFICATION OF MODELS

TYPE OF MODEL	EXAMPLE
Iconic	Architects' models of houses, engineering drawings, maps, organization charts
Analog	Network flow analyzer using electricity as an analog for water or gas; hydraulic model of river basin coastal area
Symbolic	Mathematical equations, mathematical programming, digital simulation

TABLE 1.2   A PARTIAL LISTING OF METHODOLOGICAL TECHNIQUES EMPLOYED IN SYSTEMS ANALYSIS

Mathematical programming: linear, nonlinear, dynamic	Multivariate analysis
Control theory	Regression theory
Calculus of variations	Factor analysis
Benefit-cost analysis	Principal component analysis
Input-output analysis	Sampling theory
Search procedures	PERT/CPM
Inventory analysis	Simulation
Lagrangian analysis	Queuing theory
	Information theory

Table 1.2 contains a partial listing of some of the more common models employed in systems analysis.

MODELING TECHNIQUES

So far, this discussion of modeling techniques has been quite general. In this section, however, groups of quantitative techniques are described.

Analytical Optimization Models and Techniques

This set of techniques includes optimization methods using calculus as well as mathematical programming and control theory. These modeling techniques are both descriptive and normative. They are descriptive since they usually incorporate quantitative relationships between variables of the system and describe their interactions. They are normative since they provide an optimal solution.

Probabilistic Models and Techniques

This group of techniques includes and builds on the elementary techniques for describing probabilistic (stochastic) systems with appropriate statistical parameters. Important techniques in this set are those associated with waiting-lines theory and inventory theory, which concern service and storage capacities. Waiting-line theory itself is strictly descriptive; it does not produce decision solutions. Rather, it contributes important information required for decision-making by predicting such characteristics as the average waiting time of a customer in a facility. Often waiting-line models are combined with other optimization methods, including analytical techniques and simulation and search approaches. The combination of techniques provides the normative function. Many operations management problems are inventory problems of a sort, and a number of them have been solved by using approaches that combine various techniques. Probabilistic techniques are discussed in detail separately in this book.

Statistical Techniques

Statistical techniques comprise a class of techniques that include such methodology as multivariate analysis, hypothesis testing, and decision theory. These techniques are primarily descriptive, and are used mostly for design and planning. However, many of the techniques have prescriptive characteristics in the sense of the decision-making that is concerned with selecting the elements, data sets, and functions appropriate to describe a system. The techniques of multivariate analysis, including discriminate analysis, have had numerous applications in operations management, primarily in describing inventory, assembly line, and work measurement phenomena. These techniques are discussed later in the book.

Simulation and Search Procedures

Simulation is a descriptive technique. A simulation model incorporates the quantifiable relationships among variables and describes the outcome of operating a system under a given set of inputs and operating conditions. Most simulation models do not contain algorithms for seeking optimal solutions.

Often a simulation model is run many times with various input and parameter data. The outputs of these runs describe the response of the system to variations in inputs and parameters. If the simulation model includes an objective function, the values of the objective function for the several runs produce a "response surface." Simulation is discussed in detail in the Technical Note to Chapter 8. Search techniques explore the response surface and seek near-optimal or optimal solutions by applying a set of logically developed rules.

Operations managers typically use a combination of qualitative and mathematical approaches, and many important decisions are based on qualitative approaches. The reason for the emphasis on mathematical approaches is that such approaches are usually more difficult to understand without an extensive presentation and training.

THE USE OF COMPUTERS

Many operations management problems are rather complex, involving numerous interrelated variables. The search for and evaluation of alternative solutions, especially when sophisticated models are involved, may become a gigantic computational project. In many cases, a manual or hand-calculator approach to the analysis is impractical or even impossible. Many problems are solvable only with the aid of high-speed computational devices. The use of computers has thus become closely associated with operations management. Computers have the important advantage of being a relatively inexpensive means of rapid calculation, possessing the accuracy and flexibility that are invaluable in experimenting with solving managerial decision models.

The computer (whether available in-house or through an outside service agency) has provided a means for solving those problems that have long been quantifiable but computationally too complex or time-consuming for manual calculation. Problems that would take months to solve manually can be solved in seconds by using computers. Production and personnel scheduling, allocation of resources, blending of raw materials, investment, ordering of materials, and other managerial activities can be reevaluated daily in the light of current information. Previously such activities could be reevaluated only weekly, monthly, or even annually. By the time decisions were made, the information on which they were based was often obsolete, so that undesired consequences occurred.

As time passes, the availability of computers will increase and the cost of processing data and computing results will decrease. Thus, more and more use will be made of computers in operations management.

Throughout this book a conversational (interactive-mode), real-time approach to computer use is assumed. For this, the operations manager should have a computer terminal on his desk, ready for use. All operational problems should be solved with short and frequent question-and-answer sessions (between the operations manager and the computer). The old, rule-of-thumb, haphazard approach to operational decisions must be replaced by computer-aided decision making.

In the next section, we present a simple model, called the "decision tree," which is used for decisions in the design, planning, organizing, and controlling of operations.

DECISION SITUATIONS IN OPERATIONS MANAGEMENT

The operations manager often deals with decisions that are of a sequential nature—that is, a sequence of decisions that should be made one by one, over time, as the operation evolves. Decision trees may be used to structure and analyze such decision situations as size of a hospital facility, number of seats in a medical clinic, etc. Decision trees are useful as models for two reasons:

1. Through the construction of a decision tree, decision alternatives and chance occurrences (or events) are identified. This in itself is a helpful planning aid.
2. The results of a decision tree analysis identify the best decision under the circumstances.

There are four steps in decision-tree analysis:

Step 1. Draw a tree diagram complete with alternative decisions and the payoff (outcome) of each decision.
Step 2. Define probability estimates for chance occurrences (events) and the payoff (outcome) of each chance occurrence.
Step 3. Calculate the expected payoff of all decisions.
Step 4. Select the decision with the highest expected payoff.

Let us consider a decision tree analysis that pertains to petroleum exploration. In our example, the Management of Wildcat Exploration Company is considering a drilling project for gas off the California coast. There is a probability of 70% that the drilling project will find a dry hole, in which case Wildcat Exploration will lose $50,000; there is a 20% probability of finding a gas reserve of 2 billion cubic feet (BCF), in which case the company will make a profit of $100,000; there is a 10% probability of finding a gas reserve of 5 billion cubic feet, in which case the company will make a profit of $250,000. What is the best decision?

This example is simple because it involves only an initial decision either to drill or not drill. And, in fact, we can compute the expected monetary values (EMV) of the two possible decisions, as shown in Table 1.3. Based on step 4, described above, the choice would be to drill.

This simple problem could be solved using decision-tree analysis. The first step would be to draw a diagram of the decision alternatives and the possible outcomes. The diagram, or tree, for this example is shown in Figure 1.10.

A decision tree is merely a pictorial representation of a sequence of events and possible outcomes. The decision tree in Figure 1.10 illustrates the decision alternatives "drill" and "don't drill." If the well is drilled, there are three possible outcomes: a dry hole, finding reserves of 2 BCF, or finding reserves of 5 BCF.

The point from which two or more branches emanate is called a *node*. A node surrounded by a square denotes a *decision node,* a point at which the decision-maker dictates which branch is followed. An encircled node is called a *chance node,* a point at which chance determines the outcome. These nodes are indicated in Figure 1.11.

The next step in constructing a decision tree is to associate probabilities of occurrence with all the branches radiating from chance nodes and to specify values received at the endpoint of each "open" branch. These values are shown on the tree in Figure 1.12.

In this example, the values received are expressed as profits. However, we could use costs or opportunity losses. The decision tree as drawn in Figure 1.12 is interpreted as follows: there is probability of 0.7 of drilling a dry hole with a resulting loss of $50,000; a 0.2 probability of finding 2 BCF of reserves valued at a net profit of +$100,000; and so on.

TABLE 1.3   DATA FOR DRILLING PROSPECT

		DECISIONS			
		DRILL		DON'T DRILL	
Possible Occur- rences	*Probability of Occurrence*	*Conditional Monetary Profits*	*Expected Monetary Values*	*Conditional Monetary Profits*	*Expected Monetary Values*
Dry Hole	0.7	− $ 50,000	− $35,000	0	0
2 BCF	0.2	+ 100,000	+ 20,000	0	0
5 BCF	0.1	+ 250,000	+ 25,000	0	0
	1.0		EMV* = + $10,000		EMV = 0

*EMV = (0.7)(−$50,000) + (0.2)(+$100,000) + (0.1)(250,000) = +$10,000

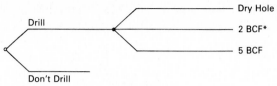

*BCF = billion cubic feet of gas reserves

Figure 1.10 Partially Completed Decision Tree for Example of Table 1.3

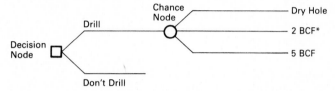

Figure 1.11 Partially Completed Decision Tree with Chance and Decision Nodes Indicated

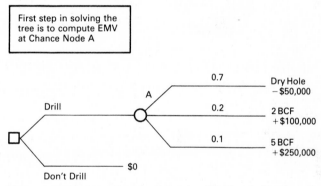

Figure 1.12 Decision Tree for Example of Table 1.3, Showing the First Step in the Solution of the Tree

When indicating probabilities on a decision tree, we must adhere to two important rules. First, the sum of the probabilities emanating from a given chance node must add to 1.0. Second, no probabilities may be shown on the branches emanating from a decision node. The probabilities emanating from a chance node indicate the relative likelihood of each outcome (branch) occurring.

The ends of a decision tree are called *terminal* points. Use of the adjective "terminal" indicates that there are no further decisions, or chance events, beyond that point. There are four terminal points on the tree of Figure 1.13. The terminal points of a decision tree are all said to be mutually exclusive. This means that we will ultimately end up at one, and only one, terminal point on the tree.

Once the decision tree has been drawn and we have indicated all of the probabilities and terminal point values, we are ready to solve it. We start by making an expected value computation using the terminal points around the last chance node in the tree. For our simple example, we first make an EMV computation at the chance node labeled A in Figure 1.12.

This EMV computation involves multiplying the probabilities of occurrence of each possible outcome (branch) by the corresponding terminal point values. For the example in Figure 1.13, the computation is as follows:

$$EMV_A = (0.7) (-\$50,000) + (0.2) (+\$100,000) + (0.1) (+\$250,000)$$

$$EMV_A = +\$10,000$$

This expected value is written above chance node A in Figure 1.13.

Next we proceed backward (to the left) in the tree to the next node, which in this case is a decision node. Now we make a decision as if the decision-maker were actually standing in the square. His choices are summarized as having an expectation of +\$10,000 if he drills, and an expectation of zero if he doesn't drill. That is, his choices at decision node B could be represented schematically as in Figure 1.14. Note that the EMV of +\$10,000 at chance node A is used to represent, or replace, all of the tree beyond that point. It is as if the chance node and its branches are completely blanked out and replaced with their equivalent—the EMV at chance node A.

The decision rule at any decision node is to select the alternative (branch) that has the highest EMV. In this case, it would be to drill. Hence, we cross out the ''don't drill'' branch as being a suboptimal strategy and move the expected value for the alternative selected back to the decision node, as in Figure 1.15. Now everything to the right of decision node B is replaced by the expectation shown above the node, +\$10,000. Next we would continue backward in the tree to the next node.

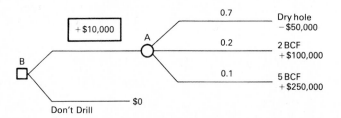

Figure 1.13   Decision Tree Showing the Expected Value at Chance Node A

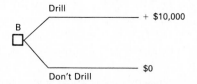

Figure 1.14   Schematic Drawing of Decision-Maker's Choices at Decision Node B

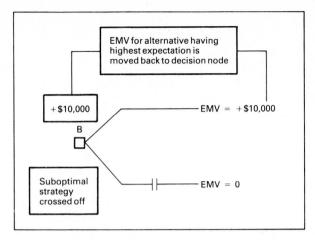

Figure 1.15   Schematic Drawing Showing the Decision that Is Made at Decision Node B

Each time we come to a chance node we make an EMV calculation, and each time we come to a decision node we make a hypothetical decision according to our decision rule. This process is continued until the initial, current decision node is reached, at which time the tree has been solved. In our simple illustration, there was nothing to the left of decision node B, so our tree was solved at that point. The decision, based on the tree, was to "drill"—exactly the same solution we found on the basis of the EMV calculation of Table 1.3.

Decision-tree analysis is simple and logical—as far as the definitions and mechanics of solution are concerned. The difficulties usually arise in correctly organizing and drawing the trees for decisions of a more complex nature.

The advantages of decision-tree analysis for operational decisions include the following:

1. All contingencies and possible decision alternatives are defined and analyzed in a consistent manner. The complex decision is broken into a series of small parts; then the parts are "reassembled" piece by piece to provide a rational basis for the initial decision.
2. Such an analysis provides a better chance for consistent action in achieving a systems goal than does a series of decisions. That is because each step in the sequence has been analyzed ahead of time. This reduces the likelihood of the operations manager's ending up at some future option point and wondering how the sequence of events ever led him to that point and what should be done next (such as drilling a second wildcat or quitting).
3. Any operational decision, no matter how complicated, can be analyzed by this method.
4. The entire sequential course of action is set out prior to the initial decision. This is a good feature in cases in which authority is to be delegated.

SUMMARY

Operations management is the process of obtaining and utilizing resources to provide goods and services so as to meet customer wants and organizational goals.

Operations management is one of the six management activities found in virtually every organization. However, the term "operations management" may not be used to label the operations management function. Instead, this function is described by indicating the operation process with which the organization is involved.

The business organization is viewed as a system. A system is defined as a collection of people, resources and information that is intended to perform a specific function, or to reach a predetermined objective. As all systems are

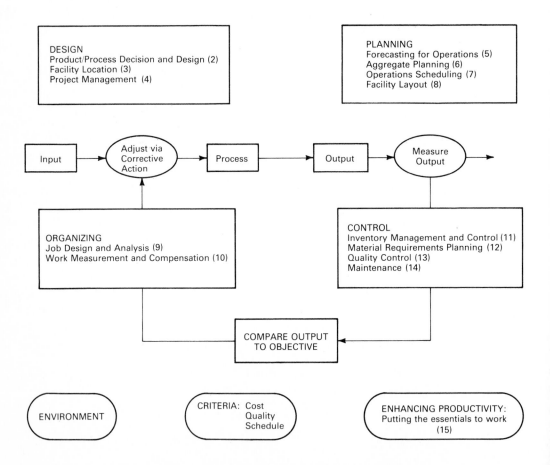

Figure 1.16 A Graphical Model of Operations Management (Note chapter numbers.)

subsystems of a larger one, the operations system is a subsystem of the business organization system.

Systems concepts are useful for understanding the role of operations systems, and modeling is an important tool in performing the design, planning, organizing and control activities. Operations management and operations managers make use of the systems approach and mathematical modeling.

One particular modeling technique—namely, decision analysis—has been discussed in detail. This technique helps managers in operational decision making.

This book presents operations management as the management of operations systems.

Figure 1.16 presents a general graphical model of operations management. This figure includes all the activities performed by the operations manager (Design, planning, organizing, control) and the elements of the operations system (Inputs, outputs, processes, control). This graphical model provides the conceptual framework which is used throughout this book.

DISCUSSION QUESTIONS

1.1 Identify the five classes of operations systems and give examples of each class.

1.2 Two definitions of operations management have been presented in this chapter. Compare and contrast them.

1.3 What are the components of an operations system?

1.4 What class of operations system would include a McDonald's restaurant?

1.5 Following Figure 1.6, generate a chart showing the resources, customers, objectives, and activities for:
a) a fire department.
b) a Chinese take-out outlet.

1.6 Discuss the impact of operations research (OR) on operations management (OM).

1.7 Define a system.

1.8 How would you identify an environmental element? Think of a specific business organization and define for it some environmental elements.

1.9 Describe the four activities performed by the operations manager.

1.10 Present the operations system for an accounting firm and a computer software house. The presentation should follow the graphical model of Figure 1.9.

1.11 What are the four necessary steps in the use of formal mathematical models in managerial decision-making?

1.12 What are analytical optimization models and techniques, probabilistic models and techniques, statistical techniques, and simulation and search techniques?

1.13 What are the four steps involved in decision-tree analysis?

1.14 Present a decision problem as a tree diagram.

PROBLEMS AND SOLUTIONS

1.1   Western Steel Mill, Inc., is considering an expansion of its facilities. The expansion success depends highly on the market conditions in the coming years. Management assumes that there is a 0.01 chance of a major recession and a 0.99 chance of a boom. The net profit figures (in millions of dollars) appear in the following table.

Alternatives	Recession	Boom
No Expansion	100	100
Expansion	50	120

Use decision-tree analysis to determine whether an expansion of the facilities is warranted.

Solution

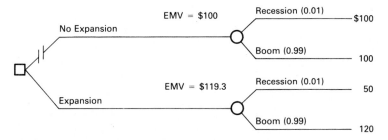

(Figures in millions of dollars)

For No Expansion: EMV = (100)(0.01) + (100)(0.99) = $100

For Expansion   EMV = (50)(0.01) + (120)(0.99) = $119.3

Decision: Western Steelmill should expand to maximize expected monetary value (EMV)

1.2   The growth rate of Betterway Supermarkets, Inc., in the past several years has been of concern to the management. Betterway is considering two alternatives for enhancing growth:
a) Expand the number of brand names carried
b) Increase the size of inventories
        There is a 60 percent chance that the economy will boom, in which case there is a 70 percent chance for increased demand. If demand increases, a profit of $2,000,000 is expected; however, if demand remains stable, only $1,000,000 profit is expected. If the size of inventories is increased, a profit of $900,000 is anticipated in case of increased demand; otherwise, $800,000 will be the profit.
        If the economy enters recession, there is a 50 percent chance for high demand, and 50 percent for low demand. The profits for each possibility are estimated to be:

Expand the number of brand names and high demand	$800,000
Expand the number of brand names and low demand	$500,000

| Increase the size of inventories and high demand | $550,000 |
| Increase the size of inventories and low demand | $300,000 |

Expanding the number of brand names involves a cost of $150,000. Expanding the size of inventories involves $90,000. Should Betterway Supermarkets, Inc., expand the number of brand names or increase the size of its inventory?

$$EMV_A = (0.70) (2,000,000) + (0.30) (1,000,000) = \$1,700,000$$
$$EMV_B = (0.50) (800,000) \quad + (0.50) (500,000) \quad = \$650,000$$
$$EMV_E = (0.60) (1,700,000) + (0.40) (650,000) \quad = \$1,280,000$$

Expanding the number of brand names will result in an expected monetary value (EMV) of $1,280,000 less than the required $150,000, or $1,130,000.

$$EMV_C = (0.70) (900,000) + (.30) (800,000) = \$870,000$$
$$EMV_D = (0.50) (550,000) + (.50) (300,000) = \$425,000$$
$$EMV_F = (0.60) (870,000) + (.40) (425,000) = \$692,000$$

Increasing the size of inventories will result in an expected monetary value (EMV) of $692,000 less the required $90,000, or $602,000. Decision: Betterway Supermarkets, Inc., should expand the number of brand names.

Solution

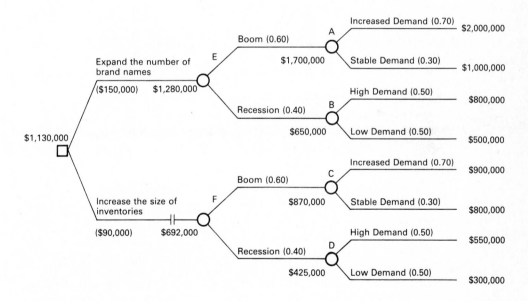

CHAPTER REVIEW PROBLEMS

1.1   Sheldon-Gear, Inc., a producer of automatic transmissions, anticipates a receipt of an order of Model AE-1 automatic transmissions. The order has to be processed on a numerically controlled machine that is prone to failure. Management has to decide whether to spend $600 to upgrade the machine performance before the new order is processed. As the due date for the order will determine the load on the machine, the management has assumed various loads probabilities and revenue figures. The complete decision tree is presented below:

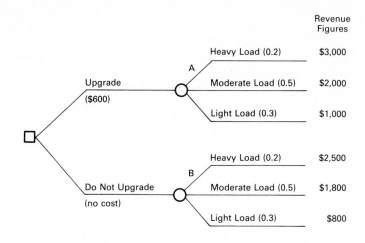

Revenue Figures

Heavy Load (0.2)	$3,000
Moderate Load (0.5)	$2,000
Light Load (0.3)	$1,000
Heavy Load (0.2)	$2,500
Moderate Load (0.5)	$1,800
Light Load (0.3)	$800

Should Sheldon-Gear, Inc. upgrade the Numerically Controlled machines?

1.2 COMPU-XI, Inc., a computer service company, is in the process of selecting a new computer system. The alternatives are:
a) Lease a large computer system
b) Lease a medium-size computer system
c) Lease a small computer system
The market acceptance of their services is anticipated to be high with a probability of 0.4, and low with a probability of 0.6.
    The net profits are stated below:

	MARKET ACCEPTANCE	
Alternative	*High*	*Low*
Large System	$350,000	($40,000)
Medium-Size System	$250,000	$30,000
Small System	$150,000	$60,000

Use a decision-tree analysis to determine which computer system COMPU-XI, Inc., should lease.

1.3 Given the following decision tree for an expansion of Baxter Hospital, find the best alternative and its expected value. The outcomes shown are costs and the investment expenses are in brackets.

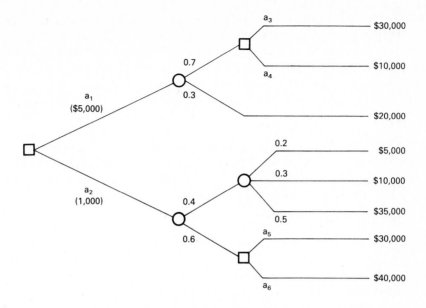

Factors: Risk analysis begins in the field, where local managers are constantly on alert for subtle signs of instability. The information is sometimes supplemented by expensive risk-analysis surveys that corporations regularly buy. But the final analysis is based on business and political factors unique to the country—and company—in question. A firm interested in processing foods in Mexico, for example, has to consider that the government is under some pressure to nationalize the food industry. And while an auto manufacturer will primarily want to analyze a country's regulatory atmosphere and labor militancy, a bank looking to invest in the same country will be more concerned with the government's ability to service debt.

An analysis sometimes will trigger withdrawal from a troubled nation, but less drastic measures will often protect a company's assets. American Can, for example, was advised to form a partnership with a native firm to insulate itself from the instability of the South Korean dictatorship. Occasionally the advice is ignored—in part because businessmen find the abstract art of risk analysis difficult to grasp. But corporations usually take whatever precautions are necessary, including taking out high-priced political-risk insurance policies.

But risk analysts don't just spread doom and gloom. Sometimes they help a company make the best of it, especially mining and oil firms that don't have the luxury of moving elsewhere. After all, says consultant Jan Dauman of the InterMatrix Group, "a very unstable environment may be one in which you can make a lot of money." That's something very few corporations are willing to pass up—no matter what the risks.

Questions

1. Which mathematical models can be used by risk analysts?
2. "Major corporate decisions may be reached at by using decision trees." Qualify this statement in light of the reading above.

BIBLIOGRAPHY

AARON, J. D., "Information Systems in Perspective," *Computing Surveys,* December, 1969, pp. 213–36.

ACKOFF, R. L., "Management Misinformation Systems," *Management Science,* December, 1967, pp. B147–B156.

ADAM, E. E., and R. T. EBERT, *Production and Operations Management.* Englewood Cliffs, New Jersey: Prentice-Hall, Inc., 1978.

BIERMAN, H., C. P. BONINI, and W. H. HAUSMAN, *Quantitative Analysis for Business Decisions,* 5th ed., Chaps. 1–6. Homewood, Ill.: Richard D. Irwin, 1977.

BRITNEY, R. R., and E. F. P. NEWSON, *The Canadian Production/Operations Management Environment: An Audit.* School of Business Administration Research Monograph, London, Ontario: University of Western Ontario, April, 1975.

BUDNICK, F. S., R. MOJENA, and T. E. VOLLMAN, *Principles of Operations Research for Management.* Homewood, Ill.: R. D. Irwin, 1977.

BUFFA, E. S., *Modern Production Management,* 5th ed. New York: John Wiley and Sons, 1977.

CHASE, R., and N. AQUILANO, *Production and Operations Management,* 3rd ed. Homewood, Ill.: R. D. Irwin, 1981.

COOK, T. M., and R. A. RUSSELL, *Contemporary Operations Management.* Englewood Cliffs, New Jersey: Prentice-Hall, Inc., 1980.

DEARDEN, J., "MIS is a Mirage," *Harvard Business Review,* January–February 1972, pp. 90–99.

EBERT, R. J., and T. R. MITCHELL, *Organizational Decision Processes: Concepts and Analysis.* New York: Crane, Russak and Co., Inc., 1975.

GAITHER, N., "The Adoption of Operations Research Techniques by Manufacturing Organizations," *Decision Sciences,* 6, No. 4, October, 1975, pp. 797–813.

HEAD, R. V., "The Elusive MIS," *Datamation,* September 1, 1970, pp. 22–27.

KOONTZ, H., and C. O'DONNELL, *Principles of Management: An Analysis of Managerial Function,* 5th ed. New York: McGraw-Hill, 1972.

LEE, S. M., and L. J. MOORE, *Introduction to Decision Science,* Chaps. 1 and 3. New York: Petrocelli/Charter Publishers, 1975.

LEVITT, T., "Production-Line Approach to Service," *Harvard Business Review* 50, No. 5, September–October, 1972.

MICHAEL, G. C., "A Review of Heuristic Programming," *Decision Sciences* 3, No. 3, July, 1972, pp. 74–100.

MONKS, J. G., *Operations Management: Theory and Problems.* New York: McGraw-Hill, 1982.

MORRIS, W. T., "On the Art of Modelling," *Management Science* 13, No. 2, August, 1967, pp. 707–17.

ROSENZWEIG, J. E., "Managers and Management Scientists (Two Cultures)," *Business Horizons* 10, No. 3, Fall, 1967, pp. 79–86.

SCHUMACHER, C. C., and B. E. SMITH, "A Sample Survey of Industrial Operations Research Activities II," *Operations Research,* December, 1965, pp. 1023–27.

SKINNER, W., "Manufacturing—Missing Link in Corporate Strategy," *Harvard Business Review* 47, No. 3, May–June, 1969.

SMITH, A., *The Wealth of Nations.* New York: Random House, Inc., 1937.

SMITH, D. E., *Quantitative Business Analysis,* Chaps. 3 and 4. New York: John Wiley, 1977.

STARR, M. K., *Operations Management.* Englewood Cliffs, New Jersey: Prentice-Hall, Inc., 1978.

STEVENSON, W. J., *Production/Operations Management.* Homewood, Ill.: R. D. Irwin, 1982.

TAYLOR, F. W., *Scientific Management.* New York: Harper and Row, 1919.

———, *Shop Management.* New York: Harper and Row, 1911.

2

Product and Process Decision and Design

INTRODUCTION

New products and services are vital to the economic survival of business organizations. Most companies have continually to redesign existing products to reflect market demands, changing technologies, and changing costs of raw material and other inputs. New products and services are created by using new or improved processes.

Product decision, product design, process decision, and process design are important functions in every organization and greatly affect the operations system. The word "product" refers to the output of the operations systems, and describes both goods and services. The *product decision* involves the systematic gathering of several product ideas and the choosing of the product that will meet the organization's goals. *Product design* involves the development of the best design of the new product.

The *process decision* (sometimes referred to as process selection) involves the choice of the methods by which raw materials inputs are transformed into product outputs. The *process design* involves the development of the chosen method by which raw materials inputs are transformed into product outputs.

Successful product and process decision and design ensures the economic viability of the operating system and, in turn, the economic viability of the business organization.

THE PRODUCT LIFE CYCLE

As has just been suggested, new products and services are vital to the economic survival of business organizations. The continued introduction of new products or services assures the maintenance of the sales volume over a period of time as old products age through the product life cycle. The *product life cycle* relates the volume of sales of a product to the time that has elapsed since its introduction into the market place. The product life cycle involves four stages:

Stage 1   Introduction
Stage 2   Acceptance
Stage 3   Maturity
Stage 4   Decline

The stages for two products, A and B, are presented in Figure 2.1. In stage 1, the introduction stage, the product A is still new and unknown to the general public. There may be field troubles that call for redesign or production changes, and the product generally is high priced.

In stage 2, the acceptance stage, the product is improved, and its sales volume increases at an accelerated pace. Also, in many cases, the product price decreases, reflecting production efficiencies and reduced costs, effects of learning curves (discussed in Chapter 8), and, possibly, competition in the market place.

In stage 3, the maturity stage, the product is dependable and the product's trade name becomes accepted. During this stage, the company should be engaged in an effort to decide on, design, and start marketing a new and different product that will be able to sustain the production capacity and sales volume. In Figure 2.1, a new product, B, is entering stage 2 while product A is entering stage 3.

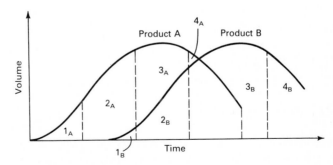

Figure 2.1   Product Life Cycle

In the fourth stage, the decline stage, the product is faced with new competition that may have benefited from new technological breakthroughs. Its popularity and sales volume decline. However, since the company has been involved in research and development of new products, sales of the new product replace those of the old product, as can be seen in Figure 2.1. Product B is entering stage 3, while product A is entering stage 4.

NEW PRODUCT DECISION AND DESIGN

Figure 2.2 shows the steps of the new product decision and design process. In any one of the stages described in Figure 2.2, the product or service could be scrapped. In the following sections, we shall concentrate on the description and demonstration of the steps involved in this process.

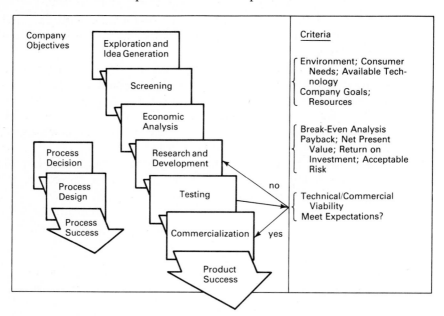

Figure 2.2 Stages in New Product Decision and Design

EXPLORATION AND IDEA GENERATION

Ideas for new products and services are generated both from within the organization (operations, marketing, finance, personnel, engineering departments) and from outside agencies and forces (government, customer/market needs).

While the actual process of exploration and idea generation varies from one organization to another, it is highly influenced by three major variables:

1. The nature of the organization's business operations.
2. The major competence or comparative advantage of the organization.
3. The organization's stated goals.

EXAMPLE   Consider as an example an increasingly energy-minded consumer market that has motivated General Electric to come up with a new low-energy light bulb. The product is a light bulb for the home that uses one third the energy of bulbs currently in use. The organization is the General Electric Lighting Division. Light bulbs fit well into the company's operations, as the General Electric Lighting Division is a leader in the production of light bulbs and other lighting devices. The division has been operated successfully for many years, and it makes a continuous effort to maintain its leadership. The production of a new type of light bulb is compatible with the company's comparative advantage and stated goals.

Figure 2.3 is a statement of goals for a light bulb manufacturer. It is this statement of goals that dictates the long- and short-term decisions in regard to the organization's operations.

A major competence and comparative advantage of General Electric is its extensive research and development capability which makes viable the most innovative product ideas. For the moment, assume that, using this capacity, General Electric has generated an idea to develop a light bulb that produces light in a manner different from the usual. We shall refer back to this example throughout this chapter.

SCREENING

In order to stimulate new ideas generation a checklist may be used, similar to the one presented in Figure 2.4. Using the checklist is a systematic way of stimulating creative thinking.

While there could be numerous ideas for new products/services, not all of these ideas will be developed. New product/service ideas should be screened and selected. The purpose of screening is to select the most promising ideas for further economic analysis, research and development, testing, and eventual commercialization. Extensive analysis may be conducted through test markets before a final decision is reached.

To assist in product screening, several techniques may be used. One is a scoring method that includes a list of factors, along with a weight for each. To evaluate a product idea, each factor is rated on a scale from 1 to 5, and a total weighted score is calculated. If the total score is above a certain level, the new

1. Maximize return on investment, consistent with growth objectives, and operate to protect that investment. The Company has as its objective 25% profit before tax and 45% return on stockholders' equity and long-term debt in order to maximize long-term growth and profitability, and remain a leader in the lighting industry in advanced technology, device development, and engineering.

2. Provide a productive and satisfying work environment for employees, offering career opportunities for personal development and advancement.

3. Remain an ethical manufacturer of lighting devices, providing customers with full value and establishing and maintaining a reputation for fair and honest business practices.

4. Maintain a basic technological capability permitting the company to develop, produce, and market a specific product within two years. Development is directed toward products that will have a significant market within 3 to 5 years.

5. Attain a sales volume adequate for a leader in the lighting industry, participating with a broad line of products and competing for a minimum of 30% in each market.

6. Participate in industrial, military, and consumer markets, with emphasis on the consumer market.

7. Manufacture lighting devices in high quantity and at minimum cost consistent with customer quality, volume, and energy requirements. Continue to develop, produce, and market high-performance lighting devices.

8. Maintain a standard performance product line that can be produced and marketed at low cost and high volume. This product line will employ the technology developed for the high-performance products and will depend upon new technology.

9. Obtain more contract sales, particularly in areas in which contract programs parallel company programs and product plans.

10. Consider domestic and foreign markets as one integrated world market, with interrelated technical, manufacturing, and marketing opportunities. The company will exploit the advantages of foreign manufacturing and marketing.

Figure 2.3   Light Bulb Manufacturer's Corporate Goals

idea may be selected for economic analysis. The total score may also be used to rank-order several new ideas to determine which are the best candidates for further development. An example of this scoring is presented in Figure 2.5.

The total weighted score is computed by multiplying the rating by the respective weight and adding, as follows:

1. Have I pinpointed the problem?
2. Have I searched books, reports, trade magazines, patents?
3. How would I design the product if I were to build it in my workshop at home?
4. Have I considered the physical, thermal, electrical, chemical, and mechanical properties of this material?
5. What other materials have the same required properties?
6. Have I looked for electrical, electronic, optical, hydraulic, mechanical, or magnetic ways of doing this?
7. Have I blindly followed tradition, custom, authority, opinion?
8. Have I looked at analogs for parallel problems?
9. Is this function really necessary?
10. How would other experts look at this problem?
11. Have I made this design accomplish its purpose?
12. Could I alter something already available to do the job?
13. Have I analyzed this in several ways?
14. Could I construct a model?
15. Why must it have this shape?
16. Could it be speeded up or slowed down?
17. Could this be turned inside out, upside down, or reversed?
18. Could this be changed to more of a three-dimensional object, or could it be flattened out?
19. Could this be made cheaper, or should it be made more expensive?
20. What if this were made larger, higher, longer, wider, thicker, or lower?
21. What could be substituted? For what?
22. How could I rearrange or alter the parts, the subassemblies?
23. Has it been simplified as much as possible?
24. In what new ways could it be used as it is?
25. What other forms of power would make it work better?
26. Where else can this be done?
27. Would this work better in the day, in the night, intermittently, or continuously?
28. Could this be put to other uses if it were modified?
29. Could several parts be combined?
30. Could standard components be substituted?
31. Could this be made easier to operate?
32. What if the order of the process were changed?
33. Can materials be salvaged or reclaimed?
34. Suppose this were left out?

Figure 2.4 Checklist for New Product Idea Stimulation

Figure 2.4 *(Cont.)*

> 35. How can this be made to appeal to the senses? How can its appearance be improved?
> 36. Can it be made safer?
> 37. Can it be made more compact?
> 38. Should it be made more symmetrical or more asymmetrical?
> 39. Can I forget the specifications and get a better performance?

FIGURE 2.5 NEW PRODUCT/SERVICE SCORING METHOD

PRODUCT/ SERVICE CHARACTER- ISTICS	RATING					WEIGHT
	Poor = 1	*Fair = 2*	*Good = 3*	*Very Good = 4*	*Excel- lent = 5*	
Meets Customer Expectations			X			15%
Technology Compatibility		X				15%
Sales Volume Potential					X	20%
Fit with Corpo- rate Goals				X		20%
Quality				X		10%
Revenue Potential			X			20%
					Total Weight	100%

Total Weighted Score (TWS) = (0.15)3 + (0.15)2 + (0.20)5 + (0.20)4 + (0.10)4

+ (0.20)3

= 0.45 + 0.30 + 1.00 + 0.80 + 0.40 + 0.60 = 3.55

Obviously, the ratings are subjective and should be used cautiously.

ECONOMIC ANALYSIS

Following the screening stage, the proposed products/services are subjected to an economic analysis. There are several techniques that may be used. This is a very important stage, as it determines the economic viability of the business organization. One simple method, entitled break-even analysis, is discussed in the following section. More complex techniques will be discussed and demonstrated in the Technical Note to this chapter.

Break-Even Analysis

The break-even point is the minimum volume of sales, in units of output or in dollar amount, that must be produced and sold in order for the firm to break even after paying all expenses. This volume is called the break-even point. Obviously, the firm is interested in producing and selling more than the break-even point in order to make a profit.

Let us first define two terms: fixed costs and variable costs. *Fixed costs* are the expenses that remain constant regardless of the volume of products or services. Examples of fixed costs are rent, property taxes, depreciation, insurance, and salaries to permanent staff. *Variable costs* are the expenses that fluctuate directly with changes in the output volume of products or services. Examples of variable costs are labor and material.

The break-even point is calculated as follows:

$$\frac{\text{Break-even point}}{\text{(in units)}} = \frac{\text{Fixed costs}}{\text{Unit selling price} - \text{Variable cost per unit}}$$

The difference between the unit selling price and the variable cost is the contribution of each unit sold toward covering the fixed costs or its "contribution to fixed costs and profit."

The break-even point is reached when the sales produce just enough revenue to equal the sum of all variable and fixed costs. One may like to include overhead expenses in the numerator of the break-even-point expression above. In this case, the difference between the unit selling price and the variable cost is the contribution of each unit sold to fixed costs, overhead expenses, and profit.

EXAMPLE General Electric is considering the production of the new, energy-saving light bulb. The selling price is $10.00, and the variable cost is about $2.00 per light bulb. If total fixed costs are $20 million, the break-even point, in units of output sold, or light bulbs, is

$$\text{Break-even point} = \frac{\$20,000,000}{\$10.00 - \$2.00} = 2,500,000$$

Thus, when General Electric produces 2,500,000 light bulbs, total costs equal total revenue. Let us check this result. Total costs are:

$$\$20,000,000 + \$2(2,500,000) = \$25,000,000.$$

The total revenue is:

$$\$10 \times 2,500,000 = \$25,000,000.$$

What will happen if the selling price of the light bulb is set by General Electric at $12? Obviously, the break-even point (volume of production) will be lower:

$$\text{Break-even point} = \frac{\$20,000,000}{\$12.00 - \$2.00} = 2,000,000 \text{ light bulbs.}$$

The selling price is subject to market constraints, and perhaps cannot be raised. However, the break-even point can be lowered by reducing production costs. This can be achieved through reduced scrap, and more efficient use of machines and labor. These topics are discussed elsewhere in this book.

Figure 2.6 presents a graph of the General Electric break-even point for a selling price of $10.00. The curves indicate the total variable costs, total fixed costs, the sum of variable and fixed costs, and the total revenue as a function of the volume of production. The presentation assumes that all the light bulbs will be sold. The break-even point is the point at which total costs equal revenues.

General Electric could use this break-even analysis to decide on a price for the light bulb. At a selling price of $10.00, GE must sell 2,500,000 light bulbs to break even. At a selling price of $12.00, GE must sell only 2,000,000 light bulbs. Obviously, the question is how much of the market share GE can get at each price. The total annual demand for light bulbs in the U.S. is three billion, or approximately $1.5 billion.

Which price is chosen depends on GE's estimated demand curve for energy-saving light bulbs. Beyond 2,000,000 light bulbs, sales volume yields greater profits if a $12.00 price is used. But suppose GE feels that it can sell 2,000,000 light bulbs when the price is $12.00, and 3,000,000 if the light bulb is priced at $10.00. GE will break even using a $12.00 price, and earn a profit at the $10.00 price.

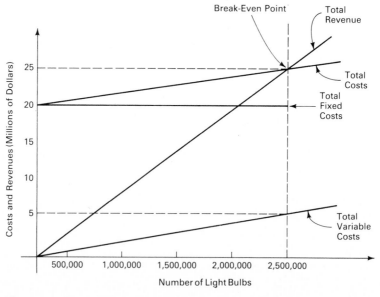

Figure 2.6   General Electric Break-Even Point (at $10.00/Light Bulb)

Alternatively, suppose 3,000,000 light bulbs can be sold at $12.00, and the sales volume will be 3,500,000 light bulbs if the price is $10.00. In this case, a larger profit can be earned at a price of $12.00, even though 500,000 additional light bulbs could be sold if the price were $10.00.

At a selling price of $12.00, profit is

$$(3,000,000) (\$12.00) - 20,000,000 - (3,000,000) (\$2.00)$$

$$= \$36,000,000 - 20,000,000 - 6,000,000 = \$10,000,000$$

At a selling price of $10.00, profit is

$$(3,500,000) (\$10.00) - \$20,000,000 - (3,500,000) (\$2.00)$$

$$= \$35,000,000 - 20,000,000 - 7,000,000 = \$8,000,000$$

The fixed and variable costs, as well as the expected selling price, is determined by the actual selection and design of the product as well as the actual choice and design of the production process, the type of machinery, material handling equipment, and raw material used, and other characteristics of the operations system. A more complex economic analysis treatment is included in the Technical Note to this chapter.

RESEARCH AND DEVELOPMENT

Research and development (R&D) is the next stage that was shown in Figure 2.2. This stage involves all the activities necessary to design a product prototype that will be tested and, if successful, commercialized.

This stage entails the preliminary product design and the prototype construction. *The preliminary product design* involves the development of the best design for the new product idea. When the new product design is approved for performance, cost, and quality, several alternative *prototypes* of the new product are constructed and the economic viability is checked for each prototype.

It should be noted here that business R&D spending has grown substantially in the past two decades (consult the reading at the end of this chapter), but spending on basic[1] research has declined. In addition, many companies now apply the same standard to R&D that they apply to capital investment: proceed only if the payoff is prompt and the risks are minor.

On the other hand, the U.S. Government spent roughly twice as much on R&D during the 1960's as the private sector spent. This spending peaked in 1966 and then declined, as can be seen in Figure 2.7. This decline led to a decline in productivity, as will be explained later.

[1] A distinction should be made between basic and applied research. Basic research entails the discovery of major chemical or physical relationships and processes. Applied research deals with the application of available and known relationships and processes to the development of new products and services that can be commercially produced and applied.

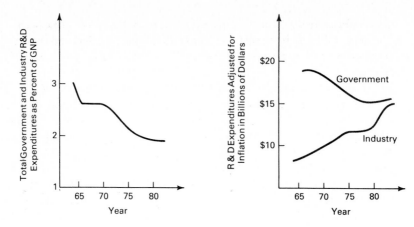

Figure 2.7   Government and Industry Research and Development Expenditures

Let us introduce two examples of R&D efforts that have led to successful new products.

EXAMPLE   *Powder Paint*

A manufacturer of paints was interested in finding a substitute for oil paint that was pollution free, replaced oil, which was becoming scarce, and was more resistant. The manufacturer created a team of six people who were continuously involved in this effort.

The team came up with a powder paint. Appearance-wise, the product is a very fine powder, similar to flour or baby powder, and is applied by an electrostatic process in an enclosed system consisting of a spray gun. The powder is heated to the melting point and after application it has a very quick jelling paint, which gives it its glossy extra-smooth finish. The principle of the electrostatic application consists of charging the object to be painted with a high electric voltage. The difference in voltage creates an attraction between the two bodies, and the powder is melted to form a glossy finish which is used on chain saws, generators, and the like. The advantages are:

1. 2% waste, as compared to waste from regular oil paint, which may be up to 50% when smaller objects are painted.
2. The powder paint is more resistant to wear, tear, chipping and corrosion than is any other type of paint known today.

Obviously, because of its sophistication and the cost of equipment, powder paint is only suitable for industrial applications.

EXAMPLE   *Disposable Lighter*

During the early '60's, Gillette Co. was caught off-guard by Wilkinson's Sword's introduction of the stainless-steel blade, which slashed Gillette's American market share from 72 to 50 percent. Aware of the short product life cycle of its products, Gillette has formed a new R&D unit (called Advanced Technology Laboratory) to seek new products outside the company's traditional product areas.

The disposable lighter came to Gillette through the social contacts of one of its managers with a member of the S. T. Dupont Company of France. The French manufacturer, S. T. Dupont, was the maker of elegant, lacquered lighters selling for $180 and up. But we consumers wanted a cheap lighter, since most of us are forgetful, often leaving our expensive lighters behind and upsetting the loved ones who gave them to us. S. T. Dupont was the first company in the world to introduce, in addition to its expensive lighters, a disposable model that it called Cricket. This development came at a time when in North America the trend to the "throw-away article" was already becoming a way of life.

Dupont was having trouble at the time keeping pace with its success. The market was growing explosively and the small French company had neither the capital necessary to expand production nor the distribution network needed to increase sales. It was in danger of losing the benefits of its innovation, and already Cricket had lost the lead to Feudor, which was owned by the much wealthier Swedish Match Company. This was when Dupont and Gillette discovered each other in what seemed to be the perfect mix. From Dupont's point of view, it had developed an idea, and produced and tested the disposable lighter in the home market with great success. Gillette needed such products to add to its line and could offer the necessary capital, management, distribution channels, and further monies needed for the development of a second generation of Cricket lighters. The disposable lighter idea fitted the companies' objectives. Its president said recently that Gillette is looking at things from an increasingly worldwide prospective and welcomes all products from here and abroad that fit its general line. Gillette will use its resources wherever they can be found. The disposable lighter suited Gillette very well. It obtained a product with repetitive demand, equalled, in terms of business, only by its razor blade.

The financial risks and payback criteria (see the Technical Note) were found to be entirely satisfactory, and Cricket is being sold through the same channels as blades, and offers scope for Gillette's famed ability to mass-produce.

Dupont has helped develop the Wild Cricket, a table-top model of the disposable lighter, and the Super Cricket, a higher-priced version of the lighter, to be brought to the market soon. Dupont also plans to undercut competitors by introducing an economy model.

Since acquisition in 1971, Dupont quintupled the size of its French plant and built four new ones, but it still cannot keep up with the demand for Gillette's highest selling product, the highly profitable Cricket Disposable Lighter. Demand for this item will be kept up unless some basic raw material becomes too expensive or the basic consumer makeup changes (as would happen if, for example, everybody quit smoking).

TESTING

The testing of newly developed products is aimed at confirming their performance. The extent of the testing depends greatly on the kind of product.

A now-well-known remark was made by David Scott, an Apollo-15 astronaut, when questioned about the blastoff: "You just sat there thinking that this piece of hardware had 400,000 components, all of them built by the lowest bidder. . . ."[2]

Obviously, the more critical a product failure may be, the more effort is invested in prototype testing. If the testing shows that the product does not meet expectations, engineering changes are initiated (see Figure 2.2), and the final design is based on the information gathered throughout the testing stage.

Several major considerations play a very important role in regard to the testing and, thus, the final design. The first consideration is *compatibility*, which refers to the fitting together of parts during operation. All parts should fit, as well as respond similary to conditions of stress. The second consideration is *simplification*, which refers to the exclusion of features that raise manufacturing costs as well as "after-sale" field service costs. The computer-assisted design (CAD) approach has been useful in enabling designers to rough out a particular product configuration and receive immediate feedback, insofar as compatibility and simplification are concerned, by using a computer. In this approach, designers use "light-pens" on a computer-controlled cathode ray tube (CRT) while the computer interprets these drawings through a conversational computer program. The computer may display the drawing on the screen to the designer from any desired angle for further inspection. This technique has been used extensively in the design and testing of aircraft, cars and electronic products.

Third is the *reliability* of new products, which refers to the extent to which the products may perform their functions during a specific period of time. The reliability consideration, as it is related to product liability, is so important in today's market that a more extended look is offered below.

Reliability

Reliability is the probability that a product (goods or services) will perform its mission during a given length of time. The higher the reliability of a product, the more expensive the design and the manufacturing process are. However, a lower reliability carries a cost penalty. A trade-off situation exists, in which the cost of reliability, together with costs resulting from failure, is minimized. The relation between design and manufacturing costs and reliability is shown in Figure 2.8. Also shown is the effect of reliability on the after-delivery (field service) costs.

---

[2] D. F. Linowes, "How Databanks Get the Goods on Everybody," *Business and Society Review*, 26, 54–57.

Obviously, lower reliability might result in field troubles, and thus might require a recall and might result in other manufacturer's and user's expenses. For example, the shedding of turbine blades due to a design error in the ship Queen Elizabeth II caused its owners a loss of revenue measured in millions of dollars. Repair of cracks in the roof of a nuclear reactor cost three quarters of a million dollars in capital and two million dollars in lost revenue.

In Figure 2.9, customer's costs are related to reliability. Both the price of a product and the costs after delivery carried by the customer are affected by the product's reliability.

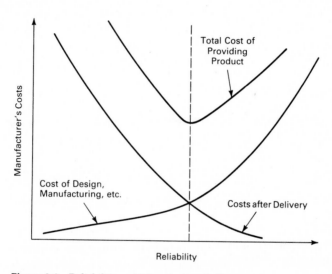

Figure 2.8   Reliability and Manufacturer's Costs

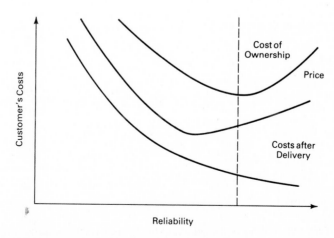

Figure 2.9   Reliability and Customer's Costs

1. The length of operating time
2. The condition of use
3. The reliability of the product's subparts
4. The seriousness of failure
5. The trim required to repair or replace failed parts
6. The cost of increased reliability
7. The nature of what constitutes a failure in the particular case: is poor performance acceptable, or is it considered a failure?

EXAMPLE   Let us assume a new product that consists of parts A and B. Both A and B must work in order for the product to work. Part A has a reliability of 0.90, part B has a reliability of 0.95. The cost of a failure is $1,000. The designer would like to determine the average cost of failure. The average cost of failure is found by multiplying the individual reliabilities by the cost of failure.

$$\text{Reliability of the product} = 0.90 \times 0.95 = 0.855$$

$$\text{Average failure cost} = \$1,000 \times (1 - 0.855) = \$145$$

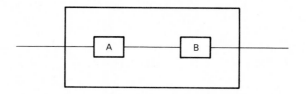

Figure 2.10   A Product Consisting of Parts A and B

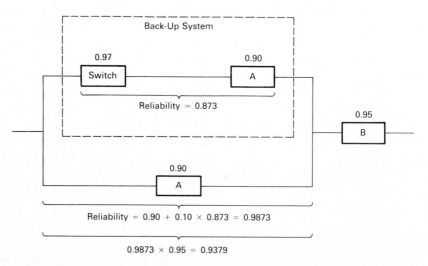

Figure 2.11   Reliability Calculation of the Product with a Back-Up System

The manufacturer considers instituting an alternative product design that includes a back-up system. This back-up system consists of a switch with reliability of 0.97 and of another part that is of type A (the reliability of A is 0.90, as before). Note that the switch activates the back-up system when Part A fails. The cost of the back-up system is $350. The question is whether it is economical to institute the back-up system. The reliability of the new configuration would be calculated as in Figure 2.11. The reliability of the total system is:

[(Reliability of part A) + (1 − Reliability of part A)(Reliability of the switch)(Reliability of part A)][Reliability of part B]

= [0.90 + (1 − 0.90)(0.97)(0.90)][0.95]

= 0.9379

The reliability of the system with the back-up is 0.9379, and the probability of failure is 0.0621. Thus,

Average cost of the failure = $1,000 × 0.0621 = $62.1

The total average cost of failure in the product with the back-up system is

$350 + $62.1 = $412.10

This cost is much higher than $145; thus, the new product should not include the back-up system. Note that the implicit assumption here is that after each failure the entire product is replaced.

COMMERCIALIZATION

The culmination of the series of stages in Figure 2.2 is the actual marketing of the new product. A study conducted in 1969[3] indicated that only one out of 60 new product ideas results in a successfully commercialized product. Obviously, this high rate of mortality of product ideas indicates the risk involved in new product decision and design. As can be seen in Figure 2.12, the chances of successful commercialization increase as the product is going through the various stages described in Figure 2.2. For example, after a period of time, one out of 60 products has been successfully commercialized.

EXAMPLE   At the beginning of this chapter, we presented a new product idea formulated by General Electric. After the various stages of product decision and design described in Figure 2.2 had been gone through, the announcement came of the upcoming commercialization of the new energy-saver's light bulb during 1981.

---

[3] D. B. Uman, *New Product Programs: Their Planning and Control* (New York: American Management Association, 1969), p. 67.

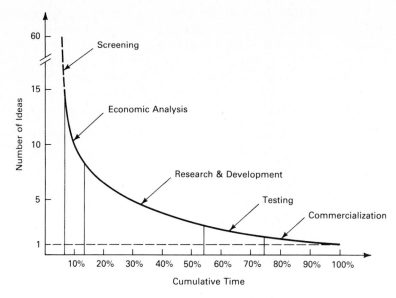

Figure 2.12 Mortality of New Product Ideas

PROCESS DECISION AND DESIGN

The manufacturing process for the new product is decided upon and designed in parallel with the new product design, as Figure 2.2 demonstrated. In the following paragraphs, we shall be dealing with the manufacturing process (or, simply, the process). This is the domain of operations management, and, thus, it is important that operations managers be involved in the product decision and design stages.

A "process" accepts inputs and transforms them into outputs that are of greater value to the organization than were the original inputs. All products decided upon and designed are subjects of a process or operating system. A car assembly plant accepts raw materials in the form of parts and subassemblies. These materials, along with labor, capital equipment, and energy, are transformed into a car. The transformation is called final assembly, and the output is a car. A McDonald's outlet takes inputs in the form of unprocessed or semiprocessed agricultural products and energy. These, together with labor (the cook) and capital equipment (a stove), result in the output, a hamburger or a fishburger.

Both these processes produce products as an output. However, the output of some operating systems is a service. Consider an airline. The inputs are capital equipment in the form of airplanes and ground equipment, labor in the form of flight crews, ground crews, and maintenance crews, and energy in the form of fuel and electricity. These are transformed into a service—namely, a

GE SAYS LIGHT BULB
IT DESIGNED CUTS USE
OF ENERGY TO A THIRD

*Firm Plans $10 Selling Price
and Sees Saving of $20;
It Also Cites Durability*

Wall Street Journal, June 15, 1979.

NEW YORK—General Electric Co. says it developed a light bulb for the home that, the company claims, uses one-third the energy of bulbs currently in use.

The new bulb, which fits into existing electric sockets, also is designed to last about four times longer than ones currently in use, GE said.

The suggested retail price of the bulb, which is expected to be on the market in early 1981, will be about $10, compared with about $1.50 for the conventional, three-way bulb it is designed to replace, GE said. However, because of its durability and lower energy use, the new bulb is expected to produce a net savings of about $20 to the consumer over its projected life, the company asserted.

Light in the new bulb is produced by an arc of electricity in a quartz tube using a metal halide vapor. It is similar to the technology used in some industrial lighting. The standard incandescent home light bulb produces light by running electricity through a metal filament.

GE said development of the Electronic Halarc bulb cost about $20 million, and the company expects to spend a similar amount in preparation for manufacturing. The company estimated it would make one million of the bulbs during the first year of production, with the aim of sharply increasing output after that. About 1.5 billion incandescent light bulbs are sold annually in the U.S., GE said.

Figure 2.13 A New Product Commercialization Announcement—An Energy-Saver Light Bulb
Source: Reprinted by permission of the Wall Street Journal © Dow Jones Company, Inc. (1979). All rights reserved.

means of transportation between cities. Another process with a service output is that found in a university. Here capital, labor, and energy are applied to another output, the graduating student, in order to transform him or her into a degreed professional or academician.

More formally, a process is a *collection of tasks connected by a flow of goods or services, and information that transforms various inputs into useful outputs.* A task is a small part of the total process. A process has the capability to store both the goods and information during the transformation. To analyze a process, it is useful to have a simple method of describing the process and some standard definitions for its components. One way to describe a process is with a *process flow diagram.*

Figure 2.14 shows the process flow diagram for a hypothetical process. The operating system is represented by the large rectangle. Inputs enter at the left and are converted into useful goods or services that leave the system as outputs at the right. Tasks in the process are shown as circles, flows as arrows, and the storage of goods as triangles. Information is shown stored in the square in the upper center. In this hypothetical process, goods are being produced. Raw materials flow to Task A and Task C from a storage called the raw materials inventory. Task B cannot start until Task A is completed. Two such tasks are defined as being in a *series* relationship. Tasks C and D are also in series. Task D and Task B are not dependent on each other and as such are defined as *parallel* tasks. Task E cannot be started until all the others are finished; thus a work-in-process storage is shown before Task E, in case Tasks B and D are not completed simultaneously. After Task E, work flows into a finished goods inventory and from there the output flows out of the system.

Once you have described a process using a process flow diagram, you must then analyze its components. After that analysis, it should be possible to draw some conclusions about the process as a whole. Let us discuss each component and some of the problems you will encounter when you try to measure and analyze them.

Inputs

The *inputs* to a process can be grouped into at least four categories: labor, materials, energy, and capital. To analyze an operations system it is necessary to measure these inputs and to determine the amount of each output. It would be

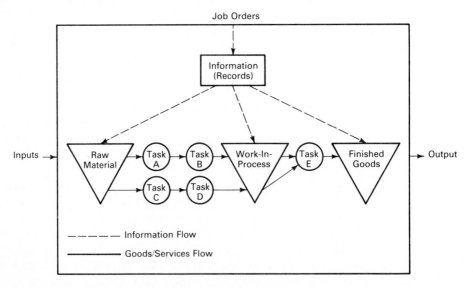

Figure 2.14 Process Flow Diagram for a Hypothetical Process

possible to use physical units to measure the inputs—for example, manhours for labor, and BTUs for energy. However, it is often more convenient to measure the input in dollars by determining prices. Thus, in most analyses, it is necessary to consider the economic conditions that influence the cost of labor, materials, energy, and capital.

There are varying degrees of difficulty in determining how much input is needed to make a given output (product). Some inputs, such as direct labor and materials, are fully consumed to produce an output and thus are easily assigned values. For example, it is easy to measure how many minutes of labor a barber uses in producing a haircut or how many ounces of beef are used in making a hamburger. Other inputs are utilized in the production of an output, but are not fully consumed—for example, the chef's stove or the barber's chair. The capital input is often the most difficult to assign to specific output because it is almost impossible to measure how much capital is consumed by a product. It is important to be able to determine the amount of each input consumed per product if we are to calculate the cost of providing a desired output. We will return to this problem later in this chapter.

Output

The *output* of a process is either goods or a service. The process flow diagram in Figure 2.14 shows a storage and finished goods inventory, before the output leaves the system. In some organizations, this finished goods inventory is kept at zero units and the process is made to produce to order.

In fact, this is an important characteristic of processes that provide service as their final output because it is often impossible to store a service for later distribution. In some organizations, the finished goods inventory is kept apart from the operating system that produces the goods and is managed by a separate group, usually the sales organization.

A meaningful measure of outputs is often quite difficult to obtain. Although it is a simple matter to count the number of units produced by some manufacturing organization or to count the number of patients served by a hospital, it is much more difficult to place a value on such outputs. The question of output valuation can be approached from an economic point of view if it is assumed that a market places a value on the output through the pricing mechanism. Thus, the revenue that can be obtained from selling the goods or service should serve as a measure of value. For this reason, it is necessary to have a good understanding of what the market pays for a comparable product or service.

The question of what price will be paid for the output is difficult to answer unless some other information is known about the output. For our purposes, three output characteristics will be considered: the cost of providing the output, the quality of the output, and the timeliness of the output. So far we have discussed what goes in and what comes out of a process. It is also necessary to understand *what goes on inside a process.* The specifics of every process are different, but there are three general categories of activities within the process: *tasks, flows, and storage.*

Tasks

A *task* is a small part of the whole process. Some examples of tasks are: operating a drill press to change the form of a piece of metal; inspecting a part to make sure it meets some standard; flying an airplane; and anesthetizing a patient before an operation. A task may take the form of labor added to the product, with or without the use of capital. In cases in which the process is partially or completely automated, capital, material, and energy may have been substituted for the labor in a task.

Flows

There are two types of *flows* to be considered in each process: the flow of goods and the flow of information. Figure 2.14 showed the goods flow in solid lines and the information flow in broken lines. The first results when goods are moved from task to task or from a task to storage, or vice versa. Labor or capital is added during a flow because workers or equipment are required in order to move the goods. The difference between flows and tasks is that flows merely change the position of goods or services in the process, while a task changes their characteristics. The flow of information initiates and aids in the production of goods or a service. This flow results when the necessary records or instructions move from their point of origin or storage to the task, in time to be used in the task. Quite often the information will physically move through the process with the goods or service. This happens when a routing slip or job ticket is attached to the physical goods. In other situations, workers must go to some central location to obtain the information in writing or orally before performing the task. In yet other situations, the information arrives by a flow independent of the flow of the goods or service being processed. It is important, in analyzing a process, to consider the information flows in addition to the physical flow of goods or services.

Storage

A *storage* results when no task is being performed and the goods or services are not being transported. In other words, a storage is anything that is not a task or flow. In Figure 2.14, we have shown the storage of goods as triangles. Technically, there should be a triangle between successive tasks. If there is no delay in starting the task after the flow has been finished, the storage will have zero units in it. If there is no storage between two successive tasks, there must be a planned continuous flow between these tasks. Figure 2.14 showed only one in-process storage (commonly known as work-in-process inventory).

It is also possible, and in fact necessary, to store information. This storage was shown as a rectangle in Figure 2.14, with an arrow entering the information. There are two functions of the information box: records and control. Records are general instructions, such as blueprints and maintenance documents. Control indicates information specific to a given order, such as the due dates and the routing procedure for the particular order, or special instructions that make processing of this order different from the generally accepted procedures explained in the records.

Technology

Two major areas of the *environment* should be considered in analyzing operating systems. We have already mentioned that the *economic conditions* in the environment are important and that an analysis of them is necessary in order to determine the costs of the inputs and the value of the output. The second environmental area, which we will call the *state of technology*, is more difficult to explain. *The state of the technology can be defined as the set of knowledge regarding processes, methods, techniques, and capital goods by which products are made or services rendered.* The choice of process technology will determine the relationship between the tasks and flows and determine the inputs needed to provide the process output.

As an example, consider two alternatives for providing copies of some information, one using a printing press and the other using a Xerox copying machine. The printing press requires several tasks in order to produce the information (typesetting, proofreading, press operation, etc.). The Xerox copying machine, on the other hand, requires only an operator and an original document containing the information. The cost of providing the information is also different for each technology. The Xerox has a small cost per copy, but this cost is about the same for each copy, regardless of how many are produced. The printing press has a very high setup cost but each additional copy is very cheap. Thus for large numbers of copies the press has an economic advantage, and the technology used will be determined by the number of copies desired.

As the state of technology changes, it may be possible to change a process and achieve the same output with fewer inputs or to use the same inputs to achieve more output. This will alter the costs of inputs and may improve the quality and timeliness of the output. Changes in technology may allow a process to make entirely new outputs. For these reasons, it is necessary to give consideration to the state of technology when analyzing a process.

CHARACTERISTICS OF A PROCESS

So far we have defined a process in general terms and defined the various components of the process—namely, the tasks, flows, and storages within the process. We have also noted that the process is affected by the environment.

Economic conditions influence the values of inputs and outputs, and the state of technology influences the nature of the tasks and flows. Using these concepts as a basis we can now discuss four important characteristics of a process: capacity, efficiency, effectiveness, and flexibility.

Capacity

Capacity is the (designed) rate of output from the process. This characteristic is measured in units of output per unit of time. For example, a steel mill can produce a certain number of tons of steel per year, and an insurance office can process a certain number of claims per hour. Capacity is easy to define and hard to measure. It is often possible to determine the theoretical maximum capacity of a process—the most output it could generate under ideal conditions over some short period of time. For planning purposes and management decisions, it is more useful to know the effective capacity of a process. To measure effective capacity, it is necessary to know a great deal about the process, and to analyze carefully the particular situation at hand.

Quite often, managers believe that the capacity of a process is an absolutely fixed quantity. This is not true. The capacity of a process can change for many reasons, and we will encounter several cases in which this is a key problem facing the manager. For example, a steel mill may be designed for some ideal capacity of x tons of steel per year. However, the actual capacity may be more or less than x, due to such factors as the nature of the raw materials being utilized, the mix of products in the output, and the quantity and nature of the labor input. Capacity is further discussed later in this chapter.

Efficiency

Efficiency is a measure that compares the value of the output of the process to the value of the input. As has been explained in Chapter 1, the concept of efficiency is widely used in considering physical processes. Every engine has a specific efficiency and it is expressed as a ratio of output energy to input energy. For example, an engine with 75-percent efficiency can deliver 75 percent of the input energy as useful output energy. The energy efficiency of a physical systems cannot exceed 100 percent; i.e., the useful output energy is always less than the input. This is not true of economic processes, for which the value of the output *should* exceed the value of the input if the process is going to generate sufficient resources to support its own continued operation. Thus, the efficiency of economic processes should exceed 100 percent. If we measure the value of output by the price or revenue it will bring in the market, and if we measure the value of inputs by their costs, one measure of efficiency is profit. Profit, which is simply revenue less cost, is the value of output minus the value of input.

Effectiveness

An important characteristic we are interested in is the effectiveness of the process. *Effectiveness* is a comparison or comparative measure of actual output against planned output. As has been explained in Chapter 1, determining effectiveness requires that some plan or standard be established before the process begins to produce output. The actual output is measured in some way and compared to the planned output. This measurement may take many forms; three that we will be interested in are cost, quality, and timeliness.

Efficiency and effectiveness are often confused. Some plant managers will state that they have reached x percent efficiency in a given week. When questioned about this they will often explain that the output that week was x percent of what they had assumed as standard. According to our definitions, they are describing effectiveness. The distinction between the two characteristics has a practical value for managers. Efficiency is more difficult to measure accurately and involves calculations of both output and input.

Flexibility

Flexibility is a measure of how long it takes to change the process to produce a different output or to use different inputs. Changes in the environment require a change in the process. Thus, the importance of flexibility should not be underestimated in a changing environment.

CAPACITY OF A FACILITY

A facility accommodates several processes. A facility's capacity is the rate of its output, indicating how many products or services (using a common measure) are turned out by the facility per unit of time. An effort is made to express the rate of output without regard to specific products. For example, the Maytag Corporation can measure its capacity as the number of tons of steel that are converted into washing machines and dryers over a year, rather than as the number of washing machines and dryers. A stock brokerage house expresses its capacity as the number of transactions processed over a specific period of time without a distinction between stocks, bonds, and other financial instruments. A hospital specifies its capacity by the number of patients treated per month, without regard to the specific kinds of sicknesses or treatments required. An airline measures its capacity in available seat miles per month. This measure is an *aggregate* measure that incorporates the effect of size, range, maintenance, and speed of the various planes owned by the airline.

Consider, as an example, the ELVO Corporation, a provider of research and development services and products to NASA. Its overall objective is to serve the aerospace industry with the highest-quality custom-made products and services. Its areas of expertise are research and development engineering, electronic component/system design and manufacture, and custom-built machine-shop products.

ELVO's capacity is being measured in terms of sales revenues. Its capacity has been growing at an accelerated rate since 1962. In 1962, its capacity was $1,000,000; now it stands at $80,000,000.

The capacity for Elvo is expressed in dollars, because no other measure can better reflect the level of activity for such research and development organizations. However, capacity can be measured in production units, man-hours or machine-hours per period.

When expressing capacity, one has to include the time dimension. For example, the number of beds in a hospital or seats in a bar represent the size of the facility and not the rate of output. One also has to be careful not to confuse *actual capacity* with *design capacity*. The actual capacity might be lower than the design capacity due to a lower demand for products or services. The actual capacity may change from one time period to another, whereas design capacity, which is the *potential* rate of output, is constant over a longer period of time.

The design capacity may be changed only through expansion or displacement of the available facilities. *Capacity expansion* involves adding new facilities to existing facilities. This may also be done through subcontracting, overtime, and the increased efficiency of the currently existing production processes. *Capacity displacement* involves replacing the currently existing facilities with new facilities that are more economical and technologically advanced. Since it is not always possible to sell the ousted facility (for example, an older machine tool), it may be diverted to some secondary use in operations or placed on standby. Since such a facility is not sold, it has not been replaced. Thus, this change in the design capacity is termed "displacement."

In discussing capacity, there is one final comment that should be made. This is that the actual capacity may, at times, reach a maximum level that will be maintained for a short time and that is termed *peak capacity*. For service organizations, like hospitals and electrical utilities, peak capacity is a common phenomenon, as services may in some cases not be stored.

It is appropriate at this time to present a specific example of a facility that accommodates several processes in sequence: a bakery.

EXAMPLE

POM (Pride of Montana) Bakery, Limited, was founded on September 22, 1937, by Mr. Dent Harrison and his three sons. The first mechanical dough mixer in Montana was introduced by Mr. Harrison. He had also made great contributions to the baking industry by cooperating in the development of the first travelling oven.

POM Bakery Ltd. is one of the largest independent bakeries in the northwestern U.S.A. and employs a total of 365 permanent employees. It produces bread, rolls, English muffins, crumpets, cakes, biscuits, cookies, pies, and donuts. But it is mainly concerned with the production of bread.

POM serves a metropolitan area and distributes to jobbers located within a radius of approximately 80 miles. Its target markets are grocers, including convenience stores and restaurants, and institutions, such as hospitals and schools. The company has total annual sales of over $11 million, mostly from the bread department (about $10 million) with the remainder from the cake department. POM also spends about $25,000 annually to purchase from other bakeries certain kinds of bread, such as rye bread, the sales of which are so small that it is unprofitable for the company to produce it. The rye bread is purchased for resale mainly to satisfy customers (restaurants) who want a wider product line to satisfy their clients.

The *production process* of POM Bakery involves the transformation of raw materials (flour, water, yeast, salt, milk, sugar, malt, etc.) into ready-to-consume products (breads, rolls, English muffins, crumpets, cakes, pies, cookies, etc.).

Basically, the process of bread production can be presented as the following series of steps:

After the raw materials are received from the suppliers, the materials are stored in bins or tanks in the basement. Flour, the main raw material, comes in bulk trucks and is blown by air into the bins. There are two bins, each with a capacity of 50,000 lbs. The flour will be transferred (blown by air through a pipe) into a use-bin whenever required.

During mixing, all the ingredients necessary are combined to form the dough. At POM, there are three mixers, situated on the top (third) foor of the plant. Amounts of flour, water, yeast, and liquid sugar are set by dial, and are sent to the mixer through pipes by pressing a button, while salt, milk, and malt are weighed and put into the mixer by hand.

After 15 minutes of mixing, the dough is sent to the ferment room (also on the top floor) for fermentation. The fermentation time is $4\frac{1}{2}$ hours, after which time the dough is sent back to the mixer for another 15 minutes. The dough that comes out will then be transferred into a container and pushed by hand through a pipe down to the make-up area (on the second floor).

At the proof stage, the dough is divided into equal parts, rounded to the shape of bread, proofed up (given a short rest period), and then made up in pans. All this is done automatically. It takes approximately 30 minutes for the dough to be ready in the pans. Then the pans are individually put on ten-shelf racks and pushed into the proof box, where they are left for 70 minutes. The proof box is necessary for further fermentation of the raw bread, which begins to rise under controlled conditions of heat and humidity.

After the proof time, the racks are removed from the proof box and brought to the oven. At the baking stage, the pans are removed from the racks and introduced into the oven by hand.

The oven stage is the bottleneck of the bread production (the oven used at POM is a travelling oven—that is, an oven in which the bread goes in one end, travels on a moving hearth through a baking chamber, and comes out, baked, at the other end. The baking time for a loaf of bread is approximately 25 to 30 minutes.

The bread is removed from the pans automatically by vacuum. The bread then continues on a conveyor belt to the cooling section, where an employee places them on racks to cool.

The cooling stage is very important because a hot loaf of bread cannot be sliced. The cooling time is about $2\frac{1}{2}$ hours, after which the loaves are introduced by hand to the automatic slicing machine.

The loaves then go into the bag wrapper, and then move on a conveyor belt to the shipping room (on the first floor), where a general bakery helper takes the bags of bread and places them on pallets. Finally, the bread is put on racks, according to the salesmen's orders.

The process we have described shows that the POM Company is a combination semiautomatic/manual plant. All the machines and the feeding to machines are controlled by employees.

Because of the perishable nature of the product, POM cannot carry any inventory. POM has to produce as close as possible to its demand. This affects the process and the production plan.

"Cripples" (breads coming out of the oven underbaked or overbaked, too big or too small, or damaged by faulty handling) are treated like unsold bread. There is no definite permissible level at which bread could be considered to be in a saleable state. It is up to the worker (usually an experienced person) to detect any cripples. As the bread moves along the conveyor belt, just before it is sliced, the cripples are removed by the worker. Quality judgment depends entirely on the individual doing the job. The actual percentage of cripples is between 1.2% and 1.5% (this is considered too high, as the company's target is 0.33%). Because of the nature of the product, an inspection of the quality can only be made after baking. Again, the quality of the outgoing product or service depends on the process. Obviously, the production process chosen by POM as well as the changes in the process machines have an impact on the per-unit production costs involved.

Other processes will be described in this book. Whatever the process may be, the basic presentation of Figure 2.14 will be applicable. Namely, the process will consist of inventories (raw material, in-process, and finished goods), process tasks (or stages), and information flows and center.

SUMMARY

An operations system, whether manufacturing or service, starts with an idea. The idea serves as a basis for the design, planning, organizing, and control functions.

After the idea stage, the operations manager is faced with two major decisions: the product decision and the process decision. The product decision involves the systematic gathering of several product ideas and the choosing of a product that meets all the organization's goals. The process decision involves the choice of methods by which raw material inputs are transformed into product outputs.

Economic analysis is used in assessing the viability of a new product and process. In particular, this chapter has covered break-even analysis. The Technical Note will deal with capital budgeting techniques.

The product life cycle relates the volume of the sales of a product to the time that has passed since its introduction into the market place. It shows what happens to the product after it is introduced. By keeping up its research and development (R&D) efforts, the company is able to introduce new products to replace older ones, and thus is able to maintain a constant level of revenues.

Once the product decision has been made, the design of the product starts. The process design is related and executed parallel to the product design.

DISCUSSION QUESTIONS

2.1 Describe the product decision and the process decision.

2.2 What are the variables affecting the product or service decision?

2.3 In the light of your answer to question 2.2, can you explain the reason behind General Electric's move, described in the chapter?

2.4 Describe the use of break-even analysis.

2.5 Choose any product (such as Texas Instruments electronic calculators) and try to assess its product life cycle.

2.6 Describe the steps that might be required to establish a new fast-food item. Compare these steps with the steps described in Figure 2.2.

2.7 How can research and development (R&D) sustain the company's level of revenue?

2.8 Define reliability, and explain its importance in product design.

2.9 What are the main components of any process?

PROBLEMS AND SOLUTIONS

2.1 Two new product ideas, for products A and B, have been conceived. These ideas have been rated for their characteristics, as shown in the table below. Rank the products and recommend the product idea that should be further investigated.

PRODUCT A RATINGS

PRODUCT CHARACTER- ISTICS	Poor = 1	Fair = 2	Good = 3	Very Good = 4	Excel- lent = 5	WEIGHT
Meets Customer Expectations		X				15%
Technology Compatibility			X			10%

PRODUCT CHARACTER-ISTICS	Poor = 1	Fair = 2	Good = 3	Very Good = 4	Excel-lent = 5	WEIGHT
Sales Volume Potential				X		25%
Fit with Corporate Goals			X			20%
Quality		X				10%
Revenue Potential					X	20%
					Total Weight	100%

PRODUCT B RATINGS

PRODUCT CHARACTER-ISTICS	Poor = 1	Fair = 2	Good = 3	Very Good = 4	Excel-lent = 5	WEIGHT
Meets Customer Expectations			X			15%
Technology Compatibility		X				10%
Sales Volume Potential			X			25%
Fit with Corporate Goals		X				20%
Quality					X	10%
Revenue Potential		X				20%
					Total Weight	100%

Solution

Total Weighted Score (TWS) for product idea A is

$$TWS_A = (0.15)2 + (0.10)3 + (0.25)4 + (0.20)3 + (0.10)2 + (0.20)5$$

$$= 0.30 + 0.30 + 1.00 + 0.60 + 0.20 + 1.00 = 4.40$$

Total Weighted Score (TWS) for product idea B is

$$TWS_B = (0.15)3 + (0.10)2 + (0.25)3 + (0.20)2 + (0.10)5 + (0.20)2$$

$$= 0.45 + 0.20 + 0.75 + 0.40 + 0.50 + 0.40 = 2.70$$

Product idea A is ranked first, and should be further investigated.

2.2   A new word-processing machine is contemplated by Short-Life Underwriters, Inc., to accommodate insurance policy typing and printing. The fixed costs of energy, depreciation, labor, printing paper, and disc supply amount to $19,700, and the variable costs are $3/policy. The average revenue from an insurance policy drafted is $200.
a) How many policies should be drafted in order to break even?
b) What is each policy's contribution to fixed costs and profit?

Solution

a) Break-even point $= \dfrac{\$19,700}{\$200 - \$3} = 100$ policies

b) Contribution $= \$200 - \$3 = \$197$

CHAPTER REVIEW PROBLEMS

2.1 In order to facilitate a faster return of rented cars, Hertz Rent-A-Car has installed a special express counter with a capability of handling 60 car returns/hour. The fixed costs involved are $5,000. The variable cost of direct labor, depreciation, and material (including computer terminal charges) amounts to $1.30/car return. The surcharge to the customer using this express counter is $1.40/car return.
a) What is the break-even point, expressed in number of returns?
b) Graphically present the break-even point?
c) What is the break-even point in hours?

2.2 The following table presents a major decision that an oil company has to make. The company could develop either as an integrated resource company that includes exploration, drilling, production, refining, and distribution functions (Alternative A), or could specialize in exploration and drilling only (Alternative B). The impact on fixed and variable costs, as well as a selling price per barrel, is provided:

	Alternative A	*Alternative B*
Fixed Costs	$50,000,000	$20,000,000
Variable Costs	$25/barrel	$18/barrel
Selling Price	$35/barrel	$25/barrel

If the company is interested in realizing a profit with a smaller break-even volume, which alternative should be chosen?

READING
Business to Hike R&D Spending 17%

NEW YORK (AP)—Indicating that U.S. business is looking somewhat optimistically at the future, business plans to hike research and development spending 17 percent this year, to $59.7 billion, according to a survey released by the McGraw-Hill Publications Co.

R&D spending rose 16 percent in 1981 from the previous year and is expected to be up at least 37 percent, to $81.9 billion, by 1985, the survey said.

Historically, companies have reacted to recession by cutting spending that isn't tied to current operations—that is, capital spending and R&D.

SOURCE: *Los Angeles Herald Examiner*, May 31, 1982, p. 7.

R&D spending has been on the rise since the mid-1970s. The McGraw-Hill report suggested the growth reflects shifting corporate strategy in the face of an energy crisis, a technological challenge from Japan and an inflation-plagued economy.

The economic recovery tax act of 1981 also provides incentives for R&D spending. The act allots companies a 25 percent tax credit for R&D expenditures in excess of the average spent in the previous three years.

McGraw-Hill said all industries surveyed forecast increases in R&D this year.

The electrical machinery industry, which includes high-technology electronics and communications equipment manufacturers, had the largest R&D budget and also planned the largest percentage increase in spending this year—23.2 percent to more than $12.9 billion. The industry plans to raise R&D spending to $18.9 billion in 1985, a 46 percent jump from 1982.

The non-electrical machinery industry anticipates 21 percent growth in R&D spending in 1982 to more than $8.9 billion.

The aerospace industry, second to electrical machinery in R&D spending, projects a 12.8 percent gain in 1982 expenditures to $11.7 billion.

READING
The String of Flops That Clogged Water Pik

The decay that remains hidden at many Teledyne Inc. operations is rapidly becoming evident at the company's Water Pik subsidiary, maker of such familiar products as the Water Pik dental appliance and the Shower Massage pulsating showerhead. After an initial success with new-product launches, Teledyne now appears to be siphoning cash from Water Pik with little regard for the offshoot's future health.

At first the 1967 purchase of the outfit, based in Fort Collins, Colo., proved to be one of the Teledyne's star acquisitions. Revenues soared to $130 million by 1976 from less than $20 million before the takeover. Sales of the Water Pik device that gave the company its name continued to grow, peaking at about 1 million units that year. The Shower Massage, launched in 1973, became one of the hottest gift items of its time, and its sales spurted to 9 million units.

Absurd device. But the company stumbled badly when it introduced a string of new products that flopped. Mothers snubbed the company's

SOURCE: Reprinted from the May 31, 1982 issue of *Business Week* by special permission, © 1982 by McGraw-Hill, Inc.

Nurtury baby food grinders, preferring household blenders. And what one former insider calls "the most absurd consumer product ever devised"—an electronic counter of a dieter's bites that signaled how fast to chew—met a quick death. Both the Instapure water filter and the One Step At A Time cigarette filter, rolled out in the mid-1970s and still being distributed, are reported to be barely profitable.

After these sorry events, Teledyne virtually shut down new-product development, leaving Water Pik dependent on two main lines: the Shower Massage, which is down about 75% from its peak sales level, and the now 20-year-old Water Pik, which has plummeted almost one-third from its high point. The only product the subsidiary has introduced recently—the Smart Tip Cigarette filter, which cuts tar and nicotine intake by 50%—has had a slow start since its debut last year.

Water Pik's sales have dropped 50%, to $65 million, since 1976. Expenses have been slashed, too. For example, advertising costs have been cut more than 80% over the past six years. Sources say Teledyne has kept the unit strongly profitable. But with aging products and weak promotional support, Water Pik is almost certainly headed for troubled times.

Questions

1. Can you relate the Water Pik sales to the "product life cycle" presented in the chapter?
2. Why has Water Pik been pushed to appear along with several new products like the baby food grinder, the dieter's electronic counter, and the cigarette filter? Can you present the respective life cycles?
3. Comment on the future of Water Pik in light of the shut-down of new-product development.

BIBLIOGRAPHY

BRITNEY, R. R., and E. F. P. NEWSON, *The Canadian Production/Operations Management Environment: An Audit*, School of Business Administration Research Monograph, London, Ontario: University of Western Ontario, April, 1975.

CHASE, R. B., and N. J. AQUILANO, *Production and Operations Management (A Life Cycle Approach)*, 2nd ed. Homewood, Ill.: Richard D. Irwin, 1977.

DONALDSON, G., "Strategic Hurdle Rates for Capital Investment," *Harvard Business Review*, March–April, 1972, pp. 50–58.

DRUCKER, P. F., *Management: Tasks, Responsibilities, Practice*. New York: Harper & Row, 1974.

Factory Report, "Picking the Right Plant Site," *Factory,* May, 1976, pp. 61–62.

FRANCIS, R. L., and J. A. WHITE, *Facility Layout and Location, An Analytical Approach.* Englewood Cliffs, N.J.: Prentice-Hall, Inc., 1974.

GRANT, E. L., and W. G. IRESON, *Principles of Engineering Economy,* 5th ed. New York: Ronald Press, 1970.

GREEN, P. E., and D. S. TULL, *Research for Marketing Decisions,* 3rd ed. Englewood Cliffs, N.J.: Prentice-Hall, Inc., 1974.

HERTZ, D. B., "Risk Analysis in Capital Investment," *Harvard Business Review,* Jan.–Feb., 1964, pp. 95–106.

KAST, F. E., and J. E. ROSENZWEIG, *Organization and Management: A Systems Approach.* New York: McGraw-Hill Book Co., 1970.

KAUFMAN, A., M. FUSTIER, and A. DREVET, *L'Inventique, Nouvelles Methodes de Creativite.* Paris: Enterprise Moderne D'Edition, 1970.

MAO, J. C. T., *Quantitative Analysis of Financial Decisions.* London, England: Macmillan & Co., Ltd., 1969.

MENIPAZ, E., "A Look at Alternative Forms of Feasibility Studies," *Canadian Consulting Engineer,* November, 1980, pp. 40–47.

_____, "Industrial Projects Feasibility Methodology," *Europe Industrial Review,* February, 1980, pp. 42–45.

MOORE, F. G., and T. E. HENDRICK, *Production/Operations Management,* 8th ed. Homewood, Ill.: Richard D. Irwin, 1980.

MORTON, J. A., *Organizing for Innovation.* New York: McGraw-Hill Book Company, 1971.

PESSEMIER, E. A., *New-Product Decisions: An Analytical Approach.* New York: McGraw-Hill, 1966.

QUIRIN, G. D., *The Capital Expenditure Decision.* Homewood, Ill.: Richard D. Irwin, 1967.

RINGBAKK, K. A., "Why Planning Fails," *European Business,* No. 29, Spring, 1971, pp. 15–26.

SCHON, D. A., *Technology and Change.* New York: Delacorte Press, 1967.

SKINNER, W., "Manufacturing—Missing Link in Corporate Strategy," *Harvard Business Review,* Vol. 47, No. 3, May–June, 1967, pp. 136–45.

SMITH, V., *Investment and Production.* Cambridge, Mass.: Harvard University Press, 1966.

STARR, M. K., "Product Planning from the Top Variety and Diversity," University of Illinois Bulletin, Vol. 65, No. 144, Proceedings, *Systems: Research and Applications for Marketing,* July 26, 1968, pp. 71–77.

_____, *Operations Management.* Englewood Cliffs, N.J.: Prentice-Hall, Inc., 1978.

VAN HORNE, J. C., *Financial Management and Policy,* 3rd ed. Englewood Cliffs, N. J.: Prentice-Hall, Inc., 1974.

WELSCH, G. A., and R. N. ANTHONY, *Fundamentals of Financial Accounting.* Homewood, Ill.: Richard D. Irwin, 1974.

WESTON, J. F., and E. F. BRIGHAM, *Essentials of Managerial Finance,* 3rd ed. Hindsdale, Ill.: Dryden Press, 1974.

```
┌─────────────────────────────────────────────────────────────┐ ┌─┬─┬─┐
│                                                             │ │ │ │ │
│  TECHNICAL NOTE:  Capital Budgeting                         │ │ │ │ │
│                   and Financial Investment Analysis         │ │ │ │ │
│                                                             │ │ │ │ │
└─────────────────────────────────────────────────────────────┘ └─┴─┴─┘
```

INTRODUCTION

Capital budgeting and financial investment analysis are used to make decisions involving product and process decisions and design—decisions, for example, on which product to produce, which production process is most economical, which machines should be replaced, which facilities should be bought, and which piece of equipment should be acquired. In all of the above examples, funds are committed in the present in return for an expected steam of future benefits. These decisions are important not only because they require a sizable commitment of capital, but also because such a commitment, once made, is largely irreversible.

The concept of the *time value of money* is important in capital budgeting decisions. A consequence of the time value of money is that a dollar today is worth more than a dollar a year from now. Thus, the value of dollars received or spent during later periods should be discounted accordingly.

As many capital budgeting decisions involve tools, machines and other physical assets, the value of which decrease over time, we shall first discuss the concepts of economic life, accounting life, productive life, and depreciation. The *economic life* of an asset or other investment is the period of time during which it performs a useful service to the organization. Economic life differs from accounting life. *Accounting life* is the period of time over which the asset is depreciated.

Productive life of an asset is the period of time during which the asset can perform. The productive period of equipment often exceeds its economic life because of technological changes that make the equipment obsolete. The accounting life changes according to tax laws and tax provisions.

Related to the accounting life is depreciation. *Depreciation is an accounting term that expresses the annual reduction in the value of an asset on the accounting records of the company.* Since a capital good provides benefits for many years, its cost is averaged over many years. Depreciation is very important because of its effect on income tax payments. Higher depreciation expense means lower profit and therefore lower taxes. Different depreciation methods can substantially alter the patterns of cash flows and thus influence the capital investment decision. The three most widely used depreciation methods are: straight line, sum-of-years'-digits, and double-declining balance. These methods are first explained and then demonstrated in an example.

The simplest method of computing depreciation is the *straight-line method*. The original cost of the asset is allocated evenly over its accounting life. The annual depreciation is obtained from the following formula.

$$\text{Straight-line depreciation} = \frac{\text{Cost} - \text{salvage value}}{\text{Lifetime}} = \frac{C - S}{n}$$

The *salvage value, S,* is the estimated income that will be received from the sale of an asset. C is the original cost of the asset and n is the accounting life of the asset, expressed in years.

Sum-of-years'-digits (SYD) is an accelerated depreciation method that results in a declining amount of depreciation expense each year of an asset's accounting life. It assigns depreciation to the current year in proportion to the number of years of an asset's accounting life that remain at the beginning of the current year. A consequence of this method is that taxes are paid later than they otherwise would be. The taxes are not avoided, but they are delayed. Thus, the after-tax returns on a project are higher in the earlier years. The annual depreciation is obtained from the following formula:

$$\text{SYD depreciation} = \frac{(\text{No. of years remaining}) (\text{Cost} - \text{Salvage})}{\text{Total of digits of years of life}}$$

If the asset's lifetime is 4 years, the denominator has a value of $1 + 2 + 3 + 4 = 10$. The depreciation for the first year would be 4/10 of the cost minus salvage. The second year would have a factor of 3/10; the third year, a factor of 2/10; and the final year, a factor of 1/10.

The double-declining balance method achieves an accelerated rate of depreciation, as does the sum-of-years'-digits method, but the pattern is different. With this method, the annual rate of depreciation is derived by doubling the straight-line rate and applying it, year by year, to the portion of the asset value still not depreciated. Salvage value is not subtracted from cost, as it is in the straight-line and sum-of-years'-digits methods. With a 10-year depreciation period, the depreciation rate would be 2(1/10), or 0.20. If the book value indicates the value of the asset less the accumulated depreciation, the annual depreciation is obtained from the following formula:

$$\text{Double-declining balance depreciation} = \frac{2(\text{Book value})}{\text{Lifetime}}$$

This calculation is done for each year over the lifetime of the asset.

EXAMPLE A new machine costs $20,000 and has a depreciable (accounting) life of 5 years, with a salvage value of $5,000. What are the values of the: a) annual straight line depreciation, b) annual sum-of-years'-digits depreciation, and c) annual double-declining depreciation?

a) Straight-line $= \dfrac{C - S}{n} = \dfrac{20{,}000 - 5{,}000}{5} = \$3{,}000$ per year

b) Sum-of-years'-digits (SYD):

Year	Depreciation Rate		Depreciation Amount		Depreciation Charge
1	5/15	×	$15,000	=	$5,000
2	4/15	×	15,000	=	4,000
3	3/15	×	15,000	=	3,000
4	2/15	×	15,000	=	2,000
5	1/15	×	15,000	=	1,000
				Total	$15,000

c) Double-declining balance:

Year	Depreciation Ratio		Beginning Book Value		Depreciation Charge	Accumulated Depreciation	Ending Book Value
1	2/5 = 0.40	×	20,000	=	$8,000	$8,000	12,000
2	0.40	×	12,000	=	4,800	12,800	7,200
3	0.40	×	7,200	=	2,200*	15,000	5,000*
4	0	×	5,000	=	0	15,000	5,000
5	0	×	5,000	=	0	15,000	5,000
				Total	15,000		

*Note that in the double-declining-balance method, one does not depreciate beneath the salvage value. Since the machine is fully depreciated by the third year, depreciation must be 0 in years 4 and 5.

Let us discuss now the time value of money and its effect on the capital budgeting decision.

PRESENT VALUE OF A SINGLE PAYMENT

Money to be received in the future is worth less in the present. This is true since the money could have been invested in a financial institution and interest earned on it.

A principal sum P, invested at interest rate i, will yield a future sum S in n years if all the earnings are retained and compounded. The amount P in the present is equivalent to S in the future, by virtue of the compound amount factor.

$$S = P(1 + i)^n$$

$(1 + i)^n =$ compound amount factor.

Thus the present value of a single payment, S, received n years hence is:

$$P = \frac{S}{(1 + i)^n} = S(PV_{SP});$$

PV_{SP} = present value factor for a single payment.

It is not necessary to calculate the present value factor PV_{SP} in determining present values. Tables have been developed that permit a quick and easy solution to the problem (see Table A in the Appendix).

EXAMPLE How much money must you invest in a savings bank that pays interest at 12 percent compounded annually, to have $10,000 in your account five years from the date of the lump sum deposit?

We calculate the present value of $10,000 by using the PV_{SP} taken from Table A:

$$P = S(PV_{SP}) = 10,000 \ (0.567) = \$5,670.00$$

That is, we should deposit $5,670.00 in the savings account in order to have $10,000 five years later.

PRESENT VALUE OF AN ANNUITY

An annuity is a series of equal payments (or receipts) to be paid (or received) at the end of successive periods of equal length. The notation PV_a represents the present value factor of an annuity, and S_a represents the yearly annuity payments. If n is the total number of years of the investment and i is the interest rate charged in the bank, it can be shown that the present value of an annuity payment of size S_a is as follows:

$$P_a = \frac{S_a}{i} \left(1 - \frac{1}{(1 + i)^n} \right) = S_a \ (PV_a)$$

It is not necessary to calculate the present value factor for an annuity PV_a. Tables of these factors have been developed for quick and easy computation (see Table B in the Appendix).

EXAMPLE A new word processor will save $1,000 a year after depreciation and taxes for the next five years. If the minimum rate of return allowed by management is 12 percent, what is the most that should be spent to purchase the word processor (WP)?

$$P_a = S_a(PV_a) - 1,000 \ (3.605) = \$3,605.$$

Thus, a maximum of $3,605 should be spent on the WP.

PAYBACK PERIOD

The payback period is the length of time required for the profits to equal the investment. It is also known as the cash breakeven period. Thus, the payback period is not a gauge of prospective profitability, but rather a measure of the rate of turnover or liquidity of an investment. If a firm is desperately short of cash, but is able to make an investment, the financial manager uses the payback method to emphasize investments that produce a quick return of cash funds. The liquidity objective is stressed at the expense of the profit objective. Industries characterized by instability, uncertainty, and rapid technological change may adopt this approach for capital budgeting on the grounds that the future is too unpredictable. This method does not consider the time value of money. The following formula can be used to determine the payback period if earnings after taxes and depreciation are uniform (do not change from year to year).

$$\text{Payback period} = \frac{\text{Investment}}{\text{Net cash flow}} = \frac{I}{E + D}$$

where E is the earnings after taxes and D is depreciation.

EXAMPLE A new production line used to produce a product costs $30,000 and has an estimated life of 10 years, with no salvage value. Annual savings after taxes that accrue due to use of the new production line will be $2,000. What is the payback period if straight-line depreciation is used?

$$\frac{I}{E + D} = \frac{30,000}{2,000 + 3,000} = 6 \text{ years}$$

EXAMPLE A project requires an investment of $24,000 at the beginning of the first year. The earnings from the project are not uniform from year to year. From the information given below, what would be the payback period for the project? (Assume no salvage value.)

Year	Earnings after Taxes	Depreciation	Cumulative Total
1	$1,000	$4,000	$5,000
2	3,000	4,000	12,000
3	4,000	4,000	20,000
4	5,000	4,000	29,000
5	2,000	4,000	35,000
6	1,000	4,000	40,000
7	0	0	40,000

$$\text{Payback} = 3 + \frac{24,000 - 20,000}{29,000 - 20,000} = 3 \ 4/9 \text{ years}$$

Note that after 3 years, we recover $20,000. In order to recover the balance of $4,000, we need to interpolate between $20,000 and $29,000.

PAYBACK RECIPROCAL

Under certain conditions the payback reciprocal is an adequate approximation to the internal rate of return, which is discussed later. These conditions are:

1. The useful life of the machine or other investment is at least twice the payback period.
2. Benefits are constant over the investment life.
3. There is no salvage value.

If these conditions are not met, the payback reciprocal is, at best, a very rough estimate of the internal rate of return (IRR), which is discussed later.

EXAMPLE   A new machine costs $30,000 and has an estimated life of 10 years, with no salvage value. Annual savings after taxes will be $2,000. What is the approximate internal rate of return?

$$\text{Internal rate of return} = \frac{1}{\text{Payback}} = \frac{1}{6} = 16\tfrac{2}{3} \text{ percent}$$

NET PRESENT VALUE (NPV) METHOD

The net present value (NPV) method considers the time value of money by giving greater weight to income received during the earlier years of a project. The more distant in the future the income is, the lower is the weight assigned to it. The weights assigned are called present value factors. Present value factors are contained in Tables B and C in the Appendix.

The NPV method assumes some minimum desired rate of return or a cost of capital to the firm. In this method, the future cash inflows are discounted at a predetermined discount rate (cost of capital), and the sum of the present values of the cash inflows over a specified period is compared with the cost of the investment. All expected cash flows are discounted to the present, using the minimum desired rate of return. If the NPV is positive, the project is desirable because its return exceeds the desired minimum. If the result is negative, the project is undesirable. Assuming:

NPV = new present value

I_0 = investment required at time 0

F_j = net cash flow in time period j (earnings after taxes plus depreciation)

k = minimum required rate of return (cost of capital)

S_n = salvage value in time period n

n_j = lifetime of the project

The formulation of the present value is:

$$\text{NPV} = -I_0 + \frac{F_1}{1 + k} + \frac{F_2}{(1 + k)^2} + \cdots \frac{F_n}{(1 + k)^n} + \frac{S_n}{(1 + k)^n}$$

$$= -I_0 + \sum_{j=1}^{n} \frac{F_j}{(1 + k)^j} + \frac{S_n}{(1 + k)^n}$$

Fortunately, it is not necessary to work with the formula above. The weights or present value factors are contained in Table B in the Appendix.

If the net cash flows are the same for each year, the appropriate present value factor can be found in Table C in the Appendix.

$$\text{Present value factor} = \frac{1}{1 + k} + \frac{1}{(1 + k)^2} + \cdots \frac{1}{(1 + k)^n}$$

$$= \sum_{j=1}^{n} \frac{1}{(1 + k)^j}$$

To determine the net present value, the minimum required rate of return is established and used in calculating the expected net cash flows to determine their present value.

EXAMPLE   A new computer used in Northwest General Hospital costs $30,000 and has an estimated life of ten years with no salvage value. It will produce annual savings after taxes of $2,000. What is the net present value of the investment if the required rate of return is 10 percent with straight-line depreciation?

Since the annual net cash flow is constant for each year, the present value factor from Table C in the Appendix is used (6.145) for ten years at 10%. The net cash flow is the annual savings after taxes ($2,000) plus the depreciation charge ($30,000 ÷ 10 = $3,000).

$$\text{NPV} = -I_0 + \sum_{j=1}^{10} \frac{F_j}{(1 + k)^j} = -\$30,000 + (6.145)(\$2,000 + \$3,000) = \$725$$

Since the net present value (NPV) is positive, the computer should be bought.

Profitability Index

A *profitability index* is frequently used for ranking different projects by the net present value method. The index is calculated by dividing the gross present value of a project by the required investment. The index makes different sized projects comparable. Projects with the highest profitability index are the most desirable.

$$\text{Profitability index} = \frac{\text{Gross present value}}{\text{Investment}} = \frac{\text{NPV} + I_0}{I_0}$$

EXAMPLE Based on the preceding example:

$$\text{Profitability index} = \frac{\text{NPV} + I_0}{I_0} = \frac{725 + 30,000}{30,000} = 1.02$$

EXAMPLE A project requires an investment of $24,000 at the beginning of the first year. The minimum required rate of return is 10 percent, with straight line depreciation. From the data given below, determine the net present value of the investment, as well as the profitability index.

Year	Earnings after Taxes	Depreciation	Salvage Value	Earnings after Taxes and Depreciation
1	$1,000	$3,000		$4,000
2	3,000	3,000		6,000
3	4,000	3,000		7,000
4	5,000	3,000		8,000
5	2,000	3,000		5,000
6	1,000	3,000	$6,000	4,000

Since the net cash flow is not uniform, the present value factors from Table B in the Appendix are used.

$$\text{NPV} = -24,000 + 0.909(4,000) + 0.826(6,000) + 0.751(7,000)$$
$$+ 0.683(8,000) + 0.621(5,000) + 0.564(4,000) + 0.564(6,000)$$
$$= \$4,058$$

Since the net present value is positive, the project should be undertaken.

$$\text{Profitability index} = \frac{4,058 + 24,000}{24,000} = 1.16$$

If we have to decide between this project, with a profitability index of 1.16, and the computer used in Northwest General Hospital of the preceding example, with a profitability index of 1.02, the project should have first priority.

Internal Rate of Return (IRR)

The internal rate of return (IRR) method is a method for deriving the rate of return implicit in a set of forecasted future cash flows. It is that rate of return which equates the present value of cash inflows to the present value of cash outflows. If the cost of capital is higher than the rate of return, the receipts generated from the investment would be insufficient to cover costs.

Projects are ranked in descending order of IRR, and priority is given to projects with a higher IRR. The internal rate of return can be determined from the following formula. Assume:

$$I_0 = \text{investment required at time } 0$$
$$F_j = \text{net cash flow in the time period } j$$
$$r = \text{internal rate of return}$$
$$S_n = \text{salvage value in time period } n$$
$$n = \text{lifetime of the project}$$

Then:

$$I_0 = \frac{F_1}{1 + r} + \frac{F_2}{(1 + r)^2} + \cdots \frac{F_n}{(1 + r)^n} + \frac{S_n}{(1 + r)^n}$$

$$I_0 = \sum_{j = 1}^{n} = \frac{F_j}{(1 + r)^j} + \frac{S_n}{(1 + r)^n} = F(PV_a)$$

Present value tables make available a method of solution that does not require mathematical solution from the above formula. To obtain the internal rate of return from the present value tables, it is necessary to use a trial-and-error approach and interpolate between the respective returns to equate outflows to inflows.

EXAMPLE   A new laundry machine for Central Hilton Hotel costs $30,000 and has an estimated life of ten years, with no salvage value. If annual savings after taxes are $2,000, what is the internal rate of return with straight line depreciation?

$$I_0 = F(PV_a)$$
$$30,000 = 5,000 \, PV_a$$
$$PV_a = 6.000$$

From Table C of the Appendix, for ten years, you find 6.000 is between 10% and 12%. Interpolating between 6.145 and 5.650, you obtain:

$$r = 10.0\% + (0.02)\frac{(6.145 - 6.000)}{(6.45 - 5.650)} = 10.6\%$$

The following example will demonstrate the various techniques discussed so far.

EXAMPLE You are considering the purchase of a new production line that would cost $12,000 installed. The pertinent data are as follows.

(1)	(2)	(3) Earnings before Taxes	(4) = (3) ÷ 2 Taxes 50% Rate	(5) = (3) − (4) Earnings after Taxes	(6) = (2) + (5) Net Cash Flow
Year	Depreciation				
1	$3,000	$6,000	$3,000	$3,000	$6,000
2	3,000	4,000	2,000	2,000	5,000
3	3,000	2,000	1,000	1,000	4,000
4	3,000	0	0	0	3,000

If cost of capital is 12 percent, what are: (1) the payback period, (2) the net present value (NPV), and (3) the internal rate of return (IRR)?

(1) We have to recover the investment of $12,000 through the annual net cash flows:

$$\$6,000 + \$5,000 + \tfrac{1}{4}(4,000) = \$12,000$$

Thus,

$$\text{Payback period} = 2\tfrac{1}{4} \text{ years}$$

Thus, the investment will be recovered in just over two years.

(2)   Net present value: $\text{NPV} = -I_0 + \sum_{j=1}^{n} \frac{F_j}{(1 + k)^j} + \frac{S_n}{(1 + k)^n}$

The appropriate present value factors are found in Table B of the Appendix.

$\text{NPV} = -12,000 + 6,000(0.893) + 5,000(0.797) + 4,000(0.712) + 3,000(0.636)$

$\text{NPV} = +\$2,099$

Thus, the new production line should be constructed.

(3) Calculating the internal rate of return (IRR):

$$I_0 = \sum_{j=1}^{n} \frac{F_j}{(1 + r)^j} + \frac{S_n}{(1 + r)^n}$$

$$12,000 = \frac{6,000}{(1 + r)} + \frac{5,000}{(1 + r)^2} + \frac{4,000}{(1 + r)^3} + \frac{3,000}{(1 + r)^4} + \frac{0}{(1 + r)^4}$$

$$12,000 = 6,000(PV_{SP}) + 5,000(PV_{SP}) + 4,000(PV_{SP}) + 3,000(PV_{SP})$$

From the Table B of the Appendix, one gets the PV_{SP} values for various r's and substitute these values into the above equation. For $r = 18\%$; $I_0 = \$12,656$; and for $r = 20\%$, $I_0 = \$11,230$. Since we have to recover exactly $12,000, we have to interpolate between 18% and 20%.

$$r = 0.18 + \frac{12,656 - 12,000}{12,656 - 11,230}(0.02) = 18.9\%$$

Thus, the Internal Rate of Return (IRR) for the new production line is 18.9%. If this IRR is greater than the firm's cost of capital, the new production line is desirable.

SUMMARY

In this Technical Note, we have presented several techniques that can be used in the economic analysis of new product and process decision and design.

Whereas in Chapter 2 we covered the break-even analysis, this Technical Note has presented important capital budgeting techniques that are more involved and that consider explicitly, among other things, the time value of money, tax effects, and depreciation charges.

TECHNICAL NOTE PROBLEMS

2.1 Compute the present value of the following stream of payments, assuming a 10 percent rate of return.

Year	Amount
1	$1,000
2	2,000
3–5	4,000
6	10,000

2.2 Compute the internal rate of return on a $10,000 investment, assuming the following cash flow benefits;

Year	Cash Flow
1	$2,000
2	2,000
3	2,500
4	4,000
5	6,000

2.3 Compute the average rate of return on a $20,000 investment, assuming the following benefits:

(1)	(2)	(3)	(4) = (2) − (3)	(5) = (4)(.50)	(6) = (4) − (5)	(7) = (3) + (6)
Year	Earn-ings	Depre-ciation	Earnings before Taxes	Taxes	Earnings after Taxes	Cash Flow
1	$7,000	$5,000	$2,000	$1,000	$1,000	$6,000
2	9,000	5,000	4,000	2,000	2,000	7,000
3	11,000	5,000	6,000	3,000	3,000	8,000
4	15,000	5,000	10,000	5,000	5,000	10,000

2.4 An apartment building can be acquired for $60,500 and then leased for the next 10 years at annual payments of $10,000 to be paid at the end of each year. What is the internal rate of return?

2.5 A planted acre of timber is estimated to be worth $25,000 in 20 years. How much can you invest per acre if you are to realize a 10 percent rate of return?

2.6 You have the opportunity to invest a sum that is expected to return $13,000 at the end of the first year, with subsequent annual receipts decreasing by $500 each year. Compute the value of the investment if it is expected to last 6 years and the minimum required rate of return is 7 percent.

2.7 Your great-aunt, having a life expectancy of 15 more years, promises to leave you $1,000 in her will if you will give her a car you are about to sell.
a) If money is worth 12 percent to you, at what price would you have to sell your car in order to beat her offer?
b) Would you be better off if she gave you $500 now and left you $500 in her will?

2.8 A production department is contemplating the purchase of a new milling machine at a cost of $13,000. Expenses to install the new machine are $440. Its estimated life is 6 years, with no salvage value. Annual savings are expected to equal $4,126. Using straight-line depreciation and a tax rate of 50 percent:
a) What is the payback period?
b) What is the average rate of return?
c) What is the internal rate of return?

2.9 The Capital Gains Investment Company must choose between two mutually exclusive investment proposals. Each would cost $6,000, have a 4-year life, and generate earnings before depreciation and taxes as shown below. Assuming a 50 percent tax rate and straight-line depreciation, compute the payback period and average rate of return.

	PROJECT	
Year	A	B
1	$2,000	$2,000
2	3,000	2,000
3	1,500	2,000
4	1,500	4,000

2.10 Two mutually exclusive proposals of equal risk have been made for the purchase of a new machine. Data on the two proposals are as follows:

PROJECT

	A	B
Net Investment	$8,500	$6,000
Salvage Value	0	0
Estimated Life	5 years	5 years
Earnings before taxes and depreciation:		
1–3 years	3,500	1,800
4–5 years	3,000	1,800

Assume straight-line depreciation, a corporate tax rate of 40%, and 10% cost of capital. Rank each project according to:
a) Internal rate of return (IRR)
b) Net present value (NPV)
c) Payback period.

2.11   A lathe costs $50,000, is expected to last 5 years, with a salvage value of $5,000. Its pattern of benefits is as follows:

Year	EBT & Depr.
1	$29,000
2	25,000
*3	(3,000)
4	25,000
5	15,000

A major overhaul will be required. Assuming straight-line depreciation, a 50 percent tax rate, and a 10 percent cost of capital, determine:
a) Payback period
b) Average rate of return
c) Internal rate of return
d) Net present value.

2.12   Allstate Manufacturing Company purchased a planer 5 years ago at a cost of $7,500. The machine had an expected life of 15 years at the time of purchase and no salvage value at the end of this period. It is being depreciated on a straight-line basis and has a book value of $5,000 at present. The production manager reports that he can buy a new planer for $10,000. The new machine will reduce operating expenses by $2,000 and have a 10-year life with no salvage value. The old machine's current market value is $1,000. Corporate taxes are 50 percent, and the firm's cost of capital is 10 percent.
a) Using net present value, would you recommend purchasing the new machine?
b) Explain your recommendation in part (a).

2.13   The Griffin Company is considering bidding on a contract to manufacture a special fixture for the government. This would require the purchase of a new mold that would cost $50,000, have a freight and setup expense of $5,000, and a $10,000 scrap value at the end of its 5-year life. The machine would be depreciated on a straight-line basis. If the company is successful in obtaining the contract, there would result an increase in gross revenue of $70,000 and an increase in cash expenses of $30,000 during each of the 5 years. An additional investment in inventory of $25,000 will be required during the 5-year life of the contract. If the tax rate is 50 percent and the cost of capital is 12 percent, determine

a) the average rate of return

b) the net present value of the project.

2.14 The Allied Company is considering two exclusive proposals for the purchase of a new machine. Data on each are as follows:

	Machine A	Machine B
Original Cost	$18,000	$27,000
Freight	1,000	500
Installation Cost	1,000	500
Additional Working Capital	0	6,000
Salvage Value	2,000	0
Estimated Life in Years	3	4
Net Cash Benefits Before Depreciation and Taxes,		
Year 1	10,000	17,000
Year 2	10,000	17,000
Year 3	10,000	17,000
Year 4	0	17,000

The financial manager estimates that the working capital investment for Machine B will be recovered in full at the end of the fourth year. The corporation employs the straight-line method of depreciation. The cost of capital is 6 percent, and the tax rate is 50 percent. What is the best machine to select using the net present value method?

3

Facility Location

INTRODUCTION

Very early in the planning phase, the operations manager is faced with a facility location decision. The small entrepreneur, when considering a location for his welding shop, is concerned with easy access to the shop by potential clients and with building costs and rental rates. The major national producer of chain saws considers his markets, the availability of skilled personnel, the supply of raw materials, energy, and so on. The property and liability insurance company, when considering the location of service offices, is concerned with the locations of its insurers, the communication of the offices with headquarters, and the price of proper housing.

The location of a facility is a major decision and is affected by many factors, both internal and external to the organization's operations. Internal factors include the technology used, the capacity, the financial position, and the work force required. External factors include the economic, political, and social conditions in the various localities.

Most of the fixed and some of the variable costs of the operation are determined by the location decision. Thus, the efficiency, effectiveness, productivity, and profitability of the facility are affected by the location decision. While some aspects of location analysis can be dealt with quantitatively, the final decision is based largely on informed qualitative judgment.

FACILITY LOCATION FACTORS

The location of a facility, be it manufacturing or service, is largely affected by the following factors:[1]

Process inputs
Process outputs
Process characteristics
Personal preferences
Tax incentives and legal aspects
Site, community, and building availability

Process inputs involve raw materials, personnel, and other inputs. So far as raw materials are concerned, transportation costs are of importance. These costs are significant when bulky and heavy raw materials are involved in the process.

When there is only one major raw material source and many dispersed markets, one considers locating the facility near the raw material source. However, when there are various raw materials that are to be used for the production of one single marketable product, one considers locating the facility near the market.

Inputs other than raw materials are also involved in the operation process. For example, work force availability and wages are, at times, of far more importance to an operation than are raw materials. Service organizations and labor-intensive industries in general, are very sensitive to the availability, the skill level, and the pay rate of the work force. A lower wage scale as well as a nonunion environment has led to the move of labor-intensive manufacturing companies (such as textile manufacturers) from New England to the Sun Belt area. However, to a certain extent increased mechanization has contributed to the reduced importance of the labor aspect of location analysis.

Another consideration in the context of human resources is the availability of manpower. Generally speaking, the work force consists of skilled, semi-skilled, and unskilled personnel. All of these skill levels are represented in organizations. For example, if a plant is to be located in a low-skill, low-wage area, the degree of mechanization must be increased. The number of vocational schools as well as primary and secondary schools is of importance, too, as are the work attitude and habits of locally recruited personnel. Right-to-work laws, the wage scales, and the local average income are to be considered as well.

Process outputs involve distribution costs. The more bulky and heavy the finished product is, the more costly becomes the distribution. Also, the more service-oriented the operation is, the more important it is that it be located near its market. For industries whose *services are not directly consumed*, such as

---

[1] For a coverage of related topics, see E. Menipaz, "Industrial Projects Feasibility Methodology," *Europa Industrial Review*, Vol. 1, Feb., 1980, pp. 18–21, 42–45.

automative repair shops and headquarters of mortgage and trust companies, location is not so crucial. However, for *services that are directly consumed*, such as those of bank branches, theatres, restaurants, apartment buildings, and public parks, locations near the consuming public is crucial. As a matter of fact, proximity to the market is possibly the *most* important consideration in location services that are directly consumed.

When the process requires a great deal of energy, as does the steel industry, it should be located next to a major source of power. When the process requires a great deal of water, as does the sugar industry, it should be located where water is available in ample supply.

Process characteristics are concerned with environmental conditions. Very noisy or odor- or chemical-producing plants should be located far from urban or suburban communities. Certain weather conditions are advantageous for various processes. For example, a certain humidity level is favorable for knitting operations. A certain humidity level is required for the printing industry because of the paper-sheet feeding technology which is based on vacuum cups. A certain humidity, temperature, and rainfall is favored by health spa clients. The facility location is thus affected by the process requirements.

Personal preferences of the entrepreneur or the top executives of the company also affect the location decision.

Tax incentives and legal aspects are very important factors. Corporate tax, personal income taxes, sales tax, and gasoline and tobacco taxes all affect the location decision. Obviously, the corporate tax structure is built into any location feasibility study made by the corporation. Personal taxes determine how attractive the move to the new location is and what the wage structure should be. Various communities, states, and governments offer incentives for facility location by providing industrial parks, properly zoned land at favorable tax rates, and rebates based on capital allowances and per worker outright grants. At times, loans and loan guarantees are offered.

Certain industries are barred from certain localities. Others are most favorably looked upon. Certain products might be legally banned from certain localities. These aspects of facility location should be checked and confirmed.

STEPS IN THE FACILITY LOCATION STUDY

In most cases, a location analysis should begin with a preliminary survey of the factors indicated above to determine whether or not the use of new facility sites might be justified. When it is not justified, the study simply ends. If the survey indicates that new sites may be desirable, a detailed analysis that carefully evaluates all possible alternatives should be undertaken.

Usually, the analysis is undertaken in several stages. First, the general area or region is selected. Second, a specific community is selected. Third, a specific site is selected. Sometimes, the second and third stages are combined.

The selection of factors to consider at each stage is to an extent arbitrary. Some factors may be evaluated at different stages and some are evaluated in all three stages. What is important is that all the factors be considered at some point in the analysis.

Numerous sources of information are available to assist the firm with the analysis. These include federal, state, and local governments, chambers of commerce, chartered banks, railways, utility companies, and management consultants.

Step 1. Area Selection

In this initial phase, management is involved in selecting the region or general area in which the plant should be located. The following are some of the important factors that influence its selection.

LOCATION OF MARKETS   Locating plants near the markets for their products and services is of primary importance in a plant location decision, particularly if the manufacturing process increases the bulk or weight of the product, renders it more fragile, or makes it susceptible to spoilage. Besides adding transportation cost, distance adds to transit time and slows down deliveries, thus affecting promptness of service.

If the product is relatively inexpensive and transportation costs (e.g., of bricks, cement) add substantially to the price, a location near the markets is desirable. Also, if the product is custom-made, close customer contact is essential. Assembly-type industries (in which many raw materials are gathered together from diverse locations and assembled into single units) tend to locate near markets.

LOCATION OF MATERIALS   Ease of access to suppliers of raw materials, parts, supplies, tools, equipment, etc., may be acutely important. Promptness and regularity of delivery from suppliers and minimization of freight costs are at issue.

In general, this factor is most likely to be important if transportation of materials and parts represents the major portion of unit costs and/or these inputs are available only in a particular region. If the raw material is bulky or low in cost, if it is greatly reduced in bulk (transformed into various products and byproducts) in processing, or if it is perishable and processing makes it less so, then location near raw-material sources is important (e.g., locating a nickel smelter in Columbus, Ohio, is not feasible, as the cost to transport such bulky material—much of which is lost in processing—from the nickel mines in Idaho would be astronomical and would price the product out of the market). If raw materials come from a variety of locations, the plant may be situated so as to minimize total transportation cost.

In calculating transportation costs, one should be aware of the fact that these costs are not simply a function of distance, but vary depending upon specific routes and specific product classifications. Two locations may be in close proximity, yet freight rate differentials can be substantial. Later in this chapter, quantitative approaches to transportation costs are discussed.

TRANSPORTATION FACILITIES   Adequate transportation facilities are essential for the economic operation of a production system. The bulk of all freight shipments is made by rail, and although the cost per ton-mile is greater than by water transport, rail offers a great deal of flexibility and speed. Most firms require access to railways, which they consider to be essential carriers of their products.

For companies that produce or buy heavy, bulky, and low-value-per-ton commodities (especially those that are imported or exported), water transportation is an important factor in locating plants.

Truck transport is also important, particularly for intercity transport. Availability of pipelines may also influence location. Use of air freight and executive aircraft is rapidly expanding, so proximity to airports may be vital.

Traveling expenses of management and sales personnel should also be considered.

LABOR SUPPLY   Manpower is one of the most important and costly inputs in production systems. An ample supply of labor is essential. Firms often look to areas in which there will be three or four times as many permanent job applicants than will be required. General Electric, for example, attempts to locate where it will absorb less than 10 to 12 percent of the local labor force. It is also advantageous to locate in places where there is diversification between industry and commerce (it is not desirable to have more than 50 percent of the available work force in manufacturing).

The type and level of skills possessed by the labor force is important. If a company requires particular skills that are not widespread, it may have to locate near the particular areas where these skills are prevalent; otherwise, training costs might be prohibitive and inadequate productivity would result. In other cases, skilled labor is desirable but not essential, as all the workers will require some training anyway. It should be noted that a firm can relocate from a high-skill/high-cost to a low-skill/low-cost operation if sufficient process mechanization is achieved to permit trading off the higher investment in machinery for less manpower and lower wages and level of skills.

The existence of regional wage rate differentials may be important, particularly in those cases in which labor costs represent the bulk of total production costs (e.g., in textiles). This factor must be considered in light of the skills available in the area, the size of labor force, productivity levels, etc. The extent of unionization, prevailing labor-management attitudes, history of labor relations, turnover rates, absenteeism, etc., should also be considered.

LOCATION OF OTHER PLANTS AND WAREHOUSES   Firms always try to place new plants where they will complement sister plants and warehouses and minimize total system costs. They look for market needs and supply-and-demand disparities, and locate where major markets have been served by long-distance hauls. The locations of competitors' plants and warehouses must also be considered, the object being to obtain an advantage in both freight costs and the level of customer service.

Step 2. Community Selection

The choice of a community depends upon the region already chosen. Most community selection factors cannot be quantified and can only be evaluated subjectively.

MANAGERIAL PREFERENCES   These often play an important role in plant location decisions. Many times, due to community ties, companies will not relocate. When firms do relocate, the location selection in some cases is heavily influenced by the preferences of the managers who will be transferred.

COMMUNITY FACILITIES   These involve such factors as quality of life, which in turn is a function of the availability of such facilities as schools, churches, medical services, police and fire protection, cultural, social, and recreational opportunities, housing, good streets, and highways. Also important are the community's communication facilities and the range, frequency, and reliability of transportation facilities.

COMMUNITY ATTITUDES   These can be difficult to evaluate. Unless the industry is for some reason of an offensive nature, most communities welcome new industry. However, the formation of antiindustrial pressure groups, or a lack of cooperation, interest, and enthusiasm on the part of the community can result in poor relations between the relocating firm and local government, labor, and the general public.

COMMUNITY, GOVERNMENT AND TAXATION   Stable, honest, and cooperative government officials are an important asset, as most of the local legislation affecting industry is under their control. Restrictive, unreasonable local ordinances concerning building codes, zoning, pollution control, etc., can seriously inhibit operations.

Tax rates are important, but must be considered in terms of the services provided. There should be some attempt to forecast these charges; if future expansion of community services and facilities is likely, taxes will probably increase.

FINANCIAL INDUCEMENTS   Many local and state governments offer financial inducements to companies to influence them to build plants in their areas. The federal departments concerned with regional economic expansion have programs to entice industry to designated slow-growth regions. On the state level, organizations may provide loans for plants newly established within their region. However, companies should not allow temporary inducements to overshadow the basic merits of any location.

PROFILE OF PRESENT INDUSTRY   The kinds and quality of industrial concerns already in the community are pertinent factors.

Step 3. Site Selection

This is the final stage in the plant location analysis. When choosing a site, the following factors should be investigated. (Many of these categories may also be considered when selecting the community.)

SIZE OF SITE   The plot of land must be large enough to hold the proposed plant and parking and access facilities, and provide room for future expansion. Industrial parks are often an excellent choice (except for heavy industry).

TOPOGRAPHY   The topography, soil mixture, and drainage must be suited to the type of building required and must be capable of providing it with a proper foundation. If considerable land improvement is required, low-priced land may turn out to be expensive.

UTILITIES   The cost, adequacy, and reliability of the supply of power, water, and fuel must be evaluated. These are sizeable and constantly recurring costs. Variations in utility expenses may be as high as 100 percent, depending upon locality, demand, and use. Accurate cost determination requires contact with the local utility company. Use restrictions may be imposed, and there may be wide variations in availability. The water supply must be sufficient to meet peak needs and compensate for dry spells. If the water is of poor quality, it may require chemical treatment or purification. The cost of connecting these services to the plant must not be overlooked; sometimes it can be done only at high cost.

WASTE DISPOSAL   This must be considered when selecting the site. The plant should be positioned so that prevailing winds carry any fumes away from populated areas and so that waste may be disposed of properly and at reasonable expense.

TRANSPORTATION FACILITIES   Railroads and highways should be close by in order to minimize the cost of rail spur lines and access roads. There must be enough through-highways and railroads to serve the community itself. Special requirements for water or air transport must be considered. The plant itself should be easily accessible by car or (preferably) public transport.

Intangible factors to consider include the dependability and character of the available carriers, frequency of service, and freight and terminal facilities. Cost and time required to transport the finished product to market, and the time required to contact or service a customer must also be considered. (See the Heuristic Model section of this chapter, which deals with the quantitative treatment of service area determination.)

LAND COSTS   These are generally of minor importance, as they are nonrecurring and make up a relatively small proportion of the total cost of locating a new plant. Generally speaking, the site will be in a city, suburb, or country location. Some of the industrial needs and characteristics that tend to flavor each of these locales are:

> Country location
>> Large land requirements
>> Production processes/products that are dangerous or objectionable
>> Requirements for large volumes of relatively pure water
>> Need for favorable property tax
>> Need for protection against sabotage or observation of secret processes/ inputs
>
> Suburban location
>> Requirement that a relatively large site be close to transportation and population
>> Freedom from strict city building and zoning codes, and other restrictions
>> Need for large female labor supply
>> Freedom from high taxes
>> Desire to locate near employees' homes
>
> City location
>> High proportion of highly skilled employees
>> Requirements for rapid transportation or quick contact with customers and suppliers
>> Small plant sites or possible multifloor operations
>> Large variety of materials and supplies, but each in relatively small quantities
>> City facilities and utilities at reasonable rates
>> Need to start production with minimum possible investment in land, buildings, etc., which usually can be rented in the city.

It should be emphasized that plant location analysis is a periodic task. The world is rapidly changing and management should not expect a location to remain optimal forever. Every organization should periodically reassess its environment to determine whether long term changes have occurred that may make it advantageous for the organization to alter or possibly relocate some portion of its facilities. For example, some aircraft factories were originally located on waterways because they were to produce seaplanes. Seaplanes are no longer produced, and thus such locations may no longer be optimal.

COMMON ERRORS IN FACILITY LOCATION ANALYSIS

Not infrequently, the location selected is poorly suited to the company's needs. Among the more common causes of failure to make a proper location decision are the following:

1. Labor cost miscalculations (it is important to check not only hourly wage differences between two possible locations but other contributions to cost, such as local patterns in incentive systems, strikes, and labor disturbances)
2. Inadequate labor reservoir
3. Failure to anticipate growth (firms overly influenced by short-term considerations find expansion restricted by natural boundaries, residential or commercial encroachment, limited utilities, etc.)
4. Carelessness in checking site
5. Lack of distribution outlets
6. Failure to predict local impact of new plant
7. Lack of supporting facilities
8. Misinformation on utility costs and problems
9. Underestimated importance of taxes
10. Failure to identify critical costs
11. Choosing a community in which living conditions are substandard
12. Yielding to the desire to locate near home, friends, and relatives
13. Allowing the personal opinions and prejudices of company officers to influence the decisions
14. Purchase of an existing building due to low price, even though it is unsuited to the firm's process.

FACILITY LOCATION—INDUSTRIAL CASE

As has been indicated, the location decision is a very individualistic process with no hard and fast rules. What factors are to be evaluated and how they are to be evaluated vary from situation to situation.

Case studies are perhaps more illustrative of the problems and implications of plant moves. Let us describe one such case.

General Foods is one of the largest producers of packaged foods in the United States.

In the 'seventies, the Jello Division manufacturing facilities of General Foods were located in five plants, in Dorchester, Massachusetts; Orange, Massachusetts; Le Roy, New York; Hoboken, New Jersey; and Chicago, Illinois. All had been acquired in the 1920's, all were to varying degrees old and outmoded, and none was at a location chosen by General Foods. Some of the plants had been expanded over the years by tacking on additions. The plants were inefficient, multi-storied, located in crowded urban areas with no further room for expansion except at high cost, and were divided or hemmed in by railway lines, streets, rivers, etc. Thus, General Foods was faced with the problem of a growing, dynamic business with no room to grow. Production facilities had to be extensively revamped and revitalized if a competitive position was to be maintained and provisions were to be made for new processes and products.

Studies began with the establishment of a task force to make an exploratory investigation. Various alternatives and cost projections were developed; the most favorable alternative was the construction of one new Eastern plant combining all four of the older Eastern plants. Many advantages were cited, including cost and flexibility for future expansion and adaptation to unforeseen conditions. Disadvantages included placing all the production "eggs" in one basket, and closing up long-established plants upon which small communities were dependent.

Based on these studies, management decided to proceed with a six-phase program that was to carry the work forward through construction of the new plant, shutdown of the old one, and start-up of the consolidated facility. Savings and cost verification studies confirmed impressive savings in property taxes, utilities, labor rates, insurance, direct labor and benefits (fewer workers were required), and indirect labor and benefits (there was no duplication of services).

A more detailed study to identify a location was now required. This was assigned to a consulting firm, Fantus Company. Several initial requirements were imposed. The new plant had to be built within the range of the primary market served by the four old plants and, preferably, within 250 miles of New York City. It had to be near an adequate ocean port or ports, since large quantities of raw materials would come from overseas. It was necessary that the plant be close to a sugar refinery (consumption of sugar would amount to ½ million pounds per day), and it had to be located in a receptive community.

In its report to GF, Fantus focused on the Philadelphia-Wilmington-Baltimore area and gave detailed figures and specific site recommendations. The report consisted of three important parts:

1. A review of the cost factors influencing choice of location
2. A delineation of the areas considered and the reasons for their selection
3. A comparison of operating costs in present plants and in the considered locations.

In arriving at its conclusions, Fantus first studied process output (finished goods) and process input (raw materials, especially sugar) freight costs. Consideration was given to a waterfront site but savings were not sufficient to offset the capital outlay for waterfront facilities. Labor availability and the probable cost of labor were investigated (based on the net employee requirements expected). It was found that the widest differentials in wages among the various localities were in the unskilled labor categories, whereas highly skilled employees' wages did not differ as much. This alleviated the anticipated problem of transferring highly skilled employees from two of the present plants, which were located in relatively high-wage areas.

Construction costs in each area were studied, as well as state income and franchise taxes, local taxes (it was decided to avoid any community that taxed property such as machinery), variations in premiums for workman's compensation insurance, unemployment insurance rates, and utilities (in terms of cost, capacity, and reliability of service).

After considering all factors, the following conclusions were reached:

1. Finished goods freight costs would be minimized for a site in the Philadelphia-Wilmington-Baltimore vicinity.
2. General Foods must locate close to an existing sugar refinery, as no new refinery would be built on the East coast.
3. Heavy movement of raw materials (other than sugar) from overseas suggests a location oriented to a general cargo port.
4. Combined freight costs favor the Philadelphia-Wilmington-Baltimore area.
5. The General Foods decision to pay local wages suggests potential selection of an outlying, low-cost community in the Philadelphia-Wilmington-Baltimore area.
6. Combined state and local taxes are lowest in Delaware.
7. Construction costs would be lowest in the southern portions of the area under consideration.

The report concluded with an estimate of operating cost savings for the three proposed plant sites in Philadelphia, Baltimore, and Dover, Delaware. Dover emerged as the definite winner because, in addition to tax attractions, it offered the following unique advantages:

1. Wage differentials have persisted for decades.
2. Most of the local industries, including the largest (2,100 employees), enjoy good management-labor relations.
3. Within a 30-mile radius the estimated supply of workers seeking industrial employment is 5,000 males and 3,000 females.
4. Living conditions are superior to those in typical cities in its class, reflecting the combined presence of the state offices, a college, and an air force base.
5. Good freight transportation services are available, including an active line of the Pennsylvania Railroad.
6. Excellent sites served by rail and all utilities could be acquired at low cost.

Fantus specifically recommended one site of ample size that had all utilities in place and was bounded on one side by a railroad.

Some of the potential problems in Dover were:

1. Little skilled labor is available, necessitating an extensive training program.
2. Housing, though modern, is in short supply. Some company aid may be necessary.
3. Upon completion of their 33,000-kW municipal power plant, Dover officials cancelled a power supply contract with the Delaware Power & Light Company. Negotiations would be necessary to ensure service by the utility company.
4. Some surplus capacity is available in the water system and sewage treatment plant. Plans for their expansion should be expedited to correspond with General Foods production schedules.

General Foods' management decided to take a closer look at Dover and took an option to purchase the land. In addition to information about zoning and utilities, further data were required on the Dover area labor pool, especially in the skilled craft categories. A survey research firm was commissioned to make a Dover community study to answer the following:

1. What are the attitudes and feelings of people in the area that bear on whether General Foods should locate there? Would people in the area be desirous of working in the plant? Would the company be welcomed? What are the union attitudes in the community?
2. What is the availability of skilled-craft labor? How many such workers live in the area? How skilled are they? Would they be interested in working for GF?

The survey interviews were of three types: interviews with community leaders, interviews with more than 300 adult residents, and interviews with 43 skilled craftsmen. The interviews with community leaders revealed a unanimous desire to have General Foods locate in Dover. The community leaders were neither for nor against unions as there had been very little experience with them in the area.

Local residents were also overwhelmingly in favor of having General Foods move to Dover, and thought the community would be better for it. The vast majority thought the plant would be a good place to work, with one third expecting to apply for jobs. Questionnaires revealed that 270 of the 304 respondents were employed or employable. The public was noncommittal on the subject of unions.

The survey of craftsmen revealed that, contrary to what the Fantus report stated, there seemed to be a good many skilled workers, some of whom seemed to have the necessary qualifications. Moreover, many planned to apply at the new plant. Additional skilled labor could be recruited from surrounding counties. Also, the State Vocational Training Department and a local junior college had offered their services in helping develop training programs. Thus, there appeared to be a stable, skilled, productive work force.

The only occasional negative comments were that the plant might cause general wage levels to increase, some farm land would be taken out of production, "Old Doverites" might be against the plant, the plant might cause some pollution, and it might use excessive amounts of water.

Thus, General Foods now had two reports favoring Dover. The only outstanding matters blocking a final decision were soon cleared up. With respect to electric power, an agreement was reached to tie the plant to Delaware Power & Light facilities, but with the city selling the power. The city agreed to speed up planned expansion of sewage treatment facilities and expand the water system to meet plant requirements. The city also arranged to annex the General Foods property so that it would be part of the city and thus protected by city regulations.

At a meeting of the General Foods Board of Directors, the final decision was made to move to Dover.

FACILITY LOCATION MODELS

Various types of quantitative models have been used to help determine the best facility location. Many of these models have been devised for use in specific instances.

A quantitative model was developed to determine the locations of regional service offices for a large New England homeowner and automobile insurance company.[2] These offices were to serve as first-line administrative centers for sales support and claims processing. The criteria and constraints of the model reflected capital and operating costs, budget considerations, and a measure of service level provided. The location of the regional service offices has been determined using multiple objective models.

In New York City, a quantitative model was developed for use as a fire department planning tool. The major concern was the optimal location of fire companies.[3] The objective was to balance available fire companies to reduce risks of property damage and fatalities. The model devised was capable of handling different decision criteria as they were generated by the operations manager. A relationship was developed between expected travel time (to be minimized) and the following: the region's area, the number of fire companies allocated to the region, the average number of companies busy in the region, the

---

[2]See G. R. Bitran, and K. D. Lawrence, "Locating Service Offices for a Property and Liability Insurer: A Multicriteria Approach," unpublished paper, Sloan School of Management, MIT, Cambridge, Massachusetts.

[3]K. L. Rider, "A Parametric Model for the Allocation of Fire Companies in New York City," *Management Science*, Vol. 23, No. 2, October, 1976, pp. 146–158.

street configuration, the company placement in the region, and the travel characteristics of the companies. It should be understood that the model was not necessarily applicable to other operating systems.

There are some general models that have been devised and adapted to the wide range of facility location problems. Most of these models use cost as a single criteria for choosing an optimal location. Let us examine in detail several facility location models.

THE MEDIAN MODEL

The Median Model determines the facility location that minimizes the annual transportation costs for the entire production and distribution system.

Let us assume that a new processing plant is to be built. It is scheduled to receive raw materials from two sources, S_1 and S_2, and sends its finished products to two distribution points, M_1 and M_2. The locations are plotted on a map, using an arbitrarily placed origin. The units on the axes may be miles or other scale units. The location of the new facility will be indicated by using the same axis as a reference. Given the current locations of the raw material sources and the distribution points, the question is, what should the location of the new facility be? The locations of the existing facilities are presented in Figure 3.1, and the number of loads moved are presented in Figure 3.2.

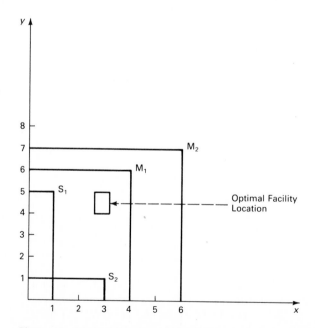

Figure 3.1 Current Location of Raw Material Sources (M_1, M_2) and Distribution Points (S_1, S_2)

FIGURE 3.2 LOCATION AND LOADS TRANSPORTED BETWEEN SOURCES/
DESTINATIONS AND THE NEW FACILITY

CURRENT FACILITIES	TOTAL ANNUAL NUMBER OF LOADS (L_i) MOVED TO/FROM NEW FACILITY	CUMULATIVE LOADS	LOCATION OF COORDINATES OF FACILITIES	
			x_i	y_i
S_1	60	60	1	5
S_2	70	130	3	1
M_1	40	170	4	6
M_2	50	220	6	7

The median model weighs the volume of loads and distance, assuming orthogonal (vertical and horizontal) paths. Diagonal paths are not allowed.

The total transportation cost is the distance moved times the load among the facilities and, thus:

$$C = \sum_{i=1}^{n} L_i D_i \qquad (3.1)$$

where n is the total number of paths, D_i is the travel distance between the new plant and existing facility i, and L_i is the number of loads moved between the new plant and existing facility i. As all loads are moved in orthogonal paths, the total travel distance is measured as:

$$D_i = |x - x_i| + |y - y_i| \qquad (3.2)$$

where x and y are the coordinates of the proposed new facility location point.

The following solution method determines the values for x and y of the new facility that result in minimum transportation cost.

1. *Find the value of the total number of loads moved and the median value.* The total number of loads moved to and from the new facility is 220. The median number of loads is the value that has half an equal number of loads above and below it. When the total number of loads is odd, the median load is the middle load. When the total number of loads is even, the median loads are the two middle loads. For 220 loads, the median loads are 111 and 110, since there are 109 above and below this pair of values.

2. *Find the x-coordinate of the median load.* Let us move from the origin of Figure 3.1 to the right along the x-axis. The number of loads moved to or from the existing facility can be observed in Figure 3.2. Loads 1 to 60 are shipped by source S_1 at $x_1 = 1$. Loads 61 to 130 are shipped by source S_2 at $x_1 = 3$. Since the median loads (110 and 111) fall in the interval 61–130, $x = 3$ is the best x-coordinate location for the new location.

3. *Find the y-coordinate of the median load.* Let us move from the origin of Figure 3.1 upwards along the y-axis. The number of loads moved to or from the existing facility can be observed from Figure 3.2. Loads 1 to 70 are shipped by source S_2 at $y_2 = 1$. Loads 71 to 130 are shipped by source S_1 at $y_1 = 5$. The best y-coordinate location for the new facility is $y = 5$.

The optimal facility location point is $x = 3$ and $y = 5$. Location at this point minimizes annual transportation costs for the production-distribution system. The total transportation cost is:

$$C = \sum_{i=1}^{n} L_i(|x - x_i| + |y - y_i|) \tag{3.3}$$

The total cost is calculated in Table 3.1. As distance is assumed to be proportional to transportation costs, the total distance loads may be regarded as dollar units. The total (minimum) cost of transportation is $690.

The media model is very simple to operate. However, it has some disadvantages. The major disadvantages are:

1. Only one new facility is added to existing facilities. This assumption can be relaxed for a multiple new facility case.[4]

2. Every point in the x,y plane has been assumed to be an eligible point for location of the new facility.

3. Topography, work force, and many other criteria that have been discussed earlier in the chapter are not considered by the model.

TABLE 3.1   TOTAL COST CALCULATION FOR OPTIMAL FACILITY LOCATION

(1) Facility	(2) x_i	(3) x of New Facility	(4) $|x - x_i|$	(5) y_i	(6) y of New Facility	(7) $|y - y_i|$	(8) Total Distance (4) + (7)	(9) L_i	(10) $D_i \times L_i$ (8) × (9)
S_1	1	3	2	5	5	0	2	60	120
S_2	3	3	0	1	5	4	4	70	280
M_1	4	3	1	6	5	1	2	40	80
M_2	6	3	3	7	5	2	5	50	250

Total Cost $= \sum_{i=1}^{4} L_i D_i = 730$

NOTE: If each distance unit costs $1/load, the total cost is $730

[4]R. A. Johnson, W. T. Newell, and R. C. Vergin, *Operations Management: A Systems Concept* (Boston: Houghton Mifflin Co., 1972). See also R. C. Vergin and J. D. Rogers, "An Algorithm and Computational Procedure for Locating Economic Facilities," *Management Science*, Vol. 13, No. 6, February, 1967, pp. 240–254.

THE DISTRIBUTION MODEL

The distribution model determines the new facility location by permitting a check of the annual transportation costs of each of the alternative locations, one at a time. It minimizes the annual transportation costs by changing the amount of units shipped from sources to destinations. It considers the facilities' capacities and various market demands.

The distribution model is a special case of linear programming, which will be discussed in the Technical Note to Chapter 6. The following is an example that shows the steps involved in choosing a facility location based on the distribution model. The mechanics involved in operating the model itself are covered in the Technical Note to this chapter.

EXAMPLE American Paper Box, Inc., was incorporated in 1925. Plants were established in 1947 in New York and Dallas. The company manufactures folding paper boxes for the shoe, clothing, and pharmaceutical industries. The Dallas and New York plants have the capacity to process 200,000 and 300,000 paper boxes, respectively, each year. The company has established three distribution centers, in Los Angeles, Louisville, and Denver. The cities represent an annual demand of 150,000, 250,000, and 200,000 paper boxes, respectively. The company realized that demand exceeded capacity of 100,000 paper boxes annually. Thus, it is considering the construction of a new plant with a higher capacity. Preliminary screening by American Paper Box has narrowed the possible locations to two alternatives: Cincinnati, Ohio, and San Antonio, Texas. American Paper Box decided to select the new plant location on the basis of minimizing transportation costs. Estimates of the transportation costs from each plant, existing or proposed, to each distribution center are presented in Table 3.2.

The distribution model can be used to determine the better location for the new plant, Cincinnati or San Antonio:

> *Step 1.* Find the lowest total distribution cost possible when the facility is located in Cincinnati.
> *Step 2.* Find the lowest total distribution cost possible when the facility is located in San Antonio.
> *Step 3.* The optimal site location is the better of the two alternatives calculated in Steps 1 and 2.

The lowest cost of transportation for each one of the stages is presented in Figure 3.3 in a tabular format. The procedure involved in finding the lowest cost possible for the alternative sites is described in the supplement to this chapter.

In Step 1, the new plant is assumed to be in Cincinnati. The analysis provides us with the least cost transportation arrangement, in which the Dallas plant ships 150,000 boxes to Los Angeles and 50,000 boxes to Denver. The New

TABLE 3.2 PLANTS TO DISTRIBUTION CENTERS TRANSPORTATION COSTS AND RESPECTIVE CAPACITIES

PLANT	DISTRIBUTION CENTER			NO. OF LOADS CAPACITY (000's)
	Los Angeles	Louisville	Denver	
Dallas	$200*	$100	$300	200
New York	500	200	400	300
Cincinnati	300	100	200	100
San Antonio	170	250	375	100
NO. OF LOADS DEMANDED (000's)	150	250	200	

*Cost of shipment of one thousand paper boxes from Dallas to Los Angeles.

York plant sends 250,000 boxes to Louisville and 50,000 boxes to Denver, and the Cincinnati plant sends 100,000 boxes to Denver. The total cost of this transportation schedule is $135,000. In Step 2, the new plant is assumed to be in San Antonio. The transportation schedule annual cost is now $142,000. Thus, American Paper Box, Inc., should build the new plant in Cincinnati, and follow the transportation schedule recommended in Step 1.

The distribution model provides an easy way to calculate the optimal facility location, based on transportation and production costs. However, other

FIGURE 3.3 MINIMUM TRANSPORTATION COST EVALUATIONS FOR TWO ALTERNATIVE SITE LOCATIONS

Step 1

PLANT	DISTRIBUTION CENTER			CAPACITY
	Los Angeles	Louisville	Denver	
Dallas	$200 150	$100 0	$300 50	200
New York	$500 0	$200 250	$400 50	300
Cincinnati	$300 0	$100 0	$200 100	100
DEMAND	150	250	200	

Total Cost = 200 × 150 + 300 × 50 + 200 × 250 + 400 × 50 + 200 × 100 = $135,000

Step 2

PLANT	DISTRIBUTION CENTER			CAPACITY
	Los Angeles	*Louisville*	*Denver*	
Dallas	$200	$100	$300	
	50	0	150	200
New York	$500	$200	$400	
	0	250	50	300
San Antonio	$170	$250	$375	
	100	0	0	100
DEMAND	150	250	200	

Total Cost = 200 × 50 + 300 × 150 + 200 × 250 + 400 × 50 + 170 × 100 = $142,000

variables that should be considered as part of the location analysis are disregarded. This is the major disadvantage of the distribution model.

THE SIMULATION MODEL

For more involved location problems, computer simulations have been devised. Many of the simulations have been custom tailored to fit one specific problem; others may be implemented for other contexts as well. While an exhaustive presentation of simulation will be made in the Technical Note to Chapter 8, a simulation model dealing with the operational problems of a service-type industry will be described at this point. Specifically, this example of a simulation model has to do with snow and ice removal. One of the most acute problems of city operation is the snow emergency problem.[5] Snow emergency routes (a major highway, for example) are identified by using traffic counts and other criteria and are divided into segments for plowing or salt-spreading operations. The objective is to minimize the time required to clear the snow routes by a given number of spreader trucks, while balancing the work load among the trucks. The basic technique used by various cities is to divide the snow routes into a set of preassigned segments. One truck is assigned to each segment. In dividing the routes, an attempt is made to balance the routes with respect to the time required and distance travelled. This balancing is complicated by the load

[5]T. M. Cook and B. J. Alprin, "Snow and Ice Removal in an Urban Environment," *Management Science*, Vol. 23, No. 3, November, 1976, pp. 227–234.

capacities of the trucks, which require several trips to the salt pile in order to be fully loaded.

Using computer simulation, that is, assuming different real life conditions using a computer, a rule to assign the trucks is devised. The rule that was checked through simulation was as follows. When a spreader truck has been checked out and loaded with salt and is available for a salting operation, it is assigned to a segment that:

1. Can be covered with one truckload of salt
2. Has not yet been salted, and
3. Is the closest unassigned street segment to the starting point (salt pile facility) for the truck.

A street segment is defined as the length of the street that can be salted on both sides at the desired application rate with one truckload of salt. The simulation flow chart in Figure 3.4 depicts the sequence of events as they occur in reality. The simulation model was used to check the salt-spreading operations in Tulsa, Oklahoma. The results showed that by using the rule, the productivity of spreader truck operations increased and, thus, no further increase in truck fleet size was contemplated.

Many simulation studies have been made in order to locate or assign a facility in an optimal manner.[6]

THE HEURISTIC MODEL

In many modern service type operations, the facility is mobile and is dispatched from job to job or customer to customer. Some examples are:

1. Material handling equipment (such as a fork-lift truck) that serves a job shop by moving processed batches from one work center to another
2. A telephone service and maintenance crew that responds to trouble calls
3. A quality control inspector who responds to inspection calls, and emergency units (ambulance, fire engine) that respond to urban community calls.

In these cases, the location problem is transformed into an area problem—namely, the question of what the size of the area that is to be serviced should be.

In determining the area that is to be served by a mobile service facility, two kinds of errors may be made:

---

[6] R. E. Markland, "Analyzing Geographically Discrete Warehousing Networks by Computer Simulation," *Decision Sciences*, Vol. 4, No. 2, April, 1973, pp. 216–236.

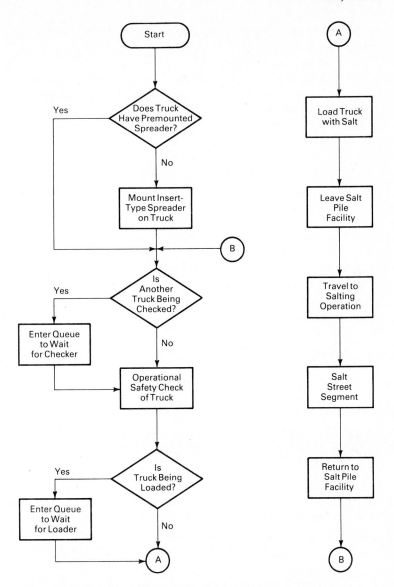

Figure 3.4 Simulated Operations of a Salt-Spreader Truck

1. The service area chosen is too small, causing underutilization of the service facility and, thus, higher operating costs
2. The service area chosen is too large, causing demand for the services to exceed the service capacity and, thus, increasing customer dissatisfaction and causing overutilization of the service facility.

The management of the service facility is interested in choosing service areas that will generate sufficient but not excessive demand, keeping in mind two important parameters:

1. The service level, which is the percentage of calls responded to over a unit of time (e.g., a day)
2. The time after placing the call that the customer has to wait until he/she gets service.

A heuristic method—that is, a formalized rule of thumb—has been devised[7] to determine the optimal service area. Basically, one increases the service area till the service level falls below a certain limit. The assumptions are:

1. The single mobile service unit is centered
2. The area served is a square
3. Customers are uniformly distributed throughout the region
4. Travel to a customer is made through orthogonal movements or on a straight-line path
5. The service unit travels at a constant speed.

Let us define some variables:

T_t = Mean travel time to a customer

T_r = Mean customer service time

t = Mean time en route—that is, total time associated with a customer

N = Number of customers serviced during one day

W = Length of a working day (hours)

D = Total distance travelled

s = Speed of a service unit

$P(n)$ = The probability of n customers calling for service over one day

Ps = Service level

R = Length of side of the service area

A = Service area = R^2

The total time required to service one customer is

$$t = T_t + T_r \qquad (3.4)$$

The capacity of the service facility is:

$$N = \frac{W}{t} \qquad (3.5)$$

[7] E. Menipaz and E. Enns, "On Mobile Service Units: Some Mathematical Considerations," *Journal of Optimization and Decision Sciences*, Vol. 2, No. 3, Sept., 1981, pp. 221–235.

As to the travel of the service unit, one may assume either an orthogonal path or a diagonal path.

Orthogonal Path

Let us assume a square of side R and travel on an orthogonal path parallel to the square sides (see Figure 3.5). The distance travelled is $D = D_x + D_y$, where D_x and D_y are, respectively, the distances travelled in the x and y directions. D_x and D_y each have a probability density function

$$f(x) = \frac{2}{R^2} (R - x) \quad 0 \le X \le R$$

The average travel distance in both vertical and horizontal directions is:

$$E(D_y) = E(D_x) = R/3$$

Hence, the expected travel distance between service points is:

$$E(D) = \frac{2R}{3} \tag{3.6}$$

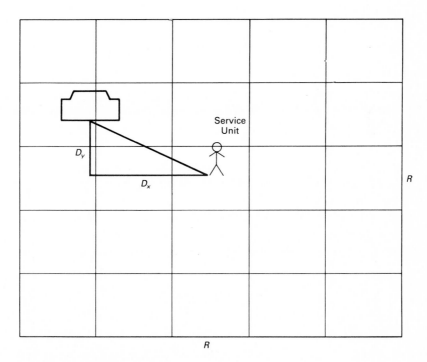

Figure 3.5   A Mobile Service Unit

Diagonal Path

Sometimes the travel to a customer can be on a straight line—e.g., if a helicopter is used (see Figure 3.6). The two points in the square have a distance D between them.

Let us develop the decision rule that may be applied for orthogonal and diagonal paths. For the orthogonal path of travel,

$$E(D) = \frac{2R}{3} \tag{3.7}$$

$$T_t = \frac{2R}{3s} \tag{3.8}$$

$$t = \frac{2R}{3s} + T_r \tag{3.9}$$

and

$$N = W/((2R/3s) + T_r) \tag{3.10}$$

The calculations for the straight-line diagonal path are similar. They lead to

$$N = W/(0.5214R/s + T_r) \tag{3.11}$$

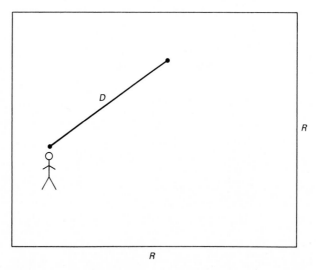

R

R

Figure 3.6 A Diagonal Pattern of Travel

The decision rule for determining the size of R is as follows. Expand the service area until the probability that demand will not exceed an assigned N (capacity) does not fall below a certain chosen service level, P_s; that is,

$$\sum_{n=0}^{[N]} P(n) \geq Ps. \tag{3.12}$$

where [N] is the largest integer less than or equal to N.

The method of solution for service area is as follows:

1. Choose a certain service level, Ps.
2. Start with some R.
3. Calculate [N] from (3.10) or (3.11), depending on the travel path used by the service unit.
4. Calculate $\sum_{n=0}^{[N]} P(n)$.

   If it is less than Ps, increase R and go to (3). Otherwise, go to (5).
5. Stop. The service area has been determined; it is equal to R^2.

The results for the orthogonal travel path are presented in Figure 3.7, when the service calls that arrive follow a Poisson Distribution. As can be seen from

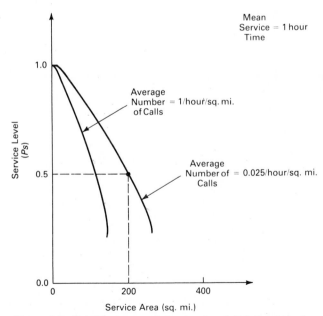

Figure 3.7 Service Area and Service Level Relationships for a Poisson Distribution

Figure 3.7, the smaller the average number of service calls per hour per area unit, the larger the area that can be served by the mobile service unit.

It has been shown, furthermore, that if several service units are available, the best policy is to divide the region assigned into an equal optimal area subregions, each served by a single service unit.

BEHAVIORAL ASPECTS OF FACILITY LOCATION

In almost all the quantitative models described above, the location problem has been treated as a cost problem or a minimum travel problem. In other words, it has been treated as a one-dimensional problem, which it obviously is not. Most location problems entail a variety of important implications.

A new location for a facility requires establishing relationships with a new environment and new employees. Employees are recruited from the new community.

To be successful at location change endeavors, the organization must recognize the specific circumstances that can exist in different locations. Nationally, differences in regional subcultures exist. Acceptable behavior patterns differ in urban settings, suburban areas, and rural areas. That means that the managerial style and organizational structure must be adapted to the social, economic, political, and religious differences at different locations. The manager must be aware of, and adapt to, the norms and customs of local subcultures. An authoritarian leadership and managerial style may be well suited to one location, whereas a democratic-participative approach may be appropriate in another.

The individual employee's personality is greatly affected by the environment within which the employee is living, and by his or her heredity. The potential for the employee's physical and intellectual growth is developed or hindered by environmental factors. The environmental factors that affect physical potential are: heat, cold, nutrition, economic conditions, and geography.

Customs, values, and standards are transmitted from generation to generation. The elements that condition the human personality affect the employee's behavior, attitudes, and ways of viewing the self, as well as others. For example, an individual may be born with the capacity to become a great scientist. However, if this person's culture stresses athletic achievement, the development of the potential for scholastic achievement may be reduced.

Within the United States, one finds employees from different subcultures bringing their own value systems into the job setting—values shaped by family, religion, school, and state. The individual's disposition toward accepting responsibility and exercising independent thought and initiative, as well as developing an appropriate style of interpersonal interaction with others and life-long goals and aspirations, are all tempered by cultural influences. For example, family structures and role relationships differ across subcultures. The family experience can mold one's views on the "proper" role of man and woman. These views are carried over into the work place in the form of employee attitudes toward men or women doing certain jobs. Employee acceptance of superior-subordinate relationships and varying degrees of authority may vary according to whether family relationships in the subculture are male dominant, female dominant, or egalitarian.

Age distribution of the population often varies with geographical area, and is a factor that can affect worker behavior. The Vega plant in Lordstown, Ohio, had a pervasive labor problem. The intensity of labor's protest depended on the general age of the plant work force—the lower the age, the more intense and frequent the outcries. During the dispute, UAW Vice President Ken Bannon commented: "The traditional concept that hard work is a virtue and a duty, which older workers have adhered to, is not applicable to younger workers and the concepts of the younger labor force must be taken into account." In the future, the younger generation is bound to be more militant, and the age-old tradition of unquestioned commitment to the plant might be disrupted.

Workers' life-goals, beliefs about the role of work, career aspirations, and perceptions of opportunity vary, resulting in different on-the-job behaviors. These cultural differences, in turn, have implications for staffing, training, and job mobility, as well as for managerial style.

Greater cultural differences exist at the international level. As more multinational companies establish organizations in third-world countries, it becomes obvious that an organization cannot change overnight the centuries of custom and tradition that influence these countries. Instead, companies must be prepared to adapt to existing cultural patterns.

As suggested above, the new location for a facility requires establishing relationships with a new environment and employees. Adding or deleting facilities also requires adjustment in the organization's management system. More facilities mean more complex systems to manage, and the decision-making procedure becomes more involved. The behavioral aspects of this dimension of the location problem should be recognized.

SUMMARY

The problem of facility location is a most important one and falls into the category of long-range planning. It entails a multiplicity of technological, economic, and behavioral dimensions. The problem of selecting a proper facility location calls for a detailed study of the cost aspects as well as the behavioral aspects. The data that are required for a location study should be collected from a variety of sources, including government, local municipalities, transportation authorities, potential customers, and suppliers and internal sources (engineers, planners, executives). The effectiveness, efficiency, productivity, and profitability of the operations are affected by the facility location decision. Several location cases have been presented in this chapter, along with several quantitative models. These latter models are, in general, one-dimensional and treat only cost, time, or distance as the sole criterion for locating a facility. The decision-maker, however, should recognize the behavioral aspects of location analysis and use informed judgement in making the location decision.

Facilities location planning entails consideration of the technology of the process, the behavior of potential employees, and the economic impact of the location. Such planning obviously represents a major effort. However, this effort is justified, as the operations manager might remember from the slogan: "The three most important decisions in the life of a business are: location, location, and location."

DISCUSSION QUESTIONS

3.1 "The location of a facility is a major decision affected by many factors, both internal and external to the organization's operations." Explain.

3.2 List and describe the facility location factors.

3.3 What are the steps of a facility location study?

3.4 What are the common errors in facility location analysis?

3.5 What are the various facility location quantitative models?

3.6 Describe the solution procedure for the median model.

3.7 How would you use the distribution model to find the best facility location? What are the conditions under which one can use the distribution model?

3.8 Describe the advantages of the heuristic model. Can you think of cases in which the heuristic model can be put to use?

3.9 What are the major behavioral aspects of facility location?

PROBLEMS AND SOLUTIONS

3.1 The location of a Caterpillar plant in a Southern California community will result in certain annual fixed costs, variable costs, and revenue. The figures are different for a Southern Florida community. If the expected sales volume is as specified below:
a) What is the best location for the Caterpillar plant?
b) Why are there differences in costs and revenues for the two locations?

Crawler/Track Type Tractor	Expected Volume	Southern California Price per Unit	Southern Florida Price per Unit
Bulldozer	95	$37,949	$41,000

	Southern California	Southern Florida
Fixed Costs	$2,000,000	$3,000,000
Variable Costs	15,000	12,000

Solution

$$\text{Break-Even (BE)} = \frac{\text{Fixed Costs}}{\text{Revenue per unit} - \text{Variable cost per unit}}$$

At the Southern California location:

$$\text{BE} = \frac{2,000,000}{37,949 - 15,000} = 87.1497 \sim 88 \text{ bulldozers}$$

At the Southern Florida location:

$$\text{BE} = \frac{3,000,000}{41,000 - 12,000} = 103.448 \sim 104 \text{ bulldozers}$$

At the expected volume of 95 units, the profit or loss for the two communities are:

	Southern California	*Southern Florida*
Revenue	3,605,155	3,895,000
Costs		
Variable	1,425,000	1,140,000
Fixed	2,000,000	3,000,000
Profit	180,155	(245,000)

The Southern California community is preferable, even though the revenues are lower, since the company will lose money by locating in Florida.

3.2 Bullshovel, an international earth-removal-equipment manufacturer is currently contemplating the location for its new assembly plant. At present, three processing and machining plants are located throughout the United States. The locations are marked on a graph like the one presented below.

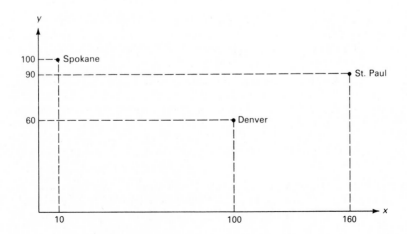

Location	x	y
Spokane, Washington	10	100
Denver, Colorado	100	60
St. Paul, Minnesota	160	90

The number of crawlers' assembly loads shipped annually to the assembly plant is 90 from Spokane, 120 from Denver, and 150 from St. Paul.

What is the best Bullshovel assembly plant location?

Solution

Location	Number of Crawlers	x-axis Cumulative
Spokane	90	90
Denver	120	210
St. Paul	150	360

The median $\left(\dfrac{360}{2}\right)$ is 180 and 181.

First, let us move along the x-axis. Loads 1–90 are shipped from Spokane, loads 91–210 are shipped from Denver. Since the median loads fall in the interval 91–210, $x = 100$ is the x-coordinate location of the assembly plant.

Second, let us move along the y-axis. Loads 1–120 are shipped from Denver. Loads 121–270 are shipped from St. Paul. The median load falls in St. Paul. Thus, $y = 90$ is the best y-coordinate location of the assembly plant. In conclusion, the plant should be built at $(x = 100, y = 90)$, a location in or near Montana.

3.3 How could you change problem 3.2 to make it soluble by means of distribution model analysis?

Solution

a) Assume several alternative sites for the assembly plant.

b) Find the minimum transportation schedule and cost involved in moving loads from each of the processing and machining plants to the assembly plant for each alternative site. This is done by using the distribution model analysis for each proposed site.

c) One has to choose the assembly plant site that carries the minimum transportation cost, as has been determined in (b).

3.4 Caterpillar Corporation has established plants in San Diego, California, and Saint Lucia, Florida. The assembled crawlers are sent to customers in Toronto, New York, and Los Angeles. The San Diego plant has the capacity to assemble 50 crawlers annually; the Saint Lucia plant has the capacity to assemble 70 crawlers annually. Costs for transportation from San Diego are $1,000 to Toronto, $1,500 to New York, and $300 to Los Angeles. Transportation costs from Saint Lucia are $600 to Toronto, $500 to New York, and $900 to Los Angeles. The demand for crawlers is 40 in Toronto, 50 in New York, and 50 in Los Angeles. Caterpillar is going to build another plant with an annual capacity of 20 crawlers in either Dallas or Denver. From Dallas, transportation costs are $600 to Toronto, $500 to New York, and $300 to Los Angeles. From Denver, transportation costs are $200 to

Toronto, $400 to New York, and $500 to Los Angeles.

a) Set up this problem as a distribution model.

b) What are the steps involved in solving the location problem?

a) *Solution*

PLANT	MARKET			CAPACITY
	Toronto	*New York*	*Los Angeles*	
San Diego	$1,000	$1,500	$300	50
St. Lucia	$ 600	$ 500	$900	70
Dallas	$ 600	$ 500	$300	20
DEMAND	40	50	50	

PLANT	MARKET			CAPACITY
	Toronto	*New York*	*Los Angeles*	
San Diego	$1,000	$1,500	$300	50
St. Lucia	$ 600	$ 500	$900	70
Denver	$ 200	$ 400	$500	20
DEMAND	40	50	50	

b)

Step 1. Find the lowest cost possible when the facility is located in Dallas.

Step 2. Find the lowest cost possible when the facility is located in Denver.

Step 3. The optimal location is the lesser of the alternatives calculated in Steps 1 and 2.

CHAPTER REVIEW PROBLEMS

3.1   Location A results in annual fixed costs of $30,000, variable costs of $6.30/unit, and revenues of $6.90/unit.

Location B results in annual fixed costs of $80,000, variable costs of $3.20/unit, and revenues of $6.90/unit. Sales volume is forecast at 30,000 units/year.

Which location should be chosen?

3.2 Los Angeles city officials are trying to determine the best location for a major solid-waste collection station. Currently, there are four minor solid-waste collection stations:

Minor Station	x	y	Daily Loads
1	4	12	30
2	6	4	120
3	11	9	30
4	1	13	40

Use the median model to find the best locations for the major solid-waste collection station.

3.3 Set up the Los Angeles city location problem of 3.2 as a linear programming problem, if possible. (For a complete description of linear programming, consult the Technical Note in Chapter 6.)

3.4 American Paper Box Company has plants in Atlanta and Cincinnati. The transportation costs per Model K paper box are as follows:

From	To Montana	To Indiana	To Texas
Atlanta	6¢	8¢	5¢
Cincinnati	10¢	3¢	10¢

The demand and capacities are listed below:

Plant	Capacity	Production Cost per Unit	Warehouse	Monthly Demand
Atlanta	1,600	20¢	Montana	1,500
Cincinnati	1,700	18¢	Indiana	1,000
			Texas	800

Set up the problem as a distribution model in order to find the best shipment and production schedule.

READING
Too Many Lunches

By April, 1984, in a move that will affect 1,600 of the publisher's 8,200 employees, Jovanovich will have relocated much of HBJ Publishing Company out of New York City to offices in Orlando, Fla., and San Diego. The company's major nonpublishing subsidiary, Sea World Enterprises Inc., owns marine parks in both cities. "We're moving because the continued profitability of publishing is in jeopardy," concedes Jovanovich. "I hope we will be able to make as much per share this year as last year."

SOURCE: Reprinted from the May 31, 1982 issue of *Business Week* by special permission, © 1982 by McGraw-Hill, Inc.

The chairman adds that "it's a risky move, but it is not capricious." And several experts agree that the shift of operations may work as a defensive tactic because of the savings in rent and other operational expenses. "We think the move will mean at least $20 million a year in operating income," Jovanovich says. "We had to see how much of our business was people-intensive." Although some critics believe that transplanting the parent company could be harmful because of the difficulty of finding experienced publishing personnel, Jovanovich disagrees. He derides the notion that publishing companies must be in New York. "Too much time is spent lunching, and not enough is spent reading. Many of our writers don't live in New York anyway," he notes. He is betting that the savings made by the move will result in the creation of a more successful publishing operation.

Questions

1. Are the services of HBJ Publishing House directly consumed?
2. Can you relate HBJ's decision to move to process inputs and outputs?
3. What are the adjustments that HBJ will have to make by moving from one location to two locations?
4. What are the major considerations in the move?

BIBLIOGRAPHY

ADAM, E. E., JR., and R. J. EBERT, *Production and Operations Management.* Englewood Cliffs, N.J.: Prentice-Hall, Inc., 1978.

BAUMOL, W. J., and P. WOLFE, "A Warehouse-Location Problem," *Operations Research,* Vol. 6, No. 2, March–April, 1958, pp. 252–263.

BUFFA, E. S., and J. S. DYER, *Management Science/Operations Research; Model Formulation and Solution Methods.* Santa Barbara, Calif.: Wiley/Hamilton, 1977.

CHUANG, Y. H., and W. G. SMITH, "A Dynamic Programming Model for Combined Production, Distribution and Storage," *The Journal of Industrial Engineering,* Vol. 17, No. 1, January, 1966, pp. 7–13.

COOPER, L., "Location-Allocation Problems," *Operations Research,* Vol. 11, No. 3, May–June, 1963, pp. 331–343.

COOPER, L., "Heuristic Methods for Location-Allocation Problems," *SIAM Review,* Vol. 6, No. 1, January, 1964, pp. 37–52.

COOPER, L., "Solutions of Generalized Location Equilibrium Models," *Journal of Regional Science,* Vol. 7, No. 1, Spring, 1967, pp. 1–18.

EFROYMSON, M. A., and R. L. RAY, "A Branch-Bound Algorithm for Plant Location," *Operations Research,* Vol. 14, No. 3, May–June, 1966, pp. 361–368.

EILON, S., and D. P. DEZIEL, "Siting a Distribution Centre, An Analogue Computer Application," *Management Science,* Vol. 12, No. 6, February, 1966, pp. B245–B254.

FELDMAN, E., F. A. LEHRER, and T. L. RAY, "Warehouse Location Under Continuous Economies of Scale," *Management Science,* Vol. 12, No. 9, May, 1966, pp. 670–684.

FORRESTER, H., *Industrial Dynamics.* Cambridge, Mass.: Massachusetts Institute of Technology Press, 1961.

GERSON, M. L., and R. B. MAFFEI, "Technical Characteristics of Distribution Simulators," *Management Science,* Vol. 10, No. 1, October, 1963, pp. 62–69.

HALEY, K. B., "The Siting of Depots," *International Journal of Production Research,* Vol. 2, No. 1, March, 1963, pp. 41–45.

HAMMOND, R. A., "Reducing Fixed and Variable Costs of Distribution," *Management Technology,* Vol. 3, No. 2, December, 1963, pp. 119–127.

KUEHN, A. A., and M. J. HAMBURGER, "A Heuristic Program for Locating Warehouses," *Management Science,* Vol. 9, No. 4, July, 1963, pp. 643–668.

McHOSE, A., "A Quadratic Formulation of the Activity Location Problem," *Journal of Industrial Engineering,* Vol. 12, No. 5, September–October, 1961, pp. 334–337.

MANNE, A. S., "Plant Location Under Economies-of-Scale—Decentralization and Computation," *Management Science,* Vol. 11, No. 2, November, 1964, pp. 213–235.

MARKLAND, R. E., and R. J. NEWETT, "Optimizing Food Product Distribution by Computer Simulation," *Proceedings of the 1970 Summer Computer Simulation Conference,* Vol. II, pp. 1103–1109.

MENIPAZ, E., "Industrial Projects Feasibility Methodology," *Europa Industrial Review,* Vol. 1, Feb., 1980, pp. 18–21, 42–45.

MENIPAZ, E., and E. ENNS, "On Mobile Service Units: Some Mathematical Considerations," *Journal of Optimization and Decision Sciences,* Volume 2, No. 3, Sept., 1981, pp. 221–235.

REED, R., JR., *Plant Location, Layout and Maintenance.* Homewood, Ill.: R. D. Irwin, 1967.

SHYCON, H. N., and R. B. MAFFEI, "Simulation—Tool for Better Distribution," *Harvard Business Review,* Vol. 38, No. 6, November–December, 1960, pp. 65–75.

SPIELBERG, K., "Plant Location with Generalized Search Origin," *Management Science,* Vol. 15, No. 3, November, 1969, pp. 165–178.

SPIELBERG, K., "An Algorithm for the Simple Plant Location Problem with Some Side Conditions," *Operations Research,* Vol. 17, No. 1, January–February, 1969, pp. 85–111.

SWEENEY, D. J., and R. L. TATHAM, "An Improved Long-run Model for Multiple Warehouse Location," *Management Science,* Vol. 22, No. 7, March, 1976, pp. 748–758.

VERGIN, R. C., and J. D. ROGERS, "An Algorithm and Computational Procedure for Locating Economic Facilities," *Management Science,* Vol. 13, No. 6, February, 1967, pp. B240–B254.

TECHNICAL NOTE: THE DISTRIBUTION MODEL OF LINEAR PROGRAMMING

INTRODUCTION

The distribution model, sometimes termed the transportation model, is a special case of linear programming. Linear programming is discussed later in the book.

The basic conditions that must prevail in order to analyze a distribution or location problem using the distribution model are as follows:

1. There should be a finite number of sources and destinations with specific demand and capacity (supply).
2. All shipped units should be identical.
3. The transportation costs should be known and constant.
4. All capacities and demand needs must be met.
5. No negative shipment can be made.

The solution method follows the following steps:

Step 1. Arrange the problem in tabular form.
Step 2. Balance the table.
Step 3. Find initial feasible solution.
Step 4. Test the solution for optimality.
Step 5. Improve the nonoptimal solution and repeat Step 4.

Let us present the method in detail.

ESSENTIALS OF THE DISTRIBUTION METHOD

EXAMPLE Plant A has a capacity of 20 units, Plant B has a capacity of 10 units. The demand for units is 8 at destination E, 12 at destination F, and 6 at destination G. The cost, in dollars, of shipping one unit between each plant and each destination is marked at the upper left corner of each cell. What is the shipping schedule that minimizes total shipping costs?

The solution procedure involves several steps.

TABLE TN3.1 AN UNBALANCED MATRIX (EXCESS CAPACITY)

Plant \ Destination	E	F	G	Capacity
A	1	2	3	20
B	4	5	6	10
Demand	8	12	6	30 / 26

Step 1. Arrange the Problem in Tabular Form

The transportation problem must first be arranged in tabular form. An example of such an arrangement is given in Table TN3.1. The costs involved in moving one unit from a plant to a destination point is noted at the upper left corner of each cell. The capacity for each plant, as well as the demand, is entered as shown.

Step 2. Balance the Table

The use of the solution technique requires that the table be *balanced;* that is, the total capacity must equal the total demand.[1] If the matrix is not already balanced, this must be done first. Two causes of imbalance are excess capacity and excess demand.

1. *Excess supply*   Table TN3.1 shows an example of an unbalanced matrix in which the total capacity, 30, exceeds the total demand, 26. In this case, there will be 4 unshipped units. This matrix is balanced by adding a column for excess capacity (sometimes labelled a "dummy" destination). The amount in this column equals the excess capacity, as shown in Table TN3.2. The cost of

TABLE TN3.2   A BALANCED MATRIX

Plant \ Destination	E	F	G	D (dummy)	Capacity
A	1	2	3	0	20
B	4	1	5	0	10
Demand	8	12	6	4 (excess supply)	30 / 30

[1] This requirement can be written as:

$$\sum_{i=1}^{m} b_i = \sum_{j=i}^{n} d_j$$

where:

m	is the number of plants
n	is the number of destinations
b_i	is plant i's capacity
d_j	is destination j's demand

"shipments" to the dummy is usually set at zero; this ensures that all excess capacity will be absorbed by the dummy.

2. *Excess demand*   When the total demand exceeds the total supply (see Table TN3.3), a dummy row for the excess demand (5, in this case) is added. Again, the per-unit shipping costs for the dummy row are set to zero. The results are shown in Table TN3.4. Once the matrix is balanced, an initial feasible solution can be generated.

TABLE TN3.3   AN UNBALANCED MATRIX (EXCESS DEMAND)

Plant \ Destination	E	F	G	Capacity
A	1	2	3	10
B	1	1	5	11
Demand	8	12	6	21 / 26

TABLE TN3.4   A BALANCED MATRIX

Plant \ Destination	E	F	G	Capacity
A	1	2	3	10
B	4	1	5	11
D (dummy)	0	0	0	5 (excess demand)
Demand	8	12	6	26 / 26

TABLE TN3.5   INITIAL SOLUTION BY THE NORTHWEST CORNER RULE

Plant \ Destination	E	F	G	Capacity	Remaining Capacity
A	1 8	2 2	3	10	0
B	4	1 10	5 1	11	0
D (dummy)	0	0	0 5	5	0
Demand	8	12	6	26	
Remaining Demand	0	0	0		

Step 3. Find Initial Feasible Solution

An initial feasible solution can be found by the northwest corner rule or by the Vogel's approximation method (VAM).

NORTHWEST CORNER RULE   This rule is applied in Table TN3.5.

1. Starting with the northwest corner (left uppermost corner in the table), allocate the *smaller amount* of either the row capacity or the column's demand. In Table TN3.5, it is 8 units for cell AE.
2. Subtract from the row capacity *and* from the column demand the amount allocated in (1).
3. If the column demand is zero, move to the next cell on the right; if the row demand is zero, move down to the cell in the next row. If both are zero, move first to the next cell on the right, then down one cell.
4. Once a cell is identified as per step (3), allocate to it an amount as per step (1).
5. Repeat the above (1–4) until all capacity and demand are zero.

The advantage of this rule is that it is a simple mechanical process. We use this rule on the data of Table TN3.4. Table TN3.5 illustrates the assignment by the northwest corner rule.

Initially, an amount of 8 units is allocated to cell AE, out of the 10 available in source A, meeting all the demand of destination E. The remaining capacity of 2 units at source A is then allocated to cell AF, since that is the closest in the A row to AE.

The capacity of row A has now been exhausted, but the demand of F has not yet been fully satisfied. Therefore, 10 units of the 11-unit capacity of source B is allocated to cell BF in order to meet the entire demand of destination F. Then, moving to the right in row B, the remaining capacity of B (1 unit) is allocated to cell BG. This exhausts the capacity in row B, but the destination G still needs 5 units. Moving down column G, the remainder (5 units) is allocated to cell DG. In this fashion, the entire capacity has been used and the entire demand has been satisfied. Cells that receive allocations are called *occupied* cells to distinguish them from the remaining empty, or unoccupied, ones.

The initial solution shown in Table TN3.5 calls for shipments of:

8 units from A to E at a cost of $8 \times 1 = \$\ 8$
2 units from A to E at a cost of $2 \times 2 =\ \ \ 4$
10 units from B to F at a cost of $10 \times 1 =\ \ 10$
1 unit from B to F at a cost of $1 \times 5\ \ =\ \ \ 5$
5 units from D to G at no cost $\ \ \ \ \ \ \ \ \ \ \ =\ \ \ 0$

  Total $27

Note that destination G supposedly obtains 5 units from D (dummy); that is, there is a shortage (an unsatisfied demand of 5 units at destination G).

Another method that may be used to find an initial feasible solution is the least-cost method.

THE VOGEL'S APPROXIMATION METHOD (VAM)   The VAM yields not only an initial feasible solution but also one that is close to optimal for most problems. The method is heuristic in nature. To illustrate the method, an example is shown in Table TN3.6.

1. The difference between the two smallest numbers in each row and column are calculated and registered at the margins.
2. The least cost cell at the column or row corresponding to the largest difference marked with a circle receives a shipment allocation (ties may be broken arbitrarily).
3. If a demand or a capacity is exhausted, the corresponding row or column is not considered any longer.
4. The procedure is repeated until all demand and capacity requirements are exhausted.

In Table TN3.6, row and column differences are calculated. The maximum difference was 3 at row B or column G. The tie is broken arbitrarily, and row B is marked for an allocation. In that row, cell BF is the least-cost cell, and it receives the allocation of the 11 units of capacity. Row B is exhausted and will not be considered further. A new set of differences is calculated. Column G has the maximum difference. A maximum allocation of 5 units is made to the least-cost

TABLE TN3.6 INITIAL SOLUTION BY THE VOGEL'S APPROXIMATION METHOD

Plant \ Destination	E	F	G	Capacity			
A	1 8	2 1	3 1	10	1	1	①
B	4	1 11	5	11	③		
D	0	0	0 5	5	0	0	
Demand	8	12	6	26			
	1	1	3				
	1	2	③				

cell, DG, and row D is not considered any more. The procedure is repeated until one arrives at the initial feasible solution:

    8 units from A to E
    1 unit from A to F
    1 unit from A to G
  11 units from B to F
    5 units from D to G

Step 4. Test for Optimality

The purpose of the optimality test is to determine whether the proposed solution, just generated, is optimal or not.

The procedure for testing optimality is analogous to that of the simplex method. A distinction is made between *basic* variables (those associated with the occupied cells), and *nonbasic* variables (those associated with the empty cells). The effect of changing each empty cell to an occupied cell is examined. If any of the changes are favorable, the solution is not optimal and a new solution must be designed.

Two general methods for calculating the effect of such a change are the stepping stone method and the Modified Distribution Procedure (MODI). In both bases the solution to be checked for optimality must be nondegenerate; that is, the number of occupied cells must be $m + n - 1$ (where m = number of sources, and n = number of destinations).

THE STEPPING-STONE METHOD The name "stepping stone" derives from the similarity of the procedure to crossing a shallow pond by stepping from stone to stone. In the stepping-stone method, one evaluates the savings accrued by changing the allocation in an empty cell from zero units to one unit. This is done by drawing a closed loop. If the closed loop identifies an allocation that provides cost savings, an allocation is made; otherwise, it is an optimal solution.

In order to draw a closed loop, one starts with the empty cell to be evaluated, and draws an arrow from it to an occupied cell in the same row (or column). Only occupied cells are used; otherwise, it would not be clear which unoccupied cell the evaluator corresponded to. Next, move vertically or horizontally (*never* diagonally), to another occupied cell. Follow the same procedure to another occupied cell until returning to the original empty cell. At each turn of the loop (the loop may cross over itself at times), plus and minus signs are alternately placed in the cells, starting with a + sign in the empty cell. One further important restriction is that there must be exactly one positive cell and exactly one negative cell in any row or column through which the loop happens to pass. This restriction is imposed to ensure that the requirements of supply and demand will not be violated when the units are shifted. Note that an even number of at least four cells must participate in a loop and that the occupied cells can be visited only once.

Let us apply the stepping-stone method on the initial feasible solution of Table TN3.6. As can be seen from Table TN3.7, when all empty cells are evaluated, none is seen to present savings over the initial feasible solution. Therefore, the solution is optimal.

TABLE TN3.7 THE STEPPING-STONE METHOD

Plant \ Destination	E	F	G	Capacity
A	1 − 8	2 + 1	3 1	10
B	4 +	1 − 11	5	11
D	0	0	0 5	5
Demand	8	12	6	26

For Cell BE: $4 - 1 + 2 - 1 > 0$
For Cell BG: $5 - 1 + 2 - 3 > 0$
For Cell DE: $0 - 1 + 3 - 0 > 0$
For Cell DF: $0 - 2 + 3 - 0 > 0$

THE MODIFIED DISTRIBUTION PROCEDURE (MODI) This method for improving the initial feasible solution uses the following notation

C_{ij} = the cost of shipping a unit from source i to destination j (e.g., C_{AH} is the cost of shipping a unit from source A to destination H)

U_i = a constant value assigned to row i and used for solution identification

V_j = a constant value assigned to column j and used for solution identification.

The method involves several steps that are demonstrated by using the initial solution of Table TN3.8(a).

We start by marking each occupied cell with a star ($\star$), disregarding the actual assignment. (See Table TN3.8(b).)

Next, all values of U_i and V_j are calculated. This calculation is based on the fact that, for each *occupied cell*, $U_i + V_j = C_{ij}$. The calculation starts by assigning a value of zero to the U_i or V_j of a row or column with the highest number of positive assignments. Since the third row has the highest number of positive assignments, $U_c = 0$.

We know that $C_{CF} = U_C + V_F$. Substituting $C_{CF} = 1$ (as per Table TN3.8(b)) and $V_C = 0$ gives $1 = 0 + V_F$. Solving for V_F, $V_F = 1$. This result is entered in Table TN3.8(b). Similarly, $C_{CG} = U_C + V_G$; substituting $C_{CG} = 2$ (as per Table TN3.8(b)) and $U_C = 0$ gives $2 = 0 + V_G$. Solving for V_G, $V_G = 2$. This result is entered in Table TN3.8(b). Let us continue:

$$C_{CH} = U_C + V_H, 4 = 0 + V_H, V_H = 4$$

$$C_{AH} = U_A + V_H, 4 = U_A + 4, U_A = 0$$

$$C_{AE} = U_A + V_E, 1 = 0 + V_E, V_E = 1$$

$$C_{BG} = U_B + V_G, 2 = U_B + 2, U_B = 0$$

Having found all U_i's and V_j's, we are ready to test the solution for optimality. The procedure involves the calculation of the cell evaluators $C_{ij} - (U_i + V_j)$ for each *unoccupied* cell.

$$\text{For cell AF, } C_{AF} - (U_A + V_F) = 5 - (0 + 1) = 4$$

$$\text{For cell AG, } C_{AG} - (U_A + V_G) = 3 - (0 + 2) = 1$$

$$\text{For cell BE, } C_{BE} - (U_B + V_E) = 4 - (0 + 1) = 3$$

$$\text{For cell BF, } C_{BF} - (U_B + V_F) = 2 - (0 + 1) = 1$$

$$\text{For cell BH, } C_{BH} - (U_B + V_H) = 5 - (0 + 4) = 1$$

$$\text{For cell CE, } C_{CE} - (U_C + V_E) = 3 - (0 + 1) = 2$$

All the calculations of the cell evaluators are shown, in the respective cells, in Table TN3.8(b). In the test for optimality, if, for each unoccupied cell, cell evaluators $C_{ij} - (U_i + V_j)$ are positive or zero, an optimal solution has been achieved. Otherwise, one must assign the maximum feasible shipment to the cell with the most negative cell evaluator.

TABLE TN3.8(a)   INITIAL SOLUTION BY THE VOGEL'S APPROXIMATION METHOD

Plant \ Destination	E	F	G	H	Capacity				
A	1 — 7	5	3	4 — 3	10	②	1	1	1
B	4	2	2 — 6	5	6	0	0	③	
C	3	1 — 5	2 — 4	4 — 3	12	1	1	2	②
Demand	7	5	10	6	28 / 28				
	2	1	0	0					
		①	0	0					
			0	0					
			1	0					

TABLE TN3.8(b)   MODI TEST FOR OPTIMALITY

	Plant \ Destination	$V_E = 1$ — E	$V_F = 1$ — F	$V_G = 2$ — G	$V_H = 4$ — H	Capacity
$U_A = 0$	A	1 — *	5 — $5 - (0 + 1) = 4$	3 — $3 - (0 + 2) = 1$	4 — *	10
$U_B = 0$	B	4 — $4 - (0 + 1) = 3$	2 — $2 - (0 + 1) = 1$	2 — *	5 — $5 - (0 + 4) = 1$	6
$U_E = 0$	C	3 — $3 - (0 + 1) = 2$	1 — *	2 — *	4 — *	12
	Demand	7	5	10	6	28 / 28

Note: *indicates occupied cell

As for the example here, all the $(C_{ij} - (U_i + V_j))$ values are positive, indicating that Table TN3.8(a) provides us with the optimal solution. Let us summarize the MODI for the test of optimality.

1. All rows and columns are assigned constants, U_i and V_j respectively. A value of zero is assigned to U_i and V_j in a row or column with the most number of shipments.
2. All U_i's and V_j's are calculated. This is done by using the fact that $C_{ij} = U_i + V_j$ for each occupied cell.
3. For each occupied cell, cell evaluators, $C_{ij} - (U_i + V_j)$ are calculated and the test of optimality is applied.

Step 5. Improving a Nonoptimal Solution

Having discovered that a solution is *not* optimal, the next step in the distribution algorithm is to find a better solution. The operations in this step are:

1. Identify the "incoming" cell (empty cell to be occupied). In a minimization case, the "incoming" cell is located by identifying the *most negative* cell evaluator. In the preceding example, all cell evaluators are positive. Thus, the solution in Table TN3.8(b) is optimal.
2. Design an improved solution. This is done by assigning the maximum feasible shipment to the most negative $C_{ij} - (U_i + V_j)$ cell, and adjusting the other cells on the closed loop accordingly.

THE AMERICAN PAPER BOX CASE

Let us solve the American Paper Box case by using the Northwest corner rule for the initial solution and the MODI for improving the solution. Here again is the essential information on the American Paper Box, Inc., case.

American Paper Box, Inc., was incorporated in 1925. Plants were established in 1947 in New York and Dallas. The company manufactures folding paper boxes for the shoe, clothing, and pharmaceutical industries. The New York and Dallas plants have the capacity to process 200,000 and 300,000 paper boxes, respectively, each year. The company has established three distribution centers, in Los Angeles, Louisville and Denver, representing an annual demand of 150,000, 250,000, and 200,000 paper boxes, respectively. The company realized that demand exceeded supply by 100,000 paper boxes annually. Thus it is considering construction of a new plant with higher capacity. Preliminary screening by American Paper Box has narrowed the possible locations to two alternatives: Cincinnati, Ohio, and San Antonio, Texas. American Paper Box decided to select the new plant location on the basis of minimizing transportation costs.

In Table TN3.9, we assume that the third plant is located in Cincinnati, and the initial feasible solution is found by using the Northwest method. Using the

TABLE TN3.9 INITIAL SOLUTION USING THE NORTHWEST CORNER RULE FOR THE CINCINNATI-LOCATED PLANT

Plant \ Destination	Los Angeles	Louisville	Denver	Capacity
New York	$200 150	$100 50	$300	200
Dallas	$500	$200 200	$400 100	300
Cincinnati	$300	$100	$200 100	100
Demand	150	250	200	600 / 600

TABLE TN3.10 USING MODI TO CHECK FOR OPTIMALITY FOR THE CINCINNATI-LOCATED PLANT

	Plant \ Destination	Los Angeles $V_1 = 200$	Louisville $V_2 = 100$	Denver $V_3 = 300$	Capacity
$U_1 = 0$	New York	$200 *	$100 *	$300 300 − (300 + 0) = 0	200
$U_2 = 100$	Dallas	$500 500 − (200 + 100) = 200	$200 *	$400 *	300
$U_3 = -100$	Cincinnati	$300 300 − (200 − 100) = 200	$100 100 − (100 − 100) = 100	$200 *	100
	Demand	150	250	200	600 / 600

MODI, one finds that for all cells $C_{ij} - (U_i + V_j)$ is nonnegative, which means that it is an optimal solution. This procedure is presented in Table TN3.10. Note that for the cell New York to Denver, the $C_{ij} - (U_i + V_j) = 0$, which means that there is another optimal solution to the problem. This alternative solution was presented in Figure 3.3 in Chapter 3. Both solutions involve the same total transportation costs, $135,000.

In Table TN3.11, one makes the assumption that the plant is built in San Antonio, and the initial feasible solution is found using the Northwest method (the total transportation costs are $152,500). In Table TN3.12, the $C_{ij} - (U_i + V_j)$ values are calculated. One of the cells presents a $C_{ij} - (U_i + V_j) = -105$. That means that it is not an optimal solution. A closed loop is formed, and the resulting solution is presented in Table TN3.13, with a total transportation cost of $142,000. The question is: Is this an optimal solution? The MODI is used again to check for optimality, as shown in Table TN3.14.

As all cell evaluators are positive or zero, Table TN3.14 is the optimal solution. Again, the $C_{ij} - (U_i + V_j) = 0$ for the New York to Denver cell, which means another optimal solution. This solution is presented in Figure 3.3 in Chapter 3.

It is obvious that locating the plant in Cincinnati, which involves $135,000 in transportation costs, is preferred.

Maximizing Profit Problems

At times, the problem is to maximize profit rather than minimize costs. In these circumstances the same procedure is followed. A positive $C_{ij} - (U_i + V_j)$

TABLE TN3.11   INITIAL SOLUTION USING THE NORTHWEST CORNER RULE FOR THE SAN ANTONIO–LOCATED PLANT

Plant \ Destination	Los Angeles	Louisville	Denver	Capacity
New York	$200 / 150	$100 / 50	$300	200
Dallas	$500	$200 / 200	$400 / 100	300
San Antonio	$170	$250	$375 / 100	100
Demand	150	250	200	600 / 600

indicates that the solution is not optimal. The most positive $C_{ij} - (U_i + V_j)$ cell gets the allocation.

Degeneracy

We have seen that drawing a closed loop in order to evaluate or improve cell allocation uses occupied cells as stepping stones. A condition of *degeneracy* exists if there are not enough occupied cells to allow the necessary closed loop to be constructed. This occurs when allocation (other than the last) exhausts both the row and the column quantities. Degeneracy may occur in the initial or subsequent solutions. Thus, after each iteration, it is necessary to test for degeneracy by comparing the number of occupied cells to $(m + n - 1)$. As has been explained, if fewer than $(m + n - 1)$ cells are occupied, degeneracy exists.

In Table TN3.15, degeneracy is shown to have developed. $3 + 3 - 1 = 5$ occupied cells are required for evaluation. However, only four cells are occupied. The evaluation is facilitated by placing a very small quantity, ϵ (epsilon), in cell CE. This very small quantity, makes the cell an occupied cell for evaluation purposes, but will be regarded as having a value of zero in the final solution.

The allocation of ϵ should be to the cell that will permit evaluation of all remaining empty cells. This is done in Table TN3.16.

Some experimentation is required in order to find the best cell for ϵ, as not every cell will permit the construction of closed loops. One should not place ϵ in a cell that calls for a reduction in the quantity assigned to this cell, because that would mean no change in the allocations (ϵ is essentially zero).

TABLE TN3.12   USING MODI TO CHECK FOR OPTIMALITY FOR THE SAN ANTONIO–LOCATED PLANT

	Destination / Plant	Los Angeles $V_1 = 200$	Louisville $V_2 = 100$	Denver $V_3 = 300$	Capacity
$U_1 = 0$	New York	$200	$100	$300 $300 - (300 + 0) = 0$	200
$U_2 = 100$	Dallas	$500 $500 - (100 + 200) = 200$	$200	$400	300
$U_3 = 75$	San Antonio	$170 $170 - (200 + 75) = -105$	$250 $250 - (100 + 75) = 75$	$375	100
	Demand	150	250	200	

TABLE TN3.13   AN IMPROVED SOLUTION FOR THE SAN ANTONIO–LOCATED PLANT

Plant \ Destination	Los Angeles	Louisville	Denver	Capacity
New York	$200 50	$100 150	$300	200
Dallas	$500	$200 100	$400 200	300
Cincinnati	$170 100	$250	$375	100
Demand	150	250	200	600 / 600

TABLE TN3.14   OPTIMAL SOLUTIONS FOR THE SAN ANTONIO–LOCATED PLANT

$V_1 = 200$ $V_2 = 100$ $V_3 = 300$

	Plant \ Destination	Los Angeles	Louisville	Denver	Capacity
$U_1 = 0$	New York	$200 *	$100 *	$300 $300 - (300 + 0) = 0$	200
$U_2 = 100$	Dallas	$500 $500 - (100 + 200) = 200$	$200 *	$400 *	300
$U_3 = -30$	San Antonio	$170 *	$250 $250 - (100 - 30) = 180$	$375 $375 - (300 - 30) = 105$	100
	Demand	150	250	200	600 / 600

The reader is encouraged to evaluate the cells in Table TN3.16 and to verify that the solution is optimal. Cell CE is not to be evaluated, as it is an occupied cell.

TECHNICAL NOTE PROBLEMS

3.1   What are basic conditions that must prevail in order to present a distribution problem as a distribution model?

TABLE TN3.15 DEGENERACY: THERE ARE NOT ENOUGH OCCUPIED CELLS TO ALLOW EVALUATION AND SOLUTION IMPROVEMENT

Plant \ Destination	E	F	G	Capacity
A	$6 30	$4	$10	30
B	$16	$12 60	$8 10	70
C	$14	$14	$12 20	20
Demand	30	60	30	120 / 120

TABLE TN3.16 A VERY SMALL ALLOCATION ϵ IS ADDED TO CELL CE TO ALLOW EVALUATION

Plant \ Destination	E	F	G	Capacity
A	$6 30	$4	$10	30
B	$16	$12 60	$8 10	70
C	$14 ϵ	$14	$12 20	20
Demand	30	60	30	120 / 120

3.2 How does one check for degeneracy of solutions?

3.3 What should be done if the total capacity is greater than the total demand?

3.4 What should be done if the total demand is greater than the total capacity?

3.5 How would you find an initial feasible solution?

3.6   Will the optimal solution have $m + n - 1$ occupied cells?

3.7   Why are dummy cells assigned a transportation cost of zero?

3.8   How would you identify an optimal solution?

3.9   How would you identify other optimal solutions?

3.10   Give examples in which the distribution method can be used.

3.11   Consider the following costs for transporting one mail service order from regional warehouses to regional distribution centres.

Source \ Destination	D	E	F	Units Available
A	$10	$30	$20	2750
B	$20	$40	$10	3250
C	$30	$20	$30	3000
Units Requested	3500	4000	1500	

a) Use the Northwest corner method to find an initial feasible solution.

b) What is the total cost involved in (a)?

c) Use the VAM method to find an initial feasible solution.

d) What is the total cost involved in (b)?

3.12   For problem TN3.11, find:

a) The optimal transportation schedule

b) The optimal total cost

c) Any alternative optimal schedules of transportation that may exist.

3.13   Let us assume that in problem TN3.11, the data indicate the profit/unit shipped. Find the transportation schedule that maximized profit.

3.14   Costs of shipping a unit from a source to a destination is given below:

Source \ Destination	D	E	F	Units Available
A	40	70	30	25
B	50	60	20	15
C	30	70	50	25
D	60	10	40	20
Units Requested	35	30	20	

a) Develop an initial feasible solution using the Northwest corner rule.

b) Develop an initial feasible solution using the VAM.

c) Find the optimal solution and indicate the total cost involved.

3.15 A large department store is planning to open a new store. Two locations are currently considered, Century Plaza and Culver Mall. Shipping costs for these locations are given below.

From Warehouse	To Century Plaza	To Culver Mall
A	$.04	$.08
B	$.11	$.05
C	$.04	$.04
Demand	300	300

Current costs, demands and supplies for existing stores and warehouses (sources) are:

Warehouses \ Stores	D	E	Supply
A	$.15	$.90	600
B	$.10	$.70	400
C	$.14	$.18	200
Demand	400	500	900 / 1200

a) Find the initial feasible solution using the VAM for each new location alternative.

b) Which is the best location alternative?

c) What is the cost of transportation for the alternative chosen in (b)?

BIBLIOGRAPHY

ANDERSON, D. R., D. J. SWEENEY, and T. A. WILLIAMS, *An Introduction to Management Science*, 2nd ed. St Paul: West Publishing, 1979.

BIERMAN, H., JR., C. P. BONINI, and W. H. HAUSMAN, *Quantitative Analysis for Business Decisions*, 5th ed. Homewood, Ill.: R. D. Irwin, 1977.

WAGNER, H. M., *Principles of Management Science*. Englewood Cliffs, N.J.: Prentice-Hall, Inc., 1970.

4

Project Planning and Management

INTRODUCTION

A project is a *one-time* set of activities with clearly defined beginning and ending points. The building of a new facility, the introduction of a new service, major oil exploration and drilling ventures, the building of the Alaska pipeline, major maintenance and overhaul activities, the introduction of a new machine into the production process, the construction of a warehouse, and the construction of an urban light-rail transit system are all examples of projects.

Simply put, project planning and management involves planning and administering work that is done only once.

Project situations present the operations manager with some unique problems with regard to planning, organizing, and controlling the conversion process of inputs into finished goods or services since a given project occurs only once.

Besides being one-time occurrences, projects have other specific characteristics that differentiate project planning and management from other types of planning and management.

First, the duration of a project may be weeks, months, or years. During this long period, project costs, technology, labor, and other resources may change and affect the project.

Second, a project is complex in nature, involving various interrelated activities. It may call for the interaction of several disciplines, various executive levels, and a myriad of outside agencies.

Third, delays in completion time may be very costly. It is customary for construction projects to carry penalties of thousands of dollars for delays—on top of which is the cost involved in the loss of good will.

Fourth, projects are of a sequential nature, with specific precedence requirements. Thus, certain activities have to be completed before others can start.

Fifth, large projects involve large investments. The decision to go ahead with a large project means that corrective actions cannot readily be taken, and the feedback of information is slow and often late. The nonreversibility of the project as opposed to a job-shop order makes such a project extremely complex to plan and manage.

Consequently, the planning, scheduling, and control of projects is unique and complicated. In this chapter, we shall examine the essentials of project planning and management and present some qualitative and quantitative guidelines with which the operations manager should be familiar when planning a project.

ROUTINE PLANNING VERSUS PROJECT PLANNING

Project-related decisions result in actions that are not to be repeated under similar circumstances. Thus, as each activity is accomplished, it is unlikely to be repeated. Developing the space shuttle involved a long-term nonrepetitive set of activities—namely, a project. However, in routine planning, such as a case of a job-shop order processing, the decisions are made repeatedly. The job shop has a set of outstanding scheduling rules, which repeat themselves time and again. Furthermore, corrective action can be effected easily. For example, if the operations manager of a job shop notes that customer returns, liability claims, and back orders are on the increase, steps are taken to correct the cause in subsequent orders. This cannot be done in a project environment, since each project occurs under different circumstances.

In Chapter 7 we shall discuss assembly line balancing, and in Chapter 8 we shall discuss job-shop scheduling. The question at this point is whether or not project scheduling is similar to these. Let us compare these types of scheduling with project scheduling.

Assembly line balancing (ALB) is concerned with repetitive operations and large numbers of identical products, whereas the project scheduling problem is usually a one-time, one-of-a-kind operation. On the other hand, the two problems may be formulated in such a manner as to emphasize their similarities. For example, the precedence list of a project representation could illustrate an assembly problem in which nodes represent work elements and arrows indicate precedence of the various operations (this is, in fact, the normal means of representing the ALB problem). The following analogies exist:

Assembly Line Balancing	Project Scheduling
work elements	activities
work element times	activity resource requirements (time or money)
work stations	days
cycle time	maximum available units of resource (time or money)

The job-shop scheduling problem has been described as: a number of jobs, each comprising one or more operations that are to be performed in specified sequence on specified machines, and that require certain amounts of time. The operations are to be scheduled such that due dates associated with each job will be met, or, failing this, such that some measure, such as the mean lateness time, will be minimized. We would add that, typically, the jobs are assumed to be one-of-a-kind orders, with simple (serial) precedence orderings among operations, and requirements of only 1 resource unit (machine) for each operation.

In practice, one of the major differences between job-shop scheduling and the project scheduling problem is the continuous nature of work input and flow in the job shop. New orders are continuously entering the system, and, within the system, queues of jobs may form between processing operations. Thus, from a managerial point of view, there is no end to the scheduling effort. This has led to sequencing rules that are statistically superior over the long run (i.e., in terms of average resource utilization, average delay, etc).

MODELS FOR PROJECT PLANNING

Various kinds of models can be used for project planning. A lawyer who sends a secretary to the bank to make a deposit and tells her exactly what to do, is using a verbal model of a "project." However, the most common type of models used for project planning are schematic models. The schematic models are simple to understand and to follow. Among these are the Gantt chart, the critical path method (CPM), and the program evaluation and review technique (PERT). In Table 4.1, the features and suggested uses of the three models are presented. Let us describe them in detail.

Gantt Chart

The Gantt chart was developed in the early 1900's by Henry L. Gantt. Obviously, the projects that Mr. Gantt faced were of less complexity than the ones many operations managers are faced with today. However, the Gantt chart still provides a good trial-and-error method for planning small-scale projects. It is also used extensively for job-shop scheduling. Many computerized project systems are still based on the principles laid out by Mr. Gantt.

TABLE 4.1   FEATURES AND SUGGESTED USES OF SCHEMATIC MODELS

	GANTT CHART	PERT	CPM
Features	Easiest to assemble and update Least sophisticated Activity- and time-oriented Does not clearly show relationships between activities Least costly scheduling technique	Event (milestone) oriented Use of multiple estimates that increases validity Most complex and difficult to implement Very good for simulating alternative plans, resource allocations Most costly system to maintain Best for forecasting and monitoring completion dates Best for scheduling projects where work content is not well-defined	Activity-oriented Best for identifying and following critical path Easy to update and correct logic Can be manually calculated with ease Best for scheduling highly sequential work with parallel, independent chains Best for showing work by area, type Outputs can be used as "working schedules" Excellent for simulating alternatives May be costly to maintain
Suggested Uses	Short-term projects with under 50 activities Projects with few interorganizational relationships Projects with activities that are easy to estimate (well-known state-of-the-art) Making "explosions" of project phases for a large, complex project	First-of-a-kind or state-of-the-art projects (e.g., research) Very complex programs with critical completion times and costs	Long-term programs with highly predictable activities (e.g., construction, development) Programs where scarce resources must be efficiently allocated

A Gantt chart is presented in Figure 4.1. The project described is the production of a household lamp. This is obviously a small-scale project that has been chosen for demonstration purposes only.

Before turning to Figure 4.2, let us check the symbols used for the schematic presentation of the Gantt chart.

First, brackets, [   ], indicate the beginning and the end of an activity. Solid areas, ▬▬▬, indicate the amount of work that has been completed in units of production. A crossed out area, [><], indicates the time period during which no execution is possible because of maintenance, material shortage, nonavailability of tools, operator absenteeism, power failure, and the like. The triangle, ∇, indicates the present time.

Referring back to Figure 4.1, one can see that currently we are shown to be at the end of the second week. Most of the raw materials have been purchased.

FIGURE 4.1   GANTT CHART FOR THE PRODUCTION OF A HOUSEHOLD LAMP

PROJECT ACTIVITY	WEEK 1	WEEK 2 ▽	WEEK 3	WEEK 4
Purchase Raw Material	[▬]			
Produce Plug No. M-3		[▬▬]	[▷◁]	
Produce Metal Base		[▬▬]		
Produce Stem			[ ]	
Produce Socket		[▬]		
Produce Wiring		[	]	
Assemble and Package				[ ]

However, several raw material units have not yet arrived as scheduled. Plug No. M-3 has been produced on time and in the right quantity. Also noted is the fact that Plug No. M-3 cannot be produced during the third week. The production of the socket is somewhat behind. The assembled and packaged order should be ready on the last day of the fourth week.

Network Analysis

The use of the Gantt chart is limited, as the chart is very simple and cannot describe the interrelationships among very many activities. It may thus be used only in scheduling very simple projects. A method was required to permit the description of the sequencing of activities and utilization of resources for complex projects. The methodology that was found useful has been entitled *network analysis* or network modeling.

Network analysis allows the operations manager to address the problem of project scheduling in a formal manner.

During the late 1950's, a number of different network approaches evolved. The method and approaches are based on an extensive theory; however, we shall confine our discussion to the essentials of the theory.

Program evaluation and review technique (PERT), which is used to control time of projects, and critical path method (CPM), which is used to control both time and cost of projects, are the two most common network analysis techniques.

Terminology of PERT and CPM

An *activity* is a distinct part of the project whose completion requires a certain amount of time. Examples of activities are: preparing a purchase order, excavating, backfilling, and starting up a car.

An event is a specific completion or starting-up instant. All activities will have a starting-up event and a completion event. Events do not have a time duration. In order to reach an event, all the activities preceding the event must

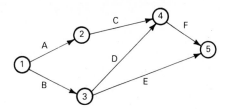

Figure 4.2   A Network Presentation of Activities

have been completed. Examples of events are: starting up excavations of a house, completing work on a college degree, and shut-down of a jet engine.

A *critical activity* is an activity that, if delayed, holds up the completion of the entire project.

A *path* is a series of sequential activities that provides an access from one event to another.

A *critical path* is a continuous series of critical activities that stretches between the start and the completion of the project. The total activity times for this path are longer than those of any other path through the network.

We may use Figure 4.2 to demonstrate the terms mentioned above. The circles indicate events. The arrows indicate activities. An arrow's length has no significance.

In Figure 4.2, event 1 indicates the start-up of the whole project, as well as the starting of activities A and B. Activities D and E follow the completion of activity B. Activity C follows the completion of activity A, and activity F follows the completion of both activities C and D. The project ends at event 5—that is, at the completion of activities F and E.

Comparing PERT and CPM

PERT and CPM are similar in that both are network techniques used to manage and control a project. However, there are two differences between the two techniques.

First, in PERT three time estimates are used to calculate a weighted average of the expected activity time. In CPM, only one time estimate is used. Thus, PERT is considered to be a probabilistic tool, whereas CPM is considered to be a deterministic tool.

Second, only CPM allows an explicit estimate of costs. Thus, while PERT allows control of time only, CPM allows control of both time and cost of a project.

Both PERT and CPM are used to determine which activities should be completed on time to assure completion of the whole project on schedule, and which activities can be permitted to take longer without affecting the completion time of the whole project. Both techniques are used to determine the earliest expected completion date of the project and the best way to handle delays during the execution of the project. Both techniques are used to determine management flexibility in executing noncritical activities (this flexibility is otherwise known as slack).

PERT AND CPM ANALYSIS PROCEDURE

PERT and CPM require the operations manager to go through the following procedure:

Construction of the Network. This stage involves the following steps:

Step 1. Analyze the project and break it down into specific activities and events.

Step 2. Determine the sequence of activities and events.

Step 3. Construct a diagram (network) of the project.

Step 4. Estimate the time (in CPM, cost also) of all activities.

Planning. This stage involves finding the critical path and slacks.

Step 5. Identify the critical events and activities.

Step 6. Identify the critical path(s) (containing critical events and activities).

Step 7. Compute the slacks on all events and activities.

Step 8. Establish a complete project plan.

Monitoring and Control. Once the project is on its way, the project plan may be used for monitoring and control.

Step 9. Monitor all activities and their execution times and compare them with the plan.

Step 10. Identify all deviations from the original plan.

Step 11. When delays in critical events are identified, replan and reconstruct the entire network.

Step 12. Transfer resources, if possible, from activities with slack, to lagging, critical activities in order to expedite completion and avoid potential delays.

Let us demonstrate the use of the models in the construction of a house. We start by breaking the construction project into specific activities and determining the sequence of activities. This is done in Figure 4.3.

To construct the network, one starts by identifying an activity as an arrow between two events (circles). For example, the first activity, "clear lot", is shown in Figure 4.4.

The arrow points in the direction of the time flow, but its length is *not* related to the duration of the activity; rather it is arbitrarily set at a suitable length for the purpose of drawing the diagram. The number circled in front of

Figure 4.3   ACTIVITIES AND THEIR SEQUENCE FOR HOUSE CONSTRUCTION

ACTIVITY*	DESCRIPTION	PRECEDING ACTIVITIES
A	Clear lot	None
B	Excavate	A
C	Pour footing	A
D	Do plumbing rough-in	C
E	Lay block walls of cellar and house	A
F	Do electrical rough-in	C
G	Complete roof	D, B
H	Tile walls	E
I	Clean and rough-grade lot	F, G
J	Install trims and inspection	I, H

*Note that the list of activities is by no means complete, as it is being used for demonstration purposes only.

the arrow, 1, in Figure 4.4, is the start-up event that *precedes* the activity. The number circled after the arrow, 2, in Figure 4.4 is the completion event. That is, event 1 indicates the start-up of lot clearing and event 2 indicates the completion of lot clearing and the start-up of excavating.

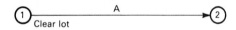

Figure 4.4   An activity

The construction of the network starts with activity A. The first activity will always be the one that *does not* require any preceding activity. It is placed at the left side of the diagram.

Figure 4.3 showed that activities B, C, and E must all be preceded by activity A, whose conclusion is event 2. Therefore, these three activities can start only after event 2 has occurred. This is shown as in Figure 4.5.

At the end of each activity, a number is assigned to designate the completion of the activity and the start-up of the next activity. The representation in Figure 4.5 shows that activities B, C, and E can be conducted simultaneously but that none can start until activity A has been completed.

The construction of the network continues in the same manner. The diagram is built from left to right until all activities and events are drawn as shown in Figure 4.6.

DUMMY ACTIVITIES   In the construction of a network, care must be taken to assure that the activities and events are in proper sequence. One technique that helps in proper sequencing involves the use of dummy activities.

Dummy activities are characterized by the use of zero time and zero resources; their only function is to designate a precedence relationship. Graphi-

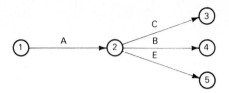

Figure 4.5   Precedence Requirements

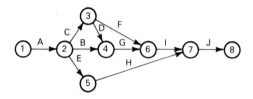

Figure 4.6   A Network for a House Construction Project

cally, such activities are shown as broken lines. For example, given a network with:

Activity	Required Preceding Activities
A	None
B	None
C	B
D	A, C
E	A
F	D, E

the diagram of this network can be presented as in Figure 4.7.

As one can see from the example, activity D cannot start until both activities A and C are completed. However, the completion events of activities A and C are different (For A, event 2 indicates completion and for C, event 4 indicates completion).

We could use the same event to indicate the completion of both activities. However, activity E should follow activity A only; thus, there should be separate events, 2 and 4. In order to assure start-up of D after completion of A and C, one should indicate the dummy activity, as marked.

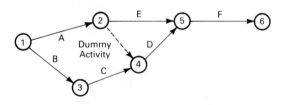

Figure 4.7   A Network with Dummy Activity

Calculation of Project Duration

Once the network is completely drawn, the activity times, designated as T_e's, are entered on the diagram, as shown in Figure 4.8. Now the first stage of the procedure is complete, and the planning stage begins, as will be shown shortly.

In order to understand the planning stage, the reader should be familiar with some network analysis terminology. A short glossary is presented in Table 4.2

In order to identify a critical path, we must present two important quantities: T_E and T_L.

The first quantity, T_E, is the earliest date. By definition, the earliest date an event can occur is the instant after all the preceding activities are completed. For example, let us assume the following: a certain event is preceded by three activities and the earliest date that activity A can be completed is 2 weeks; the earliest date that activity B can be completed is 4 weeks; and the earliest date that activity C can be completed is 5 weeks. In this case the earliest date that the event can occur is at the end of 5 weeks. It follows from the above definition that the earliest possible date for the completion of the entire project is the earliest date of the last event.

The second quantity, T_L, is the latest date. By definition, T_L is the latest date that an event can occur without causing a delay in the project's earliest completion date.

We shall now find the critical path by identifying the critical events (and thus the critical activities). First, we shall compute T_E for each of the events. Second, we shall compute T_L for each of the events. Third, we shall compute ($T_L - T_E$). The events for which ($T_L - T_E$) is equal to zero (that is, events for which there is no slack) are the critical events. The critical path is the path that will connect all critical events.

We will now find T_E for all events. To begin with, the information in Figure 4.8 is included in Figure 4.9.

Event 1 is the event at the beginning of the project. The T_E for this event is set equal to zero. This information is written above the event (in Figure 4.8). There is only one activity from event 1 to event 2; its duration is thirty days. The

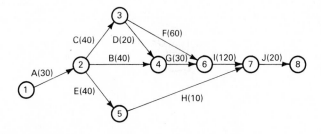

Figure 4.8 Time Estimates for the Project (in days)

TABLE 4.2   NETWORK ANALYSIS GLOSSARY

SYMBOL	TERM	DESCRIPTION
	Critical path	The path through the network consisting of several activities whose total activity times are longer than those of any other path through the network; the most risky path through the network; usually denoted by heavy lines through the activities on that path.
	Critical path time	Total time of all activities on the critical path.
t_o	Optimistic time	Time estimate for fast activity completion. There is very little chance of completing the activity in less than this time.
t_p	Pessimistic time	Time estimate for slow activity completion. There is very little chance of completing the activity in more than this time.
t_m	Most likely time	Time estimate that is the single best guess for activity completion. The most likely time is the mode of the distribution of activity times.
t_e	Expected time of an activity	Expected completion time of an activity. The time estimate with a 50-50 chance of being over- or under-achieved; the mean time for the activity; t_e is given in the case of CPM, or calculated (using t_o, t_p, and t_m) in the case of PERT.
T_E	Earliest expected time	Summation of t_e times up to that event; calculated at an event; earliest time expected to complete all previous activities.
T_L	Latest allowable time	Latest time an activity can be started and that still allows the project to be completed on time; calculated at an event that designates the start of an activity.
T_S	Slack time	Difference between T_L and T_E; $T_S = T_L - T_E$; the amount of freedom or latitude available in deciding when to start an activity without jeopardizing the timely completion of the overall project.

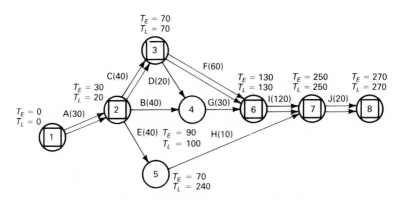

Figure 4.9   Computation of T_E and T_L

T_E for event 2 is thus 30. Similarly, T_E for event 3 is seventy days and for event 5 is seventy days.

Note that T_E is to be determined by the longest path leading to an event. However, it is not necessary to compute all paths leading to an event to figure the longest one.

One can use existing information by applying the following formula: T_E for current event = Duration of the last activity on the path + T_E of the preceding event.

When there are several activities leading to a single event, the maximum T_E computed by this formula is the current event's T_E.

For event 4, both activities D and B must be completed. The length of the path connecting events 1, 2, 3, and 4 is 70 + 20 = 90. The length of the path connecting events 1, 2, and 4 is 30 + 40 = 70. The two possible T_E's are compared, and, since 90 is the larger, T_E for event 4 is 90.

For event 6, one compares 70 + 60 = 130, and 90 + 30 = 120. The T_E for event 6 is thus 130.

The rest of the T_E values are obtained in the same manner (shown in Figure 4.9). Event 8 designates the end of the project, since no activities emerge from it. Therefore, the earliest date for this event, 270 days, is the earliest date on which the entire project can be completed.

To compute each T_L, one starts from the last event (8) and works all the way back to event 1. T_L for the last event (8) is set equal to the computed completion time for the project (270 days). Since the latest that event 8 can occur is 270 days, and since it takes 20 days to complete activity J, the latest allowable date event 7 can occur is 270 − 20 = 250 days. Since the latest that event 7 can occur is 250 and since activity I lasts 120 days, then the latest time for event 6 is 250 − 120 = 130. In a similar manner T_L for event 5 is found to be 240 (T_L for 7 is 250 minus 10 days for activity H, or 240). In a similar manner T_L for event 4 is computed as 100.

For event 3, two activities, D and F, must be considered. Since activity D lasts 20 days, and since it must be completed no later than the 100th day (the latest allowable time for event 4), then activity D must start not later than 100 − 20 = 80. Activity F takes 60 days; it must be completed, at the latest, by day 130 (which is T_L for event 6). Therefore, activity F must be started *not later* than 130 − 60 = 70. Now, to enable both activities to start on time so that there will be no delay in the entire project, event 3 must occur, *at the latest*, by day 70, which is the *smaller* of the two T_L's.

Computation is continued in the same manner, event by event, until event 1 is reached. Of special interest is event 2. Here three activities must be considered. For C, 70 − 40 = 30; for B, 100 − 40 = 60; and for E, 240 − 40 = 200. The smallest value, 30 days, is selected as T_L for event 2. For event 1, T_L is zero.

The *critical events* can now be identified. They are all those events for which $(T_L - T_E)$ equals zero. A box is drawn to indicate these critical events (see Figure 4.9).

Once the *critical events* are determined, the critical path can be constructed. The critical path goes through all critical events. Starting with event 1, which is always critical, one goes to the next critical event: 2 in our example. Since there is only one way to go from event 1 to event 2, activity A, which is between events 1 and 2, is a critical activity. It is so designated by a double-shafted arrow in Figure 4.9.

In a similar manner, activities C, F, I, and J are found to be critical. Activities B, D, E, G, and H are not critical because they are not between critical events. The critical path goes through all the critical activities and events. In our example, it is the path through 1, 2, 3, 6, 7, 8.

The importance of critical activities and events is that, by definition, a delay in any activity (or event) on the critical path will delay the entire project. Thus, these activities and events must be carefully monitored and controlled. Before getting into the topics of monitoring and control, let us examine those events, activities, and paths that are *not critical*.

Slack of Events and Activities

A critical event was defined as an event for which $(T_E - T_L)$ equals zero. In all other cases, the events are not critical and T_L is larger than T_E. The difference between T_L and T_E is called *slack*, T_S.

$$T_S = T_L - T_E$$

What is the meaning of slack? Since T_E is the earliest that an event can occur and T_L is the latest that the event can occur without delaying the entire project, then the difference, the slack, tells how long the activity can "linger" *without* delaying the entire project. In a critical event, the slack is zero. Therefore, any delay in the event will cause a delay in the entire project.

Critical activities, by definition, also have zero slack. These are the activities that should be closely watched. However, management is also interested in noncritical activities, or those activities with slack. The reason is that management, in order to catch up, can transfer resources from the noncritical activities to others that need to be expedited. It is important, therefore, to know the exact amount of slack on each noncritical activity.

The amount of slack in an activity is determined by how much the activity can linger before it becomes critical. There are two kinds of slack: regular slack and floating slack.

A *regular slack* is a slack related to one activity only. As shown in Figure 4.10, activity A has a duration of 7 days, while the path B—C has a duration of 15 days. Therefore, activity A can linger $15 - 7 = 8$ days; that is, there is an eight-day slack on the activity.

Whenever there are two or more noncritical activities or noncritical events connected in a series, the slack is said to be *floating*. An example of floating slack is shown in Figure 4.11. Activities E and H are connected in series. The critical

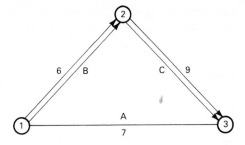

Figure 4.10   Regular Slack

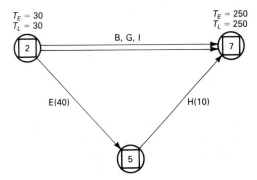

Figure 4.11   Floating Slack

portion of the path (which is not shown in detail) between events 2 and 7 requires 220 days.

Activity E requires forty days and activity H requires ten days: a total of fifty days. Therefore, there is a slack of 220 − 50 = 170 days, which can be used on both E and H (for example, a slack of 160 on E and 10 on H, 150 on E and 20 on H, and so on).

CONTROLLING PROJECTS BY PERT AND CPM

Let us assume that the construction started on schedule. However, the completion of the first activity is delayed. Although the duration time of this critical activity has been estimated to be thirty days, it is determined that forty days will be required to handle all the administrative details. Thus, when the time comes for event 2 its T_E will be 40, rather than 30. The slack in event 2 will be:

$$T_S = T_L - T_E = 30 - 40 = -10$$

The slack will have a negative value, and is labeled as *negative slack*. A negative slack value means that the project is behind schedule. If T_Es are now computed for all the remaining critical events, including the ending event, there will be a negative slack of 10. This implies that the entire construction project will be delayed by ten days. The network should be studied carefully to determine how the various activities could be expedited to assure completion on time.

Let us study event 5, which is not critical. The previous slack for this event was computed as $240 - 70 = 170$; now it will be $240 - 80 = 160$, still a positive slack.

Activities B, E, and H likewise possess positive slack. This means that these activities can be delayed without delaying the entire project. Slowing down noncritical activities may release resources (such as labor, tools, and equipment) that may then be transferred to one (or more) of the critical activities. If such a transfer could reduce the time required to complete any critical activity, such as G or F, by 10 days, the delay could be eliminated and the project could be completed on schedule.

A noncritical activity might also cause a delay. For example, if activity G requires 70 rather than 30 days, a negative slack of 30 days is realized for event G. The T_E for this event is now 160 days. The critical path now includes activities A, C, B, D, F, G, I, and J. That is, activities D and G become critical.

Any change in the time of an activity from what was planned should be reported to the project manager, who is to recalculate the critical path. In recalculating it, some noncritical activities might become critical, and vice versa. The project manager may consider: expediting some activities by transferring resources from one activity to another, changing technical specifications, changing quality requirements, changing sequencing of several activities, or allocating additional resources to the project.

The next several sections will deal with some specific characteristics of PERT and CPM.

ACTIVITY TIME ESTIMATES FOR PERT

As has been explained earlier, one major difference between PERT and CPM analysis is that PERT allows for three time estimates (see Table 4.2):

Optimistic time (t_o), the estimated shortest possible time for completion of the activity. The chances of completing the activity in less time are slim.

Pessimistic time (t_p), the estimated longest possible time for completion of the activity. The chances of completing the activity in more than that time are slim.

Most likely time (t_m), the single best estimate for activity completion. This is the time that would be most often estimated by the experts.

The three time estimates are entered in Table 4.3. At times, as can be seen in this table, the three time estimates are identical, indicating that the activity time is known with certainty.

TABLE 4.3   PERT INFORMATION FOR HOUSE CONSTRUCTION

ACTIVITY	t_o	t_m	t_p	t_e
A	10	30	50	30
B	10	30	110	40
C	30	40	50	40
D	10	20	30	20
E	30	30	90	40
F	20	50	140	60
G	20	30	40	30
H	10	10	10	10
I	120	120	120	120
J	10	20	30	20

EXPECTED TIME CALCULATION

Based on the three time estimations, t_o, t_p, and t_m, a weighted average is computed. This weighted average is called the *expected time of an activity, t_e*:

$$t_e = \frac{t_o + 4t_m + t_p}{6} \tag{4.1}$$

The formula assigns four times more weight to the most likely estimate than to the pessimistic or optimistic estimates.

For example, for activity B, in Table 4.3, the expected time is calculated as follows:

$$t_e = \frac{10 + 4(30) + 110}{6} = 40 \text{ days}$$

This t_e is then added to Table 4.3 in the t_e column, which is used as the data for Figure 4.9.

Obviously, the determination of the critical path follows the same procedure whether one uses one time estimate, as in the case of CPM, or three time estimates, as in the case of PERT.

PROJECT RISKS USING PERT

PERT is a unique planning and control tool for project management, as it can be used to determine the risks in terms of project delay. More specifically, management can use the three time estimates to determine the chance of completing the project on, before, or after a specific scheduled date.

It has been determined that the three estimates of activity duration in PERT—t_o, t_m, and t_p—follow a frequency distribution called the beta distribution, shown in Figure 4.12 for activity B, as an example ($t_o = 10$, $t_m = 30$, $t_p = 110$, and their average $t_e = 40$).

While the specifics of the beta distribution are beyond the scope of this book, there is an interesting relationship that is useful for assessing project risks.

Even though estimates of each activity duration follow the beta distribution, the combined duration of several activities (such as those on the critical path) approaches the *normal* distribution, and its mean is the earliest expected time (T_E) of the project. It has been determined for the normal distribution that there is a 50-percent chance that the entire project will be completed by its earliest expected time (270 days, in our construction project). However, "50-percent chance" may not constitute sufficient information for management. Management may want to know the duration that has a larger chance of completion (say, 60 percent). Similarly, management may want to know the chances of completing the project in a given amount of time, say 200 or 250 days. To answer such questions, an analysis involving the uncertainty associated with the duration times is presented.

As each activity's duration involves three time estimates, it is possible to calculate a *standard deviation* for the activity. The standard deviation of the beta distribution of activity durations is as follows:

$$\text{Standard deviation of an activity} = \sigma = \frac{t_p - t_o}{6} \qquad (4.2)$$

The variance of the activity's distribution is given by:

$$\text{Variance of activity} = \sigma^2 = \left(\frac{t_p - t_o}{6} \right)^2 \qquad (4.3)$$

For example, for activity B the standard deviation is:

$$\sigma_B = \frac{110 - 10}{6} = 16.7 \text{ days}$$

and the variance, V, is:

$$V = \sigma_B^2 = 16.7^2 = 278 \text{ days}$$

For activities H and I, the variance is zero, since $t_p = t_o$ for these activities. This means that no uncertainty is involved in their estimates. The larger the variance, the greater the degree of uncertainty involved in estimating the duration of the activity.

Assuming that the durations of the activities are independent of each other, the variance, V, of a *group* of activities can be computed by adding the variances of the activities in that group. The value of V is then expressed as

$$V = \sigma_1^2 + \sigma_2^2 + \ldots + \sigma_n^2 \qquad (4.4)$$

where n is the number of activities in the group.

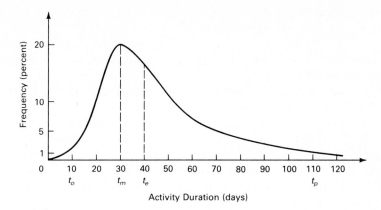

Figure 4.12   Activity Time Distribution for Activity B

Of special interest are the activities that comprise the critical path. For example, in the construction project of Figure 4.8, the variance for the critical path is given as:

$$V = \sigma_A^2 + \sigma_G^2 + \sigma_F^2 + \sigma_I^2 + \sigma_J^2$$
$$= 44 + 11 + 400 + 0 + 11 = 466$$

The value of the variance, V, can be computed for any event by considering the group of critical activities that lead to that event. The chance of completing the project in a certain desired time and the duration related to any desired probability of completion can now be calculated. Let:

S = scheduled project completion time, 270 days in the following example.

D = the desired completion time, 300 days in the following example.

Z = the number of standard deviations of a normal distribution (see Appendix Table A) corresponding to the probability of completing the project on time:

$$Z = \frac{D - S}{\sqrt{V}} \tag{4.5}$$

EXAMPLE   Suppose management wishes to know the probability of completing the construction project on or before the 300th day.

Thus: $D = 300$, $S = 270$, $V = 466$.

Therefore:

$$Z = \frac{300 - 270}{\sqrt{466}} = \frac{30}{21.6} = 1.39$$

The probability equivalent to $Z = 1.39$ can be found in Table A in the Appendix. Its value is 0.91774. Therefore, there is a 91.77-percent chance of completing the project in 300 days. One should remember that there is only a 50-percent chance of completing the construction project in 270 days.

EXAMPLE Suppose now that management wants to estimate a completion time that they can be at least 80 percent sure of attaining.

The value of Z associated with a probability of 80 percent is searched for. From Table A in the Appendix, $Z = 0.845$. We obtain:

$$0.845 = \frac{D - 270}{21.6}, \text{ or } D = 0.845 \times 21.6 + 270 = 288.3 \text{ days}$$

That is, there is an 80-percent chance of completing the project in 288.3 days. The computation of D enables management to make delivery commitments while being aware of the risks involved.

COST AND TIME TRADEOFFS USING CPM

In many project scheduling cases, management wants to reduce critical path times, even if it might involve added costs.

Cost-Time Tradeoff for an Activity

Figure 4.13 presents the relationship between cost and time for an activity. T_n is the normal activity duration; C_n is the normal cost requirements; T_c is the crash activity duration and C_c is the crash activity cost. Obviously, in order to shorten the project duration, more costs are required.

The crash activity and the normal activity are connected by a linear line. Any intermediate activity involves T_x time units and C_x cost expressed through a slope of a linear line. The relationship between time and cost is:

$$\text{Slope} = \frac{C_c - C_n}{T_n - T_c} \tag{4.6}$$

The slope gives the cost increase associated with a reduction of one unit in time.[1]

For example, activity A takes 50 days and costs $100,000 under normal conditions. Under crash conditions, it takes 40 days and costs $120,000. The slope is:

$$\text{Slope} = \frac{120,000 - 100,000}{50 - 40} = \$2,000/\text{day}$$

It costs $2,000 to expedite the activity by one day, $4,000 to expedite the activity by two days, etc.

---

[1] In some cases, the relationship between cost and time is not linear. However, the linear relationship can be used as an approximation to the nonlinear curve.

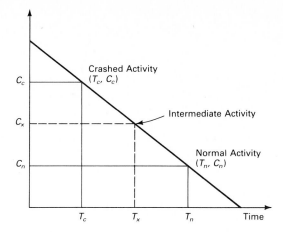

Figure 4.13   Cost-Time Tradeoffs

While expediting activities requires additional resources that add to the project's cost, considerable savings may be realized in finishing the project ahead of scheduled completion time. The decision on how much to expedite is an important management decision.

The cost-time tradeoff, traditionally a part of the CPM analysis, is a formal approach to reducing critical path times.

Cost-Time Tradeoffs for a Project

Management should examine the total cost involved in executing the project at several scheduled times, from the least-expensive–longest-time alternative up to the most-expensive–shortest-time alternative. The added cost of expediting the project is compared with possible savings from the expedited completion. The savings might be made to accrue by releasing resources for early completion.

The cost-time tradeoff for a project involves three steps.

Step 1. The CPM network is solved for critical path using normal times, and the total normal cost is computed.

Step 2. The CPM network is solved for critical path using crash times, and the total crash cost is computed.

Step 3. The cost-time tradeoffs are used to find the least-cost plan for any desired number of days between crash and normal schedules.

A construction activity list is shown in Table 4.4. The problem is to find the least-cost plan for various project durations. The normal and crash time in days and the cost are shown in Table 4.4, together with the network. The "slope" column shows the incremental increase in the cost when the duration of the

TABLE 4.4 ACTIVITY LIST FOR TIME-COST TRADEOFF

ACTIVITY	T_n (DAYS)	C_n	T_c	C_c (DAYS)	SLOPE ($/DAY)
A	50	$1,000	40	$1,400	40
B	90	2,000	70	3,000	50
C	70	2,500	40	3,400	30
D	90	2,800	70	3,400	30
E	50	2,500	20	4,600	70
F	110	4,000	70	7,200	80
G	60	3,000	40	4,200	60
H	80	800	60	1,400	30
		$18,600		$28,600	

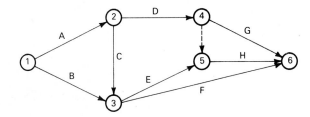

activity is decreased by one day. The slope is computed using equation (4.6). For example, for activity D:

$$\text{Slope} = \frac{3,400 - 2,800}{90 - 70} = \frac{600}{20} = \$30/\text{day}$$

It is obvious from Table 4.4 that if all activities are performed in normal duration, the total cost is $18,600. However, if all activities are performed in crash duration, the total cost is $28,600. Let us follow the three steps of the analysis as mentioned above.

STEP 1 The critical path using normal times is found (see Figure 4.14). The critical path is 1-2-3-5-6, with total duration of 250 days and total cost of $18,600.

STEP 2 The critical path using crash times is found (see Figure 4.15). The critical path is 1-2-4-5-6, with total duration of 170 days and total cost of $28,600.

STEP 3 Now one has to find the least-cost plan for any desired number of days between crash and normal schedules. Let us assume that management would like to find the least-cost plan for 220 days.

This is accomplished by compressing the project duration from 250 days (with all activities performed in normal times) to 220 days. We shall list all critical activities for the normal time schedule (see Figure 4.14) and their slopes:

Critical Activity	Slope
A	40
C	30
E	70
H	30

The activity with the smallest slope should be compressed first, since decreasing the project by one day will result in the smallest increase in total cost. Thus, activities C and/or H are to be compressed (ties may be broken arbitrarily).

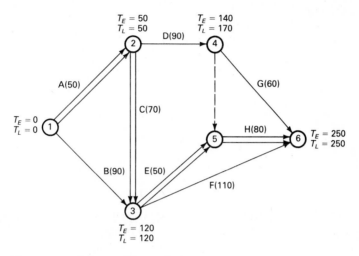

Figure 4.14 Solution When All Activities Are Performed in Normal Times

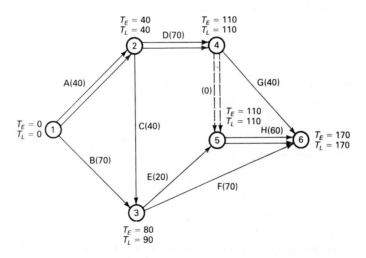

Figure 4.15 Solution When All Activities Are Performed in Crash Times

Let us compress activity C. The most that activity C can be compressed is equal to its crash time (forty days, in our example), cutting the duration of the project from 250 days to the desired 220 days. However, this reduction creates two additional critical paths, as shown in Figure 4.16.

The least-cost plan for 220 days involves crashing activity C by 30 days at a total project cost of

$$\$18,600 + (30 \text{ days}) (\$30/\text{day}) = \$18,600 + \$900 = \$19,500.$$

The cost-time tradeoffs can be developed the same way as above, and are summarized in the table below.

Project Duration	Least Total Project Cost
250	$18,600
240	$18,900
230	$19,200
220	$19,500
210	$19,800
200	$20,100
190	$21,000
180	$22,800
170	$24,600

The reader is encouraged to find the least total project cost by compressing the activities using the procedure above. Please note that the least total project cost is $24,600, whereas when one crashes *all* the activities the total cost is

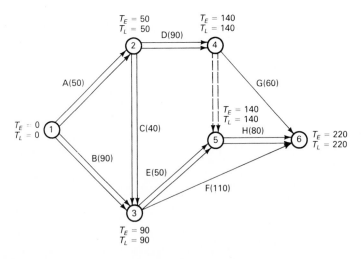

Figure 4.16   A Least-Cost Schedule for 220 Days

$28,600 (as per Table 4.4). This means that it is possible to perform the project in 170 days but at a cost lower than $28,600.

PERT/COST

CPM/COST analysis, which has been presented in the preceding section, is used mainly for minimum cost scheduling. PERT/COST analysis is used mainly for budgetary control.

The objectives of PERT/COST are:

1. To develop a realistic initial cost estimate
2. To meet or improve the initial cost estimate through detailed cost monitoring.

The components of a PERT/COST system are:

1. *A modified PERT/TIME network.*   The modification is done by adding cost estimates for each activity based upon the expected completion time (ET) of each project activity.
2. *Work breakdown structure.*   The work breakdown structure specifies which organizational units are responsible for each project activity.
3. *Cost work packages.*   A work package refers to a group of activities that are combined for purposes of budgetary control. A work package is determined either on the basis of time or on the basis of expenditures. For example, three consecutive activities costing $2,000, $4,500, and $1,500, respectively, might be included in one package. In this case, the work package equals $8,000 in cost.
4. *Reports.*   The more involved PERT/COST systems issue reports that go to various levels of the work structure, including accounting, finance, and personnel staffs. These reports include manpower availability and use, the financial status of the project, the trends and prediction of deviations of cost and time from the plan.

It should be noted that PERT/COST is an expensive system because of the extensive information requirements and is to be used only for extensive and complex projects.

Other Project-Oriented Techniques

The basic PERT and CPM approaches have been extended. Several authors[2] have elaborated on the fact that costs in a project are controlled on a project level

---

[2] See, for example, J. Wiest and F. Levy, *Management Guide to PERT-CPM*, (Englewood Cliffs, N.J.: Prentice-Hall, Inc., 1972).

(where each activity serves as a cost center for both accounting purposes and management control) rather than on a department level.

The line of balance (LOB), which is covered in Chapter 8, is also a project-oriented technique. It is used for monitoring previously identified critical activities by graphically investigating deviations from the schedule.[3]

The graphical evaluation and review technique (GERT) is another technique that relaxes some of the PERT assumptions. In particular, it assumes that not all activities are completed before an event is realized and that events can be repeated. Also, time estimates are not necessarily assumed to be beta-distributed. This enables the planning to be more responsive to real-life constraints.[4]

PROJECT PRODUCTIVITY

As we have so far stated throughout this book, any operation is judged by three criteria: cost, schedule, and quality. A project is no exception. It should be judged according to the above criteria. A multiplicative relationship between schedule (time), cost, and quality levels can be used to judge project productivity. Let us look at the following project productivity index (PPI):

$$\text{PPI} = \left(\frac{\text{Time from start as scheduled}}{\text{Time from start minus slack}}\right) \times \left(\frac{\text{Budgeted costs}}{\text{Actual costs}}\right)$$
$$\times \left(\frac{\text{Actual quality}}{\text{Planned quality}}\right) \tag{4.7}$$

If a positive slack accumulates as a result of good performance, the denominator of the first term is smaller, and the PPI increases. If the actual costs are low compared to budgeted costs, the PPI increases. If actual quality is rated high compared with the planned quality, the PPI will be higher than it otherwise would be. Therefore, the higher the PPI, the better is the actual project performance compared to the planned performance.

Obviously, there are tradeoffs. For example, the actual quality could be increased with added costs. However, at one point, the increase of the PPI due to higher quality will be offset by the decrease of PPI due to the increase in actual costs that are accrued in order to improve project quality. Government contracts sometimes call for such an extensive quality/audit schedule that the overall PPI is decreased.

The PPI is helpful, as it provides the project manager with a basic tradeoff tool as well as a control mechanism. The PPI can be part of the project milestone

[3] See, for example, E. Turban, "The Line of Balance—A Management by Exception Tool," *The Journal of Industrial Engineering*, Vol. 19 (1968), pp. 440–448.

[4] E. R. Clayton and L. J. More, "PERT vs. GERT," *Journal of Systems Management*, Vol. 23 (1972), pp. 11–19; G. E. Whitehouse, *Systems Analysis and Design Using Network Techniques*, (Englewood Cliffs, N.J.: Prentice-Hall, Inc., 1973).

checklist report or other reports on budget and schedule presented to top management.

EXAMPLE Assume that two major activities in a construction project are completed fifty days after the project started. Activity A has a positive slack of 10 days, with budget-to-date of $4,000 and actual costs of $4,000. Activity B has a negative slack of 5 days, with a budget-to-date of $5,000 and actual costs of $3,000. Also, the actual project quality has been equal to the planned quality. Let us compare the performances of the activities. The productivity index for A and for B can be calculated:

$$PPI(A) = \frac{50}{50 - (+10)} \times \frac{4,000}{4,000} \times 1.00 = 1.25$$

$$PPI(B) = \frac{50}{50 - (-5)} \times \frac{5,000}{3,000} \times 1.00 = 1.51$$

Obviously, activity B is performing better in terms of budget. Activity A is performing better in terms of schedule. However, the combined effect of both budget and schedule seems to indicate that activity B performs better overall.

COMPUTERS IN PROJECT MANAGEMENT

As a result of the Navy's successful application of PERT on the Polaris program, and other similar applications, there is a common impression that PERT is applicable only when large-scale data-processing equipment is available. This is certainly true for large networks, or aggregations of networks, where critical path and slack computations are involved for several hundred or more events. It is as desirable to have a computer handle a PERT problem when a large volume of data is involved as it is to use a computer in any extensive data-processing assignment.

Probably equally significant is the fact that several ingenious manual methods have been developed in industry by those organizations that have become convinced of PERT's usefulness. These manual methods range from simple inspection on small networks to more organized but clerically oriented routines for determination of critical path, subcritical path, and slack times on networks ranging from fifty to several hundred events.

This is sufficient proof that PERT can be applied successfully to smaller programs wherever the degree of interconnection and problems of uncertainty warrant it. For those organizations that are practiced in the technique, both the creation of small networks and the formation of time estimates and their reduction to critical path and slack analyses can be carried out in a matter of hours.

It seems clear that the small business organization that wishes to partici-pate in national defense and space programs or to improve its own internal schedule planning and control should not hesitate to adopt PERT merely because of a lack of large-scale data-processing equipment. However, larger-scope projects should take advantage of the numerous commercially available project management programs.

In particular, one should recognize the importance of conversational project management programs like the one used to produce the printout presented in Figure 4.17. (See pages 159–60.)

Here, a network analysis is being done on a project having 12 activities. The project manager is encouraged to respond to a set of questions that the computer initiates. Based on the answers provided, the computer provides the earliest time, the latest time, and the slack (entitled the "float" in the output), and indicates the critical path.

SUMMARY

Project planning and management is a unique problem of operations management. A project is a one-time set of activities with clearly defined beginning and ending points.

Project situations are commonplace in industry today. Various techniques are used in project planning and management. In this chapter, we have covered bar and network analysis techniques, specifically: The Gantt chart, the critical path method (CPM), and the program evaluation and review technique (PERT). Other techniques may also be used, most notably, assembly line balancing (ALB) and line of balance (LOB), which are covered in chapters 7 and 8, respectively. Using these techniques, project risks are assessed, major mile-stones are identified, and resources are allocated.

As with any operating system, the productivity of a project should be measured by a combination of cost, time, and quality characteristics. To this end, a project productivity index (PPI) has been devised and explained.

The use of computers for project planning and management is explained. One should recognize the importance of conversational project management programs. These programs enable the project or operations manager to create a network of activities, consider resource allocations, and identify critical paths while sitting at his or her desk, and without an extensive knowledge of computer programming or computer operations.

DISCUSSION QUESTIONS

4.1   Define the term "project" and give several examples of projects.

4.2   What are the differences between project planning and routine planning?

Figure 4.17 Project Management Conversational Program (user's entries are underlined)

```
enter your name and program title or (stop)
(max of 80 characters)
? test, run one

program critical path for test, run one
how many activities are there (max 150) ?  12

enter the preceding and succeeding node # (prec, succ)
activity  1 ?  1,2
activity  2 ?  2,3
activity  3 ?  2,4
activity  4 ?  3,5
activity  5 ?  4,5
activity  6 ?  5,6
activity  7 ?  2,6
activity  8 ?  6,7
activity  9 ?  7,8
activity 10 ?  8,10
activity 11 ?  8,10
activity 12 ?  9,10

enter (1) if one time estimate
enter (3) if three time estimates
?  3

enter time data for 3 estimates
optimistic time, likely time, pessimistic time
activity  1 ?  2,2,2
activity  2 ?  30,40,55
activity  3 ?  50,65,68
activity  4 ?  20,40,50
activity  5 ?  35,45,55
activity  6 ?  110,120,125
activity  7 ?  70,75,85
activity  8 ?  20,30,35
activity  9 ?  80,85,90
activity 10 ?  20,25,30
activity 11 ?  2,3,4
activity 12 ?  3,4,5

program crit for test, run one input network of 12 activities
```

Figure 4.17 (Cont.)

act #	pred	suc	to	tm	tp
1	1	2	2.00	2.00	2.00
2	2	3	30.00	40.00	55.00
3	2	4	50.00	65.00	68.00
4	3	5	20.00	40.00	50.00
5	4	5	35.00	45.00	55.00
6	5	6	110.00	120.00	125.00
7	2	6	70.00	75.00	85.00
8	6	7	20.00	30.00	35.00
9	7	8	80.00	85.00	90.00
10	8	10	20.00	25.00	30.00
11	8	10	2.00	3.00	4.00
12	9	10	3.00	4.00	5.00

check input data: is it correct (y/n) ? <u>y</u>

events (nodes) are

1	2	3	4	5	6	7	8	9	10

critical path analysis for events is

event	earliest time	latest time	slack
1	0.00	0.00	0.00
2	2.00	2.00	0.00
3	42.83	71.67	28.83
4	65.00	65.00	0.00
5	110.00	100.00	0.00
6	229.17	229.17	0.00
7	258.33	258.33	0.00
8	343.33	343.33	0.00
10	368.33	368.33	0.00
9	0.00	364.33	364.33

the critical path in order is as follows . . .

1	2	4	5	6	7	8	10

critical path analysis for activities is

predecessor	successor	te	te + slack	
1	2	2.00	2.00	crit path
2	3	40.83	69.67	
2	4	63.00	63.00	crit path
3	5	38.33	67.17	
4	5	45.00	45.00	crit path
5	6	119.17	119.17	crit path
2	6	75.83	227.17	
6	7	29.17	29.17	crit path
7	8	85.00	85.00	crit path
8	10	25.00	25.00	crit path
8	10	3.00	25.00	
9	10	4.00	368.33	

4.3 What are the steps involved in the project "going to a bank to deposit a check"? Identify the beginning and ending points, the activities, and the sequencing of the activities.

4.4 Is a Gantt chart a schematic model for planning? How can it be used as a planning tool?

4.5 Describe and contrast the Gantt chart, PERT, and CPM.

4.6 Define the PPI and explain its importance.

4.7 List the stages involved in finding a critical path for a project.

4.8 How can PERT help management in evaluating project risks?

4.9 Describe the computer uses in project planning and management.

PROBLEMS AND SOLUTIONS

4.1 Walita Company, a producer of small domestic appliances, in contemplating the change from a job shop to an assembly line operation, noted the following phases in the project, along with the corresponding numbers of weeks:

> Planning (2)
> Demolishing partitions and machinery removal (7)
> Concrete pad pouring (2)
> Electrical wiring (2)
> Line construction (3)
> Employee training (1)

All phases are sequential except electrical wiring and line construction. Both of these can be done only after concrete pad pouring.
a) Present a Gantt chart for Walita's project.
b) Present a PERT chart for Walita's project.
c) Which one of the charts would you recommend for Walita's project?

Solution

a)

Activities	0	1	2	3	4	5	6	7	8	9	10	11	12	13	14	15
Planning (P)	[		]													
Demolishing (D)			[							]						
Concrete Pouring (CP)										[		]				
Electrical Wiring (EW)												[		]		
Line Construction (LC)												[			]	
Employee Training (ET)															[	]

b)

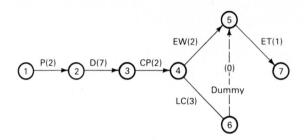

4.2 The following is a list of maintenance activities made on a wire rope used for a construction site crane. The lubrication activities are performed as part of an experiment.

Activity	T_e (hours)	Precedence
Heated oil bath	30	None
Bath casing use	60	None
Pouring of oil	80	None
Dripping of lubricant	70	After heated oil bath
Swabbing with lubricant rags	50	After bath casing use
Brushing-on	100	After pouring oil
Spraying with lubricant	50	After: dripping of lubricant, swabbing with lubricant rags, and brushing-on
Inspection	40	After pouring of oil
Report writing	60	After inspection

Note: The first three activities should start from the same event.
a) Draw the experiment network.
b) Find T_E, T_L, and the slack for each of the events.
c) Identify the critical path.
d) Identify activity slacks.
e) Calculate the total slack in the network.

Solution
Let us identify the activities in letters:

Activity	T_e (hours)	Precedence
A = Heated oil bath	30	—
B = Bath casing use	60	—
C = Pouring of oil	80	—
D = Dripping of lubricant	70	A
E = Swabbing with lubricant rags	50	B
F = Brushing-on	100	C
G = Spraying with lubricant	50	D, E, F
H = Inspection	40	C
I = Report writing	60	H

a)

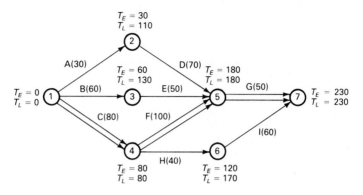

b)

Event	T_E	T_L	Slack
1	0	0	0
2	30	110	80
3	60	130	70
4	80	80	0
5	180	180	0
6	120	170	50
7	230	230	0

c) The critical path is 1-4-5-7 or activities C-F-G.

d) Activities A and D have a (combined) floating slack of 80 hours. Activities B and E have a floating slack of 70 hours. Activities H and I have a floating slack of 50 hours.

e) As per (d), the total slack in the network is 80 + 70 + 50 = 200 hours.

4.3   Wilshire Department Stores, Inc., is currently redesigning its main floor. The following activities, precedence list, and times are involved:

		TIME (DAYS)		
Activity	Precedence	Optimistic	Most Likely	Pessimistic
A	—	5	11	11
B	—	10	10	10
C	—	2	5	8
D	A	1	7	13
E	B	4	4	10
F	B	4	7	10
G	B	2	2	2
H	C	0	6	6
I	D, E	1	4	7
J	G, H	2	8	14

a) Find T_E, T_L, and slack for all events.

b) Find the critical path.

Solution (Find the T_E for the activities.)

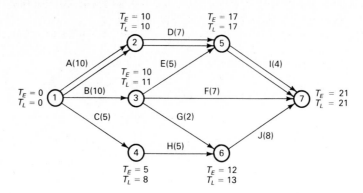

Event	Slack
1	0
2	0
3	1
4	3
5	0
6	1
7	0

B. The critical path: events 1-2-5-7 (or activities A-D-I)

4.4 a) For Problem 4.3, find the probability of finishing the main floor relayout in 24 days.
   b) Wilshire Department Stores, Inc., is interested in the date in which, with at least 80 percent probability, the relayout will be completed. What is this date?

Solution

a) The variance for the critical path is:

Activity	Standard Deviation
A	$\dfrac{11-5}{6} = 1$
D	$\dfrac{13-1}{6} = 2$
I	$\dfrac{7-1}{6} = 1$

V critical path $= 1^2 + 2^2 + 1^2 = 6$
σ critical path $= \sqrt{V}$ critical path $= \sqrt{6} = 2.449$

$$Z = \frac{24 - 21}{2.449} = 1.225$$

As per the Cumulative Normal Distribution Table (Table A in the Appendix) the corresponding probability is 89 percent. Thus, there is 89-percent probability that the relayout will be completed on or before 24 days.

b) For a probability of 80 percent, the Cumulative Normal Distribution Table A indicates Z value of:

$Z = 0.84$

Thus, $0.84 = \dfrac{D - 21}{2.449}$

and

$D = (0.84)(2.449) + 21 = 23.06$ days.

There is an 80-percent probability that the relayout will be completed on or before 23 days.

4.5 The Los Angeles–based accounting firm of Alder, Gensen, & Hasson, Ltd., is engaged in an audit program of a major client. Mr. Hasson, knowledgeable in operations management subjects, has constructed a list of related activities, and their precedence requirements and duration.

Activity Code	Activity	Precedence	Expected Time (days)	Cost of Expediting (per day)
A	Study operations	None	2	$1,000
B	Select audit personnel	None	4	800
C	Systems audit	None	5	700
D	Effectiveness audit	A, B	3	1,000
E	Production-cycle audit	C	11	1,000
F	Cash-cycle audit	D	6	1,500
G	Inventory audit	F	2	500
H	Statements audit	E, G	2	1,000

a) Design an audit network.
b) Calculate T_E, T_L, and slack for all events.
c) Determine the critical path and explain its importance to Alder, Gensen, & Hasson, Ltd., audit project.
d) Mr. Hasson has indicated the availability of $1,700 of expediting monies. Where would you think they should be invested?

Solution

a)

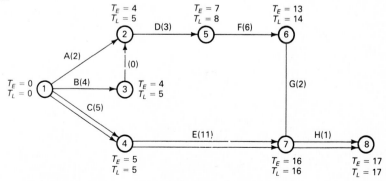

b) T_E and T_L are indicated on network.

Event	Slack
1	1
2	1
3	1
4	0
5	1
6	1
7	0
8	0

c) The critical path by events is: 1-4-7-8.
The critical path by activities is: C-E-H.

d) Mr. Hasson should spend the first \$700 on activity C, reducing it by one day. This will change the audit project duration from 18 to 17 days. Let us examine the network now.

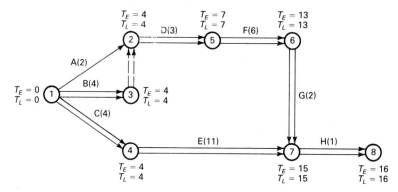

Now there are two critical paths: A-D-F-G-H and C-E-H. The next \$1,000 should be spent on activity H, reducing total project time to 16 days.

CHAPTER REVIEW PROBLEMS

4.1 Jim is required to complete a term paper for his operations management course that involves the following steps:

1. Do a library search.
2. Gather reference materials.
3. Survey reference materials.
4. Prepare, outline, and define scope of discussion.
5. Read reference materials.
6. Make notes on reference materials.
7. Write rough draft from notes.
8. Prepare final draft.

The term paper was assigned at the beginning of the semester, and is due in six weeks. Prepare a Gantt chart for this procedure.

4.2   The Midwest Gas Transmission Company must build a pump station on one of its major pipelines. The activities involved in completing this project are given in the following table:

Activity	Description	Required Preceding Activities
A	Carry out project administration	None
B	Hire pipeline construction personnel	A
C	Purchase pump station equipment	A
D	Transport pump station equipment to pipeline location	C
E	Run simulation of pump station operation	A
F	Inspect equipment	C
G	Construct pump station	B, D
H	Perform production tests of completed pump station	E
I	Start up pump station	F, G
J	Carry out performance evaluation	I
K	Complete accounting data	H, J

Construct a network diagram for this Project.

4.3   Construct a network analysis diagram for a major project with the following activities:

Activity	Required Preceding Activities
A	None
B	None
C	B
D	A, C
E	A
F	D, E

4.4   For the project network shown below, the number alongside each of the activities designates the number of weeks required to complete the activity:

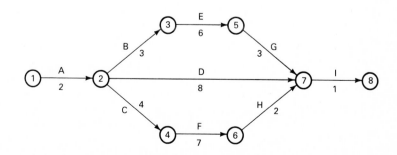

Determine:
a) The T_E and T_L for each event
b) The slack on all events
c) The earliest time that the project can be completed
d) The critical path on the project network diagram, and the critical events.

4.5   A major construction project involves the following activities:

Activity	Time Required to Complete	Required Preceding Activities
A	5 weeks	None
B	4 weeks	None
C	6 weeks	None
D	3 weeks	B
E	6 weeks	A
F	8 weeks	C
G	4 weeks	C
H	5 weeks	D, E, F
I	10 weeks	G
J	7 weeks	A
K	5 weeks	H, I
L	3 weeks	J, K

If the project is completed within 26 weeks, a substantial cash rebate will be rewarded. Using CPM network analysis, determine whether the project can be completed by this deadline. Also, calculate the total slack for the project.

4.6   Given the following activities of a proposed construction project, draw a network diagram showing the project's critical path, and determine the total slack for the project.

Activity	t_e (weeks)	Required Preceding Activities
A	3	None
B	5	None
C	13	A
D	4	A
E	8	A
F	7	B
G	10	D
H	3	E, F
I	6	C, G, H
J	14	B

4.7   The construction manager of CanMar Developers has received three time estimates for the activities involved in an urban development project. The first time estimates were provided by an idealistic MBA student and were considered very optimistic. The second set of time estimates was given by an experienced manager who is known to have good judgment with respect to the company's business. His time estimates were considered the most likely to be correct. Finally, the third set of estimates was provided by a manager who has been against the project since its inception. He gave relatively pessimistic time estimates for each activity. These time estimates are summarized in the following table:

Activity	Expected Completion Times			Precedence of Activities
	Optimistic	Most Likely	Pessimistic	
A	30	32	34	—
B	28	44	60	—
C	52	72	94	—
D	36	65	112	A
E	31	56	81	B
F	63	80	127	C
G	70	100	142	A
H	18	44	70	D, E, F
I	36	50	64	G, H
J	48	77	84	D, E, F
K	12	42	60	C
L	6	21	30	I, J, K

a) Determine the earliest completion date based on PERT.
b) Determine the variance of the project's critical path.

4.8   Repeat Problem 4.7, determining the earliest project completion time based on CPM, using the "most likely" time estimates for each activity's expected completion time. Compare the two solutions.

4.9   Given the following information:

Activity (noted by events)	Crash Time	Crash Cost	Normal Time	Normal Cost
1-2	30 days	$600	50 days	$400
1-3	10 days	$500	50 days	$300
2-4	50 days	$700	100 days	$400
3-4	20 days	$600	70 days	$400
2-6	20 days	$500	60 days	$300
4-6	50 days	$900	110 days	$600
4-5	40 days	$600	60 days	$300
6-7	10 days	$400	50 days	$200
5-7	10 days	$500	40 days	$200

a) Find the normal schedule and cost.
b) Find the schedule and cost when all activities are crashed.
c) Find the total cost required to expedite all the activities from normal times to crash times.
d) Find the least cost plan for a scheduled completion time of 170 days.

4.10 The Big City U.S.A. is engaged in the following urban development projects. Using a project productivity index, what is the project that causes greatest concern for the city manager?

Project	Start (weeks)	Slack	Budget (000's)	Actual Cost (000's)	Planned Quality*	Actual Quality
Light Rail Transit	100	(−16)	$7,000	$10,000	10	9
Exhibition Complex	80	(+5)	3,000	2,500	10	8
High 295 Overpass	50	(+15)	2,000	3,000	10	10

*Quality is measured on a scale from 1 to 10

4.11   Given the following Gantt schedule chart for tent trailer A200:

	Day 1	2	3	4	5	6	7
Order wheels	[━]				[ ]		
Order sheet steel	[━]	[━]					
Order tent	[━]					[ ]	
Fabricate steel			[━]				
Assemble steel					[ ]		
Assemble running gear						[ ]	
Paint						[ ]	
Do final assembly and test							[ ]

What remains to be done after day 4?

4.12   The Walita Company, a producer of small domestic appliances, is in the process of changing its job shop into a continuous assembly-line operation. Two activities are currently scheduled for fifty days after the start of the project: the pouring of heavy duty concrete pads for the presses, and the electric wiring of the assembly department. The concrete-pouring activity is ten days ahead of schedule, with budget-to-date of $40,000 and actual costs of $40,000. The electrical wiring activity is five days behind, with budget-to-date of $5,000 and actual costs of $3,000. The laboratory reports indicate that both activities are performed at the desired quality levels. Measure the project productivity and draw conclusions.

4.13   In a drive-in restaurant construction project, the following network applies:

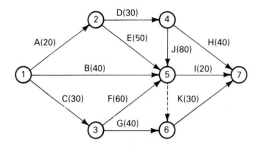

NOTE: Times are in days.

Find:

a) The T_E, T_L, and slack for each event.

b) The completion time of the project.

c) The critical activities.
d) The critical events.

BIBLIOGRAPHY

BAUMGARTNER, J. S., *Project Management*. Homewood, Ill.: Richard D. Irwin, 1963.

BIERMAN, H., JR., C. P. BONINI, and W. H. HAUSMAN, *Quantitative Analysis for Business Decisions*, 6th ed. Homewood, Ill.: R. D. Irwin, 1981.

BROWN, R. A., "Probabilistic Models of Project Management with Design Implication," *IEEE Transaction on Engineering Management*, Vol. EM-25, No. 2, May, 1978, pp. 43–48.

BUFFA, E. S., *Modern Production Management*, 4th ed. New York: John Wiley & Sons, 1973.

BUFFA, E. S., *Operations Management: The Management of Productive Systems*. New York: John Wiley & Sons, 1976.

CHASE, R. B., and N. T. AQUILANO, *Production and Operations Management: A Life Cycle Approach*, 3rd ed. Homewood, Ill.: R. D. Irwin, 1981.

CORMAN, J., *Managing the Productive Process*. Morristown, N.J.: General Learning Corporation, 1974.

DAVIS, E. W., "Project Scheduling under Resource Constraints—Historical Review and Categorization of Procedures," *AIIE Transactions*, Vol. 5, No. 4, Dec., 1973, pp. 297–313.

DONNELLEY, J. H., J. L. GIBSON, and J. M. IVANCEVICH, *Fundamentals of Management: Functions, Behavior, Models*, rev. ed. Dallas: Business Publications, Inc., 1975.

GARRETT, L. J., ET AL., *Production Management Analysis*. New York: Harcourt Brace Jovanovich, 1966.

GAVETT, J. W., *Production and Operations Management*. New York: Harcourt Brace Jovanovich, 1968.

GEORGE, C. S., JR., *Management for Business and Industry*. Englewood Cliffs, N.J.: Prentice-Hall, Inc., 1970.

GREENE, J. H., *Production and Inventory Control*. Homewood, Ill.: R. D. Irwin, 1974.

GROFF, G. K., and JOHN F. MUTH, *Operations Management Analysis for Decision*. Homewood, Ill.: R. D. Irwin, 1972.

HOROWITZ, J., *Critical Path Scheduling*. New York: Ronald, 1967.

IANNONE, A. L., *Management Program Planning and Control with PERT, MOST, and LOB*. Englewood Cliffs, N.J.: Prentice-Hall, Inc., 1967.

JOHNSON, L. A., and D. C. MONTGOMERY, *Operations Research in Production Planning, Scheduling and Inventory Control*. New York: John Wiley & Sons, 1974.

LAUFER, A. C., *Operations Management*. Cincinnati: South-Western Publishing, 1975.

LEVIN, R. I., and C. A. KIRKPATRICK, *Quantitative Approaches to Management*, 4th ed. New York: McGraw-Hill, 1978.

LEVY, R. K., ET AL., "The ABC's of the Critical Path Method," *Harvard Business Review*, Sept.–Oct., 1963, pp. 98–108.

MacCrimmon, K. R., and C. A. Ryavec, "An Analytical Study of the PERT Assumptions," *Operations Research*, January–February, 1964.

Malcolm, D. G., et al., "Application of a Technique for Research and Development Program Evaluation," *Operations Research*, September–October, 1959, pp. 646–669.

Marshall, P. W., et al., *Operations Management, Text and Cases*. Homewood, Ill.: R. D. Irwin, 1975.

Mayer, R. R., *Production and Operations Management*, 3rd ed. New York: McGraw-Hill, 1975.

Menipaz, E., *Automated Production: Decision Support Systems Approach*, Ottowa: Randcomp, 1984.

Michael, S. R., and H. R. Jones, *Organization Management: Concepts and Practices*. New York: Intext Publishers Group, 1973.

Neel, C. W., "Evaluation of Network Models Use in Industrial Construction," *IEEE Transactions on Engineering Management*, Vol. EM-18, No. 1, February, 1971, pp. 7–11.

Niland, P., *Production Planning, Scheduling, and Inventory Control*. New York: Macmillan, 1970.

Olson, R. A., *Manufacturing Management*. Scranton, Pa.: Intext, 1968.

Schoderbek, P. P., "A Study of the Applications of PERT," *Academy of Management Journal*, Sept., 1966, pp. 199–210.

Starr, M. K., *Systems Management of Operations*. Englewood Cliffs, N.J.: Prentice-Hall, Inc., 1971.

Wiest, J. D., "Heuristic Programs for Decision Making," *Harvard Business Review*, Sept.–Oct., 1966, pp. 129–143.

Wiest, J. D., et al., *A Management Guide to PERT/CPM*, 2nd ed. Englewood Cliffs, N.J.: Prentice-Hall, Inc., 1977.

Zimmerman, H. J., and M. G. Sovereign, *Quantitative Models for Production Management*. Englewood Cliffs, N.J.: Prentice-Hall, Inc., 1974.

5

Forecasting
for Operations

INTRODUCTION

In general, planning involves the following steps:

1. *Goal Determination*   Goals must be established, so that detailed planning can take place.
2. *Events Forecast*   In an effort to assess product or service demand, the general business forecast and specific item demand should be made. Future demand sets the requirements in regard to the various planning areas.
3. *Generation of Alternatives*   Alternatives must be generated in order to attain the desired operations level.
4. *Choosing an Alternative*   This may be done by using a cost criterion. The alternatives are budgeted and the one that involves the least amount of expense is adopted.
5. *Determine a Plan of Action*   Once an alternative is determined, a plan of action is structured. This involves the preparation of detailed budgets, establishing standard-data for the operation, establishing management controls, etc.
6. *Implementation*   The plan of action is implemented and proper controls are placed in order to make sure that the goals are indeed attained.

The more carefully operations are planned and organized, the easier and less expensive is control of those operations. Forecasting can reduce the costs of adjusting operations in response to deviations in the performance of the system. With fewer and smaller adjustments, operating efficiency increases.

In virtually every decision, the operations manager considers some kind of forecast. The fast-food-outlet operator is interested in the number of sandwiches he or she may sell next week. In planning a production schedule, the linen manufacturer is interested in the demand for each grade, size, color, design, and quality of linen during the next twelve months. The university physical plant manager is interested in determining the number of mechanical emergency calls he or she might receive during the coming academic year.

In this chapter, we shall discuss the essential aspects of forecasting, with emphasis on item demand forecasts, the most common type used in operations management. Item demand indicates the demand on the operating system and is used for both short-, intermediate-, and long-range planning.

TYPES OF FORECASTS

Different organizations require different types of forecasts, depending on other objectives and the context in which the forecast is used. The types of forecasts are: technological forecasts, economic forecasts, and demand forecasts.

A *technological forecast* is an estimate of the rate of technological change. It is related to long-range planning activities. Technological changes affect operations management in profound ways. For example, many products that were once made from wood are now being made from plastics, requiring a different operations system: a different set of tools, new design of work stations, and a different set of quality control standards. The development of solar energy photovoltaic cells will greatly affect the energy production capacity of the electric utilities, which follow the development in this field very closely.

Technological development can affect product decision and design as well as the processes used to make these products. This forecasting is best performed by specialists in the field of long-range technological forecasts.

An *economic forecast* is an estimate of expected future business conditions. Various government departments publish estimates and predictions of such economic factors, like levels of unemployment, inflation rates, and balance of trade. Various models employed by the University of Chicago, The Chase Manhattan Bank, and others help in calculating these forecasts. These models are called econometric models. Economic consulting companies provide access to several of these forecasting models that are useful in determining long-range and intermediate-range business growth.

The *item demand forecast*, or simply demand forecast, is an estimate of the expected demand for an organization's goods or services in future periods. The item demand forecast is treated extensively in this chapter. It is obtained by analyzing the sales quantities of individual items and casting actual sales figures forward into the future. The demand forecast serves as a basis for capacity planning, as it can be translated into numbers of direct labor hours and machine hours, number of subcontracted units, level of inventory, etc. It also serves as a basis for financial planning and marketing planning.

DEMAND FORECASTING AND PREDICTION

For operations management, the definition of forecasting is as follows: *Forecasting is the procedure for estimating a future event by casting forward past data that are combined in a predetermined way.*

The forecasting procedure should be distinguished from the prediction procedure, which is not based on past data only. *Prediction is a procedure of estimating a future event using subjective considerations other than simply past data.*

Thus, the distinction between forecasting and prediction involves the use and the availability of past data. The manager usually uses a combination of forecasting and prediction to estimate future demand for his products or services. The objective calculations made while forecasting are augmented based on the manager's subjective judgments.

Usually, forecasts made by staff personnel are augmented to reflect management "feeling" as to the market potential. By incorporating this subjective information in an unstructured manner into the forecasting, the latter is turned into prediction.

It is important to note that virtually all the departments represented in an organization should be and are involved in various degrees in the preparation of the demand forecast.

Table 5.1 represents the responses of 126 companies to a survey in which they were asked to indicate the department or individual that is responsible for the demand forecast. Although most of the companies assign the responsibility to a sales or marketing department, departments other than these do become involved.

TABLE 5.1   FORECASTING RESPONSIBILITY

DEPARTMENT RESPONSIBLE FOR DEMAND FORECAST	PERCENT OF COMPANIES RESPONDED
Sales	32
Marketing	29
Economic planning	13
General management	11
Finance	6
More than one department	9

Source: Adapted from Robert S. Reichard, *Practical Techniques of Sales Forecasting* (New York: McGraw-Hill Book Company, 1966), p. 21. Reproduced with permission.

FACTORS AFFECTING DEMAND

The business environment is an extremely demanding one. Many different variables affect the demand for a product or a service. The general business cycle has an impact on the disposable income of individuals and, thus, on the consumption pattern. In addition, each product or service proceeds through several stages of acceptance and sales, called its life cycle, as has been discussed in Chapter 2. The actual duration of the life cycle varies. For hot pants, for example, the entire cycle lasted for only several months in the early 1970's; for disposable lighters, it has been with us since the early sixties, and sales are still growing. Other variables that affect demand are advertising, marketing efforts, after-sale service, product and service design, credit policy, quality, and competing products (see Figure 5.1). This multiplicity of variables make the forecasting a difficult task.

Most companies revise their demand forecasts every month; others do so quarterly, semiannually, or annually. Most companies use five-year and ten-year forecast horizons, whereas others use one-, two-, or fifteen-year forecast horizons.

There are two reasons for the differences in forecast horizons for different organizations. First, the forecast may be used for short- or longer-term decision. A decision to expand an existing facility should be based on a longer-term forecast horizon. A decision to increase the work force temporarily may require a forecast horizon of only several months. Second, the nature of demand growth may indicate the necessity for a shorter or longer forecast horizon. Thus, if the organization expects erratic changes in demand that should be followed, it might prefer a shorter forecast horizon.

INDEPENDENT AND DEPENDENT DEMAND

The demand for end item products or completed services is affected by the variables presented in Figure 5.1. This demand is termed *independent demand,* as it is determined by variables that are only partially controlled by the organization. For example, the organization has no control on competing products, and the credit policy is highly affected by the acceptable marketwide credit policy.

The demand for subassemblies (otherwise called components) or partially completed services depends on the demand for end products and completed services. This demand is termed *dependent demand,* as it is controlled by the

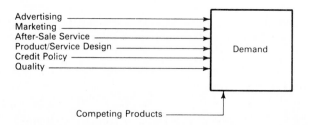

Figure 5.1 Variables Affecting Demand for Product or Service

organization. Obviously, in the dependent demand case, the forecast of the demand can be determined with certainty.

Not only are the quantities of subassemblies known, but also the schedule can be better set based on data available from former production runs. If the fast-food-outlet operator expects to sell 1600 hamburgers on Sunday, he or she knows that 1600 buns, 1600 beef patties, 400 tomatoes (at four slices per tomato), and so on, must be in stock. In this situation, one might claim that the number of tomatoes required is derived from the number of hamburgers to be sold and that the demand for tomatoes is dependent on the demand for hamburgers, the end item. The fast-food operator is required to forecast only the end item demand (that for hamburgers).

The material requirement planning (MRP) concept, presented later in the book, deals with dependent item demand forecasting, whereas this chapter deals with independent demand forecasting.

FORECASTING METHODS

Basically, there are three families of forecasting techniques. *Qualitative techniques* use qualitative data, such as expert opinions, and information regarding special events that might influence the item demand. These techniques do not necessarily imply that the past demand pattern is taken into consideration. Thus, qualitative techniques are prediction techniques. *Time series analysis and projection techniques* focus on the analysis of historical demand patterns and pattern changes. *Causal models* are based on the identification of specific relations between system elements; these, too, rely heavily on historical data.

Tables 5.2, 5.3, and 5.4 summarize the major forecasting methods included in these groupings. In the following sections, we shall examine in detail some of the frequently used forecasting methods.

QUALITATIVE TECHNIQUES

These techniques are used when historical data are not available—e.g., when the demand for a new product is forecasted. They make use of human judgment and rating schemes in order to turn qualitative information into quantitative estimates.

The objective is to incorporate, in a logical, unbiased, and systematic way, all information and judgments that relate to the product. These techniques are useful mostly for new technological products, where development of the product idea may have required several scientific breakthroughs, and where market acceptance and penetration rates are highly uncertain.

One of the most common qualitative techniques is the Delphi technique, which will be described in detail. The Delphi technique is a group process that strives for a consensus forecast, rather than a compromise or average forecast.

TABLE 5.2 FORECASTING TECHNIQUES—QUALITATIVE METHODS

TECHNIQUE	DELPHI METHOD	MARKET RESEARCH	PANEL CONSENSUS	VISIONARY FORECAST	HISTORICAL ANALOGY
Description	A panel of experts is interrogated by a sequence of questionnaires in which the responses to one questionnaire are used to produce the next questionnaire. Any set of information available to some experts and not others is thus passed on to the others, enabling all the experts to have access to all the information for forecasting. This technique eliminates the bandwagon effect of majority opinion.	The systematic, formal, and conscious procedure for evolving and testing hypotheses about real markets.	This technique is based on the assumption that several experts can arrive at a better forecast than one person. There is no secrecy, and communication is encouraged. The forecasts are sometimes influenced by social factors, and may not reflect a true consensus.	A prophecy that uses personal insights, judgment, and, when possible, facts about different scenarios of the future. It is characterized by subjective guesswork and imagination; in general, the methods used are nonscientific.	This is a comparative analysis of the introduction and growth of similar new products, that bases the forecast on similarity patterns.

Accuracy					
Short-term	Fair to very good	Excellent	Poor to fair	Poor	Poor
Medium-term	Fair to very good	Good	Poor to fair	Poor	Good to fair
Long-term	Fair to very good	Fair to good	Poor	Poor	Good to fair
Identification of Turning Point	Fair to good	Fair to very good	Poor to fair	Poor	Poor to fair
Typical Application	Forecasts of long-range and new-product sales, forecasts of margins.	Forecasts of long-range and new-product sales, forecasts of margins.	Forecasts of long-range and new-product sales, forecasts of margins.	Forecasts of long-range and new-product sales, forecasts of margins.	Forecasts of long-range and new-product sales, forecasts of margins.
Data Required	A coordinator issues the sequence of questionnaires, editing and consolidating the responses.	As a minimum, two sets of reports over time. One needs a considerable collection of market data from questionnaires, surveys, and time series analyses of market variables.	Information from a panel of experts is presented openly in group meetings to arrive at a consensus forecast. Again, a minimum is two sets of reports over time.	A set of possible scenarios about the future prepared by a few experts in light of past events.	Several years history of one or more products.
Is Calculation Possible without a Computer?	Yes	Yes	Yes	Yes	Yes

TABLE 5.3 FORECASTING TECHNIQUES—TIME SERIES ANALYSIS AND PROJECTION

	MOVING AVERAGE	EXPONENTIAL SMOOTHING	BOX-JENKINS	X-11	TREND PROJECTIONS
Description	Each point of a moving average of a time series is the arithmetic or weighted average of a number of consecutive points of the series, where the number of data points is chosen so that the effects of seasonals or irregularity or both are eliminated.	This technique is similar to the moving average, except that more recent data points are given more weight. Descriptively, the new forecast is equal to the old one plus some proportion of the past forecasting error. Adaptive forecasting is somewhat the same except that seasonals are also computed. There are many variations of exponential smoothing; some are more versatile than others; some are computationally more complex, some require more computer time.	Exponential smoothing is a special case of the Box-Jenkins technique. The time series is fitted with a mathematical model that is optimal in the sense that it assigns smaller errors to history than any other model. The type of model must be identified and the parameters then estimated. This is apparently the most accurate statistical routine available but also one of the most costly and time-consuming ones.	Developed by Julius Shiskin of the Census Bureau, this technique decomposes a time series into seasonals, trend cycles, and irregular elements. Primarily used for detailed time series analysis (including estimating seasonals); but we have extended its uses to forecasting and tracking and warming by incorporating other analytical methods. Used with special knowledge, it is perhaps the most effective technique for medium-range forecasting—three months to one year—allowing one to predict turning points and to time special events.	This technique fits a trend line to a mathematical equation and then projects it into the future by means of this equation. There are several variations: the slope-characteristic method, polynomials, logarithms, and so on.

Accuracy					
Short-term	Poor to good	Fair to very good	Very good to excellent	Very good to excellent	Very good
Medium-term	Poor	Poor to good	Poor to good	Good	Good
Long-term	Very poor	Very poor	Very poor	Very poor	Good
Identification of turning point	Poor	Poor	Fair	Very good	Poor
Typical Application	Inventory control for low-volume items, forecasts of margins.	Production and inventory control, forecasts of margins and other financial data.	Production and inventory control for large volume items, forecasts of cash balances.	Tracking and warning, forecasts of company, division, or department sales.	New-product forecasts (particularly intermediate and long-term).
Data Required	A minimum of two years of sales history, if seasonals are present. Otherwise, less data. (Of course, the more history the better.) The moving average must be specified.	The same as for a moving average.	The same as for a moving average. However, in this case more history is very advantageous in model identification.	A minimum of three years history to start the complete history.	Varies with the technique used. However, a good rule of thumb is to use a minimum of five years' annual data to start and, thereafter, the complete history.
Is Calculation Possible without a Computer?	Yes	Yes	Yes	No	Yes

Source: Reprinted by permission of the *Harvard Business Review*. An exhibit from "How to Choose the Right Forecasting Technique" by J. C. Chambers, S. K. Mullick, and D. D. Smith (July/August 1971). Copyright © 1971 by the President and Fellows of Harvard College. All rights reserved.

TABLE 5.4 FORECASTING TECHNIQUES—CAUSAL MODELS

	REGRESSION MODEL	ECONOMETRIC MODEL	INTENTION-TO-BUY & ANTICIPATIONS SURVEYS	INPUT-OUTPUT MODEL
Description	This functionally relates sales to other economic, competitive, or internal variables, and estimates an equation using the least-squares technique. Relationships are primarily analyzed statistically, although any relationship should be selected for testing on a rational ground.	An econometric model is a system of interdependent regression equations that describes some sector of economic sales or profit activity. The parameters of the regression equations are usually estimated simultaneously. As a rule, these models are relatively expensive to develop and can easily cost between $5,000 and $10,000, depending on detail. However, due to the system of equations inherent in such models, they will better express the causalities involved than will an ordinary regression equation, and hence will predict turning points more accurately.	These surveys of the general public (a) determine intentions to buy certain products or (b) derive an index that measures general feeling about the present and the future and estimates how this feeling will affect buying habits. These approaches to forecasting are more useful for tracking & warning than forecasting. The basic problem in using them is that a turning point may be signaled incorrectly (and hence never occur).	A method of analysis concerned with the interindustry or interdepartmental flow of goods or services in the economy or a company and its markets. It shows what flows of inputs must occur to obtain certain outputs. Considerable effort must be expended to use these models properly, and additional detail, not normally available, must be obtained if they are to be applied to specific businesses. Corporations using input-output models have expended as much as $100,000 and more annually to develop useful applications.

Accuracy				
Short-term	Good to very good	Good to very good	Poor to good	Not applicable
Medium-term	Good to very good	Very good to excellent	Poor to good	Good to very good
Long-term	Poor	Good	Very poor	Good to very good
Identification of turning point	Very good	Excellent	Good	Fair
Typical Application	Forecasts of sales by product classes. Forecasts of margins.	Forecasts of sales by product classes, forecasts of margins	Forecasts of sales by products.	Forecasts of company sales and division sales for industrial sectors and sub-sectors.
Data Required	Several years' quarterly history, to obtain good, meaningful relationships. Mathematically necessary to have two more observations than there are independent variables.	The same as for regression.	Several years' data are usually required to relate such indexes to company sales.	Ten or fifteen years' history. Considerable amounts of information on product and service flows within a corporation (or economy) for each year for which an input-output analysis is desired.
Is Calculation Possible without a Computer?	Yes	Yes	Yes	No

183

TABLE 5.4 (Cont.)

	ECONOMIC INPUT-OUTPUT MODEL	DIFFUSION INDEX	LEADING INDICATOR	LIFE-CYCLE ANALYSIS
Description	Econometric models and input-output models are sometimes combined for forecasting. The input-output model is used to provide long-term trends for the econometric model; it also stabilizes the econometric model.	The percentage of a group economic indicators that are going up or down, this percentage then becoming the index.	A time series of an economic activity whose movement in a given direction precedes the movement of some other time series in the same direction is a leading indicator.	This is an analysis and forecasting of new-product growth rates based on S-curves. The phases of product acceptance by the various groups such as innovators, early adapters, early majority, late majority, and laggards are central to the analysis.
Accuracy				
Short-term	Not applicable	Poor to good	Poor to good	Poor
Medium-term	Good to very good	Poor to good	Poor to good	Poor to good
Long-term	Good to excellent	Very poor	Very poor	Poor to good
Identification of turning point	Good	Good	Good	Poor to good
Typical Application	Company sales for industrial sectors and subsectors.	Forecasts of sales by product class.	Forecasts of sales by product class.	Forecasts of new-product sales.
Data Required	The same as for a moving average and X-11.	The same as an intention-to-buy survey.	The same as an intention-to-buy survey + 5 to 10 years history.	As a minimum the annual sales of the product being considered or of a similar product. It is often necessary to do market surveys.
Is Calculation Possible without a Computer?	No	Yes	Yes	Yes

Source: Reprinted by permission of the *Harvard Business Review.* An exhibit from "How to Choose the Right Forecasting Technique" by J. C. Chambers, S. K. Mullick, and D. D. Smith (July/August 1971). Copyright © 1971 by the President and Fellows of Harvard College. All rights reserved.

Delphi has been employed in many different settings. Originally, it was used as a process for technological forecasting. For example, Delphi was used to obtain predictions concerning the impact of a new land-use policy upon population growth, pollution, agriculture, taxes, etc.

There are three critical conditions necessary to complete a successful Delphi process:

1. Adequate time (a session can last several weeks)
2. High participant skill in written communication
3. High participant level of motivation.

The Delphi process is conducted by the Delphi coordinator. The steps in the process are as follows:

1. Develop the objective of the forecast requested.
2. Determine the number of participants. When the group of people is homogeneous, ten to fifteen participants are enough. However, when various reference groups are involved, several hundred people may participate.
3. Select and contact the participants. All the participants should be familiar with the objective of the forecast, should have pertinent information to share, and should feel that the process will provide them with information they value and to which they would not otherwise have access.
4. Develop the first questionnaire and submit it to the participants. Unlike other group techniques (e.g., nominal group techniques), where the coordinator is present at a meeting with the participants, in the Delphi process a cover letter and questionnaire are the only means by which the work team can communicate at this stage. This initial questionnaire consists of rather open-ended questions.
5. The Delphi coordinator analyzes the responses to the first questionnaire and constructs a summary list of items identified and comments made.
6. Construct a second questionnaire, accurately conveying the meaning that the participants attempted to communicate by means of the first questionnaire. Indicate areas of disagreement and agreement, items requiring clarification, and emerging priorities. Send the second questionnaire to participants.
7. Analyze the responses to the second questionnaire. This questionnaire's summary includes tally votes for questions presented and comments made about the questions in a form that is both thought-provoking and easy to understand.
8. Repeat this process until the Delphi coordinator can identify a forecast's consensus.

The author has had the opportunity to recommend the use of the Delphi method to a commercial catering operation for identifying key service characteristics, and to a large linen manufacturer for determining next year's product mix. The technique has proven to be easy to understand and carry out and has facilitated the complete participation of many of the line and staff members of the organization.

TIME SERIES ANALYSIS AND PROJECTION TECHNIQUES

These techniques use available historical data concerning a product's demand for forecasting. They are most effective when trends are clear and seem to be stable.

A *time series* is a set of chronologically ordered points of data taken at regular intervals over a period of time (daily, monthly, annually, etc.). As an example, a masonry levels manufacturer may have the monthly shipping figures recorded in the last several years. These data may be used to forecast the sales into the future. The main theme of time series analysis is that future values of a series can be estimated from past values of the series. There is no attempt to identify variables that might affect the time series.

The *projection technique* calls for a development of a trend line that fits into the data, and the extension of the data into the future by use of this trend line.

Both techniques require the plotting of demand data on a time scale. Through the graphical presentation, a pattern of demand over time emerges. We might find that every summer in the past the demand for a particular product has peaked and, thus, we can assume that the same will happen during the coming summer.

Decomposition of a Time Series

The demand consists of several components that interact in some manner to create the general form of the demand pattern. The components of demand are:

1. Average demand
2. Trends
3. Seasonal variation
4. Cyclic variation
5. Random and irregular variation
6. Auto correlation.

A *trend* refers to a gradual, long-term movement in the data. Population growth and inflation impact on incomes often account for this movement.

Seasonality refers to short-term, fairly regular, periodic changes in demand that are generally related to weather or holidays.

Cyclic variations are ups and downs in demand of more than one year's duration, and are related to a variety of economic and political factors. For an example, one can refer to the recessions of the early 'seventies and early 'eighties. It is difficult to determine cyclic variation, as the length or the cause of a cycle may be unknown.

Random and irregular variations are the residual variations left after all known components (i.e., average demand, trends, seasonal and cyclical variations) of the demand pattern are detected and removed from the total demand. What remains is the unexplained part of the demand.

Auto correlation is the extent to which the current period demand is related to the immediate past values of demand. When high auto correlation exists, the demand from one time period to another will not change much.

The pattern of demand may be described as either *stable* or *unstable*. The term *stability* is used to describe the tendency of the demand to retain a specific profile over time. The greater the random variation around the average, the more unstable the demand pattern is and the more difficult it is to cast forward the demand pattern with minimum error.

Obviously, all time series analyses and projections are based on the assumption that existing demand patterns will continue into the future. Thus, the use of time series analysis should include a consultation of leading indicators whenever possible in order to identify a change of direction in the trend (up or down).

EXAMPLE: POM Bakery, Inc.   POM Bakery, Inc., is a large bakery that produces breads, rolls, English muffins, cupcakes, biscuits, cookies, and doughnuts. Tables 5.5, 5.6, and 5.7 describe the unit demand for three different products in terms of number of baking trays. We assume that demand equals sales and we use the two terms interchangeably. The data contained in the tables have been graphed in Figures 5.2, 5.3, and 5.4 as time series. We shall use these data to exemplify time series analysis and projection techniques.

From Figure 5.2, one can detect no generally stable pattern for white bread, with variation around the *average demand* of 104.48 baking trays of white bread per month (the calculation of average demand is shown later). Furthermore, while the minimum demand was 30 trays in December, 1976, the maximum demand was 160 units in August, 1976, indicating a spread or range of 130 trays. This is a large spread if one considers an average monthly demand of 104.48 trays.

From Figure 5.3, one can detect a moderately increasing demand for cupcakes over the period of five years. That is, a *trend* is detected—in this case, an upward trend. The average monthly demand for the first year was 48.50 units, the average demand for the second year was 50.08, and the average monthly demand for the fifth year was 68.75 units.

From Figure 5.4, one can see that, in spite of a significant variation around the average, there is a *seasonal pattern* in the demand for rolls. The unit demand seems to peak around the summer months of June, July, and August and to drop significantly during the following month. Any projection into the future for this item should take the seasonality into account.

Note that by simply presenting the time series graphically, one may draw some important conclusions regarding the demand.

TABLE 5.5   MONTHLY DEMAND FOR WHITE BREAD

YEAR	MONTH	DEMAND, IN NUMBER OF TRAYS		YEAR	MONTH	DEMAND, IN NUMBER OF TRAYS
1975	J	120		1978	J	122
	F	80			A	75
	M	140			S	125
	A	110			O	110
	M	100			N	115
	J	150			D	75
	J	90			J	105
	A	130			F	65
	S	110			M	80
	O	105			A	75
	N	50			M	60
	D	90			J	122
1976	J	130			J	90
	F	120			A	125
	M	125			S	120
	A	125			O	125
	M	110			N	115
	J	120			D	120
	J	100		1979	J	150
	A	160			F	80
	S	125			M	100
	O	90			A	70
	N	80			M	100
	D	30			J	120
1977	J	125			J	70
	F	90			A	60
	M	80			S	150
	A	110			O	140
	M	130			N	90
	J	70			D	120

Average Demand 6,269 ÷ 60 = 104.88 Trays

TABLE 5.6 MONTHLY DEMAND FOR CUPCAKES

YEAR	MONTH	DEMAND, IN NUMBER OF TRAYS
1975	J	40
	F	38
	M	50
	A	48
	M	65
	J	62
	J	40
	A	43
	S	56
	O	58
	N	42
	D	40
1976	J	43
	F	53
	M	50
	A	51
	M	42
	J	50
	J	52
	A	50
	S	50
	O	58
	N	50
	D	52
1977	J	42
	F	40
	M	65
	A	67
	M	69
	J	40
	J	46
	A	48
	S	42
	O	44
	N	60
	D	58
1978	J	40
	F	38
	M	65
	A	67
	M	38
	J	65
	J	67
	A	38
	S	58
	O	60
	N	62
	D	65
1979	J	78
	F	82
	M	65
	A	67
	M	69
	J	58
	J	64
	A	66
	S	68
	O	60
	N	96
	D	52

Average Demand 3,292 ÷ 60 = 54.87 Trays

TABLE 5.7 MONTHLY DEMAND FOR ROLLS

YEAR	MONTH	DEMAND, IN NUMBER OF TRAYS
1975	J	95
	F	105
	M	95
	A	80
	M	105
	J	110
	J	115
	A	130
	S	70
	O	95
	N	100
	D	97
1976	J	95
	F	102
	M	100
	A	106
	M	80
	J	130
	J	125
	A	140
	S	65
	O	125
	N	100
	D	98
1977	J	96
	F	94
	M	92
	A	93
	M	106
	J	100

YEAR	MONTH	DEMAND, IN NUMBER OF TRAYS
	J	140
	A	142
	S	80
	O	100
	N	98
	D	105
1978	J	107
	F	105
	M	103
	A	101
	M	100
	J	130
	J	140
	A	142
	S	65
	O	100
	N	96
	D	102
1979	J	96
	F	106
	M	102
	A	104
	M	96
	J	98
	J	130
	A	110
	S	75
	O	80
	N	100
	D	96

Average Monthly Demand = 6,088 ÷ 60 = 101.47 Trays

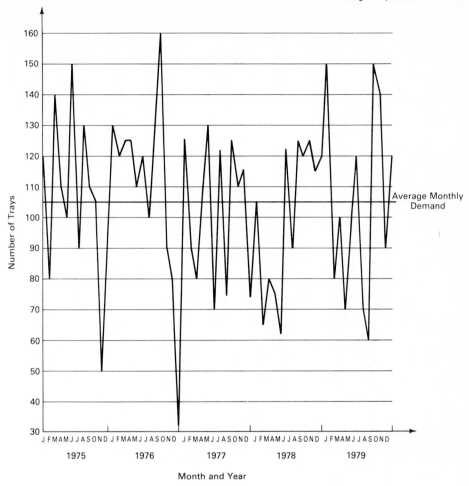

Figure 5.2   Monthly Demand for White Bread

Simple Average

The simplest and crudest indicator of future demand is the arithmetic average, taken over several past periods. In using this technique, one assumes that the average demand over past periods represents the demand during those periods accurately enough to be extended into the future. The arithmetic average gives equal weight to the demands of all the past periods used in calculating that average. Recent data have no more weight in the projection than much older data. The calculation is:

$$F_{n+1} = \frac{D_1 + D_2 + \cdots + D_n}{n} = \frac{\sum\limits_{t=1}^{n} D_t}{n} \tag{5.1}$$

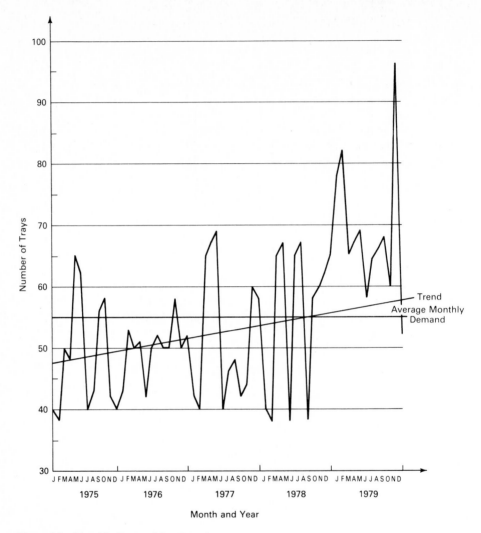

Figure 5.3   Monthly Demand for Cupcakes

where F_{n+1} = the demand forecast for the next period
         D_t = demand during period t
         n = number of historical periods from which the average is calculated.

That is, the average of the previous n demands is used as the forecast of the $(n+1)$st demand.

EXAMPLE   To forecast the demand for bread trays during January, 1979, POM Bakery uses a simple average over the twelve preceding months (January–December, 1978). That average is

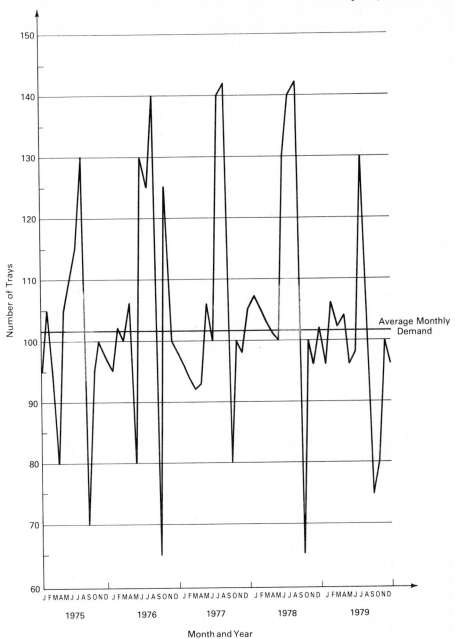

Figure 5.4 Monthly Demand for Rolls

$$F_{\text{Jan.}} = \frac{105 + 65 + 80 + 75 + 60 + 122 + 90 + 125 + 120 + 125 + 115 + 120}{12}$$

$$= 100.17 \text{ units}$$

Thus, POM forecasts a unit demand (in bread trays) of 100 units for the month of January, 1979. The actual sales figures in Table 5.5 show for January, 1979, a demand of 150 units. The difference between the calculated forecast and the actual sales figure is 50 units.

This example emphasizes a major disadvantage of the simple average as a forecasting tool. When the unit demand fluctuates or shows a trend over time, this change is lost when the simple average is calculated. The reason for this lack of sensitivity is the fact that all the periods entering into the calculation are equally weighted in the forecasting formula.

This lack of sensitivity is also one of the advantages of the technique, since random variations in the demand pattern will have only minimal effect on the forecast.

Simple Moving Average

In the simple moving average, one calculates the average of the unit demand data for a specific number of recent periods. As a new sales figure becomes available, the earliest sales figure is dropped and the new figure is included in the average. Thus, the number of most recent periods represented in the calculation of the average stays constant.

The computation is the same as that for the simpler average:

$$F_{n+1} = \frac{D_1 + D_2 + \cdots + D_n}{n} = \frac{\sum_{t=1}^{n} D_t}{n} \tag{5.2}$$

where n is the number of most recent periods on which the moving average is based.

EXAMPLE POM Bakery considers the use of three-, six- and nine-months' moving averages in forecasting demand for bread-baking trays.

The calculations lead to the forecasts in Table 5.8 for the month of January, 1979. As one can see, the shortest (three months') moving average gives us the best forecast, in that it is closest to the actual sales figure for the month of January (150 units). This results from the elimination of earlier low-sales periods from the calculation.

By the end of January, with the January actual sales figure at hand, POM Bakery is in a position to forecast the February demand. The calculations (see Table 5.9) lead again to three forecasts for February, 1979. Actual sales for the month of February, 1979, from Table 5.5, were 80 units; thus, the best forecast was that of the nine-months' moving average.

One can conclude that variations around the average, such as those in Figure 5.2, defeat any effort to obtain a reasonable forecast through averaging. However, by including a larger number of periods in calculating the average,

TABLE 5.8 SIMPLE MOVING AVERAGE USED TO FORECAST THE JANUARY DEMAND FOR WHITE BREAD

MONTH	LAST NINE MONTHS' SALES	LAST SIX MONTHS' SALES	LAST THREE MONTHS' SALES
April, 1978	75		
May	60		
June	122		
July	90	90	
August	125	125	
September	120	120	
October	125	125	125
November	115	115	115
December, 1978	120	120	120
January, 1979 (Forecast)	105.78	115.83*	120

*The calculation for the six-months' moving average forecast is

$$F_{\text{Jan.}} = \frac{90 + 125 + 120 + 125 + 115 + 120}{6} = 115.83 \text{ units}$$

TABLE 5.9 SIMPLE MOVING AVERAGE USED TO FORECAST THE FEBRUARY DEMAND FOR WHITE BREAD

MONTH	LAST NINE MONTHS' SALES	LAST SIX MONTHS' SALES	LAST THREE MONTHS' SALES
May, 1978	60		
June	122		
July	90		
August	125	125	
September	120	120	
October	125	125	
November	115	115	115
December	120	120	120
January, 1979	150	150	150
February (Forecast)	114.11	125.83*	128.33

*The calculation for the six-months' moving average forecast is

$$F_{\text{Feb.}} = \frac{125 + 120 + 125 + 115 + 120 + 150}{6} = 125.83 \text{ units}$$

one dampens the effect of random variation and the general trend becomes more obvious.

The choice of the number of periods to include in a moving average will depend on such things as the degree to which random variations are present, as well as the cost of not reacting quickly to changes compared to the cost of reacting when no real changes are present.

Weighted Moving Average

The weighted moving average is an average in which each of the items D_t is given a weight that is proportional to its assumed effect on the forecast. As in the simple average, each sales period carries the same weight in a simple moving average. However, recent periods often provide more accurate information and should be weighted more heavily than remote periods. The weighted moving average technique allows one to take into consideration the effect of each past period on future periods. The computation is

$$F_{n+1} = W_1 D_1 + W_2 D_2 + \cdots + W_n D_n = \sum_{t=1}^{n} W_t D_t \qquad (5.3)$$

where W_t is the weight assigned to period t. W_t is between 0 and 1, inclusive, and $\sum_{t=1}^{n} W_t = 1.0$. Thus, if one would like to average four periods, the two most recent of which should be weighted equally and most heavily, one might assign the following weights: $W_1 = 0.15$, $W_2 = 0.15$, $W_3 = 0.35$, $W_4 = 0.35$. Note that this allocation of weights implies that periods 3 and 4 are more than twice as important in the forecast as are periods 1 and 2.

EXAMPLE   POM Bakery uses a four-months' weighted moving average for forecasting sales of cupcakes. The operations manager considers the previous month's demand to be most important and assigns the weights $W_1 = 0.10$, $W_2 = 0.10$, $W_3 = 0.10$, $W_4 = 0.70$. Based on the information contained in Table 5.6 for product B, the manager calculates, for January and February, 1979,

$$F_{\text{Jan.}} = 0.10(58) + 0.10(60) + 0.10(62) + 0.70(65) = 63.5$$

$$F_{\text{Feb.}} = 0.10(60) + 0.10(62) + 0.10(65) + 0.70(78) = 73.3$$

The actual demand for cupcakes was 78 units in January, compared with a forecast of 63.5; and 82 units for February, compared with a forecast of 73.3.

The choice of weights is critical to proper forecasting using this method. The weights should be chosen so that a change of demand upwards or downwards may be identified, while weights assigned to earlier periods will dampen the effects of random variations.

Exponential Smoothing Technique

In the calculation of moving average, each item in the averaging period is assigned a specific weight, while all items outside the averaging period are assigned a weight value of zero. For example, in a three-months' moving average, only the three most recent periods are assigned a nonzero weight (1/3 each).

In exponential smoothing, the weights assigned to the sales periods in the computation of the forecast decrease exponentially as they become less recent.

The forecasted demand value F_t is thus a weighted average of the demand figures for *all* previous periods. The exponential weighting, however, emphasizes the most recent periods.

There are several exponential smoothing techniques. We shall describe first-order exponential smoothing, as well as some other techniques.

First-order exponential smoothing is based on the following equation:

$$F_t = \alpha D_{t-1} + (1 - \alpha)F_{t-1} \tag{5.4}$$

where F_t = forecast for period t

D_{t-1} = demand for period $t - 1$

F_{t-1} = forecast for period $t - 1$

α = smoothing constant, $0.0 \leq \alpha \leq 1.0$

Here we are including both the forecast and the actual demand of the last period, to improve our forecasting equation as well as our forecast.

In using this technique, only three pieces of data are required in order to forecast (unlike the previous methods, for which we had to carry continually a large amount of data): the most recent forecast, the actual demand that occurred for that forecasted period, and a smoothing constant, α. This constant determines the level of smoothing and the speed at which differences between forecasts and actual occurrences are accounted for. The value of this constant is determined by management, based on the product and what management considers a good response rate. If the firm produces a standard item with a stable demand, the response rate to differences between actual and forecasted demand should be small, indicating a smaller α. However, if the firm is experiencing growth, it should use a larger value for α, which enables a faster response rate, in order to account for the recent growth in demand.

For example, suppose management uses this method to make a forecast $F_{\text{Dec.}}$ of December sales (this forecast is made at the end of November). At the end of December, management knows the actual December sales figure, $D_{\text{Dec.}}$ as well. Their exponentially smoothed forecast for the month of January is then:

$$F_{\text{Jan.}} = \alpha D_{\text{Dec.}} + (1 - \alpha)F_{\text{Dec.}}$$

where the weight α has been decided on and is used for all such forecasts.

The forecasts for preceding months can be written as:

$$F_t = \alpha D_{t-1} + (1 - \alpha)F_{t-1} \tag{5.5}$$

$$F_{t-1} = \alpha D_{t-2} + (1 - \alpha)F_{t-2} \tag{5.6}$$

$$F_{t-2} = \alpha D_{t-3} + (1 - \alpha)F_{t-3} \tag{5.7}$$

Substituting equation (5.6) into equation (5.5) gives:

$$F_t = \alpha D_{t-1} + (1 - \alpha)[\alpha D_{t-2} + (1 - \alpha)F_{t-2}]$$

Or,

$$F_t = \alpha D_{t-1} + \alpha(1-\alpha)D_{t-2} + (1-\alpha)^2 F_{t-2} \qquad (5.8)$$

Furthermore, substituting equation (5.7) into equation (5.8) gives:

$$F_t = \alpha D_{t-1} + \alpha(1-\alpha)D_{t-2} + (1-\alpha)^2[\alpha D_{t-3} + (1-\alpha)F_{t-3}]$$

Or,

$$F_t = \alpha D_{t-1} + \alpha(1-\alpha)D_{t-2} + \alpha(1-\alpha)^2 D_{t-3} + (1-\alpha)^3 F_{t-3}$$

By extending the expression for F_t to include explicitly the forecasts for preceding months, one arrives at

$$F_t = \alpha(1-\alpha)^0 D_{t-1} + \alpha(1-\alpha)^1 D_{t-2} + \alpha(1-\alpha)^2 D_{t-3}$$
$$+ \alpha(1-\alpha)^3 D_{t-4} + \cdots + \alpha(1-\alpha)^{t-1} D_0 + (1-\alpha)^t F_0 \qquad (5.9)$$

Thus, the forecast for period t, calculated according to equation (5.4), includes all past actual demands, weighted exponentially, and some initial forecast F_0, also weighted. Note that

$$\sum_{n=0}^{t} \alpha(1-\alpha)^n = 1$$

That is, the sum of the weights is one and the weights decrease with age.

When the exponential smoothing is first used by the organization, the value of F_0 or the initial forecast may be obtained by using an estimate or an average demand during preceding periods.

EXAMPLE   POM Bakery is interested in forecasting the demand for cupcakes for January, 1979. The forecast for the month of December was 68 units. Actual demand in December was 65 units.

If POM's management is under the impression that the forecast for January, 1979, is highly related to the demand during the preceding month, December, then it will choose a high value of α, say $\alpha = 0.80$. Then

$$F_{\text{Jan.}} = \alpha D_{\text{Dec.}} + (1-\alpha)F_{\text{Dec.}}$$

$$= (0.80)(65) + (1 - 0.80)68 = 65.6 \text{ units}$$

This forecast is considerably below the actual demand; however, it does indicate an upward trend from December demand.[1]

Let us examine the weights that have been assigned to the different sales periods by the choice of $\alpha = 0.80$. As per our extended equation (5.9), the weight assigned to the month of December, which is the term indicated as D_{t-1} in the equation, is $(1-\alpha)^0 = 0.800$; the weight assigned to the month of November, which is the term indicated as D_{t-2} in the equation, is $\alpha(1-\alpha)^1 = 0.80\,(1-0.80)$

---

[1] Note that α may be changed as the pattern of demand changes.

= 0.160; the weight assigned to the month of October, which is the term indicated as D_{t-3} in the equation, is $\alpha(1 - \alpha)^2 = 0.80 (1 - 0.80)^2 = 0.032$; and so on. Note how fast the coefficients decrease (exponentially) as the averaging periods become more remote. The choice of a value for α determines this speed of decrease of the coefficients.

When initially using the exponential smoothing technique, one should choose an initial forecast, F_0, and a smoothing constant, α. A high value of α—say 0.7, 0.8, 0.9—is justified when the product's demand is unstable. This is the case when a new product is introduced to the market, when the market experiences technological breakthroughs, or when customer preferences change and affect sales of the forecast product's demand.

A low value of α—say 0.1, 0.2, 0.3—is justified when the demand is stable and, to the best of the forecaster's knowledge, future demand will remain fairly stable. A low value of α smoothes out random variations around the average.

Midrange values of α—say 0.4, 0.5, 0.6—are justified when the demand is somewhat unstable. Subjective judgment is the basis for the choice of the smoothing constant, but, basically, the faster the forecast should react to shifts in demand, the higher the value of α should be.

Figure 5.5 demonstrates the forecasting capability of low and high values of α when the demand pattern is unstable. It depicts the actual demand for rolls as well as the forecasts for $\alpha = 0.2$ and $\alpha = 0.8$. Note that $\alpha = 0.8$ provides a

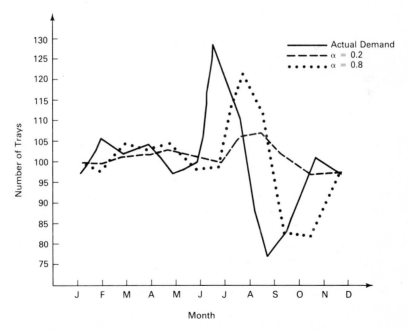

Figure 5.5 Actual Demand and Forecasts Based on Two Different Smoothing Constants for Rolls During 1979

TABLE 5.10   COMPARISON OF ACTUAL DEMAND AND FORECASTS BASED ON TWO DIFFERENT SMOOTHING CONSTANTS FOR ROLLS DURING 1979

MONTH	ACTUAL DEMAND	FORECAST ($\alpha = 0.2$)	FORECAST ($\alpha = 0.8$)
December, 1978	100	—	—
January, 1979	96	100.00*	100.00*
February	106	99.20	96.80
March	102	100.56	104.16
April	104	100.85	102.43
May	96	101.45	103.69
June	98	100.36	97.54
July	130	99.45	97.91
August	110	105.56	123.53
September	75	106.45	112.72
October	80	100.16	82.54
November	100	96.13	80.51
December, 1979	96	96.90	96.10

*The forecast for January, 1979, was assumed to be equal to the actual demand in December, 1978.

much better forecast, in that all up and down changes in the demand are identified quickly, and the actual demand can be forecasted more closely. In developing Figure 5.5, we assumed an initial forecast for January of 100 units.

The forecaster who needs to decide a value for α tests different values of α on historical data. The α that provides the best fit to the available data should be used for the actual forecasting procedure.

Simple exponential smoothing has become a widely used business forecasting technique. Many professional associations, including APICS (American Production and Inventory Control Society) and IIE (Institute of Industrial Engineers), have promoted the use of this technique through their newsletters and professional seminars.

There is another advantage of using this technique: few data points need to be kept on file. Only the last month's forecast and actual demand and the value of α are required.

Smoothing Techniques and Trend Analysis

When there is a definite trend in the data, the simple moving average and the first order exponential smoothing are not very useful. In these cases, one has to resort to some other techniques.

SECOND-ORDER (DOUBLE) EXPONENTIAL SMOOTHING TECHNIQUE
This Technique involves:

1. Computing the first-order exponentially smoothed value, as in the preceding section.

2. Computing another exponentially smoothed value using the first exponentially smoothed values as data.
3. Adjusting the value computed in (2) in order to account for the trend.

Table 5.11 shows an example of double exponential smoothing, for trays of doughnuts baked during 1979, for which a trend is realized for both the first and the second smoothing.

Column (2) shows the monthly demand for doughnuts; column (3) shows the first-order exponential smoothing forecast and column (4) shows the second-order exponential smoothing values, using the same $\alpha = 0.2$ (the appropriate value for α may be found by the criterion of minimizing the forecasting error, which is explained later in this chapter).

Column (4) gives the exponentially smoothed value of the data appearing in column (3).

The first-order exponentially smoothed value for March is:

$$F_{Mar.} = 0.2D_{Feb.} + (1 - 0.2)\,F_{Feb.} = 0.2(92) + (0.8)(87.00) = 88.00$$

If F^* will be taken to denote the second-order smoothing forecast, then for example,

$$F^*_{Mar.} = \alpha F_{Mar.} + (1 - \alpha)F^*_{Feb.}$$

$$= (0.2)(88.000) + (1 - 0.2)(87.000)$$

$$= 17.600 + 69.600$$

$$= 87.2000$$

TABLE 5.11 FORECASTING OF DEMAND FOR TRAYS OF DOUGHNUTS BAKED DURING 1979, USING SECOND-ORDER EXPONENTIAL SMOOTHING, $\alpha = 0.2$

(1) MONTH	(2) ACTUAL DEMAND	(3) FIRST-ORDER EXPONENTIAL SMOOTHING	(4) SECOND-ORDER EXPONENTIAL SMOOTHING	(5) VALUE OF A	(6) VALUE OF B	(7) VALUE OF $A + B$
J '79	87	—	—	—	—	—
F	92	87.000*	87.000	—	—	—
M	93	88.000	87.200	88.800	0.200	89.000
A	98	89.000	87.560	90.440	0.360	90.800
M	102	90.800	88.208	93.392	0.648	94.040
J	101	93.04	89.174	96.906	0.966	97.872
J	108	94.632	90.265	98.999	1.091	100.090
A	107	97.305	91.673	102.937	1.408	104.345
S	111	99.244	93.186	105.302	1.514	106.816
O	113	101.595	94.867	108.323	1.682	110.005
N	116	103.876	96.668	111.084	1.802	112.886
D	119	106.300	98.594	114.006	1.926	115.932

*The forecast for February is assumed to be equal to the actual demand in January.

Usually, if there is an upward trend, the first-order exponential forecast is below the actual values, and the second-order exponential forecast is below the first-order exponential forecast.

If there is a downward trend, then the first-order exponentially smoothed forecast is above the actual values and the second-order exponentially smoothed forecast is higher than the first-order exponential forecast.

In fact, the degree of difference between the actual values and the first-order exponential forecast is approximately the same as the difference between the first- and second-order exponential forecasts.

Next, one has to adjust the values to account for the trend. If one adds the difference between the first-order and second-order exponential forecasts (i.e., the difference between columns (3) and (4) in Table 5.11) to the first-order exponential value, one obtains a forecast that is very close to the actual demand. If there is a downward trend, one has to deduct the difference from the first-order exponential forecast. Column (5) then is calculated by adding the difference between columns (3) and (4) to column (3) (in Table 5.11). This yields a value called A.

For example:

$$A_{\text{Mar.}} = (F_{\text{Mar.}} - F^\star_{\text{Mar.}}) + F_{\text{Mar.}} = 2F_{\text{Mar.}} - F^\star_{\text{Mar.}}$$

$$= 2(88.000) - 87.200$$

$$= 88.800$$

A further refinement, which provides a more accurate forecast, involves the calculation of a value called B.

$$B = \frac{\alpha}{1 - \alpha} (F_t - F^\star_t)$$

The values of B are shown in column (6) of Table 4.11. For example:

$$B_{\text{Mar.}} = \frac{0.2}{1 - 0.2} (F_{\text{Mar.}} - F^\star_{\text{Mar.}})$$

$$= \frac{0.2}{1 - 0.2} (88.000 - 87.200)$$

$$= 0.2$$

The adjusted forecast is found by adding the value of A (column (5)) and B (column (6)), and is presented in column (7).

To forecast the demand more than one period hence, one has to multiply the adjustment factor B by the number of periods hence, and add this to A. The extension of column (7) is then:

$$F_t = A + BX$$

Where X is the number of periods hence.

For example, to forecast the demand for February of 1980 (two periods hence):

$$F_{\text{Feb.}} = 114.006 + 1.926(2) = 117.858$$

The further ahead the forecast, the greater the inaccuracy that can be expected. Again, one should experiment with several values of α and choose the one that minimizes the forecast error.

Second-order exponential smoothing is a technique superior to first-order exponential smoothing if there is a trend present in the demand pattern. It can forecast demand as well as can the first-order technique where there is no trend present.

Smoothing Techniques and Trend/Seasonality Analysis

When the demand presents a seasonal as well as a trend pattern, two alternative techniques may be used.

1. The seasonal pattern may be estimated independently, and an adjustment for the trend only can be applied to the seasonally adjusted data. This adjustment for the trend follows the first- or second-order exponential smoothing techniques described earlier.

2. Both the trend and the seasonal pattern may be adjusted (smoothed) simultaneously. This approach is preferred when the seasonality pattern is not stable.

The reader is encouraged to consult the references by Holt[2], and Winters[3] in regard to the first and second approaches.

FORECASTING TECHNIQUES—CAUSAL MODELS

These techniques are best for preparing long-range forecasts. While they are quite involved mathematically and may include considerable expense (as indicated in Table 5.4), they can follow turning points and result in more accurate forecasts than can the methods that have been covered so far.

A causal model recognizes the relationship between the forecast quantity and some other variable that accounts for the demand pattern. This other variable, which is called the independent variable, might be an economic indicator (Dow-Jones average, number of construction permits issued, etc.),

[2] C. C. Holt et al., *Planning Production, Inventories and Work Force,* (Englewood Cliffs, N.J.: Prentice-Hall, Inc., 1960).

[3] P. R. Winters, "Forecasting Sales by Exponentially Weighted Moving Averages," *Management Science,* vol. 6 (1960).

number of households, or some other market survey information. At times, one can use the calendar year as the independent variable, such as when one would like to fit an equation for a time series. The causal model takes into account events, such as strikes, promotion drives, and competitors' actions, that might have an impact on the forecast quantity. The causal model is an analytical equation that presents in a straightforward manner the relationship between underlying causes and the forecast.

Let us discuss a causal model termed Linear Regression Analysis.

Linear Regression Analysis

In regression analysis, one calculates mathematical relationships that give weights to indicators or variables. These indicators or variables are related to the product or product group's demand. For example, the number of actual air conditioning units that are sold in one year do have some relationship to the number of construction permits granted and also to the Gross National Product (GNP). Thus, it is possible to construct mathematical relationships that will take into account the number of construction permits and GNP level in order to forecast the number of air conditioning units that will be sold next year. This approach is particularly useful if the indicators, like construction permits, are "leading indicators"—that is, indicators that trend up or down before the sales of the air conditioning units react.

Instead of using an indicator as an independent variable, one may use the calendar month or the year as the independent variable. The calendar month or the year is then a surrogate variable, in that it substitutes an indicator but "behaves" in the same way. Let us discuss linear regression in such a case.

Let t represent the independent variable (the calendar month), and D_t represent the regressed (forecasted) demand. If the assumption is that the relationship between t and D_t can be described in a linear fashion, then:

$$D_t = D_0 + at \tag{5.10}$$

where D_0 is the intersection of the linear line with the demand axis and a is the slope of the line.

In order to find the best fit to the historical data, the values of D_0 and a are determined by minimizing the sum of the squares of the distances between the data points and the corresponding points on the assumed line. We demonstrate the technique in the following example.

EXAMPLE   Recapturing the data from Table 5.6, and marking the annual unit demand for cupcakes for the years 1975 through 1978, POM Bakery, Inc., is trying to forecast the 1979 annual demand using regression analysis.

The parameters of the linear line are found as follows:

$$a = \frac{\displaystyle\sum_{t=1}^{n} d_t t - n\bar{d}\bar{t}}{\displaystyle\sum_{t=1}^{n} t^2 - n\bar{t}^2} \tag{5.11}$$

$$D_0 = \bar{d} - a\bar{t} \tag{5.12}$$

where: D_0 = intercept of the y-axis (the demand axis)

a = the slope of the line

d_t = the actual annual demand in period t

$\bar{d}$ = the average of all d's

t = the time period (last two digits of the calendar year may be used without losing accuracy)

$\bar{t}$ = the average of all t's

n = the total number of periods on which the forecast is based

D_t = the annual demand in period t computed by using the regression equation (5.10)

Table 5.12 demonstrates the calculations. The results indicate that the line that can be used to forecast the annual demand is

$$D_t = -1,395.2 + 26.3t$$

If indeed that demand pattern is stable, then the forecast for the year 1979 can be found by

$$D_t = -1,395.2 + 26.3(79) = 682.5 \text{ units}$$

From Table 5.6, one can see that the actual annual demand for cupcakes was 825 during 1979, indicating a turn upwards in the demand that could not be

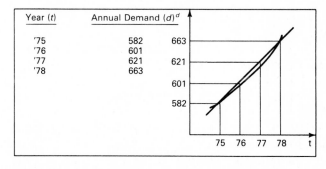

Figure 5.6   Annual Demand for POM Bakery's Cupcakes

TABLE 5.12 REGRESSION ANALYSIS OF POM BAKERY'S DEMAND FOR CUPCAKES

(1) DEMAND d_t	(2) YEAR t	(3) CALCULATIONS $(d_t)(t)$	(4) d_t^2	(5) t^2	(6) FROM EQUATION (5.10) $D_t = D_0 + at$ D
582	'75	43,650	338,724	5,625	$D_{75} = -1,395.2 + 26.3(75) = 577.3$
601	'76	45,676	361,201	5,776	$D_{76} = -1,395.2 + 26.3(76) = 603.6$
621	'77	47,817	395,614	5,929	$D_{77} = -1,395.2 + 26.3(77) = 629.9$
663	'78	51,714	439,569	6,084	$D_{78} = -1,395.2 + 26.3(78) = 656.2$
$\sum_{t=1}^4 d_t = 2,467$	$\sum_{t=1}^4 t = 306$	$\sum_{t=1}^4 (d_t)(t) = 188,857$	$\sum_{t=1}^4 d_t^2 = 1,525,135$	$\sum_{t=1}^4 t^2 = 23,414$	

$$\bar{t} = \frac{\sum_{t=1}^n t}{n} = \frac{306}{4} = 76.5$$

$$\bar{d} = \frac{\sum_{t=1}^n d_t}{n} = \frac{2,467}{4} = 616.75$$

$$a = \frac{\sum_{t=1}^n d_t - n\bar{d}\bar{t}}{\bar{t}^2 - n\bar{t}^2} = \frac{188,857 - 4(616.75)(76.5)}{23,414 - 4(76.5)^2} = 26.3$$

$$D_0 = \bar{d} - a\bar{t} = 616.75 - 26.3(76.5) = -1,395.2$$

indicated by using the historical data. One should note that the calendar year affects the sales, possibly through an increase in the size of the population. Another type of regression is obviously called for, possibly nonlinear (or curvilinear) regression, which is described later.

Even though the discussion of forecasting errors appears later in the chapter, it is of importance to take note of the following expression for standard error (SE) of the linear regression technique:

$$SE = \sqrt{\frac{\sum_{t=1}^{n} (d_t - D_t)^2}{n - 1}} \qquad (5.13)$$

Based on Table 5.12,

$$SE =$$

$$\sqrt{\frac{(582 - 577.3)^2 + (601 - 603.6)^2 + (621 - 629.9)^2 + (663 - 656.2)^2}{4 - 1}} = 7.17$$

The standard error can be alternatively expressed as

$$SE = \sqrt{\frac{\sum_{t=1}^{n} d_t^2 - D_0 \sum_{t=1}^{n} d_t - a \sum_{t=1}^{n} d_t t}{n - 1}}$$

Based on Table 5.12,

$$SE = \sqrt{\frac{1,525,135 - (-1,395.2)(2,467) - (26.3)(188,857)}{4 - 1}} = 7.17$$

The standard error expression is similar to the one used for the standard deviation. It serves as an indication of the degree of dispersion the data present around the "fitted" linear line.

Nonlinear Regression

So far we have considered linear regression—that is, data for which a linear relationship exists. However, some business variables may not have a linear form even when their logarithms are considered. Instead, they may be represented by various forms of polynomials as follows:

$$Y = a + bX + cX^2$$

$$Y = a + bX + cX^2 + dX^3$$

$$Y = a + bX + cX^2 + dX^3 + eX^4$$

where X is a variable that affects the demand, Y, and a, b, c, d, and e are coefficients.

Having established what type of relationship exists, least-square regression can then be used to establish the coefficients. For example, the regression equation may take the form

$$Y = a + bX + cX^2 + dX^3$$

where a, b, c, and d are the coefficients found by minimizing the difference between the forecast and the actual demand. If a linear relationship does not exist between the variables and if from both statistical and economic evidence it appears that a nonlinear (curvilinear) relationship may exist, then this method should be attempted for forecasting purposes.

EFFECTIVENESS OF FORECASTING TECHNIQUES

Since the forecast serves as a basis for diverse operational decisions and is, at times, crucial to the survival of the organization, forecasting effectiveness should be accounted for. Generally speaking, the very choice of the forecasting method has an impact on the forecasting error and thus on its effectiveness as is shown in Figure 5.7

The effectiveness of a forecasting technique is measured by:

1. The *bias* of the forecast, which indicates whether the forecast is too high or too low, on the average
2. The *consistency* of the forecast, which indicates the variability of the forecast error
3. The *correlation*, which indicates how strong the relationship between the forecast and the actual demand is
4. The *tracking signal*, which is used to monitor an implemented forecast technique.

Bias and Consistency

A bias error is present when a consistent difference is noted between the forecast and the actual demand. The bias error will be either an underestimation or an overestimation of the demand over several periods. Sources of bias error include using the wrong variables in the forecast, assuming the wrong relationships among variables, and disregarding a trend that influences the demand. The bias error can be calculated as follows:

$$\text{Bias} = \frac{\text{Summation of errors over all periods}}{\text{Number of periods used in forecasting}}$$

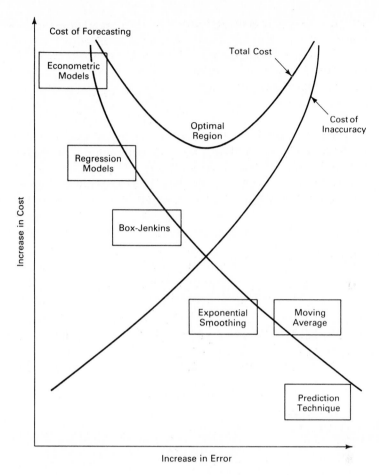

Figure 5.7   Cost of Forecasting and Cost of Error Tradeoff

$$\text{Bias} = \frac{\sum\limits_{t=1}^{n} (D_t - d_t)}{n} \qquad (5.14)$$

where:

n = number of periods used in forecasting

D_t = forecasted demand in period t, $1 \le t \le n$

d_t = actual demand in period t, $1 \le t \le n$

EXAMPLE   The regression line calculated in Table 5.12 is

$$D_t = -1,395.2 + 26.3t$$

This equation may be used to forecast the annual demands shown in Table 5.13. Let us assume that the actual demand is as listed in Table 5.13, in column (4). The calculation will follow:

$$\text{Bias Error} = \frac{-142.5 + 58.8 + 15.1 + 21.4}{4} = \frac{-47.2}{4} = -11.8$$

A negative value for the bias error indicates an underestimation of the demand. A positive value of the bias error indicates an overestimation of the demand. Thus, in the example above, an underestimation tendency is signaled, possibly because of the forecast error for 1979.

A correction for a consistent bias is easily implemented by adding or subtracting a constant from the forecast. However, when the forecast errors are not consistent, the correction becomes very involved. Most of the inconsistent forecast errors are random errors which are discussed in the following section.

RANDOM ERRORS   Random errors are errors that cannot be explained by any of the known components of demand (average, trend, seasonal variation, cyclic variation). The errors that can be measured are:

Standard error (SE)
Mean squared error (MSE)
Mean absolute deviation (MAD)

The *Standard Error* (SE) was defined earlier as

$$SE = \sqrt{\frac{\sum\limits_{t=1}^{n} (d_t - D_t)^2}{n-1}} \tag{5.15}$$

As in the case of a standard deviation, one can expect 99.7 percent of the actual demand values to fall within plus or minus three standard errors from the average demand during the period.

Another measure of error is the *mean squared error* (MSE). Simply stated, it is the mean of the squared difference of forecasted and actual demand for each time period.

TABLE 5.13   CALCULATION OF FORECAST AND BIAS ERROR

(1) CALENDAR YEAR	(2) t	(3) D_t	(4) d_t	(5) $(D_t - d_t)$
1979	79	682.5	825	−142.5
1980	80	708.8	650	58.8
1981	81	735.1	720	15.1
1982	82	761.4	740	21.4

$$\text{MSE} = \frac{\sum_{t=1}^{n} (d_t - D_t)^2}{n - 1} \tag{5.16}$$

The last measure of error to be discussed here is the *mean absolute deviation* (MAD). The MAD is the mean of the absolute value of the differences between the actual demand and the forecasted demand. The equation used to calculate the MAD is:

$$\text{MAD} = \frac{\sum_{t=1}^{n} |D_t - d_t|}{n} \tag{5.17}$$

For the last example,

$$\text{MAD} = \frac{|-142.5| + |58.8| + |15.1| + |21.4|}{4}$$

$$= \frac{142.5 + 58.8 + 15.1 + 21.4}{4} = 59.45 \text{ units}$$

The MAD does give the forecasting error to date, but it does not indicate the direction of the error. This is provided by the bias measure discussed above.

If the forecast errors are normally distributed, as they are for most forecasts, there is a relationship between the standard error (SE) and the mean absolute deviation (MAD):

$$\text{SE} = 1.25 \text{ (MAD)}$$

Therefore, only one of the two should be calculated from the raw data.

One should recall that the MAD is based on historical data. However, the forecaster is mostly interested in forecasting the next period's MAD in order to decide, for example, on a proper forecasting method. This can be done by following the simple exponential smoothing approach covered earlier:

$$\text{MAD}_t = \alpha |D_{t-1} - d_{t-1}| + (1 - \alpha) \text{MAD}_{t-1} \tag{5.18}$$

where:

MAD_t = forecast MAD for coming period t

α = smoothing constant (low values of α used)

D_{t-1} = forecast demand in period $(t - 1)$

d_{t-1} = actual demand in period $(t - 1)$

MAD_{t-1} = Forecast MAD for immediately preceding period

As in its use in forecasting, the exponentially smoothed MAD gives us a measure of the error for several periods hence. One may choose the forecasting technique that minimizes the MAD_t.

Correlation

A forecasting technique may be evaluated by checking how close the forecast is to the actual demand. The statistical tool used for that purpose is the correlation coefficient, R.

$$R = \frac{\text{covariance } (D,d)}{S_D \, S_d}$$

where:

$$d = \text{actual demand}$$

$$D = \text{the forecast}$$

$$\text{covariance } (D,d) = \frac{\sum_{t=1}^{n} (D_t - \overline{D}) (d_t - \overline{d})}{n - 1}$$

$$S_d = \sqrt{\frac{\sum_{t=1}^{n} (d_t - \overline{d})^2}{n - 1}}$$

$$S_D = \sqrt{\frac{\sum_{t=1}^{n} (D_t - \overline{D})^2}{n - 1}}$$

The value of the correlation coefficient, R, should be between $+1.00$ and -1.00. If the forecast and the actual demand are strongly correlated (that is, knowing the value of one, a person can accurately calculate the value of the second) the correlation coefficient equals $+1.00$ or -1.00. It is $+1.00$ if both move in the same direction. It is -1.00 if they move in opposite directions.

The forecast technique that should be used is the one that presents the highest correlation coefficient. Table 5.14 demonstrates the coefficient-of-correlation calculations for the data in Table 5.12.

The individual squared deviations for each variable, D and d, are summed in columns (5) and (7), and standard deviations, S_d and S_D are calculated. The product of the standard deviations divides the covariance, yielding $R = 0.978$. The value indicates a high correlation between the forecast and the actual demand.

Tracking Signal

The above measures, SE, MSE, MAD, and the correlation, are useful for choosing the forecasting technique but are computationally awkward for monitoring a forecasting technique that is already in use.

TABLE 5.14   CORRELATION COEFFICIENT CALCULATION FOR THE DATA OF TABLE 5.12

(1)	(2)	(3)	(4) FORE-CAST DEVIA-TION	(5)	(6) ACTUAL DEVIA-TION	(7)	(8) = (4) × (6)
CALEN-DAR YEAR	FORE-CAST D_t	AC-TUAL d_t	$D_t - \overline{D}$	$(D_t - \overline{D})^2$	$d_t - \overline{d}$	$(d_t - \overline{d})^2$	$(D_t - \overline{D})(d_t - \overline{d})$
1975	577.3	582	−39.45	1,556.30	−34.75	1,207.56	1,370.89
1976	603.6	601	−13.15	172.92	−15.75	248.06	207.11
1977	629.9	621	13.15	172.92	4.25	18.06	55.89
1978	656.2	663	39.45	1,556.30	46.25	2,139.06	1,824.56
TOTALS	2,467.0	2,467		3,458.44		3,612.74	3,458.45

$$\overline{D} = \frac{2,467.00}{4} = 616.75$$

$$\overline{d} = \frac{2,467}{4} = 616.75$$

$$\text{covariance } (D, d) = \frac{3,458.45}{3} = 1,152.817$$

$$S_D = \sqrt{\frac{\sum_{t=1}^{n}(D_t - \bar{D})^2}{n-1}} = \sqrt{\frac{3,458.44}{3}} = 33.95$$

$$S_d = \sqrt{\frac{\sum_{t=1}^{n}(d_t - \bar{d})^2}{n-1}} = \sqrt{\frac{3,612.74}{3}} = 34.702$$

$$R = \frac{\text{covariance } (D, d)}{S_D S_d} = \frac{1,152.817}{(33.95)(34.702)} = .978$$

The tracking signal is useful in monitoring forecast errors in an implemented forecasting technique. The calculation of the tracking signal, TS_n over n periods, is done by dividing the bias measure (equation (5.14)) by the MAD measure.

$$TS_n = \frac{\sum_{t=1}^{n}(D_t - d_t)/n}{\sum_{t=1}^{n}|D_t - d_t|/n} = \frac{\sum_{t=1}^{n}(D_t - d_t)}{\sum_{t=1}^{n}|D_t - d_t|}$$

When the forecast technique chosen is tracking the actual demand in an unbiased way, the tracking signal should be close to zero, as the numerator is close to zero.

When the forecast is consistently above the actual demand, the TS_n is $+1.0$. When the forecast is consistently below the actual demand, the TS_n is -1.0.

To summarize, the further away from zero the tracking signal, TS_n, is, the more bias exists in using the forecast techniques. The operations manager may choose maximum value for TS_n—say, TS. If the TS_n goes beyond TS, then the forecast technique is considered inadequate (biased) and should be changed. For example, the adjustment factor, α, may be restudied if the forecast technique is exponential smoothing. A common maximum value of TS is ±0.5.

Table 5.15 illustrates the use of the tracking signal. The cumulative sums of the deviation and the absolute deviation of the forecast from the actual demand are calculated. Then the ratio of the cumulative deviation in column (6) is divided by the cumulative absolute deviation in column (7), which results in the tracking signal in column (8).

The initial tracking signal value is always $+1.00$ or -1.00, and thus should be disregarded. The tracking signal is less than ±0.5 during 1976 and 1977. However, during 1978 and 1979, the actual demand changes significantly, although the forecast technique does not follow this change. This results in a TS_n value much below the maximum allowed value of TS $= (-0.5)$. One can assume that the forecasting technique should either be replaced or have its parameters changed.

CHOOSING A FORECASTING TECHNIQUE

In an effort to choose the most appropriate forecasting technique, the forecaster may compare several techniques by preparing a forecast by each of the techniques for several periods, and then comparing actual and forecasted values for the several periods. The best method is the one that minimizes the error.

However, the techniques tested should be those that have passed an initial screening performed by the forecaster and the forecast user. The screening involves answering the following questions:

1. *What is the purpose of the forecast?* The answer to this question determines the required sophistication of the technique. A most accurate forecast is required when the forecast is to be used for budgeting or costing purposes. This in turn calls for expensive forecasting techniques, such as regression analysis, that will result in a most accurate forecast. Once management has defined the purpose of the forecast, the forecasting frequency can be determined, as well as the best measure of the forecast error.

2. *What are the variables affecting demand, and how do they interact?* If there is a definite relationship among the different variables, the forecaster can recommend a causal technique as a basis for forecasting.

3. *How pertinent is past demand in forecasting the future?* Extensive promotion drives or major technological breakthroughs may change the pattern of demand

TABLE 5.15 CALCULATION OF TRACKING SIGNAL

(1) CALENDAR YEAR	(2) FORECAST D_t	(3) ACTUAL d_t	(4) DEVIATION $D_t - d_t$	(5) ABSOLUTE DEVIATION $|D_t - d_t|$	(6) CUMULATIVE DEVIATION	(7) CUMULATIVE ABSOLUTE DEVIATION	(8) = (6) ÷ (7) TRACKING SIGNAL TS_n
1975	110	100	10	10	10	10	1.00
1976	180	200	−20	20	−10	30	−3.33
1977	320	310	10	10	0	40	.00
1978	400	490	90	90	−90	130	−0.69
1979	510	590	80	80	−170	210	−0.81

$$TS_n = \frac{\sum_{t=1}^{n} (D_t - d_t)}{\sum_{t=1}^{n} |D_t - d_t|}$$

considerably. The effect of those changes and the implied demand change should be clearly defined in order to increase the reliability of the forecast.

DEVELOPING A WORKABLE FORECASTING SYSTEM

Production personnel, inventory control personnel, and marketing personnel should cooperate in determining the forecast. This cooperation provides checks and balances for the forecasting procedure. While production and inventory control personnel are able to base these forecasts on past historical demand by using techniques such as exponential smoothing or moving weighted average, the marketing people are able to base their forecast on external factors, such as promotion drives by the competition and new product-line acceptance.

In order to create a workable forecasting system, it is best to assign specific responsibilities as follows.[4]

1. The marketing people should forecast only product groups or promotion items and items for which a definite trend is expected or has been detected. (Items with no definite trend are assumed to be made for order.)

2. Production and inventory management people should be responsible for tracking forecasts, and for reporting deviations of a significant magnitude to the marketing people for interpretation.

3. Transformation of sales forecasts into production plans should be done by production and inventory control management, since, in order to level the capacity requirements, the production plan will not necessarily follow the sales forecast. Procedures to level the capacity requirements are described in chapter 6.

4. The expeditious interpretation of deviations from forecast, when reported, is the responsibility of the marketing people. Unless an interpretation has been put forward and revision was requested by the marketing people, production and purchasing will not stop.

In other words, a workable forecasting system is a system in which production and inventory personnel and marketing work together, in a coordinated effort, from the initial forecast, through actual production, down to forecasting revision, as required.

---

[4] For extended discussion, refer to Oliver W. Wight, *Production and Inventory in the Computer Age* (Boston: Cahners Books, 1974), pp. 164–167.

COMPUTERIZED FORECASTING MODELS

Forecasting is a natural tool of the operations manager. It is used to gain control, to manage, and to become prepared for the unexpected. The techniques presented in this chapter are useful but elaborate. The data base required for a decision may be large, and the calculations extensive.

Computerized, interactive, real-time programs can be useful in processing data as they come and in presenting the manager with forecasting alternatives. The computer executes all the necessary calculations and leaves to the manager the qualitative factors considerations.

Let us consider the example of an interactive computer program that has the capability of forecasting by use of five different forecasting methods. In Figure 5.8, an example presented earlier is solved using the computer.

The program indicates that the results are based on twelve periods of history, and the forecast is made for one period into the future. For period 13 (the month of January in our previous example) the forecast is 100.2 trays.

Let us summarize the forecasts made by the different methods for the 61st period for Product A. (Data provided in Table 5.5.)

Figure 5.8 An Interactive Computer Printout Using a Simple Average Forecasting Method (Note: The user entries are underlined.)

```
enter your name and the problem title or (stop)
(max of 80 characters)
? POM Bakery, Inc.

program forecasting for POM Bakery, Inc.
do you wish to change past data (y/n) ? y

same # of historical period (y/n) ? n

how many historical periods (1–99) ? 12

enter sales data for each period
period  1 ? 105

period  2 ? 65

period  3 ? 80

period  4 ? 75

period  5 ? 60

period  6 ? 122

period  7 ? 90
```

Figure 5.8 (Cont.)

period 8 ? 125

period 9 ? 120

period 10 ? 125

period 11 ? 115

period 12 ? 120

check your input: is it correct (y/n) ? y

program forecasting for POM Bakery, Inc.
history data for 12 periods

1	105.0
2	65.0
3	80.0
4	75.0
5	60.0
6	122.0
7	90.0
8	125.0
9	120.0
10	125.0
11	115.0
12	120.0

forecasting methods

(1) simple average   (2) regression
(3) seasonal average and regression
(4) moving average   (5) exponential smoothing

enter forecasting method (1–5) ? 1

enter no of future periods ? 1

forecasting results for POM Bakery, Inc.
program forecasting requests

type	future period		move	alpha
	ann	seasonal		
1	1	0	0	0.0000

mean forecast results
forecase based on 12 periods of history
forecast 1 period into future
period   forecast
  13   100.2

Method	Forecast
Simple average	104.5
Moving average (three months)	116.7
Moving average (six months)	105.0
Moving average (nine months)	102.2
Exponential smoothing ($\alpha = 0.50$)	114.0
Exponential smoothing ($\alpha = 0.80$)	115.9
Regression	100.4

Obviously, the operations manager can compute all those forecasts quickly by using his computer terminal and, after receiving the results, can make up his mind on the method. Computers are helpful in the calculation of forecasts because of the data requirements. Organizations have access to the programs that perform the techniques we have discussed.

SUMMARY

In virtually every design or planning decision made, the operations manager considers some kind of forecast. The operations manager is interested in the number of shipments that may be distributed the following week. The chain-saw manufacturer may be interested in the different item demand for each site, color, design, and price range during the next twelve months.

There are three kinds of forecasts: technological forecasts, economic forecasts, and item demand forecasts. The item demand forecast is treated extensively in this chapter.

Demand forecasting is a procedure for estimating a future event by casting forward past data that are combined in a predetermined way.

The multiplicity of variables that affect the demand for products and services makes the forecasting a difficult task. However, several forecasting methods have been presented: qualitative techniques, time series analysis and projection techniques, and causal models.

Basic to the use of forecasting methods presented in this chapter is the premise that past history is a reflection of several factors that will be at work in shaping the next period's demand.

The qualitative forecast methods should provide the manager with an initial forecast that should be augmented by using qualitative judgment that reflects accumulated experience.

The quantitative forecasting methods described in the chapter are: simple average, simple moving average, weighted moving average, exponential smoothing of the first and second order, and causal models. Each one of these techniques has its advantages and disadvantages and represent various degrees of computation complexity and data requirements.

We have also discussed effectiveness measures of forecasting techniques: bias, consistency, correlation, and tracking signals. These measures help in choosing the most adequate forecasting technique for a particular demand pattern, as well as in monitoring the performance of a forecasting technique that is currently in use.

Last, but not least, we have demonstrated the use of a conversational-mode computerized forecasting program. This program is of great help to the operations manager in designing and planning the operations system.

DISCUSSION QUESTIONS

5.1   Give five examples in which forecasting is required for operations planning.

5.2   What are the three kinds of forecasts required by the various economic sectors?

5.3   Compare and contrast the three kinds of forecasts.

5.4   What is an item demand forecast?

5.5   Define forecasting and prediction. Give examples of both.

5.6   What are the reasons for the differences in forecast horizons for different organizations?

5.7   What are the factors affecting the item demand?

5.8   What is the difference between independent and dependent demand?

5.9   Explain and name: qualitative forecasting techniques, time series analysis and projection techniques, causal models.

5.10   Explain and compare: simple average, simple moving average, weighted moving average, exponential smoothing.

5.11   Describe the linear regression analysis.

5.12   What is a bias error? Explain the physical meaning of a bias.

5.13   What are random errors? Explain the physical meaning of these errors.

5.14   What are the three questions the forecaster should answer in order to decide on the forecasting method?

PROBLEMS AND SOLUTIONS

5.1   The Carter Cartop Canoe Carrier Company experienced the following sales for their canoe carrier during their busiest time of year:

Month	Actual Demand
May	120
June	180
July	150

Forecasted demand for May was 80 units. Using exponential smoothing with $\alpha = 0.20$, forecast the demand for August.

Solution

$$F_t = \alpha D_{t-1} + (1 - \alpha) F_{t-1} \qquad\qquad \alpha = 0.20$$

$$F_{June} = 0.20(120) + 0.80(80) \quad = \ 88$$

$$F_{July} = 0.20(180) + 0.80(88) \quad = 106.4$$

$$F_{Aug.} = 0.20(150) + 0.80(106.4) = 115.12 = 115$$

5.2   A pharmaceutical company produces a costly chemical substance used in experiments conducted by medical research laboratories. The chemical is purchased by the laboratories daily, as it has a shelf life of only 24 hours. Daily required production of the substance is determined by a demand forecast. If the company underproduces and is unable to meet demand, company sales are adversely affected. If the company overproduces, extensive spoilage costs are incurred due to the substance's extremely limited shelf life. Thus, the manager of the company is highly concerned that the demand forecast be as accurate as possible.

The company presently uses a five-day simple moving average, but the manager has recently been confronted by an enthusiastic management science student who suggests that exponential smoothing may be a better approach. The manager has heard of exponential smoothing, but is still unsure of which method to use.

Using the following data, compare exponential smoothing (with $\alpha = 0.20$) to the company's present forecasting technique. Compare the two forecast methods based on the data given for Wednesday and Thursday. Justify your answer using MAD and recommend a method to the company manager.

PHARMACEUTICAL COMPANY DATA

Day	Actual Demand in Units	Company Forecast	Exponential Forecast*
Monday	260	210	
Tuesday	260	260	300
Wednesday	350	300	
Thursday	300	350	

* Initial exponential forecast assumed to be 300.

Solution

Exponential Smoothing Forecast	Company Forecast	Actual Demand
$F_{Wed.} = 0.20(260) + (1 - 0.20)\,300$ $\quad = \quad 52 \quad + \qquad 240$ $\quad = 292$	300	350
$F_{Thurs.} = 0.20(350) + (1 - 0.20)\,292$ $\quad = \quad 70 \quad + \qquad 233.6$ $\quad = 303.6$ $\quad \approx 304$	350	300

$$\text{Exponential smoothing MAD} = \frac{|292 - 350| + |304 - 300|}{2}$$

$$= \frac{58 + 4}{2} = \frac{62}{2} = 31$$

$$\text{Company forecast MAD} = \frac{|300 - 200| + |350 - 300|}{2}$$

$$= \frac{50 + 50}{2}$$

$$= 50$$

Based on Wednesday and Thursday, it is recommended that the company use the exponential smoothing method, since a MAD of 31 is lower than a MAD of 50.

5.3   Dionysus Table Wine Company experienced the following monthly demand during the first half of 1979 for two of their more successful products:

Month	Product 1 (Chateau Bleu)	Product 2 (Vintage Wednesday)
January	985	2800
February	1350	3375
March	1320	3300
April	1425	3560
May	1490	3725
June	1375	3440

Forecast the demand for July, using
a) A simple average.
b) A four-month simple moving average.
c) A four-month weighted moving average, using weights of 0.4, 0.3, 0.2, and 0.1, respectively, for the past four months (0.4 for the most recent one).
d) Single exponential smoothing with $\alpha = 0.20$, assuming actual demand for June was 1325 for Product 1 and 3305 for Product 2.
e) A linear regression analysis. Also, compute the standard error of estimate for the regression.

Solution
a) Simple average:

$$F_{n+1} = \frac{\sum\limits_{t=1}^{n} D_t}{n}$$

For Product 1:

$$F_{n+1} = \frac{985 + 1350 + 1320 + 1425 + 1490 + 1375}{6}$$

$$= \frac{7945}{6}$$

$$= 1324$$

For Product 2:

$$F_{n + 1} = \frac{2800 + 3375 + 3300 + 3560 + 3725 + 3440}{6}$$

$$= \frac{20200}{6}$$

$$= 3367$$

b) Four-month simple moving average:

$$F_{n + 1} = \frac{D_t + D_{t - 1} + D_{t - 2} + \ldots}{n} = \frac{\sum_{t = 1}^{n} D_t}{n}$$

For Product 1:

$$= \frac{1375 + 1490 + 1425 + 1320}{4}$$

$$= 1403$$

For Product 2:

$$= \frac{3440 + 3725 + 3560 + 3300}{4}$$

$$= 3506$$

c) Four-month weighted moving average:

$$F_{n + 1} = W_1 D_1 + W_2 D_2 + \ldots + W_n D_n = \sum_{t = 1}^{n} W_t D_t$$

For Product 1:

$$= (0.4)(1375) + (0.3)(1490) + (0.2)(1425) + (0.1)(1320)$$
$$= \quad 550 \quad + \quad 447 \quad + \quad 285 \quad + \quad 132$$
$$= 1414$$

For Product 2:

$$= (0.4)(3440) + (0.3)(3725) + (0.2)(3560) + (0.1)(3300)$$
$$= \quad 1376 \quad + \quad 1118 \quad + \quad 712 \quad + \quad 330$$
$$= 3536$$

d) Single exponential smoothing ($\alpha = 0.20$):

$$F_t = \alpha D_{t - 1} + (1 - \alpha) F_{t - 1}$$

For Product 1:

$$= 0.20 (1325) + [(1 - 0.20)(1375)]$$
$$= \quad 265 \quad + \quad 1100$$
$$= 1365$$

For Product 2:

$$= 0.20\ (3305) + [(1 - 0.20)(3440)]$$
$$= \quad 661 \quad + \quad 2752$$
$$= 3413$$

e) Linear regression analysis:

For Product 1:

Month (X)		Demand (Y)
Jan.:	1	985
Feb.:	2	1350
Mar.:	3	1320
Apr.:	4	1425
May:	5	1490
June:	6	1375

Calculations (numbers rounded):
D_0 : y-intercept = 1077
a : slope   = 71
Forecast for July (Period 7) = 1573

For Product 2:

Month (X)		Demand (Y)
Jan.:	1	2800
Feb.:	2	3375
Mar.:	3	3300
Apr.:	4	3560
May:	5	3725
June:	6	3440

Calculations (numbers rounded):
D_0 : y-intercept = 2916
a : slope   = 129
Forecast for July (Period 7) = 3819

Standard Error of Estimate for Linear Regression Analysis:

$$SE = \sqrt{\frac{\sum_{n=1}^{n} d^2 - D_0 \sum_{n=1}^{n} d - a \sum_{n=1}^{n} dt}{n-1}}$$

For Product 1:

Demand d	Month t	Calculations		
		dt	d^2	t^2
.985	1 (Jan.)	985	970225	1
1350	2 (Feb.)	2700	1822500	4
1320	3 (Mar.)	3960	1742400	9
1425	4 (Apr.)	5700	2030625	16
1490	5 (May)	7450	2220100	25
1375	6 (June)	8250	1890625	36
$\sum_{t=1}^{6} d = 7945$	$\sum_{t=1}^{6} t = 21$	$\sum_{t=1}^{6} dt = 29045$	$\sum_{t=1}^{6} d^2 = 10676475$	$\sum_{t=1}^{6} t^2 = 91$

$$D_0 = 1077$$

$$a = 71$$

$$SE = \sqrt{\frac{10676475 - [(1077)(7945)] - [(71)(29045)]}{6 - 1}}$$

$$= \sqrt{\frac{10676475 - 8556765 - 2062195}{5}}$$

$$= \sqrt{\frac{57515}{5}}$$

$$= 107.25$$

For Product 2:

Demand d	Month t	Calculations		
		dt	d^2	t^2
2800	1 (Jan.)	2800	7840000	1
3375	2 (Feb.)	6750	11390625	4
3300	3 (Mar.)	9900	10890000	9
3560	4 (Apr.)	14240	12673600	16
3725	5 (May)	18625	13875625	25
3440	6 (June)	20640	11833600	36
$\sum_{t=1}^{6} d = 20200$	$\sum_{t=1}^{6} t = 21$	$\sum_{t=1}^{6} dt = 72955$	$\sum_{t=1}^{6} d^2 = 68503450$	$\sum_{t=1}^{6} t^2 = 91$

$$D_0 = 2916$$

$$a = 129$$

$$\text{SE} = \sqrt{\frac{68503450 - (2916)(20200) - (129)(72955)}{6 - 1}}$$

$$= \sqrt{\frac{68503450 - 58903200 - 9411195}{5}}$$

$$= \sqrt{\frac{189055}{5}}$$

$$= 194.45$$

5.4   Calculate MAD and Bias using the following data:

Period	Forecasted Demand in Units	Actual Demand in Units
1	180	170
2	200	190
3	190	170
4	230	220
5	265	200
6	245	220

Solution

MAD = [|180 − 170| + |200 − 190| + |190 − 170| + |230 − 220| + |265 − 200| + |245 − 220|] ÷ 6 = 140/6 = $23\frac{1}{3}$.

Bias = [(180 − 170) + (200 − 190) + (190 − 170) + (230 − 220) + (265 − 200) + (245 − 220)] ÷ 6 = 140/6 = $23\frac{1}{3}$.

CHAPTER REVIEW PROBLEMS

5.1   The New Hampton General Merchandise Company had the following item demand during the past 6 months:

Month	Item Demand
July	5300
August	5422
September	5560
October	5600
November	5675
December	5784

The production manager of the company wants an item demand forecast for January based on this data, using the following forecasting techniques:

a) Simple average

b) Three-month simple moving average

c) Three-month weighted moving average, using weights of 0.25, 0.35, and 0.40 for October, November, and December, respectively.

5.2 The All-Write Pen Company manufactures gold-plated ballpoint pens that are distributed through major jewelry stores. The company has been using very subjective means of forecasting their demand. However, the current escalating fluctuations in the price of gold have resulted in the company's incurring extensive material costs and, consequently, an accurate demand forecast is essential. The company would therefore like to employ a more quantitative approach to forecasting, based on the following information for the past 12 months:

	Number of Cartons (24 pens per carton)	
Month	Forecasting Sales	Actual Sales
January	75	80
February	75	78
March	75	70
April	75	65
May	90	85
June	100	125
July	100	103
August	90	85
September	90	115
October	90	95
November	100	98
December	145	153

Forecast the demand for next month, based on the above information, using:

a) Three-month simple moving average

b) Six-month simple moving average

c) Twelve-month average. What can be concluded from including a larger number of periods in calculating the average?

d) Four-month weighted moving average using weights of 0.1, 0.2, 0.3 and 0.4 for the months of December, November, October, and September, respectively

e) Exponential smoothing, using $\alpha = 0.70$. Do you think this is a good indicator of company sales, given the above information?

5.3 A single product manufacturer makes a weekly forecast for production planning purposes. Production had been forecast for last week at 6500 units; however, only 5800 units were actually demanded.

a) Using exponential smoothing with $\alpha = 0.30$, calculate the manufacturer's production forecast for this week.

b) This week's demand turned out to be exactly 6000 units. What would the production forecast be for the following week?

c) Calculate MAD and the Bias for the two weeks forecasted.

5.4   An automobile-parts wholesaler had the following demand over the past 6 months:

Month	Number of Items Sold
July	5747
August	5361
September	5580
October	5879
November	5236
December	5083

Using regression analysis, forecast demand for the next 6 months.

5.5   A photographic processing lab must determine a demand forecast for next month. The number of batches processed over the past 6 weeks is as follows:

Week	Number of Batches
6 weeks ago	15
5 weeks ago	18
4 weeks ago	14
3 weeks ago	25
2 weeks ago	18
1 week ago	20

a) Determine a forecast for next month's production, using linear regression analysis.

b) Compute the standard error of estimate for the weekly forecast.

5.6   Tedium, Incorporated, makes boring games for active people who need to slow down. The company's quarterly demand for "Audit Trail," the party game for Accountants, was as follows:

Month	Actual Demand
January	550
February	585
March	560

Forecasted demand for the first month was 500 units.

Using exponential smoothing, with $\alpha = 0.30$, determine a demand forecast for April.

5.7   Silly Sally and Crazy Jane own a clothing store called "The Silly Sally and Crazy Jane Clothing Store." One day, Silly Sally and Crazy Jane were commenting on how fast a new shirt has been selling. "It's really crazy," said Silly Sally. "Yeah, it's really silly," said Crazy Jane. Crazy Jane and Silly Sally need a demand forecast for July, based on sales for the first six months of the current year, as shown in the following chart:

Month	Actual Demand
January	435
February	420
March	485
April	510
May	465
June	450

Prepare a demand forecast for July, using the following forecasting methods:
a) Three-month moving average
b) Six-month average
c) Four-month weighted moving average, using weights of 0.4, 0.3, 0.2, and 0.1 respectively, beginning with the most recent month (0.4 weight assigned to June)
d) Linear regression analysis.

5.8 A professor at a northern university had the following nationwide sales of his first textbook during the academic year just completed:

Month	Sales
Jan.	5000
Feb.	2000
Mar.	1000
Apr.	1000
May	3000
June	1000
July	2000
Aug.	4000
Sept.	9000
Oct.	7000
Nov.	2000
Dec.	4000

The publisher of the text anticipates enrollment in classes using this text to increase by 20 percent next year.
a) Prepare a monthly estimate of sales for next year.
b) Why is such a breakdown required?

5.9 A salesman of commercial restaurant supplies believes that the growth of his business is somehow related to the dollar volume and number of nonresidential building permits issued in his sales area. He further believes that the demand for his services will increase by 30 percent over the next year. Using the linear regression method, fit a line to the data below and project one year into the future. Is the salesman correct?

Month	$ Volume	# Permits
Jan.	75,000	6
Feb.	85,000	6
Mar.	92,000	8

Month	$ Volume	# Permits
Apr.	112,000	13
May	154,000	23
June	143,000	18
July	119,000	15
Aug.	121,000	17
Sept.	83,000	8
Oct.	68,000	7
Nov.	53,000	3
Dec.	21,000	2

5.10   In December of this year, the Corporate Planning Committee of the Atlas Corporation was trying to develop an item demand forecast for its best-selling product after January. During the current year, the company forecast the monthly demand as follows:

Month	Demand (number of units)
Jan.	185
Feb.	185
Mar.	190
Apr.	195
May	270
June	210
July	245
Aug.	200
Sept.	130
Oct.	120
Nov.	145
Dec.	185

(The number of units actually demanded in December was 170.)

Forecast the demand for January, using:
a) Simple average
b) Four-month simple moving average
c) Four-month weighted moving average, using weights of 0.4, 0.3, 0.2 and 0.1, respectively (0.4 weight to the most recent month)
d) Single exponential smoothing, with a weight factor of 0.30
e) Linear regression analysis.

5.11   The Bowmont Motorcycle Company wants a demand forecast for the seventh and eighth week, of the current period. Weekly demand for the past six weeks was:

Week	Demand
1	11
2	13
3	11
4	19
5	15
6	17

a) Calculate a three-week weighted moving average forecast for the seventh and eighth weeks. The most recent week's demand must have a weight three times as heavy as each of the previous two weeks' demands.

b) Repeat part (a), using linear regression analysis.

5.12 The Great Canadian Chinese Food and Pizza Chalet is a highly successful restaurant. Recently it has been experiencing stock shortages due to errors in forecasting. The following chart is a tally of the number of people served in June during the peak weekend periods.

Day	1st Week	2nd Week	3rd Week	Last Week
Friday	1285	1214	1411	898
Saturday	1325	1108	1649	996
Sunday	900	851	991	948

Prepare a forecast for next Friday, Saturday, and Sunday, using:

a) A simple four-week moving average.

b) A weighted average of 0.5, 0.3, 0.10, and 0.10, respectively, for the past four weeks. (0.5 assigned for the first week)

c) A linear regression analysis.

READING
Why Forecasters Really Blew It in 1982

The path of economic activity over the past few years has been sharply different from forecasters' expectations. But this past year was particularly vexing. Even as late as mid 1981, when the economy was sliding into recession, few economic shamans were expecting a recession for the second half of the year.

At yearend they generally agreed that the recession would be over by spring and that business would show a brisk second-half recovery. As it turned out, the current recession will probably go down as the worst in postwar history.

According to the concensus of last year's BUSINESS WEEK survey, real GNP was expected to grow about 3% from the fourth quarter of 1981 to the final period of 1982. However, the final tally will probably show a decline. The rise in the overall level of prices will come in at about 5%, well under the forecast rate of 7.2%. And the unemployment rate will average much higher than the projected 8.5%.

AN UNEQUAL CONTEST   The 1982 forecasts were off the mark because economists underestimated the devastating impact of the Fed's attempt to adhere to specific monetary targets. The clash between tight monetary policy and loose fiscal policy demonstrated that it was an unequal contest. Tight money policy undercut the most expansive fiscal policy of modern times.

Most forecasters remained stubborn in their belief that recovery would come in the second half. As late as July, 1982, the consensus of "blue chip" forecasters assembed by Eggert Economic Enterprises Inc. was for tidy growth of nearly 4% in both the third and fourth quarters. Growth in the second half evidently turned out to be about zero.

Not all economists followed the crowd, of course. Of 30 whose forecasts appeared in last year's compilation, Irwin L. Kellner, a senior vice-president and economist at Manufacturers Hanover Trust Co., and S. Jay Levy, who publishes an economics letter, Industry Forecast, both appreciated the effect of the Fed's policies. They accurately forecast that the second half of 1982 will be weak, with the final quarter ending on the downside. Their forecasts for 1983? Business will be sluggish in the first half and pick up moderately in the second—essentially the standard forecast of economists.

Questions

1. This chapter has described several components of demand. Which of these components have been affected by the recession of 1982?
2. Based on the article, describe how an individual organization can incorporate the general business cycle forecasts into its own demand forecast?
3. It has been stated in the chapter that the use of time series analysis should include a consultation of leading indicators whenever possible in order to identify a change of direction in the trend. Can you qualify this statement based on the article you have just read?

BIBLIOGRAPHY

ADAM E. E., JR., and R. J. EBERT, "A Comparison of Human and Statistical Forecasting," *AIIE Transactions*, Vol. 8, No. 1, March, 1976, pp 120–127.

AHL, D. H., "New Product Forecasting Using Consumer Panels," *Journal of Marketing*, Vol. 7, No. 2, May, 1970, pp. 159–67.

BARCLAY, A. G., "Easy Way to Better Trend Lines," *Industrial Engineering*, Vol. 9, No. 1, January, 1977, pp. 32–37.

BENTON, W. K., *Forecasting for Management*. Reading, Mass.: Addison-Wesley, 1972.

BOX, G. E. P., and G. M. JENKINS, *Time Series Analysis, Forecasting and Control* (revised edition). San Francisco: Holden-Day, 1976.

CHAMBERS, J. S., S. K. MULLICK, and D. D. SMITH, "How to Choose the Right Forecasting Technique," *Harvard Business Review*, Vol. 49, No. 4, July–August, 1971, pp. 55–64.

GILCHRIST, W., *Statistical Forecasting*. New York: John Wiley and Sons, 1976.

LEWIS, C., *Demand Analysis and Inventory Control*. Lexington, Mass.: Saxon House, 1975.

MABERT, V. A., *An Introduction to Short-Term Forecasting Using the Box-Jenkins Methodology*, AIIE Monograph, AIIE–PP&C–75–1, Norcross, Georgia, 1975.

MAKRIDAKIS, S., and S. C. WHEELWRIGHT, *Forecasting: Methods and Applications*. Santa Barbara: Wiley/Hamilton, 1978.

MAKRIDAKIS, S., and S. C. WHEELWRIGHT, *Interactive Forecasting* (2nd edition). San Francisco: Holden-Day, 1978.

MONTGOMERY, D. C., and I. A. JOHNSON, *Forecasting and Time Series Analysis*. New York: McGraw-Hill, 1976.

PARKER, G. C., and E. L. SEGURA, "How to Get a Better Forecast," *Harvard Business Review*, Vol. 49, No. 2, March–April 1971, pp. 99–109.

ROBERTS, S. D., and R. REED, "The Development of a Self-Adaptive Forecasting Technique," *AIIE Transactions*, December, 1969, pp 314–322.

SCHEUING, E. E., *New Product Management*. Hinsdale, Illinois: Dryden Press, 1974.

SULLIVAN, W. G., and W. W. CLAYCOMBE, *Fundamentals of Forecasting*. Reston, Va.: Reston Publishing, 1977.

WHEELWRIGHT, S. C., and S. G. MAKRIDAKIS, *Forecasting Methods for Management*. New York: John Wiley and Sons, 1973.

WHEELWRIGHT, S. C., and D. G. CLARKE, "Corporate Forecasting: Promise and Reality," *Harvard Business Review*, November–December, 1976, pp. 47–48, 47, 60, 64, 198.

WHEELWRIGHT, S. E., and S. MAKRIDAKIS, *Forecasting Methods for Management* (2nd ed.). New York: John Wiley & Sons, 1977.

WHYBARK, D. CLAY, "A Comparison of Adaptive Forecasting Techniques," *The Logistics and Transportation Review*, Vol. 8, No. 3, 1972, pp. 13–26.

WIGHT, O. W., *Production and Inventory Management in the Computer Age*. Boston: Cahhers Brooks, 1974.

WINTERS, P. R., "Forecasting Sales by Exponentially Weighted Moving Average," *Management Science*, Vol. 6, 1960.

6

Aggregate Planning

INTRODUCTION

There are three levels of planning that concern the operations manager: long-range planning (strategic decisions, such as introducing new products or processes, and locating of facilities); short-term planning (scheduling); and, between these two extremes, intermediate planning, or *aggregate planning*. Aggregate planning involves the structuring of a general plan for responding to forecasted demand through some combination of work force, output, and inventory loadings. One can perceive aggregate planning as a macro-approach to the development of a production plan. This plan allows upper-level management to make decisions regarding the use of resources without getting into the details of daily schedules and job assignments.

THE NATURE OF AGGREGATE PLANNING

Aggregate planning is the term coined to describe the formulation of general strategies by which capacity can be made to satisfy demand in a most economical way during a specific time period. The common time period is up to a year into the future.

Aggregate planning is closely related to other corporate functions, such as budgeting, personnel, and marketing. Corporate budgets are based on the aggregate output, size of work force, inventory contol, and purchasing level. An

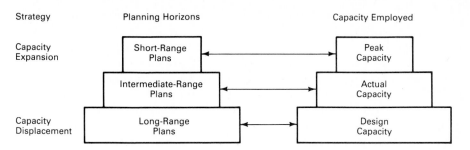

| Strategy | Planning Horizons | Capacity Employed |

Figure 6.1 The Capacity and Planning Hierarchies and the Relationship Between the Two

aggregate plan should, then, serve as the basis for budget development and budget revisions.

Personnel planning is affected by aggregate planning because aggregate planning results in hiring, firing, and overtime decisions. In service industries, where inventory of completed services cannot be stored, budgeting and personnel planning are the only two functions that are treated through aggregate planning.

The marketing function is intimately related to aggregate planning because the supply of products and services is determined through such planning. The marketing department may influence future demand and thus create aggregate planning alternatives to supply the forecasted demand.

Thus, while aggregate planning is a primary responsibility of the management department, it requires the cooperation and coordination of many other corporate departments. The remainder of this chapter is devoted to a discussion of decision options, strategies, and methods that are used in aggregate planning.

DECISION OPTIONS

The formulation of strategies by which capacity can be made to satisfy demand in a most economical way involves various decision options. These decision options are basically of two types:

1. Those that modify the demand for products and services.
2. Those that modify the supply of products and services.

The demand for products and services can be modified through differential pricing, promotion, creation of backlog, and development of complementary products and services. Let us explain each of the decision options in detail.

Differential pricing is used to level peak demand or increase demand during off-peak periods. Off-season hotel rates, airline night flight rates, and warehouse discounts for consumer products are several examples.

Promotion drives are used to increase demand during slack periods or to smooth out demand during peak periods. For example, clothing manufacturers promote the purchase of summer clothing during the winter season.

The *creation of backlogs,* in which customers are asked to wait for the delivery of products and services, shifts demand from peak periods to periods with slack capacity. At times, however, this decision option may cause customer dissatisfaction.

The development of complementary products and services that can be produced during slack periods helps smooth out capacity. A producer of water heaters may start producing air conditioners, a chain-saw manufacturer may start producing emergency generators, and a fast-food store may implement a breakfast service in order to utilize its capacity during the morning slack period.

It should be noted that since service organizations cannot carry inventory of services, they use extensively all the above mentioned options in order to influence the demand for services.

The supply of products and services can be modified through hiring and laying-off of employees, using overtime and shorter working days, using part-time labor, carrying inventory, and using subcontractors. Let us explain each of these particular decision options in detail.

Hiring and laying-off of employees affect labor relations, productivity, and workers' morale. As such, companies consider this option carefully in light of union standing and the structure of the work force.

The savings resulting from a temporary reduction in the size of the work force may be outweighed by the expense involved in rehiring and reduced morale and productivity.

Overtime and shorter working days or weeks is a common option used in cases of temporary changes in demand. Overtime is an expensive option as it costs 150 percent of regular time and 200 percent on weekends. Furthermore, workers might be reluctant to work overtime for an extended period of time. Shorter work days or work weeks, or, alternatively, a reduction of the pace of work during regular time is also termed undertime.

Part-time labor is used extensively by service organizations (such as restaurants, hospitals, and department stores) to accommodate periods of peak demand. Wages paid to part-time employees are lower and the terms of employment are flexible to accommodate varying supply requirements.

Carrying inventory is an option that is highly used by manufacturing organizations. During slack periods, production overflow is stored as subassemblies or completed products, to accommodate the supply during peak periods. Service organizations, by and large, cannot store completed services and thus cannot use this option to affect supply.

Subcontracting involves the use of other organizations to supply the entire product, subassembly, or component. For example, a linen manufacturer may use a dye-house organization as a subcontractor; a word-processing service house may subcontract some typing work; an electric utility company may be hooked up to another utility network to increase supply during peak period.

AGGREGATE PLANNING COSTS

If demand is considered given, there are several cost components that are considered when deciding on an appropriate aggregate plan. These cost components are discussed below.

Hiring and laying-off of employees costs include the cost of recruiting, screening, and training that are required to break in a new employee. For low-skill jobs this cost might be a few hundred dollars; for high-skill jobs, it might be in the thousands. The laying-off of employees includes the cost of employee benefits and severance pay.

Overtime and shorter work week costs include the extra fifty to one hundred percent added compensation for overtime and the costs of carrying full-time employees while utilizing them on a part-time basis.

Inventory carrying costs include the cost of capital, opportunity costs, variable storage costs, obsolescence, shrinkage, and deterioration. These costs are expressed as a percentage of the value of inventory, and may require from fifteen to forty-five percent a year. Thus, if the unit value held in inventory is $100 and the total carrying cost is forty-five percent of the value of the unit, it costs $45 to hold one unit in inventory for one year.

Subcontracting costs are the price paid to a subcontractor for the production of a unit to the original manufacturer's specifications.

Part-time labor costs are generally lower than the costs involved in keeping a full-time employee on a payroll. However, the amount of part-time labor should be monitored closely.

Cost of backorders includes the costs involved in reduced customer service through a loss of goodwill, possible loss of future sales, reprocessing (paperwork) costs, shipping costs, communications costs (phones, letters), expediters' costs, and customer liaison costs.

Any aggregate planning case should consider the above costs. They form the basis for the budgeting of alternative courses of action.

AGGREGATE PLANNING STRATEGIES

There are two basic aggregate planning strategies that may be used to meet fluctuating demand. One basic strategy is to *level the size of the workforce* used and the other is to *chase the demand* by varying the work force size.

When the work force is kept constant over time, any variation in demand is accommodated by using inventories, overtime, and part-time workers, and by subcontracting, as well as by advertising and promoting to influence the demand.

When the work force is changed continuously (chasing demand) to meet the variation in the demand, inventory is kept to a minimum. Overtime, part-time workers, and subcontracting are also kept to a minimum.

Obviously, any combination of the two basic strategies may be used. Different departments within the same organization may also use different approaches to meet varying demand. For example, a software and computer service house that provides systems analysis, programming, keypunching, and other computer services is using a constant number of highly skilled programmers and systems analysts for software development, and may vary the number of keypunch operators to chase the demand for keypunch services.

The particular strategy used should be selected on a basis of a cost criterion. The alternative strategies may be evaluated by using various methods. In the following section, we shall present several aggregate planning methods that can be used for the development and the evaluation of various aggregate planning strategies.

GRAPHIC AND CHARTING METHODS FOR AGGREGATE PLANNING

These methods consist of the development of simple tables and graphs that enable the operations manager to compare and contrast forecasted demand with existing capacity. This comparison gives the operations manager the basis for developing plans to achieve intermediate-range objectives. The alternative plans are evaluated in terms of their overall costs. The major disadvantage of graphic and charting methods is that they do not necessarily result in the optimum aggregate plan.

These methods involve the following steps:

1. Determine demand for each period.
2. Determine capacity for each period of regular time, overtime, and subcontracting. (The reader should consult the definitions of capacity stated in Chapter 2.)
3. Determine unit cost for regular time, overtime, subcontracting, and inventory holding cost.
4. Determine companywide or departmental policies that are followed (e.g., level of safety stock, maximum level of inventory, and preferred work force size).
5. Develop alternative plans and compute the cost of each.
6. If satisfactory plans emerge, select the best one. Otherwise, return to step 5.

A *working sheet* like the one in Figure 6.4 might be helpful in summarizing demand forecasting and capacities for each time period. The quantities are entered and the total costs are calculated based on working sheets prepared for each alternative. A comparison of total costs indicates the best alternative.

Let us work out an example to demonstrate the use of these techniques. The methods involve repeated costing of various aggregate planning strategies, in which chasing demand, level work force, and other mixed strategies are considered and the least expensive one is chosen.

EXAMPLE   The Rival Manufacturing Company, a manufacturer of can openers, is constructing an aggregate plan for the next twelve months. Although several sizes of openers are produced at the Rival plant, management has decided to use the number of can openers as the aggregate measure of capacity.

Table 6.1 depicts the fluctuating demand that is marked by a well-defined seasonal pattern with a cycle of 12 months. Management has decided to maintain always some extra openers in stock to hedge against unforeseen increases in demand. This stock is termed safety stock and is set to be 25 percent of the forecasted demand.

The safety stock in column (4) serves as the beginning inventory of the following month. It is also known that the beginning inventory for the month of January is 100 units. The cumulative demand is calculated in column (3).

The monthly production requirement in column (5) is simply the forecasted demand plus the required safety stock (4) minus the beginning inventory (1). Also given are the number of working days, excluding weekends, holidays and shut-downs for maintenance. The daily production requirements are calculated in column (9).

The management of Rival Manufacturing Company would like to consider three aggregate planning strategies:

Strategy 1. Produce each month an amount equal to the exact production requirements, by varying the size of the work force over regular hours.

Strategy 2. Maintain the work force at a level corresponding to the average monthly production requirement.

Strategy 3. Reduce the size of the work force to an arbitrary number—say, 10—of workers, and subcontract excess production required.

To evaluate the three strategies, Rival's management collected the following required costs and resource data:

Variable production cost	$200/unit
Inventory costs	$3/unit/month
Hourly wage	$12/hour
Overtime wage rate	$18/hour
Stockout cost	$10/unit/month

TABLE 6.1 PRODUCTION REQUIREMENTS BASED ON THE FORECASTED DEMAND

MONTH	(1) BEGINNING INVENTORY	(2) FORE-CASTED DEMAND	(3) CUMU-LATIVE DEMAND	(4) SAFETY** STOCK 0.25 × (2)	(5) MONTHLY PRODUCTION REQUIREMENTS (2) + (4) − (1)	(6) CUMULATIVE PRODUCTION REQUIREMENTS	(7) MONTHLY WORKING DAYS	(8) CUMU-LATIVE WORKING DAYS	(9) DAILY PRODUCTION REQUIREMENTS (5) ÷ (7)
January	100*	1,000	1,000	250	1,150	1,150	20	20	57.5
February	250	700	1,700	175	625	1,775	19	39	32.9
March	175	500	2,200	125	450	2,225	21	60	21.4
April	125	300	2,500	75	250	2,475	22	82	11.4
May	75	500	3,000	125	600	3,075	21	103	28.6
June	125	900	3,900	225	1,000	4,705	20	123	50.0
July	225	1,000	4,900	250	1,025	5,100	20	143	51.2
August	250	1,200	6,100	300	1,250	6,350	19	162	65.8
September	300	1,400	7,500	350	1,450	7,800	21	183	69.0
October	350	1,500	9,000	375	1,525	9,325	22	205	69.3
November	375	1,300	10,300	325	1,250	10,575	21	226	59.5
December	325	1,200	11,500	300	1,175	11,750	20	246	58.8

*Beginning inventory for the month of January is the closing inventory of December.

**Management decision.

240

Subcontracting cost	$212/unit
Hiring and training costs	$1,000/worker
Layoff costs	$1,800/worker
Labor content	10/hours/unit
Number of workers currently employed	40/workers

The costing of each one of the strategies is the next step. Please note that strategy 2 involves the maintenance of a work force at a level corresponding to the average monthly production requirement. Thus, the work force size required is

[Annual production requirements × Hours per unit]

÷ [Total working days × 8 Hours per day]

= [11,750 × 10] ÷ [246 × 8] = 59.7 ≈ 60 workers.

This work force size assures meeting the cumulative production requirements by the end of the planning period. However, one can expect inventory to accumulate during some months, and shortages to occur during some others. Shortages are assumed to be filled from the next month's production.

Figure 6.2 presents the daily production requirements and daily production rate of the three strategies. Figure 6.3 presents the cumulative production required. Note that whenever the cumulative production line is above the line indicating the cumulative production requirement, inventory of units is accumulated. Whenever the cumulative production line is below the line indicating the

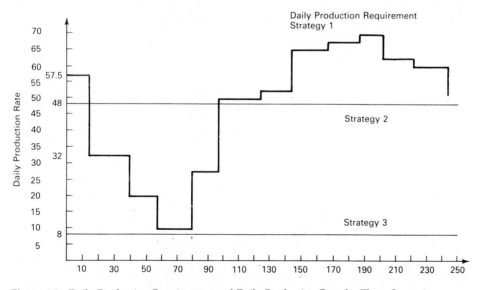

Figure 6.2 Daily Production Requirement and Daily Production Rate for Three Strategies

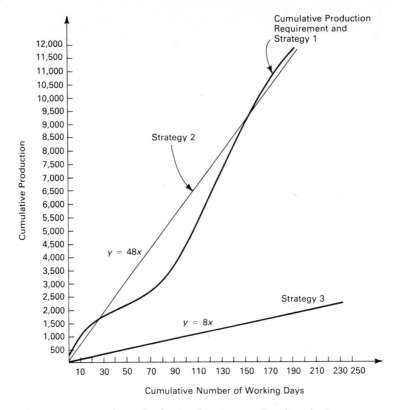

Figure 6.3 Cumulative Production Requirement Based on the Forecast

cumulative production requirement, one must deplete inventory and resort to subcontracting to supplement plant capacity.

The costs involved in each of the alternative strategies are presented in Tables 6.2, 6.3, and 6.4. The annual costs of each strategy are collected and summarized in Table 6.5. Based on the assumptions used, strategy 1, in which the work force size is varied, has the highest penalties. This could be expected. Strategy 3, in which a minimal work force is kept and overflow production requirements are subcontracted, is somewhat more economical. The best strategy is strategy 2, with a cost of $34,513.

MATHEMATICAL METHODS

There are various mathematical methods that have been developed to help in aggregate planning. In this section, we shall present some general mathematical relationships. This will be followed by some presentation and survey of specific methods.

Let us use the following symbols to formulate the aggregate planning problem:

TABLE 6.2 AGGREGATE PLAN: STRATEGY 1

	(1) MONTHLY PRODUCTION REQUIREMENT	(2) PRODUCTION HOURS REQUIRED (1) × 10	(3) AVAILABLE HOURS PER WORKER PER MONTH (days × 8)	(4) WORKERS REQUIRED* (2) ÷ (3)	(5) WORKERS HIRED	(6) HIRING & TRAINING COST (5)($1,000)	(7) WORKERS LAID OFF	(8) LAYOFF COSTS (7)($1,800)
January	1,150	11,500	160	72	32	32,000	—	—
February	625	6,250	152	42	—	—	30	54,000
March	450	4,500	168	27	—	—	15	27,000
April	250	2,500	176	15	—	—	12	21,600
May	600	6,000	168	36	21	21,000	—	—
June	1,000	10,000	160	63	27	27,000	—	—
July	1,025	10,250	160	65	2	2,000	—	—
August	1,250	12,500	152	83	18	18,000	—	—
September	1,450	14,500	168	87	4	4,000	—	—
October	1,525	15,250	176	87	—	—	—	—
November	1,250	12,500	168	75	—	—	12	21,600
December	1,175	11,750	160	74	—	—	1	1,800
						$104,000		$126,000

*Rounded to the next higher whole number.

TABLE 6.3 AGGREGATE PLAN: STRATEGY 2

	(1) CUMULATIVE PRODUCTION REQUIRED	(2) WORKING HOURS AVAILABLE (DAYS × 8 × 60 WORKERS)	(3) NUMBER OF UNITS PRODUCED (2) ÷ 10	(4) CUMULATIVE PRODUCTION	(5) NUMBER OF UNITS SHORT (1) − (4)	(6) STOCKOUT COST (5) × $10	(7) NUMBER OF UNITS TO INVENTORY (4) − (1)	(8) INVENTORY COST (7) × $3
January	1,150	9,600	960	960	190	1,900	—	—
February	1,775	9,120	912	1,872	—	—	97	291
March	2,225	10,080	1,008	2,880	—	—	655	1,965
April	2,475	10,560	1,056	3,936	—	—	1,461	4,383
May	3,075	10,080	1,008	4,944	—	—	1,869	5,607
June	4,075	9,600	960	5,904	—	—	1,829	5,487
July	5,100	9,600	960	6,804	—	—	1,704	5,112
August	6,350	9,120	912	7,776	—	—	1,426	4,278
September	7,800	10,080	1,008	8,784	—	—	984	2,952
October	9,325	10,560	1,056	9,840	—	—	515	1,545
November	10,575	10,080	1,008	10,848	—	—	273	819
December	11,750	9,600	960	11,808	—	—	58	174
						$1,900		$32,613

TABLE 6.4 AGGREGATE PLAN: STRATEGY 3

	(1) MONTHLY PRODUCTION REQUIREMENT	(2) PRODUCTION HOURS AVAILABLE (DAYS × 8 HOURS × 10 WORKERS)	(3) NUMBER OF UNITS PRODUCED (2) ÷ 10	(4) NUMBER OF UNITS SUB- CONTRACTED (1) − (3)	(5) SUBCON- TRACTING COST (4) × ($212 − 200)
January	1,150	1,600	160	990	11,800
February	625	1,520	152	473	5,676
March	450	1,680	168	282	3,384
April	250	1,760	176	74	888
May	600	1,680	168	432	5,184
June	1,000	1,600	160	840	10,080
July	1,025	1,600	160	865	10,380
August	1,250	1,520	152	1,098	13,176
September	1,450	1,680	168	1,282	15,384
October	1,525	1,760	176	1,349	16,188
November	1,250	1,680	168	1,082	12,984
December	1,175	1,600	160	1,015	12,180
					$117,384

TABLE 6.5 A TRADEOFF OF THE THREE AGGREGATE PLAN STRATEGIES

STRATEGY VARIABLE	1	2	3
Hiring and Training Cost	104,000	—	—
Layoff Cost	126,000	—	—
Inventory Cost	—	32,613	—
Stockout Cost	—	1,900	—
Subcontracting Cost	—	—	117,384
Total Cost	$230,000	$34,513	$117,384

P_t = Number of units produced during period t (P_0 initial value)

W_t = Number of workers during period t (W_0 initial value)

I_t = Number of units in inventory at the end of period t (I_0 initial value)

F_t = Demand forecast (or production requirements), in units, for period t.

The mathematical methods assume that the demand forecasts for the planning horizon, $F_1, F_2, \ldots, F_t$, are known, and the initial values of P_0, W_0, I_0 are given.

The problem is to find the values of P_t and W_t which will minimize costs while meeting the demand forecast (production requirements).

The mathematical methods provide the best values for $P_1, P_2, \ldots, P_t,$ and $W_1, W_2, \ldots, W_t$. However, only the values of P_t and W_t for the first period namely, P_1 and W_1 are implemented. The subsequent values will be implemented only if all the data given is unchanged over the planning horizon.

The mathematical methods provide the best planning decisions, as well as decision rules that are used to calculate optimal planning decisions in subsequent time periods. Two decision rules are provided, one for P_t and another for W_t. The cost data, $P_0, W_0,$ and F_t are used as inputs. Let us present examples of decision rules.

The *chase* strategy indicates the following decision rule:

$$P_t = F_t.$$

Production level would follow the fluctuating demand. That is, if forecasted demand is 250 units, then production is set to 250 units.

A *smoothed* production level is indicated by the following decision rule:

$$P_t = P_{t-1} + \alpha(F_t - P_{t-1}) \quad 0.0 \le \alpha \le 1.0$$

The production level in period t depends on the difference between the production level during the last period, plus an adjustment comparable to the exponential smoothing discussed in Chapter 5. If $\alpha = 0.0$, one adopts the pure level strategy; if $\alpha = 1.0$, one adopts the pure chase strategy. Intermediate values indicate mixed strategies.

Some other mathematical methods may include inventory levels in the decision rules.

$$P_t = P_{t-1} + \alpha(F_t - P_{t-1}) + \beta(I_N - I_{t-1})$$

Here, I_N indicates the normal inventory level, and β a smoothing constant, $0.0 \le \beta \le 1.0$. The production level, P_t, is decreased if the inventory level is above the normal, and increased if the inventory level is below normal. The rate of response will be determined by the value of β.

Clearly, the best decision rule is chosen based on some cost structure. In the following sections we will describe in detail several mathematical methods.

THE TRANSPORTATION METHOD

In the transportation method, rows represent the available supply of regular time and overtime for each month. The columns represent the demand forecasted. Production can be scheduled in a current month to satisfy demand in a later month by carrying inventory.

Let us examine this approach by using the data given in the example above. We assume that: (a) production requirements may be satisfied by producing during regular time and overtime, (b) backorders are not allowed, (c) fifty workers are employed, and (d) overtime capacity is 40 percent of regular time capacity.

The steps involved in setting up transportation method are as follows (consult Figure 6.4):

Step 1: Register the monthly production requirements and the production quantities available from different sources. For example, monthly production capacity during regular time is

[50 workers × 8 hours/day × 20 days] ÷ [10 hours/unit] = 800 units

Production capacity during overtime is 800 × 0.40 = 320 units.

Step 2: Equate supply and demand; add a slack column if supply exceeds demand.

Step 3: Mark down the costs per unit involved in each of the spaces (cells). A unit produced in January during regular time costs [$12/hour × 10 hours/unit] = $120. If this unit was shipped in February, it has an added inventory cost of $3. If sold in March, it has an added inventory cost of $6. A unit that has been produced during overtime costs time and a half, $180.

Step 4: Find an initial solution to the transportation problem.

Step 5: Find an optimal solution to the transportation problem.

A solution, suggested in Figure 6.4 has been found. The solution procedure is explained in the Technical Note to Chapter 6. The cost involved in the aggregate production plan specified in Figure 6.4 is found by multiplying the number of units in each space (cell) by the corresponding costs.[1]

LINEAR DECISION RULES

The trial-and-error method, described earlier, is simple to understand and to apply, but it requires numerous calculations that do not necessarily assure optimality. The transportation method finds an optimum solution to the aggregate planning problem, but it assumes linear relationships—that is, that costs are related to the work force size, etc., in a linear fashion.

The linear decision rule does not assume linearity, while finding the optimum solution to the aggregate production planning problem subject to certain assumptions.[2]

---

[1] For a detailed presentation see E. H. Bowman, "Production Scheduling by the Transportation Method of Linear Programming," *Operations Research,* Vol. 4, No. 1, February, 1956, pp. 100–103; E. H. Bowman, and R. B. Fetter, *Analysis of Production and Operations Management,* 3rd ed. (Homewood, Ill. Richard D. Irwin, 1967), pp. 134–136.

[2] C. C. Holt, F. Modigliani, J. F. Muth, and H. A. Simon, "A Linear Decision Rule for Production and Employment Scheduling," *Management Science,* October, 1955, pp. 1–30; C. C. Holt, F. Modigliani, J. F. Muth and H. A. Simon, *Planning Production, Inventories and Work Force* (Englewood Cliffs, N.J.: Prentice-Hall, 1960).

FIGURE 6.4 A TRANSPORTATION METHOD OF AGGREGATE PLANNING

	JAN.	FEB.	MAR.	APR.	MAY	JUNE	JULY	AUG.	SEPT.	OCT.	NOV.	DEC.	SLACK	SUPPLY
Initial Inventory	0 100													100
January Regular	120 800	123	126	129	132	135	138	141	144	147	150	153	156	800
January Overtime	180 250	183 70	186	189	192	195	198	201	204	207	210	213	216	320
February Regular	—	120 555	123 205	126	129	132	135	138	141	144	147	150	153	760
February Overtime	—	180	183 245	186 59	189	192	195	198	201	204	207	210	213	304
March Regular	—	—	120	123 191	126 600	129 49	132	135	138	141	144	147	150	840
March Overtime	—	—	180	183	186	189 336	192	195	198	201	204	207	210	336
April Regular	—	—	—	120	123	126 600	129 280	132	135	138	141	144	147	880
April Overtime	—	—	—	180	183	186 15	189 337	192	195	198	201	204	207	352
May Regular	—	—	—	—	120	123	126 408	129 432	132	135	138	141	144	840
May Overtime	—	—	—	—	180	183	186	189 336	192	195	198	201	204	336
June Regular	—	—	—	—	—	120	123	126 482	129 318	132	135	138	141	800

June Overtime	—	—	—	—	—	180	183	186	189 / 320	192	195	198	201	320
July Regular	—	—	—	—	—	—	120	123	126 / 800	129	132	135	138	800
July Overtime	—	—	—	—	—	—	180	183	186 / 12	189 / 308	192	195	198	320
August Regular	—	—	—	—	—	—	—	120	123	126 / 760	129	132	135	760
August Overtime	—	—	—	—	—	—	—	180	183	186 / 304	189	192	195	304
September Regular	—	—	—	—	—	—	—	—	120	123 / 153	126 / 687	129	132	840
September Overtime	—	—	—	—	—	—	—	—	180	183	186 / 336	189	192	336
October Regular	—	—	—	—	—	—	—	—	—	120	123 / 227	126 / 653	129	880
October Overtime	—	—	—	—	—	—	—	—	—	180	183	186 / 352	189	352
November Regular	—	—	—	—	—	—	—	—	—	—	120	123 / 170	126 / 670	840
November Overtime	—	—	—	—	—	—	—	—	—	—	180	183	186 / 336	336
December Regular	—	—	—	—	—	—	—	—	—	—	—	120	123 / 800	800
December Overtime	—	—	—	—	—	—	—	—	—	—	—	180	183 / 320	320
Demand	1,150	625	450	250	600	1,000	1,025	1,250	1,450	1,525	1,250	1,175	2,126	13,876

The linear decision rule got its name because it results in linear equations. The first of the two equations indicates the optimum production rate, P_t; the second indicates the optimum employment level, W_t.

The rule contends that the total cost C_t of an aggregate production plan during overtime period t is:

C_t = regular time payroll + hiring and layoff costs + overtime costs + inventory costs.

Holt et al.[3] examined the various costs for several time periods in a paint factory and fitted quadratic ($z = ax^2$), as opposed to linear ($y = ax$), equations to the available data. The four cost equations for a paint factory case are presented in Figure 6.5. Let us describe each one of the cost components.

REGULAR TIME COSTS   The cost of regular time-production in period t is assumed to be $C_1(t) = CW_t$. This cost is linearly related to the size of the work force.

HIRING AND FIRING COSTS   This cost is assumed to be

$$C_2(t) = C_2(W_t - W_{t-1})^2.$$

This cost is a quadratic function of the amount of increase or decrease in the work force. This function is an approximation and is chosen for reasons of mathematical convenience.

OVERTIME COSTS   This cost has been expressed as zero cost up to 100 percent utilization of the work force, and then as a linear cost of overtime beyond 100 percent. A quadratic function is used as an approximation.

$$C_3(5t) = C_3(P_t - C_4W_t)^2 + C_5P_t - C_6W_t.$$

COST OF INVENTORIES AND BACKORDERS   Backorders are treated as negative inventory. The inventory and back orders function is:

$$C_4(t) = C_7(I_t - C_8 - C_9F_t)^2.$$

As has been explained earlier, the total cost in each time period is the sum of the above cost components:

$$C(t) = C_1(t) + C_2(t) + C_3(t) + C_4(t)$$

and the cost over the planning horizon is:

$$C = \sum_{t=1}^{T} C(t)$$

---

[3] Holt et al., *Planning Production, Inventories, and Work Force.*

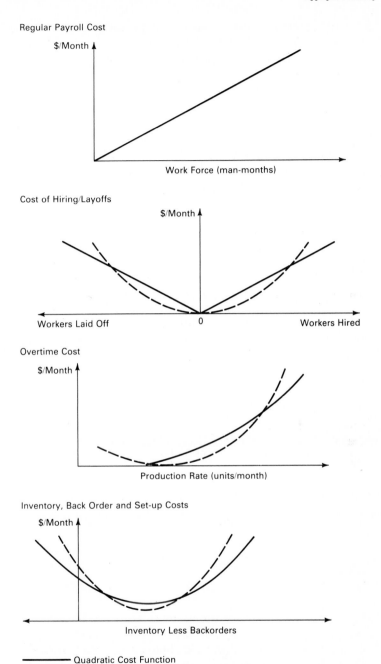

Regular Payroll Cost

$/Month

Work Force (man-months)

Cost of Hiring/Layoffs

$/Month

Workers Laid Off   0   Workers Hired

Overtime Cost

$/Month

Production Rate (units/month)

Inventory, Back Order and Set-up Costs

$/Month

Inventory Less Backorders

——————— Quadratic Cost Function

— — — — Approximate Cost Function

Figure 6.5 Cost Functions for the Linear Decision Rule *Source:* C. C. Holt, F. Modigliani, J. F. Muth, and H. A. Simon, "Cost Structure and Equations for Cost Components in the Linear Decision Rule," *Management Science*, October, 1955, pp. 8–13.

The LDR method is based on the minimization of the total cost C by choosing W_t and P_t for each period. These variables are sequentially related from period to period by the inventory relationship:

$$I_t = I_{t-1} + P_t - F_t$$

When I_t is substituted in the various cost functions, an unconstrained minimization problem results that is solved by using calculus.

The optimal solution is a linear decision rule for P_t and W_t:

$$P_t = A_0 F_t + A_1 F_{t+1} + \cdots + A_T F_{t+T}$$
$$+ B_1 W_{t-1} - D_1 I_{t-1} + E_1$$
$$W_t = A'_0 F_t + A' F_{t+1} + \cdots + A'_T F_{t+T}$$
$$+ B'_1 W_{t-1} - D' I_{t-1} + E'_1$$

where A_i, A'_i, B_1, B'_1, D_1, D'_1, E_1, and E'_1 are constants.

In the paint factory case, it has been observed that the production level was greatly affected by the demand forecast for the next three months, while the work force size was greatly affected by the long-term (12 months) demand forecast. Thus, short-term changes in demand have been accommodated by changes in the production level, and long-term changes in demand have been accommodated by changes in the work force size.

The LDR method is relatively simple and easy to use; however, it is restricted to the use of quadratic cost functions, and it reacts gradually to changing demand by means of hiring and firing a few workers each month rather than changing work force size later in larger increments. Since there are no restrictions on the size of the variables, the results may include negative work force size or an inventory size that exceeds warehouse capacity.

OTHER AGGREGATE PLANNING METHODS

Since the 1950's, aggregate planning methods have been researched extensively. Let us describe some of the methods.

LINEAR PROGRAMMING   The aggregate planning problem can be formulated as a linear programming problem.[4] Linear cost functions are used, similar to the quadratic cost functions used in the LDR. This formulation allows the use of constraints to limit inventories or overtime. The major disadvantage is the requirements that linear cost functions be used. It is more exhaustive than the transportation method and yields better results than the LDR method in cases in which the cost functions are approximately linear. The Technical Note to this chapter explains linear programming in detail.

[4] F. Haussmann and S. W. Hess, "A Linear Programming Approach to Production and Employment Scheduling," *Management Science*, Vol. 1, January, 1960, pp. 46–52.

MANAGEMENT COEFFICIENTS   Past management behavior is used to determine the appropriate coefficients of the production level and work force size decision rules.[5] Thus, costs are not utilized to set the value for these coefficients. The logic behind this technique is based on the assumption that management makes good decisions but could perhaps make them more consistent by using a mathematical decision rule. This rule has been criticized, since a good rule may be obtained only when management decisions *have been* consistent—when the rule is *not* needed! Thus, all mathematical rules should still be based on cost or profit rather than on past management performance.

SIMULATION   Simulation is used to select the parameters for aggregate planning decision rules.[6] Any desired cost structure can be evaluated. However, only a limited number of rules can be evaluated, since each rule requires a separate simulation run. This method should be considered only when complex cost structures are called for.

PARAMETRIC PRODUCTION PLANNING   This method allows the use of more general cost functions.[7] The two LDR rules presented earlier in the chapter are generalized by the introduction of two smoothing parameters for each rule. The method utilizes a grid search to find the parameter values that minimize the total cost over the planning horizon.

SEARCH DECISION RULE (SDR)   This method[8] allows the use of any mathematical form for the cost structure. Any desired cost function and decision rules may be used. The cost function is minimized by using the Hookes-Jeeves pattern-search method. The method arrives at an approximate local minimum of the cost function within a relatively short period of time.

GOAL PROGRAMMING   This method[9] suggests a multiple-criterion approach to the selection of a decision rule. Rather than relating to a single criterion of minimization of costs, multiple goals such as the following are specified in a descending order of priority:

P_1: Do not exceed production capacity

P_2: Meet delivery schedule

[5] E. H. Bowman, "Consistency and Optimality in Managerial Decision Making," *Management Science*, Vol. 9, January, 1963, pp. 310–321.

[6] R. C. Vergin, "Production Scheduling Under Seasonal Demand," *Journal of Industrial Engineering*, Vol. 17, May 1966, pp. 260–266.

[7] Curtis H. Jones, "Parametric Production Planning," *Management Science*, Vol. 13, No. 11, July, 1967, pp. 843–866.

[8] W. H. Taubert, Jr., "A Search Decision Rule for Aggregate Scheduling Problems," *Management Science*, Vol. 14, No. 6, February, 1968, pp. B343–B359.

[9] S. M. Lee, and L. J. Moore, "A Practical Approach to Production Scheduling," *Production and Inventory Management*, 1st quarter, 1974, pp. 79–92.

P₃: Keep inventory to a maximum of five units

P₄: Minimize total production and inventory costs

P₅: Hold overtime to a minimum.

The method seeks satisfaction of these goals, starting with P_1 and proceeding to P_2, P_3, etc.

PRODUCTION-SWITCHING HEURISTIC   This method[10] is based on the observation that management favors one major change in work force size over a series of smaller and more frequent changes. Thus, three-level (low, medium, high) production and work force rules were formulated. Production level is switched from one level to another, depending on the level of inventory and demand forecasts. The switching points are based on minimization of any cost function through the use of a search procedure. The major advantage of this method is that fluctuation in the production level and work force size is kept to a minimum.

THE USE OF AGGREGATE PLANNING METHODS

Although many methods have been researched, there have been only a few studies that have shown how well the methods perform in practice. The original study of the LDR paint factory showed a cost reduction of 8.5 percent. A comparison of several methods[11] revealed that the SDR method outperformed the other methods, showing a cost reduction of 13.6 percent by the best decision rule.

Although the methods can reduce costs, there are very few cases of implementation of these methods by operating managers. There are several reasons for this fact. First, the operations managers are responsible for aggregate planning decisions, but general managers often review and approve large changes in inventories or work force. Second, the marketing department controls variables that influence demand, while the operations department controls supply. Third, because of labor unions, many companies prefer to maintain a level work force whether demand is fluctuating, seasonal, or uncertain, as layoff or rehire become very expensive. Fourth, many operations managers are evaluated on the basis of meeting schedules rather than of keeping costs to a minimum. Inventory turnover and labor relations are only second in importance. Fifth, aggregate planning methods should be tailor-made for a particular situation and, as necessary, may call for the inclusion of more than

---

[10] Joseph Mellichamp and Robert Love, "Production Heuristics for the Aggregate Planning Problem," *Management Science*, Vol. 24, No. 12, August, 1978, pp. 1242–1251.

[11] W. B. Lee and B. M. Khumawala, "Simulation Testing of Aggregate Production Models in an Implementation Methodology," *Management Science*, Vol. 20, February, 1974, pp. 903–911.

one aggregate product. A considerable effort and expense is involved in either case. Sixth, management may not understand the value of a quantitative approach to the solution of planning problems.[12]

SUMMARY

Aggregate planning is one of the four major planning areas that are of concern to the operations manager. It is concerned with matching of supply and forecasted demand for products and services during a specific time period. The common time period is up to a year into the future.

Supply variables that may be changed by aggregate planning are hiring, lay-off, overtime, shorter work week, inventory, subcontracting, and part-time labor. Variables that are available to influence demand are pricing, promotion, backlog, and the production of complementary products.

When the forecasted demand is given two pure strategies are available for the supply: the level and the chase strategies. Mixed strategies are also available, the choice of which is made by determining the least cost decision rule.

All mathematical methods are based on the concept of a decision rule. The linear decision rules (LDR) method was the first method that was developed. This method minimized a quadratic cost function by using two decision rules: one for work force size and the other for production level. Later methods used generalized cost structures and various other types of decision rules.

Mathematical methods for aggregate planning have not been widely accepted in industry despite their applicability and robustness. An implementation effort should be made that includes tailor-made methods, demonstration of potential savings, and a careful definition of the decision problem in each case.

DISCUSSION QUESTIONS

6.1 What are the steps involved in planning?

6.2 What are the various capacities mentioned in Chapter 2?

6.3 What is aggregate planning?

6.4 What are the variables that can be changed to satisfy demand forecasted?

6.5 What are the methods used for aggregate planning?

6.6 What is the linear decision rule (LDR)?

6.7 What is the search decision rule (SDR)?

[12] For a comparison and categorization of several aggregate planning methods see: E. Menipaz, "Overview of Production Planning," *Journal of Information & Optimization Sciences*, Vol. 4, No. 1, January, 1983, pp. 65–72.

6.8   What are the reasons for the lack of adoption of mathematical methods for aggregate planning by industry?

PROBLEMS AND SOLUTIONS

6.1   The Arid Air Conditioning Company's demand forecast for its busiest six-month period is as follows:

Month	Demand
April	700 units
May	600
June	1100
July	1500
August	1300
September	750

Additional information:

Manufacturing cost	$100/unit
Storage costs	$5/unit/month
Stockout costs	$12/unit/month
Number of hours required to produce one unit	10
Number of hours in a working day	8
Number of working days in each month	20

The company maintains a work force size of 40 workers, except during July and August, when the work force level increases to 150. Find the cost involved in the aggregate production plan.

Solution

ARID AIR CONDITIONING COMPANY AGGREGATE PRODUCTION SCHEDULE APRIL TO SEPTEMBER

| | (1) PROD. REQ. | (2) CUMU-LATIVE PROD. | (3) WORKING HOURS AVAIL. | (4) NO. OF UNITS PROD. | (5) CUMU-LATIVE PROD. | (6) NO. OF UNITS SHORT | (7) STOCK OUT COST | (8) NO. OF UNITS TO INV. | (9) INVEN-TORY COST |
MONTH									
Apr.	700	700	6400	640	640	60	$720		
May	600	1300	6400	640	1280	20	240		
June	1100	2400	6400	640	1920	480	5760		
July	1500	3900	24000	2400	4320			420	$2,100
Aug.	1300	5200	24000	2400	6720			1520	7,600
Sept.	750	5950	6400	640	7360			1410	7,050
							$6720		$16,750

Total cost involved = 6,720 + 16,750 = $23,470

6.2   Canuck Corporation is a very successful manufacturing company, but is having difficulty in preparing a feasible aggregate production plan for the next six-month period, which begins in January. In using a trial-and-error approach, the company has formulated three alternative production strategies:

> *Strategy 1.* Produce to exact production requirements by varying the work force size on regular hours.
>
> *Strategy 2.* Maintain a constant work force level based on a six-month average. Inventory is allowed to accumulate, with shortages filled from the next month's production.
>
> *Strategy 3.* Hold the work force constant for a six-month period at a level to meet the lowest month's demand, and subcontract any monthly difference between requirements and production.

The company's safety stock policy, as determined by management, is 30 percent of the month's demand forecast. The monthly demand forecast, the current inventory stock level, the safety stock policy of requiring 30 percent of the month's forecast, and the number of working days available each month are required in order to compute the cumulative production requirements, and are shown in the following table.

CANUCK CORPORATION AGGREGATE PRODUCTION SCHEDULING REQUIREMENTS
FOR THE NEXT SIX-MONTH PERIOD

BEGINNING INVENTORY	FORE-CASTED DEMAND	CUMULATIVE DEMAND	SAFETY STOCK	MONTHLY PRODUCTION REQUIREMENT	CUMULATIVE PRODUCTION REQUIREMENT	MONTHLY WORKING DAYS
400	2200	2200	660	2460	2460	22
660	1900	4100	570	1810	4270	19
570	1400	5500	420	1250	5520	21
420	1100	6600	330	1010	6530	21
330	1400	8000	420	1490	8020	22
420	2100	10,100	630	2310	10,330	20

The following additional information was taken from company records:

Manufacturing cost	$125/unit
Storage costs	$1.25/unit/month
Standard pay rate	$5.00/hr, 8 hr/day
Overtime rate	$7.50/hr
Marginal cost of stockout	$6.00/unit/month
Hiring and training cost	$250/man
Layoff costs	$300/man
Manhours required per unit	6

Determine the optimal production strategy.

Solution

STRATEGY 1

Month	(1) Monthly Production Required	(2) Production Hours Required (1) × (6)	(3) Available Hours per Worker per Month days × 8	(4) Workers Required (2) ÷ (3)	(5) Workers Hired	(6) Hiring and Training Cost (5) × $250	(7) Workers Laid Off	(8) Lay-off Cost (7) × $300	Total Cost
January	2460	14,760	176	84	—	—	—	—	
February	1810	10,860	152	71	0	0	13	3900	
March	1250	7500	168	45	0	0	26	7800	
April	1010	6060	168	36	0	0	9	2700	
May	1490	8940	176	51	15	1250	0	0	
June	2310	13,860	160	87	36	9000	0	0	
						10,250		14,400	$24,650

STRATEGY 2

Month	(1) Cumulative Production Required	(2) Working Hours Available* (days × 8 × 62 workers)	(3) Number of Units Produced (2) ÷ 6	(4) Cumulative Production	(5) Number of Units Short (1) − (4)	(6) Stockout Cost (5) × $6	(7) Number of Units to Inventory (4) − (1)	(8) Inventory Cost (7) × ($1.25)	Total Cost
January	2460	10,912	1819	1819	641	3846			
February	4270	9424	1571	3390	880	5280			
March	5520	10,416	1736	5126	394	2364			
April	6530	10,416	1736	6862			332	415	
May	8020	10,912	1819	8681			661	826	
June	10,330	9920	1653	10,334			4	5	
						11,490		1246	$12,736

*Calculation of constant work force level (62 workers): (10,330 units × 6 hrs each) ÷ (125 days × 8 hrs/day) = 62 workers.

STRATEGY 3

Month	(1) Monthly Production Requirement	(2) Production Hours Available (days × 8 × 25)	(3) Number of Units Produced (2) ÷ 6	(4) Number of units subcontracted (1) − (3)	(5) Subcontracting Cost (4) × $2.50
January	2460	4400	733	1727	4318
February	1810	3800	633	1177	2943
March	1250	4200	700	5500	1375
April	1010	4200	700	310	775
May	1490	4400	733	757	1893
June	2310	4000	667	1643	4108
					$15,412

Based on cost, the most feasible alternative is strategy 2, which is to maintain 62 workers. (Note that in strategy 1 the initial work force size is assumed to be 84. Thus, no expense is involved in hiring or laying-off workers.)

6.3   A toy manufacturer wants to determine an aggregate production plan for May, June, July and August. Production cost during regular hours is $8 each, and the cost of production during overtime is $12. Units that are produced in one time period but that are carried forward to satisfy future demand cost $1.00 per unit per time period held. The inventory on hand at the beginning of the planning period is 50 units. The following matrix contains the available production capacities and the demands for each period.

PRODUCTION SOURCES		SALES PERIOD				INVEN-TORY	UNUSED CAPAC-ITY	TOTAL CAPAC-ITY
		MAY	JUNE	JULY	AUG.			
Beginning Inventory								50
May	Reg. Time							105
	Overtime							40
June	Reg. Time							105
	Overtime							40
July	Reg. Time							105
	Overtime							40
Aug.	Reg. Time							105
	Overtime							40
Total Requirements		120	120	120	120	75	75	630

Using the above matrix and the transportation method of aggregate planning, develop a feasible production plan. Indicate the appropriate costs on the matrix.

Solution

PRODUCTION SOURCES		SALES PERIOD				INVEN-TORY	UNUSED CAPAC-ITY	TOTAL CAPAC-ITY
		MAY	JUNE	JULY	AUG.			
Beginning Inventory		0 50	1	2	3	4	0	50
May	Reg. Time	8 70	9	10	11	12	0	105
	Overtime	12	13 40	14	15	16	0	40
June	Reg. Time	✕	8 45	9 60	10	11	0	105
	Overtime	✕	12	13 40	14	15	0	40
July	Reg. Time	✕	✕	8 20	9 85	10	0	105
	Overtime	✕	✕	12	13 35	14 5	0	40
Aug.	Reg. Time	✕	✕	✕	8	9 70	35	105
	Overtime	✕	✕	✕	8	9	40	40
Total Requirements		120	120	120	120	75	75	630

CHAPTER REVIEW PROBLEMS

6.1 The Business Policy and Strategy Committee of the National Appliance Company has met in order to determine a feasible production plan for the following year. Present at the meeting were the company's president, the administration manager, the marketing manager, the production manager, and the quality control manager. The production manager suggested that the company produce to exact monthly requirements by varying the work force size. He commented that the company's greatest manufacturing cost is the cost of labor; he felt that the size of the work force should therefore be based on each month's production requirements, thus resulting in hiring or laying-off of workers accordingly. However, the administration manager stated that the company was constrained by a strict labor union, and the imposed regulations would result in the company's incurring lay-off costs. Moreover, the technical nature of each worker's job required considerable hiring and training costs.

The administration manager then suggested that the company maintain a constant work force based on the average monthly production required, and allow inventory to accumulate, with shortages filled for the following month's production. However, the marketing manager was a bit apprehensive about this idea, pointing out that it would result in either storage costs for units produced in excess of requirements, or stockout costs for units short. The marketing manager said that a better approach would be to maintain a constant work force level of 55 workers, which is approximately the level required to meet the lower monthly demands, and subcontract to satisfy total production required each month. The committee seemed to think that this was a feasible alternative, until the quality control manager pointed out that the company has no control over quality standards when production is in the hands of an outsider.

After the committee had finished discussing alternative production strategies, the president provided the following information in order that a decision be made.

Month	Beginning Inventory	Forecast Demand	Cumulative Demand	Safety Stock	Monthly Production Required	Cumulative Production Required	Monthly Working Days	Cumulative Working Days
Jan.	678	3730	3730	746	3798	3798	20	20
Feb.	746	3220	6950	644	3118	6916	18	38
Mar.	644	2375	9325	475	2206	9122	20	58
Apr.	475	2065	11,390	413	2003	11,125	20	78
May	413	2250	13,640	450	2287	13,412	20	98
June	450	2350	15,990	470	2370	15,782	20	118
July	470	2400	18,390	480	2410	18,192	20	138
Aug.	480	2400	20,790	480	2400	20,592	20	158
Sept.	480	3000	23,790	600	3120	23,712	20	178
Oct.	600	3200	26,990	640	3240	26,952	20	198
Nov.	640	3250	30,240	650	3260	30,212	20	218
Dec.	650	3350	33,590	670	3370	33,582	20	238

The following additional information was taken from company records:

Manufacturing cost	$250/unit
Storage costs	$2.00/unit/month
Standard pay rate	$8.00/hr, 8 hr/day
Overtime rate	$12/hr
Stockout cost	$3.00/unit/month
Hiring and training cost	$150/worker
Lay-off costs	$300/worker
Subcontracting cost	$3.50/unit
Number of workers currently employed	95

From the committee's discussion, develop alternative production strategies for National Appliance Company and determine the optimal production strategy.

6.2   The item demand forecasts for a product for October, November, and December are 2000, 3000, and 2500 units, respectively. Safety stock policy, as determined by management, is 25 percent of the forecast for that month. There is no beginning inventory. Additional information for this product is as follows:

Manufacturing cost	$250/unit
Storage costs	$100/unit/month
Standard pay rate	$8.00/hr, 8 hr/day
Overtime rate	$12.00/hr
Cost of stockout	$10.00/unit/month
Cost of subcontracting	$10.00/unit
Hiring and training cost	$200/worker
Lay-off costs	$200/worker
Production man-hours required per unit	12 hrs
Number of working days in each month	20

a) Develop a production schedule to produce the exact production requirements by varying the work force size.

b) Calculate total hiring and lay-off costs.

6.3   Given the information in problem 6.2, develop a production schedule that holds the work force level constant for the three-month period corresponding to the lowest month's demand, and subcontract any monthly difference between requirements and production.

6.4   The Staff Recruiting Officer of the A&M Corporation wants to know how many workers will be needed each month for the next six-month production period. The following is a monthly demand forecast for the six-month period:

Month	Forecasted Demand
January	1250
February	1100
March	950
April	900
May	1000
June	1150

Beginning inventory for the period is 500 units. The company's safety stock policy is 20 percent of the current month's forecasted demand. Each unit requires five man-hours to produce. There are 20 working days each month, and the company works an 8-hour day. There are presently 35 workers employed by the company. How many workers will be hired or layed off each month?

6.5   The No-Slack Company needs an aggregate production plan for October, November, and December for Model 1, Model 2, and Model 3. The cost to produce each model is $10 per unit during regular hours and $15 per unit during overtime shifts. Units that are produced in one time period but that are carried forward to satisfy future demand cost $2 per unit per time period held. There is no beginning inventory on hand and the company is operating at total capacity. The following chart gives the production requirements for the three-month period:

Month	Product	Production Required
October	Model 1	255
	Model 2	275
	Model 3	350
November	Model 1	255
	Model 2	275
	Model 3	350
December	Model 1	300
	Model 2	375
	Model 3	550
	Total	2985

595 units can be produced during regular hours and 400 units can be produced during overtime.

a) Set up a production planning matrix, following the transportation method of aggregate planning.

b) Find an initial solution to the production planning problem.

6.6 The Stuffco Manufacturing Company makes several kinds of VCR's and must come up with a production plan for the next 12 months. The company must comply with labor union regulations, which dictate that the work force level can only be changed at the beginning of the year, and that no further changes can be made. Additionally, all employees are to put in full work weeks. The item demand forecast for the next 12 months is as follows:

January	750 units	July	250
February	1000 units	August	250
March	1200 units	September	400
April	750 units	October	900
May	500 units	November	1000
June	400 units	December	1200

Manufacturing cost is $25 per unit. Inventory storage costs are $1.00 per unit per month. A shortage of units results in lost sales, and the loss is estimated at $3.00 per unit short. There is no beginning inventory. Ten hours are required to produce one unit, and the working day is 8 hours. Assume 20 working days in each month. Develop a feasible aggregate production plan for the company.

6.7 The production manager of the Marabell Manufacturing Corporation wants to determine an optimal production strategy for the first quarter of the year. The company has extremely high production control standards and will not subcontract any work. Therefore, the company must determine a production plan taking this constraint into account.

Beginning inventory for the first month of the quarter period is 200 units, and, for each subsequent month, the beginning inventory for that month is equal to the safety stock of the preceding month. The company's safety stock policy is 25 percent of the month's demand forecast. The demand forecast for each month of the quarter period is 700, 900, and 875 units, respectively. The corresponding monthly production requirements are 670,990, and 800 units, and the number of working days in each month is 21, 22, and 20.

The following additional information was also made available:

Manufacturing cost	$100/unit
Storage costs	$1.00/unit/month
Standard pay rate	$5.00/hr, 8 hr/day
Overtime pay	150% of standard
Marginal cost of stockout	$4.00/unit/month
Hiring and training cost	$150/man
Lay-off costs	$200/man
Man-hours required per unit	4
Number of workers currently employed	15
Marginal cost of subcontracting	$1.75/unit

Determine the production costs if the company wants to carry out the strategy of:

a) Producing to exact production requirements by varying the work force size on regular hours.

b) Maintaining a constant work force level based on a quarterly (3-month) average. Inventory is allowed to accumulate, while shortages may be filled from next month's production.

BIBLIOGRAPHY

ARMSTRONG, T. B., "Job Content and Content Factors Related to Satisfaction for Different Occupational Levels," *Journal of Applied Psychology*, 54, No. 1, February, 1971, pp. 57–65.

BOWMAN, E. H., "Consistency and Optimality in Managerial Decision Making," *Management Science*, Vol. 9, No. 2, January, 1963, pp. 310–21.

BUFFA, E. S., "Aggregate Planning for Production," *Business Horizons*, 10, No. 3, Fall, 1967, pp. 87–97.

BUFFA, E. S., and W. H. TAUBERT, *Production-Inventory Systems: Planning and Control*, rev. ed. Homewood, Ill.: Richard D., Irwin Inc., 1974.

CHASE, R. B., and N. J. AQUILANO, *Production and Operations Management*, 3rd ed. Homewood, Ill.: Richard D. Irwin, 1981.

EBERT, R. J., "Environmental Structure and Programmed Decision Effectiveness," *Management Science*, Vol. 19, No. 4, December, 1972, pp. 298–307.

EBERT, R. J., and T. R. MITCHELL, *Organizational Decision Processes: Concepts and Analysis*. New York: Crane, Russak & Co., Inc., 1975.

EBERT, R. J., and D. PIEHL. "Time Horizon: A Concept for Management," *California Management Review*, 15, No. 4, Summer, 1973, pp. 35–41.

HENDERSON, W. B., and W. L. BERRY, "Heuristic Methods for Telephone Operator Shift Scheduling: An Experimental Analysis," *Management Science*, Vol. 22, No. 12, August, 1976, pp. 1372–80.

HOLT, C. C., F. MODIGLIANI, J. F. MUTH, and H. A. SIMON, *Planning Production, Inventories and Work Force*. Englewood Cliffs, N.J.: Prentice-Hall, Inc., 1960.

LEE, W. B., and B. M. KHUMAWALA, "Simulation Testing of Aggregate Production Planning Models in an Implementation Methodology," *Management Science*, Vol. 20, No. 6, February, 1974, pp. 903–11.

MENIPAZ, E., "Overview of Production Planning," *Journal of Information & Optimization Sciences*, Vol. 4, No. 1, January, 1983, pp. 65–72.

————. *Automated Production: A Decision Support Systems Approach*. Ottawa: Randcomp Company, 1984.

MOSKOWITZ, H., "The Value of Information in Aggregate Production Planning, *AIIE Transactions* 4, No. 4, December, 1972, 290–97.

STARR, M. K., *Production Management: Systems and Synthesis*, 2nd ed. Englewood Cliffs, N.J.: Prentice-Hall, Inc., 1972.

TAUBERT, W. H., "Search Decision Rule for the Aggregate Scheduling Problem," *Management Science*, Vol. 14, No. 6, February, 1968, pp. 343–59.

TECHNICAL NOTE: Linear Programming

INTRODUCTION

Linear programming is a method used to allocate scarce resources in a manner that will optimize certain output criteria. Linear programming is the most popular of mathematical optimization techniques.

The linear programming method determines nonnegative values for a set of n decision variables $x_1, x_2, x_3, \ldots x_n$, so as to optimize (maximize or minimize) an objective function in the following form:

$$\text{Maximize (minimize) } Z = C_1X_1 + C_2X_2 + \ldots + C_nX_n.$$

Subject to resource constraints:

$$A_{11}X_1 + A_{12}X_2 + \ldots A_{1n}X_n \leq B_1$$
$$A_{21}X_1 + A_{22}X_2 + \ldots A_{2n}X_n \leq B_2$$
$$\vdots$$
$$A_{m1}X_1 + A_{m2}X_2 + \ldots + A_{mn}X_n \leq B_m$$
$$X_1, \qquad X_2, \qquad \ldots, \qquad X_n \geq 0$$

where:

C_j =Cost (profit) constants per product type produced, sold, or transported.

A_{ij} =Utilization rate of resource i when used to produce unit type j constants.

B_i =Total amount of resource type i (constants).

m =Number of different resources available.

n =Number of different product types.

The constraints may be stated as less than ($\leq$), equal to ($=$), or greater than ($\geq$), as per the particular problem.

The linear programming method is based on the following assumptions:

1. The objective function and the constraints should be linear.
2. The constants, C_j, A_{ij} and B_i should be known and deterministic—that is, nonprobabilistic.
3. The decision variables, X_j, should be divisible—that is, be able to assume fractional values.

The following are some typical problems in which linear programming can be used.

1. A manufacturer wants to develop a production schedule and an inventory policy that will satisfy sales demand in future periods. Ideally, the schedule and policy will enable the company to satisfy demand and at the same time minimize the total production and inventory costs.
2. A financial analyst must select an investment portfolio from a variety of stock and bond investment alternatives. The analyst would like to establish the portfolio that maximizes the return on investment.
3. A marketing manager wants to determine how best to allocate a fixed advertising budget among alternative advertising media, such as radio, television, newspaper, and magazine. The manager would like to determine the media mix that maximizes advertising effectiveness.
4. A company has warehouses in a number of locations throughout North America. Given a set of customer demands for its products, the company would like to determine which warehouse should ship, how much product should be shipped, which customers should receive the product from a given warehouse, so that the total transportation costs are minimized.

FORMULATION OF THE LINEAR PROGRAMMING PROBLEM

Rival Company, a small manufacturer of home appliances, is considering the production of a medium- and a high-power food processor. Each processor made will require the following operations: molding, assembly, and finishing.

The operations manager has estimated the hours required in each department for the medium-priced, standard model and for the more expensive, deluxe model (see Table TN6.1).

The accounting department has assigned all relevant variable costs, and has arrived at prices for both processors that will result in a profit of $20 for every medium-power processor and $15 for every high-power processor.

TABLE TN6.1 PROCESSES, PRODUCTION REQUIREMENTS, AND PROFIT PER FOOD PROCESSOR

PRODUCT	MEDIUM POWER	HIGH POWER	HOURS AVAILABLE
Molding Hours	3	10	1,500
Assembly Hours	1	2	400
Finishing Hours	1	0	300
Profit	$20	$15	

In addition, after studying departmental production plans, the operations manager estimates 500 hours of molding time, 400 hours of assembly time, and 300 hours of finishing time available during the next month. The problem is to determine how many medium-power and how many high-power processors should be produced in order to maximize profit during the coming month. Let:

x_1 = the number of medium-power processors

x_2 = the number of high-power processors

Total profit = $z = 20x_1 + 15x_2$.

Since there is a limited amount of production time available for each of these operations, the next step in the linear programming approach will be to specify the constraints associated with the problem.

From the production information (in Table TN6.1), we know that the total number of hours of molding time used in the manufacture of x_1 processors will be $3x_1$ and the production of x_2 high-power processors will use $10x_2$ hours of molding time.

Total molding time required = $3x_1 + 10x_2$.

Since the operations manager has stated that there are at most 1,500 hours of molding time available, it follows that the product mix selected must satisfy the constraint

$$3x_1 + 10x_2 \leq 1500$$

From Table TN6.1 we also see that

$$1x_1 + 2x_2 \leq 400$$

The constraint for finishing capacity is

$$1x_1 \leq 300$$

We now have specified the constraints associated with the production process. In order to prevent the decision variables x_1 and x_2 from having negative values, one adds two constraints:

$$x_1 \geq 0 \text{ and } x_2 \geq 0$$

To conclude: the mathematical statement or mathematical formulation of a production plan is:

$$\max \{Z = 20x_1 + 15x_2\}$$

subject to (s.t.):

$3x_1 + 10x_2 \leq 1500$	molding
$1x_1 + 2x_2 \leq 400$	assembly
$1x_1 \leq 300$	finishing

$$x_1, x_2 \geq 0$$

Rival has to find the product mix (that is, the combination of x_1 and x_2) that satisfies all the constraints and, at the same time, yields a maximum value for the objective function that is greater than or equal to the value given by any other feasible solution. (A feasible solution is a solution that satisfies all the constraints.) The above mathematical formulation of the Rival Company's problem is a *linear program*.

THE GRAPHICAL SOLUTION METHOD OF THE LINEAR PROGRAMMING PROBLEM

An easy way to solve a linear programming problem having only two decision variables is the graphical solution procedure. Although the graphical method is awkward in solving three-variable problems and cannot be used for problems involving more than three variables, the insight gained from studying this method will help in understanding some of the more advanced concepts to be discussed later. The graphical method also provides an intuitive basis for a more practical solution method (the simplex method), which will be discussed in the following section.

Let us begin our graphical solution procedure by developing a graph that can be used to display the possible solutions (x_1 and x_2 values) for the problem. The graph (see Figure TN6.1) has the values of x_1 on the horizontal axis and the values of x_2 on the vertical axis. Every point (x_1, x_2) corresponds to a possible solution, and is called a *solution point*. The solution point for which $x_1 = 0$ and $x_2 = 0$ is referred to as the origin.

The next step is to show which of the solution points correspond to feasible solutions for the linear program. Since both x_1 and x_2 must be nonnegative, one needs to consider points where $x_1 \geq 0$ and $x_2 \geq 0$. This is indicated in Figure TN6.2 by arrows pointing in the direction of production combinations that will satisfy the nonnegativity constraints.

Earlier, we saw that the inequality representing the molding constraint was

$$3x_1 + 10x_2 \leq 1500$$

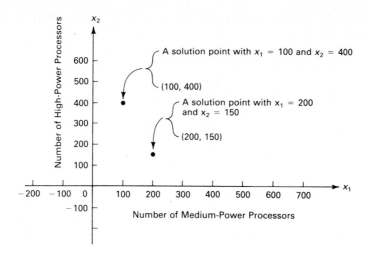

Figure TN6.1 Graph of Solution Points for the Two-Variable Problem

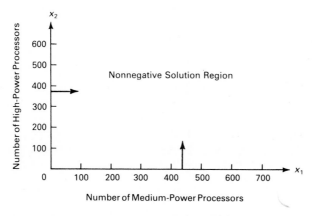

Figure TN6.2 The Nonnegativity Constraints

To show all solution points that satisfy this relationship, one starts by graphing the line corresponding to the equation

$$3x_1 + 10x_2 = 1500$$

This line, the molding constraint line, is shown in Figure TN6.3. Any point below the molding constraint line satisfies the constraint. We treat all the other constraints in a similar fashion.

Figure TN6.4 presents all the constraints and the feasible solution region for Rival's problem. A graph of the profit function (or profit line) is presented in Figure TN6.5. From this graph, one can see that there are an infinite number of feasible production combinations that will provide a $1500 profit.

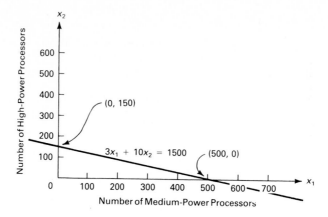

Figure TN6.3   The Molding Constraint Line

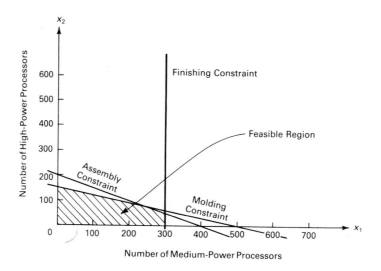

Figure TN6.4   Feasible Solution Region for Rival's Problem

Since the objective is to find the feasible solution that has the highest profit, we proceed by selecting higher profit values and finding the feasible solution points that yield the stated profits. We have drawn $3000 and $6750 profit lines on the graph in Figure TN6.6. From Figure TN6.6, one observes the following: the profit lines are parallel and profit lines farther from the origin represent higher profits.

By continuing to move parallel profit lines away from the origin, one can obtain solution points that yield higher and higher values for the objective function. *The point in the feasible region that lies on the highest profit line is the optimal solution to the linear program.* This optimal point is shown in Figure TN6.6. It is customary to note the optimal values with a star.

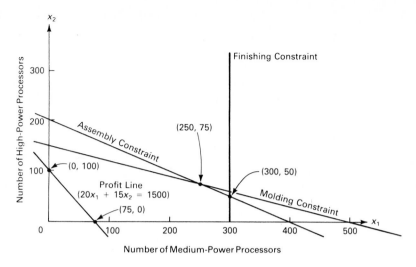

Figure TN6.5 $1500 Profit Line

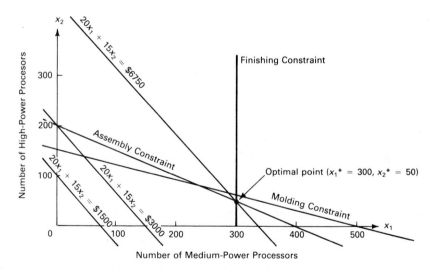

Figure TN6.6   Selected Profit Lines and Optimal Solution Point for Rival's Problem

The x_1 and x_2 values at the optimal solution point are $x_1{}^* = 300$ and $x_2{}^* = 50$, a combination that yields a profit of $Z^* = 20(300) + 15(50) = 6750$.
This calls for the following production times:

$$3(300) + 10(50) = 1400 \qquad \text{hours of molding time.}$$

$$1(300) + 2(50) = 400 \qquad \text{hours of assembly time.}$$

$$1(300) = 300 \qquad \text{hours of finishing time.}$$

While all available assembly and finishing time is consumed, the molding department is going to be idle (1500 − 1400 =) 100 hours during the coming month.

The 100 hours of unused molding time are referred to as *slack* for the department. In linear programming, any unused or idle capacity for a ≤ constraint is referred to as the slack associated with the constraint.

The solution for minimization problems is identical to the above, except that the cost lines should be moved leftwards and downwards as far as possible.

THE SIMPLEX SOLUTION METHOD OF THE LINEAR PROGRAMMING PROBLEM

The graphical solution method is a convenient way to find optimal extreme point solutions[1] for two-variable linear programming problems. For problems having more than two decision variables, however, this method is awkward. The simplex method can be used to find optimal extreme point solutions for linear programming problems having any number of decision variables.

Standard Form

The mathematics of the simplex method is based upon concepts associated with the study of simultaneous linear equations. Since linear programming problems almost always contain some constraints with inequality relationships—that is ≤ and/or ≥ relationships—one needs a standard procedure for converting each inequality constraint to an equality. When all the constraints of a linear programming problem have been written as equalities, the problem is said to be in standard form. Only then is the simplex solution method applied.

The Rival Company example is recalled as:

$$\max \{z = 20x_1 + 15x_2\}$$

subject to:

$$3x_1 + 10x_2 \leq 1500$$

$$1x_1 + 2x_2 \leq 400$$

$$1x_1 \leq 300$$

$$x_1, x_2 \geq 0.$$

In order to transform the above formulation into standard form, one must write the constraints corresponding to the three production operations as equalities. In order to do that, three *slack variables* are used: s_1, s_2, and s_3,

---

[1] An extreme point is a point of intersection of two constraints on the edge of the feasible region.

indicating the unused portion of resources associated with each of the constraints.

Since three new variables have been added to the problem, these variables must be incorporated into the objective function. Since the unused or idle capacity makes no contribution to profit, the profit coefficient associated with each slack variable will be zero. Thus the linear programming problem can be written in standard form as follows:

$$\max \{20x_1 + 15x_2 + 0s_1 + 0s_2 + 0s_3 + 0s_4\}$$

subject to

$$3x_1 + 10x_2 + 1s_1 \qquad\qquad = 1{,}500$$
$$1x_1 + 2x_2 \qquad + 1s_2 \qquad\quad = 400$$
$$1x_1 \qquad\qquad\qquad + 1s_3 \quad = 300$$

$$x_1, x_2, s_1, s_2, s_3 \geq 0.$$

Note that we have expanded the nonnegativity constraints to include the four new slack variables.

Greater-than-or-equal-to constraints are converted to the standard form by subtracting *surplus variables*. As an example, a problem such as:

$$\min \{z = 10x_1 + 20x_2\}$$

subject to:

$$1x_1 + 2x_2 \geq 50$$
$$1x_2 \geq 30$$
$$x_1, x_2 \quad \geq 0,$$

can be rewritten in the following standard form:

$$\min \{z = 10x_1 + 20x_2 + 0s_1 + 0s_2\}$$

subject to:

$$1x_1 + 2x_2 \qquad - 1s_1 \qquad\qquad = 50$$
$$1x_2 \qquad\qquad - 1s_2 \quad = 30$$
$$x_1, x_2, s_1, \geq 0.$$

THE SIMPLEX PROCEDURE

Step 1. Formulate a linear programming model of the real-world problem. That is, obtain a mathematical representation of the problem, as has been done for Rival Company.

Step 2. Define an equivalent linear program by:

    a.) Multiplying negative right-hand side constraints by 1 and changing the direction of the inequalities;

    b.) If it is a min (z) problem, change to max (−z) by multiplying the objective function by −1. This will result in an equivalent mathematical representation that is ready for the maximization simplex procedure.

Step 3. Set up the standard form representation of the linear program. That is, change every constraint to an equality by introducing slack/surplus variables.

Step 4. Set up the simplex table (which is discussed later). This table is used to keep track of the calculations made. The initial solution to the linear programming problem, when using the simplex procedure, is zero for all the decision variables; thus, the value of the objective function is also zero.

Step 5. Choose the variable with the largest $C_j - z_j$ to introduce into solution. (The column corresponding to this variable in the simplex table is marked as A_{ij}.) The value of $C_j - z_j$ tells us the amount by which the value of the objective function will increase for every unit of x_j introduced into the solution.

Step 6. Choose as the pivot row that row with the smallest ratio of B_i/A_{ij}, $A_{ij} > 0$. (B_i is the column of the solution values on the right of the simplex table.) This determines which variable will leave the basis when x_j enters. (A variable that leaves the basis receives a value of zero.) This also tells us how many units of x_j can be introduced into the solution before the basic variable in the ith row equals zero.

Step 7. Perform the necessary row operations to convert column j to a unit column.

    a.) Multiply the pivot row by the constant necessary to make the pivot element a unit (1).

    b.) Obtain zeros in all the other rows for the pivot's column by multiplying the new pivot row by an appropriate constant and adding it to the appropriate row.

Once these row operations have been performed, we can read the values of basic decision variables from the B column (solution values) of the simplex table.

Step 8. Test for optimality. If $C_j - z_j \leq 0$ for all columns, the current solution is the optimal solution. If not, return to step 6. If $C_j - z_j \leq 0$ for all variables, there is no variable that one can introduce that will cause the objective function to increase; hence, one has the optimal solution.

Let us demonstrate the initial simplex procedure for Rival Company. The initial simplex table, based on the standard form, is:

BASIS	C_j	x_1 20	x_2 15	s_1 0	s_2 0	s_3 0	SOLUTION VALUES B_i
s_1	0	3	10	1	0	0	1500
s_2	0	1	2	0	1	0	400
s_3	0	1	0	0	0	1	300
z_j		0	0	0	0	0	$\Sigma(C_j)(B_i) = 0$
$C_j - z_j$		20	15	0	0	0	Profit

In this table, one sees a 0 in the z_j row in the last column. This zero represents the profit associated with the current basic solution. The value was obtained by multiplying the values of the basic variables s_1, s_2, s_3, which are given in the last column, by their corresponding contribution to profit, as given in the C_j column.

By looking at the $C_j - z_j$ row, one sees that every medium-power processor produced will increase the value of the objective function by $20, and every high-power processor will increase the value of the objective function by $15. Given this information, it would make sense to produce as many medium-power processors as possible.

Considering all the constraints together, one sees that the most restrictive constraint on x_1 is the finishing constraint. That is, making $x_1 = 300$ will use all the finishing capacity available. Thus, if the maximum value of x_1 is introduced into the solution, Rival will produce 300 medium-power processors and will leave no slack time in the finishing department ($s_3 = 0$).

In making the decision to produce as many medium-power processors as possible, one has changed the set of variables in the basic feasible solution. The previous nonbasic variable x_1 is now a basic variable with $x_1 = 300$, while the previous basic variable s_3 is now a nonbasic variable with $s_3 = 0$. This interchange of roles between two variables is the essence of the simplex method. That is, the simplex method moves from one basic feasible solution to another by means of a selection of a nonbasic variable to replace one of the current basic variables. This process of moving from one basic feasible solution to another is called an *iteration*.

In determining which variable should leave the current basis, we only need to consider rows of our table in which the coefficient of the incoming nonbasic variable is strictly positive, $A_{ij} > 0$. With this additional consideration in mind, one can present the general simplex rules for selecting a nonbasic variable to enter the basis and a current basic variable to leave the basis.

The criterion for entering a new variable into the basis is as follows. Look at the net evaluation in row $(C_j - z_j)$ and select as the variable to enter the basis that variable that will cause the largest per-unit increase in the objective function. Let us assume that this variable corresponds to column j in the table.

The criterion for removing a variable from the current basis is as follows. For each row i, compute the ratio B_i/A_{ij}, $A_{ij} > 0$. This ratio tells us the maximum amount of the variable x_j that can be brought into the solution and still satisfy the constraint equation represented by that row. The minimum of these ratios determines which constraint will be most restrictive when x_j is introduced into the solution. Hence, one recognizes the following rule for selecting the variable to remove from the current basis. *For all the ratios* B_i/A_{ij}, $A_{ij} > 0$, *select the basic variable corresponding to the minimum value of these ratios as the variable to leave the basis.*

Let us return to the Rival Company example problem. For illustration purposes, we have added an extra column showing the B_i/A_{ij} ratios for the initial simplex table associated with the problem.

BASIS	C_j	A MATRIX					B MATRIX	$\dfrac{B_i}{A_{i1}}$
		x_1	x_2	s_1	s_2	s_3	SOLUTION VALUES B_i	
		20	15	0	0	0		
s_1	0	3	10	1	0	0	1500	$\dfrac{1500}{3} = 500$
s_2	0	1	2	0	1	0	400	$\dfrac{400}{1} = 400$
s_3	0	1	0	0	0	1	300	$\dfrac{300}{1} = 300$
	z_j	0	0	0	0	0	0	
	$C_j - z_j$	20	15	0	0	0		

Note that $C_1 - z_1 = 20$ is the largest positive value in the $C_j - z_j$ row. Hence, x_1 is selected to become the new basic variable. Checking the ratios B_i/A_{i1} for $A_{i1} > 0$, we see that $B_3/A_{31} = 300$ is the minimum of these ratios. Thus, the current basic variable associated with row 3 (s_3) is the variable selected to leave the basis. In our table, we have circled $A_{31} = 1$ to indicate that the variable corresponding to the first column is to enter the basis and to indicate that the basic variable corresponding to the third row is to leave the basis. We refer to this circled element as the *pivot element*.

In order to improve the current solution of $x_1 = 0$, $x_2 = 0$, $s_1 = 500$, $s_2 = 400$, $s_3 = 1500$, we should increase x_1 to 300. This would call for the production of $x_1 = 300$ at a corresponding profit of $\$20 \times 300$ units $= \$6000$. In doing so, we will use all the available finishing capacity, and thus s_3 will be reduced to zero. Hence, x_1 will become the new basic variable replacing s_3 in the old basis.

We saw that the initial basic feasible solution could be improved by introducing x_1 into the basis to replace s_3. Before we can determine whether this new basic feasible solution can be improved upon, it will be necessary to develop the corresponding simplex table.

We will formulate a new table such that all the columns associated with the new basic variables are unit columns, and such that the value of the basic variable in row i is given by B_i.

There were two row operations that we could perform on a system of linear equations and still retain an equivalent system: (1) we could multiply any row by a nonzero number, and (2) we could multiply any row by a nonzero number and add it to another row.

Following the above-mentioned row operations, one gets the following simplex table:

BASIS	C_j	x_1 20	x_2 15	s_1 0	s_2 0	s_3 0	SOLUTION VALUES B_i
s_1	0	0	10	1	0	-3	600
s_2	0	0	2	0	1	-1	100
x_1	0	1	0	0	0	1	300
z_j							6000
$C_j - z_j$							

Since s_1, s_2, and x_1, are the basic variables in this table, x_2 and s_3 are set equal to 0, and we can read the solution for s_1, s_2, and x_1 directly from the table: $s_1 = 600$, $s_2 = 100$, $x_1 = 300$.

The profit corresponding to this solution is $6000. Note that the value for profit was obtained by multiplying the solution values for the basic variables in the B_i column by their corresponding objective function coefficients as given in the C_j column, that is, $0(600) + 0(100) + 20(300) = 6000$.

Moving toward a Better Solution

The next question we must ask ourselves is, can we find a new basic feasible solution (extreme point) that will increase the value of the objective function above $6000? To answer this, we need to calculate the z_j and $C_j - z_j$ rows for the current simplex table.

The elements in the z_j row can be calculated by multiplying the elements in the C_j column of the simplex table by the corresponding elements in the columns of the A matrix and summing.

Subtracting z_j from c_j to obtain the net evaluation row, one gets the complete simplex table:

		A					B
		x_1	x_2	s_1	s_2	s_3	SOLUTION VALUES
BASIS	C_j	20	15	0	0	0	B_i
s_1	0	0	10	1	0	−3	600
s_2	0	0	2	0	1	−1	100
x_1	20	1	0	0	0	1	300
	z_j	20	0	0	0	20	6000
	$C_j - z_j$	0	15	0	0	−20	

One should note that at each iteration of the simplex method

1. The value of the current basic feasible solution can be found in the B column of the simplex table
2. The value of $C_j - z_j$ for each of the basic variables is equal to zero
3. The coefficients in a particular column of the A portion of the simplex table indicate how much the current basic solution will change if one unit of the variable associated with that column is introduced.

Let us now analyze the net evaluation row $(C_j - z_j)$ to see whether we can introduce a new variable into the basis and continue to improve the objective function. Using the rule for determining which variable should enter the basis next, we select x_2, since it has the highest positive coefficient in the net evaluation row.

In order to determine which variable will be removed from the basis when x_2 enters, we must compute for each row i the ratio B_i/A_{i2} (note that one only computes this ratio if A_{i2} is greater than zero) and then select the variable corresponding to the minimum ratio as the variable to leave the basis. The table becomes:

BASIS	C_j	x_1 20	x_2 15	s_1 0	s_2 0	s_3 0	SOLUTION VALUES B_i	$\dfrac{B_i}{A_{i2}}$
s_1	0	0	10	1	0	−3	600	$\dfrac{600}{10} = 60$
s_2	0	0	②	0	1	−1	100	$\dfrac{100}{2} = 50$ →
x_1	20	1	0	0	0	1	300	Nonexistent (300)
								0
	z_j	20	0	0	0	20	6000	
	$C_j - z_j$	0	15	0	0	−20		

↑

After performing the calculations for the next iteration one obtains the following complete simplex table:

BASIS	C_j	x_1 20	x_2 15	s_1 0	s_2 0	s_3 0	SOLUTION VALUES B_i
s_1	0	0	0	1	−5	2	100
x_2	15	0	1	0	1/2	−1/2	50
x_1	20	1	0	0	0	1	300
z_j		20	15	0	7 1/2	12 1/2	6750
$C_j - z_j$		0	0	0	−7 1/2	−12 1/2	

The optimal solution to a linear programming problem has been reached when there are no positive values in the net evaluation row of the simplex table.

The complete optimal solution to the problem is thus:

$$x_1{}^* = 300, \; x_2{}^* = 50, \; s_1{}^* = 100, \; s_2{}^* = 0, \; s_3{}^* = 0$$

with a value of the objective function of $z^* = \$6750$. Thus if the management of Rival Company wants to maximize profit, 300 medium-size processors and 50 large-size processors should be produced. In addition, management should note that there will be 100 hours of idle time in the molding department.

With $s_2{}^* = 0$ and $s_3{}^* = 0$, there is no slack time available in the assembly and finishing departments. If it is possible to obtain additional man-hours for these two departments, management should consider doing so. The solution for Rival Company's problem achieved by using the simplex method is identical to the one presented earlier using the graphical method.

TREATMENT OF IRREGULARITIES

Steps 2 and 3 of the simplex procedure described in the preceding section are very important for the successful solution of the linear programming problem. Let us examine how these steps are accomplished for some irregular constraints.

If the right-hand side of a constraint is negative ($1x_1 - 11x_2 \leq -25$), the procedure of adding a slack variable ($x_1 - 11x_2 + s_1 = -25$) to obatin the table form is unacceptable since the constraint would not satisfy the table form requirement of nonnegative right-hand sides.

Sometimes a constraint may be an equality rather than an inequality.

For an equality constraint, for example,

$$1x_1 - 11x_2 = -25$$

We need only to multiply both sides of the equation by -1 in order to obtain

$$-1x_1 + 11x_2 = 25$$

which has an acceptable right-hand side.

At times, a constraint might not be less-than-or-equal-to constraint for a greater-than-or-equal-to constraint, for example,

$$1x_2 - 11x_2 \geq -25$$

we multiply both sides of an inequality by a negative number, and change the direction of the inequality. Thus,

$$-1x_1 - 11x_2 \leq 25$$

This constraint can now be treated in the same way as any ordinary less-than-or-equal-to constraint by adding a slack variable to the left-hand side.

What if there is a less-than-or-equal-to constraint?

For a less-than-or-equal-to constraint, for example,

$$1x_1 - 11x_2 \leq -25$$

we multiply both sides by -1 and change the direction of the inequality to obtain

$$-1x_1 + 11x_2 \geq 25$$

All one needs to do now to obtain the standard form is to subtract a surplus variable from the left-hand side.

Let us present an example that includes the irregularities mentioned above.

EXAMPLE

$$\max \{z = 10x_1 + 19x_2\}$$

subject to:
$$7x_1 + 1x_2 \leq 700$$

$$1x_1 + 5x_2 \leq 600$$

$$1x_1 + 2x_2 \leq 800$$

$$-1x_1 \qquad \leq -200$$

$$x_1, x_2 \qquad \geq 0$$

Using slack and surplus variables, the standard form is obtained.

$$\max \{z = 10x_1 + 19x_2 + 0s_1 + 0s_2 + 0s_3 + 0s_4 \quad -Ma_1 \quad \}$$

$$7x_1 + 1x_2 + 1s_1 \qquad\qquad\qquad = 700$$

$$1x_1 + 5x_2 + \qquad + 1s_2 \qquad\qquad = 600$$

$$1x_1 + 2x_2 + \quad\quad + 1s_3 \quad\quad\quad\quad = 800$$

$$1x_1 - \quad\quad\quad\quad\quad -1s_4 + a_1 = 200$$

$$x_1, x_2, s_1, s_2, s_3, s_4, a_1 \geq 0$$

Since for the initial basic feasible solution, one needs to set $x_1 = x_2 = 0$ and use four variables as the basis, we have added an artificial variable (a_1). The artificial variable has been introduced into the objective function with a very large negative coefficient M. This makes sure that the artificial variable will be driven out of the solution (i.e., will receive a value of zero) eventually.

From the standard form presented above, one proceeds to the construction of the simplex table and subsequent solution.

SHADOW PRICES

Shadow price is worth of an additional unit of a resource capacity. The information is obtained from the $C_j - z_j$ values associated with slack variables. In the final table for the Rival Company example, the shadow price for s_1 is $0.00; for s_2 it is $7.50; and for s_3 it is $12.50. This means that management should be willing to pay up to $7.50 for an additional hour of capacity in the assembly department (the constraint associated with s_2), and up to $12.50 for an additional hour in the finishing department, and nothing for additional capacity in the molding department.

TECHNICAL NOTE PROBLEMS

6.1 State the linear programming assumptions

6.2 What is a nonnegativity requirement?

6.3 What is a decision variable?

6.4 State the areas of application for linear programming.

6.5 Describe the graphical solution procedure of linear programming problems.

6.6 What type of information is provided by shadow prices?

6.7 How does one deal with negative right-hand-side coefficients?

6.8 Given

$$\min \{z = -2x_1 + x_2\}$$

subject to:

$$5x_1 - x_2 \leq 20$$

$$x_1 \quad\quad \leq 5$$

$$x_1, x_2 \quad \geq 0$$

solve the problem graphically.

Solution

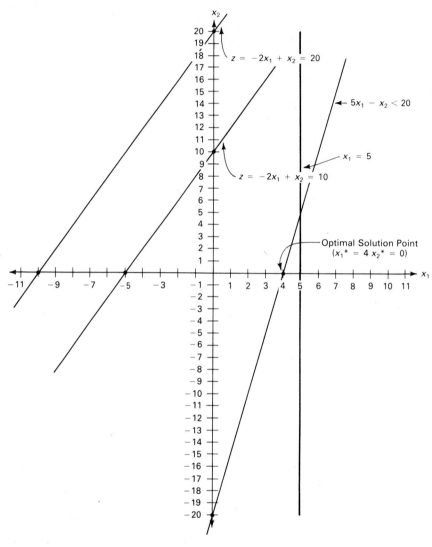

6.9 Given

$$\max \{z = 2x_1 + x_2\}$$

subject to:

$$5x_1 - x_2 \leq 20$$

$$x_1 \quad \leq 5$$

$$x_1, x_2 \quad \geq 0$$

solve using the simplex method.

Solution

$$\max \{z = -2x_1 + x_2 + 0s_1 + 0s_2\}$$

subject to:

$$5x_1 - x_2 + s_1 \quad = 20$$

$$x_1 \qquad\quad + s_2 = 5$$

$$x_1, x_2, s_1, s_2 \qquad \geq 0$$

		x_1	x_2	s_1	s_2	B_i	SOLUTION VALUES
BASIS	C_j	-2	$+1$	0	0	0	
s_1	0	5	-1	1	0	20	20/-1
s_2	0	1	0	0	0	5	5/0
	z_j	0	0	0	0	0	
$C_j \quad - \quad z_j$		-2	$+1$	0	0		

Please note that since all A_{i2} are less than or equal to zero, no variable in the basis is driven to zero as x_2 increases. $x_1{}^*$ and $x_2{}^* = \infty$, an unbounded solution for which $z^* = \infty$.

6.10 Maximize

$$z = 3x_1 + 2x_2$$

subject to:

$$3x_1 + 5x_2 \leq 60$$

$$6x_1 + 4x_2 \leq 48$$

$$x_1, x_2 \geq 0$$

Is there more than one solution to this problem? Check it graphically. (Solutions of this and the following problems appear in the Instructor's Manual.)

6.11 Maximize

$$z = x_1 + 2x_2$$

subject to:

$$2x_1 + 4x_2 \leq 9$$

$$3x_1 + x_2 \leq 12$$

$$x_1, x_2 \geq 0$$

6.12 Maximize

$$z = 3x_3 + 5x_2$$

subject to:

$$6x_1 - 4x_2 \geq 24$$

$$-4x_1 + 2x_2 \leq 12$$

$$x_1, x_2 \geq 0$$

a) Solve graphically.

b) What is the conclusion?

c) Solve graphically the same problem when z has to be minimized.

6.13 The Bombastic Oil Ventures (BOV) Company has in the past contracted out the shipment of its heavy oil from its oil fields to its refineries. The volume of deliveries is measured in ton-miles (the tons of oil times the number of miles over which the oil should be delivered).

Currently, BOV is paying Greek Marine Line (GML) $0.50 per ton-mile to deliver the product. BOV is considering purchasing a fleet of tankers to take over a part or all of this delivery service.

Three types of tankers are under consideration: large tankers, medium-size tankers, and small tankers. Details of each are given:

Tanker Type	Purchase Cost	Operating Cost (per ton-mile)	Capacity
Large Tanker	$15,000	$0.28	10,000
Medium Size Tanker	$8,000	$0.32	8,000
Small Tanker	$5,000	$0.40	6,000

GML has indicated that it would be willing to continue to deliver any excess of heavy oil not delivered by BOV's own tankers at the rate of $0.50 per ton-mile.

The budget for tankers' purchasing is in short supply, $380,000 in all. Because of the marine dock limitations, not more than 28 tanker spaces are available. A medium-size tanker and large tanker each use one space. Two small-size tankers use one space. At least two thirds of the tankers purchased would have to be either large or medium-size tankers. BOV wants to maximize the savings below the current $0.50 per ton-mile. Formulate as a linear programming problem; define all variables; explain the constraints.

BIBLIOGRAPHY

Management, Production, and Scheduling

Aarvik, O., and P. Randolph, "The Application of Linear Programming to the Determination of Transmission Fees in an Electrical Power Network," *Tims-ORSA Interfaces*, Vol. 6, No. 1, Nov., 1975, pp. 47–49.

Advant, S., "A Linear Programming Approach to Air Cleaner Design," *Operations Research*, Vol. 22, Mar.–Apr., 1974, pp. 295–97.

Chappel, A. E., "Linear Programming Cuts Costs in Production of Animal Fees," *Operational Research Quarterly*, Vol. 25, No. 1, Mar., 1974, pp. 19–26.

DE WET, G. L., "Comparative Costs, Linear Programming and the Decentralization of Industries," *South African Journal of Economics,* Vol. 40, June, 1972, pp. 152–62.

DYSON, R. G., and A. S. GREGORY, "The Cutting Stock Problem in the Flat Glass Industry," *Operational Research Quarterly,* Vol. 25, No. 1, Mar., 1974, pp. 41–45.

GLASSEY, C. R., and V. K. GUPTA, "A Linear Programming Analysis of Paper Recycling," *Management Science,* Vol. 21, Dec., 1974, pp. 392–40.

GOYAL, S. K., "A Decision Rule for Producing Christmas Greeting Cards," *Operations Research,* Vol. 22, July–Aug., 1974, pp. 795–801.

KRAJEWSKI, L. J., and H. E. THOMPSON, "Efficient Employment Planning in Public Utilities," *The Bell Journal of Economics,* Vol. 6, No. 1, Spring, 1975, pp. 314–26.

MAY, J. G., "A Linear Program for Economic Lot Sizes Using Labor Priorities," *Management Science,* Vol. 21, No. 3, Nov., 1974, pp. 277–85.

SZPIGEL, B., "Optimal Train Scheduling on a Single Track Railway," *Operational Research,* Vol. 20, 1972, pp. 343–51.

Accounting

CARSBERG, B., "On the Linear Programming Approach to Asset Valuation," *Journal of Accounting Research,* Vol. 7, Autumn, 1969, pp. 165–82.

CHARNES, A., C. COLANTONI, W. W. COOPER, and K. O. KORTANEK, "Economic Social and Enterprise Accounting and Mathematical Models," *The Accounting Review,* Vol. 47, Jan., 1972, pp. 85–108.

DEMSKI, J. S., "An Accounting System Structured on a Linear Programming Model," *The Accounting Review,* Vol. 42, Oct., 1967, pp. 701–12.

HARTLEY, R. V., "Linear Programming: Some Implications for Management Accounting," *Management Accounting,* 51, Nov., 1969, pp. 48–51.

SAMUELS, J. M., "Opportunity Costing: An Application of Mathematical Programming," *Journal of Accounting Research,* Vol. 3, Autumn, 1965, pp. 182–91.

SUMMERS, E. L., "The Audit Staff Assignment Problem: A Linear Programming Analysis," *The Accounting Review,* Vol. 47, July, 1972, pp. 443–53.

Administration, Education, and Politics

BARKAN, J. D., and J. E. BRUNO, "Operations Research in Planning Political Campaign Strategies," *Operations Research,* Vol. 20, Sept.–Oct., 1972, pp. 925–41.

BOWLES, S., "The Efficient Allocation of Resources in Education," *Quarterly Journal of Economics,* Vol. 81, May, 1967, pp. 189–219.

FRANKLIN, A. D., and E. KOENIGSBERG, "Computer School Assignments in a Large District," *Operations Research,* Vol. 21, Mar.–Apr., 1973, pp. 413–26.

KOCH, J. V., "A Linear Programming Model of Resource Allocation in a University," *The Journal for the American Institute for Decision Sciences,* Vol. 4, Oct., 1973, pp. 494–504.

MCKEOWN, P., and B. WORKMAN, "A Study in Using Linear Programming to Assign Students to Schools," *Tims-ORSA Interfaces,* Vol. 6, No. 4, Aug., 1976, pp. 96–100.

Advertising and Marketing

ENGEL, J. F., and R. WARSHAW, "Allocating Advertising Dollars by Linear Programming," *Journal of Advertising Research*, Vol. 4, No. 3, Sept., 1964, pp. 42–48.

GENSCH, D. H. , "Computer Models in Advertising Media Selection," *Journal of Marketing Research*, Vol. 5, Nov., 1968, pp. 414–24.

KOTLER, P., "Toward an Explicity Model for Media Selection," *Journal of Advertising Research*, Vol. 4, Mar., 1964, pp. 34–41.

YOUNG, L. F., "Media Buying Controlled by Sales Territories," *Journal of Advertising Research*, Vol. 9, No. 4, Dec., 1969, pp. 11–14.

Finance

BRADLEY, S. P., and D. B. CRANE, "A Dynamic Model for Bond Portfolio Management," *Management Science*, Vol. 19, Oct., 1972, pp. 139–51.

KROUSE, C. G., "Optimal Financing and Capital Structure Programs for the Firm," *The Journal of Finance*, Vol. 27, Dec., 1972, pp. 1057–71.

FELDSTEIN, M., and H. LUFT, "Distributional Constraints in Public Expenditure Planning," *Management Science*, Vol. 19, Aug., 1973, pp. 1414–22.

HEROUX, R. L., and W. A. WALLACE, "Linear Programming and Financial Analysis of the New Community Development Process," *Management Science*, Vol. 19, Apr., 1973, pp. 857–72.

LEE, S. M., and A. J. LERRO, "Optimizing the Portfolio Selection for Mutual Funds," *The Journal of Finance*, Vol. 28, Dec., 1973, pp. 1087–1101.

MASSE, P., and R. GIBRAT, "Application of Linear Programming to Investments in the Electric Power Industry," translated by G. B. Dantzig, *Management Science*, Vol. 3, Jan., 1957, pp. 149–66.

SHARPE, W. F., "A Linear Programming Algorithm for Mutual Funds Portfolio Selection," *Management Science*, Vol. 13, No. 3, Nov., 1967, pp. 499–510.

WARREN, J. M., and J. P. SHELTON, "A Simultaneous Equation Approach to Financial Planning," *The Journal of Finance*, Vol. 26, Dec., 1971, pp. 1123–42.

WEINGARTNER, H. M., *Mathematical Programming and the Analysis of Capital Budgeting Problems.* Englewood Cliffs, N.J.: Prentice-Hall, Inc., 1963.

7

Facility Layout

INTRODUCTION

Once a proper location for a facility is found, the various functions must be located inside the facility. This procedure is termed facilities layout, plant layout, plant design, or facilities design.

The planning of a layout is a task that has profound implications on the profitability and the operational efficiency of service and manufacturing organizations. The layout is studied in the following cases:

1. When a new facility is designed to replace an old one: *capacity displacement*
2. When an existing facility is expanded to increase its operational output: *capacity expansion*
3. When a new process or method that reduces costs, increases quality, etc., is found to replace the current one: *capacity change*
4. When a change in capacity is effected to produce a change in the mix of goods or services: *capacity mix*

By definition, *layout planning is comprised of all the activities involved in selecting locations for and transportation routes among departments, processes, work centers, machines, and service functions.* Layout planning is multidimensional in that it must satisfy various—and often conflicting—objectives and wants. Some of the objectives of layout planning are:

1. To minimize materials-handling costs among different functions
2. To reduce congestion of personnel and material

3. To increase safety of personnel
4. To increase labor efficiency
5. To improve morale
6. To facilitate communication and coordination, as required
7. To provide operations flexibility
8. To increase quality of working life through better physical (light, temperature, noise) and psychological (possibility of socializing and communicating) conditions.

As layout planning involves a multiplicity of objectives, it is apparent that informed judgment is the best tool with which to attack the problem, as most quantitative tools are limited in their ability to bring about all the objectives.

Let us consider the impact of input, process, and output on layout planning. From the input end of operations, capacity dictates specific quantities of raw materials received, stored, retrieved, and transported. The sizing and location of the storage areas is considered part of the layout problem. In a service operation, such as a bank, the waiting customers are "stored" in line.

On the process end, several items are considered. For example, inventories should be built up between successive operations to reduce disruption of work due to breakdowns. The in-process inventory storage area is a layout problem. The location of various departments, including the service departments (such as maintenance, quality control, and first aid), is a layout problem. The maintenance department should be located near failure-prone areas or machines, and the quality control department next to the most critical processing unit.

On the output end, finished goods storage areas and the conveyors that deliver finished goods into storage must be considered in the layout decision. The size of the product, the capacity of production, and the transportation requirements will dictate the need for a warehouse or access to a rail car. This is part of the layout problem.

We shall use informed judgment aided by quantitative and computerized techniques to arrive at an acceptable, if not optimal, layout. The next section presents, through an industrial case, the relationship between technology, capacity and layout planning.

TECHNOLOGY, CAPACITY AND LAYOUT PLANNING: AN INDUSTRIAL CASE

We shall demonstrate that the technology used and the capacity required have a major impact on the layout planning, by considering the planning of a potato chip plant. In order to be competitive in producing potato chips, a continuous and automated process is selected by the management. The process starts with raw potatoes and ends with potato chips in bags and/or boxes, with no handling in between.

The operation is completely automated with two control devices. First, the temperature is controlled automatically to provide the required cooking-oil temperature. Second, the rate at which the sliced potatoes are fed into the cooker is controlled.

The main operations involved are peeling, slicing, frying, seasoning, and packaging. The process is illustrated in Figure 7.1.

PEELING   Raw and dirty potatoes are fed into a hopper. Then, the potatoes are thoroughly washed to remove dirt and to prevent the particles from damaging the equipment. The potatoes are then transferred to the peeler. There are three common peeling methods: abrasion, lye immersion, and steam. In the abrasion method, potatoes are peeled by disks or rollers with abrasive coating. In lye peeling, pressure spray washers remove the surfaces and eyes already softened and loosened by a hot caustic solution. Steam peeling is a very efficient process, but it has the disadvantage of cooking the potato surface, which will affect the appearance of the potato chip.

SLICING   Potatoes are then cut into slices of various thickness (1/15 to 1/4 inch), according to the type of potatoes, frying temperature, and time.

FRYING   Frying is the core of the process. The frying equipment may vary from one manufacturer to another, but the basic elements remain the same: a tank of hot oil in which the chips are cooked; a reservoir in which hot oil is heated to the desired temperature; a conveyor that carries the cooked chips out of the tank; a filtering unit that remove particles from the oil used for cooking; a heating and circulating oil unit; and vapor-collecting hoods over the tank.

It is important to recoup oil because it is a very costly ingredient. The oil used in the process transfers the heat to the potato slices and becomes part of the potato chips. That is why it is important to use a high-quality oil. When the chips are completely cooked, they come out on a conveyor.

SEASONING   The next step involves adding special flavor to the chips. Powders are dropped onto the chips at this point to provide special taste to meet consumer requirements.

PACKAGING   The finished product is transferred to the packaging area. In some instances, the potato chips are dumped into large containers that are unloaded to the packaging machines when needed. Since this process involves handling and interruptions, most plants are equipped with machinery that can accumulate potato chips before switching to the packaging equipment. This kind of conveyor permits the packaging process to be stopped during breaks and lunches while the cooking process continues.

The shelf-life of potato chips is from four to six weeks, provided the frying oil is stabilized and the packaging is opaque.

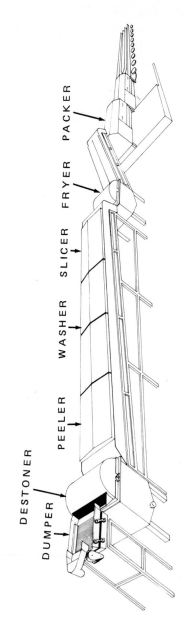

Figure 7.1 Potato Chip Production Line

The main reasons for loss of quality or freshness are breakage, absorption of moisture, or fat oxidation that leads to rancidity.

The typical equipment capacity is 1500 pounds per hour, which has implications for storage before packaging and after packaging. This and other machinery specifications, including dimensions, are given in Figure 7.2.

LAYOUT   One must provide for a minimum storage area for raw materials and equipment. Potato chip producers tend to try to receive continuous shipments of fresh potatoes, thus avoiding warehousing costs and handling. The management has provided (see Figure 7.3) 7000 square feet for this purpose.

In some of the newest installations, cooking takes place "on the mezzanine," a cooker having been installed on a structure above the floor. The conveyor and the packaging systems are located on the ground floor. This system provides economy of space.

Space for the installation and operation of the complete chip line is estimated to be 16,000 square feet. Space is available for the addition of a second cooker.

Another area of 7000 square feet has been allocated for the shipping area and the storage of finished product. The office could be located on the second floor above this area.

The total building area is to 30,000 square feet. This space allows for production, shipping, and receiving areas. Building costs for such a type of structure (30 feet high) is about $10/square foot. A total area of one and a half acres (65,000 square feet) would be suitable for these purposes.

FIGURE 7.2   SPECIFICATIONS—POTATO CHIP FRYER MODELS: THE INFORMATION
USED TO DESIGN THE LAYOUT

Cooker Model Number	DIMENSIONS			SPECIFICATIONS	
	Length	*Width*	*Height*	*Capacity*	*Heating Surface Area*
M60	62'3"	4'6"	4'0"	500–600 lb/hr	336 sq. ft
	18.97 m	1.37 m	1.22 m	227–272 kg/hr	31 sq. m
M100	62'3"	4'10"	4'0"	900–1000 lb/hr	798 sq. ft
	18.97 m	1.46 m	1.22 m	408–454 kg/hr	74 sq. m
M150	64'3"	5'4"	5'4"	1400–1500 lb/hr	1196 sq. ft
	19.58 m	1.63 m	1.62 m	635–680 kg/hr	111 sq. m
M220	64'3"	6'7"	6'6"	2000–2200 lb/hr	1596 sq. ft
	19.58 m	2.0 m	1.98 m	907–998 kg/hr	148 sq. m
M260	70'3"	6'7"	8'0"	2400–2600 lb/hr	1995 sq. ft
	21.41 m	2.0 m	2.44 m	1088–1179 kg/hr	185 sq. m
M320	74'3"	6'7"	8'0"	3000–3200 lb/hr	2270 sq. ft
	22.63 m	2.0 m	2.44 m	1361–1451 kg/hr	211 sq. m

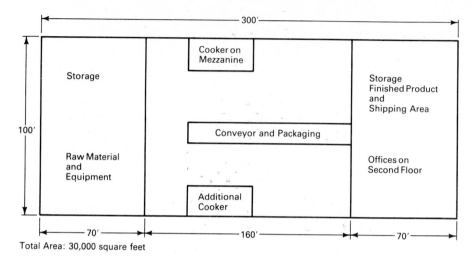

Figure 7.3   Potato Chip Plant Layout

Actual costs for land in a medium-sized town have been estimated at $25,000 per acre. It is difficult to determine a precise figure since the cost of land can often be negotiated with the selected city. The $25,000-per-acre figure includes installation of services by the city.

The layout determines the size of the building and the area of land that is required. Based on this data, an estimate of total capital outlay and break-even point may be established.

An efficient layout will result in a lower break-even point and will help increase profits. A poor layout will result in a higher break-even point and will decrease profits. This is shown in Figure 7.4 (there, a poor layout is shown to increase variable costs by 25 percent).

Because of the automated technology and large capacity requirement, the potato chip manufacturer has decided to use the product-type layout for his plants. This is one of the layout types found in operating organizations. Let us examine the various types of layouts.

OPERATION TYPES

The layout type depends on the operation type. There are basically two kinds of operations: process oriented (intermittent operation process) and product oriented (continuous operation process).

Process-oriented operations are characterized by low production volume, general-purpose equipment, labor-intensive activities, frequent schedule changes, complex product mix, made-to-order products, and interrupted product flow.

Product-oriented operations are characterized by high product volume, special purpose machinery, capital-intensive activities, continuous product

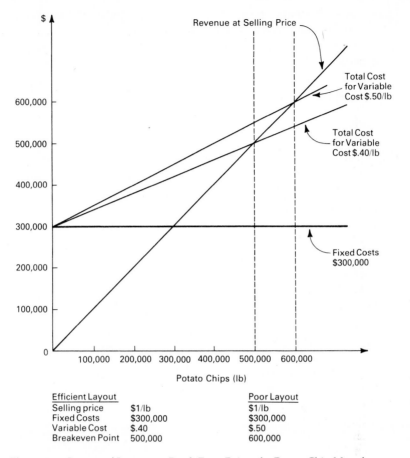

Figure 7.4   Impact of Layout on Break-Even Point of a Potato Chip Manufacturer

flow, minimum schedule changes, limited product mix, standardization, and made-for-inventory products.

LAYOUT TYPES

The layout type used for an operation depends to a high degree on the operation type. There are four different layout types:

Process Layout

In a process layout, the work centers are grouped together according to the type of function performed. Similar general-purpose machines are grouped together. Process layouts are found in those cases where the work flow is not standardized for all products, as in a job shop or a medical clinic. Hospitals have all x-ray machines grouped in one department. Banks have all loan officers grouped together in one area. A job shop will have all machining done in one department and all assembly done in a separate department. An example of a process layout in a library operation appears in Figure 7.5. The process layout is applicable to the job shop as well. For example, see Figure 7.6.

Product Layout

In a product layout, where each of the products requires the same sequence of operations, work centers are grouped in sequence to accommodate the specific product needs. Every work center provides a highly specialized service or

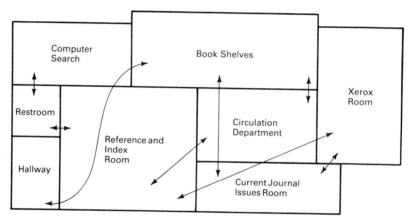

Figure 7.5   Process Layout in a Library (arrows indicate flow of people between departments)

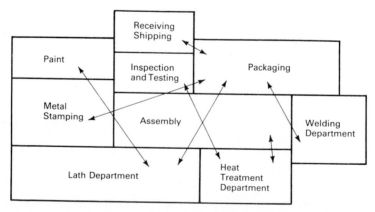

Figure 7.6   Process Layout in a Job Shop (arrows indicate flow of products)

process. For example, a university registration operation, a car wash, and a car assembly line are arranged as a product layout. Figure 7.7 demonstrates a product layout for a potato chip operation, and Figure 7.8 demonstrates a product layout for a university registration operation.

Fixed Position Layout

The following layout types are used in special cases of process-type operations. In a fixed position layout, the product remains in one location, while tools, materials, and labor are brought to it, as required, to perform the appropriate operations. Layouts for building airplanes, submarines, and missiles are of this type, as are those for agricultural work in which labor and material are brought to the field. An example of a fixed position layout as used in a foundry to produce molten iron appears in Figure 7.9.

Project Layout

A project layout is similar to a fixed position layout in that the tools, materials, and labor are brought to the product, as required, to perform the appropriate operations. However, unlike the site for the fixed position layout, the site changes from product to product. For example, in a building construction project, after construction is completed, the next product (building) is built in another location.

Most layouts are a mixture of the layouts discussed above. As the volume of operations increases, a layout design will change. More specialized equip-

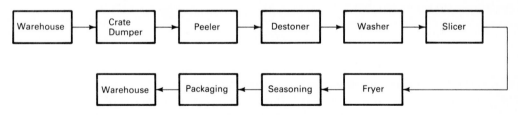

Figure 7.7 Product Layout for a Potato Chip Manufacturer

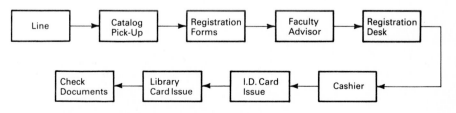

Figure 7.8 Product Layout for a University Registration Operation

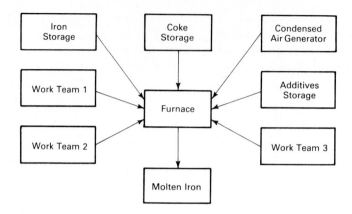

Figure 7.9   Fixed Position Layout in a Foundry

ment will be used, and the variety of products will decrease. This will effect a gradual change from a process to a product layout.

LAYOUT DESIGN COMPARISON

As discussed in the potato chip processing case, the layout type chosen has a great impact on the capacity of the plant, its product standardization, flexibility, and profitability. The potato chip manufacturer has decided, based on the technology available, that product-type layout best suits his needs.

At times, there are several technologies available, and thus several types of layouts may be considered. The decision should be based on economic trade-offs and availability of financial resources. Table 7.1 presents a taxonomy of layout types and their characteristics.

Naturally, there are always exceptions. For example, the construction of a small private residence or an office building might be enhanced by using prefabricated material. The product becomes standardized, interchangeable, and high volume. Low-skilled personnel could be used, and high-capital investment is called for to build a plant that produces prefabricated material. This will change the nature of the project layout to resemble somewhat the product layout.

ESSENTIALS OF LAYOUT ANALYSIS

Most layout analyses are based on informed judgments and past experience. However, there are various formal methodologies that can be used for the analysis.

The traditional approaches to facilities layout problems seem to follow a common path. First, layout problems are categorized as manufacturing or

TABLE 7.1 LAYOUT TYPES AND THEIR CHARACTERISTICS

DESIGN CHARACTERISTICS / LAYOUT TYPE	PRODUCT CHARACTERISTICS	PRODUCT FLOW	WORK CONTENT AND LABOR SKILLS	INCENTIVE APPROACH
Product Layout	Standardization; interchangeable parts; high volume; stable demand	Same sequence of operations on each product	Specialized work content; unskilled or low-skill workers; routine repetitious tasks	Group incentives
Process Layout	Nonstandardized—made to order; diversified product mix	Changing flow pattern; sequence of operations changes from order to order	Diversified work content; skilled personnel; minimal supervision	Individual incentive plans based on quantity, quality or some combination of both
Fixed Position Layout	Low volume; unique product unit	Minimal product flow; all resources brought to the product	Location constant; work content varied and often complex; high-skilled personnel	Group incentives
Project Layout	Low volume; unique product unit	No product flow—all resources brought to the product	Location varied from project to project; work content varied; high-skilled personnel	Group incentives based on measured units

TABLE 7.1 (Cont.)

LAYOUT TYPE \ DESIGN CHARACTERISTICS	MATERIALS HANDLING	INVENTORY AND SUPPLY REQUIREMENTS	CAPITAL REQUIREMENTS	PRODUCTION COSTS
Product Layout	Predictable flow; conveyor belt and other fixed material-handling equipment	Steady supply of raw material; high turnover of in-process inventory	High capital investment in specialized equipment and fixed material-handling equipment	High fixed costs; low variable costs
Process Layout	Nonpredictable flow; type and volume of handling changes from order to order	Varied requirements; fluctuating supply; low turnover of in-process inventory	Relatively low capital investment in general-purpose machinery	Relatively low fixed costs of material, labor, and material handling
Fixed Position Layout	Low-volume material handling; heavy-duty general-purpose equipment	Low turnover of inventory; intermittent flow of raw material	Varied; general-purpose heavy-duty equipment	Relatively low fixed costs; high cost of materials, labor, and material handling
Project Layout	Low-volume material handling; heavy-duty general-purpose equipment	Low turnover of inventory; intermittent flow of raw and semi-processed material	Varied; depends on size of the project	Relatively low fixed costs; high cost of material, labor, and material handling

nonmanufacturing, product or process, and initial or relayout. The nonmanufacturing layout is frequently regarded as being analogous to manufacturing layout, with recommendations to adapt the tools of the one to the other. Product layout is typically considered elementary insofar as the location of the various work centers or machines is concerned, because of the severe restrictions arising from sequential constraints. The problem of balancing the work load among the various work centers assumes primary consideration in a product layout with the assumption of standardized methods. Relayout is considered to be the same as initial layout with added constraints (e.g., existing offices, buildings, service facilities). This traditional approach leads to the determination of the initial, manufacturing, process layout as the most complex case.

The measure of effectiveness for layout problems traditionally has been concerned with the flow of materials. Changes in manufacturing methods have complicated the determination of this flow, and new techniques have evolved for better examination of complex flow situations. The criterion for quantitative layout models is now frequently stated as the minimization of materials-handling cost, which is assumed to be an incremental linear function of the distances between the work centers, machines, or departments of the system under study.

Graphic and Schematic Analysis

The most familiar tools utilized for the solution of layout problems have been graphic and schematic models, particularly two-and-three-dimensional templates, product flow process charts, assembly charts, and operation process charts.

Recent improvements in graphic and schematic layout techniques include the load-distance model and systematic layout planning. They call for the use of data collected on the amount of materials flowing from each department to every other department for some time period. The data are accumulated into a matrix form that is frequently referred to as a from-to-chart, load chart, or flow matrix. The methodology for reducing materials flow is to locate departments in such a way as to minimize the volume of non-adjacent departmental flow.

One should remember, however, that graphic and schematic analysis becomes virtually unmanageable when the number of departments becomes at all large (say above 10) unless the flow has a dominant pattern. In the following sections, we shall cover some of the most common analysis techniques for process and product layout planning.

Load-Distance Analysis

The process layout has been characterized as a layout that accommodates varied work flows, different products, and high material-handling volume. A workpiece is moved from one work center to another at intermittent intervals. In a library, for example, books are moved from the circulation center back to the shelf.

The most acute problem in the process-type layout is, thus, the material-handling cost. The layout of work centers would be arranged to minimize the total cost of moving units between work centers. A long move costs more than a short move. A move of a larger quantity costs more than a move of a smaller quantity.

The load-distance analysis is the most common approach to process-type layout. This analysis considers the number of interdepartmental moves of a product, as well as the distances over which the moves are made. Let

$$N = \text{the number of work centers (departments)}$$

$$P_{ij} = \text{the number of products moved between work centers } i \text{ and } j$$

$$D_{ij} = \text{the distance between work centers } i \text{ and } j$$

$$M = \text{the cost of moving one product one distance unit.}$$

The total cost (C) involved in all moves between all the departments can be expressed as

$$C = \sum_{i=1}^{N} \sum_{j=1}^{N} P_{ij} D_{ij} M \qquad (7.1)$$

The first step of the analysis is to determine the number of products, P_{ij}, that should be moved between all pairs of work centers during a certain period. The usual length of this period is one year. The estimated number of moves is summarized in a load matrix, as in Figure 7.10. The numbers for the P_{ij} are obtained from production control or work flow observations.

Work Center / Work Center	1	2	3	4	5	6
1	—	150	110	300	150	140
2	—	—	120	50	70	80
3	—	—	—	120	90	100
4	—	—	—	—	80	60
5	—	—	—	—	—	70
6	—	—	—	—	—	—

The number of products moved from work center 3 to work center 4 over one year.

Figure 7.10   Load Matrix Showing Expected Number of Products, P_{ij}, Moved Between all Pairs of Work Centers

In the second step of the analysis, the distances D_{ij}, among all pairs of work centers, is determined. In order to start the procedure, one must assume some initial layout configuration. Work centers are positioned in some way to accommodate available space. The cost of that configuration is then calculated. Since we are trying to minimize material-handling costs, the work centers are relocated in such a way that the costs are decreased. The process is repeated, using equation (7.1) until no further reduction in cost is found. The final arrangement is the one that should minimize the total cost of products movement.

In a rectangular building, the six departments of Figure 7.9 may be placed in $6! = 6 \times 5 \times 4 \times 3 \times 2 \times 1 = 720$ ways. However, many of these configurations are equivalent in regard to cost, since the relative positioning of work centers is the same. As an example, the four configurations in Figure 7.11 are virtually equivalent, in that the same departments are adjacent to each other.

Let us assume that the move from one work center to an adjacent center costs $M = \$1$ per product and an extra $M = \$1$ per product to cross over a department. Let us examine the two configurations in Figure 7.12 by using a cost matrix.

The figures in the cost matrix of Figure 7.12(a) are found by multiplying the loads of Figure 7.10 by the appropriate material-handling costs. For example, since work centers 1 and 2 are adjacent, one multiplies $150 \times \$1$, to get $150. Similarly, the load between work centers 1 and 3 is multiplied by $2, for a total of

1	2	3
4	5	6

4	5	3
1	2	6

4	2	3
1	5	6

4	5	6
1	2	3

Figure 7.11 Different But Equivalent Relative Positioning of Work Centers

	1	2	3
	4	5	6

	1	2	3	4	5	6
1		150	220	300	150	280
2			120	50	70	80
3				240	90	100
4					80	120
5						70
6						

(a) Initial Layout Cost Matrix   Total Cost = $2120

	1	3	2
	4	6	5

	1	2	3	4	5	6
1		300	110	300	300	140
2			120	100	70	80
3				120	90	100
4					160	60
5						70
6						

+ 150 + 110 + 150 − 140 =   270

+ 50   =   50

− 120   =   −120

+ 80 − 60   =   20

Total cost = $2340

(b) Revised Layout Cost Matrix

Figure 7.12   The Use of the Cost Matrix for Layout Analysis

$220. The total cost is calculated by summing all the cost figures in the cost matrix.

As one can see, the initial layout resulted in a total annual cost of $2,120. Repositioning work centers 2, 3, 5, and 6 results in a higher annual cost: $2340. Obviously, configuration 7.12(b) is less desirable than 7.12(a). The search to find the optimal configuration should continue.

The limitations of the load-distance model approach are:

1. Since the only criterion for location of work centers is the material-handling cost, no consideration is given to the particular work center function. In the optimal layout, shipping and receiving, for example, could be positioned between the assembly and machining departments. This is an operationally unacceptable solution, however, since the assembly and machining departments should be adjacent for better communication and coordination.
2. The assumption is made that departments are equal in size.
3. Work center areas are assumed to have unlimited access.
4. No regard is given to stairs, posts, columns, walls, and other obstacles.
5. No alternative material-handling equipment is considered. A costly fork lift truck might, for example, be replaced by a manual delivery system, by a belt or a roller conveyor. These alternatives might change the material-handling cost, affecting the cost matrix.

Systematic Layout Planning

In various instances, the number of products moved between work centers is either impractical to obtain or does not express the qualitative factors that are important to the relative positioning decision. In these cases, systematic layout planning, which was first suggested by Muther,[1] is used.

Systematic layout planning (SLP) is based on a relationship chart that shows the degree of importance of having each work center positioned adjacent to another. From this chart an activity relationship diagram is developed.

The activity relationship diagram is adjusted by trial and error until a satisfactory positioning is obtained. This positioning is modified to meet space limitations. Figure 7.13 is an illustration of the technique in a case of a library layout. In Figure 7.13(a), a relationship chart is developed. The closeness of various work centers in the library is assessed using the following legend: Absolutely Necessary (AN), Important (I), Closeness Preferred (O), Unimportant (U), and Undesirable (X). The reason for the closeness rating is specified on the relationship chart and is coded as well. For example, closeness is preferred (O) between circulation and the photo duplication service because it provides better supervision (Code 1) of the latter work center by the circulation supervisor. The circulation department could not be close (X) to the computer search department, since the circulation department is a relatively noisy area (Code 5), and so on.

Based on the relationship chart, an initial relationship diagram is developed in Figure 7.13(b). In a graphical manner, the closeness ratings are marked and consulted. An initial layout, based on the initial relationship diagram and

[1] See R. Muther and J. D. Wheeler, "Simplified Systematic Layout Planning" *Factory*, Vol. 120, Nos. 8, 9, 10 (August, September, October, 1962), pp. 68–77, 111–119, 101–113.

TO FROM	2	3	4	5	Area
1. Circulation	O --- 1	I --- 3	X --- 5	U --- 	400
2. Photoduplication	---	U ---	U ---	AN --- 2	100
3. Information	---	---	O --- 1	I --- 2	200
4. Computer Search	---	---	---	I --- 2	100
5. Book Shelves	---	---	---	---	100

Closeness Rating (Letter)

Reason for Rating (Number)

Legend—Reason for Rating

Code	Reason
1	Supervision
2	Accessibility
3	Share Some Space
4	Psychology
5	Environmental (Noise)

Legend—Closeness Rating

Value	Closeness	Line Code*
AN	Absolutely Necessary	═══════
I	Important	════
O	Closeness Preferred	────
U	Unimportant	
X	Undesirable	XXXXXXXXX

*In practice, will be "Color code"

Figure 7.13 Systematic Layout Planning for a Library

ignoring work center areas, is developed. Finally, as shown in Figure 7.13(c), a final layout is presented, based on the initial layout and work center areas.

One should note that the closeness rating can be expanded to include other ratings as well. However, as this technique is a manual technique, the number of work centers, closeness ratings, and reasons for rating are limited.

By resorting to computer programs, a more complete set of considerations could be treated. Various measurements of flow and a variety of constraints, such as stairwells and elevators, could be taken into account.

COMPUTER MODELS FOR PROCESS LAYOUT

CRAFT, which stands for computerized relative allocation of facilities technique,[2] requires as input an initial block diagram, a load matrix, and a material-

[2] E. S. Buffa, G. C. Armour, and T. E. Vollman, "Allocating Facilities with CRAFT," *Harvard Business Review*, March–April, 1964, pp. 136–150.

(a) Relationship Chart

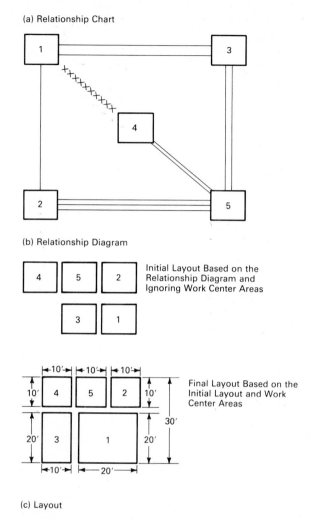

(b) Relationship Diagram

Initial Layout Based on the
Relationship Diagram and
Ignoring Work Center Areas

Final Layout Based on the
Initial Layout and Work
Center Areas

(c) Layout

Figure 7.13   (Cont.)

handling cost matrix. It can handle up to 40 work centers and outputs block layout, conforming to building dimensions. It also provides the cost of each solution computed.

The minimum total material handling cost is the criterion used by CRAFT to find the optimal solution. However, the final solution is a function of the initial layout, and instances are computed between work center centroids. The CRAFT program is limited to single-story buildings, and departments can be fixed in location.

CORELAP, which stands for computerized relationship layout planning,[3] is not confined to any particular building shape. It can handle up to 70 work centers, with up to 1,000 relationships. As input, CORELAP requires a reference table giving relative department location preferences, building width-length ratio, departmental area restrictions, and size of work centers. The output consists of a numerical layout matrix printout. The criterion for optimality is the maximum total closeness rating for all layouts calculated.

ALDEP, which stands for automated layout design program,[4] can layout a multistory building of up to 3 floors, that houses up to 63 work centers. As input, the program requires the size and number of like work center, building dimensions (including aisles and stairwells), and a preference table like the one used by CORELAP. As output, the program provides the layout matrix with work centers and aisles drawn by plotter, and a preference score for each layout. The criterion for optimization is the maximum preference score for all layouts generated.

The characteristics of the three programs are presented in Table 7.2.

OTHER ASPECTS OF PROCESS LAYOUT ANALYSIS

Now that we have covered several techniques for layout analysis, there are two questions that come to mind:

1. Which technique should be used under a given set of circumstances?
2. Are quantitative/computer derived layouts superior to the traditional designs developed without computers?

In trying to develop the best technique to use in a specific case, the following steps[5] might be helpful:

STEP 1: DETERMINE THE COMPATIBILITY OF THE MATERIALS-HANDLING LAYOUT WITH THE PROBLEM UNDER STUDY Examine the specific problem at hand, and attempt to determine what factor can be modeled as materials flow. Traditional plant layout approaches have been constrained in their definition of the term "materials." Existing techniques provide useful results by utilizing any factor as a criterion that varies as a function of the distance between work centers. If in the problem under study any factor can be

---

[3] R. S. Lee, and J. M. Moore, "CORELAP—Computerized Relationship Layout Planning," *Journal of Industrial Engineering*, Vol. 18, No. 3, March, 1967, pp. 195–220.

[4] J. M. Sheehof, and W. O. Evans, "Automated Layout Design Programs," *Journal of Industrial Engineering*, Vol. 18, No. 2, December, 1967, pp. 690–95.

[5] For an extended treatment of this subject consult T. E. Vollman, and E. S. Buffa, "The Facilities Layout Problem in Perspective." *Management Science*, Vol. 12, No. 10, June, 1966, pp. B-461–465.

identified as being influenced by the relative location of work centers, the analysis can proceed to step 2. If, on the other hand, no factor exists in the problem that can conceivably be treated as "materials," the investigation should proceed to step 6.

STEP 2: DETERMINE THE BASIC SUBUNITS FOR ANALYSIS Identify what is to be the basic work center or department subunits in the particular problem. The layout problem typically assumes that each subsystem is specified and that the grouping process itself is not a part of the layout problem. However, departmental organization may in fact be determined by layout. For any particular problem, answers to the following questions may provide considerable insight. Is the present grouping system (assuming one exists) to dictate future grouping? What changes in work methodology are expected to occur?

   For a given problem, the salient question is whether or not the departmentation is fixed. If the answer is fixed, the analysis can proceed to step 3. If the departmentation is not fixed, two things may be done. First, the existing departments may be subdivided into smaller units. Second, the departmentation bases themselves can be evaluated by treating them as variables to be investigated by simulation.

STEP 3: DETERMINE THE COMPATIBILITY OF THE PROBLEM COST WITH THE MODEL COST Determine whether the materials-handling cost is linear, incremental, and assignable for the particular problem. Materials-handling cost models necessarily assume these cost characteristics. Is the materials-handling cost of an incremental nature? If so, can the cost be readily assigned to particular activities or must the assignment process necessarily become arbitrary, as is true for overhead allocation? Is the cost selected linear? If not, is linear approximation satisfactory? Is the cost significant—i.e., how does the cost under study compare to other system costs?

   The major question for any particular problem situation is whether the problem cost is consistent with the above concepts. If the answer is a clear-cut yes, the interrogation process can move to step 4. If the answer is a clear-cut no, the process can proceed to Step 6. If the answer is not clear-cut, the costs may be evaluated by treating them as variables to be investigated by simulation.

STEP 4: EXAMINE THE IMPACT OF LOAD-DATA ASSUMPTIONS Examine the specific problem and attempt to ascertain how sensitive the final results are to load-data changes. In this pursuit, answers to the following questions may provide considerable insight. To what extent will future load data differ from the data used for model input? Are existing data representative? How sensitive to random changes in the data is a layout generated on the basis of existing data? What change in load data would occur if production of some product were to change by some factor? Which products would cause the most difference? Is

TABLE 7.2 CHARACTERISTICS OF COMPUTERIZED LAYOUT MODELS

INPUT	PROBLEM SIZE HANDLED	OUTPUT	CRITERION OF EFFECTIVENESS	REMARKS
ALDEP (Automated Layout Design Program) 1. Size and number of each department to be located in the building 2. Description of building dimensions, which must include areas assigned to specific building features (aisles, stairwells, etc.); these data are fed into program in form of a matrix 3. Preference table giving relative department location preferences, denoted by letters A, B, C, V, F, X, which range from "absolutely essential" (A) to "undesirable" (F) 4. Control cards to activate subroutines, such as "number of layouts to be tried" CORELAP (Computerized Relationship Layout Planning)	1. 63 departments	1. Layout matrix with departments and aisles drawn by plotter 2. Preference score for each layout	1. Maximum preference score (for all layouts generated)	1. Program can layout a multistory building up to 3 floors 2. Departmental exchanges may be made randomly or according to criteria 3. Departments are exchanged 2 at a time 4. Authors favor using the program in concert with a layout planner who, at various stages, inserts departments into intermediate layouts 5. Best suited for relayout

308

1. Relationship chart similar to preference chart used in ALDEP 2. Building width-length ratio 3. Departmental area restrictions 4. Size of area modules to be manipulated to form each department 5. Number of modules per department	1. 70 departments with over 1000 interdepartmental relationships	1. Numerical layout matrix printout 2. Can use digital plotter as CALCOMP plotter	1. Maximum total closeness rating (for all layouts tested)	1. Not confined to any particular building shape 2. Yields near optimum solutions according to authors 3. Requires little computer time

CRAFT (Computerized Relative Allocation of Facilities Technique)

1. Initial block layout 2. Load matrix (tabulation) of loads, e.g., materials, that flow between all combinations of departments 3. Material-handling cost matrix (handling costs between departments)	1. 40 departments	1. Block layout, shaped to conform to building dimensions	1. Minimum total material-handling cost	1. Final solution is function of initial layout 2. Later versions exchange departments 3 at a time rather than 2 at a time, as in ALDEP and CORELAP 3. Distances computed between department centroids 4. Limit—1-story building 5. Departments can be fixed in location

there some layout that will provide superior results for several alternative load data?

Determine the coefficient of variation of the load data. (The coefficient of variation has been presented in Chapter 4.) At this point in the analysis, the decision has been made that materials-handling cost is an appropriate measure of effectiveness for the particular problem under study. This does not mean, however, that a computerized model is necessarily required in order to determine the best layout. Before the decision is made to use a sophisticated model, the load data should be subjected to an investigation for dominance.

The use of layout by inspection of the load matrix or some other shortcut technique is largely determined by whether or not the criterion is relatively straightforward with no real need for the simulation of assumption changes. If the criterion is straightforward *and* the load data has a relatively large coeffcient of variation, it would seem appropriate to consider the particular problem as capable of solution by some shortcut technique. The analysis could then proceed to step 6. If high dominance is not the case, and/or simulation seems called for, the problem should be tentatively considered as amenable to analysis by CRAFT. The flow data should also be assessed in terms of how they are grouped relative to future material handling, inventory, and lot-splitting conventions.

STEP 5: RECOGNIZE THE MODEL IDIOSYNCRASIES, AND LOOK FOR POSSIBLE IMPROVEMENTS Most heuristic models have certain idiosyncrasies that affect the final solution values obtained. For example, several idiosyncrasies in the CRAFT model presented earlier can be highlighted. First, the CRAFT heuristic rule always selects the largest potential cost reduction as the basis for exchange. Initial iterations usually cause relatively large reductions in the objective function, thereby allowing certain iterations to be ignored where the change in the objective function is trivial. Second, the CRAFT model necessarily approximates departmental areas by centroids. It is possible to achieve suboptimal improvements in the objective function by the use of odd-shaped areas—e.g., with all departments laid out as long, thin strips.

Search for potential improvement in the model. No model is perfect, and improvements are always possible.

STEP 6: DETERMINE THE LONG-RUN IMPLICATIONS OF THE PROBLEM Several steps in the guide have provided for proceeding to step 6. The primary reason for this branching from these steps is that the problem under study is not compatible with model assumptions. The problem may be compatible, however, if it is considered in a larger context. Minor changes in the layout may be best treated as major changes in the layout in cases in which we recognize that the minor layout problem is not compatible with the model (or technique) assumptions. If a major case (or for that matter, a more inclusive minor case) approach seems justified, the problem should be restated, and the analysis should proceed back to step 1. If, on the other hand, the present delineation of the problem seems appropriate, the analysis can move to step 7.

STEP 7: EXAMINE THE LAYOUT PROBLEM AS A SYSTEMS PROBLEM Determine the relative importance of this particular layout problem with respect to other system problems. Answers to the following questions will aid in this determination. Is excess capacity purposely built into the materials handling system? What is the present and probable future plant utilization? Is excess space available? Is more space needed? Is the layout question critical? What is the minimum cost method of alleviating the problem? Will refinements be worth their incremental cost or should a "rough-and-ready" approach be adopted?

If a significant change in plant activity is anticipated, perhaps the analysis should branch back to step 6. If a more detailed study of the layout problem would provide for significant slack in other system problem areas, perhaps the problem should be restated, with the analysis proceeding back to step 1. If proceeding to step 1 or step 6 cannot be justified, the analysis should proceed to step 8.

STEP 8: WEIGH THE QUALITATIVE FACTORS Determine the role of qualitative factors in this particular problem. If a materials-handling model fits the problem well, qualitative factors perhaps may not be worthy of pursuit. As qualitative factors increase in significance, their effect on the objective function may be determined by simulation (e.g., using the CRAFT model). As materials-handling-model approaches become less important, qualitative factors perhaps may become all-important and may be analyzed by a technique such as systematic layout planning or, indeed, perhaps by no formalized approach.

STEP 9: SELECT THE APPROPRIATE TOOL FOR ANALYSIS Only at this point should analytical procedures be started. Let the choice of analytical procedure, as well as the detail, be dictated by the unique considerations of the problem at hand.

There still remains the second question, of whether the quantitative/computer-derived layouts are superior to the traditional designs. A study revealed that both large and small layout problems have been solved significantly better by people than by computer programs. The researchers concluded the following:

> A comparison of the results of CRAFT with the results of experiments which required human subjects to solve the same plant layout problems used in the test of the computer algorithms indicates that the human subjects performed significantly better than the computer programs in the eight problems in general and in the largest, twenty department problem, in particular, where the ability of human subjects to recognize and visualize complex patterns seems to give them an edge over the essentially mechanical procedures followed by the computer programs. Moreover, this occurred even with each computer process given five runs on each problem with five different starting layouts.
>
> The results also show that in five computer runs of each of the algorithms, optimal solutions to the ten, fifteen, and twenty department problems were

not reached, and the likelihood of achieving an optimal solution through the use of one of these algorithms declines rapidly with an increase in problem size.

The foregoing results indicate that present attempts to use fully automated computer algorithms to solve the plant layout problem should be reexamined with a view to incorporating human beings' visual capability into the procedures, especially since the real layout problem involves many factors which cannot readily be incorporated into a computer program, but which a human being can take into account while designing a layout.[6]

This quotation may indicate that the best approach to use in processing layout planning is CAD (computer-aided design), in which a continuous dialogue is maintained between operations managers and computer programs during the planning phase.

AN INDUSTRIAL CASE: RELAYOUT AND LOCATION OF A HIGH-SPEED N/C TURRET PUNCH PRESS

A manager at the Dominion Steel and Coal, Inc., had to decide where to locate a new high-speed numerically controlled (N/C) turret punch press in the sheet-metal department. The following is the analysis carried out to find a location.

Management wanted to locate manually the new machine, so that the resultant layout improves material flow and considers future requirements. Without this study, the new punch press would probably have been located in the present punch department.

An attempt was made to layout the departments involved using as much of a scientific approach as possible, considering the general lack of production data available. The flow of material and usual machine utilization was based on experience. The blueprints and machine drawings were supplied by the company. A major constraint on the study was a request by the management not to move any walls, and to keep the polishing and grinding departments away from the painting area. The findings were as follows.

1. Approximately 95 percent of all materials follow the normal sequence from department to department (see Figure 7.14).
2. The present layout causes much backtracking and 454 feet of travel (see Figure 7.15).
3. 276 feet, or 61 percent, of the travel is between departments and is due to the poor present layout.
4. Since sheetmetal is received a maximum of twice per week, it could be received through the shipping door.

---

[6] M. Scriabin, and R. C. Vergin, "Comparison of Computer Algorithms and Visual Based Methods for Plant Layout," *Management Science*, October, 1975, pp. 172–181.

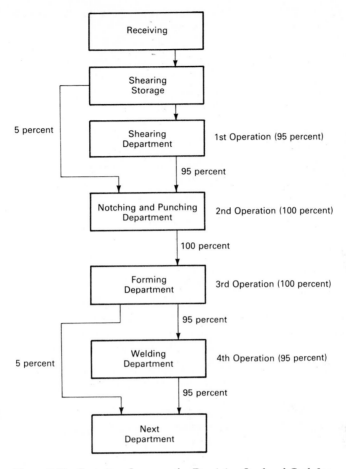

Figure 7.14   Operation Sequence for Dominion Steel and Coal, Inc.

5. The new N/C punch press will improve the throughput and allow removal of three obsolete machines (see Figure 7.15).

The *recommendations* included the relayout of various machines, the location of the new machine, and some changes in material flow.

1. Relocation of the various machines allows material to move from start to finish in 303 feet, which is a reduction in travel of 33 percent. Distances travelled are shown in Figure 7.16.

2. Utilizing the existing forklift and overhead crane, sheet metal should be received at the shipping door and stored in new cantilever racks adjacent to the shears.

FIGURE 7.15   PRESENT DISTANCE TRAVELLED IN MAJOR VOLUME

TRANSPORTATION	DISTANCE
Receiving to shearing storage	104' (1)
Shearing storage to shearing	26'
Shearing storage to notch/punch storage	65' (2)
Notch/punch storage to notch/punch stations	16'
Notch/punch stations to forming storage	20'
Forming storage to forming stations	26'
Forming stations to welding storage	20'
Welding storage to welding station #1	12'
Welding station #1 to welding station #2	20'
Welding station #2 to storage	18'
Storage to welding station #3	20'
Welding station #3 to paint line storage	107'
Total Travel	454'

FIGURE 7.16   PROPOSED DISTANCE TRAVELLED IN MAJOR VOLUME

TRANSPORTATION	DISTANCE
Receiving to shearing storage	33' (1)
Shearing storage to shearing	40'
Shearing storage to notch/punch storage	31' (2)
Notch/punch storage to notch/punch department	11'
Notch/punch department to forming storage	20'
Forming storage to forming department	10'
Forming department to welding storage	72'
Welding storage to welding station #1	11'
Welding station #1 to welding station #2	16'
Welding station #2 to paint line storage	59'
Total Travel Distance	303'

It was proposed that the entire sheet metal department be rearranged. This layout is highly recommended, since the study showed that 95 percent of all materials follow the normal sequence through the four departments. The new layout also allows a smooth flow of materials, eliminates all backtracking, and reduces material movement 151 feet, or 33 percent. Storing the sheet metal in racks frees up needed floor space and makes retreiving easier, using either the forklift truck or overhead crane.

Summarizing, the relayout and new machine location in the sheetmetal department improves material handling, reduces input storage, reduces material handling costs, reduces machine setup time, and reduces the amount of rejected material.

PRODUCT LAYOUT ANALYSIS

Product layouts are used in almost all industries and many service organizations. Various registration systems, component parts fabrication, paper-work processing, car assembly lines, jet-engine assembly, continuous food-processing plants, etc., are all designed for product layouts.

As has been discussed earlier, the use of product layout is called for when:

1. High volume of production is required
2. The product is standardized
3. The parts are interchangeable
4. The raw material supply is continuous
5. Product demand is stable.

Once the product layout is adopted, a sequence of processing steps is determined. The sequence of machines or work centers that results from a product layout is termed "line."

The decision to use a product layout is followed by other important decisions, such as:

1. Types of machinery and tools to be used on the line
2. Required output rate
3. Size and location of in-process inventories
4. Pace (flexible or constant) of movement of parts between work centers

The total job to be done on the line is divided into *work elements*. The work elements are small tasks that have to be performed on every product that passes through the line. The work elements should be grouped into *work stations*. Each work station is manned by one or more workers. The procedure is summarized in Figure 7.17.

Grouping the work elements into stations is called *line balancing*. The objective is to equalize the amount of work assigned to the stations. This equalization objective can be achieved in two alternative ways:

1. Given a desired cycle time, equalize the work load in such a way that the number of work stations is minimized.
2. Given an allowable number of work stations, equalize the work load in such a way that the cycle time is minimized.

In the next section, we use an example to show the actual procedure of line balancing, following the first approach. Namely, we assume that the desired cycle time or output rate is given, and strive to minimize the number of work stations and idle time.

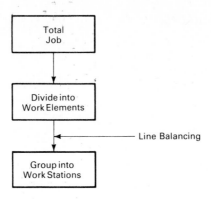

Figure 7.17   The Line-Balancing Problem

LINE BALANCING

When the cycle time is given, the first step in line balancing is to decide on the rule by which work elements (tasks) will be allocated to the various work stations. The rules that are used for line balancing are heuristic decision rules. A line-balancing heuristic rule is a selection criterion for assigning work elements to stations. There are several line-balancing heuristics.[7] We choose two relatively simple rules to demonstrate the line-balancing procedure.

> *Rule 1.* Allocate first the work elements that have the largest number of following elements.
>
> *Rule 2.* Allocate first the work elements that have the longest processing time.

We shall further decide that all ties that occur while using rule 1 are broken with rule 2. All ties that occur while using rule 2 are broken with rule 1.

The information in regard to the assembly of a videotape recorder (VTR) is given in Figures 7.18 and 7.19. Figure 7.18 lists the assembly steps, processing times, and precedence requirements. Figure 7.19 presents as an arrow diagram the precedence requirements, which constitute a useful graphical tool.

The cycle time, which is the time elapsed between the completion of two successive VTR's, can be determined based on the daily demand for VTR. Let us assume that demand per day, D, is 450 VTR/day, and that working time per day, T, is 420 minutes/day. Total processing time for all elements, P, is 205 seconds.

---

[7] G. M. Buxley, N. P. Slack, and R. Wild, "Production Flow System Design—A Review," *AIIE Transactions*, Vol. 5, No. 1, March, 1973, pp. 37–48; E. J. Ignall, "A Review of Assembly Line Balancing," *Journal of Industrial Engineering*, Vol. 16, No. 4, July–August, 1965, pp. 244–254; A. A. Mastor, "An Experimental Investigation and Comparative Evaluation of Production Line Balancing Techniques," *Management Science*, Vol. 16, No. 11, July, 1970, pp. 728–746.

FIGURE 7.18 ASSEMBLY STEPS, TIMES, AND PRECEDENCE REQUIREMENTS OF A
VTR

ELEMENT	PROCESSING TIME (SECONDS)	DESCRIPTION	ELEMENTS THAT MUST PRECEDE
A	55	Position Capstan Idler	—
B	42	Assemble Head Drum Motor	A
C	20	Assemble Video Head Drum	A, B
D	10	Mount Erase and Control Track Heads	—
E	12	Mount Audio Track Head	D
F	15	Position Idler	A, B, C
G	12	Position Self-Aligning Post A	A, B, C
H	8	Position Self-Aligning Post B	A, B, C
I	9	Mount Supply Reel	D, E
J	10	Mount Take-up Reel	A, B, C, D, E, F, G, H, I
K	12	Mount Head Assembly onto VTR Top Plate	J
Total Processing Time	205 seconds		

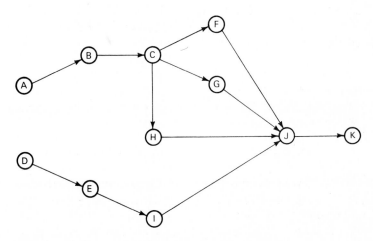

Figure 7.19 Precedence Relationships for VTR Assembly

(See Fig. 7.18.) The cycle time is indicated by the letter C. From Figure 7.18, it is
obvious that we could assign all elements to one work station, with a resulting
cycle time of $C = 205$ seconds and a daily output of (420 minutes $\times$ 60) $\div$ 205 =
122.92 VTR's. Since this amount is considerably less than the required 450
VTR's, one work station is not a proper solution. On the other hand, the shortest
possible cycle time is 55 seconds (the longest elemental processing time). Thus,
if we would have assigned each element to a separate work station, the daily

output could have been (420 minutes × 60) ÷ 55 = 458.18 VTR's. However, the number of work stations might not be minimized this way and, furthermore, there might be a large idle time.

In order to balance the line for the desired demand per day (output rate) one should calculate C and N, as follows:

$$C = \frac{60 \times \text{Working time per day (in minutes)}}{\text{Demand per day}} = \frac{60 \times 420}{450} = 56 \text{ seconds} \qquad (7.2)$$

The *theoretical* number of work stations can be found. However, it will differ from the *actual* number of work stations because one is planning for a number of stations. The theoretical number of work stations (N) is:

$$N = \frac{\text{Demand per day} \times \text{Total processing time}}{60 \times \text{Working time per day}} = \frac{450 \times 205}{60 \times 420}$$

$$= 3.66 \text{ work stations} \qquad (7.3)$$

The actual number of work stations should be 4.

In order to use rule (1), we start with the following "popularity poll" that lists the number of following work elements for each work element.

Element	Number of Following Elements
A	6
B	5
C	4
D	3
E	2
F, G, H, I, J	1
K	0

Now is the time to start allocating work elements to stations, following the precedence requirements and subject to the maximum cycle time of 56 seconds found in equation (7.2). To start the procedure, one sets up a table with the following headings, and assigns work element A to station 1 (no element precedes element A).

Station	Work Element	Element Time (seconds)	Unassigned Time (seconds)	Feasible Remaining Elements	Element with Most Followers	Element with Longest Processing Time
1	A	55	1	None	—	—

The excess available time for this station is the difference between the sum of the assigned work elements times and the cycle time of 56 seconds. No work element has a processing time of one second or less, so no other work element may be assigned to station 1. Station 2 must now be assigned.

Element B has the second largest number of following tasks. Thus, it is assigned to station 2. The remaining unassigned time in that station is $56 - 42 = 14$ seconds. The element with the next largest number of followers (C) has 20 seconds processing time, so we cannot assign it to station 2. Thus, we assign element D to station 2, and so on. The assignment results are shown in Table 7.3.

As one can see, we have arranged the elements in four work stations. The cycle time is 56 seconds at the required output rate of 450 VTR/day, which means that every 56 seconds a completed VTR can leave the assembly line. However, we can have a cycle time of 55 seconds (cycle time in station 1) if we so desire.

Using rule (2), the elements are assigned as in Table 7.4. The cycle time of each station is found by adding the elemental processing times.

Analyzing the two balances achieved, one sees that rule (1), supplemented with rule (2), has achieved the same assignment as rule (2), supplemented with rule (1). Both have yielded a four-station (actual number of work stations) balance. The question is: Would one expect to have the same results using the two rules in other balancing problems? The answer is: Not always. The best strategy is to check several rules and choose the one that gives the minimum number of work stations at minimum balance delay.

TABLE 7.3 LINE BALANCING ACCORDING TO THE LARGEST NUMBER OF FOLLOWING ELEMENTS (NOTE: BLOCKED FIGURES INDICATE IDLE TIME)

STA-TION	WORK ELE-MENT	ELEMENT TIME (SECONDS)	REMAINING UNASSIGNED TIME (SECONDS)	FEASIBLE REMAINING ELEMENT	ELEMENT WITH MOST FOLLOWERS	ELEMENT WITH LONGEST PROCESSING TIME
1	A	55	1	None	—	—
2	B	42	14	D	—	—
	D	10	4	None	—	—
3	C	20	36	E, F, G, H	E	—
	E	12	24	F, G, H, I	F, G, H, I	F
	F	15	9	H, I	H, I	I
	I	9	0	None	—	—
4	G	12	44	H, J	H, J	J
	J	10	34	H, K	H	—
	H	8	26	K	—	—
	K	12	14	None	—	—

TABLE 7.4 LINE BALANCING ACCORDING TO THE LONGEST PROCESSING TIME
RULE (NOTE: BLOCKED FIGURES INDICATE IDLE TIME)

STATION	WORK ELEMENT	ELEMENT TIME (SECONDS)	REMAINING UNASSIGNED TIME (SECONDS)	FEASIBLE REMAINING ELEMENT	ELEMENT WITH LONGEST TIME	ELEMENT WITH MOST FOLLOWERS
1	A	55	1	None	—	—
2	B	42	14	D	—	—
	D	10	4	—	—	—
3	C	20	36	E, F, G, H	F	—
	F	15	21	E, G, H	E, G	E
	E	12	9	H, I	I	
	I	9	0	—	—	—
4	G	12	44	H	—	—
	H	8	36	J	—	—
	J	10	26	K	—	—
	K	12	14	—	—	—

Balance Delay and Effectiveness

Balance delay is an efficiency indicator. It indicates the amount of idle time on the assembly line due to the imperfect assignment of work elements among the work stations. The balance delay is the ratio of the total idle time at all work stations to the total work time.

$$\text{Balance Delay} = \frac{\text{Total idle time}}{\text{Total work time}} \times 100 \text{ percent} \qquad (7.4)$$

where:

Total idle time = Number of work stations × Cycle time − Total work elements time

Total work time = Number of work stations × Cycle time

For the videotape recorder line, the balance delay is as follows:

Total idle time = 4 × 56 − 205 = 224 − 205 = 19 seconds

Total work time = 4 × 56   = 224

Balance delay = (19 ÷ 224) × 100 = 8.48 percent

The work element assignment for the VTR case has a balance delay of 8.48 percent. This balance delay is used as a measure of how well the assignment allocates the work load among the work stations. The optimal balance allocates equal work loads to the various work stations, with a resulting balance delay of zero.

Sometimes, the efficiency of the line is expressed as the number complementary to the balance delay. Thus, the efficiency of the VTR line is 100 percent − 8.48 percent = 91.52 percent.

The *effectiveness* of the line is the degree to which the desired capacity is achieved. For example, with a 56-second cycle time, the total daily output is

$$\frac{60 \times 420}{56} = 450 \text{ VTR/day}$$

The effectiveness is measured as

$$\text{Effectiveness} = \frac{\text{Achieved daily output}}{\text{Desired daily output}} \times 100 \text{ percent} \quad (7.5)$$

$$= \frac{450}{450} \times 100 \text{ percent} = 100 \text{ percent}$$

So the effectiveness of the VTR Line is 100 percent.

COMPUTER MODEL FOR LINE BALANCING

As happens in so many other areas of production and operations management, the problem of line balancing gets out of hand once the number of work elements and work stations increases. The number of combinations of work elements that may be assigned to work stations is such that a computer must be used to operate the line-balancing heuristic.

Furthermore, the operations manager can use the computer more efficiently if the line balancing program is conversational—that is, programmed so that no excessive background in computer operation is required—and the hardware requirement is a small, mobile terminal like a cathode-ray-tube type of terminal.

For demonstration purposes, let us use the example given for the VTR assembly. To use the program, the operations manager must first enter his or her name and the program name. This information will be used in descriptive titles for the output that is generated. The user will then be asked to enter the number of work elements for the particular problem. For the VTR assembly, there are eleven work elements, which are entered as shown in Figure 7.20.

For each of the work elements, the program requires that the operations manager enter the element time and the preceding elements of that work element. The allowable number of preceding elements is 10, and each must be greater than 1 and less than the work element. At the completion of the input process, the program prints a table containing the data entered. The operations manager is asked to check the values and indicate whether they are correct. This phase is presented in Figure 7.21. If the operations manager indicates that there

balw

note: all numeric values entered must be separated by a comma and/or a space.

enter your name and program title or (stop)
? program run one

program balance for program run one
how many elements ? 11

enter work element time and the preceding element data
WORK ELEMENT 1 :
  time ? 55

   enter the preceding element; (0) when finished
   or if no preceding elements, enter (0)
   prec. (1) ? 0

WORK ELEMENT 2 :
  time ? 42

   prec. (1) ? 1
   prec. (2) ? 0

WORK ELEMENT 3 :
  time ? 20

   prec. (1) ? 1
   prec. (2) ? 2
   prec. (3) ? 0

WORK ELEMENT 4 :
  time ? 10

   prec. (1) ? 0

WORK ELEMENT 5 :
  time ? 12

   prec. (1) ? 4
   prec. (2) ? 0

WORK ELEMENT 6 :
  time ? 15

   prec. (1) ? 1
   prec. (2) ? 2
   prec. (3) ? 3
   prec. (4) ? 0

Figure 7.20   (Cont.)

WORK ELEMENT 7 :
  time ? 12

     prec. (1) ? 1
     prec. (2) ? 2
     prec. (3) ? 3
     prec. (4) ? 0

WORK ELEMENT 8 :
  time ? 8

     prec. (1) ? 1
     prec. (2) ? 2
     prec. (3) ? 3
     prec. (4) ? 0

WORK ELEMENT 9 :
  time ? 9

     prec. (1) ? 4
     prec. (2) ? 5
     prec. (3) ? 0

WORK ELEMENT 10 :
  time ? 10

     prec. (1) ? 1
     prec. (2) ? 2
     prec. (3) ? 3
     prec. (4) ? 4
     prec. (5) ? 5
     prec. (6) ? 6
     prec. (7) ? 7
     prec. (8) ? 8
     prec. (9) ? 9
     prec. (10) ? 0

WORK ELEMENT 11 :
  time ? 12

     prec. (1) ? 1
     prec. (2) ? 0

Figure 7.21 Check Data for Line-Balancing Program

program balance for program run one
11 work elements as read

no.	time	******************Predecessors***********************									
1	55.0	0	0	0	0	0	0	0	0	0	0
2	42.0	1	0	0	0	0	0	0	0	0	0
3	20.0	1	2	0	0	0	0	0	0	0	0
4	10.0	0	0	0	0	0	0	0	0	0	0
5	12.0	4	0	0	0	0	0	0	0	0	0
6	15.0	1	2	3	0	0	0	0	0	0	0
7	12.0	1	2	3	0	0	0	0	0	0	0
8	8.0	1	2	3	0	0	0	0	0	0	0
9	9.0	4	5	0	0	0	0	0	0	0	0
10	10.0	1	2	2	4	5	6	7	8	9	0
11	12.0	10	0	0	0	0	0	0	0	0	0

is an input error, the program will start a correction process. This process enables the operations manager to make spot changes to his/her input data without re-entering all the data.

To use the program, the operations manager must indicate a choice in two areas: first, whether to enter the actual number of stations or to enter the cycle time; second, to indicate which of the four different line-balancing heuristics is to be used in the evaluation of the problem:

1. Largest processing time rule
2. Smallest processing time rule
3. Random device rule
4. "First available" rule.

The operations manager may also change the work elements as desired.

An example of the run and results using the first heuristic is provided in Figure 7.22. The results are identical to those achieved manually in Table 7.4. This illustration of the solution to the VTR case includes summary information, such as:

1. Final cycle time
2. Final number of stations
3. Balance delay for the solution
4. Station-by-station assignment of work elements and the idle time at each station.

Figure 7.22 Line-Balancing Results Using a Conversational Computer Program (user's entries underlined)

---

check your input; is it correct (y/n) ? y

enter (1) for station or (2) for cycle time ? 2

LINE BALANCING HEURISTICS

(1) Largest Time
(2) Smallest Time
(3) Random
(4) First available
(5) Change work elements or stop

enter the index no. of the desired choice ? 1

enter cycle time (time units;integers) ? 56

balance results for program run one
analysis control card requests

cycl   56   larg

number of iterations required for solution = 1
final cycltime = 56.
final number of stations = 4
balance delay for the solution is 8. percent
****

station number 1

element number	time
1	55.

total number of elements in station = 1
total work time in stations =   55.00
idle time in station =   1.00
****

station number 2

element number	time
2	42.
4	10.

total number of elements in station = 2
total work time in stations =   52.00
idle time in station =   4.00
****

station number 3

element number	time
3	20.
6	15.

Figure 7.22 (Cont.)

```
                          5                    12.
                          9                     9.
total number of elements in station = 4
total work time in stations =      56.00
idle time in station =         0.00
*************************************************************************************
                      station number  4
             element number              time
                      7                  12.
                      8                   8.
                     10                  10.
                     11                  12.
total number of elements in station = 4
total work time in stations =      42.00
idle time in station =        14.00
```

When the operations manager has completed the run, the program returns and requests the next choice of options. To stop the program, one has to enter the number "5." The program then returns to the beginning, and the word "STOP" is entered.

SUMMARY

Layout is the set of activities involved in selecting locations for and transportation routes among departments, processes, work centers, machines, and service functions. The layout decisions are made in the planning stage and occur periodically. As the layout decisions have long-run implications, they must be made carefully. The capacity, the technology, and the profitability of an organization depend on the layout planned.

This chapter presented four layout types: process, product, fixed-position, and project layouts. Process and product layouts were treated at length. Process layout conforms to process-type operations: work centers are grouped together according to the type of function performed. Product layout conforms to product type operations: specialized work centers are arranged in a line to conform to product processing sequence.

Each layout plan starts with a definition of optimality criteria. Based on an initial layout, improvements that improve the operational criteria are recommended. At times, informed judgment and manual planning are aided by quantified measures, and often a computer helps with the computations.

Process layout analyses strive to minimize load-distance-moved criteria. Product layout models strive to minimize idle labor time and maximize effectiveness.

The conversational computer heuristic models are of great help to the operations manager as he or she tries various layout configurations. Once a solution is arrived at, behavioral aspects should be considered, as they have an impact on the quality of working life.

DISCUSSION QUESTIONS

7.1 What is layout?

7.2 What are the circumstances in which a layout study is called for?

7.3 Discuss the relationship between layout and technology, and between layout and capacity. Give examples.

7.4 Discuss layout and its relationship to the conversion process (input, process, and output).

7.5 Compare and contrast process- and product-oriented processes.

7.6 Compare and contrast the various layout types.

7.7 Give examples of organizations that have predominantly product, process, fixed position, and project layouts.

7.8 Discuss the essentials of traditional, graphic, and schematic layout analysis.

7.9 Do quantitative layout models consider behavioral aspects of layout planning?

7.10 Define and discuss the applicability of the load-distance model.

7.11 What are the paramount problems in product and process layouts?

7.12 Discuss the behavioral aspects of product layout and assembly-line planning.

7.13 Identify the limitations of the load-distance model in the context of process layout planning.

7.14 Under what circumstances will we use systematic layout planning (SLP)? Give an example.

7.15 Describe and compare layout computer programs.

7.16 Discuss various line-balancing rules.

7.17 Define and explain the balance, delay, and effectiveness measures.

7.18 Define and explain job enlargement, job rotation, and job enrichment.

PROBLEMS AND SOLUTIONS

7.1 Dominion Steel and Coal, Inc., has fixed costs of $700,000 annually, variable costs of $20 per unit produced, and $30 revenue per unit sold. The company is considering two alternative layout designs.

The first alternative involves receiving the sheet-metal department's raw material directly from company-owned trucks at a large receiving facility. Annual fixed costs of operating a large truck fleet are $250,000. The material-handling costs, including an overhead crane, are $200,000.

The second alternative involves building a large warehouse to accommodate inventory of the sheet-metal department's raw material (see Figure 7.15). The truck fleet would cost only $100,000 per year, and inventory costs would be $150,000, including a conveyor belt that connects the warehouse with the sheet-metal department.

Determine the impact of the two layout alternatives on Dominion's break-even point. (Disregard the cost of building the warehouse.)

Solution

Let: r = Revenue per unit, V = Variable cost per unit, F = Fixed costs, n = Number of units produced.

$$rn = F + vn$$

$$F = n(r - v)$$

$$\text{Break-even point } n = \frac{F}{r - v}$$

Extensive Truck Fleet (first alternative)

Fixed costs	$700,000
Truck fleet fixed costs	250,000
Material-handling fixed costs	200,000
Total fixed costs	$1,150,000

$$\text{Break-even point} = \frac{1,150,000}{30 - 20} = 115,000 \text{ units}$$

Warehouse Construction (second alternative)

Fixed costs	$700,000
Truck fleet fixed costs	100,000
Inventory fixed costs	150,000
Total fixed costs	$950,000

$$\text{Break-even point} = \frac{950,000}{30 - 20} = 95,000 \text{ units.}$$

Dominion should prefer building a warehouse, as the break-even point is much lower than that for operating an extensive truck fleet.

7.2 Western Cable Harness and Crimping, Inc., is designing a one-floor operation that is 1200 ft. long and 800 ft. wide. Six operating departments, each 400 × 400 ft., should be located on this floor. The number of loads transported among departments over one year is as presented in the following table. What should be the recommended process layout?

ANNUAL LOAD NUMBERS AMONG DEPARTMENTS

Department	Receiving (1)	Band/ Circular Saw (2)	Wire Bundling (3)	Cutting/ Stripping (4)	Painting (5)	Shipping (6)
Receiving (1)	—	100	50	50	25	25
Band/Circular Saw (2)	—	—	150	25	50	100
Wire Bundling (3)	—	—	—	50	50	100
Cutting/Stripping (4)	—	—	—	—	50	—
Painting (5)	—	—	—	—	—	200
Shipping (6)	—	—	—	—	—	—

Assume that moves between adjacent departments (horizontally or diagonally) do not cost money. Moves between non-adjacent departments cost $1 per load.

Solution

Initial layout (arbitrary):

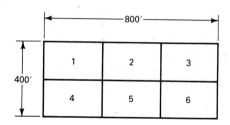

The nonadjacent department cost matrix is:

	1	2	3	4	5	6
1			50			25
2						
3				50		
4						0
5						
6						

Total = $125

The solution is found through trial and error. The optimal solution:

The nonadjacent department cost matrix is:

	1	2	3	4	5	6
1					25	25
2						
3						
4					50	0
5						
6						

Total = $100

7.3 The following assembly elements and times are given:

Work Element	Time (minutes)	Precedence
A	4.5	—
B	1.1	A
C	0.9	A, B
D	5.0	—
E	1.5	D
F	1.2	A, B, C
G	1.2	A, B, C
H	1.2	D, E
I	1.2	D, E
J	0.8	A, B, C, D, E, F, G, H, I
K	0.9	J

Assuming the required cycle time is 5.0 minutes:
a) Build an arrow diagram showing precedence.
b) What is the minimum number of work stations required, using the "largest-number-of-following-elements" rule?
c) What is the minimum number of stations required, using the "longest-processing-time" rule?
d) Calculate the balance delay for (b) and (c).

Solution

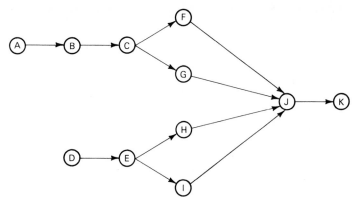

b) One starts by taking a "Popularity" poll:

Work Element	"Popularity"
A	5
B	4
C	3
D	4
E	3
F	1
G	1
H	1
I	1
J	1
K	0

Now the "largest number of following elements" rule may be applied.

STA-TION	WORK ELE-MENT	ELEMENT TIME (MIN.)	REMAINING UNASSIGNED TIME (MIN.)	FEASIBLE REMAINING ELEMENTS	ELEMENT WITH MOST FOLLOWERS	ELEMENT WITH LONGEST PROCESSING TIME
1	A	4.5	0.5	—		
2	D	5.0	0.0	—		
	B	1.1	3.9	C, E	C, E	E
	E	1.5	2.4	C, H, I	C	
3	C	0.9	1.5	F, G, H, I	F, G, H, I	F, G, H, I
	F	1.2	0.3	—		
	G	1.2	3.8	H, I	H, I	H, I
	H	1.2	2.6	I		
4	I	1.2	1.4	J		
	J	0.8	0.6	—		
5	K	0.9	4.1	—		

The minimum number of working stations according to this rule is five.

c)

STA-TION	WORK ELE-MENT	ELEMENT TIME (MIN.)	REMAINING UNASSIGNED TIME (MIN.)	FEASIBLE REMAINING ELEMENTS	ELEMENT WITH MOST FOLLOWERS	ELEMENT WITH LONGEST PROCESSING TIME
1	D	5.0	0.0	—		
2	A	4.5	0.5	—		
3	E	1.5	3.5	B, H, I	H, I	H, I
	H	1.2	2.3	B, I	I	
	I	1.2	1.1	B		
	B	1.1	0.0	—		
4	C	0.9	4.1	F, G	F, G	F, G
	F	1.2	2.9	G		
	G	1.2	1.7	J		
	J	0.8	0.9	K		
	K	0.9	0.0	—		

The minimum number of working stations according to this rule is four.

d) Balance delay for (b) = $\dfrac{(5 \times 5.0 - 19.5)}{5 \times 5.0} \times 100$ percent = 22 percent

Balance delay for (c) = $\dfrac{(4 \times 5.0 - 19.5)}{4 \times 5.0} \times 100$ percent = 2.5 percent

CHAPTER REVIEW PROBLEMS

7.1 Standard Industries, Ltd., manufactures various electrical products that are sold through three local retail outlets. The company has fixed costs of $500,000 annually, variable costs of $17 per unit produced, and $25 revenue per unit sold. The plant manager of Standard Industries, Ltd., is unhappy with the present facility layout, and has suggested an alternative layout design. Her proposed layout design would result in a $200,000 increase in fixed costs; however, variable costs would decrease by $4.50 per unit. Compare the present layout to the proposed layout using break-even analysis.

7.2 A diesel engine manufacturer wants to determine whether the present process layout of six departments can be rearranged in order to minimize total handling costs. These six departments are of equal size and are situated in a rectangular building, as shown in the following diagram:

5	1	3
6	4	2

The annual number of interdepartmental moves of units in production among the departments is given in the following table:

	1	2	3	4	5	6
1	—	60	80	35	60	75
2		—	100	120	120	65
3			—	115	85	95
4				—	90	105
5					—	80
6						—

The cost of moving one unit from one work center to another is $5, and an extra $3 per unit to cross over one or more departments.
a) Calculate the materials handling cost of the present layout.
b) Can you suggest any changes in the present layout in order to reduce materials-handling cost?

7.3 Hercules Manufacturing Company, Inc., a producer of corrugated card boxes, is planning a 3600 sq.-ft. floor layout. The operations manager has obtained SLP ratings for locating departments next to each other, as well as for their respective areas.

FROM \ TO	STORAGE	CORRU-GATOR	FLEXO FOLDER/ GLUER	TAPER/ BAILER	INSPEC-TION	SHIP-PING	AREA (SQ. FT.)
Storage	—	AN	U	U	I	U	1200
Corrugator	—	—	I	U	U	X	400
Flexo Folder/Gluer	—	—	—	AN	I	U	400
Taper/Bailer	—	—	—	—	U	I	400
Inspection	—	—	—	—	—	AN	400
Shipping	—	—	—	—	—	—	800

What should be the layout used by Hercules Manufacturing Company, Inc.?

7.4 Terry Industries, a producer of chain saws, is planning its XL-200 model assembly line. The work elements as they are assigned to work stations are presented as follows (assume 480 minutes/day working time):

Work Station	Work Element	Element Time (sec.)
1	A	12
	B	9
2	C	24
3	D	12
	E	12
4	F	18
5	G	15
6	H	18

a) What is the cycle time?
b) What is the daily output of chain saws?
c) What is the efficiency of the line?
d) What is the daily idle time for each work station?
e) What is the daily idle time for the line?

7.5 Rival Manufacturing Company, Inc., a producer of can openers, has to balance its line. Given below are the work elements, their times, and their precedence requirements:

Work Element	Time (sec.)	Precedence
A	30	—
B	60	A
C	70	A
D	50	A
E	20	A
F	40	A, B, C
G	50	A, C
H	50	A, B, C, D, E, F, G
Total	370 seconds	

Demand per day is 400 can openers. Working time per day is 8 hours.
a) Build an arrow diagram showing precedence.
b) What is the theoretical number of work stations?
c) What is the minimum number of work stations needed to achieve a cycle time of 70 seconds, using the "largest-number-of-following-elements" rule?
d) What is the minimum number of stations needed to meet a cycle time of 100 seconds, according to the "longest-processing-time" rule (assuming demand is no longer 400/day)?
e) What are the balance delays in parts (c) and (d)?

7.6 A young entrepreneur has found a vacant building on the main street of a summer resort, and wants to develop a small to medium-sized grocery store. The major "departments" that are required correspond to the major food types—namely, meats, produce, dairy products, frozen foods, and canned goods. In addition, a shipping-receiving dock, a refrigerated storage room, and a section for cashiers will be required. Using the systematic layout planning technique, construct a relationship chart to determine a feasible layout of the required departments and to determine the importance of having the various departments positioned adjacent to each other.

7.7 The Good Sport Manufacturing Company is a national distributor of electric golf carts. The cart is assembled mostly from prefabricated components. The following chart lists the procedure, processing times, and precedence requirements in assembling the cart on the company's assembly line:

ELE-MENT	PROC-ESSING TIMES (MIN.)	DESCRIPTION	REQUIRED PRECEDING ELEMENTS
A	25	Assemble steel-frame chassis	
B	15	Mount electric engine to assembled steel-frame chassis	A
C	20	Install rear axle assembly and drive train mechanism	A
D	15	Install accelerator and transmission assembly	A, B, C
E	12	Mount front end mechanism, steering and brake assembly	A
F	22	Mount molded fiberglass body to chassis	A, B, C, D, E
G	10	Install electrical connections	F
H	8	Attach wheels	F
J	5	Attach seats and cosmetic accessories	H

Demand is 15 carts per day and the company's productive time is 420 minutes per day. The company wants to balance the electric cart assembly line.

a) Draw a precedence relationship chart for the electric cart assembly.
b) Calculate the cycle time.
c) Determine the theoretical number of work stations.
d) Determine the actual number of work stations by allocating first the work elements having the largest number of following elements. Should a tie occur, allocate first the element with the longest processing time.
e) Determine the efficiency of the line by calculating balance delay.

7.8 Perry Industries, Inc., a producer of chain saws, wishes to locate seven departments on one floor that is 100 ft. long and 80 ft. wide. The department sizes are:

Department	Length (ft.)	Width (ft.)
Receiving	20	20
Electroplating	40	20
Machining	20	20
Assembly	30	30
Test Room	35	45
Packaging	45	35
Shipping	40	40

The annual number of loads moved between departments is as specified in the table below. Assume that moves between adjacent departments cost zero. The cost of moving a load between non-adjacent departments is proportional to the distance travelled. Terry Industries prefers to have the receiving and shipping departments at corners of the building, and to have the assembly and test-room departments adjacent to each other. What is your recommended layout?

ANNUAL LOAD NUMBERS BETWEEN DEPARTMENTS

Department	Receiving (1)	Electroplating (2)	Machining (3)	Assembly (4)	Test Room (5)	Packaging (6)	Shipping (7)
Assembly (1)	—	—	—	—	—	—	—
Electroplating (2)	—	—	—	200	—	800	—
Machining (3)	—	—	—	1000	—	—	—
Receiving (4)	—	1200	200	—	800	200	—
Test Room (5)	—	—	—	—	—	2400	200
Packaging (6)	—	200	2000	—	400	—	—
Shipping (7)	—	200	—	—	200	—	—

7.9   Western Cable Harness and Crimping, Inc. (see problem 7-2 in "Problems and Solutions"), has revised its transportation costs. Now, moves between adjacent departments cost as indicated in the table below. Moves between non-adjacent departments cost $1 in addition.

COST PER LOAD MOVED

Department	Receiv- ing (1)	Band/ Circular Saw (2)	Wire Bundling (3)	Cutting/ Stripping (4)	Painting (5)	Shipping (6)
Receiving (1)	—	$4.00	$2.00	$2.00	$2.00	$1.00
Band/Circular Saw (2)	—	—	$1.00	—	—	—
Wire Bundling (3)	—	—	—	$2.00	$1.00	$3.00
Cutting/Stripping (4)	—	—	—	—	$1.00	$1.00
Painting (5)	—	—	—	—	—	$1.00
Shipping (6)	—	—	—	—	—	—

Find the optimum process layout and total material-handling costs.

READING
La Jolla: A Nice Place for Signal to Weather Recession Problems

LA JOLLA   The floors feature terra cotta brick, deco ceramic tile, oak borders and, in the hallways, Oriental carpeting in autumn tones and deep blues.

The walls on the first floor are rough plaster, in keeping with the Spanish Mediterranean motif. On the second floor, they're covered with a rough-textured fabric.

Almost everywhere, the ceilings feature oak "box beams" and custom-made lighting fixtures of brass, marble and oak.

The 110 employees who work in the large (77,000 square feet) building eat in a handsome dining room they've nicknamed the Oak Room. The tables are covered with linen.

Outside, there are two tennis courts, a racquetball court, a swimming pool, a workout room and a clubroom. They're available free of charge during non-working hours. On weekends and holidays, employees are encouraged to bring their families to enjoy them.

These are among the first things that impress a visitor to Signal Inc.'s new corporate headquarters in the Torrey Pines area of La Jolla.

After a while, one notices other, more subtle attractions. Throughout the building, for instance, the windows—many of which look out onto a large courtyard complete with fountain—actually open. It's an innovation that would be unthinkable to many architects these days.

After a while, too, you realize why it's so quiet: Everybody in the building has his own private office. Independent-minded Forrest N. Shumway, Signal's chairman and chief executive, has turned his back on yet another fad—that of worker togetherness.

It's been a year and a half since Shumway and two-thirds of his corporate staff left their old headquarters in Beverly Hills and moved 120 miles down the coast.

"A third of them decided not to go—mainly people whose spouses had jobs in the L.A. area or who were getting ready to retire," he recalled during an interview in his new office. "But I think I can say those who made the move are glad they did."

Shumway decided to leave Los Angeles mainly because of the traffic and smog—especially West Side Traffic.

"When we first moved to Beverly Hills in '72, our employees took 20 to 30 minutes to drive to work from places like Redondo Beach and the (San Fernando) Valley. By the time we left, people living in those same areas were commuting a total of three hours a day. It was an awful waste of time that

SOURCE: *Los Angeles Herald Examiner*, June 1, 1982, p. 9.

they could have been devoting to business, the community and their families."

In the San Diego area (the new building is officially in the city of San Diego), Shumway said, his staff members have had little trouble finding desirable housing within 15 minutes' drive of the office.

Shumway, who's 55, has joined his aides in making good use of the new building's recreation center. He plays racquetball on the company court. "But nobody's allowed to use those facilities during working hours," he hastened to point out.

All staff members are encouraged to set up an exercise program with the help of a physician who's on duty full time. The doctor treats employees as well as their families; Signal pays the bill.

Little by little, Shumway has cut most of his ties with Los Angeles, though he still drives or takes Amtrack up north to attend meetings of USC's Board of Trustees and the board of First Interstate Bank. More and more, he says, he and the others who made the move have become involved in San Diego's civic and cultural activities.

With $5.3 billion in sales and nearly 60,000 employees, Signal is the largest concern headquartered in San Diego.

That's right—only 110 persons man the nerve center of this worldwide conglomerate. From Shumway and Signal's president, Daniel Derbes, on down, they provide planning, financial, legal and public-relations guidance to subsidiaries that are giants in their own right.

Questions

1. What prompted Signal's move from Los Angeles to La Jolla?
2. What was the impact of the relocation decision on the work force? On the chief executives?
3. Comment on the major layout features of the new building?
4. Identify the type of layout Signal has followed in the design of the building.
5. How does the layout affect working conditions, productivity, and morale, according to the article?

BIBLIOGRAPHY

ARCUS, A. L., "COMSOAL: A Computer Method for Sequencing Operations for Assembly Lines," *International Journal of Production Research,* 4(4), 1966.

BIEGEL, J. E., *Production Control: A Quantitative Approch* (2d ed.). Englewood Cliffs, N.J.: Prentice-Hall, Inc., 1971.

BOWMAN, E. H., and R. B. FETTER, *Analysis for Production and Operations Management.* Homewood, Ill.: Richard D. Irwin, 1967.

BUFFA, E. S., *Modern Production Management* (4th ed.). New York: John Wiley, 1973.

BUFFA, E. S., G. C. ARMOUR, and T. E. VOLLMANN, "Allocating Facilities with CRAFT," *Harvard Business Review*, 42, March–April, 1964, pp. 136–158.

BUFFA, E. S., and W. H. TAUBERT, *Production and Inventory Systems: Planning and Control.* Homewood, Ill.: Richard D. Irwin, 1972, pp. 303–366.

BUXEY, G. M., N. D. SLACK, and R. WILD, "Production Flow Line System Design—A Review," *AIIE Transactions*, Vol. 5, No. 1, March, 1973.

CHASE, R. B., "Strategic Considerations in Assembly-Line Selection," *California Management Review*, Fall, 1975, pp. 17–23.

COOK, T. M., and R. A. RUSSELL, *Introduction to Management Science.* Englewood Cliffs, N.J.: Prentice-Hall, Inc., 1977.

FRANCIS, R. L., and J. A. WHITE, *Facility Layout and Location: An Analytical Approach.* Englewood Cliffs, N.J.: Prentice-Hall, Inc., 1974.

FREEMAN, D. R., and J. V. TUCKER, "The Line Balancing Problem," *Journal of Industrial Engineering*, Vol. 18, 1967, p. 361.

GAVETT, J. W., *Production and Operations Management.* New York: Harcourt Brace Jovanovich, 1968.

HICKS, P. E., and T. E. COWAN, "CRAFT-M for Layout Rearrangement," *Industrial Engineering*, Vol. 8, May, 1976, pp. 30–35.

IGNALL, E. J., "A Review of Assembly Line Balancing," *Journal of Industrial Engineering*, 16, July–August, 1965, pp. 244–254.

JOHNSON, L. A., and D. C. MONTGOMERY, *Operations Research in Production Planning, Scheduling and Inventory Control.* New York: John Wiley, 1974.

JOHNSON, R. A., W. T. NEWELL, and R. C. VERGIN, *Operations Management: A Systems Concept.* Boston: Houghton Mifflin Co., 1974.

LEE, R. C., and J. M. MOORE, "CORELAP—Computerized Relationship Layout Planning," *Journal of Industrial Engineering*, 18, March, 1967, pp. 195–200.

MARIOTTI, J., "Four Approaches to Manual Assembly Line Balancing," *Journal of Industrial Engineering*, June, 1970, pp. 35–40.

MARSHALL, P. W., et al., *Operations Management, Text and Cases.* Homewood, Ill.: Richard D. Irwin, 1975.

MASTOR, A. A., "An Experimental Investigation and Comparative Evaluation of Production Line Balancing Techniques," *Management Science*, Vol. 16, No. 11, July, 1970.

MAYNARD, H. B., *Industrial Engineering Handbook.* New York: McGraw-Hill, 1963.

MOORE, J. M., "Computer Program Evaluates Plant Layout Alternatives," *Industrial Engineering*, Vol. 3, No. 8, 1971, pp. 19–25.

MOORE, J. M., *Plant Layout and Design.* New York: The Macmillan Company, 1962.

MUTHER, R., and K. MCPHERSON, "Four Approaches to Computerized Layout," *Industrial Engineering*, February, 1970, pp. 39–42.

MUTHER, R., and J. D. WHEELER, "Simplified Systematic Layout Planning," *Factory*, 120, August, September, and October 1962, pp. 68–77, 111–119, 101–113.

PARSONS, J. A., "A Technique for Suboptimal Solutions to the Facilities Layout Problem," *Journal of Systems Management*, Vol. 25, No. 7, July 1974, pp. 42–43.

REED, R., *Plant Location, Layout, and Maintenance.* Homewood, Ill.: Richard D. Irwin, 1967.

RIGGS, J. L., *Production Systems: Planning Analysis and Control* (2d ed.). New York: John Wiley, 1976.

SAPHIER, M., *Office Planning and Design.* New York: McGraw-Hill, 1968.

SCRIABIN, M., and R. C. VERGIN, "Comparison of Computer Algorithms and Visual Based Methods for Plant Layout," *Management Science,* October, 1975, pp. 172–81.

STARR, M. K., *Systems Management of Operations.* Englewood Cliffs, N.J.: Prentice-Hall, Inc., 1971.

TERRY, G. R., *Office Management and Control* (7th ed.). Homewood, Ill: Richard D. Irwin, 1975.

VOLLMANN, T. E., and E. S. BUFFA, "The Facilities Design Problem in Perspective," *Management Science,* Vol. 12, No. 10, June, 1966, pp. 450–468.

VOLLMANN, T. E., *Operations Management, A Systems Model Building Approach.* Reading, Mass.: Addison-Wesley, 1973.

ZIMMERMAN, H. J., and M. G. SOVEREIGN, *Quantitative Models in Production Management.* Englewood Cliffs, N.J.: Prentice-Hall, Inc., 1974.

8

Operations Scheduling

INTRODUCTION

Operations scheduling involves the allocation of available resources (equipment, labor, time) to products, jobs, activities, or customers. Since scheduling is a resource allocation decision, it uses the resources made available by other planning decision areas: capacity, location, and layout planning. Scheduling results in a time-phased plan of activities that indicates what is to be done and when and with what equipment it should be started.

It is important to differentiate between aggregate (capacity) planning and scheduling. Aggregate planning results in gross production requirements. These requirements specify the number of pseudoproducts or services that should be provided over a period of time, without regard to the sequencing of jobs or activities, and without regard to the starting times of the processing of different job orders. In this sense, scheduling is a refined procedure and, chronologically, follows aggregate planning.

Several conflicting objectives are to be accommodated through proper scheduling:

1. High efficiency of operations, by maintaining high utilization of equipment, labor and time
2. Low inventories, which might undermine objective 1, since a subassembly may not be available when required if inventories are too low
3. Short flow time (flow time is the time a product or a customer spends in processing and in waiting till completion; keeping flow time to a minimum is in conflict with objectives 1 and 2).

Thus, scheduling involves a trade-off of conflicting objectives, such that a proper balance is achieved.

It is best to treat scheduling for various types of operations by following a classification of continuous, high-volume operations systems, versus intermittent, low-volume operations systems. Continuous and high-volume operations systems involve the provision of identical products or services in large quantities. Intermittent, low-volume operations systems involve the provision of a variety of products and services in limited quantities.

Intermittent, low-volume operations systems are of three kinds:

1. Closed job shop, which produces items to inventory
2. Open job shop, which produces custom-made products to order
3. The single project, which is usually large scale, and consists of numerous activities that should be coordinated and sequenced.

This chapter covers intermittent systems of types 1 and 2. It describes accepted techniques and suggests the implementation of several methodologies. Scheduling for an intermittent, low-volume operations system of type 3 is discussed in Chapter 4.

Scheduling entails allocating work loads to specific work centers and determining the sequence in which operations are performed. Continuous, high-volume systems are characterized by standardized activities and equipment. Such systems provide the customer with identical or similar operations for service organizations (examples: cafeteria lines, mass immunizations, and university registration) or identical production routine for a manufacturing organization (examples: production of cars, washing machines, stereos, potato chips—refer back to Chapter 7). The use of highly specialized tools, the arrangement of equipment, and the use of specialized material-handling equipment are designed to smooth the flow of work through the system.

A major problem in the design of flow systems is line balancing, which deals with the allocation of the required tasks to work stations so that they satisfy sequencing constraints and provide equal work times among stations. A high degree of work balancing provides for maximum output and maximum utilization of resources. Line balancing was discussed in Chapter 7.

SCHEDULING FOR CONTINUOUS, HIGH-VOLUME SYSTEMS

Continuous, high-volume, mass-production operations systems found in assembly lines and process industries present the scheduler with some difficult problems. First (as in the car assembly plant, or the potato-chip plant described in Chapter 7), the production rate is high. High cost is associated with each minute during which the production line is down due to scheduling problems. This cost includes direct idle labor cost, wasted material costs and any emergency costs involved in rushed-in parts and expedited subassemblies. Thus, the schedule has to assume the continuous availability of raw materials, subassemblies and finished goods.

Second, several work stations arranged in sequence are involved in such operations. While some inventory should be kept as a buffer, one would like to avoid excessive inventory build-up of raw materials at the initial work station, in-process inventory at the stations along the line, and finished goods inventory at the end of the process.

Scheduling for continuous, high-volume systems has to address these two problems, and necessitates the development of detailed schedules relating to raw-materials ordering, subassemblies production times, and the hauling of finished products to storage areas.

In this context, we present two techniques that are useful in dealing with high-volume systems:

1. The line of balance (LOB) helps in ensuring availability of parts and subassemblies without using a computer. Materials requirements planning (MRP), which is covered in Chapter 12, performs the same function, but requires the use of a computer. For manual scheduling, the LOB is a good traditional approach.
2. The learning curve helps in determining schedules for larger production batches. This technique may be used for lower-volume systems as well.

The Line-of-Balance (LOB) Technique

The LOB method was developed at the Goodyear Company and was subsequently supported by the U.S. Navy Special Service Project Office. It is particularly useful in operation scheduling whenever the finished product or service is composed of a number of components or subassemblies and when delivery of these products or services is scheduled over some time period.

LOB is a "management-by-exception" technique. It identifies the steps of the operation that call for expediting. LOB compares actual progress with planned progress of an operation. It considers planned production, actual production, the assembly flow, and component lead times.

LOB identifies control points, such as completion of an assembly operation, along the production operation. At these control points, physical inventory count takes place. This inventory represents a cumulative recording of all units that have successfully passed through a control point. A control point can be any selected work station or warehouse. The LOB calls for the use of three major graphical aides:

1. *The Assembly Chart* (see Figure 8.1(a)), which is an event-oriented chart. This chart arranges activities by precedence and notes lead times. It shows how the

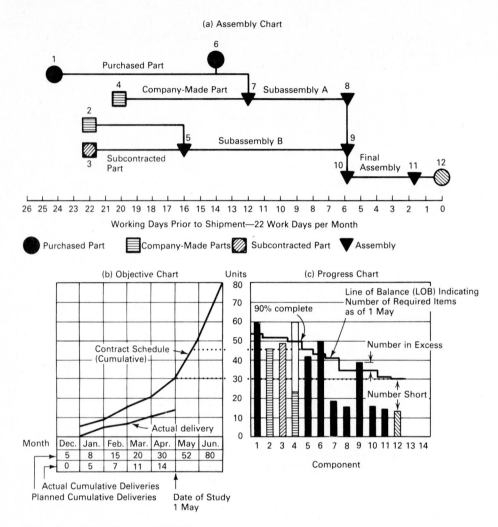

Figure 8.1 Line of Balance (LOB) Charts

different components are grouped together to form the subassemblies and the final product. A characteristic of the control points on the assembly chart is that they not only indicate starting and ending of an operation, but also "have an inventory as if [they] were a work station."[1] The chart is developed before the operation has started, as part of planning.

[1] Peter P. Schoderbek and Lester A. Digman, "Third Generation, PERT/LOB," *Harvard Business Review*, Vol. 45, No. 5, Sept.–Oct., 1967, pp. 100–110.

2. *The Objective Chart* (Figure 8.1(b)) is a weekly or monthly plan of production output. It is a plot of accumulated planned output and actual output. The presentation allows an easy comparison between planned and actual output. This chart is updated on a monthly basis.

3. *The Progress Chart* (Figure 8.1(c)), shows the cumulative number of units that have passed through a control point on a particular date. This inventory count should be executed each time the line of balance is developed.

The Line of Balance (LOB) represents, for a particular date, how many units should have passed through a control point. The LOB is compared with the progress chart bars, and balances the two against each other. This comparison indicates overages and shortages in the inventory of units at the various control points.

Let us describe the example in Figure 8.1. According to Figure 8.1(a), there are 12 control points. The product consists of two subassemblies, A and B. Subassembly A, in turn, consists of purchased parts 1 and 6, and company-made part 4. Assembly B consists of subcontracted part 3 and company-made part 2. The total lead time for the production of the different components, as indicated in Figure 8.1(a), is 24 days before delivery. As of the first of May, only fourteen of thirty planned products have actually been produced. This is shown in Figure 8.1(b).

The line of balance as of May 1 is determined by extending the intermittent, horizontal line at the level of 30 onto the progress chart in Figure 8.1(c). The solid line at control point 12 at the level of 30 in the progress chart 8.1(c) indicates a shortage at that conrol point. Although 30 units are scheduled, only 14 are available.

The line of balance, a stair-step function increasing to the left as time goes by, is used to see whether progress is adequate to achieve the rate-of-delivery schedule. Figure 8.1 shows that production is behind schedule. Purchased parts 1 and 6 are in ample supply, company-made part 4 is only 90 percent completed. Thus, subassembly A is much behind schedule. Control point 8 indicates a wide gap between plan and actual delivery. The operations manager, in turn, should expedite the production of subassembly A by completing the production of item 4, which is only 90 percent completed. Several examples of LOB are treated in the problems at the end of this chapter.

It has been suggested that material requirements planning (MRP), discussed elsewhere in the book, should replace the LOB technique. Although they are both concerned with the production and delivery of the final products, the MRP is product oriented, whereas the LOB is mostly customer oriented. The LOB technique is used primarily to control progress on a particular order. MRP is used for aggregate scheduling by systematically grouping like parts and subassemblies. In summary, the line-of-balance technique helps to monitor a production schedule by using graphical aids.

Learning Curves

In high-volume operations, the direct labor hours required to produce a unit decrease as more units are produced. This decrease in labor input is of such magnitude that it should be taken into account in scheduling and capacity planning.

The expertise gained over time in the process of production and operation suggests that the second unit produced requires less direct labor time than the first. This reduction in time has been proven to continue for many units. The phenomenon can be described by using a *learning curve*, or, alternatively, a "manufacturing process function" or "progress curve."

A worker at a work station may become more familiar with a given job and may introduce changes. Examples of such changes are: improved tooling in the machining phase of a gearbox, improved material handling system in the assembly department at a chain-saw manufacturer, and better-designed form for patients' admission in a hospital. Such changes result in reduced processing time per unit. These improvements affect learning curves that show the rate of improvement in productivity.

The unit production times may be reduced abruptly or slowly, as more products are produced. A rather erratic learning curve may therefore result. However, for a particular type of product, a rather consistent relationship between unit production time and the number of units produced is present: namely, the direct labor time per product is reduced by a consistent percentage each time the cumulative number of units produced is doubled. The consistent percentage by which the direct labor hours are reduced or production quantity is doubled is called the *learning curve rate,* ϕ.

A learning curve rate of 90 percent means that only 90 percent of the time required to process the first unit is required to process the second unit. The twentieth unit requires 90 percent of the time required to process the tenth unit, and so on. In other words, there is a 10 percent improvement ratio, termed *progress ratio.*

The relationship between the direct hours required to process the nth unit and the direct hours required to process the first unit is expressed as:

$$W_n = (W_1)(n)^R \tag{8.1}$$

where:

W_n = Direct hours required to process the nth unit. (unit time)

W_1 = Direct hours required to process the first unit.

n = Chronological number of the unit for which the direct hours are to be established.

R = Ratio of the logarithm of the learning curve rate to the logarithm of

$$2, R = \dfrac{\log \phi}{\log 2}$$

ϕ = Learning rate

$1 - \phi$ = Progress ratio.

One can avoid using logarithms by using Table D in the Appendix at the end of this book. For some selected learning curve rates, the *unit time* and *total time* is given as well as the unit time, W_n. The total time is the cumulative time it takes to complete the batch. In order to find unit time, W_n, one multiplies the table value, K, by the time required for the first unit:

$$W_n = (W_1)(K)$$

EXAMPLE   A producer of home appliances is experiencing a 90 percent learning curve rate for the toaster-ovens line. It took 30 hours to process the first unit, and management wants to estimate how many hours of processing the twentieth unit will take. Here, using a table of logarithms,

$$R = \frac{\log 0.90}{\log 2} = \frac{\log 9 - \log 10}{0.3010} = \frac{0.9542 - 1.000}{0.3010} = -0.1522$$

$$W_{20} = (W_1)(n)^{-0.1522} = (30)(20)^{-0.1522}$$

Using generally accepted logarithm rules:

$$\log W_{20} = \log 30 - 0.1522 \log 20$$

$$= \log 3 + \log 10 - 0.1522 (\log 2 + \log 10)$$

$$= 0.4771 + 1.0000 - 0.1522 (0.3010 + 1.000)$$

$$= 1.2791$$

$$W_{20} = \text{antilog } 1.2791 = 19.02 \text{ hours}$$

Thus, the twentieth unit will require about 19 direct hours of processing.
When using Table D in the Appendix:

$$W_{20} = (30 \text{ hours})(0.634) = 19.02 \text{ hours}$$

EXAMPLE   A new mortgage department in the bank is to determine the time it takes to process twenty identical mortgage applications. Assuming a learning rate of 80 percent and 400 labor-minutes of direct labor for the first mortgage application,

a) What are the expected labor-minutes required for the twentieth application?

b) What is the expected time required for all twenty applications?

Using Appendix Table D, for $n = 20$ and $\phi = 80$ percent,

a) Expected time for the twentieth application
$W_{20} = (400)(0.381) = 152.4$ labor-minutes
b) Expected total time for all twenty applications
$(400)(10.485) = 4{,}194$ labor-minutes

At times, the direct hours required to process the first unit is not known. Or, alternatively, management believes that the completion time for a later unit is more reliable. In these cases, the table can help in determining the direct hours required for the first unit.

EXAMPLE   The bank manager believes that processing the first application was unusually delayed and would like to revise the first unit estimate, based on a completion time of 250 labor-minutes for the fourth application. Now $n = 4$, $W_4 = 250$, $\phi = 80$ percent (from Table D) the unit time is 0.640. Divide the actual time, 250 labor-minutes, for the fourth application by the value from Table D to get the revised estimate for the first application:

$$250 \div 0.640 = 390.6 \text{ labor-minutes}$$

Equation (8.1) is exponential and, plotted on logarithmic-scale ("log-log") paper, appears as a straight line.

$$\log W_n = \log W_1 + R \log n \tag{8.2}$$

In Figure 8.2(b) the abscissa is marked as the log of the number of units produced ($\log n$), and the ordinate is marked as the logarithm of number of direct hours of processing required ($\log W_n$).

The learning curve rate, R, is the slope of the straight line. The logarithm of the number of direct hours required to process the first unit denotes the intersection point of the learning curve with the ordinate.

From Figure 8.2, one can see that the lower the learning curve rate, the higher the impact of the volume of processed units on the schedule.

The Use of Learning Curves

Learning curves are used for contract negotiations. The time required to produce a unit becomes smaller as experience accumulated. Thus, contract negotiators first settle on the number of units and then negotiate price on that basis. The government requests learning-curve data on contracts that involve large and complex products. If a contract is terminated before production and delivery of all products, the supplier can use the learning-curve argument to support an increase in the unit price for the smaller order size. The government can use

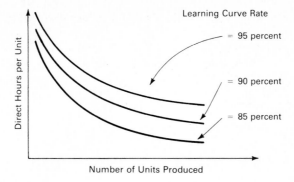

Figure 8.2(a)   Learning Curve on a Regular Scale Paper

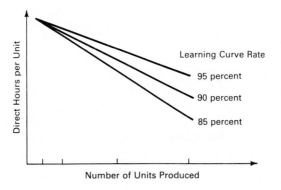

Figure 8.2(b)   Learning Curve on a Logarithmic Scale Paper

learning curves to negotiate lower prices per unit for late orders of the same product.

2 Learning curves are used for pricing purposes of new products and services. Simply projecting the cost of the first few units will result in a higher price than would be expected after several units have been delivered.

3 Learning curves help operations managers to plan labor, purchasing, and inventory costs. The initial cost per unit is high and the production rate is low, so labor, purchasing, and inventory should match the low rate of output. As productivity increases, labor, purchasing, and inventory should allow for increased cost of raw materials and purchased parts. Learning curves should be consulted for projected rates of production. Otherwise, one may face overestimation of labor needs and underestimation of raw material and parts requirements. It should be noted that learning curves may also be used at times for intermittent, low-volume operations systems. Learning curves may also be used to evaluate new workers during training periods. This is done by comparing the worker's performance to an expected rate of learning.

Learning curves should be used with caution. First, operations that are controlled largely by machine capacity and not by operator skill and dexterity are characterized by a higher learning curve rate. That is, they are less influenced by the learning curve phenomenon. Second, the use of learning curves for special projects is somewhat restricted. Special projects are characterized by untried processes, designs, and raw materials. As such, the learning curve rate should be studied carefully. Third, because the learning curve flattens out after a while, its effects should be considered mostly during the start-up phase of operations.

SCHEDULING FOR INTERMITTENT, LOW-VOLUME SYSTEMS

Intermittent, low-volume systems are characterized by the variety of processes or services offered. There are three types of intermittent systems: the closed job shop, which produces items to stock; the open job shop, which produces custom items to order; and the large-scale, one-time project. The large-scale-project scheduling problem was dealt with in Chapter 4. Closed and open job shop scheduling are dealt with in this section.

Job shop scheduling is recognized as very complex, for several reasons:

1. Product design and processing times must be flexible.
2. Routes through the system may change as processing proceeds.
3. Job arrival pattern, number of machines in the shop, and number of workers in the shop all have an impact on the schedule.

The rules of assigning jobs to machines and the criteria for assignment is the most important topic in job shop scheduling.

Job Shop Scheduling Rules

The priority rules governing the assignment of single jobs to machines affect the time the individual orders spend on the floor as well as shipment dates. The underlying assumption is that job processing would not be pre-empted—that is, once a job is started, it is worked on until completion.

The priority rules that are most common in industry are:

1. Highest priority is given to the job with the shortest processing time.
2. Highest priority is given to the job with the earliest due date.[2]
3. Highest priority is given to the job with the least slack, where slack is defined as the time remaining until due date after deducting the remaining processing time.

---

[2] Richard W. Conway, "Priority Dispatching Rules and Job Lateness in a Job Shop," *Journal of Industrial Engineering*, Vol. 16, No. 4, July–August, 1965, pp. 228–237.

4. Slack is divided by the number of remaining operations. Highest priority is assigned to the job that has the least slack per remaining operations.

Priority Value =

$$\frac{[\text{Due date}] - [\text{Time now}] - [\text{Remaining machine processing time}]}{[\text{Number of operations to be done}]}$$

The last priority rule is the most frequently used.[3] This rule suggests changing priorities as due dates get closer. As an example, suppose jobs A and B have the same due date of 220 days hence and await processing on the same machine group. The priority values are presented in Table 8.1 for four different dates: 80, 90, 100, and 110 days hence.

Table 8.1 demonstrates the dynamic nature of the priority rule. As one can see, if a machine becomes free 80 days or 90 days hence, then Job B is loaded first. If a machine becomes free 100 days hence, the options have equal priority values. If a machine becomes free 110 days hence, job A is loaded first.

TABLE 8.1 THE DYNAMIC NATURE OF A PRIORITY RULE

JOB	DUE DATE	REMAINING MACHINE TIME	NUMBER OF REMAINING OPERATIONS	PRIORITY VALUE WHEN TIME NOW IS:			
				80	90	100	110
A	220	90	4	12.50	10.00	7.50	5.00
B	220	60	8	10.00	8.75	7.50	6.25

SINGLE FACILITY SCHEDULE

Assume that several jobs are awaiting processing by a single facility. The facility can handle only one job at a time. Further, the processing time and due date are predetermined and do not change. What should be the sequencing of the jobs through the single facility? This problem is known as the "*n*-jobs–one-machine problem," or "*n*/1 problem," where *n* can take any finite value.

Any of the priority rules covered earlier may be used to establish a schedule. Furthermore, there are other rules that have been recommended, but that are not as popular as those described.[4]

---

[3] C. Colin New, "Job Shop Scheduling: Who Needs a Computer to Sequence Jobs?" *Production and Inventory Management,* 4th quarter, 1975, pp. 38–45.

[4] R. E. Larson and M. I. Dessouky, "Heuristic Procedures for the Single Machine Problem to Minimize Lateness," *AIIE Transactions,* Vol. 10, No. 2, pp. 176–183.

EXAMPLE Four mortgage agreements are to be drawn by Mr. Honest, the well-known real-estate lawyer. The due date and processing time for each of the agreements are listed in Table 8.2.

The schedule will be developed by using various priority rules as shown in Table 8.3. The priority rules are evaluated by using two criteria: mean flow time, which is the average time a job requires from scheduling day ("today") until completion; mean lateness, which is the average number of days a job is late.

As per the following table, it is interesting to note that no one priority rule provides the best schedule. While the shortest-processing-time rule performs best according to the mean-flow-time criterion, the earliest-due-date rule performs best according to the mean-lateness criterion.

Rule	Flow Time Criterion	Lateness Criterion
Shortest Processing Time	9 days	4 days
Earliest Due Date	9 1/2 days	3 1/2 days
Least Slack	11 1/2 days	5 1/2 days

However, some rules perform better under certain conditions. Studies have shown that the shortest processing time rule yields the lowest mean flow time. That results in low in-process inventory, and a faster delivery schedule for most customers. The earliest-due-date and least-slack rules become effective when one tries to reduce the lateness of jobs. A random sequence generally performs worst under any of the criteria.

It is interesting to examine a graph in which we rank-order the jobs by ascending order of processing times. Figure 8.3 is a plot of the jobs against flow time. The *x*-axis specifies the flow time, and the *y*-axis presents the jobs.

The area under the graph, which indicates the total flow time of all scheduled jobs, is minimized when we rank-order the jobs by ascending order of processing times. Any other sequence—random, for example—results in a larger area under the curve.

Two-Facility Schedule

Assume that several jobs are awaiting processing by a sequence of two facilities. Once a job is processed on one facility, it proceeds directly to the second, with

TABLE 8.2   DATA FOR SCHEDULING OF MORTGAGE PROCESSING

(1) MORTGAGE	(2) REMAINING PROCESSING TIME	(3) DUE DATE	(4) = (3) − (2) SLACK TO DATE
A	2	6	4
B	5	8	3
C	4	2	0
D	6	8	2

TABLE 8.3 SCHEDULING USING VARIOUS PRIORITY RULES

a) Using the Shortest-Processing-Time Rule:

(1) MORTGAGE	(2) SEQUENCE	(3) REMAINING PROCESSING TIME	(4) FLOW TIME	(5) DUE DATE	(6) = (4) − (5) LATENESS
A	1	2	2	6	0
C	2	4	6	2	4
B	3	5	11	8	3
D	4	6	17	8	9
			Σ = 36		Σ = 16

Mean Lateness 16/4 = 4 days
Mean Flow Time = 36/4 = 9 days

b) Using the Earliest-Due-Date Rule:

(1) MORTGAGE	(2) SEQUENCE	(3) REMAINING PROCESSING TIME	(4) FLOW TIME	(5) DUE DATE	(6) = (4) − (5) LATENESS
C	1	4	4	2	2
A	2	2	6	6	0
B*	3	5	11	8	3
D*	4	6	17	8	9
			Σ = 38		Σ = 14

Mean Lateness 14/4 = 3.5 days
Mean Flow Time = 38/4 = 9.5 days

*Ties are broken following the shortest-processing-time rule

c) Using the least slack rule:

(1) MORT-GAGE	(2) SE-QUENCE	(3) REMAINING PROCESSING TIME	(4) DUE DATE	(5) SLACK TO DATE	(6) FLOW TIME	(6) = (4) − (5) LATENESS
C	1	2	2	0	4	2
D	2	6	8	2	10	2
B	3	5	8	3	15	7
A	4	2	6	4	17	11
					Σ = 46	Σ = 22

Mean Lateness 22/4 = 5.5 days
Mean Flow Time = 46/4 = 11.5 days

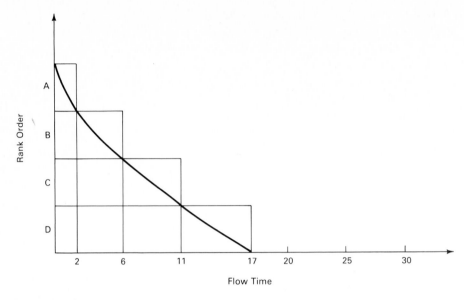

Figure 8.3 Mortgage Sequence and Flow Time

no interruption. How should a schedule be set if the same processing sequence must be maintained by both facilities? A simple two-facility rule that performs well under the mean-flow-time criterion has been conceived by Johnson:[5]

1. List jobs, showing the processing time required by each facility.
2. Choose the job with the shortest processing time. If the shortest time is with facility A, assign it as early as possible (on facility A); if the shortest time is with facility B, assign it as late as possible (on facility B).
3. Eliminate the job already scheduled; then, repeat (b). (Ties are broken arbitrarily.)

This priority rule maximizes the concurrent processing time by both facility A and B, and thus minimizes the overall flow times.

EXAMPLE   Two major processing centers are involved in the production of chain saws: machining center (A) and assembly center (B). Orders X100, X200, X300, and X400 carry the following processing times.

Order	Machining Center (A)	Assembly Center (B)
X100	9 days	2 days
X200	1	5
X300	7	3
X400	6	4

[5] S. M. Johnson, "Optimal Two and Three Stage Production Schedules with Set-Up Time Included," *Naval Research Logistics Quarterly*, Vol. 1, No. 1, March, 1954, pp. 61–68.

What should the processing schedule be? Order X200 has the shortest processing time at the machining center (A). It is therefore scheduled first to the machining center (A) and first to the assembly center (B). Order X100 has the shortest processing time at the assembly center (B); thus, it is scheduled last to the assembly center (B) and last to the machining center (A). This procedure continues until all orders are scheduled, yielding the sequence presented in Figure 8.4 (number of days in process appears in brackets).

The flow times for the various orders are as follows:

Order	X100	X200	X300	X400
Flow Time	25 days	6 days	17 days	11 days

The mean flow time is $(25 + 6 + 17 + 11)/4 = 14.75$ days.

Three-Facility Schedule

Under certain conditions, a three-facility schedule may be treated as a two-facility schedule. Let us assume processing times on three facilities as follows:

Order	Facility A	Facility B	Facility C
X100	8 days	9 days	12 days
X200	9	3	12
X300	7	8	10
X400	14	2	9
X500	7	3	13

If the minimum processing time on facility C is greater than or equal to the maximum processing time on facility B, or if the minimum processing time on facility A is greater than or equal to the maximum processing time on facility B, then the triple-facility case can be treated as a double-facility case by summing all processing times on facilities A and B and summing all processing times on

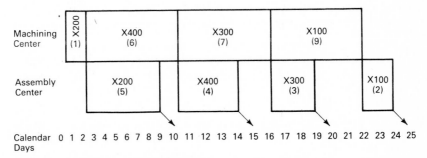

Figure 8.4   Sequencing Jobs for Processing

facilities C and B, to arrive at a double-facility presentation. From that point, the solution follows as in the two-facility schedule. The transformed problem is:

	A*	B*
Order	Facilities A + B	Facilities B + C
X100	8 + 9 = 17	9 + 12 = 21
X200	9 + 3 = 12	3 + 12 = 15
X300	7 + 8 = 15	8 + 10 = 18
X400	14 + 2 = 16	2 + 9 = 11
X500	7 + 3 = 10	3 + 13 = 16

The problem now is to schedule the two orders on the two facilities, A* and B*, where the processing times are the corresponding summations, (A + B) and (B + C). The sequence, following Johnson's rule from the preceding section, is X500, X200, X300, X100, X400.

Facility Loading

Facility loading is different from facility scheduling. Facility scheduling deals with the sequencing of jobs through a facility after the jobs have been assigned to it. Facility loading deals with the assignment of jobs to facilities, taking into account the efficiency with which the various facilities can perform a particular job.

For example, a numerically controlled lathe can achieve higher accuracy and speed than a manually operated lathe. This affects the costs involved in processing. The jobs should be assigned to minimize the total costs involved in the assignment without regard (as yet) to the actual scheduling (sequencing) of jobs.

When alternative facilities exist for processing jobs, a technique called the assignment method can be used. This method helps in assigning jobs to machines or workers to jobs, while minimizing costs. In order to operate the technique one assumes a certain cost, called the cost coefficient, that involves the assignment of a job to a machine. The method requires that the number of jobs be equal to the number of facilities. If this is not true, a dummy job or facility should be added with zero cost coefficient. If any job to facility assignment is nonfeasible, the cost coefficient is given an extremely high value. Let us describe the assignment-method procedure and then demonstrate its used through an example.

Step 1. Construct a square matrix. Indicate the cost coefficient values (other kinds of criteria may be used, such as profit, for example).

Step 2. Subtract the smallest cost coefficient in each row from all coefficients in the row. Form a new matrix.

Step 3. Using the new matrix, subtract the smallest cost coefficient in each column from all coefficients in the column. Form a new matrix.

Step 4. Draw the minimum number of lines necessary to cover all zero-entries in the matrix.

Step 5. If the number of lines is equal to the number of rows (or columns), assign jobs to facilities based on the zero-entries; if the number of lines is less than the number of rows (or columns), add the smallest uncovered cost coefficient to all coefficients at line intersections, and subtract it from each uncovered coefficient, including itself, and go back to step 4.

EXAMPLE   The operations manager has four jobs that can be processed by any of four facilities. The costs involved in the processing of the various jobs by the four facilities is given in the appropriate cells. How should the jobs be loaded to facilities to minimize cost? (Note: costs are given in thousands of dollars.)

Step 1

Job \ Facility	1	2	3	4
A	4	5	7	6
B	9	10	11	7
C	9	7	12	5
D	7	6	3	2

Step 2

Job \ Facility	1	2	3	4
A	0	1	3	2
B	2	3	4	0
C	4	2	7	0
D	5	4	1	0

Step 3 and Step 4

Job \ Facility	1	2	3	4
A	0	0	2	2
B	2	2	3	0
C	4	1	6	0
D	5	3	0	0

As one can see, the number of lines necessary to cover all zero-entries (three lines) is less than the number of rows or columns (four). Thus, the solution should be improved.

Step 5

Job \ Facility	1	2	3	4
A	0	0	3	3
B	1	1	3	0
C	3	0	6	0
D	4	2	0	0

Now we shall try to cover all zero-entries with the minimum number of lines.

Step 4

Job \ Facility	1	2	3	4
A	0	0	3	3
B	1	1	3	0
C	3	0	6	0
D	4	2	0	0

Since the number of lines required to cover all zeros is equal to the number of jobs and facilities, this is an optimal solution.

Step 5

Now we are ready to assign jobs to facilities. The assignment will be based on the zero entries. The first assignment should be made to cells with zero cost coefficients (in the last table) that stand alone in their respective row or column. Thus, the first assignment should be made of job A to facility 1. This is marked with a square. Since only one job can be assigned to a facility, row A and column 1 would no longer be considered for an assignment. The next assignment will be made of job C to facility 2, which now, after the first assignment, presents a lone zero-entry in its column. In the same manner we assign job B to facility 4, and job D to facility 3.

Job \ Facility	1	2	3	4	Optimal Assignment
A	☐0	0			A—1
B				☐0	B—4
C		☐0		☐0	C—2
D			☐0	0	D—3

The symbol ☐ indicates an optimal assignment.

Thus, job A should be assigned to facility 1, job B to facility 4, job C to facility 2, and job D to facility 3. The total cost involved in this assignment is 4000 + 7000 + 3000 + 7000, or $21,000.

Computer Systems Considerations

As the amount of information required for proper planning increases, and as the operations become more involved, greater importance is placed on computerization of the scheduling function, especially in concert with capacity planning. One such program[6] aims at meeting due dates and cutting down flow time, which in turn cuts down the amounts of in-process inventory and lead time. It also aims at minimizing idle time. Let us describe the stages involved in using this computer program (see Figure 8.5).

Capacity Requirements Planning. This stage plans the output by helping to establish a period-by-period capacity capable of covering production requirements. Planning the capacity starts with determining detailed capacity requirements (work loads). The planner then plans capacity adjustments to overloaded

[6] International Business Machines, *Communications Oriented Production Information and Control System,* (White Plains, N.Y.: IBM, 1972), Vol. I, pp. 44–46.

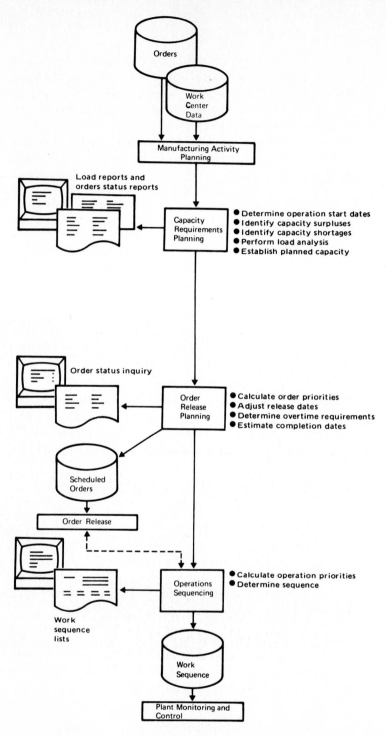

Figure 8.5 Three Stages of Operations Activity Planning *Source:* IBM *COPICS*, Vol. 1, p. 45 Courtesy of International Business Machines Corporation.

or underloaded work centers. Analysis of the load by means of a terminal (see Figures 8.5, 8.6) enables.him or her to make recommendations, such as on the need for hiring production workers, subcontracting or performing work for other plants, planning extra shifts, or planning overtime work.

Order Release Planning. This second stage may adjust the date on which the planned order is to be released to the shop floor. Together with OPERATION SEQUENCING, it levels the planned load on each mine center. It also determines which orders should be released early to prevent idle time. These decisions are based on calculated order priorities. At this stage the system also estimates the completion time for each shop order and customer order.

Operation Sequencing. The third stage of manufacturing activity planning produces a work sequence list, which is the basis for assigning work to machines and operators. The sequence reflects the decisions made in the previous

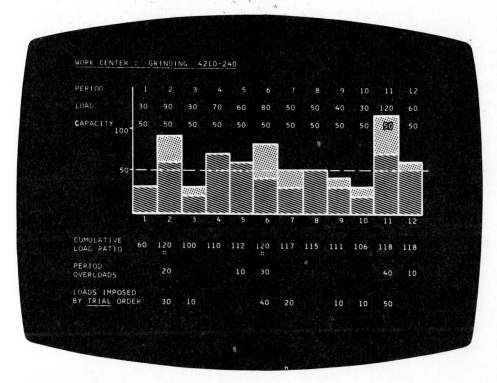

Figure 8.6   Example of the Type of Load Report That Can Be Displayed To Analyze Critical Load Situations   *Source:* IBM *COPICS,* Vol. 1, p. 46. Courtesy of International Business Machines Corporation.

planning phases, and takes into account the latest conditions on the shop floor. By simulating the minute-by-minute situation in the factory, operation sequencing attempts to keep machines from running out of work or becoming bottlenecks.

The program described above produces a centralized, detailed schedule. However, loading systems have generally emphasized the decentralization of detailed scheduling. In a decentralized scheduling system, job starting times, assignment of jobs to workers, and the assignment of jobs to specific machines are determined locally by the individual foremen, while the priority rules are stated by management on a plant-wide basis.

United Aircraft Company operates such a system. This system consists of a shop with approximately 3000 job orders in process, and employs roughly 5000 workers daily. It has about 130 work centers. The schedule, which is developed by using an involved priority rule, is served as a guideline to the individual foremen. However, the foremen are not obliged to use that schedule.

Apparently, the use of this system has helped to cut down flow time and lateness. This is extremely important as the assembly of a jet engine, United Aircraft's major product, cannot begin unless all subassemblies have been forwarded from the machining area. Before the installation of the system, the assembly area was frequently idle, while the machining department was overloaded with expedited jobs.

Another example of a successful scheduling system is Hughes Aircraft Company.[7] This job shop fabricates a variety of products, such as machine subassemblies, waveguides, and printed circuit boards. At any time, there are some 2000 to 3000 job orders processed in the shop. The shop consists of 1000 machines that are grouped into 120 functional work centers. There are 400 direct workers, and the average flow time per completed job is three to four weeks.

The schedule is compiled by an extensive, integrated computer-based scheduling and control system. A simulator incorporates a priority scheduling rule and develops a detailed schedule for the following day for each foreman. The results of installing the system have been reported to be successful; the number of job orders completed by due date have increased; average order cycle time has been reduced; in-process inventory has declined and less expediting has been required.

SCHEDULING OF SERVICE OPERATIONS

Scheduling of service operations is rather an involved procedure. Service operations are characterized by:

[7] Michael H. Bulkin, and H. Steinhoff, Jr., "Load Forecasting Priority Sequencing and Simulation in a Job Shop Control System," *Management Science*, Vol. B, No. 2, October, 1966, p. 13–29.

1. Lack of inventory of processed units, as the service is provided, when required, "to order"
2. Generally, minimized flow time, as the customer is present as the process goes on
3. Multiple objectives present, such as the requirement of high-quality service (which takes time) and the need for fast service
4. Random number of customer requests for service.

There are basically two kinds of service operations:

1. Standardized service operations that are facilities-oriented. The schedule is vigorously adhered to, and there is little flexibility to meet any individual customer's need. Mail delivery, street cleaning, solid-waste collection, school-bus scheduling, and airline scheduling are examples of standardized services.
2. Customized service operations that are customer-oriented. Flexibility is built into the scheduling system to accommodate the individual customer's needs. Hospital admission and surgery scheduling are examples of customized service scheduling.

An important objective of the scheduling system is to match the flow of customers and service capabilities. A smooth flow with no delays and waiting can be effected if a new customer arrives at the instant that the preceding customer's service is completed, as is often the case in a dentist's office. A smooth flow also results if, for example, the demand for service exactly equals the number of seats available, as in an airplane. Smooth flow results in zero waiting time for the customer and full utilization of the service facility. Unfortunately, the random nature of customers' requests for service will undermine an exact match of capacity with demand. There are also random variations of the service rate, due to sickness, current conditions, servers' moods, variations in customers' requirements for service, etc.

Determining the capacity and scheduling of service systems can be facilitated by using waiting-lines theory, which is covered in the Technical Note to Chapter 14. It can help in cases such as repair service of equipment breakdowns, hospital emergency rooms, gas stations, and theaters.

In the following sections, a description of proposed scheduling systems for some service operations is presented.

School-Bus Schedules

The multiple objectives involved in school-bus scheduling make it a complicated scheduling problem. The objectives are as follows:

1. The number of routes (buses) should be minimized.

2. The time required to traverse any route cannot exceed a maximum allowed by the scheduler.
3. A bus cannot be overloaded.

There are several methods for satisfying this objective. An optimal assignment of routes and loading times can be obtained by the calculation of each possible loading pattern. However, this approach is very expensive and time consuming.

A computer-assisted school-bus scheduling was proposed.[8] The data required was of three kinds:

1. Stop-loading information that includes number of students to be scheduled at each stop
2. A matrix that contains the shortest path in time between any pair of bus stops
3. Decisions relating to the value of the following parameters: number and capacity of buses, maximum route time (in minutes), loading time per student, and allowance for extra time for each stop.

The schedule output identifies the number of students, arrival time of the bus, and the time required to load the bus for each stop. It also contains data on route time, loading time, driving speed, total students, total stops, and miles driven.

Figure 8.8 shows the actual results of the bus-scheduling method. The utilization of buses has been increased by 6.45 percent, as is evidenced by a higher average load of number of students per bus. The number of routes has been decreased by 4.17 percent.

This scheduling system was questioned, and other (manual scheduling) systems, have been proven to be closer to optimal in many instances. At any rate, the benefits of somewhat higher utilization rate should be weighed against the cost of implementing a scheduling system.

Hospital Admission Scheduling

The more expensive the idle time and the opportunity costs of operating a service, the more sophisticated should be the scheduling system. Such is the case in airline scheduling, emergency services scheduling (fire, ambulance, police), and hospital admission scheduling.

Current hospital admission practices, surgical operations scheduling, and nurse staffing often result in inefficient use of resources. Costs of these activities can be reduced through more effective administrative planning and control.

---

[8] R. D. Angel, W. L. Caudle, R. Noonan, A. Whinston, "Computer Assisted School Bus Scheduling," *Management Science*, Vol. 8, No. 6, February, 1973, pp. B279–B288.

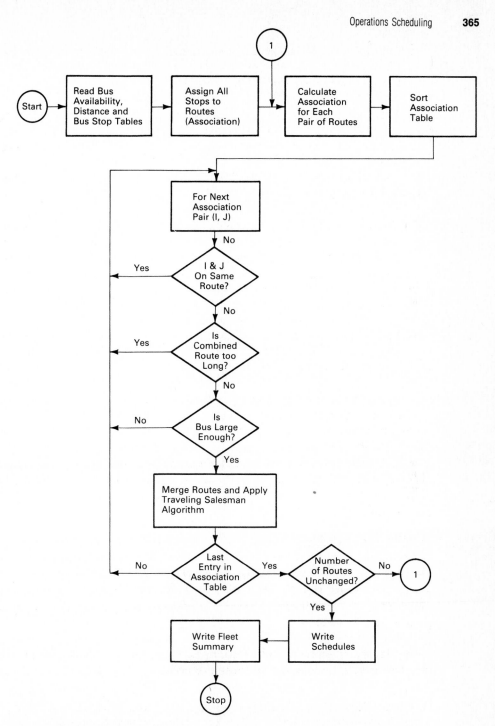

Figure 8.7 Bus-Scheduling Approach *Source:* A. D. Angel, W. L. Caudle, R. Noonan, A. Whinton, "Computer Assisted School Bus Scheduling," *Management Science,* Vol. 18, No. 6, Feb. 1973, p. 288. Used with permission.

School System Information
Number of students: 1500
Number of routes: 24
Average load size: 62
Load-size range: 39–81
Computer Assisted Routes
Number of routes: 23
Average load size: 66
Load-size range: 57–72
Maximum riding time: 58 minutes

FIGURE 8.8 DETAILS ON COMPUTER-ASSISTED ROUTES

Route Number	Scheduled Quantity	Number of Stops	Number of Miles	Maximum Riding Time (min.)
1	67	32	13	43
2	65	26	13	38
3	72	37	12	50
4	69	38	14	52
5	72	20	13	31
6	71	33	12	48
7	65	30	8	40
8	71	26	11	40
9	65	33	12	46
10	70	26	10	37
11	61	24	11	33
12	72	31	25	47
13	64	13	15	25
14	66	32	15	25
15	70	46	7	41
16	62	30	8	40
17	63	33	24	44
18	60	27	28	44
19	57	22	12	31
20	70	21	13	34
21	70	37	25	47
22	61	29	21	45
23	57	30	17	47

Routes 9, 18, 19, 20 have additional transit times of either 9 minutes or 12 minutes.

Source: R. D. Angel, W. L. Caudle, R. Noonan, A. Whinston, "Computer Assisted School Bus Scheduling," *Management Science*, Vol. 8, No. 6, February, 1973, p. 284.

Several researchers have addressed the problems of hospital admission scheduling,[9] surgery scheduling,[10] and nurse scheduling.[11,12]

[9] J. H. Milsum, E. Turban, I. Vertinsky, "Hospital Admission Systems: Their Evaluation and Management," *Management Science*, Vol. 19, No. 6, February, 1973, pp. 646–666.

[10] N. K. Kwak, J. Kuzdrall, H. H. Schmitz, "The GPSS Simulation of Scheduling Policies for Surgical Patients," *Management Science*, Vol. 22, No. 9, May, 1976, pp. 982–989.

TABLE 8.4 DECISION VARIABLES AND ANALYSIS TECHNIQUES USED IN STUDIES
OF HOSPITAL ADMISSION SCHEDULES

DECISION VARIABLES	POLICIES	QUANTITATIVE TECHNIQUES	EFFECTIVENESS MEASURE
Number of Patients to be Scheduled Daily	1. Scheduling of a constant number every day 2. Scheduling of a variable number each day as a function of bed occupancy	Waiting Lines Simulation	1. Occupancy level 2. Overload 3. Stabilization in bed occupancy
Feasible Admission Date	1. Analysis of each application 2. Several patients with same health needs to be assigned to an admission date	Linear Programming	1. Deviation from ideal admission date, vs. turning a patient away
Scheduling of Operations in Operating Rooms	1. First come, first served 2. Longest operations first 3. Shortest operations first	Simulation	1. Facilities utilization 2. Average number of patients waiting 3. Delayed operations 4. Average overtime/day
Scheduling of Standby Emergency Hospital	Every nth day, or k_1 consecutive days on, k_2 consecutive days off.	Simulation	Stabilization of bed occupancy

Table 8.4 summarizes decision variables and quantitative techniques used
in order to improve hospital admission practices. Generally, simulation is used
since the complexity of the variable interrelationships calls for renumeration
rather than analytical solution for optimal admission scheduling. The reader is
encouraged to consult the Technical Note to this chapter, which presents the
essentials of simulation.

SUMMARY

This chapter has provided an insight into the nature of scheduling
methodologies and aids. The area of scheduling has been studied extensively in
the context of a job shop.[13] The solutions recommended for a job shop have been

[11] D. Michael Warner, Juan Prawda, "A Mathematical Programming Model for Scheduling
Nursing Personnel in a Hospital," *Management Science*, Vol. 19, No. 4, Part I, December, 1972, pp.
411–422.

[12] W. J. Abernathy, N. Baloff, J. C. Hershey, "The Nurse Staffing Problem: Issue and
Prospects," *Sloan Management Review*, Fall, 1971, pp. 87–99.

[13] For a categorization and comparison of several scheduling methodologies consult Menipaz,
E., "Scheduling Models: Shibboleth and Operating Characteristics," *Journal of Information and
Optimization Policies*, Vol. 4, No. 1, January 1983, pp. 49–64.

extended to analogous situations. Several of the scheduling methods are actually visual presentations of jobs and activities that facilitate monitoring (LOB, Gantt chart). Others involve more of a system-based philosophy, and are generally computerized (MRP).

It seems that many scheduling problems, especially in the service area, call for custom-built scheduling techniques. Ths is attributed to the number of the variables affecting schedule and the complexity of the interrelationships among the variables. This complexity makes analytical solutions impossible and calls for a trial-and-error approach that is assisted by the simulation technique. The essentials of the simulation technique are described in the Technical Note to this chapter. It should be noted that the schedule's user—the foreman or the operations manager—should be familiar with the technique employed and should trust it.

DISCUSSION QUESTIONS

8.1 What are the scheduling problems that are peculiar to high-volume systems?

8.2 What are the components of the line-of-balance (LOB) technique?

8.3 What is a learning curve? Is a learning curve of 90 percent "better" or "worse" than a learning curve of 80 percent?

8.4 What are the three types of intermittent systems?

8.5 What priority rules are most common in industry?

8.6 List the steps involved in the double-facility priority rule.

8.7 List the steps involved in the assignment-method procedure.

8.8 Compare and contrast line of balance, and the material requirements planning (MRP).

8.9 What are the stages involved in computerized operations scheduling?

8.10 What are the characteristics of service operations scheduling?

PROBLEMS AND SOLUTIONS

8.1 A maintenance department currently has four jobs that it must process on a single machine. Given the information in the following table, compare the scheduling priority rules for assigning jobs according to the "minimum-slack-time" rule and for assigning jobs according to the "shortest-processing-time" rule. Evaluate your comparison by using the criteria of "minimum mean flow time" and "minimum mean lateness."

Job	(1) Due Date	(2) Time Required to Repair	(3) Job Slack (1) − (2)
A	3 days hence	2 days	1
B	8 days hence	5 days	3
C	6 days hence	6 days	0
D	10 days hence	8 days	2

Solution

Jobs Assigned According to Minimum Slack Time:

Sequence: C − A − D − B

6 + 2 + 8 + 5 = 21 days

Evaluation:

Job	(1) Flow Time	(2) Time Available	(3) Lateness (1) − (2)
A	8	3	5
B	21	8	13
C	6	6	0
D	16	10	6
	51		24

Mean Flow Time: 51/4 = 12.75

Mean Lateness: 24/4 = 6.00

Jobs Assigned According to Shortest Processing Times:

Sequence: A − B − C − D

2 + 5 + 6 + 8 = 21 days

Job	(1) Flow Time	(2) Time Available	(3) Lateness (1) − (2)
A	2	3	0
B	7	8	0
C	13	6	7
D	21	10	11
	43		18

Mean Flow Time: 43/4 = 10.75

Mean Lateness: 18/4 = 4.50

    As would be expected, the "shortest-processing-time" rule yields the optimal solution.

8.2   Dr. Band is a well-known management consultant who specializes in developing management information systems for production facilities. Currently, Dr. Band has 6 data processing jobs, each of which requires flowcharting and writing of the actual computer program. Band must complete these jobs within 36 hours. Given the following processing times, use Johnson's method to determine whether Band can meet the 36-hours processing time.

Job	Flowcharting Time	Program-Writing Time
A	9 hrs	1 hr.
B	8	3
C	5	4
D	7	11
E	6	8
F	2	9

Solution

Order of Job Performance

A	6th
B	5th
C	4th
D	3rd
E	2nd
F	1st

Graph of Johnson Solution:

	F	E	D	C	B	A
Flowcharting	(2)	(6)	(7)	(5)	(8)	(9)

		F	E	D	C	B	A
Program-Writing		(9)	(8)	(11)	(4)	(3)	(1)

Elapsed Time: 38 hours

Thus, Dr. Band cannot meet the 36 hour deadline. (The moral of this story is that management consultants should realize that things do not always get done on time.)

8.3 George Williams, production and operations management instructor at York College, determined that the "learning rate" of his students is 80 percent. If these students were put to work on an assembly line, how many direct labor hours do you think they would need in order to make the 96th item, assuming that it took them 120 hours to make the 3rd item.

Solution

Unit	Man-Hours
3rd Item	120
	× .80
6th Item	96
	× .80

Unit	Man-Hours
12th Item	76.8
	× .80
24th Item	61.4
	× .80
48th Item	49.15
	× .80
96th Item	39.32 hours

8.4 A professor in the geology department was enjoying some liquid sunshine in the faculty club with a colleague from the faculty of management when the topic of conversation swung around to cost reduction in their respective offices. "Max," said the geologist, "maybe you can help me. I've got four duplication systems in the office, and for each duplication job that must be done, the price is different. Perhaps you can show me how you would select the process to minimize the cost." Here's what his cost structure looked like:

	Newsprint	#4 Bond	#7 Bond	Fine Bond
Machine 1	5	8	5	4
2	8	1	3	1
3	2	4	9	9
4	6	1	3	2

Note: these costs are in cents per page.

If you were the professor in the faculty of management, what would you advise the geologist to do?

Solution
Set up a square cost matrix.

Machine / Job	1	2	3	4
Newsprint	5	8	2	6
#4 Bond	8	1	4	1
#7 Bond	5	3	9	3
Fine Bond	4	1	9	2

Subtract the smallest number in each row from all others in the row. Form a new matrix.

3	6	0	4
7	0	3	0
2	0	6	0
3	0	8	1

Using the new matrix, subtract the smallest number in each column from all others in the column. Form a new matrix.

1	6	0	4
5	0	3	0
0	0	6	0
1	0	8	1

Draw the minimum number of lines necessary to cover all zero-entries in the matrix.

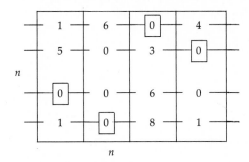

This solution is now optimal because the minimum number of lines necessary to cover each zero is "n" in the "$n \times n$" matrix, $n = 4$ in this case.

Therefore, the optimal assignments and their costs are as follows:

Job # 1	Newsprint	to machine 3	$0.02
Job # 2	#4 Bond	to machine 4	$0.01
Job # 3	#7 Bond	to machine 1	$0.05
Job # 4	Fine Bond	to machine 2	$0.01

Job \ Machine	1	2	3	4
Newsprint			2¢	
#4 Bond				1¢
#7 Bond	5¢			
Fine Bond		1¢		

8.5 In a new manufacturing process, the Lakeside Manufacturing Company produced the first batch of a new product, at a cost of $100,000, which consisted of $30,000 for materials, and $70,000 for labor. The production manager has received a contract to produce three batches. He has agreed to a 10 percent profit, based on cost, and is willing to contract on the basis of an 80 percent learning curve. Using Table D in the Appendix, determine the contract price for the three production batches.

Solution

Cost of 1st Batch		$100,000
Cost of 2nd Batch		
Materials	$30,000	
Labor 0.80 × 70,000	56,000	86,000
Cost of 3rd Batch		
Materials	$30,000	
Labor		
From Table D in the Appendix		
(0.702) × ($70,000)	49,140	79,140
Total Cost		$265,140
Add: Markup		26,514
Selling Price		$291,654

8.6   Given the following line-of-balance assembly chart:

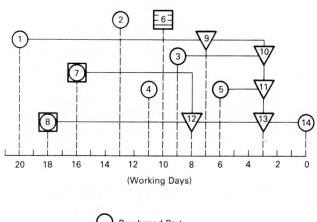

(Working Days)

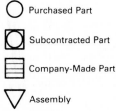

○ Purchased Part

▣ Subcontracted Part

▤ Company-Made Part

▽ Assembly

a) When is the first part ordered?
b) How many components are involved at event 9? What are the lead times before assembly?
c) How many major subassemblies are there?
d) What is significant about day 3?

Solution

a) The first part is ordered 20 working days before completion.

b) There are 3 components involved at event 9: purchased parts numbers 1 and 2, and a company made part 6. The assembly of parts numbered 1, 2, and 6 takes place 7 days before completion. Part number 6 must be begun 3 days before assembly (at day 10). Part number 2 must be requisitioned 6 days before assembly (at day 13), and part number 1 must be ordered 13 days before assembly (at day 20).

c) There are two major subassemblies: the first is composed of purchased parts number 1 and 2, plus company-made part number 6; the second is composed of subcontracted parts number 7 and 8, plus purchased part number 4. The latter assembly is begun on the 8th day before completion.

d) Day 3 marks the time that final assembly of the two major subassemblies, plus purchased parts numbers 3 and 5, is begun. The final assembly takes 3 days to complete.

8.7   Given the line of balance objective chart and progress chart, which component, as of March 21st, is causing the delivery problem? (Use the assembly chart of problem 8.6.)

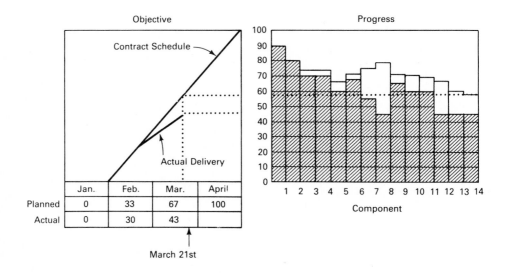

Solution

Component number 8, a subcontracted part, is the cause of the delay in actual deliveries. According to the assembly chart, in problem 8.6, this part should be started 18 days before completion. According to the objective chart, 57 units should be available on March 21st. In fact, only 43 are completed.

CHAPTER REVIEW PROBLEMS

8.1   During the busiest time of the year, the assembly-line workers at the Westmount Manufacturing Company walked off the job as a result of a labor dispute with upper management. Consequently, the production supervisor of the company recruited some temporary workers. These workers were considered to be quite efficient, having a manufacturing progress rate of 95%. It was found that these workers required a total of 100 man-hours to manufacture the first to the eighth batch, inclusive. From this information, determine how long it will take this staff to manufacture the 128th batch.

8.2   The processing time required to manufacture the first unit of production on a new assembly line with a learning-curve rate of 80 percent was 12 hours. How many hours will the 24th item take to process?

8.3   A repair service facility currently has four jobs to be processed. The due date and remaining processing time for each of the jobs are given below:

Job	Remaining Processing Time	Due Date
1	3	7
2	6	9
3	5	4
4	9	14

Determine the scheduling priority by:
a) Using the shortest-processing-time rule
b) Using the earliest-due-date rule.
   Evaluate your comparison by using the criteria of minimum mean flow time and minimum mean lateness.

8.4   A company currently has four major projects that must be carried out on a single production process. Job A is due in 41 days and will require 34 days to process. Job B is due in 96 days and will take 64 days to process. Job C is due in 74 days and will require 60 days to process, and Job D is due in 100 days and will require 80 days to process. Given this information, compare the scheduling priority rules for assigning jobs according to minimum slack time and for assigning jobs according to shortest processing time. Evaluate your comparison using the criteria of minimum mean flow time and minimum mean lateness.

8.5   A machine shop fabricates and paints various household metal products. Currently, there are six items in the machine shop that must be completed. The times (in hours) required for completing the two production processes on each item are given below:

Item	Fabricating	Painting and Finishing
A	6	4
B	9	12
C	7	5
D	8	9
E	2	6
F	6	3

a) Using Johnson's method, determine the optimal time required to complete these six jobs.
b) Calculate the mean flow time.
c) Draw the Johnson processing sequence chart for this problem.

8.6   A small production facility performs three processing operations on each unit manufactured. The times required for each processing operation on three current job orders are given below:

Job Order	Operations Times Required (in days)		
	(1)	(2)	(3)
P	5	3	4
R	4	1	5
S	6	4	4

Determine the optimal time required to complete these three job orders.

8.7   The production supervisor of a machine shop has four jobs that can be processed on any one of four machines, and the cost of each job-machine combination is given below:

Job \ Machine	A	B	C	D
1	$9	8	3	5
2	7	2	1	5
3	8	4	7	3
4	9	3	5	6

Determine a minimum cost assignment of jobs to machines.

8.8   Carrington Manufacturers, Incorporated, has its factory subdivided into five work stations, each under the direction of a production supervisor. The manager of the company wants to place these production supervisors in whatever work stations they work the most efficiently. Efficiency, or lack of it, was measured by the number of defective units that came out at each work station. The matrix below gives the number of defective units in each work station for each production supervisor during one month of service:

Production Supervisor \ Work Stations	1	2	3	4	5
A	4	6	5	9	3
B	10	5	4	7	6
C	11	5	9	10	8
D	6	11	5	13	6
E	3	7	8	5	9

Using the assignment method, determine the best assignment of production supervisors to work stations. (Ignore the practical implications of assigning workers based on this criteria.)

8.9 The Azulykit Manufacturing Company is an intermittent manufacturing facility that processes jobs according to customers' specifications. Currently, five new orders, which must be processed on one machine, are awaiting processing:

Job	Processing Time	Due Date
A	17 days	30 days from now
B	18	45
C	14	25
D	35	50
E	16	35

Compare the scheduling priority rules of:
a) Assigning jobs according to "minimum slack time" rule
b) Assigning jobs according to "shortest processing time" rule.

Evaluate your comparison by using the criteria of minimum mean flow time and minimum mean lateness.

8.10 One work station in the assembly line of the Montezuma Manufacturing Company performs two operations: casting and forging. These two operations must be carried out on each unit produced. There are presently four units at the work stations, waiting to be processed. The times required in completing the two operations are listed below:

	TIME REQUIRED (IN HOURS)	
Unit	Casting	Forging
A	4	2
B	7	8
C	5	6
D	6	4

a) Using Johnson's method, determine the optimal time required to complete these four jobs.
b) Calculate the mean flow time.

8.11 The Kenworth Motor Truck repair service depot presently has three trucks that need to be repaired and returned as soon as possible. Given the following data regarding the trucks, use the priority rule of "least slack per remaining operation" to determine Kenworth's scheduling priority.

Truck	Days before Truck Is Required	Remaining Repair Time	Number of Remaining Operations
1	12	6	1
2	20	8	3
3	16	3	3

8.12 Using the rule that the job with the least slack has the highest priority, determine the priorities of assignments 1, 2, and 3, all of which are due at the end of term 33 days away. Determine the priority values from the schedule below:

Job	Due Date	Number of Remaining Operations	Remaining Machine Processing Time	Priority Value When Time Now Is			
				25	18	11	4
1	33	3	12				
2	33	2	7				
3	33	6	4				

8.13 Glen Davron has 4 term papers to complete before the end of the semester. The details of each are contained in the schedule below. Determine the best schedules using
a) The shortest-processing-time rule
b) The earliest due date rule
c) The least slack rule.
d) Which method is preferable?

	(1)	(2) Remaining Processing Time	(3) Due Date	(4) = (3) − (2) Slack to Date
	Term Paper			
	Math	4	3	0
	Statistics	5	6	1
	Accounting	9	5	0
	Finance	8	10	2

8.14 A contractor has received tender applications for 4 major projects. Each project must go through a 2-stage evaluation process: design analysis and financial analysis. Since time is critical, how might this scheduling problem be solved? The data are given below.

Project	Design Analysis	Financial Analysis
A	12	8
B	15	9
C	13	5
D	9	7

BIBLIOGRAPHY

ABERNATHY, W. J., "The Limits of the Learning Curve," *Harvard Business Review*, Sept.–Oct., 1974, pp. 109–119.

BAKER, K. R., *Introduction to Sequencing and Scheduling*. New York: John Wiley and Sons, 1974.

Buffa, E. S., *Operations Management: The Management of Production Systems.* New York: Wiley/Hamilton, 1976.

Buffa, E. S., and W. H. Taubert, *Production-Inventory Systems: Planning and Control* (rev. ed.), Chapters 11 and 12. Homewood, Illinois: R. D. Irwin, 1972.

Buffa, E. S., and J. G. Miller, *Production-Inventory Systems: Planning and Control* (3rd ed.). Homewood, Illinois: R. D. Irwin, 1979.

Chase, R., and N. Aquilano, *Production and Operations Management* (3rd ed.). Homewood, Ill.: R. D. Irwin, 1981.

Conway, R. W., W. L. Maxwell, and L. W. Miller, *Theory of Scheduling.* Reading, Mass.: Addison-Wesley Publishing Company, Inc., 1967.

Day, J. E., and M. P. Hottenstein, "Review of Sequencing Research," *Naval Research Logistics Quarterly,* Vol. 27, No. 1, March, 1970, pp. 11–39.

Fabrycky, W. J., P. M. Ghare, and P. E. Torgensen, *Industrial Operations Research.* Englewood Cliffs, N.J.: Prentice-Hall, Inc., 1972.

Ferguson, R. L., and C. H. Jones, "A Computer-Aided Decision System," *Management Science,* Vol. 5, No. 10, June, 1969, p. B-550.

Fischer, W. A., "Line of Balance: Obsolete After MRP?" *Production and Investor Management,* 4th Quarter, 1975, pp. 63–77.

Hershauer, J. C., and R. J. Ebert, "Search and Simulation of a Job-Shop Sequencing Rule," *Management Science,* Vol. 21, No. 7, March, 1975, pp. 833–43.

Holdham, J. H., "Learning Curves—Their Applications in Industry," *Production and Inventory Management,* Fourth Quarter, 1970, pp. 40–55.

Holtz, J. N., "An Analysis of Major Scheduling Techniques in the Defense Systems Environment," in Cleland, D. I., and W. R. King, *Systems, Organizations, Analysis, Management: A Book of Readings,* pp. 317–355. New York: McGraw-Hill Book Co., 1969.

Larson, R. E., and M. I. Dessouky, "Heuristic Procedures for the Single Machine Problem to Minimize Maximum Lateness," *AIIE Transactions,* Vol. 10, No. 2, pp. 176–183.

Magee, J. F., and D. M. Boodman, *Production Planning and Inventory Control.* New York: McGraw-Hill Book Co., 1967.

Maxwell, W. L., "On Sequencing in Jobs on One Machine to Minimize the Number of Late Jobs," *Management Science,* Vol. 18, No. 5, January, 1970, p. 295.

McClain, J. O., and L. J. Thomas, *Operations Management: Production of Goods and Services.* Englewood Cliffs, N.J.: Prentice-Hall, Inc., 1980.

Menipaz, E., "Scheduling Models: Shibboleth and Operating Characteristics," *Journal of Information & Optimization Sciences,* Vol. 4, No. 1, January 1983, pp. 49–64.

Muth, J. F., and G. L. Thompson, *Industrial Scheduling.* Englewood Cliffs, N.J. Prentice-Hall, Inc., 1963.

Niland, P., *Production Planning, Scheduling and Inventory Control,* Chapter 3. New York: Macmillan Co., 1970.

Nanot, Y. R., "An Experimental Investigation and Comparative Evaluation in Job Shop-Like Sequencing Networks," unpublished Ph.D. dissertation. Los Angeles: UCLA, 1964.

O'Brien, J. J., *Scheduling Handbook.* New York: McGraw-Hill Book Co., 1969.

PANWALKER, S. S., "A Survey of Scheduling Rules." *Operations Research*, Vol. 25, No. 1, January–February, 1977, pp. 45–61.

RATCLIFF, H. D., "Network Models for Production Scheduling Problems with Convex Cost and Batch Processing," *AIIE Transactions*, Vol. 10, No. 1, 1978, pp. 104–108.

REITER, S., "A System for Managing Job-Shop Production," *The Journal of Business*, Vol. 39, No. 3, July, 1966, pp. 371–93.

SCHONBERGER, R. J. *Operations Management: Planning and Control of Operations and Operating Resources.* Planto, Tex.: Business Publications, 1981.

SHORE, B., *Operations Management*, Chapter 5. New York: McGraw-Hill Book Co., 1973.

STARR, M. K., *Systems Management of Operations.* Englewood Cliffs, N.J.: Prentice-Hall, Inc., 1971, Chapters 10, 11.

STINSON, J. P., E. W. DAVID, B. M. KHUMAWALE, "Multiple Resources Constrained Scheduling Using Branch and Bound," *AIIE Transactions*, Vol. 10, No. 3, 1979, pp. 252–259.

TERSINE, R. J., *Production/Operations Management: Concepts, Structure, and Analysis.* New York: Elsevier North-Holland, 1980.

VOLLMAN, T. E., *Operations Management: A Systems Model Building Approach.* Reading, Mass.: Addison-Wesley, 1973.

VOLLMAN, T. E., "A User Approach to Production Scheduling," *American Institute for Decision Sciences Conference Proceedings.* St. Louis, Missouri, 1971, pp. 153–157.

WAGNER, H. M., *Principles of Operations Research*, Chapter 13. Englewood Cliffs, N.J.: Prentice-Hall, Inc., 1969.

WEEKS, J. K., and J. S. FRYER, "A Methodology for Assigning Minimum Cost Due-Dates", *Management Science*, Vol. 23, No. 8, April, 1977, pp. 872–81.

WEEKS, J. K., and J. S. FRYER, "A Simulation Study of Operating Policies in a Hypothetical Dual-Constrained Job Shop," *Management Science*, Vol. 22, No. 12, August, 1976, pp. 1362–71.

WOOLSEY, R. D., and H. S. SWANSON, *Operations Research for Immediate Application, A Quick and Dirty Manual.* New York: Harper & Row, 1975.

TECHNICAL NOTE: Essentials of Simulation

INTRODUCTION

Simulation has been used extensively to develop and test alternative schedules. Simulation is used also in aggregate planning, assembly-line balancing, plant location, warehouse location, inventory control, product and process design, and other areas of operations management.

Simulation is a technique that can be used to formulate and solve a variety of operational problems. As planning becomes more complicated, mathematical models expressed as equations or functions become less useful. Simulation is a numeric-solution procedure that develops numerical relationships among the various decision variables, tests them on a case-by-case basis, and draws general conclusions as to the behavior of these decision variables, based on these cases.

With bigger and faster computers, the use of simulation techniques to analyze complex planning systems has been almost routine since the late 1950's. Rather than simplifying a complex planning system—in order to solve it with known analytical techniques—simulation techniques describe systems as exactly as possible. The simulation technique finds approximate answers to exact planning questions, whereas analytical models find exact answers to simplified questions.

MONTE CARLO SIMULATION

Monte Carlo simulation is a discrete simulation method that was used originally in the 1940's to solve problems in nuclear physics. To discuss this simulation technique, let us consider the problem of calculating the total sales over the lifetime of a product. The product's sales curve is shown in Figure TN8.1. The area under the curve represents the total sales over the lifetime of a product.

The mathematical equation describing the area under the curve may be unknown or complicated. Simulation can help us to find the area. To simulate that area let us first place the curve within a known area—say, an area representing a square, as shown in Figure TN8.2. Now let us imagine a "machine" that throws darts aimed randomly at the square area. (We will develop specifics on the "machine" later.) "Randomly aimed" means in this case

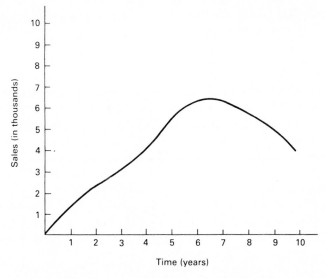

Figure TN8.1   Area under Curve to be Calculated by Simulation

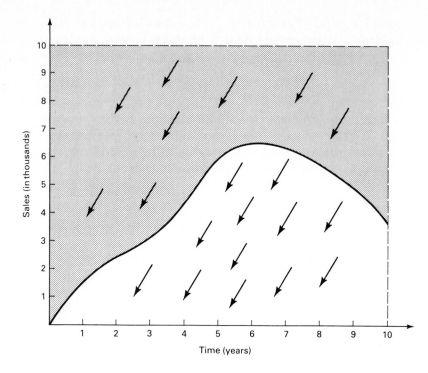

Figure TN8.2   Simulating the Area Under the Curve by Throwing Randomly Aimed Darts

that each dart has an equal chance of hitting any point on the square surface. Figure TN8.2 shows the landing points for 20 randomly aimed darts. The ratio of the number of darts that landed in the unshaded area to the total number of darts thrown is an approximation of the ratio of the area under the curve to the total area of the square. Therefore, the ratio of darts hitting the unshaded area to the total number of darts thrown is a simulated estimate of the sales. For example, 12 darts out of 20 thrown landed in the area under the curve; therefore, our estimate of the area equals 12/20 of the total square area. Then sales are 12/20 $(10,000 \times 10) = 60,000$ units.

Rather than actually throwing darts, we can use 40 spins of a roulette wheel to determine where the darts might land, or, for that matter, 20 randomly chosen points of the square (40 spins provide 20 points). The roulette wheel is a simple *random number generator,* which is why this simulation technique is called the Monte Carlo simulation. Random numbers are generated by spinning the wheel; that is, the roulette ball is equally likely to land on any number between 1 and 36.

Any point on the square in Figure TN8.3 can be represented by a horizontal and a vertical coordinate. We divide both the horizontal and vertical axes of the figure into 36 equal parts (a roulette wheel has 36 possible outcomes). Two roulette wheels are used to simulate a point at random: one is spun to find the horizontal coordinate, and the other to find the vertical coordinate. Table TN8.1 lists 20 pairs of random numbers that were produced by spinning two roulette wheels. These points are plotted in Figure TN8.3. For example, point 8 is defined by a horizontal coordinate value of 11 (the random number from roulette wheel #1) and a vertical coordinate value of 10 (the random number from roulette wheel #2).

Of the 20 points selected randomly with the roulette wheels, eleven points are in the unshaded area. Therefore, the area under the curve is estimated to represent 11/20, or $0.55 \times 10,000 \times 10 = 55,000$ units, if the total area of the square represents 100,000 units. Remember that this is not an exact solution; it is a simulated measure of the area and, therefore, an *estimate* of the true area. In comparing this with the results obtained by throwing 20 randomly aimed darts into the square area, we notice a difference: 55,000 units versus 60,000 units. At this point, it is difficult to judge which estimate is better; however, in general, we may say that the more points established, the better will be the resulting estimate.

GENERATING RANDOM NUMBERS

We have shown how a roulette wheel can be used to generate random numbers. In the early 1950's, scientists built complex and expensive mechanical and electromechanical devices to generate random numbers at relatively high speed. In 1955, the Rand Corporation published a book containing one million random numbers. The computers presently used in business and industry can be programmed to generate random numbers. These random numbers are either integers (say, from 000 to 999) or decimal numbers between 0 and 1. Each number is as likely to occur as any other number. Integer random numbers can be transformed to decimal numbers (and vice versa) simply by shifting the decimal point.

For example, the following integer random numbers:

7345	2747	3421	6207	0271

can be converted to the following decimal random numbers by dividing by 10,000:

0.7345	0.2747	0.3421	0.6207	0.0271

The use of simulation in the planning and control of operations is extensive. Good computer random number generators have been created, and users of digital computers usually have access to a well-tested random number generator. One should note that computer-generated random numbers are called pseudorandom numbers because ultimately the generated sequence of random numbers will be repeated. The quality of a random number generator is

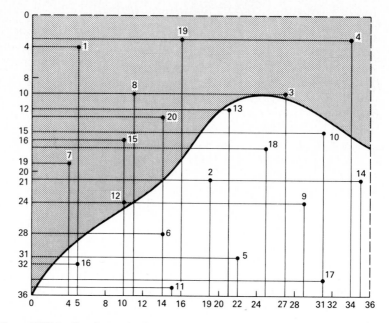

Figure TN8.3 Simulating the Area Under the Curve by the Use of a Roulette Wheel

TABLE TN8.1 SIMULATION OF 20 POINTS BY TWO ROULETTE WHEELS

POINT	HORIZONTAL COORDINATE: RANDOM NUMBER 1	VERTICAL COORDINATE: RANDOM NUMBER 2
1	5	4
2	19	21
3	27	10
4	34	3
5	22	31
6	14	28
7	4	19
8	11	10
9	29	24
10	31	15
11	15	35
12	10	24
13	21	12
14	35	21
15	10	16
16	5	32
17	31	34
18	25	17
19	16	3
20	14	13

generally measured by the length of the sequence of random numbers before repetition occurs; the longer that sequence, the better the random number generator. Henceforth, we shall use the term "random number" to indicate only those random numbers that are uniformly distributed (a uniformly distributed random number is a number that has an even chance to appear between 0 and 1) and that are drawn from a pseudorandom number generator. We shall use the random number table, Table E in the Appendix of this book, to solve problems.

Use of Decimal Random Numbers to Simulate the Area Under the Curve

Recall our earlier effort to find the area under the curve in Figure TN8.1 by simulation. Rather than subdividing the horizontal and vertical axes into 36 equal parts, we subdivided them according to the outcomes of a decimal random number generator—that is, to correspond to the decimal numbers between zero and one. Twenty pairs of decimal random numbers were then generated to represent the coordinates of twenty points. The computer-generated pairs of random numbers are listed in Table TN8.2 and plotted in Figure TN8.4. Since 11 points are enclosed under the curve, we estimate sales as $11/20 \times 100,000 = 55,000$ units.

TABLE TN8.2 SIMULATION OF 20 POINTS BY TWO RANDOM NUMBER GENERATORS

POINT	HORIZONTAL COORDINATE: RANDOM NUMBER 1	VERTICAL COORDINATE: RANDOM NUMBER 2
1	2217	5325
2	6413	6371
3	8607	8299
4	4199	3477
5	8511	1453
6	9637	6469
7	6277	4193
8	1371	1167
9	4193	0793
10	4813	5273
11	2453	8631
12	2507	3715
13	8301	3217
14	8473	5431
15	3777	6501
16	4897	7827
17	6191	1873
18	3897	2197
19	1427	7435
20	7435	2791

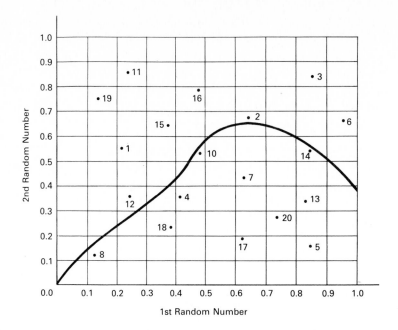

Figure TN8.4   Simulating the Area under the Curve by the Use of a Random Number Generator

CASE: SIMULATING AN OUTPATIENT CLINIC

Patients arrive at the General Hospital Outpatient Clinic according to an appointment schedule. The medical nurse schedules a constant 18 patients a day. The number of patients that are treated during each day varies according to the data in Table TN8.3. That is, the number of patients treated in one day is 16 in 15 out of 100 days; It is 17 in 20 out of 100 days, and so on. The number of patients treated would never, according to Table TN8.3, be less than 16 or more than 21. If a scheduled patient has not been treated during the day, he or she returns the next day for treatment. Using Monte Carlo simulation, one may determine the average number of patients that are left untreated by the end of a day.

The solution involves: first, calculating the cumulative probabilities, as in Table TN8.4; and, second, assigning a range of random numbers to each possible number of patients treated. Thus, in Table TN8.4, random numbers between 00001 and 14999 correspond to probability 0.15 (for 16 patients); random numbers between 15000 and 34999 correspond to probability 0.20 (for 17 patients), and so on.

The sequence of operations necessary to generate the number of waiting patients at the end of the day is as follows:

TABLE TN8.3 PROBABILITIES OF NUMBERS OF PATIENTS TREATED PER DAY

NUMBER OF PATIENTS TREATED PER DAY	PROBABILITY
16	0.15
17	0.20
18	0.25
19	0.20
20	0.10
21	0.10
	1.00

TABLE TN8.4 RELATIONSHIP BETWEEN NUMBER OF TREATED PATIENTS AND RANDOM NUMBERS

NUMBER OF PATIENTS TREATED PER DAY	PROBABILITY	CUMULATIVE PROBABILITY	RANDOM NUMBER
16	0.15	0.15	00001–14999
17	0.20	0.35	15000–34999
18	0.25	0.60	35000–59999
19	0.20	0.80	60000–79999
20	0.10	0.90	80000–89999
21	0.10	1.00	90000–99999

1. Enter 18 patients (initial number of waiting patients), and update the number of waiting patients.
2. Generate a random number between zero and one.
3. Use Table TN8.4 to find the number of treated patients corresponding to that random number.
4. Update the number of patients waiting at the end of the day by subtracting the number treated from the beginning number of waiting patients (1 minus 3).

The results are shown for the next 20 days in Table TN8.5 (the assumption is that the number of waiting customers for day 0 is zero).

The sequence of operations used for the simulation is usually presented in a flow chart, similar to the one appearing in Figure TN8.5.

By reading across Table TN8.5, one can follow the simulation. For example, on day 12 at 9 a.m., the number of patients is 19; the random number 15513 (taken from Table E in the Appendix) represents 17 treated patients, which leaves two untreated patients by the end of the day at 6 p.m. The next day, day 13, 18 new patients arrive. Therefore, on day 13, the starting number of waiting

TABLE TN8.5 SIMULATION OF NUMBER OF PATIENTS BY THE END OF THE DAY

DAY	NUMBER OF PATIENTS AT 9 A.M.	RANDOM NUMBER	SIMULATED NUMBER OF TREATED PATIENTS	NUMBER OF UNTREATED PATIENTS BY THE END OF THE DAY, 6 P.M.	AVERAGE NUMBER OF UNTREATED PATIENTS BY THE END OF THE DAY, 6 P.M.
1	18	21787	17	1	1/1 = 1
2	19	76774	19	0	(1 + 0)/2 = 1/2
3	18	79319	19	0	(1 + 0 + 0)/3 = 1/3
4	18	80436	20	0	(1 + 0 + 0 + 0)/4 = 1/4
5	18	88711	20	0	(1 + 0 + 0 + 0 + 0)/5 = 1/5
6	18	28248	17	1	(1 + 0 + 0 + 0 + 0 + 1)/6 = 1/3
7	19	87973	20	0	2/7
8	18	42377	18	0	1/4
9	18	08911	16	2	4/9
10	20	90991	21	0	2/5
11	18	21539	17	1	5/11
12	19	15513	17	2	7/12
13	20	04005	16	4	11/13
14	22	31221	17	5	8/7
15	23	96440	21	2	6/5
16	20	52150	18	2	10/8
17	20	28667	17	3	23/17
18	21	54989	18	3	16/9
19	21	28811	17	4	30/19
20	22	81695	20	2	8/5

	(1)	(2)	(3)	(4)	(5)	(6)	(7)
Week	Beginning Inventory	RN	Weekly Demand*	Number of Units Short	Ending Inventory	RN	Supply
1	30	21	25	0	5	76	60
2	65	79	40	0	20	80	60
3	80	88	40	0	40	28	30
4	70	87	40	0	30	42	30
5	60	08	25	0	35	90	60
6	95	21	25	0	70	15	30
7	100	04	25	0	75	31	30
8	105	96	50	0	55	52	30
9	85	28	25	0	60	54	30
10	90	28	25	0	65	81	60
11	125	95	40	0	85	38	30
12	115	64	35	0	80	32	30
13	110	78	40	0	70	77	60
14	130	31	25	0	105	43	30
15	135	71	40	0	95	24	30
16	125	97	50	0	75	37	30

$$\Sigma = 965$$

*Including Back orders

Average Inventory $= \dfrac{965}{16} = 60.31$ units

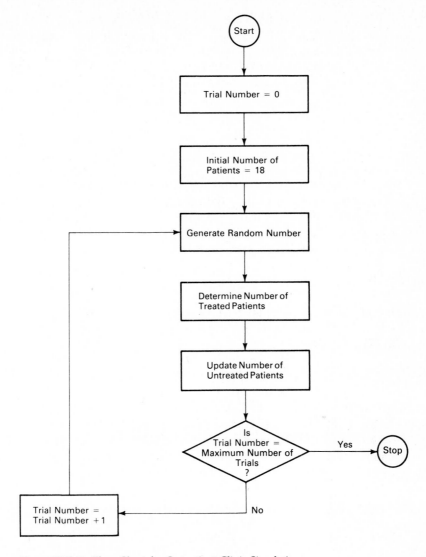

Figure TN8.5 Flow Chart for Outpatient Clinic Simulation

patients is 20. The random number 04005 (Taken from Table E) represents treatment of 16 patients, which leaves four untreated patients. Analysis is similar for the other days.

The simulated average number of end-of-the-day patients after 20 days is 8 ÷ 5 = 1.6 patients. The maximum number of customers waiting at the end of the day is 5 (on day 14), and there were 5 days (25 percent of the time) on which all patients were treated.

The number of trials used for the simulation affects the average number of patients by the end of the day. For example, in Table TN8.5, if we had stopped after 10 trials (days), the average would have been $2 \div 5 = 0.4$ patients, which is much smaller than the 1.6 found after 20 trials. The more trials we go through, the more precise are the results of the simulation.

SIMULATION WITH CONTINUOUS PROBABILITY DISTRIBUTION

There may be cases in which we would like to assume that the variables in the simulation are random variables drawn from a continuous probability distribution. Suppose, for example, that the number of emergency room patients in the General Hospital is normally distributed with mean $\mu = 3,000$ patients and standard deviation $\sigma = 500$ patients. We can generate the random values of numbers of patients by using a graphical method and an algebraic method.

Graphical Method

In this method, we plot a cumulative distribution function. The cumulative distribution function for the normal distribution mentioned above is presented in Figure TN8.6.

In order to use the cumulative function, we first use Table E in the Appendix to generate a random number between zero and one. This is done by taking, for example, the first three digits of any of the numbers, say 736, and using the corresponding decimal number, 0.736. Next, the cumulative curve of Figure TN8.6 is marked on the vertical axis at the level of this decimal number, 0.736. A horizontal line at the level is extended to the right until it intersects the curve. Then, a projection of that point is found on the x-axis. This projection is the particular random value of x. In Figure TN8.6, the value of the random number of emergency patients is 3300. This method is general, and is used for continuous or discrete probability distributions. The method works because the choice of a random decimal between zero and one is equivalent to the choice of a random percentile of the distribution. The cumulative probability figure (such as Figure TN8.6) is used to convert the random percentile (73.6 percentile) to a particular value of the random variable (3300 patients).

Algebraic Method

For cases in which the cumulative probability distribution function can be presented as a function of x without integration signs, the graphical method can be replaced by the algebraic method.

For example, if the random variable follows an exponential probability density function:

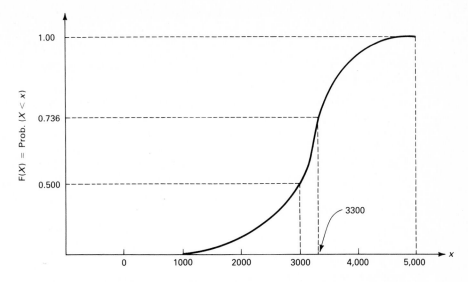

Figure TN8.6   Cumulative Normal Distribution Function ($\mu = 3,000$; $\sigma = 500$ parts)

$$f(x) = Ae^{-Ax} \qquad 0 < x < \infty$$

The cumulative probability distribution function is:

$$F(x) = 1 - e^{-Ax}$$

Let us define a hypothetical random decimal (R.D.) that is equal to the cumulative distribution function, and solve it for x:

$$R.D. = 1 - e^{-Ax}$$

$$e^{-Ax} = 1 - R.D.$$

Since the random decimal we are looking for is between zero and one, so is $(1 - R.D.)$. Thus, $(1 - R.D.)$ can be considered also as a random decimal, which means:

$$e^{-Ax} = R.D.$$

If one takes a natural logarithm from both sides of the equation, $-Ax = \log_e(R.D.)$

$$x = -(1/A) \log_e(R.D.)$$

This last relationship is used to generate values from an exponential distribution with parameter A. First, a random decimal (R.D.) is found from Table E in the Appendix. Second, the value of the random variable, x, is found by substituting the R.D. into the right-hand side of the equation. For example, if

$A = 5$ and the random decimal $R.D. = 0.475$, then from the table of natural logarithms, $\log_e (0.475) = -0.744$ and $x = -(1/5)(-0.744) = 0.1488$.

COMPUTER SIMULATION

Most complex simulations require the use of the computer, and simulation has become an increasingly popular technique, with the advent of bigger and faster computers. Computer simulation has, of course, many advantages over hand calculation, not the least of which is the speed with which large amounts of data can be manipulated. With computers, simulation is no longer considered a second-best alternative to mathematical models, because sophistication and variety can be built into the model. Programs have been written in general purpose languages such as FORTRAN (a well-known language available on practically all computer systems). However, progamming in FORTRAN is time consuming, and so special simulation languages have been developed. In general, these special languages provide standard terminology to describe the problem and program it into a computer. The computer program, in turn, performs the simulation, and the user or programmer avoids detailed programming efforts.

Of the many computer simulation languages developed, the ones used frequently are GASP, SIMSCRIPT, and GPSS (General Purpose Simulation System). GASP and SIMSCRIPT are both general in nature and have capabilities similar to those of FORTRAN. The SIMSCRIPT language was developed by Rand Corporation and is a rich and versatile computer programming language designed primarily for discrete-event (as opposed to continuous) simulation applications. It is available for use on several different types of computers and requires a great deal of programming skill.

The most widely used language is the GPSS developed by the IBM Corporation. It is a problem-oriented language with a wide range of applications, now being used extensively in business to simulate production systems, and the job-shop-type scheduling problems. The GPSS user develops a block diagram that represents the system to be modeled, and then translates that block diagram into GPSS statements. GPSS automatically generates certain statistics and updates all pertinent information. Little or no computer knowledge is required in order to program in this language.

SIMULATION AND OPERATIONS MANAGEMENT

Simulation is now well established as a management science technique and a powerful tool of analysis for decision making. Approximately 25 percent of the operations management projects involving operations research methodology are now solved via simulations. Simulation is used when other quantitative tools are less desirable due to the number of variables involved, or the size of the problem. It is the only way to test the effect of certain decision rules, called heuristics or rules of thumb. All functional areas of operations use decision rules that can be tested through simulation.

Simulation of a model does not necessarily yield an optimal solution. However, if the simulation is well done, the results are generally satisfactory and better than any intuitive solution. A simulation user will typically run the model repeatedly, each time making small changes and measuring the differences in output, and each time getting a little nearer to the optimal solution. It is important to realize, however, that simulation seeks a good alternative and that simulation models can evaluate only the alternatives given in the program; the optimal alternative may not have been conceived and programmed, and it therefore may be missed. Also, an unusual sample of random numbers may produce a poor alternative that may be mistakenly selected as the best one.

Any application of simulation for operations management should be justified based on a sound analysis of simulation cost versus payoff of simulation results. Unfortunately, the amount of available information on the economics of simulation is limited. While it is relatively easy to quantify the cost of the simulation project itself, it is increasingly difficult to assess the savings that result from the use of simulation. On one hand, this is understandable since the savings are often measured by taking the difference between operating costs incurred before and after the use of the simulation results, under the assumption that all other elements are held constant. However, since there are always changes in a dynamic operation, elements rarely remain constant. On the other hand, not all benefits are tangible and therefore cannot be measured in dollars and cents. For example, what is the value associated with the ability to make better decisions, or with the ability to obtain a better understanding of the environment and the variables affecting an operations problem?

APPLICATIONS OF SIMULATION

The applications of simulation in production and operations management include inventory management and control, material handling, job shop and general scheduling, assembly-line balancing, warehouse location, and plant allocation. Let us briefly describe some well-known applications:

SCHEDULING Simulation has been used to evaluate alternative scheduling rules. In scheduling courtrooms for trial, for example, should the potentially longest trial be scheduled first or last? In Chapter 8, the scheduling rules of jobs in intermittent, low-volume operations systems have been discussed. These alternative scheduling rules are evaluated by simulation. It has been found that selecting rules is relatively unimportant, but that combining a few heuristics with certain rules results in highly efficient schedules.

AGGREGATE PLANNING   For aggregate (capacity) planning, simulation models are used to find the cost of alternative strategies. This is especially true for cases in which there are some uncertainties as to demand, work force size, and production capacity.

FACILITIES DESIGN   These applications include the calculation of the size of facilities and the number of services required. Examples include the number of customs officers to be used at the airport, the number of runways in an airport, and the number of checkout stands in a supermarket. The use of simulation in waiting line situations using simulation is mentioned in the Technical Note to Chapter 14.

INVENTORY MANAGEMENT AND CONTROL   Most complex inventory models may be evaluated using simulation. Various reordering rules, unit costs, carrying costs, and the like may be tested, before they are actually implemented, by using simulation.

MATERIALS REQUIREMENT PLANNING (MRP)   When MRP is used to plan and control production, simulation is used to evaluate changes in the production plan before the changes are actually implemented. These applications are discussed in Chapter 16.

ASSEMBLY-LINE BALANCING   Simulation has been used extensively to balance an assembly line. Assembly-line balancing is the process of assigning assembly work elements to work stations located along a continuous conveyor line so that the sums of the work element times at each station are approximately equal. The literature reveals many assembly-line balancing rules that have been developed and evaluated by simulation. For these and other useful applications of simulation, the reader is encouraged to consult the bibliography appearing at the end of this Technical Note.

SUMMARY

Simulation is a technique for modeling reality or developing a model of a real phenomenon in order to formulate and solve a variety of operational problems. It is a numerical (as opposed to mathematical) solution procedure that seeks the best of several alternatives through repeated trials. Simulation is used when planning problems, such as aggregate planning, scheduling, and facilities layout and location, become so involved that one cannot solve them by the use of mathematical closed form (equations or models). Simulation is also used when it is the only technique for testing the effect of certain decision rules of thumb or heuristics.

We have described and demonstrated the simulation procedure for both discrete and continuous probability distribution functions, and have presented several examples. The reader is encouraged to become familiar with simulation techniques by using them wherever possible to solve problems given in this text.

TECHNICAL NOTE PROBLEMS

8.1 Give several examples of problems for which solution using simulation is preferable to an analytical (mathematical) technique.

8.2 Describe the use of random numbers in simulation.

8.3 How does one decide how long to run a simulation model?

8.4 Describe how random values for a random variable are developed from a normal distribution using the cumulative normal distribution function.

8.5 Describe some applications of simulation for production/operations management problems.

8.6 What are the advantages and disadvantages of making a simulation model completely realistic?

8.7 Present a flow chart for a simulation of making a breakfast, where the random variables are the time of making a scrambled egg and of preparing coffee.

8.8 A warehouse has one dock that is used to unload railroad cars. Incoming freight cars are delivered to the warehouse during the night. It takes half a day to unload a car. If more than two cars are waiting to be unloaded on a given day, some of the unloading is postponed until the following day. Past experience has indicated that cars arrive during the night with the frequencies shown below:

x Number of Cars Arriving	f(x) Relative Frequency
0	0.23
1	0.30
2	0.30
3	0.10
4	0.05
5	0.02
6 or more	0.00

Average = $E(x)$ = 1.5 cars per night

Furthermore, the number arriving on any night is independent of the number arriving on any other night. Simulate the performance of this dock during twenty days of operations, accounting for the number of railroad cars that are delayed for the following day. Use two-digit random numbers from the table in the Appendix.

Solution

Let us start by assigning two-digit random numbers to each possible outcome (i.e., to the number of arrivals).

Number of Cars Arriving	Random Digits	Relative Frequency
0	00 to 22	0.23
1	23 to 52	0.30
2	53 to 82	0.30
3	83 to 92	0.10
4	93 to 97	0.05
5	98 to 99	0.02
		1.00

Let us simulate twenty days:

Day Number	Random Number	Number of Arrivals	Total Number to Be Unloaded	Number Unloaded	Number Delayed to Following Day
x	21	0	0	0	0
x	76	2	2	2	0
x	79	2	2	2	0
1	80	2	2	2	0
2	88	3	3	2	1
3	28	1	2	2	0
4	87	3	3	2	1
5	42	1	2	2	0
6	08	0	0	0	0
7	90	3	3	2	1
8	21	0	1	1	0
9	15	0	0	0	0
10	04	0	0	0	0
11	31	1	1	1	0
12	96	4	4	2	2
13	52	1	3	2	1
14	28	1	2	2	0
15	54	2	2	2	0
16	28	1	1	1	0
17	81	2	2	2	0
18	95	4	4	2	2
19	38	1	3	2	1
20	64	2	3	2	1
Total:		$\Sigma = 32$			$\Sigma = 10$

During most of the period, there is little delay. The average number of arrivals per day (1.60) over the sample period of twenty days is somewhat smaller than the expected number per day (1.50). On the average, 0.50 cars are delayed per day. In this way, we can compare the effects of various unloading alternatives upon waiting time and cost. For more accurate results, the simulation could be extended beyond twenty days. Note that the first three simulation runs are not part of the calculated averages, and are used simply to "break in" the simulation.

Sometimes, initial conditions have such an impact on the simulation results that it is best to run the simulation several times (in this case, three times) before starting to calculate averages. In professional language, this means that the process reaches a steady state after an initial transient state.

8.9 On any given day, the Let Them Eat Cake Bakery has a 40 percent chance of selling 15 cakes, a 30 percent chance of selling 25 cakes, a 20 percent chance of selling 30 cakes, and a 10 percent chance of selling 40 cakes. The cakes sell for $9.00 each. It costs $5.00 to make one cake.
a) Use a 20-trial simulation to determine the average profit (use two-digit random numbers from the table in the Appendix).
b) Calculate the expected profit using the probabilities given.
c) Compare the results of parts (a) and (b).

Solution
a) Representative numbers of units sold:

Sales	RN Range
15	01–40
25	41–70
30	71–90
40	91–00

Trial	RN Generated	Units Sold	Cumulative	Daily Average	Difference of Daily Averages
1	21	15	15	15	—
2	76	30	45	22.5	7.5
3	79	30	75	25	2.5
4	80	30	105	26.25	1.25
5	88	30	135	27	0.75
6	28	15	150	25	2.00
7	87	30	180	25.71	0.71
8	42	25	205	25.625	0.62
9	08	15	220	24.44	1.18
10	90	30	250	25.00	0.56
11	21	15	265	24.09	0.81
12	15	15	280	23.330	0.76
13	04	15	295	22.692	0.64
14	31	15	310	22.142	0.55
15	96	40	350	23.333	1.19
16	52	25	375	23.437	0.104
17	28	15	390	22.941	0.496
18	54	25	415	23.055	0.114
19	28	15	430	22.631	0.424
20	81	30	460	23.000	0.369

Average Sales = 23.000
Average Profit = 23.000 × $4.00 = $92.00

b) $E(x) = (0.40)(15) + (0.30)(25) + (0.20)(30) + (0.10)(40) = 6 + 7.5 + 6 + 4 = 23.50$
Expected Profit $= (23.50)(4) = \$94.00$

c) The results of (a) and (b) are close. This reveals that twenty trials might be enough. This fact is further substantiated by the last column, "Difference of Daily Averages," in which values become smaller and smaller with more trials.

8.10   Use a 20-run simulation to determine the chance of getting a 7 in one roll of two dice.

Solution

Number of Dots on One Die	Probability (%)	Cumulative Probability Distribution	Assigned Representative Numbers
1	16.67	16.67	0001–1667
2	16.67	33.34	1668–3334
3	16.67	50.00	3335–5000
4	16.67	66.67	5001–6667
5	16.67	83.34	6668–8334
6	16.67	100.00	8335–0000
Total	100.0		

| | Die 1 | | Die 2 | | Total | | |
Run Number	RN	Dots	RN	Dots	Dots	Ratio	Percent
1	2178	2	9558	6	8	0/1	0
2	7677	5	3882	3	8	0/2	0
3	7931	5	6438	4	9	0/3	0
4	8043	5	3235	2	7	1/4	0.25
5	8871	6	6962	5	11	1/5	0.20
6	2824	2	8293	6	8	1/6	0.17
7	8797	6	6449	4	10	1/7	0.14
8	4237	3	9924	6	9	1/8	0.13
9	0891	1	6627	4	5	1/9	0.11
10	9099	6	1557	1	7	2/10	0.20
11	2153	2	1861	2	4	2/11	0.18
12	1551	1	2267	2	3	2/12	0.16
13	0400	1	2329	2	3	2/13	0.15
14	3122	2	0446	1	3	2/14	0.14
15	9644	6	0910	1	7	3/15	0.20
16	5215	4	9847	6	10	3/16	0.19
17	2866	2	7459	5	7	4/17	0.23
18	5498	4	8505	6	10	4/18	0.22
19	2881	2	4647	3	5	4/19	0.21
20	8169	5	4025	3	8	4/20	0.20

8.11   Two public transit buses are scheduled to arrive regularly at a downtown bus stop. However, if the bus is full, it will not stop to pick up passengers. The first bus, the Blue Streakliner, is full about 45 percent of the time. The second bus, the Red Flash Express, is full about 30 percent of the time.

a) Draw a simulation flow chart for a 15-trial simulation.

b) Manually simulate for 15 trials.
c) Calculate the probability of the passengers' boarding either of the two buses.

Solution
a) *Simulation Flowchart*

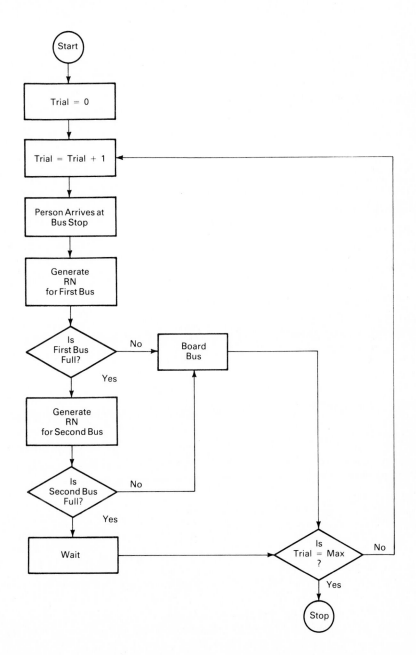

b) *15-Run Simulation: Assignment of Representative Numbers*

	Blue Streakliner	Red Flash Express
Full	01–45	01–30
Not Full	46–00	31–00

Run Number	Blue Streakliner RN	Blue Streakliner Situation	Red Flash Express RN	Red Flash Express Situation	Bus Available	Percent Available
1	21	Full	76	Not Full	Yes	1/1 = 100%
2	79	Not Full			Yes	2/2 = 100%
3	80	Not Full			Yes	3/3 = 100%
4	88	Not Full			Yes	4/4 = 100%
5	28	Full	87	Not Full	Yes	5/5 = 100%
6	42	Full	08	Full	No	5/6 = 83.3%
7	90	Not Full			Yes	6/7 = 85.7%
8	21	Full	15	Full	No	6/8 = 75%
9	04	Full	31	Not Full	Yes	7/9 = 77.8%
10	96	Not Full			Yes	8/10 = 80%
11	52	Not Full			Yes	9/11 = 81.2%
12	28	Full	54	Not Full	Yes	10/12 = 83.3%
13	28	Full	81	Not Full	Yes	11/13 = 84.6%
14	95	Not Full			Yes	12/14 = 85.7%
15	38	Full	64	Not Full	Yes	13/15 = 86.7%

c) Assuming events B and C are independent,
   A = Event of boarding the bus
   B = Event of having the Blue Streakliner empty
   $\overline{B}$ = Event of having the Blue Streakliner full
   C = Event of having the Red Flash Express empty

$P(A) = P(B) + P(C \cap \overline{B}) = p(B) + P(C)P(\overline{B})$
$P(A) = .55 + (0.70)(0.45) = 0.55 + 0.315 = 0.865$
Thus, there is an 86.5 percent chance of the customer's boarding one of the two buses.

8.12 *Simulation and Inventory Control*
    The Compu-Shop sells mini-computers for home and small business applications. The weekly demand for their BASIC business computer is according to the following distribution:

Weekly Demand	Probability
25	0.40
35	0.30
40	0.25
50	0.05

Inventory is replenished by an independent wholesaler at the close of business at the end of each week. There is a 55 percent chance that the wholesaler supplies 30 units, and a 45 percent chance that he supplies 60 units. Due to storage limitations, inventory in excess of 70 units must be sent back to the wholesaler. Back orders are allowed to accumulate, with weekly shortages filled from the following week's inventory. Beginning inventory to the current week is 30 units. Simulate 16 weeks of operation to find the average inventory on hand at the beginning of each week.

Solution

Weekly Demand	Representative Numbers
25	01–40
35	41–70
40	71–95
50	96–00

Weekly Supply	Representative Numbers
30	1–55
60	56–00

8.13 Suppose that the demand for a product is distributed according to the following probability distribution:

Demand	Probability
13	0.05
14	0.07
15	0.10
16	0.20
17	0.25
18	0.15
19	0.10
20	0.08

a) Derive the cumulative probability for the demand.
b) What is the average demand calculated by simulation using the first ten five-digit random numbers from Table E in the Appendix?
(The solutions for this problem and the following problems are contained in the instructor's manual.)

8.14 Consider the following probability distribution for the time needed to tune a passenger car engine.

Time	Probability
25 minutes	0.10
30 minutes	0.20
35 minutes	0.25
40 minutes	0.30
45 minutes	0.10
50 minutes	0.05

a) Construct the cumulative probability distribution.
b) Simulate the tune-up time for 25 cars (use Table E in the Appendix).
c) Calculate the expected tune-up time and compare it with the simulated time.

8.15 Consider the following probability distribution representing Toyland's daily demand for the "Walk and Talk" doll.

Demand	Probability
6	0.10
7	0.20
8	0.30
9	0.25
10	0.15

a) Prepare these data for simulation of the demand by the use of random numbers.
b) Use Table E in the Appendix to generate the demand for 10 days. How well is the demand simulated?
c) Continue simulating for another 40 days. How well is the demand simulated with 50 random numbers?
d) Compare your answers to parts (b) and (c). What can you conclude?

8.16 A bookstore lot has spaces for 8 cars. Starting at 10 a.m., cars arrive according to the following distribution:

Time between Arrivals (minutes)	Probability
1	0.20
2	0.30
3	0.25
4	0.15
5	0.10

The distribution of the time that a car is parked in the lot is as follows:

Parking Time (minutes)	Probability
10	0.05
12	0.20
14	0.30
16	0.25
18	0.15
20	0.05

Simulate the arrivals and departures of cars until the bookstore lot is filled. At what times does this happen?

8.17 Simulation has been used frequently to control inventory. Consider the control of one specific inventory item for which the daily demand distribution is as follows:

Demand	Probability
0	0.10
1	0.40
2	0.35
3	0.15

At the end of any day on which the inventory drops to 5 units, an order of 12 units is placed. The time to deliver goods is also a random variable, and its distribution is as follows:

Number of Days to Deliver	Probability
2	0.25
3	0.60
4	0.15

a) Simulate the inventory activity for 50 days, and for each day record the following items in a table: day, inventory received (assume that every delivery is received in the morning before the shop opens), starting inventory, random number for daily sales, ending inventory, lost sales, random number when an order needs to be placed (to determine when the order will arrive), and number of days to deliver. Start with an inventory on hand of 10 units.

b) Simulate the inventory for another 50 days, under the assumption that an order is placed when the inventory reaches 4 units.

c) Compare the results of parts (a) and (b) with respect to: simulated distribution of demand, simulated distribution of delivery time, maximum and average inventory level.

8.18 General Appliance Manufacturing, Inc., is designing a new kitchen appliance. The product design department has estimated that the capital investment is 1.5 million dollars, and submits the following distribution of variable costs:

Variable Cost/Unit	Probability
$200	0.20
220	0.50
340	0.30

The marketing department provides the following data:

Selling Price	Probability	Demand	Probability
$440	0.30	7,000	0.30
450	0.60	10,000	0.45
460	0.10	14,000	0.25

a) Use the expected value approach to calculate the profit. Remember that the profit, in general, is calculated as:

Profit = (Selling Price − Variable Cost) × Demand − Investment

b) Simulate 40 profit values by simulating the selling price, the variable cost, and the demand (use the profit formula to calculate the simulated profit).

c) Compare the results of parts (a) and (b), and discuss any differences.

8.19 A dental office opens at 8:30 a.m., and the dentist starts working at 9 a.m. He has scheduled patients to arrive every half hour from 9 a.m. until 12 noon and from 2 p.m. until 5 p.m. Patients may not necessarily arrive exactly on time; they may be as much as 10 minutes early or 10 minutes late. The following table shows the probability distributions for patients' being early, on time, and late.

Patient Arrival	Probability
10 minutes early	0.10
5 minutes early	0.30
On time	0.40
5 minutes late	0.15
10 minutes late	0.05

The distribution for the appointment duration is as follows:

Appointment Duration	Probability
15 minutes	0.05
20 minutes	0.15
25 minutes	0.20
30 minutes	0.20
35 minutes	0.15
40 minutes	0.15
45 minutes	0.10

a) Simulate for one day the arrival times of patients and their appointment durations.

b) Use the simulated information to find each patient's waiting time, the starting time of treatment, and the ending time of treatment.

c) How much time does the dentist have for lunch?

d) At what time will the office be closed?

BIBLIOGRAPHY

ARMOUR, G. A., and E. S. BUFFA, "A Heuristic Algorithm and Simulation Approach to the Relative Location of Facilities," *Management Science*, 9, January, 1963, pp. 294–309.

BARTION, R. F., *Primer on Simulation and Gaming.* Englewood Cliffs, N.J.: Prentice-Hall, Inc., 1972.

BUFFA, E. S., G. A. ARMOUR, and T. E. VOLLMAN, "Allocating Facilities with CRAFT," *Harvard Business Review*, 42, March–April, 1964, pp. 136–58.

CARLSON, J. G., and M. J. MISSHAUK, *Introduction to Gaming: Management Decision Simulations.* New York: John Wiley & Sons, Inc., 1972.

DREYFUS, H. L., *What Computers Can't Do: A Critique of Artificial Reason.* Scranton, Penn.: Harper & Row, Publishers, 1972.

FINDLER, N., and B. MELTZER, *Artificial Intelligence and Heuristic Programming.* New York: American Elsevier Publishing Co., Inc., 1971.

FLAUGH, R. S., and R. W. DEPORTO, "Simulation of Automated Material-Handling Systems Using GPSS," *Simulation,* 17, August, 1971, pp. 65–69.

FORRESTER, J. W., *Industrial Dynamics.* Cambridge, Mass.: Massachusetts Institute of Technology Press, 1961.

———, *World Dynamics.* Cambridge, Mass.: Write-Allen Press, 1971.

FREEMAN, D. R., et al., "Solving Machine Interference by Simulation," *Journal of Industrial Engineering,* 5, July, 1973, pp. 32–38.

GAVETT, J. W., "Three Heuristic Rules for Sequencing Jobs to a Single Production Facility," *Management Science,* 11, 1965, pp. B166–76.

GENSCH, D. H., "A Computer Simulation Model for Selecting Advertising Schedules," *Journal of Marketing Research,* VI, May, 1969, pp. 203–14.

GERE, W. S., JR., "Heuristics in Job Shop Scheduling," *Management Science,* 13, November, 1966, pp. 167–90.

GITLOW, H. S., "Methodology for Determining the Optimal Design of a Free Standing Abortion Clinic," *Management Science,* 22, August, 1976, pp. 1289–98.

GODIN, V. B., "The Dollars and Sense of Simulation," *The Journal of the American Institute of Decision Sciences,* 7, April, 1976, pp. 331–42.

GRAHAM, R. G., and C. F. GRAY, *Business Games Handbook.* New York: American Management Association, Inc., 1969.

GRASHOF, J. F., "Supermarket Chain Product Mix Decision Criteria: A Simulation Experiment," *Journal of Marketing Research,* VII, May, 1970, pp. 235–42.

GRINYER, P. H., and J. WOOLER, "Computer Models for Corporate Planning," *Long-Range Planning,* 8, February, 1975, pp. 14–25.

GROSS, D., and A. SORIANO, "The Effect of Reducing Leadtime on Inventory Levels— Simulation Analysis," *Management Science,* 16, October, 1969, pp. B61–B76.

GUETZKOW, H., et al., *Simulation in Social and Administrative Science.* Englewood Cliffs, N.J.: Prentice-Hall, Inc., 1972.

HELGESON, W. B., and D. P. BIRNIE, "Assembly Line Balancing Using the Ranked Positional Weight Technique," *The Journal of Industrial Engineering,* 12, November– December 1961, pp. 394–98.

HINKLE, C. L., and A. A. KUEHN, "Heuristic Models," *California Management Review,* 10, Fall, 1967, pp. 59–68.

HOLZMAN, A. G., and D. B. JOHNSON, "A Simulation Model of the College Admission Process," *Interfaces,* 5, May, 1975, pp. 55–64.

HURST, E. G., JR., and A. B. MCNAMARA, "Heuristic Scheduling in a Woolen Mill," *Management Science,* 14, December, 1967, pp. 182–203.

JONES, C. H., "An Economic Evaluation of Job Shop Dispatching Rules," *Management Science,* 20, November, 1973, pp. 293–307.

KARG, R. L., and G. L. THOMPSON, "A Heuristic Approach to Solving Traveling Salesman Problems," *Management Science,* 10, January, 1964, pp. 225–48.

KILBRIDGE, M. D., and L. WEBSTER, "A Heuristic Method of Assembly Line Balancing," *The Journal of Industrial Engineering,* 12, July–August, 1961, pp. 292–98.

KING, W. R., "Methodological Simulation in Marketing," *Journal of Marketing,* 34, April, 1970, pp. 8–13.

KUEHN, A. A., *Heuristic Programming: A Useful Technique for Maketing, Marketing Precision and Executive Action,* ed. by Charles H. Hindersman. Chicago: American Marketing Association, 1962.

KUEHN, A. A., and M. J. HAMBUREGER, "A Heuristic Program for Locating Warehouses," *Management Science,* 9, July, 1963, pp. 643–66.

LEE, W. B., and B. M. KHUMAWALA, "Simulation Testing of Aggregate Production Models in an Implementation Methodology," *Management Science,* 20, February, 1974, pp. 903–11.

LEVY, F. K., "An Application of Heuristic Program Solving to Accounts Receivable Management," *Management Science,* 12, February, 1966, pp. 236–44.

MEIER, R. C., W. T. NEWELL, and H. L. PAZER, *Simulation in Business and Economics.* Englewood Cliffs, N.J.: Prentice-Hall, Inc., 1969.

MICHAEL, G. C., "A Computer Simulation Model for Forecasting Catalog Sales," *Journal of Marketing Research,* VIII, May, 1981, pp. 224–79.

———, "A Review of Heuristic Programming," *The Journal of American Institute of Decision Sciences,* 3, January, 1971, pp. 74–100.

MINSKY, M. L., "Artificial Intelligence," *Science American,* 215, September, 1966.

MOBERLY, L. E., and F. P. WYMAN, "An Application of Simulation to the Comparison of Assembly Line Configurations," *The Journal of the American Institute for Decision Sciences,* 4, October, 1973, pp. 505–16.

NAYLOR, T. H., *Computer Simulation Experiments and Models of Economic Systems.* New York: John Wiley & Sons, Inc., 1971.

ODOM, P. R., and R. E. SHANNON, "Monographs for Computer Simulation," *Journal of Industrial Engineering,* 5, November, 1973, pp. 34–38.

REITMAN, J., *Computer Simulation Applications.* New York: John Wiley & Sons, Inc., 1971.

SIMON H. A., and A. NEWELL, *Human Problem Solving.* Englewood Cliffs, N.J.: Prentice-Hall, Inc., 1971.

SLAGE, J., *Artificial Intelligence, The Heuristic Programming Approach.* New York: McGraw-Hill Book Co., 1972.

THEIRAUF, R. J., *Systems Analysis and Design of Real-Time Management Information Systems.* Englewood Cliffs, N.J.: Prentice-Hall, Inc., 1975.

TONGE, F. M., "Summary of a Heuristic Line Balancing Procedure," *Management Science,* 7, October, 1960, pp. 21–42.

———, "The Use of Heuristic Programming in Management Science," *Management Science,* 7, April, 1961.

WEIST, J. D., "A Heuristic Model for Scheduling Large Projects with Limited Resources," *Management Science,* 13, February, 1967, pp. 359–77.

WEITZ, H., "The Promise of Simulation in Marketing," *Journal of Marketing,* 31, July, 1967, pp. 28–33.

9

Job Design
and Analysis

INTRODUCTION

In this and the following chapter, we shall concentrate on the organizing function of operations management. Organizing is the process by which individuals, groups, and facilities are combined in a formal structure of tasks and authority. The organization of work systems is based on the fact that an organization depends on human resources to accomplish its goals. Work systems organizing has tended to be de-emphasized in operations management courses.

However, recently there has been a move toward a renewed interest in the area, for several reasons: First, some studies suggested that many workers become dissatisfied with their work environment. Second, there has been a general concern over faltering productivity and quality of products and services. Ironically, jobs organized to yield the highest productivity levels are the ones that appear to generate the most worker dissatisfaction. Third, societal changes evolved that brought about a high demand for college education and a general quest for financial independence. Fourth, trade unions supported by extensive legislation were formed and extensively developed. Fifth, an increase in government welfare legislation helped secure a minimum level of security on and off the job. Sixth, a "quality-of-working-life" type of professional, including psychologists, behavioral scientists, and industrial engineers, emerged.

In this chapter, we shall be dealing with job design, which is an element of work systems organizing. Job design is concerned with specifying the contents and methods of jobs. The goal of job design is to create a work system that is productive and efficient, taking into account costs and the benefits of various alternatives.

Three questions are to be answered through job design: *Who* performs the job? *Where* is it performed? *How* is it performed?

Job design must be carried out by personnel who have the necessary training and experience. It should be documented in a written form and have the support and endorsement of both the management and labor.

Two different schools of thought guide the job design task. One is the *scientific management school,* which emphasizes a systematic, logical approach to job design that results in the most efficient job, from the point of view of management. The other one is the *behavioral school,* which emphasizes the wants and needs of the individual employee.

The latter school has made managers aware of the fact that efficiency is not all that counts, and that in the long run it is best to consider the effects of specialization on workers' morale and productivity. The degree of specialization is a major question. Too much specialization generates a high degree of dissatisfaction in workers.

SPECIALIZATION AND JOB DESIGN

Specialization is the restriction of the scope of a job. Examples range from specialist physicians, through hair dressers, to workers on assembly lines. The rationale for specialization is that it enhances the degree of proficiency of the individual involved, since the scope of the job becomes restricted. This might still leave enough scope and glamor for physicians, lawyers, or professors, but for the assembly-line worker it represents a great potential for boredom, low productivity, low morale, and a high degree of dissatisfaction.

Job Simplification

In many professions, job specialization means job simplification. *In job simplification the job is divided into the shortest and most trivial possible work cycles in such a way as to minimize workers' decision-making requirements and to maximize repetition of the work.*

For example, Henry Ford, through assembly-line methods (which simplified the job), was able to assemble a car in one hour and 33 minutes instead of the twelve hours and 28 minutes required prior to the introduction of the assembly line.

The number of advantages in job simplification and specialization may be listed, including the following:

1. A high degree of specialization enables management to hire workers at lower costs.

2. A high degree of specialization enables workers to learn a task in a shorter period of time; hence, less money has to be spent on training each worker, and higher productivity may be achieved earlier.

3. More people are capable of performing highly repetitive short-cycle operations, thus providing employment opportunities to less capable and disabled workers.

4. Due to high standardization and repetitiveness of operations, less supervision is required per worker; hence, a supervisor can supervise more workers, which reduces supervision cost.

5. A high degree of specialization enables more effective use of equipment, tools, and buildings, thus reducing overhead costs.

6. A high degree of specialization provides economically favorable conditions for use of specialized equipment.

7. Short-cycle, high-volume jobs can be performed either in a technology-paced (e.g., conveyor-belt) or a self-paced work situation.

However, these advantages may be outweighed by major *disadvantages:*

1. For smaller quantities, job simplification of higher repetitive short-cycle operations are frequently not justifiable economically.

2. When job simplification is performed in a conveyor-based operation, it is rarely possible to derive a perfect line balancing of the labor force. This results in economic loss, as the conveyor must be operated to suit the operator who has the longest standard cycle time.

3. Simplified jobs, requiring short-cycle operations, frequently involve the repeated use of the same muscle grouping. This results in high and early onset of fatigue, which necessitates the provision of additional fatigue allowances.

4. The most significant objections to job simplification come from behavioral scientists who argue that job simplification does not allow the development and use of participative management; hence, workers can rarely make decisions on variables that, according to some behavioral scientists and engineers, are vital to job satisfaction and productive performance. These variables include determination of production methods, of the internal distribution of tasks, of recruitment, of internal leadership, of additional tasks to be performed, and of hours of work.

5. Job simplification, according to some behavioral scientists, decreases for the workers the possibilities of being the masters of their immediate environment, or doing meaningful and interesting work (simplified jobs are typically monotonous), of exercising judgment, and of learning and being promoted.

Job Enrichment/Job Enlargement

In order to reduce or eliminate the above limitations, it has been suggested that the solution to the problem lies in enriching and enlarging the job. *Job enrichment is an intentional modification of the content of jobs toward the end of providing the opportunity for the employee's psychological growth.* Additions to jobs typically have included inspection; setup; maintenance by the worker of his or her equipment and control of his or her own work; combining of several jobs that together constitute a whole task; and formation of autonomous work groups that are responsible for assigning, rotation (in which workers take turns at various jobs by periodicaly exchanging them), scheduling, and completion of the whole task.

Job enlargement is achieved by adding more operations of a similar nature to the job, rather than by adding more responsibility to the job, which is characteristic of job enrichment. It is not as effective an approach to job design as is job enrichment.

The benefits of job enrichment suggest drastic improvements in productivity, such as: increase in production output of between 6 and 20 percent; increase in quality of production of between 4 and 2300 percent; and reduction of absenteeism of between 25 and 800 percent. Examples of enriched jobs[1] are presented in Table 9.1.

Grouping workers into integrated assembly clusters where the workers perform enriched jobs with larger cycle times increases responsibility for quality and provides a better working environment. This indicates an effort to improve the *quality of working life.* In addition, companies may experiment with choice of locations (smaller cities, park-like settings), flexible work hours, and quality circles (which are described in Chapter 13).

Automation

Automation refers to the use of mechanical or electrical devices to help or to replace human beings. Under this title one includes data processing computers, microswitches, microprocessors, industrial robots, and the like. All of these devices have the abiliity to exert a varying degree of control over a process. Major advantages of automation include the following:

1. Human beings are replaced in jobs that are boring, repetitive, monotonous, and difficult to carry out (such as carrying a heavy load).
2. Automation yields an extremely uniform output with less variation in quality characteristics.
3. Automation yields a higher rate of output.

There are several *disadvantages* to automation:

1. It results in displacement and retraining of workers, which some union officials might resist.
2. It involves a major capital expense and a higher break-even point.
3. It restricts the flexibility of the process and makes it more susceptible to technological obsolescence.

[1] These examples are presented in G. Salvendy, "An Industrial Engineering Dilemma: Simplified versus Enlarged Jobs," *4th International Conference on Production Research Proceedings,* August, 1977, Tokyo, Japan, pp. 22–30.

TABLE 9.1   ENRICHMENT OF SIMPLIFIED JOBS: A SAMPLE OF TYPICAL CHANGES

JOB CATEGORY	SIMPLIFIED	ENLARGED
Spot Welding	Operator inserts wires to jog and spot, welds shelves, and stores welded shelves on rack.	In addition to the simplified job, operator is also responsible for filing electrodes, adjusting the voltage of spot-welding generators, and fitting jigs.
Power Press	Operator inserts items to power press, activates the power press, and removes the pressed item.	In addition to the simplified job content, the operator is responsible for bringing the material to the power press work station and removing the pressed items from the work station.
Metal Platers	Each worker is responsible for only one job. For example, one worker's job is only to mix chemicals for plating; another operator only puts items on a conveyor line that travels through plating. A total of three operators work at each machine.	Each of the three workers arranges his or her own work, and rotation from job to job occurs.
Wire Cutters	Worker aligns machines, inserts wires and empties bins.	Work content is exactly the same, but worker can choose his or her own working hours, providing the machines are manned a total of at least 23 hours a day.
Time-Study Engineering	Engineer documents current methods and establishes time standards, using stopwatch.	In addition to documenting current methods and establishing time standards he or she is responsible for developing improved methods (previously developed by production engineer) and handles time-study grievances (previously handled by personnel manager).

Robotics

Industrial robots are part of the automation phenomenon. Many companies in Europe, Japan, and North America are using such robots. All robots have armlike projections and grippers that perform jobs traditionally performed by workers. Most of them contain built-in control systems and are either manipulated by workers or are capable of hand-alone operations.

A pick-and-place robot, which is quite a common type is mostly used for material handling. It has the ability to move in two or three directions (up and down, in and out, left and right). It is controlled by an electromechanical system.

A servo robot is the most common industrial robot. The one or more servo mechanisms enable the arm and gripper to change direction continuously without tripping a mechanical switch. Five to seven directional movements can be accomplished, depending on the number of "joints."

A *programmable robot* is a servo robot that can be programmed by memorizing a sequence of arm and gripper movements through which the robot is led initially. Any change calls for the whole sequence to be reprogrammed.

A *computerized robot* is a servo robot that receives instruction not by being led through a sequence, but by means of transmission of computer commands electronically. Thus, the robot can be instructed to improve its work routine sequence.

A *sensory robot* is a computerized robot that has one or several senses. Sight and touch are the most common of these senses.

An *assembly robot* is a sensory robot designed specifically for assembly operations. It may cost $100,000, whereas a pick-and-place robot may cost as little as $10,000.

Sociotechnical Systems

The sociotechnical systems approach is concerned with the human-technology interface. It recognizes that the choice of technology has an impact on the social structure within an organization, and that technological changes (e.g., automation, relayout) have an impact on worker productivity and morale.

The approach suggests that there are technological alternatives that produce desired results but that are consistent with sociological considerations. The approach is similar to job enrichment, calling for task variety, skill variety, and increased autonomy. However, it goes beyond job enrichment in promoting self-organization by the workers and self-determination on how the work is actually done. No definitive conclusions on using this approach have been reached, and so its use is somewhat limited.

Job Environment

Job environment is an important part of job design. Physical factors, such as temperature, humidity, ventilation, lighting, color, noise, work-breaks, and safety have an impact on workers' productivity, output quality, health, and accident rates.

Temperature should be kept within the comfort band, which is the most comfortable range for workers. For office employees, the comfort band is between 65°F and 72°F (18°C and 22°C). For moderately strenuous activities, the comfort band is between 55°F and 65°F (13°C and 18°C).

Relative Humidity level should be kept between 30 percent and 50 percent. One should remember that the higher the humidity, the more cooling is required in the summer and the more heating is required in the winter. This is because the *effective temperature* is affected by the humidity.

Ventilation should be adequate to remove odors, smoke and dust. Remember, for example, the potential hazards of asbestos particles and coal particles for the lungs.

Ample Lighting without glare and much contrast is needed for good performance. For psychological and monetary reasons, daylight is recommended.

Color is used to effect moods and feelings. Red, yellow, blue, green, brown, and orange promote stimulation, cheerfulness, thoughtfulness, calm, peacefulness, and action, respectively. It is also used to designate safe and hazardous zones and to code/identify various equipment pieces.

Noise should be kept to a minimum. Carefully selected machinery, partitions and layout can help control noise.

Work-breaks placed carefully during the day help in increasing productivity. Usually a period of increased productivity follows a break.

Safety plays a major role in job design. Accidents are undesirable not only for the employee involved but also for the employer involved. Worker carelessness contributes to accident rates. All the aforementioned environmental factors affect worker carelessness. Accident hazards are to be recognized and measures should be taken to protect the worker. Workers cannot be productive if they feel that they are in danger. The Occupational Safety and Health (OSHA) Act of 1970 is intended to ensure that workers have a healthy and safe job environment. The Act provides specific safety regulations that are audited by OSHA inspectors. OSHA officials are authorized to make unannounced inspections, issue warnings, impose fines, and invoke shutdowns for safety reasons.

JOB ANALYSIS

Job analysis (sometimes termed method analysis) involves the overall operation. It starts with identification of the overall operation to be performed, the product to be produced, or the service to be performed. Subsequently, it involves a presentation of the details of each job that concentrates on arrangements of the work place and the movements of the worker involved.

Job analysis is carried out in four steps:

1. Identification of the operations and the jobs to be analyzed. This is done by using flow process charts and flow diagrams, described below.
2. Documentation of job content and method as it is currently done. For new jobs, this step is omitted.
3. Analysis of the job content and method or the tasks (smaller elements of the job involved). This is done by using operation charts and multiple activity charts (described below).
4. Development of an improved job content and/or method. For new jobs, this step involves initial development of job content and/or method.

Sometimes jobs can be broken down to smaller elements (tasks) so that each one of them can be studied and documented in detail. The actual assignment of these tasks to individual workers in an assembly-line setting was discussed in Chapter 7.

Table 9.2 lists the various methods of job analysis and the circumstances under which they are to be used.

Flow Process Charts

There are two types of flow process charts: employee flow process charts and product flow process charts. The two are identical except for the fact that one treats the employee as the subject of analysis and the other treats the product as the subject of analysis. Let us confine our presentation to the employee flow process chart.

An employee flow process chart analysis is a graphic means of presenting the separable steps that a worker performs when doing a job that requires him or her to move from place to place in the course of the work. The employee flow process chart analysis is an analysis of what the person does and not of the sequential steps performed on the product or material. The chart is an aid in clearly identifying activities of persons performing jobs that require them to move from place to place. Care must be exercised not to confuse this analysis

TABLE 9.2 METHODS OF JOB ANALYSIS

JOB ANALYSIS METHOD	SITUATIONS WHEN APPLICABLE
Operation charts, principles of motion economy	Routine, repetitive jobs with short cycle times and low volumes; the worker stays in one place
Multiple activity charts (employees and machines)	Routine, repetitive jobs with long cycle times and higher volume, in which workers interact with each other and/or with machines
Flow process charts	Design of the overall production process, work setup, and work stations
Flow diagrams	Design of the overall production process, layout, and relayout

with a product flow process chart. The end result of an employee flow process chart analysis is usually an improvement: cutting down in the number of operations and the time required to do the job.

Four general types of jobs may be encountered when applying employee flow process chart–analysis techniques. The characteristics of the types of work are as follows:

1. The work has a single repeated cycle. In such cases, a single cycle will be charted, with a cycle defined as all the steps necessary to bring a unit of output to a state of completion.

2. The work is cyclic, but there are several subcycles performed with different frequency. For instance, the worker may perform subcycle A on each part and then subcycle B for 10 parts together, subcycle B occuring one tenth as often as A. In such a case, a chart will be drawn showing not only one performance of each subcycle, but also indicating the frequency of subcycles.

3. The work varies from cycle to cycle. This variation may take two forms. In some cases, the variation may be due primarily to operator habit rather than being inherent in the work; consequently, the analyst may plot several cycles, to give him or her more material from which to develop a preferable work pattern. In other cases, the variation may be inherent in the job, and each subsequent performance may differ in detail but not in general pattern. In such a case, sample cycles are drawn for study, with the general pattern indicated and the details that may change so noted. Attention is paid on a weighted basis to the factors that control the variation. In many instances a more complex type of study, memomotion study, described later, may be more useful in treating this type of work.

4. The task may be such that there is no cycle or pattern. This is usually true of supervisory and similar activities. In such cases, the study of an employee flow process chart may lead only to general suggestions. In such cases, other techniques, such as work sampling, may be much more productive of useful changes.

No matter where they occur, the jobs are usually broken down into the same types of steps. Experience has shown that with a breakdown into steps such as those shown in Figure 9.1, a considerable number of possibilities for elimination, rearrangement, combination, and facilitation are usually discernible. Hence, a breakdown of this type is often highly productive.

The graphic presentation achieved with a standardized chart is an aid to understanding, and it should be remembered that this is the main purpose of the analysis procedures. Hence, the standard steps and symbols should not be followed blindly. If circumstances arise wherein the use of other steps or other symbols appears to be of more assistance in performing the analysis, the analyst should not hesitate to use them. The format of a chart will also vary with the type of job. The example we shall use in this chapter will be of a job that has a single repeated cycle.

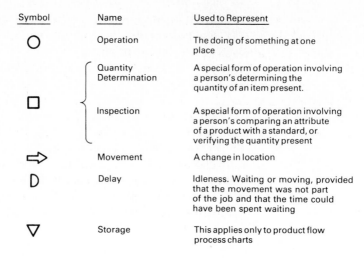

Symbol	Name	Used to Represent
◯	Operation	The doing of something at one place
☐	Quantity Determination	A special form of operation involving a person's determining the quantity of an item present.
☐	Inspection	A special form of operation involving a person's comparing an attribute of a product with a standard, or verifying the quantity present
⇨	Movement	A change in location
D	Delay	Idleness. Waiting or moving, provided that the movement was not part of the job and that the time could have been spent waiting
▽	Storage	This applies only to product flow process charts

Figure 9.1 Symbols for an Employee Flow Process Chart

Figure 9.2 presents an employee flow process chart for a change of a blow plate in a machine at a steel-casting plant.[2] It was felt that the setup took an excessive amount of time. The establishment of a new method of holding blow plates in place saved time and reduced distance, as can be seen in Figure 9.3.

The questions one should ask oneself in trying to develop a proposed process flow are noted at the upper left corner of Figure 9.2 and 9.3.

Flow Diagrams

Flow diagrams are used extensively to present the flow of material (product) and/or employees throughout an organization. Using drawings of the layout and the factors of production (desks, machines, elevators), or templates placed on magnetic board, lines indicating the flow of material and/or employees are drawn. Examples of flow diagrams for planning a library and a metal job shop were used in Chapter 7. Location of heavy traffic, "crossroads" and excessive distances become evident through the use of such diagrams.

The Operation Chart

In many manufacturing or service jobs, the workers remain at one work station. In many cases, the jobs are important enough to warrant spending time on their design or improvement. Improvements may be accomplished without disturb-

---

[2] An extended version appears in M. E. Mundel, *Motion and Time Study: Improving Productivity*, 5th ed. (Englewood Cliffs, N.J.: Prentice-Hall, Inc., 1978).

ing other aspects of the work, and thus often may be achieved more quickly. Frequently, changes may be established on the same day on which the analysis is made. The operation chart is used for this type of situation.

An operation chart is a graphic means of portraying distinct steps of the worker's body members when he or she is performing a job that takes place essentially at one location. It is a schematic model of the worker job and uses graphical symbols. The body members involved are usually the right and left hands. When the feet or eyes are important factors, they may also be charted. The operation chart shows not only the sequence performed by each body member charted, but also relationships of the members to each other during the work. It does not indicate the time or relative time for the steps.

The steps into which the work is commonly divided and the symbols used to represent these steps are given in Figure 9.4. The symbols are similar to those used for process charts (which are described later), but because of the difference in the scopes of operations and processes, the symbols are used to represent different steps.

An operation chart is easily constructed by means of direct observation of the job. When the job is not yet being performed, such a chart may readily be used to set forth in detail the contemplated method. In either case, the analyst should first familiarize himself or herself with the job cycle. The job cycle consists of all the movements required to bring a unit of the output to the stage of completion typical of the operation. It is most convenient to consider the cycle as starting with the first movement attributable to a unit of the output, and as ending with the last movement of that unit. This gives a chart that is more easily understood than one that begins and ends in the middle of work on a part.

Four types of jobs may be encountered. The types of work have the following characteristics:

1. The work has a single repeated cycle.
2. The work is cyclic, but there are several subcycles performed with different frequency.
3. The work varies from cycle to cycle.
4. The task has no regular cycle.

Jobs of type (4) may be studied more appropriately with the aid of a work-sampling study or memomotion study (which are covered later).

Figure 9.5 presents a left-hand–right-hand operation chart for drilling a hole in a 1/4" plate. Figure 9.6 presents the left-hand–right-hand operation chart after analysis has revealed a better design of the work station.

Comparing the number of operations, transportation, delays, and holds, one finds a reduction in their number over the 25 cycles (in 25 cycles, 50 sheets are drilled).

FLOW PROCESS CHART

					WHAT / WHEN / WHERE / WHO / HOW	WHY?			

Q̵uestion each step . . .

CHART IS — [X] Present Method   [ ] Proposed Method   PAGE NO **1**   NO. OF PAGES **1**

PROCESS BEING CHARTED: Change Blow Plate

SUMMARY	PRESENT		PROPOSED		DIFFERENCE	
	NO.	TIME (min.)	NO.	TIME (min.)	NO.	TIME (min.)
○ Operation	11	2.43				
⟶ Transportation	9	.64				
□ Inspection						
D Delay						
▽ Storage						
Total — Steps & Time	20	3.07				
Total — Distance		ft.		ft.		ft.

(check one and describe) [X] Employee [ ] Product

CHART BEGINS — Walk to Dolly   **CHART ENDS —** Store Dolly

CHARTED BY M. Alti   **DATE** 4/12/80

DEPT. OR DIV A100   **SECTION OR LOCATION** Building A

STEPS IN PROCESS	OPERATION	TRANSP.	INSPECTION	DELAY	STORAGE	Distance (ft.)	Time (min.)	ELIMINATE	COMBINE	SEQUENCE	PLACE	PERSON	IMPROVE	NOTES
1. To dolly		X				20	20	x						
2. Get dolly	X						05		x					
3. Carry dolly		X				20	10	x						
4. Place Dolly on Blower Table	X						05							
5. To Blower Bench		X				3	02							
6. Get Wrench	X						05							
7. Wrench to Blower		X				3	02							
8. Place wrench on top of blower head	X						02							
9. Wind up blower table	X						04							
10. Remove 3 bolts and 1 side clamp	X						73							
11. To bench		X				3	02							
12. Aside wrench-get screwdriver	X						06							
13. To rear of blower		X				6	03							
14. Pull dolly out with plate	X						13							
15. Plate to storage		X				15	20							
16. Store plate-get next one	X						16							
17. To dolly storage		X				20	10	x						
18. Store dolly	X						05		x					
19.														
20.														

Figure 9.2   Flow Process Chart—Present Method

FLOW PROCESS CHART

Q estion each step . . .   WHAT WHEN WHERE WHO HOW } WHY?

CHART IS — ☐ Present Method   ☒ Proposed Method   PAGE NO 1   NO OF PAGES 1

PROCESS BEING CHARTED
Change Blow Plate

(check one ant describe)
☐ Employee   ☐ Product

CHART BEGINS —
Get Dolly

CHART ENDS —
Hang Dolly on the side of blower

CHARTED BY
M. Alti

DATE

DEPT. OR DIV.
A100

SECTION OR LOCATION
Building A

SUMMARY	PRESENT		PROPOSED		DIFFERENCE	
	NO.	TIME (min.)	NO.	TIME (min.)	NO.	TIME (min.)
○ Operation	11	2.43	15	2.67	4	.24
⟳ Transportation	9	.64	5	.32	4	.32
☐ Inspection						
D Delay						
▽ Storage						
Total Steps & Time	20	3.07	20	2.99	0	.08
Distance	96 ft.		30 ft.		46 ft.	

STEPS IN PROCESS	OPERATION	TRANSP.	INSPECTION	DELAY	STORAGE	Distance (ft.)	Time (min.)	ELIMINATE	COMBINE	SEQUENCE	PLACE	PERSON	IMPROVE	NOTES
1. Get dolly from side of blower	⊗	⇨	☐	D	▽		.10							
2. Place on blower table	⊗	⇨	☐	D	▽		.05							
3. Wind up table	⊗	⇨	☐	D	▽		.40							
4. To bench for wedge/loosening tool	○	⊗	☐	D	▽	3	.02							
5. Get tool	⊗	⇨	☐	D	▽		.02							
6. To rear of blower	○	⊗	☐	D	▽	6	.04							
7. Strike wedge	⊗	⇨	☐	D	▽		.10							
8. To front of blower	○	⊗	☐	D	▽	3	.04							
9. Place mallet; get wrench	⊗	⇨	☐	D	▽		.05							
10. To blower	○	⊗	☐	D	▽	3	.02							
11. Off 4 nuts and front clamp	⊗	⇨	☐	D	▽		.60							
12. Pull out wedge	⊗	⇨	☐	D	▽		.16							
13. Wind down table	⊗	⇨	☐	D	▽		.13							
14. Pull bench in front of blower	⊗	⇨	☐	D	▽		.40							
15. Pull out dolly	⊗	⇨	☐	D	▽		.13							
16. Plate to storage	○	⊗	☐	D	▽	15	.20							
17. Store and get next one	⊗	⇨	☐	D	▽		.16							
18. Wind down table	⊗	⇨	☐	D	▽		.22							
19. Pull out Dolly	⊗	⇨	☐	D	▽		.05							
20. Hang dolly on side of blower	⊗	⇨	☐	D	▽		.10							

POSSIBILITIES CHANGE

Figure 9.3   Flow Process Chart—Proposed Method

Symbol	Name	Used to Represent
O	Suboperation	Body member doing something at one place, such as taking hold, lining up, assembling
⇨	Movement	A movement of a body member toward an objective or a change in the location of an object*
D	Delay	Body member idle or waiting for an action of another body member
▽	Hold	Object maintained in a fixed position by a body member so that work may be done with or on it at that location

*On very long operations, the analyst may combine some steps into larger steps, using "get" in place of terms such as "reach for, take hold of, and bring object to work area"; "aisde," in place of "move object from work area, let go of object, and return." In such a case, the chart is described as being made with a "gross breakdown," and is considerably shorter than when made with the usual steps.

Figure 9.4   Symbols for Operation Chart

In summary, an operation chart is used to reduce total steps to a minimum, arrange the steps in the best order, combine steps where feasible, make each step as easy as possible, balance the work of the hands, avoid the use of the hands for holding, and fit the work place to human dimensions.

Multiple-Activity Charts

Multiple-activity charts are used to analyze an individual who works with one or more pieces of equipment or members of a group who work together, with or without equipment. The analysis shows the sequence of steps, the amount of time they require, and how the workers and pieces of equipment interact.

There are several types of multiple-activity charts:

1. Employee and equipment activity charts.
2. Multi-employee, and multi-employee and equipment activity charts.

In a multiple-activity chart, a separate column of symbols is used for each worker or piece of equipment. For both, time for each step is indicated graphically, and the exact simultaneity of the steps is shown. Multiple-activity analyses are usually used when the objective of the study is either to design the operation or to make a change, and where an analysis showing the relative simultaneity of the two or more items charted is required for a full understanding of the job.

A multiple-activity chart is usually made in order to obtain better utilization of the equipment or workers. However, increased safety is also a common objective. The chart aids in determination of the most effective way of coordinat-

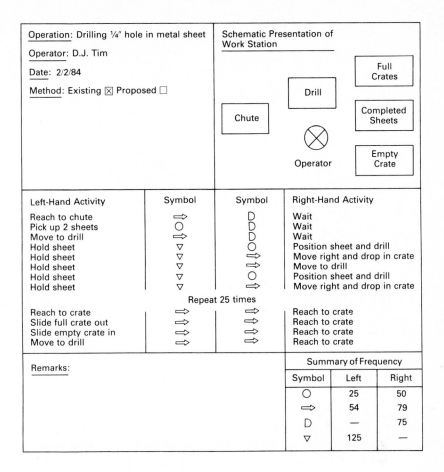

Figure 9.5   Left-Hand–Right-Hand Operation Chart

ing the work of each individual with the group as a whole or with the equipment. It may also be used to indicate how the equipment might be altered in order to accommodate the requirements of the individuals. If the chart technique is employed prior to the finalization of an equipment design, the requirements of the operator may be properly taken into account, following the intent of the sociotechnical system. As with operations charts, jobs with no cycle or pattern are usually more appropriately studied with work sampling or memomotion study.

A two-worker-and-equipment activity chart for preparing, xeroxing, collating, and stapling reports is shown in Figure 9.7. In order to increase production, a crew size change is contemplated.

Operation: Drilling ¼" hole in metal sheet	Schematic Presentation of Work Station
Operator: D.J. Tim	
Date: 2/2/84	
Method: Existing ☐ Proposed ☒	

Schematic Presentation of Work Station

Drill

Chute   Operator (⊗)   Chute

Operator

Left-Hand Activity	Symbol	Symbol	Right-Hand Activity
Reach to chute	⇒	D	Wait
Pick up 2 sheets	○	D	Wait
Move to drill	⇒	D	Wait
Hold sheet	▽	○	Position sheet and drill
Hold sheet	▽	⇒	Drop in chute
Hold sheet	▽	⇒	Move to drill
Hold sheet	▽	○	Position sheet and drill
Hold sheet	▽	⇒	Drop in crate

Repeat 25 times

Remarks:

In the improved work station, chutes are used to dispose of the completed sheets, and a material handler removes them.

Summary of Frequency		
Symbol	Left	Right
○	25	50
⇒	50	75
D	—	75
▽	125	—

Figure 9.6 Left-Hand–Right-Hand Operation Chart at the Improved Work Station

Note that if one operator carries out the whole operation, he or she will spend a total of (0.50 + 0.30 + 0.34 =) 1.14 minutes. The piece of equipment will be busy 0.34 minute of this cycle.

The proportion of the whole cycle that represents operator's busy-period is:

$$\frac{1.14}{1.14} \times 100 \text{ percent} = 100 \text{ percent}$$

The Xerox machine's busy period is:

$$\frac{0.34}{1.14} \times 100 \text{ percent} = 29.82 \text{ percent}$$

For *two operators*, the busy period (see Figure 9.7) is:

$$\frac{0.50 + 0.30 + 0.34}{0.50 + 0.30 + 0.34 + .14} \times 100 \text{ percent} = 89.06 \text{ percent}$$

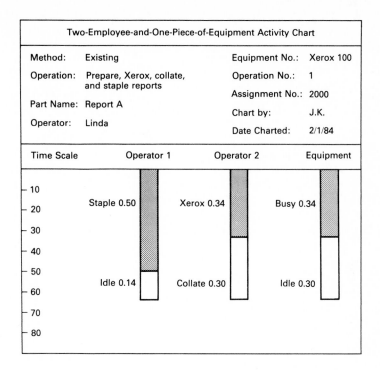

Figure 9.7 Multi-Employee-and-Equipment Activity Chart for Two-Worker Crew on Xeroxing Job

The Xerox machine's busy period (utilization) is:

$$\frac{0.34}{0.64} \times 100 \text{ percent} = 53.12 \text{ percent}$$

Figure 9.8 is a three-operations multiworker and equipment process time chart for the same job. The operator's busy period proportion (of the whole cycle) is:

$$\frac{0.50 + 0.34 + 0.30}{0.50 + 0.34 + 0.16 + 0.30 + 0.20} \times 100 \text{ percent} = 76 \text{ percent}$$

The Xerox machine's busy period (utilization) is:

$$\frac{0.34}{0.50} \times 100 \text{ percent} = 68 \text{ percent}$$

The more operators, the greater the operators' idle time and the smaller the equipment idle time.

The most desirable crew size is, of course, a function of the capacity of the Xerox machine, the amount of labor available (number of pages to be Xeroxed), the demand for reports, and the cost relationships between machine time and

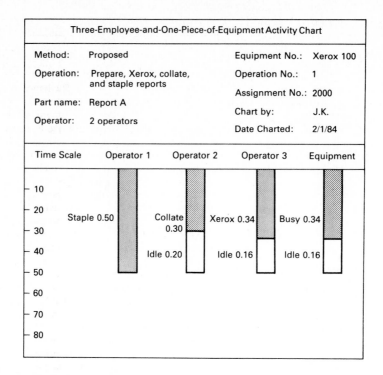

Figure 9.8 Multi-Employee-and-Equipment Activity Chart for Three-Worker Crew on Xeroxing Job

labor time. Note that this technique makes possible a good estimate of the effects of different-sized crews, and that it also provides the material for instructing the crew in the proper distribution of work, once the crew size is determined.

Motion Economy

Motion economy presents a set of guidelines for analyzing and improving jobs by a scientific use of the human body and a scientific use of tools to increase efficiency and reduce fatigue on the job. Table 9.3 presents the principles of motion economy that can be used for both manufacturing and service operations.

Two kinds of analysis are highly useful in motion economy, and are mostly suitable for improving job methods. They are based on data recorded on motion-picture film or video tape:

1. A detailed breakdown called micromotion analysis
2. A "family" of grosser breakdowns called memomotion analysis.

TABLE 9.3   PRINCIPLES OF MOTION ECONOMY

USE OF THE HANDS AND BODY	WORK PLACE ARRANGEMENT	TOOLS AND EQUIPMENT DESIGN
The two hands should begin as well as complete their motions at the same time. The two hands should not be idle at the same time except during the rest periods. Motions of the arms should be made in opposite and symmetrical directions and should be made simultaneously. Hand motions should be confined to the lowest classification with which it is possible to perform the work satisfactorily. Momentum should be employed to assist the worker wherever possible, and it should be reduced to a minimum if it must be overcome by muscular effort. Smooth continuous motions of the hands are preferable to zigzag motions or straight-line motions involving sudden and sharp changes in direction. Ballistic movements are faster, easier, and more accurate than restricted (fixation) or "controlled" movements. Rhythm is essential to the smooth and automatic performance of an operation, and the work should be arranged to permit easy and natural rhythm wherever possible.	There should be a definite and fixed place for all tools and materials. Tools, materials, and controls should be located close into and directly in front of the operator. Gravity feedbins and containers should be used to deliver materials close to the point of use. Drop deliveries should be used wherever possible. Materials and tools should be located so as to permit the best sequence of motions. Provisions should be made for adequate conditions for seeing. Good illumination is the first requirement for satisfactory visual perception. The height of the workplace and the chair should preferably be arranged so that alternate sitting and standing at work are easily possible. A chair of the type and height to permit good posture should be provided for every worker.	The hands should be relieved of all work that can be done more advantageously by a jig, a fixture, or a foot-operated device. Two or more tools should be combined whenever possible. Tools and materials should be prepositioned whenever possible. Where each finger performs some specific movement, such as in typewriting, the load should be distributed in accordance with the inherent capacities of the fingers. Handles, such as those used on cranks and large screwdrivers, should be designed to permit as much of the surface of the hand to come in contact with the handle as possible. This is particularly true when considerable force is exerted in using the handle. For light assembly work, the screwdriver handle should be so shaped that it is smaller at the bottom than at the top. Levers, crossbars, and hand wheels should be located in such positions that the operator can manipulate them with the least change in body position and with the greatest mechanical advantage.

Micromotion analysis is a detailed record of the motions involved in performing a job. The activities of the hands are usually recorded in terms of 17 separate categories. These categories are called therbligs ("Gilbreth" spelled out in reverse, after Frank B. Gilbreth, pioneer in motion and time study, who, together with his wife, Lillian M. Gilbreth, first identified these categories and

TABLE 9.4 THERBLIG DEFINITIONS AND SYMBOLS

THERBLIG	SYMBOL	COLOR	DEFINITION
Grasp	G	Lake red	Begins when hand or body member touches an object. Consists of gaining control of an object. Ends when control is gained.
Position	P	Blue	Begins when hand or body member causes part to begin to line up or locate. Consists of hand or body member causing part to line up, orient, or change position. Ends when body member has part lined up.
Preposition	PP	Sky blue	Same as position, except used when lineup is previous to use of part or tool in another place.
Use	U	Purple	Begins when hand or body member actually begins to manipulate tool or control. Consists of applying tool or manipulating control. Ends when hand or body member ceases manipulating tool or control.
Assemble	A	Heavy violet	Begins when the hand of body member causes parts to begin to go together. Consists of actual assembly of parts. Ends when hand or body member has caused parts to go together.
Disassemble	DA	Light violet	Begins when hand or body member causes parts that were integral to begin to separate. Consists of taking objects apart. Ends when hand or body member has caused complete separation.
Release load	RL	Carmine red	Begins when hand or body member begins to relax control of object. Consists of letting go of an object. Ends when hand or body member has lost contact with object.
Transport empty	TE	Olive green	Begins when hand or body member begins to move without load. Consists of reaching for something. Ends when hand or body member touches part or stops moving.
Transport loaded	TL	Grass green	Begins when hand or body member begins to move with an object. Consists of hand or body member's changing location of an object. Ends when hand or body member carrying object arrives at general destination or movement ceases.
Search	SH	Black	Begins when hand or body member gropes or hunts for part. Consists of attempting to find an object. Ends when hand or body member has found location of object.

TABLE 9.4   (Cont.)

THERBLIG	SYMBOL	COLOR	DEFINITION
Select	ST	Light gray	Begins when hand or body member touches several objects. Consists of locating an individual object from a group. Ends when hand or body member has located an individual object.
Hold	H	Gold ochre	Begins when movement of part of object, which hand or body member has under control, ceases. Consists of holding an object in a fixed position and location. Ends with any movement.
Unavoidable delay	UD	Yellow ochre	Begins when hand or body member is idle. Consists of a delay for other body member or machine when delay is part of method. Ends when hand or body member begins any work.
Avoidable delay	AD	Lemon yellow	Begins when hand or body member deviates from standard method. Consists of some movement or idleness not part of method. Ends when hand or body member returns to standard routine.
Rest for overcoming fatigue	R	Orange	Begins when hand or body member is idle. Consists of idleness that is part of cycle and necessary to overcome fatigue from previous work. Ends when hand or body member is able to work again.
Plan	PN	Brown	Begins when hand or body members are idle or making random movements while worker decides on course of action. Consists of determining a course of action. Ends when course of action is determined.
Inspect	I	Burnt ochre	Begins when hand or body member begins to feel or view an object. Consists of determining a quality of an object. Ends when hand or body member has stopped to see an object.

developed the film-analysis technique). These 17 therbligs are common to all human activity, and provide a most convenient set of categories for the classification of all physical motions and for use as a framework for the classification of basic ways of improving these motions. Table 9.4 presents the definitions and symbols of the therbligs. Note that a specific color is assigned to each therblig.

Memomotion analysis is the name given to the analysis of the special forms of film or video-tape study in which pictures are taken at unusually slow speeds. Sixty frames per minute and 100 frames per minute are the speeds most commonly used. The analysis requires three phases: filming, film analysis, and graphic presentation.

The primary fields of use of memomotion analysis is work with long or irregular cycles or with coordinated crews, for long-period studies, or for any combination of these. Memomotion study may also be used to examine the flow of material or the use of materials-handling equipment in an area, or to study simultaneously the human work, equipment usage, and flow of material. In such cases, if a time-shortened visual presentation is desired, film must be used or a special film made from the tape record. In this way, many hours of activity can be viewed in several minutes. The information contained on the film may be analyzed in numerous ways, and alternative presentations of the data in graphic form are possible, depending on the objectives of the study.

SUMMARY

Designing work systems is an important responsibility of the operations manager. Designing work systems involves job design and job analysis.

Both the scientific management school and the behavioral school influence eventual job design. The first suggests simplification and extreme specialization, the latter suggests job enrichment coupled with robotics to help alleviate boring and monotonous jobs and increase productivity. Proper job design, work environment, and safety awareness are important factors that improve the quality of working life.

Job analysis starts with the total operation, checks individual jobs, and improves methods of performing job elements, called tasks. Job analysis tools include flow process charts, flow diagrams, operation charts, multiple-activity charts, and motion economy methods. These tools help in studying and improving an existing job and in designing new jobs.

DISCUSSION QUESTIONS

9.1   What is job design?

9.2   What is job analysis?

9.3   Describe the sociotechnical systems approach.

9.4   List the methods used for job analysis.

9.5   Define "operation chart" and describe the steps involved in preparing one.

9.6   What are the symbols used in operation charts?

9.7   Define multiple-activity charts.

9.8   What are the two kinds of flow process charts?

9.9 Present a flow diagram of your typical day. Are there any conclusions that can be drawn from the flow diagram?

9.10 What are the major factors considered in motion economy?

9.11 What is job simplification?

9.12 What are the advantages of job simplification?

9.13 What are the disadvantages of job simplification?

9.14 What is job enrichment?

9.15 What are the major conclusions in regard to job enrichment?

PROBLEMS AND SOLUTIONS

9.1 The maintenance man of Western Cable Harness and Crimping, Inc., has a daily route to follow. On that route, he lubricates and inspects all machinery and structural components of the building. Based on the following figure, build an employee flow process chart. Assume that the employee stops next to each "x."

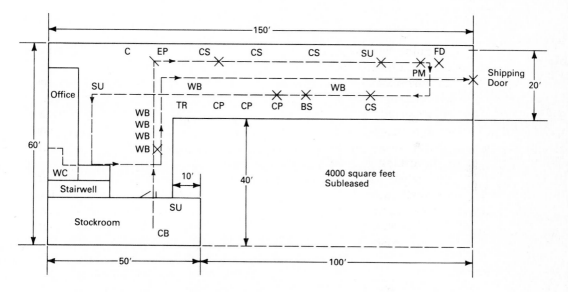

Western Cable Harness and Crimping, Inc., Plant Layout

Key:

C	Compressor		BS	Band saw
CB	Conveyor belt		CS	Cutting and stripping machine
CP	Connector press		TR	Tool rack
CS_1	Circular saw		WB	Work Bench
EP	Electrical panel		SU	Shelving Unit
FD	Fusing device for bundling wires		PM	Paint Machine

Solution

FLOW PROCESS CHART

Q *estion each step . . .*	WHAT WHEN WHERE WHO HOW } WHY?	CHART IS – [X] Present Method ☐ Proposed Method	PAGE NO / NO OF PAGES

PROCESS BEING CHARTED

SUMMARY	PRESENT		PROPOSED		DIFFERENCE	
	NO.	TIME (min.)	NO.	TIME (min.)	NO.	TIME (min.)
O Operation	9					
⟳ Transportation	9					
☐ Inspection						
D Delay						
▽ Storage						
Total Steps & Time						
Distance		ft.		ft.		ft.

(check one and describe)
☐ Employee ☐ Product

CHART BEGINS – Walk to Work Bench

CHART ENDS – Lubricate Shipping Door

CHARTED BY / DATE

DEPT. OR DIV   Western Cable

SECTION OR LOCATION

STEPS IN PROCESS	OPERATION / TRANSP / INSPECTION / DELAY / STORAGE / Distance (ft.) / Time (min.) / ELIMINATE / COMBINE / SEQUENCE / PLACE / PERSON / IMPROVE	NOTES
1. To Work Bench (WB)	O ⟳ ☐ D ▽	
2. Lubricate/Inspect Work Bench	⊗ ⟳ ☐ D ▽	
3. To Circular Saw (CS)	O ⟳ ☐ D ▽	
4. Lubricate/Inspect Circular Saw	⊗ ⟳ ☐ D ▽	
5. To Shelving Unit (SV)	O ⟳ ☐ D ▽	
6. Inspect SV	⊗ ⟳ ☐ D ▽	
7. To Paint Machine (PM)	O ⟳ ☐ D ▽	
8. Lubricate/Inspect PM	⊗ ⟳ ☐ D ▽	
9. To Cutting/Stripping Machine (CS)	O ⟳ ☐ D ▽	
10. Lubricate/Inspect CS	⊗ ⟳ ☐ D ▽	
11. To Band Saw (BS	O ⟳ ☐ D ▽	
12. Lubricate/Inspect BS	⊗ ⟳ ☐ D ▽	
13. To Connector Press (CP)	O ⟳ ☐ D ▽	
14. Lubricate/Inspect CP	⊗ ⟳ ☐ D ▽	
15. To Shipping Door (SD)	O ⟳ ☐ D ▽	
16. Lubricate/Inspect SD	⊗ ⟳ ☐ D ▽	
17.	O ⟳ ☐ D ▽	
18.	O ⟳ ☐ D ▽	
19.	O ⟳ ☐ D ▽	
20.	O ⟳ ☐ D ▽	

9.2   Prepare a right-hand–left-hand operation chart for signing a purchase order.

Solution

Left-Hand Activity	Symbol	Symbol	Right-Hand Activity
Ready for Purchase Order	⇨	⇨	Reach for pen
Wait	D	O	Grasp pen
Wait	D	⇨	Move pen to paper
Hold Purchase Order	▽	O	Position pen to sign
Hold Purchase Order	▽	O	Sign purchase order
Wait	D	⇨	Move pen to side
Wait	D	O	Put pen aside

Summary of Frequency

Symbol	Left	Right
O	—	4
⇨	1	3
D	4	—
▽	2	—

CHAPTER REVIEW PROBLEMS

9.1   Long-Haul Excavating Company is engaged in a construction project for which several dump trucks and a power shovel are used. The following is given:

Time to load a truck	15 minutes
Travel time to dump site	18 minutes
Dumping time	4 minutes
Travel time for return	14 minutes

a) How many dump trucks should be used so that the job will be finished as soon as possible?

    b) If the cost for the power shovel and operator is \$38/hour, and the cost for each truck and driver is \$24/hour, what number of trucks will minimize idle equipment cost?

    c) Construct a multiple-activity chart for (b).

9.2   Dave Hopkins, infamous management consultant specializing in simplifying work, watched an office procedure in the Marathon Manufacturing Company. He noticed that when production supplies are running low, the production supervisor fills out an order requisition form. This requisition is then placed in his out-basket, and is later picked up by the office clerk. The office clerk takes the invoice down to the plant secretary. The invoice remains in the secretary's in-basket until he is ready to type the requisition. The requisition is then typed and given to the superintendent of operations. After awaiting approval, the requisition is examined and approved by the superintendent. The office clerk then takes the requisition to the purchasing department. The requisition is examined and approved by the purchasing agent. The invoice remains on the purchasing agent's desk until picked up by the office clerk. The office clerk returns the invoice to the plant-secretary for typing of a purchase order. After typing the purchase order, the secretary attaches the order requisition to the purchase order, and drops it in his out-basket. It is later picked up by the office clerk and taken to the head office.

    a) Construct a process chart for this office procedure.

    b) Construct a process chart for an improved procedure.

9.3   Construct a right-hand–left-hand operation chart for cutting a piece of paper with scissors.

READING
France Makes Renault its Model

What is good for Régie Nationale des Usines Renault, France's Socialist government believes, is good for French industry. Like other carmakers in Europe and the U.S., Renault is suffering from the worldwide auto slump. At the company's board meeting on May 25, Chairman and Chief Executive Officer Bernard Hanon was preparing to announce a \$100 million net loss in 1981 on worldwide consolidated sales of \$16.6 billion (chart), including Renault's 46.6% interest in American Motors Corp. Yet government-owned Renault—France's second-largest industrial company and the world's No. 7 auto maker—is the model officials are holding up for emulation by five newly nationalized industrial groups. . . .

    In France, the auto maker played its role as a model company this spring by signing the largest-yet "solidarity contract," a type of agreement that the government has been urging all French companies, publicly as well as privately owned, to adopt as a means of creating new jobs. In the year that started May 1, Renault agreed to give early retirement to 3,500 employees aged 55 years or older and to replace them with an equal number of new employees. "It was a free choice to join in this national effort," Personnel Director Max Richard insists. "It will be a difficult year, and if we had been pessimistic we would not have been able to do it."

Although the government will pick up part of the tab, the operation will cost Renault at least $40 million. But Richard says the deal will enable Renault to adapt its 100,000—strong automotive work force more effectively to future conditions to reduce the average age of workers, and to allow internal promotion.

Traditionally, Renault has been a French pacesetter in improving working conditions and in labor-management relations. But "we want to do that at the same time we reduce costs," Hanon adds. Increasingly, an important part of such tradeoffs between bottom-line business calculations and progressive labor relations is a major shift to automation and robots. Thanks to 124 robots, the production line for the R-9 at Douai in northern France can produce an auto in five hours less than older factories require to make the far smaller R-5. Hanon will not reveal specific production times at Douai, but he says they are "as good as anywhere in Japan." The latest

Assembly Robots in Renault's Plant

robots, developed by a Renault subsidiary, can be reprogrammed to vary production according to demand within the same working day.

The crucial importance of good labor relations in such retooling, Hanon points out, is that "progress in automation can only be achieved with the social partners, not against them." To date, Renault's policy has allowed it to deploy 254 robots, by its own definition, or 8,000, as measured by broader Japanese criteria.

That is enough to meet even the aspirations of French Research Minister Jean-Pierre Chevenement, who is pushing to create something like Japan Inc. in high-technology areas.

Questions

1. What are the reasons for Renault to "go robotics"?
2. What are the implications of this automation decision with regard to capital investment and the work force?
3. Do you think quality of working life for Renault's workers will be improved as a result of this decision?
4. What do you think should be the role of governments in the automation transformation?

BIBLIOGRAPHY

Barnes, R. M., *Motion and Time Study* (6th ed.). New York: John Wiley, 1968.

Davis, L., "The Coming Crisis for Productive Management: Technological Organization," *International Journal of Production Research*, 1, 1971.

Davis, L., and J. C. Taylor, eds., *Design of Jobs*, Middlesex, England: Penguin, 1972.

Davis, L. E., A. B. Cherns, et al., *The Quality of Working Life*. New York: Free Press, 1975.

Dickman, R. A., *Handbook for Supporting Staff, Job Analysis and Job Evaluation*. Baltimore: Johns Hopkins Press, 1971.

Fine, S., and W. W. Wiley, *Functional Job Analysis Scales*. Kalamazoo, Mich.: W. E. Upjohn Institute for Employment Research, 1973.

Fine, S., and W. W. Wiley, *An Introduction to Functional Job Analysis*. Kalamazoo, Mich.: W. E. Upjohn Institute for Employment Research, 1971.

Ford, R. N., "Job Enrichment Lessons from AT&T," *Harvard Business Review*, 51, January, 1978, pp. 96–106.

Hackman, J. R., "Is Job Enrichment Just a Fad?" *Harvard Business Review*, 53, No. 5, September–October, 1975, pp. 129–138.

Hackman, J. R., and E. E. Lawler, "Employee Reactions to Job Characteristics," *Journal of Applied Psychology*, Monograph 55, 1971, pp. 259–86.

Herzberg, F., "Job Enrichment Admits Disparity between Promise and Reality," *Industry Week*, 187, November 24, 1975, pp. 44–45.

Journal of Contemporary Business, Spring, 1977. This issue contains several good articles related to job design.

KILBRIDGE, M., and L. WEBSTER, "An Economic Model for the Division of Labor," *Management Science*, 12, No. 6, February, 1966, pp. B255–69.

McCormick, E. J., *Human Factors Engineering* (3d ed.). New York: McGraw-Hill, 1970.

MENIPAZ, E., "Operating Service Space Determination for Higher Productivity and Satisfaction," *1980 International Congress on Applied Systems Research and Cybernetics*, Acapulco, Mexico, December, 1980.

NIEBEL, B. W., *Motion and Time Study* (6th ed.). Homewood, Ill.: Richard D. Irwin, 1976.

PARKE, E. L., and C. Tousky, "Mythologies of Job Enrichment," *Personnel*, 52, September, 1975, pp. 12–21.

POWERS, J. E., "Job Enrichment: How One Company Overcame the Obstacles," *Personnel*, 49, May, 1972, pp. 18–22.

PRICE, C. R., *New Direction in the World of Work*. Kalamazoo, Mich.: W. E. Upjohn Institute for Employment Research, 1971.

REIF, W. E., and F. Luthans, "Does Job Enrichment Really Pay Off?" *California Management Review*, 15, No. 1, Fall, 1972, pp. 30-37.

SCOTT, W. E., and L. L. Cummings, *Readings in Organizational Behavior and Human Performance* (rev. ed.). Homewood, Ill.: Richard D. Irwin, 1973, pp. 126–233.

STEERS, R. M., and R. T. Mowday, "The Motivational Properties of Tasks," *Academy of Management Review*, Vol. 2, No. 4, October, 1977, pp. 645–658.

TRESKO, J., "Myths and Realities of Job Enrichment," *Industry Week*, 187, November 24, 1975, pp. 39–43.

U.S. Department of Labor, Occupational Health and Safety Administration, *All About OSHA*, OSHA Publication No. 2056.

U.S. Department of Labor, *Handbook for Analyzing Jobs*. Washington, D.C.: U.S. Government Printing Office, 1972.

Upjohn Institute for Employment Research, *Work in America*. Cambridge, Mass.: MIT Press, 1973.

WALKER, G. R., and R. H. GUEST, *The Man on the Assembly Line*. Cambridge, Mass.: Harvard University Press, 1952.

YORKS, L., "Determining Job Enrichment Feasibility," *Personnel*, November–December, 1974, pp. 18–25.

Work Measurement and Compensation

INTRODUCTION

Job design and job analysis, covered earlier, concentrate on how, where, and when to do a job. Work measurement deals with the determination of the length of the job's time.

Work measurement is defined as a set of procedures for determining the amount of time required, under certain standard conditions of measurement, for jobs involving some human activity. The result of such a measurement is called a *standard time*.

Standard times help in developing effective methods for operating systems and constrain the use of human resources, as follows:

1. They may be used to determine the number of pieces of equipment a worker may run.
2. They may be used to balance the work on an assembly line (discussed in Chapter 7). An efficient assembly line demands an even distribution of work among the work stations. The work station with the longest job determines the output rate of the line. An unequal distribution of work among the work stations can be very costly. With a 5-man work sequencer (production line), if the job in one station requires 20 percent more work than does the next longest job in another station, the work of the equivalent of at least one whole worker may well be lost.
3. They may be used to compare methods.
4. They may be used to set schedules and, as such, are vital for aggregate planning, and capacity and operations scheduling.

5. They may be used to set labor standards. Labor standards, properly determined and properly understood, are an asset to both management and labor, since they fix a level of satisfactory activity and protect the interests of both groups.

6. They may be used to determine supervisory objectives. It will also help the foreman or supervisor to determine which workers need additional training, are misplaced, or have unusual aptitudes or apply themselves with unusual diligence.

7. They may be used to provide a basis for the setting of piece rates or incentive wages. Incentive wages are a means of automatic financial supervision for both labor and management. They reward the more productive workers in proportion to their output.

8. They may assist in comparing actual with planned performance, with respect to workload and resource usage. An organization, if profit-motivated, usually prices its output units prior to the operation. To do this, it must predict how much labor time will be expended on each phase of the work, and must have a means of continuously comparing actual performance to predicted performance. For nonprofit activities such as government agencies, the same continuous comparison of plans with performance must take place.

Standards used in comparing plans with performance are expressed in time per output unit. *Unit output* is determined differently for manufacturing and service organizations.

FOR MANUFACTURING ORGANIZATIONS   In industrial organizations, where the output is substantive (that is, it consists of goods, such as home appliances, shoes, or bakery goods, as opposed to services) the concept of output units is self-explanatory.

FOR SERVICE ORGANIZATIONS   In service-type organizations or government agencies, poor methods of quantifying the output have frequently frustrated work measurement efforts, leading many to conclude that real work measurement and, consequently, real managerial control is not possible. However, this difficulty can be avoided at times by resorting to more innovative definitions of an output. For example, the number of legal cases completed by a law office or the number of lectures given by a professor may be used as output units.[1]

LABOR STANDARDS   A standard must be defined in such a manner that consistent, reliable measurements may be made. For any job on which a large number of people work, or for a group of jobs with consistent time standards, the distribution of workers and performance is as shown in Figure 10.1. Namely,

[1] This topic is treated extensively in M. W. Mundel, *Measuring and Enhancing the Productivity of Service and Government Organizations*. (Tokyo: Asian Productivity Organization, 1975).

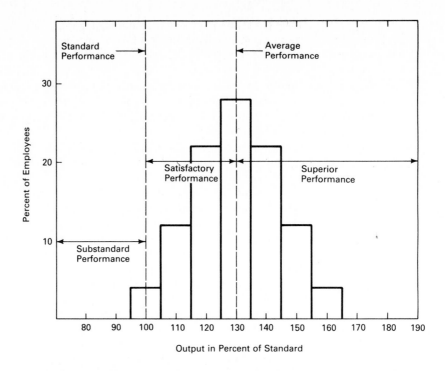

Figure 10.1. Distribution of Performance of a Large Group of Workers, with Typical Performance Denoted as 130 Percent of Standard   (Designating typical performance as 130 percent of standard is common industrial practice.)

many performances (close to thirty percent of employees), are concentrated around the average performance level, and the frequencies that are farther from the average will be lower. Only five percent of employees perform at either one hundred percent of standard or one hundred sixty percent of standard.

Once an average performance have been determined, the standard performance should be set. The operations manager is then faced with a problem. Should the standard be set at the average of total performances for the group, or at a level at which almost all workers can be expected to reach the standard?

In Figure 10.1, we define the average performance as 130 percent of standard performance. Thus, for example, if we found the average performance for a lunch-box assembly to be 130 lunch-boxes per hour, we set the standard to be 100 lunch-boxes per hour. This will assure that the majority of workers will achieve and surpass the standard.[2]

The concept of a standard time is commonly employed in work analysis, and it should be understood by both the worker and the analyst. The study of

[2] See M. E. Mundel, *Motion and Time Study: Increasing Productivity,* 5th ed. (Englewood Cliffs, New Jersey: Prentice-Hall, Inc., 1978).

jobs, and, more particularly, of tasks leads to an estimate of the time needed by an "average" person. It is assumed that figures are gathered under representative work conditions (temperature, light, work pressures, delays, etc.) and at a "normal" work pace. Thus the analyst relies on judgment or on time-value tables in at least three areas of consideration:

1. *Average person.* This seeks to take into account a fair sample of physical characteristics, intelligence, and motor abilities.
2. *Representative work conditions.* It is commonly known that work conditions can vary greatly. Such things as periodic delays involving breakdowns, lighting, temperature, shortages, absenteeism, breaks, washroom time, and meals can affect performance, and must be taken into account. Adjustments for these conditions are made by means of allowances added to the raw data, as explained later.
3. *Normal work pace.* Work analysis or tables of standard time values provide the amounts of time needed to perform operations. Such figures are based on the assumption that the pace set represents a level of energy that can be maintained over extended periods of time without undue fatigue. It is further assumed that the employee has been adequately trained for the job, and that he or she displays only those time variations in the work cycle that typically accompany work startup and fatigue.

Figure 10.2 depicts energy-time relationships for the course of a typical day of a worker who is already familiar with a job. For example, the chart indicates that many workers reach a type of daily "high" at 11 a.m. (thus the accuracy of the remark, common among workers: "I don't really wake up until 11 a.m." Time measurement does take variations like the one in Figure 10.2 into account. Time study techniques assume a fixed time to do the job without regard to the time of the day.

All time study techniques are procedures for obtaining four kinds of data. These are:

1. Work time (WT)
2. Work count associated with the work time (number of units of goods or services produced over work time) (WC)
3. A performance rating (M) used to adjust the observation of work time with respect to an "average" worker (that is, if a worker is observed to work 30 percent faster than the average worker, his or her performance rating is 1.30)
4. An allowance (A) used to adjust the standard time to accommodate for difficulty, fatigue, and rest (see Table 10.2).

Based on WT, WC, and M, one determines normal time (NT),

$$NT = \frac{WT}{WC} \times M \tag{10.1}$$

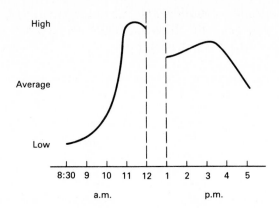

Figure 10.2 Worker-Cycle Variations (variations in worker energy expenditures over a single work day)

Based on the normal time, the standard time (*ST*) is calculated:

$$ST = NT \times A \tag{10.2}$$

The techniques of time study may be divided, in terms of general source of the necessary data, into five categories:

Direct time study—intensive sampling (sometimes called *stopwatch study*)   This is a procedure in which the performance of a job is observed directly and continuously for a limited period of time. Data concerning the work time and associated work count are recorded, together with an appraisal of the performance in comparison with the standard concept of performance. Later, an allowance for nonwork is added in conformance with the organization's policies.

Direct time study—extensive sampling (sometimes called *work sampling*)   Similar to the direct time study—intensive sampling. However, instead of continuously observing the job and recording the time at the end of each separated task element, the job is observed at intervals. Performance is rated and marked down at each observation. Later, an allowance is added.

Predetermined time standards   These standards are set by using task performance time data that have been obtained from a careful analysis of human performance. This enables the operations manager to synthesize a standard time for a job, even when the job is entirely different from those previously studied (among the most popular standard is methods-time measurement—MTM.)

Not all of these methods can be applied in all situations. As a simple illustration, a cognitive task (such as conceiving new laws) can seldom be studied by direct observational techniques; one cannot observe the thinking process. In general, the different techniques vary in:

1. Accuracy
2. Ease of studying jobs in which the cycle varies significantly
3. Manpower required to set the standard.

DIRECT TIME STUDY—INTENSIVE SAMPLING

Direct time study—intensive sampling is a procedure in which the performance of a job is observed directly and continuously for a limited period of time. Data are recorded concerning the work time (*WT*), together with an appraisal of the performance in comparison with the standard concept of performance (*M*). An allowance for nonwork time is usually added in conformance with Table 10.1 and with policies that have been established by the organization and the union. All these data are used to compute a standard time, as per equations 10.1 and 10.2.

The procedure is also termed "direct time study" or "stopwatch time study" (a misleading term, as in many cases, stopwatches are not used).

TABLE 10.1 NUMBER OF OBSERVATIONS REQUIRED FOR ±5 PERCENT, VARIABILITY OF THE DATA ABOUT ITS AVERAGE, AND 95 PERCENT CONFIDENCE LEVEL FOR INTENSIVE SAMPLING

$\dfrac{H-L}{H+L}$	DATA FROM SAMPLE OF: 5	10	$\dfrac{H-L}{H+L}$	DATA FROM SAMPLE OF: 5	10	$\dfrac{H-L}{H+L}$	DATA FROM SAMPLE OF: 5	10
0.05	3	1	0.21	52	30	0.36	154	88
0.06	4	2	0.22	57	33	0.37	162	93
0.07	6	3	0.23	63	36	0.38	171	98
0.08	8	4	0.24	68	39	0.39	180	103
0.09	10	5	0.25	74	42	0.40	190	108
0.10	12	7	0.26	80	46	0.41	200	114
0.11	14	8	0.27	86	49	0.42	210	120
0.12	17	10	0.28	93	53	0.43	220	126
0.13	20	11	0.29	100	57	0.44	230	132
0.14	23	13	0.30	107	61	0.45	240	138
0.15	27	15	0.31	114	65	0.46	250	144
0.16	30	17	0.32	121	69	0.47	262	150
0.17	34	20	0.33	129	74	0.48	273	156
0.18	38	22	0.34	137	78	0.49	285	163
0.19	43	24	0.35	145	83	0.50	296	170
0.20	47	27						

Note: For ±10 percent, variability of the data about the average, and 95 percent confidence level, divide the answers by 4.

"Direct" refers to the directness with which actual observations are recorded with motion picture, video-tape recorder, or time study device; "time study" refers to the setting of standard times. The results of direct time study—intensive sampling are sometimes referred to as "engineered standards."

Direct time study—intensive sampling is primarily employed when the job for which a standard time is sought is repetitive. Repetitive work is work with a cyclic pattern that is repeated over an extended period of time. The use of the technique is limited to manual, repetitive work that is actually being performed; the technique may not be used to set a standard prior to the start of work. However, a short experimental run may suffice to provide the necessary data. If a large variety of cycles that are not repeated in a limited time are employed, other techniques, such as direct time study—extensive sampling, may well be preferable.

There are five distinct steps in the setting of a standard time by means of direct time study—intensive sampling. They are:

1. Recording the standard practice; describing the products or services
2. Observing and recording the work time taken by a particular operator, together with data concerning the associated work count
3. Performance rating or relating performance to the standard; determining the modifier (or rating) M
4. Determining allowances; determining the adjustment factor A
5. Calculating the standard time by using equations 10.1, 10.2

Recording the Standard Practice

In actually describing a job for time study, it is usually desirable to break the job down into steps referred to as time study elements, or tasks. The use of an element breakdown, as will be seen subsequently, facilitates timing and the later use of the time for the development of standard elemental data for synthesized standards.

The elements, which will be timed separately, should be chosen so that:

1. They are easily detected and have definite end points.
2. They are as small as is convenient, in terms of timing. When stopwatches are used, the smallest practical unit is about 0.04 minute, or 3 seconds. If motion-picture films or video-tapes are taken and later analyzed, a much smaller time unit is possible.
3. They are as unified as possible. The element should consist of a well-unified group of motions, such as "reach for an object," "take hold of it," "move it," and "place it."

An operator may possess to different degrees the different skills required by the various steps of a job; thus, his or her performance on each step is best judged when the steps are separated.

4. Hand work time is separated from machine work time. Hand time is subject to the control of the operator; machine time, with automatic feeds or fixed speeds, is not.
5. Internal work time is separated from external work time. Hand work done while the machine or process controls the total elapsed time (internal time) should be separated from hand work done while only the hand work controls the total elapsed time (external time).
6. Regular and foreign elements are separated.

Foreign data may occur during time recording. Foreign data may be caused by such occurrences as: a fumble during an element, a false movement, a personal movement (such as scratching), a minor machine adjustment or repair, and faulty work due to low skill, to faulty movements, or to poor material. Any element containing such variation or any variation from the prescribed pattern of motions should be marked so as to identify it on the time study sheet.

The foreign element should be handled in the following ways:

1. If it is not a necessary part of the job or if it represents wrong movements or work improperly done, the recorded time value should be discarded and should have no influence on the final result.
2. If it is inherent in the task (e.g., fumbles with tangled material), it should be allowed to remain in the study.
3. If it is an irregular occurrence (e.g., faulty material or a machine adjustment), it should be evaluated separately and added to the final time standard in proportion to its rate of occurrence.

The data can be recorded on a form such as the one presented in Figure 10.3. R indicates the cumulative reading on the stopwatch, while T indicates the actual elemental time found by subtracting two consecutive cumulative readings.

What constitutes a representative or reliable sample is mathematically determined. We must realize that there is almost invariably some difference from reading to reading for any element, even if the worker is not attempting to vary his or her pace.

For any observed pace of performance, timings of 10 cycles will tend to produce a more stable average than will readings of five cycles; an average of 15 timings will tend to be better than an average of 10, and so forth. However, too many readings would be unduly expensive. Therefore, it would be reasonable to require only enough to ensure that the chances are 95 out of 100 that we are within ±5 percent of the true average for the element, for the pace at which it was performed. Some may prefer a looser criterion of: 95 chances out of 100, ±10 percent. In the latter case, the odds may be restated as: 68 out of 100, ±5 percent. If the time studies are to be used for incentive wages, either of these are reasonable minimum reliabilities, since ±5 or 10 percent usually approximate a

FIGURE 10.3 STOPWATCH TIME STUDY OF A KEYPUNCH OPERATION MADE BY THE CONTINUOUS METHOD

OBSERVATION SHEET

Sheet 1 of 1 sheets		Date 1/1/83
Operation Computer Card	Keypunch	Op. No. D-20
Job Name Civil Center	Payroll	Job No. MS-267
Equipment Name	IBM Keypunch	Equipment No. 3400
Operator's Name & No.	S. K. Adams 1347	Male ___ Female x
Experience on job	18 mo.	
Foreman	H. Kadz	Dept. No. DL24

BEGIN 9:15	FINISH 9:38		9:38	ELAPSED 23		CARDS FINISHED 20		ACTUAL TIME PER 100 115				NO. OF EQUIPMENT PIECES OPERATED 1		
Speed	Feed		1	2	3	4	5	6	7	8	9	10	Selected Time
Elements													
1. Pick up card place in machine		T	0.12	0.11	0.12	0.13	0.12	0.10	0.12	0.12	0.14	0.12	
		R	0.12	1.29	2.39	3.54	4.66	5.77	6.92	8.01	9.14	10.32	
2. Tighten set key		T	0.13	0.12	0.12	0.14	0.11	0.12	0.12	0.13	0.12	0.11	
		R	0.25	1.41	2.51	3.68	4.77	5.89	7.04	8.14	9.26	10.43	
3. Advance card		T	0.05	0.04	0.04	0.04	0.05	0.04	0.04	0.04	0.03	0.04	
		R	0.30	1.45	2.55	3.72	4.82	5.93	7.08	8.18	9.29	10.47	
4. Keypunch	980 Hand	T	0.67	0.54	0.56	0.51	0.54	0.58	0.52	0.53	0.59	0.56	
		R	0.87	1.99	3.11	4.23	5.36	6.51	7.60	8.71	9.88	11.03	

Element	T/R	1	2	3	4	5	6	7	8	9	10	11
5. Inspect	T	0.04	0.03	0.03	0.03	0.03	0.03	0.03	0.03	0.04	0.03	
	R	0.91	2.02	3.14	4.26	5.39	6.54	7.63	8.74	9.92	11.06	
6. Advance Card	T	0.06	0.06	0.07	0.06	0.06	0.06	0.06	0.06	0.07	0.08	
	R	0.97	2.08	3.21	4.32	5.45	6.60	7.69	8.80	9.99	11.14	
7. Eject Card	T	0.08	0.09	0.08	0.08	0.09	0.08	0.07	0.08	0.09	0.07	
	R	1.05	2.17	3.29	4.40	5.54	6.68	7.76	8.88	10.08	11.21	
8. Place card in tray	T	0.13	0.10	0.12	0.14	0.13	0.12	0.13	0.12	0.12	0.11	
	R	1.18	2.27	3.41	4.54	5.67	6.80	7.89	9.00	10.20	11.32	
9.	T											
	R											
10. (1)	T	0.12	0.11	0.13	0.14	0.12	0.12	0.11	0.13	0.12	0.12	0.12
	R	11.44	12.56	13.69	14.82	15.87	17.01	18.09	19.21	20.31	21.42	
11. (2)	T	0.12	0.14	0.12	0.11	0.12	0.10	0.13	0.15	0.12	0.11	0.12
	R	11.56	12.70	13.81	14.93	15.99	17.11	18.22	19.36	20.43	21.53	
12. (3)	T	0.04	0.04	0.04	0.03	0.04	0.04	0.04	0.04	0.04	0.04	0.04
	R	11.60	12.74	13.85	14.96	16.03	17.15	18.26	19.40	20.47	21.57	
13. (4)	T	0.54	0.53	0.55	0.52	0.57	0.54	0.50	0.53	0.55	0.54	0.54
	R	12.14	13.27	14.40	15.48	16.60	17.69	18.76	19.93	21.02	22.11	
14. (5)	T	0.03	0.03	0.03	0.03	0.03	0.03	0.03	0.03	0.03	0.03	0.03
	R	12.17	13.30	14.43	15.51	16.63	17.72	18.79	19.96	21.05	22.14	
15. (6)	T	0.06	0.06	0.06	0.07	0.06	0.05	0.06	0.06	0.06	0.06	0.06
	R	12.23	13.36	14.49	15.58	16.69	17.77	18.85	20.02	21.10	22.20	

FIGURE 10.3 (Cont.)

16. (7)	T	0.08	0.08	0.09	0.08	0.08	0.07	0.08	0.06	0.08	0.08	0.08
	R	12.31	13.44	14.58	15.66	16.77	17.84	18.93	20.08	21.18	22.28	
17. (8)	T	0.14	0.12	0.10	0.09	0.12	0.14	0.15	0.11	0.12	0.12	0.12
	R	12.45	13.56	14.68	15.75	16.89	17.98	19.08	20.19	21.30	22.40	
18.	T											
	R											1.11

Observed time 1.11	Performance Rating 100%	Normal Time 1.11	Total Allowances 15%	Standard Time 1.2765

Tools, jigs, gauges:

Hand Feed

Timed by: Joe Doe

446

bargainable increment in wages. Errors of more than this magnitude are to be avoided.

Measures have been developed for determining the probable accuracy of a sample. These may be adapted to fit this time study problem conveniently.

A certain procedure is suitable for application on the shop floor while the study is being made. In this procedure,

H = Highest value in a sample of readings of correct performances of an element.

L = Lowest value in a sample of readings of correct performances of an element.

$\overline{H\text{-}L}$ = The average difference between high and low values in samples of correct readings of an element.

Table 10.1 is used to determine the number of observations required.

To use Table 10.1, the time study observer, by inspection, takes the H and L values from either the first 5 or the first 10 readings of an element, as available, and computes the value $(H - L)/(H + L)$. (It is to be noted that 10 values form a good basis for using Table 10.1 in order to determine the appropriate number of readings, although 10 readings are seldom an adequate sample on which to base the final average.) Using the table and this value and sample size, the time study observer may derive an estimate of the required number of readings without further computation.

EXAMPLE   In the drilling operation for the element "Pick up piece and place in jig," for the first 10 times:

$$H = 0.14$$

$$L = 0.11$$

$$\frac{H - L}{H + L} = \frac{0.14 - 0.11}{0.14 + 0.11} = 0.12$$

For this value, based on a sample of 10, Table 10.1 indicates that 10 readings are required. This is fewer than the 20 readings taken on the form.

As an alternative procedure, the readings may be divided into samples of 5, and $\overline{H - L/H + L}$ used with the table.

First five times: 0.12, 0.11, 0.12, 0.13, 0.12

$$H - L = 0.13 - 0.11 = 0.02$$

$$H + L = 0.13 + 0.11 = 0.24$$

Second five times: 0.10, 0.12, 0.12, 0.14, 0.12

$$H - L = 0.14 - 0.10 = .04$$

$$H + L = 0.14 + 0.10 = 0.24$$

$$\overline{H - L} = \frac{0.02 + 0.04}{2} = 0.03$$

$$\overline{H + L} = \frac{0.24 + 0.24}{2} = .24$$

$$\frac{\overline{H - L}}{\overline{H + L}} = \frac{0.03}{0.24} = 0.125$$

The number of readings required is between 10 and 11, compared with the former 10.

In Figure 10.3, the actual element times for each element are computed by subtraction, assuming that continuous timing was used. Thus the time element 3 in the first cycle is 0.05 (0.30 − 0.25). The elemental times are added, and the total is divided by the number of observations, to yield the time for each element. The units of time used (seconds, decimal hours, or minutes) should be noted.

The statistical reliability should be calculated and used to decide whether to proceed further with the calculations.

Use of the arithmetic average (instead of other values such as median and mode, used by some time study observers) is suggested because it is the only figure that is representative of the total sample of observations. It is also simple to compute, and includes both high and low values, which, if they represent valid performances of the elements, certainly should be included in the representative measure. Also, as was shown earlier, the representativeness of this measure may be evaluated.

Performance Rating Determination (M)   It should be obvious that in practically all real situations, the observed operator is neither of the type specified by the definition of standard, nor working at the pace required for standard performance. Hence, two questions remain:

1. How should one evaluate the performance observed, as compared with the requirements given in the definition of standard used as the basis of the measurement?
2. How can one reduce this evaluation to a mathematical value (M) that will allow the adjusting (if necessary) of the average time values actually obtained, so as to determine a base for a standard time?

Solving these problems are the aims of rating.

Performance rating is determined in the following manner. A performance (speed) level is selected as a standard. An analyst compares the performance level with other performance levels and judges it in terms of the percent of standard performance level. For the example in Figure 10.3 the performance level is assumed 100 percent. Thus, marked under normal conditions at normal speed the job takes 1.2765 minutes.

The rating is determined during the actual time recording. Once the rating has been determined, the following relation applies:

$$\text{Normal time} = \{\text{Average observed time per product}\} \times \{\text{Performance rating}\}$$
$$(10.3)$$

Here we assume that performance rating is expressed in percentages.

Calculating Standard Time

$$\text{Standard time} = \text{Normal time} + \text{Standard personal allowance} + \text{Irregular occurrences allowance} \qquad (10.4)$$

In Figure 10.3, the total allowances are marked as 15 percent of normal time; thus, the standard time is:

$$1.11 \ (1.00 + 0.15) = 1.2765 \text{ minutes}.$$

DIRECT TIME STUDY—EXTENSIVE SAMPLING

In any office or plant, there are usually jobs that appear to possess no cycle or repetitive pattern. Supervisory jobs tend to fall into this category. Many clerical, service, and maintenance jobs fit into a similar classification. For jobs such as these, two techniques are available:

1. Extensive work sampling
2. Memomotion study (discussed in Chapter 9).

An extensive work sampling study, or, in short, work sampling, consists of a large number of observations taken at random intervals. In taking the observations, the state or condition of the worker is noted by using predefined categories of activity pertinent to the particular work situation (for example: work, walk, set up). From the proportions of observations in each category, inferences are drawn concerning the total work activity under study.

Work sampling observations do not record the sequence of tasks, but can be made in an intermittent fashion and do not constitute a heavy workload. Hence, work sampling studies are often used to cover an extended period. On jobs in which the daily pattern is very different from day to day, as in maintenance jobs, work sampling yields, for a given amount of study effort, a complete picture.

The technique may reveal the following:

1. The need for a change in tasks assigned to an individual
2. The parts of the job (tasks) that take up enough of the total time to merit a detailed study using other techniques, such as process charts and operation charts (see Chapter 9).

Work sampling, may be done by the worker or supervisor rather than by a staff analyst.

STEPS IN THE WORK-SAMPLING PROCEDURE

The first step in work sampling is to define and prepare a list of the states or conditions in which the worker can be found (work, walk, set up). The particular listing selected should be related to the object of the study. As a general principle, however, one should bear in mind that excess details obtained may be subsequently combined, but states that have not been separately identified when making the study cannot subsequently be separated.

The second step in work sampling is to determine a suitable number of randomized observation times. The total number of observations made must be sufficient to obtain a reliable sample of recordings. The recordings may be spread out over a number of days. The number of observations required may be computed after one has determined the objective of the study. If we are merely seeking insight into the job, low precision of the percentage may be satisfactory. Studies in which we may be seeking percentages to apply in work measurements affecting wages or job analysis and design require much more accuracy.

The basic principle behind work sampling is that the number of observations in each category is proportional to the amount of time actually spent by the worker in each category. Let:

X = number observed in that category
N = total number of observations

Thus the mean proportion $\bar{p}$ is:

$$\bar{p} = \frac{X}{N}$$

and the variability (standard deviation) of the value of $\bar{p}$, SD_p, is:

$$SD_p = \sqrt{\frac{\bar{p}(1 - \bar{p})}{N}}$$

Using Figure 10.4, one determines the number of observations required for a given value of p and the precision required at the 95 percent confidence level. For example, to maintain a precision of p within ± 1.0 percent at 95 percent

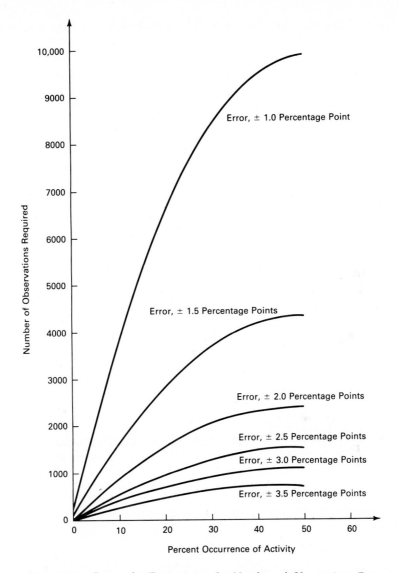

Figure 10.4 Curves for Determining the Number of Observations Required To Maintain Precision Within the Percentage Points Indicated at 95 Percent Confidence Level for Extensive Sampling

confidence level, 6000 observations are required if $\bar{p}$ is approximately 20 percent (that is, to be 95 percent sure that the actual p is between 19 and 20 percent, 6000 observations should be taken). Only 3000 observations are required if we want to be 95 percent sure that actual p is between 18.5 and 21.5 percent. In general, the lower the required precision, the fewer observations are required.

The third step in work sampling involves the planning of the observation times. When we decided upon the total number of observations to be made, we may divide this either by the number of observations that it is convenient to make per day, or by the number of days we wish to study. Dividing by the number of observations it is convenient to make per day gives us the number of days we must study. Dividing by the number of days we wish to study gives us the required number of observations per day.

The actual observation times must be arranged in a random pattern. There are several methods of doing this:

1. The first hour of the working day may be identified by the numeral 1, the second hour by the numeral 2, and so on. A table of random numbers is used to obtain a series of three-digit figures, the first digit representing the hour of the working day, and the next two digits, representing the minutes. A first digit representing hours not in the working day is discarded. Impossible minute values (whose last two digits are higher than 59) are discarded. A sufficient number is obtained to give the required number of observation times for each day of the study. Each day should have a separate list. For example, let 8 a.m. be designated by the number 1, 9 a.m. by 2, and so forth, down to 4 p.m. by 9. Now, we use Table E in the Appendix of this book to generate random numbers. Based on Table E, the following list of observation times is produced.

RANDOM NUMBERS FROM TABLE E IN APPENDIX	INTERPRETATION
217	9:17 a.m.
767	Impossible minute value; discard.
793	Impossible minute value; discard.
804	3:04 p.m.
887	Impossible minute value; discard.
282	Impossible minute value; discard.
879	Impossible minute value; discard.
423	11:23 a.m.
909	4:09 p.m.
215	9:15 a.m.
155	8:55 a.m.
040	Impossible hour value; discard.
312	10:12 a.m.
964	Impossible minute value; discard.
521	12:21 p.m.
286	Impossible minute value; discard.
549	12:49 p.m.
288	Impossible minute value; discard.
816	3:16 p.m.
955	4:55 p.m.
388	Impossible minute value; discard.

For actual use, the list of observation times should be much longer, and should be arranged in time sequence. The observation times are: 8:55 a.m., 9:15 a.m., 9:17 a.m., 10:12 a.m., 11:23 a.m., 12:21 p.m., 12:49 p.m., 3:16 p.m., 4:09 p.m., and 4:55 p.m.

2. A second method of arranging observation times in a random pattern is to specify the observation by hours. To do this, we divide the number of observations to be made per day by the number of working hours. Following this, we again use the random-number table to give us two-digit figures to represent the minutes for each hour. Using the same working day as before, and the same values from the random-number table, the following would result, for one observation per hour:

RANDOM NUMBERS	INTERPRETATION
21	8:21 a.m.
76	Impossible minute value; discard.
79	Impossible minute value; discard.
80	Impossible minute value; discard.
88	Impossible minute value; discard.
28	9:28 p.m.
87	Impossible minute value; discard.

The list is in chronological order. If more than one observation per hour is required, the values for each hour will need rearrangement for actual use. Each day should have a different list of time values.

3. If a large number of observations is required, an observer may go continuously through the area in which the observations are to be made, randomizing his or her route but constantly making observations.

4. A series of cards (i.e., 3-by-5-inch file cards) may be used. We may number these cards in order, one for each minute of the working day (8:01, 8:02, 8:03, and so on). The cards may then be shuffled, and a list prepared for a day by taking the necessary number off the top of the pile. The times are then arranged in time sequence. The cards used are then returned to the deck, and the procedure is repeated for each day to be studied.

In order to determine the labor standard based on work sampling, we have to know also the total number of pieces produced or services rendered, and the performance rating for each observation of work time. The normal time is:

$$\text{Normal time} = \frac{\begin{array}{c}\text{Total time of} \\ \text{study in minutes}\end{array} \times \begin{array}{c}\text{Proportion of work} \\ \text{time in decimals from} \\ \text{work sampling study}\end{array} \times \begin{array}{c}\text{Average} \\ \text{performance} \\ \text{rating in decimals}\end{array}}{\text{Total number of pieces produced or services rendered}}$$

$$(10.5)$$

The standard time is:

Standard time = (normal time) + (Allowances for delays, fatigue, and personal time) + (Irregular occurrences allowances)   (10.6)

EXAMPLE   A study by the AT&T regional telecommunication office determined the following:

Total time of study in minutes = 480 minutes

Proportional work time from sampling study = 84 percent

Average performance rating = 110 percent of what is expected from an average worker under normal conditions

Allowances = 20 percent

Total number of services rendered (i.e., number of cables and night letters sent) = 100

$$\text{Normal time} = \frac{(480)(0.84)(1.10)}{100} = 4.435 \text{ minutes/service}$$

$$\text{Standard time} = 4.435 + (0.20)(4.435) = 5.32 \text{ minutes/service}$$

Typical allowances applicable to both intensive and extensive sampling are given in Table 10.2. One must add all applicable allowances from the top down.

PREDETERMINED TIME STANDARDS

Such standards involve the use of published data on standard elemental times. A popular system is method-time measurement (MTM), which was developed during the 1940's by the Methods Engineering Council. MTM tables are based on research of many basic elemental motions and times. The steps involved in MTM are:

1. Divide the job into basic elements (e.g., reach, move, turn, disengage).
2. Measure the distance involved.
3. Rate the difficulty of the element.
4. Consult the appropriate table of data to obtain time for the element.
5. Find standard time for the job by adding the times for all the basic elements.

TABLE 10.2 TYPICAL ALLOWANCE PERCENTAGES FOR VARIOUS WORKING
CONDITIONS

	PERCENT
A. Constant Allowances:	
1. Personal allowance	5
2. Basic fatigue allowance	4
B. Variable allowances	
1. Standing allowance	2
2. Abnormal position allowance	
a) Slightly awkward	0
b) Awkward (bending)	2
c) Very awkward (lying, stretching)	7
3. Use of force or muscular energy (lifting, pulling, or pushing)	
Weight lifted, pounds:	
5	0
10	1
15	2
20	3
25	4
30	5
35	7
40	9
45	11
50	13
60	17
70	22
4. Bad light	
a) Slightly below recommended	0
b) Well below	2
c) Quite inadequate	5
5. Atmospheric conditions (heat and humidity)	0–10
6. Close attention	
a) Fairly fine work	0
b) Fine or exacting	2
c) Very fine or very exacting	5
7. Noise level	
a) Continuous	0
b) Intermittent-loud	2
c) Intermittent-very loud	5
d) High-pitched-loud	5
8. Mental strain	
a) Fairly complex process	1
b) Complex or wide span of attention	4
c) Very complex	8
9. Monotony	
a) Low	0
b) Medium	1
c) High	4
10. Tediousness	
a) Rather tedious	0
b) Tedious	2
c) Very tedious	5

SOURCE: B. W. Niebel, *Motion and Time Study*, 6 E (Homewood, IL: Richard D. Irwin, 1976).

The times for basic elements are measured in time-measurement units (TMU's), where one TMU equals 0.0006 minute. One minute of the job may include more than 100 elements.

In Table 10.3, we present some MTM values. Some advantages of MTM are: data are based on numerous observations, a performance rating is not necessary, there are no disruptions in the plant, and standards may be established even before the job is done.

COMPENSATION

We have already implied that compensation can be a very complex idea, so we will begin with a working definition. For our purposes, we will consider compensation as money received in the performance of work, plus any or all of the services and benefits that organizations provide to their employees. The former is called direct compensation or wages (gross pay), and the latter are called benefits (fringe benefits or indirect compensation). Benefits include life, accident, and health insurance, the employer's contributions to retirement, pay for vacation or illness, and the employer's required payments for employee welfare, such as social security.

Benefits are not "fringes" or "little extras." They are already important, and in the not-too-distant future their value may be equal to that of direct compensation. Benefits amounted to about 5 percent of direct compensation in 1940, and to about 20 percent in 1950. However, in 1975, they were almost 35 percent of direct compensation and were continuing to move upward. According to the U.S. Department of Commerce, in the period 1965–73, average factory wages rose 72 percent, while benefits increased 126 percent.

Let us discuss direct compensation as it is related to work measurement. The most common pay systems are hourly and incentive systems. In the hourly pay system, the worker receives an hourly wage with overtime payment. An incentive pay system is a compensation program designed to motivate individual or group performance. An incentive program is most frequently built on monetary rewards (incentive pay or a monetary bonus), but may include a variety of nonmonetary rewards or prizes.

The use of incentives assumes that people's actions are influenced by the incentives. Unfortunately, the issue is not always this simple. Over the years, the issue of incentives has become greatly confused as a result of the claims and denials by supporters and critics of monetary incentives, such as: "Salary is necessary to reward work, but it does not motivate people to work more effectively," "There is no direct relationship between incentives and performance, due to a variety of mediating circumstances." "One-third of all company bonus plans examined do not motivate and are quite expensive."

All of these remarks express reasons for concern, but they should not be too discouraging. Effective use of incentives depends on many situational and

TABLE 10.3 PORTIONS OF MTM TABLES

TABLE I—REACH (R)

DISTANCE MOVED (INCHES)	TIME TMU				Hand in Motion		CASE AND DESCRIPTION
	A	B	C or D	E	A	B	
3/4 or less	2.0	2.0	2.0	2.0	1.6	1.6	A. Reach to object in fixed location, or to object in other hand or on which other hand rests.
1	2.5	2.5	3.6	2.4	2.3	2.3	
2	4.0	4.0	5.9	3.8	3.5	2.7	
3	5.3	5.3	7.3	5.3	4.5	3.6	B. Reach to single object in location, which may vary slightly from cycle to cycle
4	6.1	6.4	8.4	6.8	4.9	4.3	
5	6.5	7.8	9.4	7.4	5.3	5.0	
6	7.0	8.6	10.1	8.0	5.7	5.7	
7	7.4	9.3	10.8	8.7	6.1	6.5	C. Reach to object jumbled with other objects in a group so that search and select occur
8	7.9	10.1	11.5	9.3	6.5	7.2	
9	8.3	10.8	12.2	9.9	6.9	7.9	
10	8.7	11.5	12.9	10.5	7.3	8.6	
12	9.6	12.9	14.2	11.8	8.1	10.1	
14	10.5	14.4	15.6	13.0	8.9	11.5	D. Reach to a very small object, or where accurate grasp is required
16	11.4	15.8	17.0	14.2	9.7	12.9	
18	12.3	17.2	18.4	15.5	10.5	14.4	
20	13.1	18.6	19.8	16.7	11.3	15.8	
22	14.0	20.1	21.2	18.0	12.1	17.3	E. Reach to indefinite location to get hand into position for body balance or next motion or out of way
24	14.9	21.5	22.5	19.2	12.9	18.8	
26	15.8	22.9	23.9	20.4	13.7	20.2	
28	16.7	24.4	25.3	21.7	14.5	21.7	
30	17.5	25.8	26.7	22.9	15.3	23.2	
Additional	0.4	0.7	0.7	0.6			TMU per inch over 30 inches

TABLE 10.3 (Cont.)

TABLE II—MOVE (M)

DISTANCE MOVED (INCHES)	TIME TMU				WEIGHT ALLOWANCE			CASE AND DESCRIPTION
	A	*B*	*C*	Hand in Motion *B*	Weight (pound) up to	Dynamic Factor	Static Constant TMU	
3/4 or less	2.0	2.0	2.0	1.7				
1	2.5	2.9	3.4	2.3	2.5	1.00	0	A. Move object to other hand or against stop
2	3.6	4.6	5.2	2.9				
3	4.9	5.7	6.7	3.6	7.5	1.06	2.2	
4	6.1	6.9	8.0	4.3				
5	7.3	8.0	9.2	5.0	12.5	1.11	3.9	
6	8.1	8.9	10.3	5.7				
7	8.9	9.7	11.1	6.5	17.5	1.17	5.6	
8	9.7	10.6	11.8	7.2				
9	10.5	11.5	12.7	7.9	22.5	1.22	7.4	B. Move object to approximate or indefinite location
10	11.3	12.2	13.5	8.6				
12	12.9	13.4	15.2	10.0	27.5	1.28	9.1	
14	14.4	14.6	16.9	11.4				
16	16.0	15.8	18.7	12.8	32.5	1.33	10.8	
18	17.6	17.0	20.4	14.2				
20	19.2	18.2	22.1	15.6	37.5	1.39	12.5	
22	20.8	19.4	23.8	17.0				
24	22.4	20.6	25.5	18.4	42.5	1.44	14.3	C. Move object to exact location
26	24.0	21.8	27.3	19.8				
28	25.5	23.1	29.0	21.2	47.5	1.50	16.0	
30	27.1	24.3	30.7	22.7				
Additional	0.8	0.6	0.85		TMU per inch over 30 inches			

Source: Copyrighted by the MTM Association for Standards and Research. No reprint permission without written consent from the NTM Association, 16-01 Broadway, Fair Lawn, New Jersey 07410.

TABLE 10.3   (Cont.)

TABLE IIIA—TURN (T)

WEIGHT	TIME TMU FOR DEGREES TURNED										
	30°	*45°*	*60°*	*75°*	*90°*	*105°*	*120°*	*135°*	*150°*	*165°*	*180°*
Small: 0 to 2 pounds	2.8	3.5	4.1	4.8	5.4	6.1	6.8	7.4	8.1	8.7	9.4
Medium: 2.1 to 10 pounds	4.4	5.5	6.5	7.5	8.5	9.6	10.6	11.6	12.7	13.7	14.8
Large: 10.1 to 35 pounds	8.4	10.5	12.3	14.4	16.2	18.3	20.4	22.2	24.3	26.1	28.2

TABLE IIIB—APPLY PRESSURE (AP)

FULL CYCLE			COMPONENTS		
Symbol	*TMU*	*Description*	*Symbol*	*TMU*	*Description*
APA	10.6	AF + DM + RLF	AF	3.4	Apply force
APB	16.2	APA + G2	DM	4.2	Dwell, minimum
			RLF	3.0	Release force

TABLE IV—GRASP (G)

TYPE OF GRASP	CASE	TIME TMU	DESCRIPTION	
Pick up	1A	2.0	Any size object by itself, easily grasped	
	1B	3.5	Object very small or lying close against a flat surface	
	1C1	7.3	Diameter larger than 1/2″	Interference with grasp on bottom and one side of nearly cylindrical object
	1C2	8.7	Diameter 1/4″ to 1/2″	
	1C3	10.8	Diameter less than 1/4″	
Regrasp	2	5.6	Change grasp without relinquishing control	

TABLE 10.3   (Cont.)

TABLE IV-GRASP (G)   (Cont.)

TYPE OF GRASP	CASE	TIME TMU	DESCRIPTION	
Transfer	3	5.6	Control transferred from one hand to the other	
Select	4A	7.3	Larger than 1″ × 1″ × 1″	Object jumbled with other objects, so that search and select occur
	4B	9.1	1/4″ × 1/4″ × 1/8″ to 1″ × 1″ × 1″	
	4C	12.9	Smaller than 1/4″ × 1/4″ × 1/8″	
Contact	5	0	Contact, sliding, or hook grasp	

individual factors—incentive plan, work situation, and individual. Incentives can be used effectively and productively.

Different people value things differently. An operations manager should realize that all people do not attach the same value to monetary incentives, bonuses, prizes, or trips. Employees view these things differently because of their age, marital status, economic need, and objectives. However, even though employee reactions to incentives vary greatly, incentives do have some redeeming merits. In some industries (see Table 10.4), incentive programs are a very important part of employee benefits. These programs attract many new employees.

Sales plans and programs provide a good example of how incentives can influence motivation. Some sales executives seem to have an unending number of monetary and nonmonetary incentive programs to stimulate sales. Money, trips, and gift certificates are part of the continuous parade of promotions.

However, there is such a thing as satiation (diminishing returns). Although steak is great, would you, for example, like to have it every week, or every day, for years? Even the most ardent steak-lover would throw in his knife and fork at some point along the line. Analogously, in productivity-oriented monetary incentive programs, a worker reaches a comfortable and profitable performance level and work pattern.

To be effective, incentive plans should be accurate, easy to apply, consistent, easy to understand, and fair. Incentive plans are of two kinds: individual-output-based or group-output-based. Let us discuss some examples of these kinds of plans.

TABLE 10.4 PERCENTAGE OF WORKERS PAID ON INCENTIVE BASIS IN SELECTED INDUSTRIES

INDUSTRY	PERCENTAGE OF WORKERS ON INCENTIVE BASIS
Work clothing	82
Men's and boys' shirts, except work and night wear	81
Men's and boys' suits and coats	74
Footwear, except rubber	70
Women's hosiery	70
Children's hosiery	70
Basic iron and steel	66
Men's hosiery	65
Cigars	57
Leather tanning and finishing	53
Glass containers	38
Fiber cans, tubes, drums, and similar products	37
Corrugated and solid fiber boxes	36
Glassware, except glass containers, pressed or blown	36
Cotton textiles	34
Farm machinery	34
Iron foundries	33
Motor vehicle parts	31
Meatpacking	30
Structural clay products	28
Wool, yard, and broadwoven fabrics	27
Synthetic textiles	26
Steel foundries	26
Candy and other confectionery products	25
Office and computing machines	24
Gray iron pipe and fittings foundries	23
Engines and Turbines	22
Gray iron, except pipe and fittings, foundries	21

Individual Incentive Plans

These plans are based on the amount of products or services provided by the individual employee. There are a number of types of such plans.

In *piece-rate plans*, the employee is paid for the number of units produced. If 150 units are completed in one day, and the rate is $1.50 per unit, the daily pay is:

$$150 \times \$1.50 = \$225$$

Some plans include provisions for quality level of output. For example, if there are only 130 good units in the last example, and 20 units are defective, the daily pay is:

$$130 \times \$1.50 = \$195$$

The *differential piece-rate plan* includes two rates: a low rate under an established level of number of units produced, and a high rate, above that established level. The worker is encouraged to meet the established level. Let us assume that the established level is 120 products a day. The piece rates are:

Under 120 units	$1.20/unit
120 or more units	$1.50/unit

If the worker produced 100 units, his pay would be:

$$100 \times \$1.20 = \$120$$

If the worker increased his efforts by 30 percent (and, as we have stated, 130 percent of standard is a common performance level), thus producing 130 units, his pay would be:

$$130 \times 1.50 = \$195$$

This represents an increase of 62.5 percent in pay.

The *Manchester-type plan* is another piece-rate plan. It is desirable during training periods and when conditions beyond the worker's control affect his performance. Let us assume that a worker's hourly rate is $10/hour and that he is also on a piece-rate plan of $2.50 a piece. His daily pay is the larger of the two values, piece-rate based pay and the hourly rate-based pay. Thus, if he completed 30 pieces in an 8-hour day his pay would be $80 because $80 is the larger of

$$\$10 \times 8 = \$80$$

and

$$\$2.50 \times 30 = \$75$$

Group Incentive Plans

Group incentive plans involve the sharing of productivity gains with employees. Some of these plans are strictly output related. Others reward employees for output as well as for improvement in quality and reduction in waste. Many of these plans—specifically, the participative plans—suggest that employees should participate in job design and analysis, determination of wage levels, and productivity evaluations.

Let us describe a typical calculation involved in one of these plans. During the base year:

$$\text{Sale value of production} = 1,000,000$$

$$\text{Total wage bill} = \$\ 350,000$$

Thus, the standard is 35 percent of sale value of production. During the following year (after the plan was put into effect), the actual total wage bill is $256,954.50.

$$\text{Sale value of production} = \$950,000$$

$$\text{The ``allowable'' wage bill is 35 percent of } \$950,000 = \$332,500$$

The difference between $332,500 and $256,954.50 is $75,545.50, which is the amount of the bonus. The usual practice is to distribute 25 percent of the $7555.55 to management and 75 percent to all the workers. Some well-known plans, described below, reflect the main features of group incentive plans.

The *Scanlon Plan*[3] was developed by the late Joseph Scanlon to save a company from bankruptcy. The plan encouraged reduction in labor costs by allowing workers to share in reductions achieved. The plan calls for the formation of employees' committees to search actively areas for improvement.

The *Lincoln Plan* was developed over a period of twenty years at the Lincoln Electric Company in Cleveland, Ohio. It includes profit sharing, job enrichment, and employees' committees to search for areas of improvements. The incentives include piecework system, an annual bonus, and a stock purchase option. It has been credited with an increase of Lincoln's market share and an increase in profitability and a decrease in unit costs.

The *Kaiser Sharing Plan*[4] is based on sharing cost savings rather than profits. The Kaiser plan shares not only wage-bill-cost savings, as in the Scanlon Plan, but all production-related cost savings. It establishes formulas to determine savings in production costs and prescribes how they are to be divided each month between the company and participating employees. Savings that result from decreases in material, supply and labor, costs, measured against a base year, are shared. The sharing ratio is 32.5 percent for labor and to 67.5 percent for the company. It is reported by companies using this plan that workers' attitudes and cooperation increased, absenteeism rates decreased, and wages were increased by 10 to 30 percent.

[3] See J. Geare, "Productivity from Scanlon-Type Plans," *Academy of Management Review*, Vol. 1, No. 3, July, 1976, pp 99–108.

[4] R. A. Bedolis, "The Kaiser Sharing Plan's First Year," *Conference Board Record*, Vol. 1, No. 7, July, 1964, pp. 37–42.

The *Eastman Kodak Plan* uses a combination of premium wages, as well as an annual bonus related to the company's profits. Workers are encouraged to help set goals and to recommend reasonable performance levels.

SUMMARY

After jobs have been designed and analyzed, labor standards are developed. Standards are used for evaluating performance of workers, balancing the workload among workers, scheduling work, evaluating job methods, setting incentive systems, and so on. The standards are set by work measurment.

Work measurement techniques that have been described in the chapter are direct time study—extensive sampling (work sampling), direct time study—intensive sampling (stopwatch method), and predetermined time standards (MTM).

Compensation is an involved subject. We have confined most of the discussion to hourly and incentive pay systems. Two major pay incentive systems have been described: individual plans and group plans. Organizations can choose from the various plans available. Once a plan is adopted, it is usually difficult to change it substantially.

DISCUSSION QUESTIONS

10.1   What is work measurement?

10.2   What are the uses of labor standards?

10.3   What is the basic formula for the determination of standard times?

10.4   List work measurement techniques.

10.5   What is an intensive work sampling?

10.6   When does one use an extensive work sampling?

10.7   How does one determine observation times for the work-sampling technique?

10.8   How does one treat unusual data observed during intensive work sampling?

10.9   How does one determine the number of cycles to observe in the intensive work-sampling technique?

10.10 What are the two major incentive systems?

PROBLEMS AND SOLUTIONS

10.1   a) List the activities involved in the changing of the oil in a car by a gas station attendant.

b) How do you suggest that one should determine the time standard for this job?

Solution

a) The activities are:

(1) Fill out service invoice and tell customer when it will be ready, what it will cost, and other details.
(2) Drive car into service bay, centering car over hoist.
(3) Raise car on hoist.
(4) Put oil catch bucket underneath oil pan.
(5) Remove oil pan plug.
(6) Allow car to drain.
(7) Remove oil filter.
(8) Install new oil filter.
(9) Replace oil pan plug.
(10) Remove oil catch bucket.
(11) Lower car.
(12) Raise engine hood.
(13) Remove oil cap.
(14) Add 4 quarts of oil.
(15) Replace oil cap.
(16) Record car mileage, cost, etc., on service invoice.
(17) Drive car out of service bay.

b) As it is a repetitive job with a standard sequence of activities, intensive work sampling may be used.

10.2 A management science professor would like to perform an extensive work-sampling study to analyze the performance of his research assistants with respect to the percentage of time the assistants spend studying management science. On the average, the professor's research assistants study management science about 45 percent of the time. At a 95 percent confidence level, how many observations should he make to determine the amount of time the assistants are spending studying management science, given:
a) a 1% absolute error in p
b) a 3% absolute error in p.

Solution
Using the average percentage of 45 percent as an initial estimate:
a) 9000 (from Figure 10.4)
b) 1000 (from Figure 10.4).

10.3 In making an intensive time study of a cleaning assignment, the following times were noted:

Observation Number	Amount of Time Required (in minutes)
1	2.24
2	2.24
3	1.71
4	2.14
5	2.03
6	1.71
7	2.35
8	2.14
9	2.03
10	2.03
11	1.92

Observation Number	Amount of Time Required (in minutes)
12	2.14
13	4.27
14	2.03
15	2.46
16	1.71
17	1.92
18	3.14
19	2.03
20	2.14

The worker observed works faster than normal, at about 120 percent.

a) Determine the normal time.

b) Determine the standard time (assume 10 percent allowance).

c) The worker is paid $8 per hour. What would the earned rate be under a 100 percent plan?

d) Is the number of observations sufficient?

Solutions

a) Normal time:

$$NT = \frac{44.38}{20} \times 1.20$$
$$= 2.6628$$

b) Standard time:

$ST = NT\,(1 + \text{Allowances})$
$\quad= 2.6628\,(1 + 0.10)$
$\quad= 2.9291$

c) Since the math professor is working at 120 percent, his pay under a 100 percent plan would be:

$8.00 \times 1.20 = 9.60$

d) After ten observations, the longest time observed is $H = 2.35$, and the shortest time observed is $L = 1.71$.

$$\frac{H - L}{H + L} = \frac{0.64}{4.06} = 0.157 \sim 0.16$$

According to Table 10.1, based on 10 observations, the required number of readings is 17. Thus, 20 observations made are enough.

CHAPTER REVIEW PROBLEMS

10.1   Choose a simple assembled product for which the parts can be obtained. Determine the work elements and determine standard time for assembly. (Remember to check the sample size.)

10.2 A land title office manager wishes to make an extensive work-sampling study to estimate the percent of time clerks are busy waiting on customers and the percent of time they are idle. The current best guess is that clerks are idle 30 percent of the time. Determine the number of observations required if we wish to be 95 percent confident that the result is within 1.0 percent of the true percent of idle time and work time.

10.3 From intensive work-sampling study, we found that a Xerox machine operator takes, on the average, 0.30 minutes to Xerox one page. The operator performance rating is 120 percent. If total allowance is 10 percent, what is the standard time in minutes for copying one page?

10.4 An intensive work sampling was made on a collecting job in an office, with the following results:

Element	\multicolumn{6}{c}{CYCLE (MINUTES)}	Performance Rating (percent)
	1	2	3	4	5	6	
remove rubber bands	0.04	—	0.46	—	3.10	—	120
get two pages with each hand	0.16	0.35	0.63	2.99	3.24	3.45	105
jog four sheets	0.19	0.39	2.83*	3.04	3.28	3.49	110
staple and put aside	0.22	0.41	2.86	3.07	3.30	3.52	90

*Operator dropped the four sheets on the floor.

a) Calculate the normal time per collated set.
b) If allowance for this type of work totals 10 percent, what would be the standard time per set?
c) Should the set of papers dropped be considered as a part of the study, or should the data be thrown out?

10.5 The foreman would like to determine the proportion of time a punch press operator spends in the categories of work, delay, and personal time. Initial estimates are that he spends 85 percent of his time working, 10 percent delay, and 5 percent personal time.

With 1.00 percent accuracy at 95 percent confidence level on the delay proportion, how many observations are required?

BIBLIOGRAPHY

ALFORD, L. P., and H. R. BETTY, *Principles of Industrial Management*. New York: Ronald Press, 1951.

AQUILANO, N .J., "A Physiological Evaluation of Time Standards for Strenuous Work as Set by Stopwatch Time Study and Two Predetermined Motion-Time Data Systems," *Journal of Industrial Engineering*, Vol. 19, No. 9, Sept., 1968, pp. 425–32.

BARNES, R. M., *Motion and Time Study: Design and Measurement of Work* (6th ed.). New York: John Wiley & Sons, Inc., 1968.

CARUTH, D. L., *Planning for Clerical Work Measurement*. New York: American Management Association, 1970.

CHASE, R. B., and N. J. AQUILANO, *Production and Operations Management* (3rd ed.). Homewood, Ill.: Richard D. Irwin, 1981.

DAVIS, L. E., and A. B. CHERNS, *Quality of Working Life*. New York: Free Press, Vols. 1 and 2, 1975.

DICKSON, P., *The Future of the Workplace*. New York: Weybright and Talley, 1975.

FOY, N., and H. GORDON, "Worker Participation: Contrasts in Three Countries," *Harvard Business Review*, Vol. 54, No. 3, May–June, 1976, pp. 71–83

GARNDER, D. M., and K. M. ROWLAND, "A Self-Tailored Approach to Incentives," *Personnel Journal*, Vol. 49, Nov., 1970, pp. 907–12.

GEARE, A. J., "Productivity from Scanlon-type Plans," *Academy of Management Review*, Vol. 1, No. 3, July, 1976, pp. 99–108.

GERSHONI, H., "An Analysis of Time Study Based on Studies Made in the United Kingdom and Israel," *AIIE Transactions*, Sept., 1969, Vol. 1, No. 3, pp. 244–251.

HERBST, P. G., *Socio-Technical Design: Strategies in Multidisciplinary Research*. London: Travistock, 1974.

International Labor Office, *Introduction to Work Study* (rev. ed.), Geneva, 1974.

JAMES, C. F., JR., "Incentives for Machine-Paced Operations," *Industrial Engineering*, Sept., 1975, pp. 52–55.

KILBRIDGE, M., and L. WEBSTER, "An Economic Model for Division of Labor," *Management Science*, Vol. 12, No. 6, Feb., 1966, pp. B255–69.

HERZBERG, F. W., "Does Money Really Motivate?" *Purchasing*, Vol. 69, Aug. 6, 1970, pp. 57–58.

HOPEMAN, R. J., *Production and Operations Management* (4th ed.). Columbus, Ohio: Charles E. Merrill Publishing, 1980.

"Incentive Bonuses are Great for Sales," *Advertising Age*, Vol. 41, Nov. 6, 1970, p. 66.

LAWLER, E. E., *Pay and Organizational Effectiveness: A Psychological View*. New York: McGraw-Hill, 1971.

MARTIN, N. A., "What's Wrong with Bonuses," *Dunn's Review*, Vol. 97, Apr., 1971, pp. 42–44.

MAYNARD, H. B., *Industrial Engineering Handbook*. New York: McGraw-Hill, 1963.

McMANIS, D. L., and W. G. BICK, "Monetary Incentives in Today's Industrial Setting," *Personnel Journal*, Vol. 52, May 197, pp. 37–92.

MONKS, J. G., *Operations Management: Theory and Problems*. New York: McGraw-Hill, 1977.

MOORE, F., and T. HENDRICK, *Production/Operations Management* (8th ed.). Homewood, Ill., Richard D. Irwin, 1980.

MUNDEL, M. E., "Motion and Time Study," *Handbook of Industrial Engineering and Management*, ed. William G. Ireson and Eugene L. Grant. Englewood Cliffs, N.J.: Prentice-Hall, Inc., 1955.

———, *Motion and Time Study*. Englewood Cliffs, N.J.: Prentice-Hall, Inc., 1960.

NADLER, G., "Is More Measurement Better?" *Industrial Engineering*, Mar., 1978, pp. 20–25.

NADLER, G., *Work Design: A Systems Concept* (rev. ed.). Homewood, Ill.: Richard D. Irwin, 1970.

NANCE, H. W., and R. E. NOLAN, *Office Work Managment.* New York: McGraw-Hill, 1971.

NIEBEL, B. W., *Motion and Time Study* (6th ed.). Homewood, Ill.: Richard D. Irwin, 1976.

PERHAM, J. C., "Pay Off in Performance Bonuses," *Dunn's Review,* Vol. 103, May, 1974, pp. 51–55.

PITTS, R. A., "Incentive Compensation and Organizational Design," *Personnel Journal,* Vol. 53, May, 1974, pp. 338–44.

RACHEL, F. M., and D. L. CARUTH, "Work Measurement: A Valuable Tool for Management," *Management Services,* Jan.–Feb., 1969, pp. 23–34.

RICE, R. S., "Survey of Work Measurement and Wage Incentives," *Industrial Engineering,* Vol. 9, No. 7, July, 1977, pp. 18–31.

ROBERTS, R. M., JR., "Tie Bonuses to Corporate Profits," *Financial Executive,* Vol. 41, June, 1973, pp. 12–19.

SALVENDY, G. "Hand Size and Assembly Performance," *AIIE Transactions,* Mar., 1971, Vol. 3, No. 1, pp. 32–36.

SCHRIEBER, D. E., and S. SLOAN, "Incentives: Are They Relevant, Obsolete, or Misunderstood?" *Personnel Administration,* Vol. 33, Jan., 1970, pp. 52–57.

SITNEK, L. N., "Performance Rating," *Industrial Management,* Vol. 19, No. 1, Jan.–Feb., 1977, pp. 11–16.

VAN DER ZWAAN, A. H., "The Sociotechnical Systems Approach: A Critical Evaluation," *International Journal of Production Research,* Vol. 13, No. 2, 1975, pp. 149–63.

WILSON, S. R., "The Incentive Approach to Executive Development," *Business Horizons,* Vol. 15, Apr., 1972, pp. 15–24.

11

Inventory Management and Control

INTRODUCTION

How many times have you encountered a promotion that related in some way or the other to a vast selection of items in inventory or, alternatively, to a limited amount of inventory (see Figure 11.1)? Inventory control has a significant impact on an organization, both operationally and financially. Inventory should be kept high enough to hedge against shortage and to provide product line flexibility, but low enough to minimize the capital investment in inventory.

High inventory levels represent high capital costs, high operating costs, and increased congestion in the processing area. Too low an inventory level might lead to shortages and require tight scheduling.

One fifth of the U.S. gross national product is tied up in inventories. This amounted to about 330 billion dollars in 1981. Obviously, operations managers should be aware of the potential savings and penalties involved in keeping inventory.

This chapter concentrates on inventory control and inventory management. It presents a conceptual framework for analysis of inventory systems, followed by specific quantitative models that can be used in analyzing inventory systems. Quantitative treatment of inventory systems is simple, and does not require extensive mathematical or statistical preparation. The reader is encouraged to follow the assumptions behind the practical solutions since this determines when the solutions can be applied.

Figure 11.1 Limited Quantities and Limited Time Are Inventory Characteristics *Source: The Calgary Herald,* Nov. 23, 1979.

INVENTORY: DEFINITIONS

Inventory consists of stores of goods and other stocks. Alternatively, inventory is a quantity of goods and other stocks held for a specific time period in an unproductive state, awaiting intended use or sale. Manufacturing organizations carry inventory in the form of stock items, such as:

1. Raw materials
2. Work-in-process
3. Finished but undelivered products
4. Supplies (spare parts, lubricants, etc.).

Inventory of finished services in labor-intensive services, such as restaurants or branch operations in a bank, is mostly nonexistent. The service is consumed as it is produced and is not kept as inventory. For example, a lecture at a university being delivered by a professor cannot be stocked. A lecture is consumed as it is delivered (unless it is stored on a video cassette).

In service-oriented organizations that are not labor-intensive, such as mass transportation organizations, finished stock inventories are present. Blood banks keep inventories of blood types, and the news media hold news pieces for timely release.

Inventory control is the technique of maintaining stock items at predetermined, desired levels. *Inventory management* is concerned with determining policies that set the goals for the inventory control system.

INVENTORY FUNCTIONS

The major reason for holding inventory is the impossibility of exactly matching supply and demand in terms of time and quantity. Inventory has a number of functions:

Hedge against future increases in costs and prices. An anticipated increase in labor costs causes stocking of finished goods. An anticipated increase in selling price calls for a delay in disposing of stock on hand.

Hedge against stockouts. Since demand and supply do not match and are at times unpredictable, unsatisfied orders and expediting efforts become expensive. Buffer stocks are kept to hedge against stockouts, and are determined carefully.

Decoupling of operations. Inventories break operations apart, so that one operation's demand is independent of another's supply. In this way, local material shortages or maintenance downtime do not carry throughout stages.

Leveling of production. During slack periods, inventories are built up. During high-demand periods, inventories are depleted. This is done while the production rate is kept at a constant level.

Ordering of economy. Basically, there is a trade-off between numerous low-quantity orders that present a high reordering cost and a few large orders that present a high carrying cost. The optimum-size order is a result of this trade-off and generally calls for some inventory. Besides, larger orders may entitle the buyer to a volume discount.

Control system economy. A larger inventory facilitates less control effort. Fewer review actions to determine whether reordering is necessary are required if a larger inventory is kept. Frequent review actions of this kind are costly.

Return on investment. Inventory should be carried so long as it compares favorably with other possible capital investments available to the organization. As inflation pushes purchasing costs and selling prices up, hoarding inventory presents a favorable investment.

Reducing of material-handling charges. Moving of single completed units from one process to another is costly. Moving of batches of completed units is less expensive, and can be done by means of a forklift truck, an overhead crane, or a tray. The batches, however, constitute an inventory that involves carrying costs.

Displaying to customers. Department stores, grocery stores, and car dealers hold inventory to be able to display it to the customers and to have it on hand for sale.

INVENTORY SYSTEMS: A CONCEPTUAL FRAMEWORK

Inventory control follows control theory principles. Inputs, including raw-material stocks, are converted to outputs in the form of finished, undelivered products. In order to facilitate this conversion process, operations managers keep raw materials inventory, work-in-process inventory, inventory of supplies required for the process, and inventory of finished goods. Actual inventory levels of each of the various inventories are compared with planned inventory levels. If a difference is found, an action is effected to change the actual inventory levels to match the planned inventory levels. (see Figure 11.2.) In the following sections we shall determine the optimum planned inventory levels.

The most single inventory system is one in which a single product is produced or one service provided is in one stage. In a *multistage inventory system* (see Figure 11.3), products are inventoried at more than one stage in a sequential process, or customers wait for the next stage of the service. An in-process inventory helps reduce material handling costs and smooth production, as only completed batches are moved from one stage to another, and a slowdown in one stage may not affect the next stage's rate of production for a while.

In a *multiechelon, multilevel inventory system,* products are inventoried at various distribution echelons. As shown in Figure 11.4, several institutions are involved in the distribution of a finished product. Thus, the plant is the highest

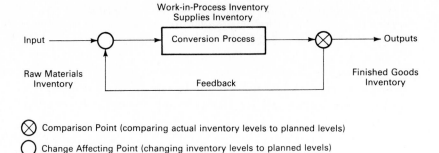

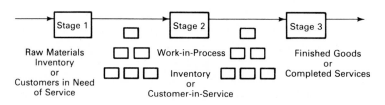

Figure 11.2   Inventory Control Process

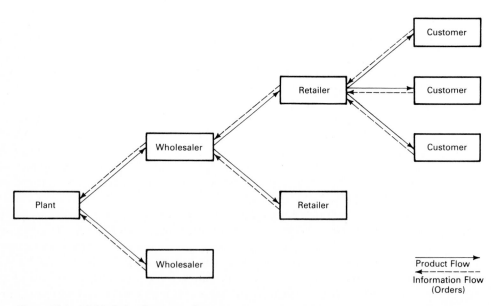

Figure 11.3   A Multistage Production Process

Figure 11.4   Multiechelon Inventory System

echelon in the system and the customer is the lowest echelon in the system. The plant supplies the product to the wholesaler who, in turn, supplies it to the retailer, who forwards it to the customer. In most cases, the higher echelons supply the items to the lower ones, and the lowest echelon satisfies the final demand for the product. Products are inventoried at the various levels, and a demand change at the customer level obviously has an impact on the inventory at the various inventory levels. Inventory management in each of the echelons engages in system-wide reordering and stock allocation in order to minimize costs. This chapter deals largely with single-stage single-echelon systems. However, the techniques recommended can be extended to include the multi-stage, multiechelon inventory systems.

THE INVENTORY DECISION

"When" and *"how much"* are the two major decisions that the operations manager should make. A decision must be made as to when to reorder inventory—namely, as to the reorder point. The reorder point is determined either in terms of the level of inventory or in terms of a calendar date. When an order is triggered, a decision must also be made as to the order size. These two decisions should be made while keeping in mind the organizational implications.

The following sections deal with economic considerations with respect to both decisions. The economic considerations are expressed in quantitative formulas, called *inventory models.* The reader is advised to pay careful attention to the assumptions behind each inventory model. Figure 11.5 shows a breakdown of the major inventory models.

Depending on the specific situation involved, the operations manager tries either to minimize inventory costs or, alternatively, to maximize profit. Whether costs or profits are concerned, inventory modes may be either of a deterministic nature (when all the variables are known with certainty), or of a stochastic nature (when some or all of the variables are probabilistic). There are two kinds of deterministic or stochastic inventory models. In periodic order quantity models, reordering is triggered by a certain date. In fixed order quantity models, reordering is triggered when a certain level of inventory is reached.

Under the periodic order quantity model, the inventory level is checked only on certain days—for example, at the beginning of the week or beginning of the month. An order is placed on these dates in such a quantity as to bring the inventory to a predetermined, optimal level. Under the fixed order quantity model, the inventory level is monitored closely (possibly every day), and as it reaches a certain level, an order of a fixed quantity is placed.

The fixed order quantity model behaves as described in Figure 11.6. The level of inventory is depleted at a certain rate until it reaches a predetermined

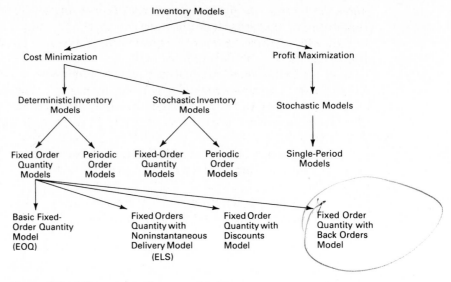

Figure 11.5 A Taxonomy of Inventory Models

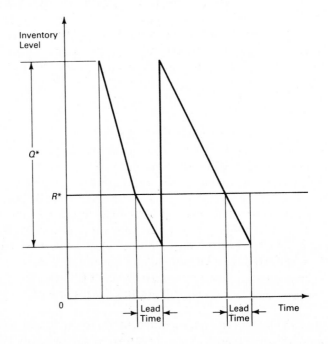

Figure 11.6 The Changes of Inventory Level for the Fixed Order Quantity Model

reordering level, R^*. At that point, an order is placed for a predetermined quantity, Q^*. Following the appropriate lead time, the order arrives and the inventory level rises by the ordered amount. (Please note that the inventory depletion rate may be different during lead times than it is at other times.)

While the fixed order quantity model requires close monitoring of inventory levels on a frequent basis, the periodic order model does not require such monitoring. At predetermined dates, an order is placed in the amount that brings the inventory level to a predetermined optimal level, R^*. This is illustrated in Fig. 11.7.

The orders are placed at equally spaced times, T_1, and T_2. For example, at time T_1, where the actual level of inventory is I_1 and order of size $(R^* - I_1)$ is placed. The chapter deals mainly with the fixed order quantity inventory model, although it should be kept in mind that the periodic order model has its merits and is used by institutions that do not stress strict inventory management procedures.

INVENTORY COSTS

As was stated earlier, inventory models are quantitative formulas. These formulas consider various inventory costs. Only those costs that vary as the inventory decisions of "when" and "how" change should be considered. Costs that are fixed and independent of how much or when to order are not considered in developing the models. Operations managers should identify these costs and then minimize their total. The costs are of five types:

1. Item cost
2. Ordering (procurement) cost
3. Costs of carrying inventory
4. Stockout costs associated with shortages
5. Fixed overhead costs.

The costs vary from one product to another but their nature stays the same.

Item cost is the purchase cost or the value of the item to the inventory holder. Whether at book value or market value, the item cost does not affect the reorder decision ("when" and "how much") if there are no quantity discounts. If there are quantity discounts, then the item cost has an impact on the reorder decision, because the larger the order is, the lower is the cost per single unit purchased.

Ordering cost includes all the necessary expenses involved in placing one order. This cost is assumed to be constant and is incurred each time an order is placed. If this cost becomes very large, one would prefer placing a large order once or twice a year. The ordering cost includes clerical and paper work

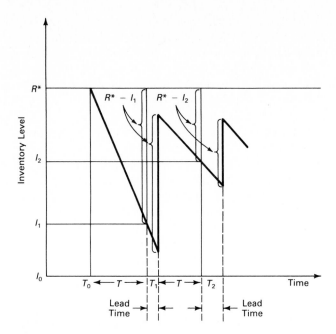

Figure 11.7   The Changes of Inventory Level for the Periodic Order Model

expenses, incoming inspection, bookkeeping, records updating, expediting expenses, postage, and delivery costs. The average procurement cost can be found from accounting records by totaling the annual costs of the above items and dividing by the number of orders placed throughout the year. It is assumed that the cost of one typed letter is approximately $35 to $40. This sets a lower limit to the procurement cost, since the least expensive order involves, minimum, the typing of a purchase order.

Carrying inventory costs are costs that reflect the investment in inventory and the costs associated with maintaining it in storage. A higher inventory level may require an expansion of the warehouse, increased material-handling costs, and increased maintenance costs. The costs may be extracted from the accounting records. Items that should be considered are:

1. Capital cost
2. Storage costs: land and building costs (depreciation, property tax, insurance, utilities) and rent
3. Service costs: (inventory taxes, insurance, material handling)
4. Risk costs: obsolescence and shrinkage (pilferage, damage, spoilage, theft).

The most significant cost among those is the capital cost. It may constitute anywhere from 49 percent to 96 percent of the total carrying costs. The capital cost is either:

1. The average cost of borrowing (interest) to the company
2. The marginal cost of borrowing to the company (that is, the interest charged on the next dollar borrowed)
3. The return on an alternative investment that is not realized due to the fact that money is tied up in inventory.

The cost associated with land and buildings is estimated by allocating total annual building costs on the basis of square footage to the inventoried items.

Obsolescence costs are obtained from write-offs by the plant department that deals with waste. Plant engineering data and public assessments information are used in the cost estimates.

Stock costs are associated with shortages. These costs occur when an item is out of stock and demand is unsatisfied. The stockout costs includes items that are specified in Table 11.1.

TABLE 11.1   ITEMS OF CARRYING INVENTORY

Cost of Raw-Material Shortage

Cost of idle production
Cost of idle labor
Premium material price
Loss of purchase quantity discount
Cost of extra ordering
Cost of expedited shipment
Cost of product spoilage

Cost of Finished-Products Shortage

Cost of ill will to the seller
Loss of good will to the seller
Premium labor rate
Cost of shift premium
Subcontracting cost
Reduced quality cost

Cost of Spare-Parts Shortage

Cost of idle machine
Cost of idle labor
Cost of expediting

A shortage may occur internally (e.g., a spare-parts shortage for maintenance) or externally (e.g., a finished-products shortage). An external shortage may be detrimental to the company, as customer dissatisfaction may develop. An internal shortage may also be detrimental to the company, since it may cause an external shortage or may become very costly, due to idle labor and equipment.

Shortage cost estimation is difficult. Shortages are a random phenomenon; thus, there is a need for estimation of the probability of the occurrence of shortages. Shortage costs are partially hidden costs, or costs that are not reflected in the accounting records.

Fixed-Overhead Costs are costs that do not change as the number and size of reorders change. These costs support the administration activities that are part of the regular operation of the organization. They may include manual or computerized records updating. These costs are fixed over a significant range of inventory volume and, thus, can be disregarded in the following discussion.

COST TRADEOFFS: MINIMUM COST INVENTORY

An inventory policy is a set of rules that assigns managerial actions to specific inventory occurrences. As has been stated earlier, one would like to try to determine the reorder point and reorder quantity that keep the total operating costs to a minimum. The optimum inventory policy is the one that minimizes the following total cost equation:

$$
\begin{Bmatrix} \text{Total} \\ \text{annual} \\ \text{inven-} \\ \text{tory} \\ \text{cost} \end{Bmatrix} = \begin{Bmatrix} \text{Item} \\ \text{cost} \end{Bmatrix} + \begin{Bmatrix} \text{Ordering} \\ \text{cost} \end{Bmatrix}
$$

$$
+ \begin{Bmatrix} \text{Carry-} \\ \text{ing in-} \\ \text{ventory} \\ \text{cost} \end{Bmatrix} + \begin{Bmatrix} \text{Stock-} \\ \text{out} \\ \text{cost} \end{Bmatrix} + \begin{Bmatrix} \text{Overhead} \\ \text{cost} \end{Bmatrix} \tag{11.1}
$$

The first four costs in equation (11.1) may be expressed in terms of reorder quantity and reorder point for a specific inventory case.

The solution for a two-variable reorder quantity and reorder point is found by three alternative methods:

1. Graphical solution
2. Trial-and-error method
3. Use of calculus.

The graphical solution, when only ordering costs and carrying costs are considered, is straightforward. Figure 11.8 illustrates this economic trade-off. When the reorder quantity is very small, the average inventory carried is small, the carrying costs are minimal, and the number of orders placed over a period is high. When the reorder quantity is very large, the average inventory carried is large and the carrying costs are high. The optimal reorder quantity is the one that minimizes the sum of both costs, and is denoted by Q^*. Q^* is found at the intersection of the curve representing the carrying costs and the curve representing the ordering costs.

When more costs are considered, the graphical cost analysis cannot be applied. However, the economic trade-off is still applicable. It is also important to understand that some inventory situations in industry have not been formally analyzed in a manner recommended here. These situations are being dealt with by operations managers on the basis of past experience. However, decisions made in this way are generally not optimal.

In the following sections, we shall develop quantitative inventory models under different assumptions. The assumptions should be remembered and checked for applicability before a given model can be used for a specific industrial case.

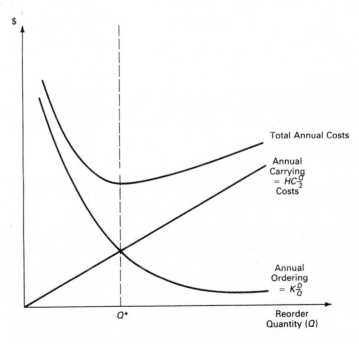

Figure 11.8 Economic Trade-offs in Inventory Control

INVENTORY MODELS

The development of inventory models consists of five straightforward steps:

1. List assumptions concerning the inventory situation. These assumptions should reflect the studied situation as accurately as possible.
2. Develop a cost equation (model) qualitatively.
3. Develop a cost equation (model) quantitatively.
4. Minimize the total cost equation (model), and find reorder quantity and reorder point.

THE BASIC FIXED ORDER QUANTITY MODEL

The basic fixed order quantity model, otherwise known as the economic order quantity (EOQ) system, was developed more than seventy years ago in the context of batch production. However, the formula has been rediscovered by several authors in different contexts. Babcock[1] in 1914, Harris[2] in 1915, Taft[3] in 1918, and other authors[4] presented extended treatments of it.

The assumptions are:

1. Demand is deterministic and a constant number of units are demanded each day.
2. No stockouts are allowed.
3. Lead time is constant and independent of demand.
4. All costs are assumed to be known and constant.
5. All orders are placed independently (there are no joint orders).
6. Orders are delivered at once.

In computing the annual total cost of applying this inventory model, only the costs that affect the reorder quantity should be included. Thus, from equation (11.1), one can exclude the annual cost of the items, since no volume discounts are applied. Furthermore, not stockout costs and no fixed costs are considered. Thus,

$$\begin{Bmatrix} \text{Total annual} \\ \text{inventory cost} \end{Bmatrix} = \begin{Bmatrix} \text{Ordering} \\ \text{cost} \end{Bmatrix} + \begin{Bmatrix} \text{Inventory} \\ \text{carring cost} \end{Bmatrix} \qquad (11.2)$$

The ordering cost is equal to the number of orders placed annually times the procurement cost per order. Carrying cost is the average number of units in

[1] G. D. Babcock, "Manufacturing With Planning Department," *Iron Age,* Vol. 97, 1914, pp. 1068–1072.

[2] F. W. Harris, *Operations and Cost* (Factory Series No. 5). Shaw: Chicago, 1915.

[3] E. W. Taft, "The Most Economical Production Lot," *Iron Age,* Vol. 101, 1918, pp. 1410–1412.

[4] R. H. Wilson, "A Scientific Routine for Stock Control," *Harvard Business Review,* Vol. 13, 1934, pp. 116–128.

inventory more than one a year, times the cost of carrying an inventory unit. Equation (11.2) then becomes:

$$\left\{\begin{array}{l}\text{Total}\\\text{annual}\\\text{inventory}\\\text{cost}\end{array}\right\} = \left\{\begin{array}{l}\text{Number}\\\text{of orders}\\\text{placed}\\\text{annually}\end{array}\right\} \times \left\{\begin{array}{l}\text{Ordering·}\\\text{cost}\end{array}\right\}$$

$$+ \left\{\begin{array}{l}\text{Average}\\\text{inventory}\end{array}\right\} \times \left\{\begin{array}{l}\text{Carrying cost}\\\text{per unit}\end{array}\right\} \qquad (11.3)$$

In order to express equation (11.3) in a more concise form, let us define symbols that will be used in developing the various models. We will only use some of these symbols at this point. The rest will be used later.

D = Annual demand in units

K = Ordering cost or setup cost per order

H = Carrying cost per unit, expressed as a fraction of cost of an individual item

Q = Reorder quantity

Q^* = Optimal reorder quantity

N = Number of orders per year

R = Reorder point

R^* = Optimum reorder point

t_L = Lead time

C = Cost of an individual item

p = Delivery rate in units per unit of time

d_L = Average demand per unit of time during lead time

D_L = Average total demand during lead time

TC = Total annual inventory cost

The total annual cost of operating the fixed order quantity system under the stated assumptions is:

$$TC = \left\{\begin{array}{l}\text{Number of orders}\\\text{placed annually}\end{array}\right\}(K) + \left\{\begin{array}{l}\text{Average}\\\text{inventory}\end{array}\right\}(HC) \qquad (11.4)$$

Let us express the total annual cost of operating the fixed order quantity model in terms of the annual demand (D), the reorder quantity (Q), and the reorder point (R). If we try to keep the excess inventory charges to a minimum with no safety stock and assume immediate delivery,

$$R^* = 0 \qquad (11.5)$$

Whenever the inventory level reaches zero (no units are in inventory), we shall place an order. But what should be the optimal size Q^*, of the order? To find it, we note that

$$N = \text{Number of orders placed annually} = \frac{\text{Annual demand}}{\text{Reorder quantity}} = \frac{D}{Q} \qquad (11.6)$$

and

$$\text{Average inventory} = \frac{\text{Highest inventory level} - \text{Lowest inventory level}}{2}$$

$$= \frac{\text{Reorder quantity} - 0}{2} = \frac{Q}{2} \qquad (11.7)$$

This means that throughout the time that the fixed order quantity model is in effect, the average inventory level is half of the reorder quantity. That is, so long as the lead time is zero, safety stock is not needed and replenishment is instantaneous. Substituting (11.6) and (11.7) into (11.4) provides us with the total annual cost:

$$TC = K\frac{D}{Q} + HC\frac{Q}{2} \qquad (11.8)$$

Figure 11.8 demonstrates the basic economic trade-off. The figure shows that the annual cost is at its minimum when the carrying costs equal the ordering costs, or when

$$K\frac{D}{Q} = HC\frac{Q}{2}$$

The optimal reorder quantity is then

$$Q^* = \sqrt{\frac{2DK}{HC}} \qquad (11.9)$$

The optimal reorder quantity, Q^* is as stated in equation (11.9). The same equation may be found by using calculus.[5] Equations (11.5) and (11.9) represent

---

[5] A necessary condition for a minimum of TC is that the first derivative equals zero.

$$(TC)' = -\frac{KD}{Q^2} + \frac{HC}{2} = 0$$

$$\frac{KD}{Q^2} = \frac{HC}{2}$$

$$Q^* = \sqrt{\frac{2KD}{HC}}$$

A sufficient condition for a minimum is that the second derivative be positive.

$$(TC)'' = \frac{2KD}{(Q^*)^3}$$

This term is always positive. Thus, ordering Q^* assures minimum total annual cost.

the operating concept of the basic fixed order quantity model. When the inventory level reaches

$$R^* = 0,$$

the operations manager should order

$$Q^* = \sqrt{\frac{2DK}{HC}}$$

The total annual cost is kept in this way to a minimum, and is equal to

$$TC^* = K\frac{D}{Q^*} + HC\frac{Q^*}{2}$$

EXAMPLE   The Buy-Bye quick-food outlet requires 120,000 buns a year. The operations manager estimates that placing an order costs him about $40. The carrying cost, including space, spoilage, and handling, amounts to 12 percent of 20 cents, the bun's price. The operations manager wishes to use the fixed order quantity model to handle inventory. Assuming that there is no safety stock and no lead time and that the replenishment is instantaneous whenever the inventory level reaches zero, what should be the characteristics of this system?

$$D = 120,000 \text{ buns}$$
$$K = \$40/\text{order}$$
$$H = 0.12/\text{bun/year}$$
$$C = \$.20/\text{bun}$$

The operations manager should order

$$Q^* = \sqrt{\frac{2DK}{HC}} = \sqrt{\frac{2\,(120,000)(40)}{(0.12)(0.20)}} = 20,000 \text{ buns/order}$$

The total optimal annual cost of operating this system is

$$TC^* = 40\,\frac{120,000}{20,000} + (0.12)(0.20)\frac{20,000}{2} = 240 + 240 = \$480.$$

The operations manager has an average inventory of 10,000 buns, and places six orders a year.

In many cases the variable values, such as annual demand, ordering cost, and holding cost, are only rough estimates, and may vary. Is there a considerable impact, then, on the operation of the system? Is the optimal order quantity affected considerably? In other words, how sensitive is the inventory system to changes in the data? This sensitivity is examined in the following section.

Sensitivity to Changes in Variable Values

To analyze the sensitivity of the system to a change in costs or demand, let us compare the optimal EOQ, Q^*, with a nonoptimal EOQ, Q. From equation (11.9), one can see that a change in any one of the variables causes a change in EOQ that equals the square root of the change in the variable.

EXAMPLE   Assume that at Buy-Bye quick-food outlet, the demand for buns actually is 12,000,000 rather than 120,000—that is, one hundred times what has been assumed in the last example. The Q^* is increased by only ten times:

$$Q^*_1 = \sqrt{\frac{2 \times 12,000,000 \times 40}{0.12 \times 0.20}} = 200,000 \text{ buns/order}$$

Looking at the sensitivity issue from another point of view, what is the impact on the total annual cost if the operations manager does not order the optimal amount, Q^*? The impact on the total cost would not be as high as one might expect. Let us look at the optimal total annual cost, and compare it to a nonoptimal total annual cost.

$$TC^* = K\frac{D}{Q^*} + HC\frac{Q^*}{2}$$

$$TC = K\frac{D}{Q} + HC\frac{Q}{2} \tag{11.10}$$

$$\frac{TC^*}{TC} = \frac{K\dfrac{D}{Q^*} + HC\dfrac{Q^*}{2}}{K\dfrac{D}{Q} + HC\dfrac{Q}{2}}$$

Since $Q^* = \sqrt{2DK/HC}$, substituting Q^* into (11.10) and solving, one gets

$$\frac{TC}{TC^*} = \frac{1}{2}\left[\frac{Q^*}{Q} + \frac{Q}{Q^*}\right] \tag{11.11}$$

EXAMPLE   Suppose that rather than ordering the optimal order quantity of 20,000 buns in each order, the operations manager orders 200,000 buns/order (ten times as much). What is the effect on the total annual cost? As per equation (11.11),

$$\frac{TC}{TC^*} = \frac{1}{2}\left[\frac{20,000}{200,000} + \frac{200,000}{20,000}\right] = \frac{1}{2}\left[\frac{1}{10} + 10\right] = \frac{1}{2} \times \frac{101}{10} = 5.05$$

Thus, while the size of the order is ten times larger, the total cost is only five times the amount determined for the optimal order size. Since

$$TC^* = (40)\frac{120,000}{20,000} + (0.12)(0.20)\left(\frac{20,000}{2}\right) = 240 + 240 = \$480$$

the cost of the nonoptimal fixed order

$$TC = 5.05 \ (TC^*) = (5.05)(480) = \$2,424.00.$$

The marginal cost of the nonoptimal order size is

$$\$2,424 - \$480 = \$1,944.$$

This relative insensitivity of total annual cost explains why businesses may survive economically without using the above inventory model.

FIXED ORDER QUANTITY WITH NONINSTANTANEOUS DELIVERY MODEL

The fixed order quantity with noninstantaneous delivery model is sometimes called the economic lot size (ELS) model. Sometimes, the actual delivery of units into the purchaser's warehouse occurs over a period of time. As is shown in Figure 11.9, as the level of inventory drops to a predetermined level, R^*, an order of size Q^* is placed, and delivery starts. However, as delivery continues, units are drawn from inventory at a rate of 1 per unit of time. If replenishment rate p exceeds the withdrawal rate d, the inventory level rises, but not up to the level of the order or lot size in the EOQ model.

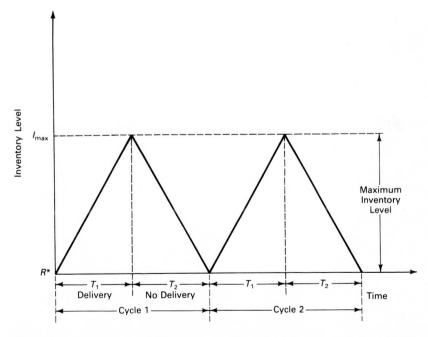

Figure 11.9 Inventory Level Changes in the Fixed Order Quantity with Usage System

Let us define symbols that have not appeared before:

$$T_1 = \text{Delivery period}$$
$$T_2 = \text{Nondelivery period}$$

During T_1, the units are delivered and consumed, while during T_2 there is no delivery, but only consumption. The delivery period T_1 is

$$T_1 = \frac{\text{Fixed order size}}{\text{Rate of delivery}} = \frac{Q}{p} \tag{11.12}$$

Q is the order size delivered or the batch size produced. During period T_1, the inventory is accumulated at a rate of $(p - d)$ per unit of time, assuming that the rate of delivery (production), p, is greater than the rate of consumption, d. The maximum level of inventory is:

$$I_{max} = (p - d)T_1 - (p - d)\frac{Q}{p} \tag{11.13}$$

The average inventory level is determined by the maximum inventory level, I_{max}, and the minimum inventory level, zero.

$$\text{Average inventory} = \frac{I_{max} - 0}{2} = \frac{(p - d)Q}{2p} \tag{11.14}$$

The annual carrying cost, then, is:

$$\text{Annual carrying cost} = \frac{(p - d)Q}{2p}(HC)$$

The total annual cost of operating this inventory model is:

$$TC = \frac{(p - d)Q}{2p}(HC) + \frac{KD}{Q}$$

D is, as before, the annual demand. Obviously, D can be found by multiplying d by the number of working days in one year.

Again, the optimal order quantity can be found by equating the carrying and procurement costs:

$$\frac{(p - d)Q}{2p}(HC) = \frac{KD}{Q}$$

$$Q^* = \sqrt{\frac{2KD}{HC}\frac{p}{p - d}} \tag{11.15}$$

The consumption or nondelivery period is

$$T_2 = \frac{I_{max}}{d} = \frac{(p - d)Q}{dp}$$

The total cycle time is

$$T = T_1 + T_2.$$

The fixed order quantity with noninstantaneous delivery model can be used to calculate optimal lot or batch sizes in manufacturing organizations. This occurs when one production department orders parts from another production department and uses the parts as soon as they arrive, on a continuous basis, rather than waiting for the whole lot to arrive. This particular use of the model is the reason for the alternative name, economic lot size (ELS). The following example demonstrates this situation.

EXAMPLE   The assembly department of cylinder brakes turns out 1600 units a month. The subassemblies are coming in at a rate of 2000 units a month. The ordering (setup) cost of a lot of subassemblies is $100, and the carrying cost per month of the subassemblies is one percent of the cost of a subassembly. The cost of one subassembly kit is $250. What is the optimum lot size of the subassembly? Here, we have:

$$K = \$100.00$$
$$d = 1600 \text{ units/month}$$
$$D = (1600)(12) = 19{,}200\text{/year}$$
$$p = 2{,}000 \text{ units/month}$$
$$H = (1\%)(12) = 12\% = 0.12$$
$$C = \$250.00$$

and Equation (11.15) applies. Thus:

$$Q^* = \sqrt{\frac{(2)(100.00)(19{,}200)}{(0.12)(250.00)} \frac{2000}{2000 - 1600}}$$

$$= \sqrt{128{,}000 \frac{2000}{400}}$$

$$= \sqrt{640{,}000} = 800 \text{ units}$$

Thus, the subassembly department should run 800 subassembly units at a time, at a minimum monthly cost of

$$TC^* = \frac{(2000 - 1600)800}{2(2000)} (0.01)(250.00) + \frac{(100.00)(1600)}{800}$$

$$= 200.00 + 200.00 = \$400.00\text{/month}$$

FIXED ORDER QUANTITY WITH DISCOUNTS MODEL

In all the systems covered so far, one important element has not been treated: the quantity discount element. It is a common occurrence that the unit price changes with order size. While trying to minimize annual carrying costs and procurement costs, one tries to take advantage of volume discounts. When this is done, the economic order quantity may be affected. In other words, the total cost equation becomes:

$$\begin{Bmatrix} \text{Total annual} \\ \text{inventory cost} \end{Bmatrix} = \begin{Bmatrix} \text{Number of orders} \\ \text{placed annually} \end{Bmatrix} \times \begin{Bmatrix} \text{Ordering} \\ \text{cost} \end{Bmatrix} + \begin{Bmatrix} \text{Average} \\ \text{inventory} \end{Bmatrix} \times$$

$$\begin{Bmatrix} \text{Carrying cost} \\ \text{per unit} \end{Bmatrix} + \begin{Bmatrix} \text{Annual purchase} \\ \text{cost (discounts} \\ \text{taken into account)} \end{Bmatrix}$$

The delivery is assumed to be instantaneous, as in the EOQ Model; however, the annual purchase cost (discounted) should be included in the calculation. Let us examine such a case in the following example.

EXAMPLE   Print-Fast, a printing shop down the street, buys paper by the box. The paper's supplier offers a volume discount:

> For quantities of 1–699: $10.00 a box
> For quantities of 700–1399: $8.00 a box
> For quantities over 1400 boxes: $6.00 a box

The printing shop consumes 5000 boxes a year. The procurement charge is $75.00 an order, and the holding cost is 20 percent of the purchase price per box per year. What is the optimal purchasing policy?

The first step is to find the EOQ for the lowest price level ($6.00 a box). Using the EOQ formula, we get:

$$Q^*_1 = \sqrt{\frac{2DK}{HC}} = \sqrt{\frac{2(5000)(75.00)}{(0.20)(6.00)}} = 791 \text{ boxes}$$

We compare Q^*_1 to the quantity that must be purchased to get the $6.00 price (1400 boxes). If Q^*_1 is larger than this quantity, the problem is solved. If Q^*_1 is smaller, the solution is not applicable. In this case, we proceed to the second step.

The second step is to select the next-higher price level ($8.00 a box) and to calculate its EOQ:

$$Q^*_2 = \sqrt{\frac{2(5000)(75.00)}{(0.20)(8.00)}} = 685 \text{ boxes}$$

Again, we compare Q^*_2 to the range of quantities required for the $8.00 price (700 to 1399). Since Q^*_2 is not within this range, the solution is not applicable.

The third step is to select the next-higher price level ($10.00 a box) and to calculate its EOQ:

$$Q^*_3 = \sqrt{\frac{2(5000)(75.00)}{(0.20)(10.00)}} = 612 \text{ boxes}$$

Compare Q^*_3 to the range of quantities required for the $10.00 price (1 to 699). Since 612 boxes is within this range, this is an applicable solution.

The fourth step is to calculate the total annual cost for each of the applicable EOQ's and for each of the cutoff points. For Q = 1400 @ $6.00/box:

$$TC = K\frac{D}{Q} + HC\frac{Q}{2} + DC$$

$$= (75.00)\frac{5000}{1400} + (0.20)(6.00)\frac{1400}{2} + (5000)(6.00)$$

$$= 267.86 + 840.00 + 30,000.00$$

$$= \$31,107.86$$

For Q = 1,399 @ $8.00/box:

$$TC = (75.00)\frac{5000}{1399} + (0.20)(8.00)\frac{1399}{2} + (5000)(8.00)$$

$$= 268.05 + 1119.20 + 40,000.00$$

$$= \$41,387.25$$

For Q = 700 @ $8.00/box:

$$TC = (75.00)\frac{5000}{700} + (0.20)(8.00)\frac{700}{2} + (5000)(8.00)$$

$$= 535.71 + 560.00 + 40,000.00$$

$$= \$41,095.71$$

For Q^*_3 = 612 @ $10.00/box:

$$TC = (75.00)\frac{5000}{612} + (0.20)(10.00)\frac{612}{2} + (5000)(10.00)$$

$$= 612.75 + 612.00 + 50,000.00$$

$$= \$51,224.75$$

Note that the total annual procurement and holding cost should be equal. However, due to a rounding in the calculation of Q^*_3, there is a small difference in the calculations of TC for Q^*_3 = 612 @ $10.00/box.

The best reorder quantity based on total annual costs comparison is 1400 boxes, for a total annual cost of $31,107.86. Let us refer to Figure 11.10 for a graphical presentation of this case. The solid lines indicate the applicable range for each price per box. The minimum TC point for each price is noted, as well as the TC for the cutoff points. Since the total annual cost of the Q^*_3 at the price of $10.00 has been checked, we should not calculate the total annual cost for the reorder quantity of 699, which is the cutoff point for $10.00.

FIXED ORDER QUANTITY WITH BACKORDERS MODEL

Until now, we have assumed that demand is known, and that if one orders in time, no back orders accumulate. In the following model, shortages are accounted for and satisfied from the next order. The system's inventory level is described in Figure 11.11.

As one can see from Figure 11.11, an order on the amount of Q is coming in, raising the inventory level to I_{max}. This I_{max} is the maximum level of inventory that is always less than or, at best, equal to Q. This inventory is consumed and, at one point, there are no more units left in inventory. From that point on, shortage occurs, at a cost of S dollars per unit per year. When an order comes in, it is used first to satisfy back orders, then builds an inventory up to a level I_{max}, and so on.

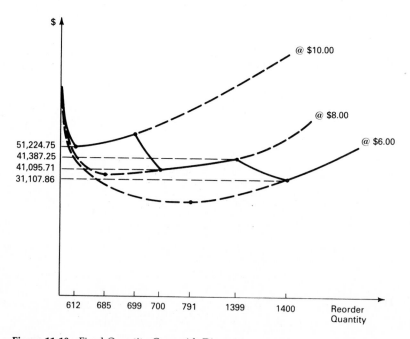

Figure 11.10 Fixed Quantity Case with Discounts

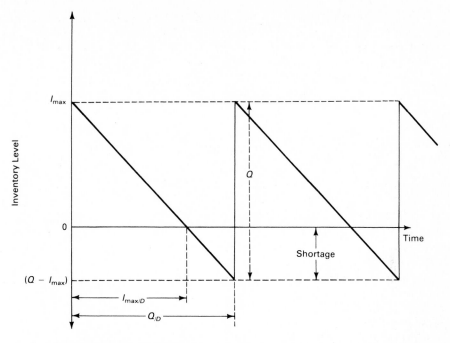

Figure 11.11   Fixed Order Quantity with Back Orders System

As for the other systems, one looks at the total annual cost of applying this inventory system:

$$\begin{Bmatrix}\text{Total annual}\\\text{inventory cost}\end{Bmatrix} = \begin{Bmatrix}\text{Number of orders}\\\text{placed annually}\end{Bmatrix} \times \begin{Bmatrix}\text{Ordering}\\\text{cost per}\\\text{order}\end{Bmatrix} + \begin{Bmatrix}\text{Average}\\\text{inventory}\end{Bmatrix} \times$$

$$\begin{Bmatrix}\text{Carrying cost}\\\text{per unit}\end{Bmatrix} + \begin{Bmatrix}\text{Annual}\\\text{shortage}\\\text{cost}\end{Bmatrix}$$

$$TC = \frac{KD}{Q} + \frac{HCI_{max}^{2}}{2Q} + \frac{S(Q - I_{max})^{2}}{2Q} \tag{11.16}$$

The best reorder quantity[6] for this system is:

---

[6] In order to find the minimum TC, partial derivatives with respect to Q and I_{max} are taken:

$$\frac{\partial TC}{\partial Q} = -\frac{KD}{Q^{2}} - \frac{HCI_{max}^{2}}{2Q^{2}} + \frac{S(Q - I_{max})}{Q} - \frac{S(Q - I_{max})^{2}}{2Q^{2}} = 0$$

$$\frac{\partial TC}{\partial I_{max}} = \frac{HCI_{max}}{Q} - \frac{S(Q - I_{max})}{Q} = 0$$

When these results are solved simultaneously, equations (11.17) and (11.18) result.

$$Q^* = \sqrt{\frac{2KD}{HC} \left(\frac{S + HC}{S} \right)} \qquad (11.17)$$

and the maximum level of inventory when one reorders quantity Q^* is:

$$I_{max}^* = \sqrt{\frac{2KD}{HC} \left(\frac{S}{S + HC} \right)} \qquad (11.18)$$

EXAMPLE Solcom, Inc., distributes solar water heaters for the residential market. Currently the company distributes 10,000 heaters a year. The carrying cost of one heater is 20 percent of its price, $2,000.00. Furthermore, the procurement cost per order is $50.00, and the shortage cost is $100.00 per heater per year. What should be the reorder quantity for Solcom, Inc.? What should be the warehouse size, assuming that the heaters cannot be piled and require 100 sq. ft. of storage space per heater?

Based on equation (11.17), the reorder quantity is:

$$Q^* = \sqrt{\frac{2(50.00)(10,000)}{(0.20)(2,000.00)} \times \left(\frac{100.00 + (0.20)(2000.00)}{100.00} \right)}$$

$$= 111.80 \cong 112 \text{ heaters}$$

Solcom, Inc., is to order 112 heaters at one time to keep total annual cost to a minimum.

$$I_{max}^* = \sqrt{\frac{2(50.00)(10,000)}{(0.20)(2,000.00)} \times \left(\frac{100.00}{100.00 + (0.20)(2,000.00)} \right)}$$

$$= 22.36 \sim 23 \text{ heaters}$$

Thus, the storage space should be $23 \times 100 = 2300$ sq. ft.

PERIODIC REORDER MODELS

Operationally, it might be easier to check the inventory level and reorder at fixed time intervals, rather than continuously. The reorder size will then vary and will be equal to the difference between the desired inventory level and the current one. Such a periodic inventory order policy requires less supervision but a higher safety stock level than does continuous observation of the inventory level.

As one can see in Figure 11.12, demand and lead time are constant and replenishment is instantaneous. However, the reorder quantity, Q, might differ from period to period, as can be seen in Figure 11.7. The reorder quantity is determined as the difference between a replenishment level, R, and the current level of inventory. The time between the placement of an order and the time of receipt is the lead time, t_L. The cycle time, the time between successive reorders,

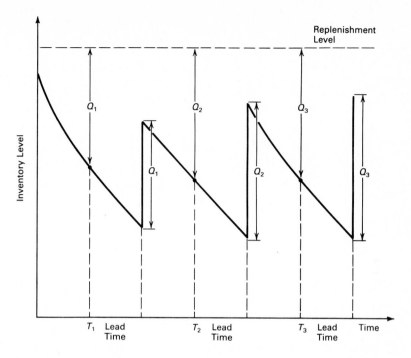

Figure 11.12   Fixed Period Case with Constant Demand, Constant Lead Time, and Instantaneous Replenishment

is termed T. The problem is to optimize the cycle time, or the time between successive reorders, T.

As can be seen from Figure 11.12, the constant lead time and constant demand result in equal reorder quantities. Thus, Q is the reorder quantity and D is the annual demand; the number of orders per year is D/Q. The cycle time, T, is equal to the ratio Q/D. (T is expressed in fractions of a year.)

Thus, DT can replace Q in the total cost equation for the fixed quantity case.

$$TC = K\frac{D}{DT} + HC\frac{Q}{2}$$

$$TC = K\frac{D}{DT} + HC\frac{DT}{2} \tag{11.19}$$

The total cost is minimal when the two right-hand terms are equal.

$$K\frac{1}{T} = HC\frac{DT}{2}$$

$$T^* = \sqrt{\frac{2K}{HCD}} \tag{11.20}$$

Once the optimal cycle time has been determined, the optimal reorder quantity can be stated as:

$$Q^* = DT^* \qquad\qquad (11.21)$$

EXAMPLE   Marble Floors, Inc., sells 2500 marble tiles a year. The cost of a production setup is $1000.00, and the annual carrying cost is 10 percent of the price of a tile. One tile is sold at $85.00. What should be the time between successive reorders, and what should be the reorder quantity that will minimize the total annual inventory cost?

Following equation (11.20), the optimal cycle time is:

$$T^* = \sqrt{\frac{2(1000.00)}{(0.10)(85.00)(2500)}} = 0.307 \text{ year}$$

Also, the reorder quantity is, as per equation (11.21):

$$Q^* = DT^* = (2500)(0.307) = 767.50 \sim 768 \text{ tiles.}$$

The operations manager should order 768 tiles every 35 days.

STOCHASTIC INVENTORY MODELS

Until now, demand has been assumed to be constant and known with certainty. An average demand is a good estimate, and many times is a basis for operational decisions. However, when the demand varies considerably from one period to another, a safety stock must be kept in order to hedge against shortages.

Let us consider the basic fixed order quantity model that was discussed earlier. When the inventory level reaches the reorder level, an order is placed, and the replenishment is carried out all at once after a certain lead time. Obviously, if the demand varies over time, or if the lead time varies, a shortage or overage might occur. These occurrences are demonstrated in Figure 11.13.

During the first cycle in Figure 11.13, the inventory level reaches the reorder level, at which time an order Q is placed. The demand during the lead time is such that the order has arrived by the time the inventory level reaches the safety stock level. Demand over lead time during the next cycle leads to an overage. The demand over the lead time during the third cycle is so intensive that the safety stock is used up and a shortage is created.

The problem is: How large should the safety stock be? In order to decide on the number of units required for a safety stock, the operations manager has to determine a "service level." A service level is the probability of not running out of stock. That is, the proportion of time in which the demand has not exceeded the available inventory. Obviously, the larger the safety stock, the smaller the probability of running out, and the better the service level, as there are no frequent stockouts. However, a large safety stock calls for higher carrying costs.

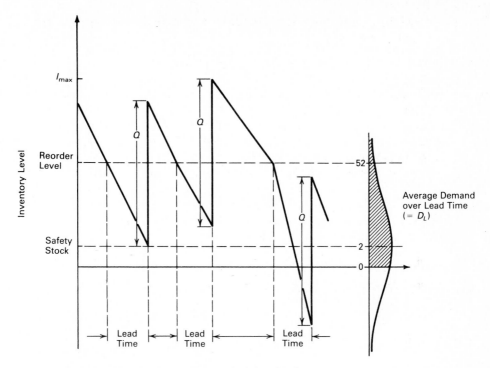

Figure 11.13   Fixed Order Quantity Case with Safety Stock

SAFETY STOCK

Let us try to determine the optimal safety stock size. As the demand for the product is affected by numerous variables, one can assume a normal distribution for the demand over lead time.

The variability of the demand over the lead time is presented as a standard deviation, σ_L. One should note the relationship between the standard deviation of demand over lead time, σ_L and the standard deviation of the daily demand σ_{daily}. This relationship is expressed as:

$$\sigma_L = \sqrt{\sum_{i=1}^{n} \sigma_{daily}^2}$$

where n is the number of days of lead time. The average demand over lead time, D_L, is the average daily demand times the number of days of lead time.

$$D_L = (n) (D_{daily})$$

The safety stock is expressed as the number of standard deviations, Z, away from the average demand over lead time, when one assumes a normal distribution of demand over lead time.

$$\text{Safety stock} = (Z)(\sigma_L)$$

This relationship is shown in Figure 11.14. The values for Z are read off Table A in the Appendix at the end of this book. The average demand over lead time is D_L, the safety stock is equal to $(Z)(\sigma_L)$, and the *reorder point* is at $D_L + (Z)(\sigma_L)$.

EXAMPLE   Etrolex, a distributor of clocks and watches, realizes an average demand over lead time of 50 stopwatches. The standard deviation of demand over lead time is 4.55 watches, found by studying historical data. Management wants to provide its customers with a service level of 67 percent.

Based on Table A in the Appendix, for 0.67, the Z value is 0.44. Thus, the safety stock is $Z \times \sigma_L = 0.44 \times 4.55 = 2.00$ watches. So, the safety stock is two watches. The average demand over lead time, D_L, as well as the safety stock, $D_L + Z\sigma_L$, is marked in Figure 11.14.

Since the average demand over lead time is 50, an order should be placed when the inventory level reaches 52 watches.

It is interesting to see how Figure 11.14 fits into Figure 11.13. (The reader is encouraged to note the superimposition of Figure 11.14 onto Figure 11.13.) The relationship between the reorder point and the safety stock then becomes clear.

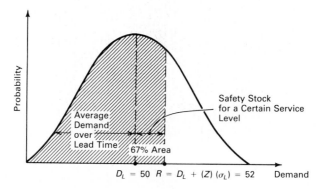

Figure 11.14   Safety Stock and Service Levels; The Safety Stock is Equal to $(Z) (\sigma_L)$

The Economical Size of Safety Stock

While the previous example determined safety stock by relating it to service level, the main problem is to decide on the economical size of the safety stock, taking into account the shortage cost and the carrying cost for various service levels.

One should look for the trade-off between shortage cost and carrying cost. Let us assume that the optimal reorder quantity, Q^*, has been determined already, and that one is interested in the optimum safety stock size.

$$\left\{\begin{array}{l}\text{Annual} \\ \text{shortage} \\ \text{cost}\end{array}\right\} = \left\{\begin{array}{l}\text{Cost of} \\ \text{one} \\ \text{shortage}\end{array}\right\} \times \left\{\begin{array}{l}\text{Number} \\ \text{of orders} \\ \text{per year}\end{array}\right\} \times \left\{\begin{array}{l}\text{Probability} \\ \text{of one} \\ \text{shortage}\end{array}\right\}$$

where

P_s = Probability of one shortage = (1 − Service level).

D/Q^* = Number of orders per year.

S = Cost of one shortage

$$\text{Annual shortage cost} = S\left(\frac{D}{Q^*}\right)(1 - \text{Service level})$$

The annual carrying cost is:

$$\text{Annual carrying cost} = (HC)(\text{Safety stock}) = (HC)(Z\sigma_L)$$

where:

Z = the number of standard deviations that provides a certain service level (read off Table A in the Appendix)

σ_L = the standard deviation of demand over lead time.

Thus, the total annual cost for a certain demand variability, σ_L, and a certain service level is:

$$TC = S\left(\frac{D}{Q^*}\right)(1 - \text{Service level}) + (HC)(Z\sigma_L)$$

In order to find the best safety stock level, $Z\sigma_L$, one should calculate the total cost, TC, for various service levels and choose the one that corresponds to the lowest total cost.

EXAMPLE Etrolex, the clock and watch distributor, has to decide between 80 percent and 90 percent service levels. It realizes a lead time of 5 days, an average daily demand of 10 stopwatches a day, and a standard deviation of demand per day over lead time of 2.035 watches. The procurement cost is $10 per order, the carrying cost is 10 percent per year, the shortage cost is $2 per shortage, and the unit price is $30. What is the recommended, most economical safety stock level for Etrolex's stopwatches?

First, assuming 250 working days, let us calculate the optimal order size:

$$Q^* = \sqrt{\frac{2(10)(250)(10)}{(0.10)(30)}} = 129.099 \sim 129 \text{ stopwatches}$$

Let us calculate the total cost for service levels of 80 percent and 90 percent:

$$\text{Lead time} = \sqrt{5\sigma^2} \text{ daily}$$

$$= \sqrt{(5)(2.035)^2}$$

$$= 4.55 \text{ stopwatches}$$

Now, let us compare the total costs for the two service levels:

80 PERCENT SERVICE LEVEL	90 PERCENT SERVICE LEVEL

From Table A in the Appendix:
$Z = 0.84$
Safety stock $= Z\sigma_L = (0.84)(4.55)$
$\qquad\qquad = 3.82 \sim 4$ stopwatches
Carrying cost $= (HC) \times$ (Safety stock)
$\qquad\qquad = (0.10)(30)(4)$
$\qquad\qquad = \$12.00$
Shortage cost $=$

$$= S\left(\frac{D}{Q^*}\right)(1 - \text{Service level})$$

$$= (2)\left(\frac{250 \times 10}{129}\right)(1 - 0.80)$$

$= \$7.75$
$TC = 12.00 + 7.75 = \$19.75$

From Table A in the Appendix:
$Z = 1.28$
Safety stock $= (1.28)(4.55)$
$\qquad\qquad = 5.824 \sim 6$ stopwatches
Carrying cost $= (0.10)(30)(6)$
$\qquad\qquad = \$18.00$
Shortage cost $=$

$$= (2)\left(\frac{280 \times 10}{129}\right)(1 - 0.90)$$

$= \$3.88$
$TC = 18.00 + 3.88 = \$21.88$

As one can see, at 80 percent service level, the carrying cost is lower than it is for the 90 percent service level, and offsets the higher shortage cost. Thus, Etrolex should order 129 stopwatches when the inventory level reaches $(5)(10) + 4 = 54$ watches. This provides for an 80 percent service level. That is, on the average, one out of every 5 units is not available when ordered.

ABC CLASSIFICATIONS

The calculations and the data required to operate the quantitative inventory models become more complex as the number of different items in inventory increases. It is not practical to calculate reorder quantities, using the models described above, for each item carried, but only for those items that call for a high degree of control.

The ABC classification is a method of identifying the degree of control required for various items. It categorizes all inventoried items into three groups, based on the annual inventory dollar value of each.

Group A includes approximately 20 percent of the items that account for approximately 80 percent of the total annual inventory. All items in this group are closely controlled and call for the use of quantitative models. The equations presented in the preceding sections should be used to determine the reorder quantity and economical safety stock.

Group B includes approximately 30 percent of the items that account for approximately 15 percent of the total annual inventory value. Less control is exercised over these items. For example, while the economic order quantity determination is recommended, safety stock considerations are somewhat less important.

Group C includes approximately 50 percent of the items that account for approximately 5 percent of the total annual inventory value. No special effort should be invested in controlling these items, as the cost of control may exceed the potential savings.

The actual percent of items and percent of total annual inventory value may vary according to the specific situation. The three groups are shown in Figure 11.15.

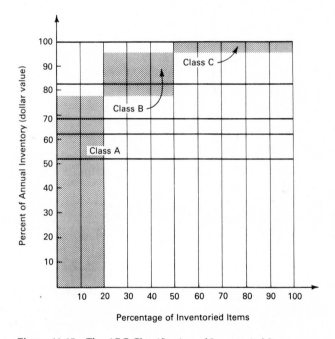

Figure 11.15   The ABC Classification of Inventoried Items

ABC Analysis Procedure

Step 1. Prepare a list of inventory items.

Step 2. Calculate the annual inventory dollar value for each item and corresponding percentage.

Step 3. Arrange the items in descending order of annual inventory dollar value.

Step 4. Compute the cumulative percentage of the annual inventory dollar value.

Step 5. Compute the cumulative percentage of the number of items.

Step 6. Determine the ABC categories.

EXAMPLE   Let us consider the example in Table 11.2. As can be seen, Class A items are: X0100 and X0200 as they are 20 percent of the items and account for 61.58 percent of the cumulative percent of value; Class B items are: X0300, X0700, and X0900, as they are 30 percent of the items and account for 21.75 percent of the cumulative percent of value; Class C items are X1000, X0800, X0600, X0500, and X0400, as they are 50 percent of the items and account for 16.67 percent of the cumulative percent of value. As one can see, a minority of items accounts for most of the annual inventory value, and requires a high degree of control. Note that the cumulative percentage of items is the benchmark, so long as the cumulative percentage of value of Class A constitutes most of the total value.

COMPUTERIZED INVENTORY SYSTEMS

Inventory systems have been subject to extensive computerization in the last several years, and by now are an integral part of inventory systems in many organizations. An illustrated example of a computerized inventory system and its integration into the organization, appears in Figure 11.16. This system is designed to perform two functions:

1. To calculate the impact of various service levels in order to support management decision
2. To calculate ordering policy that provides for a specific service level at the lowest total cost.

The system contains five lower-level systems: initializing, recordkeeping, forecasting, measuring, and ordering. The *initializing* system is used when the system is being installed or when conditions change. The system:

1. Selects the best forecast technique
2. Prepares distribution-by-value reports to serve as a guide in planning and installing an inventory management system
3. Selects the best ordering strategy to be used for each vendor and item
4. Estimates in advance the results expected from applying these decision rules.

The *recordkeeping* system keeps track of the inventory as transactions occur. It notes inventory on hand and on order, and back orders. The information accumulated is made available to the forecasting and ordering systems as it is required.

TABLE 11.2 ABC ANALYSIS EXAMPLE

ITEM	(1) UNIT VALUE ($/UNIT)	(2) UNITS USED (UNITS/YEAR)	(3) = (1) × (2) ANNUAL INVENTORY VALUE ($)	(4) PER-CENTAGE VALUE ($)	(5) ITEMS ORDERED BY PER-CENTAGE VALUE	(6) = (4) PER-CENTAGE VALUE ($)	(7) CUMULATIVE PERCENTAGE OF VALUE ($)	(8) CUMULATIVE PERCENTAGE OF ITEMS
X0100	0.60	10,000	6000.00	52.04	X0100	52.04	52.04	10.0
X0200	1.00	1100	1100.00	9.54	X0200	9.54	61.58	20.0
X0300	1.20	900	1080.00	9.37	X0300	9.37	70.95	30.0
X0400	0.80	250	200.00	1.73	X0700	7.89	78.84	40.0
X0500	0.35	1000	350.00	3.04	X0900	4.49	83.33	50.0
X0600	0.45	900	405.00	3.51	X1000	4.49	87.80	60.0
X0700	1.30	700	910.00	7.89	X0800	3.90	91.72	70.0
X0800	0.75	600	450.00	3.90	X0600	3.51	95.23	80.0
X0900	1.15	450	517.50	4.49	X0500	3.04	98.27	90.0
X1000	1.15	450	517.50	4.49	X0400	1.73	100.00	100.0
			$11,530.00	100.00				

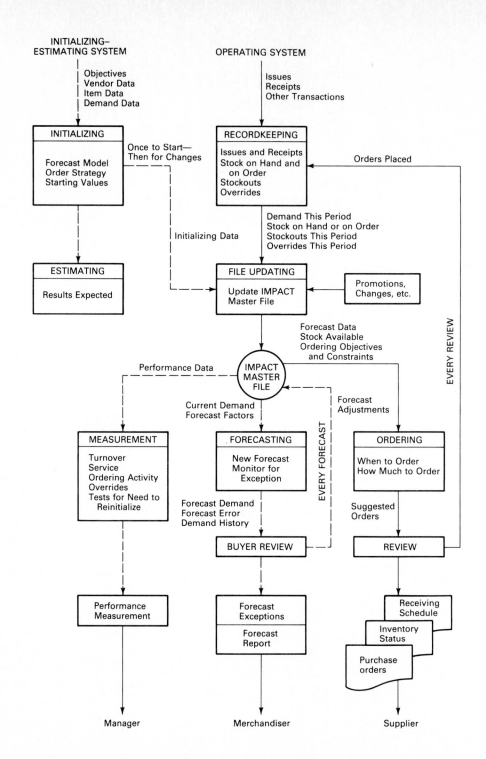

Figure 11.16 Basic Elements of an Inventory Management System *Source: Basic Principles of Wholesale IMPACT—Inventory Management Program and Control Technique,* IBM, GE 20-8105-1, p. 3. Courtesy of International Business Machines Corporation.

The *forecasting* system is used on a periodic basis, weekly or monthly, to:

1. Revise the forecast of demand
2. Revise the forecast error, as explained in Chapter 4.

The *measuring* system accumulates and analyzes performance data on a periodic basis. This enables management to determine how well the inventory system performs.

The *ordering* system is used, when inventory transactions occur on a periodic basis, to perform the following functions:

1. Determine whether an item or a vendor line should be ordered
2. Determine how much of each item or a vendor line should be ordered.

All the above systems interrelate and interact with each other on a continuous basis, as described in Figure 11.16.

COMPUTERIZED INTERACTIVE INVENTORY SYSTEMS

In this section, a computerized, interactive inventory system is described. The interactive program is accessible via a terminal that is placed on the operations manager's table. The program helps in testing various alternatives with regard to the inventory management system.

The interactive program is applicable to the fixed order quantity inventory system. The program considers price discounts, shortage costs, warehouse space limitations, and any combination of constraints. Once the input data have been entered, they are printed so that the operations manager may then inspect them. If these are errors, the operations manager types " " in answer to the question: "Check input: is it correct (y/n)?" This causes the program to return to the beginning. The operations manager has the option of changing his or her constraint choice and/or changing the base data.

When the operations manager indicates that the input is correct, the program conducts an error check itself. If any mistakes are found, messages pertaining to the problem are printed and the operations manager is required to enter the correct data.

The interactive program output includes, first, the identification information and, second, the calculated quantities. These quantities are:

1. The optimum order quantity
2. The total inventory cost
3. The number of orders to be placed annually
4. The unit price at the order quantity determined.

Let us consider the solar energy water-heater distributor, Solcom, Inc., which has been discussed earlier. The operations manager introduces the shortage costs by using index number "2" in the input phase, as shown in the computer printout in Figure 11.17. After each question mark, the operations manager responds by inserting the appropriate number. As one can see, the interactive program indicates an optimum order quantity of 111.8 heaters with a maximum inventory level of 22.38 heaters, yielding a total annual inventory cost of approximately 20 million dollars, and ninety orders per year. The operations manager may change the input to reflect the impact of various demand levels, purchasing prices, procurement costs and carrying costs.

In Figure 11.18, the operations manager considers price discounts, indicated with index 1. The data are based on the Print-Fast printing shop example discussed earlier. The computer output indicates that the optimum order quantity is 1400 paper boxes at $6.00 a box. This yields a total annual inventory cost of $31,107.86, where the number of order cycles per year is 3.57.

In Figure 11.19, warehouse space is considered, and indicated with an index 3. The input is similar to the one used for the Buy-Bye example, but the warehouse space available can accommodate up to 1000 units. The output indicates an optimum order quantity of 200,000 units. However, the order quantity is limited by the warehouse space restriction and is not an optimum. If the storage limitation is applied, the order quantity is 1000 units, yielding a higher total annual inventory cost, and increasing significantly the number of order cycles per year.

SUMMARY

This chapter has covered the essentials of inventory control and inventory management for independent demand. Inventories are used to hedge against future increases in costs and prices, to hedge against stockouts, to provide production flexibility and lot size economy, etc. The "when" and "how much" are the major questions answered through a systematic use of the analyses presented in this chapter.

We have treated quantitatively several important inventory models—in particular, the basic fixed order quantity model, sometimes termed economic order quantity (EOQ); the fixed order quantity with noninstantaneous delivery model, sometimes termed economic lot size (ELS); the fixed order quantity with back orders model that considered shortages; and the fixed order quantity with discounts model. In all of these models it was assumed that the time between orders varied while an order of a predetermined, fixed size was placed.

Periodic models, however, assume that the time between orders is constant while the order size varies and is determined by the difference between a predetermined, fixed inventory level and the level of inventory at the time an order is placed.

Figure 11.17 Interactive Program Printout for the Fixed Order Quantity with Back Orders Model (user's entries are underlined)

---

note: all numeric values entered are to be separated by a comma and/or a space

enter your name and problem title of (stop)

? *Solcom, Inc.*

program Economic Order Quantity for Solcom, Inc.

enter base data:

total annual usage in units ? 10000

cost of one purchase order ? 50.00

holding cost (of one unit price) ? .20

price per unit (regular) ? 2000.00

constraints

(1) price discounts
(2) shortage costs
(3) warehouse space limitations
(4) combination of 1, 2, and 3
(5) no constraints

enter index number of desired constraint ? 2

enter shortage cost (real #) ? 100.00

Economic Order Quantity for Solcom, Inc.

usage	order $	hold $		$/unit		
	10000.	50.00		0.20 2000.00		
shortage $	1st rate	order size	2nd rate	order size	warehouse	
100.0	0.00	0.	0.00	0.	0.	

check input: is it correct (y/n) ? y

Economic Order Quantity answer for Solcom, Inc.

optimum order quantity is	111.8
with optimum inventory of	22.36
at a price per item of	2000.00
yielding a total inventory cost of	10008944.25
where the number of order cycles per year is	89.44

change constraint type or stop (y/n) ? y

Figure 11.18 Interactive Program Printout for the Fixed Order Quantity with Discounts Model (user's entries are underlined)

enter your name and problem title of (stop)
? *Print-Fast*

program Economic Order Quantity for Print-Fast

change base data (y/n) ? y

enter base data:

total annual usage in units ? 5000

cost of one purchase order ? 75.00

holding cost (of unit price) ? .20

price per unit (regular) ? 10.00

constraints

(1) price discounts
(2) shortage costs
(3) warehouse space limitations
(4) combination of 1, 2, and 3
(5) no constraints

enter index number of desired constraint ? 1

1st discount: enter price/unit (real #) and order size
? 8.00, 700

2nd discount: enter price/unit (real #) and order size (if second discount set not desired enter (0,0))
? 6.00, 1400

Economic Order Quantity for Print-Fast

usage	order $	hold $		$/unit		
	5000.	75.00		0.20	10.00	
shortage $	1st rate	order size	2nd rate	order size	warehouse
0.00	8.00	700.	6.00	1400.	0.

check input: is it correct (y/n) ? y

Economic Order Quantity answer for Print-Fast

optimum order quantity is	1400.00
at a price per item of	6.00
yielding a total inventory cost of	31107.86
where the number of order cycles per year is	3.57

change constraint type or stop (y/n) ? y

Figure 11.19 Interactive Program Printout for the Fixed Order Quantity with Warehouse Space Limitations (user's entries are underlined)

enter your name and problem title of (stop)
? *Buy-Bye*

program Economic Order Quantity for Buy-Bye

change base data (y/n) ? y

enter base data:

total annual usage in units ? 12000000

cost of one purchase order ? 40.00

holding cost (of unit price) ? .12

price per unit (regular) ? .20

constraints

(1) price discounts
(2) shortage costs
(3) warehouse space limitations
(4) combination of 1, 2, and 3
(5) no constraints

enter index number of desired constraint ? 3

enter warehouse space available ? 1000

Economic Order Quantity for Print-Fast

usage	order $	hold $		$/unit		
12000000	40.00	0.12		0.0		
shortage $	1st rate	order size	2nd rate	order size	warehouse	
0.00	0.00	0.	0.00	0.	1000.	

check input: is it correct (y/n) ? y

Economic Order Quantity answer for Print-Fast

before the warehouse storage limitation is applied
optimum order quantity is   200000.00
at a price per item of   0.20
yielding a total inventory cost of   2404800.00
where the number of order cycles per year is   60.00
the order quantity is limited by the warehouse space restriction
  and is not at an optimum. loosen the restriction and run
  again observing the effect. after the warehouse storage limitation
  is applied optimum order quantity is   1000.00
at a price per item of   0.20
yielding a total inventory cost of   2880012.00
where the number of order cycles per year is   12000.00
this order quantity is at the maximum warehouse capacity

change constraint type or stop (y/n) ? y

Considerations of safety stock size and service levels were also treated in the chapter, as well as determination of the items that should be controlled closely based on the ABC classification.

As in all other chapters, we have covered the use of computers for inventory management and control, and, specifically, the use of conversational computer programs through a terminal that is placed on the operations manager's table.

DISCUSSION QUESTIONS

11.1 Clarify the importance of inventory and the magnitude of the problem involved.
11.2 Define the term "inventory."
11.3 State the distinction between inventory management and inventory control.
11.4 What are the functions of inventory?
11.5 What are the considerations involved in inventory systems?
11.6 What are the two inventory decisions that the operations manager should make?
11.7 What are the five types of inventory costs?
11.8 What are the three alternative solution methods used to determine reorder quantity and reorder point?
11.9 What are the steps involved in the development of inventory policy?
11.10 What are the assumptions behind the basic fixed order quantity model?
11.11 What is the basic difference between the fixed order quantity model and the periodic order model?
11.12 Describe the ABC classification system.
11.13 What are the functions of IMPACT?

PROBLEMS AND SOLUTIONS

11.1 A bakery uses 25,000 bags of flour each year for its products. It costs the company $10.50 to place an order and $1.00 to store a bag for a year.
a) Compute the optimal order quantity, Q^*, following the basic fixed order quantity model.
b) Compute total cost TC^*.

Solution
a) Optimal Order Quantity Q^*:

$$Q^* = \sqrt{\frac{2DK}{HC}} = \sqrt{\frac{2(25,000)(10.50)}{1.00}}$$

$$= 724.56 \text{ bags}$$
$$\sim 725 \text{ bags}$$

b) Total Cost TC^*:

$$TC^* = K\frac{D}{Q^*} + HC\frac{Q^*}{2}$$

$$= (10.50)\frac{25,000}{725} + (1.00)\frac{725}{2}$$

$$= 362 + 363 \qquad \text{(numbers rounded)}$$
$$= \$725$$

11.2 The Oklahoma Ranch buys 18,000 bags of fertilizer each year for its farming operation. It costs the company $7.50 to place an order, and carrying costs amount to 12.5 percent of the fertilizer's purchasing price of $6.00 per bag.
   a) Compute the optimal order quantity, Q^*, using the basic fixed order quantity model, and calculate the total annual cost TC^*.
   b) Suppose that 2000 more than the optimal order quantity calculated above is ordered. What is the impact on the total annual cost?

Solution

a) $Q^* = \sqrt{\dfrac{2DK}{HC}} = \sqrt{\dfrac{2(18,000)(7.50)}{0.75}} = \sqrt{360,000} = 600$ bags

$$TC^* = K\frac{D}{Q^*} + HC\frac{Q^*}{2}$$

$$= 7.50\frac{(18,000)}{600} + 0.75\frac{(600)}{2}$$

$$= 225 + 225$$
$$= \$450$$

b) To determine the impact on the total annual cost when 2000 more than the optimal order quantity is ordered, the total annual cost, using the optimal order quantity, is compared to the nonoptimal total annual cost:

$$\text{Optimal:} \qquad TC^* = K\frac{D}{Q^*} + HC\frac{Q^*}{2}$$

$$\text{Non-Optimal:} \quad TC = K\frac{D}{Q} + HC\frac{Q}{2}2$$

$$\frac{TC^*}{TC} = \frac{K\dfrac{D}{Q^*} + HC\dfrac{Q^*}{2}}{K\dfrac{D}{Q} + HC\dfrac{Q}{2}}$$

Substituting $\sqrt{\dfrac{2DK}{HC}}$ for Q^*, we get:

$$\frac{TC}{TC^*} = \frac{1}{2}\left[\frac{Q^*}{Q} + \frac{Q}{Q^*}\right]$$

$$= \frac{1}{2}\frac{600}{2600} + \frac{2600}{600} =$$

$$= 2.28$$

When 2000 more than the optimal order size is ordered, the total cost is 2.28 times as much as the optimal order annual cost.

11.3   A major chandlery on the West Coast manufactures a popular "self-tailing winch" for sailors. The company also manufactures several other models in the same shop. The production manager is contemplating the purchase of some new equipment for the shop and wants to calculate the new optimal production run with the new equipment. He believes that the following data are accurate, assuming 250 working days per year:

$$
\begin{array}{lll}
\text{Yearly demand} & = & 4500 \\
\text{Daily demand} & = & 18 \\
\text{Daily production} & = & 28 \\
\text{Setup cost} & = & \$25 \\
\text{Holding cost} & = & 0.021 \\
\text{Unit cost} & = & \$36.24 \text{ each}
\end{array}
$$

Calculate:
a) economic lot size
b) production run time
c) cycle period
d) period between runs
e) the economic lot size, if daily production increases to 30 units per day.

Solution

$$
\begin{array}{lll}
d & = & 4500/\text{year} \\
p & = & 7000/\text{year} \\
K & = & \$25/\text{setup} \\
HC & = & \text{holding cost per unit per year} = \$0.021
\end{array}
$$

a) Economic lot size

$$Q^* = \sqrt{\frac{2KD}{HC}\frac{p}{p-d}} = \sqrt{\frac{2(\$25)(7000)(4500)}{0.021(7000-4500)}} = 5477.22, \text{ or } 5477 \text{ units}$$

b) Production run time:

$$T_1 = \frac{Q^*}{p} = \frac{5477}{7000} = 0.7824 \text{ years}$$

$$= 0.7824 \times 250 \text{ days} = 195.6 \sim 196 \text{ days}$$

c) T = cycle period = $T_1 + T_1$, where $T_1 = Q^*/p = 0.7824$ and

$$T_2 = \frac{(p - d)Q^*}{dp}$$

$$= \frac{(7000 - 4500)5477}{(4500)\ 7000} = 0.4347 \text{ years}$$

$T = T_1 + T_2 = 0.7824 + 0.4347 = 1.2171$ years, or 304.27 working days.

d) Period between runs:

$T_2 = 0.4347$ years, or 108.67 (~109) days

e) Economic lot size, with $p = 7500$:

$$Q^* = \sqrt{\frac{2KD}{HC}\ \frac{p}{p - d}} = \sqrt{\frac{2(25)(7500)(4500)}{0.021(7500 - 4500)}}$$

$Q^* = 5175.49$, or 5175

11.4   The Security and Control (S&C) Company manufactures easy-to-install home-security systems. The company currently sells about 20,000 of these security kits each year at a price of $1200 per kit. The carrying cost of one kit is 10 percent of its price, and the procurement cost is $60. The company faces considerable competition, and the shortage cost resulting from ill will among lost customers is about $300 per unit.
a) What should the reorder quantity be?
b) What should the maximum inventory level be?
c) Calculate the total cost of this inventory system.

Solution
a) Using the formula for reorder quantity with shortages:

$$Q^* = \sqrt{\frac{2KD}{HC} \left(\frac{S + HC}{S}\right)}$$

$$= \sqrt{\frac{2(60)(20,000)}{(0.10 \times 1200)} \times \frac{300 + (0.10 \times 1200)}{300}}$$

$= 167$ units

b) $$I_{max}^* = \sqrt{\frac{2KD}{HC} \left(\frac{S}{S + HC}\right)}$$

$$= \sqrt{\frac{2(60)(20,000)}{(0.10 \times 1200)} \times \left(\frac{300}{300 + (0.10 \times 1200)}\right)}$$

$= 119.52$

~ 120 units

c) $TC^* = \dfrac{KD}{Q^*} + \dfrac{HC\,(I_{max}^*)^2}{2Q^*} + \dfrac{S(Q^* - I_{max}^*)^2}{2Q^*}$

$= \dfrac{60(20{,}000)}{167} + \dfrac{120(120)^2}{2(167)} + \dfrac{300(167 - 120)^2}{2(167)}$

$= 7185.62 + 5{,}173.65 + 1984.13$

$= \$14{,}343{,}40$

11.5   (PERIODIC ORDER SYSTEMS)

An electronics firm manufactures and sells sensitive electronic meters to public utility firms. The annual demand is one meter, which sells for $25.00. The cost of a production setup is $550.00, and the annual carrying cost is 6 percent of the price of a meter. What should be the time between successive reorders, if the company follows the basic fixed order quantity model?

Solution

For the basic fixed order quantity model,

$$Q^* = \sqrt{\dfrac{2KD}{HC}}$$

The optimal number of orders in one year is

$$N = \dfrac{D}{Q^*}$$

$$NT^* = 1 \text{ year, or } \left(\dfrac{D}{Q^*}\right)T^* = 1$$

where the optimal cycle time is expressed as a decimal fraction of a year. Thus,

$$T^* = \dfrac{Q^*}{D} = \dfrac{\sqrt{\dfrac{2KD}{HC}}}{D} = \sqrt{\dfrac{2KD}{HC(D)^2}} = \sqrt{\dfrac{2K}{HCD}}$$

$$T^* = \sqrt{\dfrac{2K}{HCD}}$$

$$T^* = \sqrt{\dfrac{2K}{HCD}} = \sqrt{\dfrac{2(550)}{(0.06)(25)(1)}} = \sqrt{733.33} = 27.15 \text{ years}$$

CHAPTER REVIEW PROBLEMS

11.1   An inventory system involves the following data:

Annual demand:	600 units
Procurement cost:	$100

Cost per unit: $350

Annual carrying cost: 20 percent of unit cost

a) Determine the economic order quantity.

b) What is the number of orders per year?

c) What is the required warehouse space?

11.2 An electrical supply firm has an annual demand of 12,000 units at a selling price of $10 per unit. The cost per unit is $6.00. When replenishing the inventory, the cost of placing an order is $45, while the annual carrying cost is 20 percent of the cost per unit. Determine the economic reorder quantity.

11.3 Umbrellas sold by the Shady Deal Company have an expected annual demand of 600 units. The cost to purchase these units from a supplier is $30 per unit, and the ordering cost is $18 per order. The annual carrying cost is 20 percent of the purchasing price.

a) Graphically display the various costs involved in this problem (e.g., cost versus order size).

b) Compute the economic order quantity.

11.4 A furniture wholesaler must supply various retail stores with 3750 sofas annually. The wholesaler's procurement cost is $60 per order. The cost of one sofa is $100, and the annual per unit carrying cost is 20 percent of the value of the product.

a) Determine how many times per year orders should be placed.

b) What should the economic reorder quantity be if demand increases fourfold? Can you draw a general conclusion?

11.5 The following data were taken from a manufacturer's accounting records:

Annual demand:	4500 units
Annual production:	6000 units
Setup cost:	$125
Annual holding cost:	10 percent of the value of the product
Unit cost:	$350
Working days per year:	225

Calculate the:

a) Economic lot size

b) Production run period

c) Period between production runs

d) Cycle period.

11.6 A bicycle manufacturer produces 1440 ten-speed bikes annually. The wheel subassembly line produces at a rate of 1500 pairs annually. The setup cost of a batch of wheel subassemblies is $100, and the annual holding cost of the subassemblies is 6 percent of the cost of one subassembly. The cost of one pair of wheels (one subassembly) is $30. Calculate the optimum batch size of the subassembly.

11.7 The assembly department is using annually 45,000 parts that are manufactured in the fabrication department. The part is valued at $115 per unit, and the total of storage and handling costs is $18 per unit per year. Total production set-up cost is $450. The assembly department requires 180 units per day, while the fabrication department can produce 360 units per day. The plant operates 250 days a year.

a) Compute the optimal order quantity.

b) How many orders will be placed each year?

c) If this component part could be purchased from another firm, with the same costs as above, what would the order quantity be?

d) If the average lead time to order from another firm is 2 days, and a safety stock level is set at 1100 units, what is the reorder point?

11.8   The Berson Propane Supply Company is a national distributor of propane and natural-gas-related equipment. It supplies several different types of customers, including commercial, industrial, farm and retail customers. The company's warehouse manager wants to employ the ABC system of inventory classification, and has provided the following list of items currently being held in inventory:

Item	Unit value	Number of Units in Inventory	Total Value of Inventory
1. Camping fridges	$120.00	125	$15,000
2. Construction heaters	150.00	125	18,750
3. 100-lb. cylinders	75.00	270	20,250
4. 20-lb. cylinders	25.00	700	17,500
5. Ranges	550.00	10	5500
6. Barbeques	30.00	750	22,500
7. Space heaters	25.00	100	2500
8. Valve fittings	3.00	1520	4560
9. Copper tubing (per ft.)	6.50	700	4550
10. Miscellaneous	10.00	(avg) 580	5800

Classify this company's inventory according to the ABC inventory classification.

11.9   The local school district requires 9000 fluorescent lights per year. It costs $55 to place an order, and it costs $.15 to store each order for a year. Find the:
a) Economic order quantity
b) Total inventory cost per year
c) Number of orders placed per year.

11.10 A university graduate, Dave Glenn, recently went into partnership in a wholesale electronics firm. The senior partner had for years ordered stock "from experience," but recently he was caught without stock on one model of amplifier. Dave wanted to check his method and came up with the following data:

$$\text{Cost per order} = \$ \; 5.00$$
$$\text{Holding cost} = \$ \quad .085$$
$$\text{Price per unit} = \$35.29$$
$$\text{Demand} = 100 \text{ per year}$$

What should Dave advise his partner with respect to ordering policy on this model of amplifier?

11.11 University Food Services is a nonprofit service of the university and operates on a fixed budget. Savings made on expenditures are permitted to be used for improvements in decor and facilities for both students and staff. The manager can save by purchasing in quantity, but the up-front purchase price is higher. His department uses 25,000 lunch bags per month. His order cost is $30.00, and his holding cost is 20 percent of the value of the item. His supplier has offered the discount schedule below for volume purchases. Based on the following discount schedule, determine the optimal purchasing policy.

Number of Cases	Price
1–99	$2.50 ea.
100–199	2.00 ea.
200–299	1.50 ea.
300 and up	1.00 ea.

11.12   The annual requirement for an item is 10,000 units, setup costs are $25, and the cost of holding the item in inventory is $.25 per year. What is the optimal economic order quantity? If the holding cost doubled to $.50 per year, what would the economic order quantity be? What is the percentage change of the order size?

11.13   The office stationery clerk in a medium-sized public accounting firm calculated the paper usage for the photocopiers to be 2000 boxes each year. The clerk is now trying to determine how many boxes of paper to order at one time. The procurement cost is $20 per order and the carrying cost is $5 per box per year. The cost in time lost as a result of running out of paper at any given time is $7.50 per box per year.
a) What is the optimal reorder quantity?
b) What should the maximum inventory level be?
c) Calculate the total cost of this inventory system.

11.14   An industrial equipment manufacturer purchases an electronic component that is required in its products. Annual production requirement for the electronic component is 10,000 units. The supplier gives quantity discounts, as follows:

Less than 600 units	$20.00 per unit
600 to 1599 units	19.80 per unit
Over 1600 units	19.60 per unit

The ordering cost is $50 and the carrying cost is 25 percent of the price paid. Determine the optimum number of units to order each time. Include in your answer any qualitative analysis that might affect your decision.

11.15   Snow White had a problem. She had only been with the seven dwarfs for a few days when she recognized that the little people had not established a level for safety stock when they ordered supplies, and as a consequence often had no supplies at all. "How can I help?" she thought. She questioned the dwarfs, and found that the demand per day for the supplies needed for their work was 7, and that 4 days lead time was usually required to acquire goods. Standard deviation of demand over lead time was 3.2 units, and lead time followed a normal distribution. What safety stock did Snow White determine was adequate for an 85 percent service level? For a 90 percent level? For a 95 percent level?

READING
U.S. Automakers See Future in Kanban

Japan's "Just-in-Time" Production System Helps to Cut Costs of Inventory.

In Japanese, kanban means "just-in-time."

Originally, it was something Japanese supermarket managers worried about: stocking their shelves with a minimum of inventory and then when a customer bought the last bottle of soy sauce, restocking it immediately.

Today, it is a term sweeping the American automobile manufacturing industry.

Suddenly, every manufacturer from the Detroit giants down to the smallest rear-view-mirror supplier in Biloxi, Miss., is trying to learn how to streamline their operations so that parts arrive kanban—just when the conveyor belt is ready for them.

Savings by Japanese carmakers have given their products an edge in American showrooms, according to William J. Harahan, director of manufacturing planning for Ford.

"Today the Japanese can land an Escort-sized vehicle in North America for $1,400 less than we can manufacture it," says Harahan. "We think $100 of that saving is attributable to lower inventories."

Kanban, as it applies to automobile manufacturing, was first introduced by Toyota about 10 years ago.

In practice, it means that attached to each container of parts is a card. As soon as the assembly line operator starts to use a part from that container, the card is sent back to the supplier, who then sends a replacement container.

"Another way to view it," says Robert B. Stone, vice-president of General Motors, "is that the U.S. auto industry pushes material through the pipeline in accordance with schedules based on forecast assembly. The Japanese "just-in-time" approach is to pull material through the pipeline based on what is actually built."

At Toyota, "just-in-time": has had two applications: On the assembly line parts manufactured in-house reach the point of assembly at nearly the exact moment they are to be installed, with virtually no stockpiling.

Outside the plant, suppliers must be told a manufacturer's need far enough in advance to truck in the needed item within hours of the time it is installed.

Either way, confirm Toyota and U.S. car executives, the rush to "kanbanize" American manufacturing will put tremendous pressure on managers and suppliers to assure quality control, because under kanban the breakdown of one part can hold up a whole assembly line for hours and cost the company thousands of dollars in downtime.

SOURCE: *The Los Angeles Herald Examiner,* June 1, 1982, p. 9.

"It's true that a breakdown can shut down our whole line," says Don Haller, general manager of Toyota's assembly and truck manufacturing plant in Long Beach. "But the object is to immediately draw attention to the defect and find out why it broke down."

Haller, who spent most of his career as a Ford assembly line supervisor, says kanban not only lowers inventory levels but forces a plant to be more efficient.

"In the typical large manufacturing plant, there is a tendency to have buffer storage, so you can overcome the breakdown. Here, instead of patching it to get through the day, we have to find out why there was a breakdown and fix it so it doesn't happen again."

Inventory costs to American car companies are tremendous. At General Motors, says Stone, the company has $9 billion tied up in stockpiling.

Harahan estimates that at Ford, every $1 spent on parts costs another 20 cents in warehousing, overhead and financing.

"There is a great motivation to reduce your inventory costs," say Harahan. "But we have had to cherry pick the Japanese, in terms of selecting which of Toyota's or Mazda's ideas are applicable to Ford. In Japan, suppliers are within 60 miles of the plant. They can make deliveries three or four times a day. Our supplier base is all over the U.S."

Even so, he said, since the peak year of 1979, Ford has been able to reduce its inventories by $2 billion. Some of that reduction was due to falling production, but some of it has been the result of a concentrated stock control system.

As an example, he cited the case of a drive shaft supplier which services a Ford truck plant in Kentucky. Before the plant might have carried 10 days worth of drive shafts; now it gives the supplier four days notice. In return the supplier guarantees delivery of the shafts needed—plus or minus a day.

"In that one plant, we were able to reduce inventory by $2 million and free up 19,000 square feet of floor space," Harahan said.

But he warns that to make the system really work, manufacturers can't just push inventory back on suppliers. "In the end you have to eliminate the whole system [of storage], otherwise there's no savings," he says.

He estimated that by 1986, Ford would have all of its 3,000 suppliers participating in a modified kanban system. "But we won't be full Japanese," says Harahan, "We will implement the system that is best for us."

"There is no question (kanban) is a better idea. And there's no question that Ford and the American manufacturers are trying to take advantage of things we've learned from the Japanese," says Harahan. "But it's not like waving a magic wand.

"We've been using the traditional assembly line methods for 20 years. If all of a sudden, you tell us no in-process inventories, no finished-part stockpiles and then a machine goes down, and there's no inventory to keep the line running, the downtime cost will be tremendous."

GM's Stone stresses this is a tough time for Detroit to regear. "We still don't have the widespread acceptance of our ability to make "just-in-time" work, but we are making progress," he told automobile industry analysts recently.

"I wish I could give you the magic formula, but one doesn't exist. But unless we, the entire auto industry, begin, the task will never be done."

Questions

1. What is the effect of the "kanban system" on the raw material and parts inventory? On the process inventory? On safety stock?

2. Why might the suppliers to the Toyota Manufacturing Company be in a better position to support the kanban system than their counterparts in the U.S.?

3. How does the "kanban system" affect efficiency? Quality control? Production scheduling?

4. How does the "kanban system" affect the final product price?

5. Can this system be applied to control inventories of service industries, such as hospitals and restaurants?

6. Cash reserves in a bank can be looked upon as an inventory of goods. Can the "kanban system" be applied in this case?

7. What are the inventory cost trade-offs related to in this article?

BIBLIOGRAPHY

AGGARWAL, S. C., "A Review of Current Inventory Theory and Its Applications," *Int. J. Product Res.*, 12, 1974, pp. 443–482.

ALJIAN, GEORGE, W., ed., *Purchasing Handbook*. New York: McGraw-Hill Co., 1958.

ARCHIBALD, B., and E. A. SILVER. "(s,S) Policies under Continuous Review and Discrete Compound Poisson Demand." *Mgmt. Sci.*, 24, 1978, pp. 899–909.

BIERMAN, HAROLD B., CHARLES P. BONINI, WARREN H. HAUSMAN, *Quantitative Analysis for Business Decisions* (5th ed.). Homewood, Ill.: Richard D. Irwin, 1978.

BROWN, R. G., *Materials Management Systems*. New York: John Wiley & Sons, 1977.

BUFFA, E. S., and J. S. DYER, *Essentials of Management Science/Operations Research*. New York: John Wiley & Sons, 1978.

COOK, T. M., and R. A. RUSSELL, *Introduction to Management Science*. Englewood Cliffs, New Jersey: Prentice-Hall, Inc., 1977.

———, *Contemporary Operations Management*, Englewood Cliffs, New Jersey: Prentice-Hall, Inc., 1980.

FETTER, ROBERT B., and WINSTON C. DALLECK, *Decision Models for Inventory Management*. Homewood, Ill.: Richard D. Irwin, 1961.

HADLEY, G., and T. WHITIN, *Analysis of Inventory Systems*. Englewood Cliffs, N.J.: Prentice-Hall, Inc., 1963.

HEINRITZ, S. F., and P. V. FARREL, *Purchasing: Principles and Applications* (5th ed.). Englewood Cliffs, N.J.: Prentice-Hall, Inc., 1971.

LITTLE, J. D. C., "Models and Managers: The Concept of a Decision Calculus." *Mgmt. Sci.*, 16, 1970, pp. 466–485.

LOVE, S., *Inventory Control*. New York: McGraw-Hill Co., 1979.

MENIPAZ, E., "A Current Taxonomy of Inventory Systems," *Journal of Information and Optimization Sciences*, Vol. 3, No. 3, September 1982, pp. 277–289.

_____, *Automated Production: A Decision Support Systems Approach*. Ottawa, Canada: RandComp, 1984.

MOORE, J. R., "Forecasting and Scheduling for Past-Model Replacement Parts," *Mgmt. Sci.*, 18, 1971, pp. 200–213.

MUCKSTADT, J. A., "NAVMET: A Four-Echelon Model for Determining the Optimal Quantity and Distribution of Navy Spare Aircraft Engines," TR 263, School of Operations Research and Industrial Engineering, Cornell University, Ithaca, N.Y., 1976.

MUCKSTADT, J. A., "A Model of a Multi-Item, Multi-Echelon, Multi-Indenture Inventory System," *Mgmt. Sci.*, 20, 1973, pp. 472–481.

NADDOR, E. *Inventory Systems*. New York: John Wiley & Sons, 1966.

_____ "Optimal and Heuristic Decisions in Single- and Multi-Item Inventory Systems," *Mgmt. Sci.*, 21, 1975, pp. 1234–1249.

_____ "Sensitivity to Distributions in Inventory Systems," *Mgmt. Sci.*, 24, 1978, pp. 1769–1772.

NAHMIAS, S., "Inventory Models," *The Encyclopedia of Computer Science and Technology*, Vol. 9, pp. 447–483, J. Belzer, A. G. Holzman, and A. Kent (eds.). New York: Marcel Dekker, 1978.

NILAND, POWELL, *Production Planning, Scheduling, and Inventory Control*. New York: The Macmillan Company, 1970.

ORLICKY, JOSEPH, *Materials Requirements Planning*. New York: McGraw-Hill Co., 1975.

PETERSON, R., and E. A. SILVER. *Decision Systems for Inventory Management and Production Planning*. New York: John Wiley & Sons, 1979.

PLOSSL, G. W., and O. W. WIGHT, *Production and Inventory Control*. Englewood Cliffs, N.J.: Prentice-Hall, Inc., 1967.

RITCHIE, E., and P. WILCOX, "Renewal Theory Forecasting for Stock Control," *Eur. J. Opnl Res.*, 1, 1977, pp. 90–93.

SCHNEIDER, H., "The Service Level in Inventory Control Systems," *Engr. Process Econ.*, 4, 1979, pp. 341–348.

SCHWARZ, L., and L. SCHRAGE. "Optimal and System Myopic Policies for Multi-Echelon Production/Inventory Assembly Systems," *Mgmt. Sci.* 21, 1975, pp. 1285–1294.

SHERBROOKE, C. C., "METRIC: A Multi-Echelon Technique for Recoverable Item Control," *Opns. Res.*, 16, 1968, pp. 122–141.

SILVER, E. A., "A Control System for Coordinated Inventory Replenishment," *Int. J. Product. Res.*, 12, 1974, pp. 647–671.

_____ "The Use of Programmable Calculators in Inventory Management," *Product. Invent. Mgmt.*, 20, 1979, pp. 64–74.

STARR, MARTIN K., and DAVID W. MILLER, *Inventory Control—Theory and Practice.* Englewood Cliffs, N.J.: Prentice-Hall, Inc., 1962.

WAGNER, H. M., "Research Portfolio for Inventory Management and Production Planning Systems," *Opns. Res.*, 28, 1980, pp. 445–475.

WAGNER, H. M., "The Design of Production and Inventory Systems for Multifacility and Multiwarehouse Companies," *Opns. Res.*, 22, 1974, pp. 278–291.

_____ *Statistical Management of Inventory Systems.* New York: John Wiley & Sons, 1962.

WARD, J. B., "Determining Reorder Points When Demand Is Lumpy," *Mgmt. Sci.*, 24, 1978, pp. 623–632.

WIGHT, OLIVER W., *Production and Inventory Management in the Computer Age.* Boston, Mass.: Cahners Books, 1974.

12

Material Requirements Planning

INTRODUCTION

In Chapter 11, the demand for a product or service was assumed to be independent of the demand for another product or service. Thus, the optimal order quantity, for example, could be calculated separately for each item.

In this chapter, we deal with situations in which the demand for one product determines the demand for its subassemblies. Once the independent demand for the final product is determined, the demand for the subassemblies is known. For example, the demand for printed circuits depends on how many completed radio transistors are produced. The required quantity of hub caps depends on how many cars are assembled by a Ford assembly plant. It is also interesting to note that the demand for subassemblies occurs in batches rather than on a unit-by-unit basis. That is, before the start of a production run *all* the parts and other subassemblies are required. Since most production runs occur in lots, the demand for subassemblies occurs at specific points in time.

AN OVERVIEW OF MATERIAL REQUIREMENTS PLANNING (MRP)

Material-requirements planning (MRP) is a computerized information system designed to handle ordering and scheduling of dependent-demand inventories (i.e., raw materials, subassemblies, parts). The MRP system is a logical sequence in which the component parts of assembled end products are identified (this indicates *what* to order). The component parts are then aggregated (this indicates *how* much to order) according to their due dates (this indicates *when* to order). The identification of the component parts is sometimes called the "explosion" of the end product.

The MRP system consists of four central subsystems:

1. The *master production schedule*, which tells how many finished products are required, and which activates the whole system
2. The *bill of materials* (BOM) file, which tells the composition of a finished product
3. The *inventory status file*, which indicates how much inventory is on hand or on order
4. The *material-requirements planning package*, which provides the explosion, aggregation, and eventual schedule of components' production, and which processes the information using various computer programs to determine the net requirements for each period of the planning horizon.

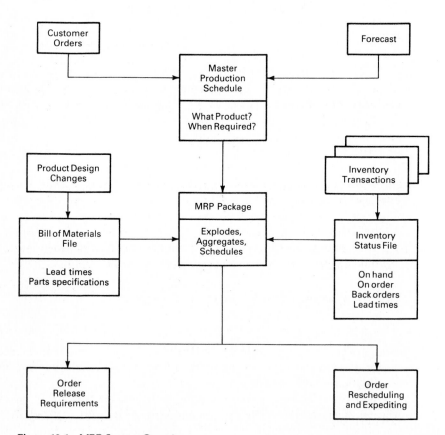

Figure 12.1 MRP System Overview

The master production schedule indicates when finished products should be assembled so that they will be available at a specified due date. The bill of materials (BOM) file captures the essence of dependent demand. This file contains a list of all parts and components, including their relationships to the subassemblies and finished products. The inventory status file contains a record of actual inventory level, lead time, ordered inventory and backorder information. A general overview of the files and systems involved in MRP is provided in Figure 12.1.

MRP Requirements

In order to employ an MRP system, the following requirements should be fulfilled:

1. A computer is available to perform the calculations and to use and update the data files.
2. A computerized, up-to-date bill of materials is available for each product.
3. The master schedule is accurate, updated, and deterministic.
4. The end product is constituted of several items or subcomponents.

In the process of developing the MRP system, one should also take into account the effort involved in creating the necessary data files. For example, preparing the bill of materials for each item may take months, and delay the activating of the MRP system.

MRP Advantages

When the above requirements are fulfilled in a company, MRP has demonstrated that it can enhance the productivity of operations. Hundreds of companies have effected cost reductions through the use of MRP by reducing inventories and improving schedules. For example, one company recorded a 12 percent reduction in finished inventories, a 30 percent reduction in work-in-process inventory, and a 35% increase in the number of on-time deliveries.[1,2]

MRP helps the operations manager by making it possible to cope with many changes relating to the scheduling of operations. Here are some specifics.

MRP helps in expediting and de-expediting orders. Consider the case of a customer who calls in to delay a due date. The final assembly operation can be delayed, consequently, the processing of individual parts can be de-expedited. This, in

---

[1] Robert A. Dennis, "Coping with the Materials Crunch", *Factory,* August, 1974, pp. 50–51.

[2] J. G. Miller, and Linda G. Sprague, "Behind the Growth in Materials Requirements Planning," *Harvard Business Review,* 52, No. 5, Sept.–Oct., 1975, pp. 83–91.

turn, releases capacity for other outstanding jobs and prevents excess in-process inventory of raw materials.

MRP helps in keeping inventories low. Since MRP points out priorities, a better schedule results, which can cut average lead times and inventories. Generally, the actual processing time of a product takes only a small fraction of the time the product stays in the plant. Most of the time it waits for parts and subassemblies to catch up. Proper priorities, provided by MRP, secure all parts and subassemblies on time. This reduces waiting times and lead times, as well as inventories.

MRP signals possible delays. Since an MRP system actually simulates alternative schedules, it can point out late deliveries or confirm promised delivery dates. The operations manager becomes aware of delays in the delivery date even before actual production of the batch starts.

MRP serves as a long-range planning tool. MRP is an effective tool for materials control and for scheduling purposes. However, it can also be used as a budgeting and long-range planning tool. For example, an appliance manufacturer may use the bill of materials, the inventory files, and the annual production requirements to simulate various annual production plans and to check budgeting, manpower, and purchasing implications. Thus, MRP is used by the appliance manufacturer as a model of manufacturing operations.

BOM and Product-Structure Tree

The computerized bill of materials allows the aggregation of identical subcomponents, even though they may be required for different end items. The BOM contains a listing of all the assemblies, subassemblies, parts, and raw materials that are needed to produce one unit of a finished product. Each finished product has its own BOM.

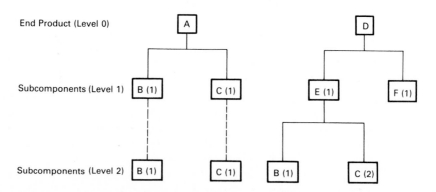

Figure 12.2   Structure Tree for Two End Products

The list on the BOM file is hierarchical—that is, it shows the type and quantity of each item needed to complete one unit of the next-highest level of assembly. The hierarchical list is facilitated by a *product-structure tree,* such as the one shown in Figure 12.2, which illustrates that for one end product A and one end product D, two B subcomponents and three C subcomponents are required.

When requirements are calculated in an MRP system, the computer scans the product structure level by level, starting at the top. In order to simplify aggregation of requirements for various items, *low-level coding* is used. This involves restructuring the BOM so that all occurrences of an item are made to coincide with the lowest level in which the item appears. As you can see from Figure 12.2, items B and C, which appear at two different levels, may be rearranged so that they appear at only one level.

For complex product configurations with thousands of subcomponents, the aggregation of subcomponents by quantity is a major task. This is the kind of task that MRP systems are presently handling efficiently.

The MRP Logic

The MRP system, often computerized, performs the logic, explodes the requirements of subcomponents into the future, offsets the lead times, and computes the on-hand and order quantities.

The logic of MRP is based on a long-time principle of production planning:

$$
\begin{Bmatrix} \text{Quality available} \\ \text{for future period} \end{Bmatrix} = \begin{Bmatrix} \text{Quantity} \\ \text{on hand} \end{Bmatrix} + \begin{Bmatrix} \text{Scheduled} \\ \text{receipts} \end{Bmatrix} - \begin{Bmatrix} \text{Current period} \\ \text{requirements} \end{Bmatrix}
$$

The requirements are exploded into the future by combining the master schedule requirements with due dates on the bill of material (BOM). The inventory file identifies lead times, so that such lead times for the required components can be calculated. Then, with the MRP system, the on-hand and planned order receipt balances are used to calculate the quantity available for future periods. A computer printout for a purchased or produced component may take the form shown in Figure 12.3. The box for planned order release for the current period (week 1, in Figure 12.3) is called the *action bucket,* since it is this box that triggers a certain amount of ordering activity.

In the following section, the use and various functions of the MRP system are demonstrated through an example. Before proceeding, study the following definitions.

> *Gross Requirements*   The total expected demand for an item or raw material during each time period. For end products, these quantities are specified in the master schedule for subassemblies or parts. These quantities equal the planned order release of their respective parents.
>
> *Quantity On-Hand*   The expected amount of inventory at the beginning of each time period.

FIGURE 12.3 MRP COMPUTER PRINTOUT

COMPONENT: _____	WEEK									
LEAD TIME (LT): ____	1	2	3	4	5	6	7	8	9	10
Gross Requirements										
Quantity On Hand										
Net Requirements										
Planned Order Receipts										
Planned Order Release	☐									

└──────── Action Bucket

Net Requirements   The difference between gross requirements and the expected quantity on-hand for each time period.

Planned-Order Receipts   The quantity expected to be received by the beginning of the period in which it is shown. If one follows lot-for-lot ordering procedure, this quantity should equal net requirements. If one follows economical-lot-size ordering procedure, this quantity may exceed net requirements. Any excess is added to projected quantity on-hand in the following time period.

Planned Order Release   Indicates the order quantity or the production lot size in each time period in order to ensure availability for the next level of production or assembly. This amount generates gross requirements at the next-lower level in the assembly or production chain.

AN EXAMPLE OF THE USE OF MRP

The assembly of the top plate of a video-tape recorder (VTR) requires several items, as specified in Table 12.1. The items are schematically described in Figure 12.4.

The weekly demand for the video-tape recorder top plate unit is:

Weeks Hence	7	8	9
Quantity	100	90	70

The Bill of Materials File

The bill of materials specifies the relationship that shows how the VTR's top plate is put together. It identifies each item and the quantity required per unit of the completed product. The VTR, as per the bill of materials (BOM) in Figure

TABLE 12.1 VTR TOP PLATE INFORMATION

ITEM	ITEM NUMBER	QUANTITY	LEAD TIME
VTR TOP Plate		1	1 week
Supply/Take-up Reel	A1	2	2 weeks
Head Assembly			
(motor, drum, track heads, idler)	B1	1	3 weeks
Idler	C1	2	1 week
Self-Aligning Post	D1	2	1 week
Head Drum Motor	E2	1	1 week
Video Head Drum	F2	1	1 week
Track Head	G2	2	2 weeks
Capstan Idler	H2	1	1 week

12.5, is made up of two units of item A1 (supply/take-up reel), one unit of item B1 (head assembly), two units of item C1 (idler), and two units of item D1 (self-aligning post). Item B1 (head assembly), in turn, consists of one unit of item E2 (head drum motor), one unit of item F2 (video head drum), two units of item G2 (track head), and one unit of item H2 (capstan idler).

Note that the tree structure of the BOM specifies levels. Level 0 corresponds to the assembled product, level 1 corresponds to the major subassemblies, and level 2 corresponds to the individual parts. The number of levels depends on the number of assembly operations involved, and can be extended beyond level 2. The required number for each part is indicated in parentheses.

There are various ways to present the relationships among the various items in the BOM. Figure 12.5 is a product structure tree of the VTR top plate. However, the same information can be presented in a tabular format.

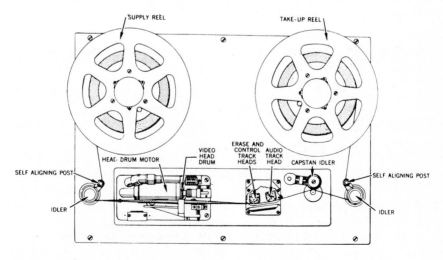

Figure 12.4 Assembly of a Video-Tape Recorder Top Plate

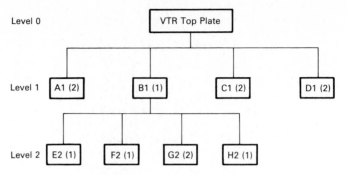

Figure 12.5   Bill of Materials (BOM) for a VTR

Material-Requirements Plan

The material-requirements plan is shown in Figure 12.6. Since we need one hundred VTR units seven weeks hence, we need to create a time schedule specifying order placement dates and planned receipt dates to meet the demand. The materials-requirements plan in Figure 12.6 is based on the independent demand for the VTR top plate, the knowledge of which parts are used for it, and the lead time required to obtain each part.

In order to be able to assemble the VTR top plate starting week six, one should have on hand 200 units of part A1, 100 units of part B1, 200 units of part C1, and 200 units of part D1. The lead time for part A1 is two weeks; thus, an order for part A1 should be placed the fourth week hence. The lead time for part B1 is three weeks; thus, an order for part B1 should be placed the third week hence. The same is done with regard to parts C1 and D1.

Subassembly B1, the head assembly, is to be ready the third week hence. Thus, it triggers order release for parts E2, F2, G2, and H2. For example, part G2 should be ordered during the first week so that it will be ready at the third week.

Once the material-requirements plan is completed and, in particular, the planned order release calculated, the plan serves as the basis for all production scheduling activities. The planned order release quantities are matched with the production capacity of each one of the parts. If the plan does not conform to the capacity constraints, it should be changed accordingly.

The VTR top plate illustration is simple. Developing a material-requirements plan manually for thousands of products is impractical. The amount of data required is large and the computations involved are tedious. Inventory status and product structure (BOM) should be known. Because of these data requirements, the operations manager is forced to use a computer, and the information should be contained in computer memory files that are updated frequently.

FIGURE 12.6 THE MATERIAL-REQUIREMENTS PLAN FOR COMPLETING 100 UNITS OF VTR TOP PLATE IN WEEK 7 (INCLUDES THE SCHEDULING OF ALL OTHER PARTS PRODUCTION FROM WEEK 1)

		WEEK							LEAD TIME (WEEKS)
		1	2	3	4	5	6	7	
VTR Top Plate	Required Date							100	1
	Order Placement						100		
A1	Required Date						200		2
	Order Placement				200				
B1	Required Date						100		3
	Order Placement			100					
C1	Required Date						200		1
	Order Placement					200			
D1	Required Date						200		1
	Order Placement					200			
E2	Required Date			100					1
	Order Placement		100						
F2	Required Date			100					1
	Order Placement		100						
G2	Required Date			200					2
	Order Placement	200							
H2	Required Date			100					1
	Order Placement		100						

PART: VTR LT: 1 WEEK TOP PLATE	WEEK									
	1	2	3	4	5	6	7	8	9	10
Gross Requirements							100	90	70	
On Hand							20	0	0	
Net Requirements							80	90	70	
Scheduled Receipts							80	90	70	
Planned Order Release						80	90	70		

FIGURE 12.6 (Cont.)

PART: A1 LT: 2 WEEKS REEL	WEEK									
	1	*2*	*3*	*4*	*5*	*6*	*7*	*8*	*9*	*10*
Gross Requirements						160	180	140		
On Hand						20	0	0		
Net Requirements						140	180	140		
Scheduled Receipts						140	180	140		
Planned Order Release				140	180	140				

PART: B1 LT: 3 WEEKS HEAD ASSEMBLY	WEEK									
	1	*2*	*3*	*4*	*5*	*6*	*7*	*8*	*9*	*10*
Gross Requirements						80	90	70		
On Hand						10	0	0		
Net Requirements						70	90	70		
Scheduled Receipts						70	90	70		
Planned Order Release			70	90	70					

PART: C1 LT: 1 WEEK IDLER	WEEK									
	1	*2*	*3*	*4*	*5*	*6*	*7*	*8*	*9*	*10*
Gross Requirements						160	180	140		
On Hand						5	0	0		
Net Requirements						155	180	140		
Scheduled Receipts						155	180	140		
Planned Order Release					155	180	140			

PART: D1 LT: 1 WEEK SELF ALIGNING POST	WEEK									
	1	*2*	*3*	*4*	*5*	*6*	*7*	*8*	*9*	*10*
Gross Requirements						160	180	140		
On Hand						0	0	0		
Net Requirements						160	180	140		

FIGURE 12.6   (Cont.)

PART: D1 LT: 1 WEEK SELF ALIGNING POST	WEEK									
	1	*2*	*3*	*4*	*5*	*6*	*7*	*8*	*9*	*10*
Scheduled Receipts						160	180	140		
Planned Order Release					160	180	140			

PART: E2 LT: 1 WEEK MOTOR	WEEK									
	1	*2*	*3*	*4*	*5*	*6*	*7*	*8*	*9*	*10*
Gross Requirements			70	90	70					
On Hand			10	0	0					
Net Requirements			· 60	90	70					
Scheduled Receipts			60	90	70					
Planned Order Release		60	90	70						

MRP PROCESSING PROCEDURE

The MRP procedure, manual or computerized, is as follows:

1. Explode the requirements into the future
2. Deal with lead times
3. Compute on-hand inventory
4. Order the balance.

As has been suggested before, the logic of MRP is simply:

$$\begin{Bmatrix} \text{Quantity available} \\ \text{for future period} \end{Bmatrix} = \begin{Bmatrix} \text{Quantity} \\ \text{on hand} \end{Bmatrix} + \begin{Bmatrix} \text{Scheduled} \\ \text{receipts} \end{Bmatrix} - \begin{Bmatrix} \text{Current period} \\ \text{requirements} \end{Bmatrix}$$

The inventory status report gives the current on-hand quantities, amount scheduled to be received, and lead times.

The assembly requirements are exploded into the future by reconciling the master schedule requirements with the due dates on the bill of materials. As lead times for subassemblies are known from the inventory file, lead times for the required parts can be calculated. With the MRP procedure, on-hand and on-order quantities are used to calculate the quantity available for the future.

This procedure performs level-by-level processing, working down through the product structure tree, beginning at the zero level, or final, assembled product. The quantity of the final, assembled product is read off the master schedule. The procedure moves backward in time by the appropriate lead time to produce it. This is done by a bill of materials (BOM)—that is, by multiplying the number of assemblies to be produced by the number of parts at the next lower level (as indicated by the BOM) that are needed for one assembly. These are the gross requirements for the parts of the assembly.

The procedure sums all the gross requirements for every product on a given level from every source within each period. This is done because a product may be used in more than one higher-level assembly or more than one final, assembled product.

The procedure determines the net requirements by checking the inventory records to see how many of each part are scheduled to be delivered or otherwise available during the period of each gross requirement. It subtracts the available inventory from the gross requirements and produces the net requirements. The net requirements are developed to a schedule of planned order releases. The net requirement at one level is the gross requirement at the next lower level.

Let us summarize the procedure:

Step 1. Take account of lead times.

Step 2. Explode the BOM.

Step 3. Accumulate gross requirements at that level.

Step 4. Find the net requirement at that level.

Step 5. Set the gross requirements at the next lower level. This value may be equal to the net requirements of the current level or to a selected lot size.

Step 6. If all levels have been dealt with, stop. Otherwise, go to step 1.

Let us refer back to the VTR top plate example. For part B1, we need: for week 6, 80 units; for week 7, 90 units; and for week 8, 70 units. We shall further assume the same scheduled receipts of products and on-hand inventory as were indicated in Figure 12.6. Figure 12.7 presents the MRP procedure for this case.

In order to have the required gross requirement of 80 units of part B1 in week 6 (and since we have 10 units of part B1 on-hand, as indicated in Figure 12.6), a planned order release of 70 B1 parts in week 3 is indicated in Figure 12.6. That means that we need 70 units of part F2 in week 3 (see Figure 12.7). Since we do not have inventory of part F2 on hand, the net requirement for F2 is 70 units. Since the lead time for F2 is one week, a planned order release of 70 units of F2 is marked in Figure 12.7. The same procedure is followed for parts G2 and H2 in Figure 12.7

The transformation of the planned order release (net requirements) at one level into gross requirements at the next-lower level does not incorporate any requirements from other comparable products. These should be incorporated as desired.

The bottom line (planned order release) for each part is of utmost importance. As has been indicated earlier, the box for the current period on the

FIGURE 12.7 MATERIAL-REQUIREMENTS PLANNING PROCEDURE

PART: F2 LT: 1 WEEK DRUM	WEEK									
	1	*2*	*3*	*4*	*5*	*6*	*7*	*8*	*9*	*10*
Gross Requirements			70	90	70					
On Hand			0	0	0					
Net Requirements			70	90	70					
Scheduled Receipts			70	90	70					
Planned Order Release		70	90	70						

PART: G2 LT: 1 WEEK TRACK HEADS	WEEK									
	1	*2*	*3*	*4*	*5*	*6*	*7*	*8*	*9*	*10*
Gross Requirements			140	180	140					
On Hand			0	0	0					
Net Requirements			140	180	140					
Scheduled Receipts			140	180	140					
Planned Order Release	140	180	140							

PART: H2 LT: 1 WEEK IDLER	WEEK									
	1	*2*	*3*	*4*	*5*	*6*	*7*	*8*	*9*	*10*
Gross Requirements			70	90	70					
On Hand			0	0	0					
Net Requirements			70	90	70					
Scheduled Receipts			70	90	70					
Planned Order Release		70	90	70						

planned order release line is called the action bucket, as it is the box that triggers the ordering activity.

For example, in week 1, 140 units of the idler (part G2) have to be ordered. In week 2, an order should be released to produce 60 motors (part E2), 70 drums (part F2), 180 track heads (part G2), and 70 idlers (part H2).

TABLE 12.2 THE PLANNED ORDER RELEASE AND COST IMPLICATIONS

(1) Week	(2) Planned Order Release	(3) Cumulative Lot Size	(4) Weeks Carried	(5) Carrying Cost	(6) Order for Weeks
4	140	140	0	0	4
5	180	320	1	$36	4 + 5
6	140	460	2	$92	4 + 5 + 6

LOT SIZING IN MRP

As can be seen from Figures 12.6 and 12.7, at each level of the exploded bill of material and for each product, a planned order release (net requirements) is developed. These requirements reflect only the time needed to secure delivery on time. However, no account is taken of the setup costs involved in each production run, or of the carrying costs of excessive inventory.

The question is, what should be the optimal batch size for each product? Grouping of requirements of like parts used is recommended, in order to spread the order cost or setup cost over more units. It might be better economically to combine several requirements and pay a holding cost until the product is needed than it would be to pay for another setup.

Let us look at the planned order release line for part A1 in Figure 12.6, and introduce the numbers into Table 12.2. During week 4, an order for 140 units is released. During week 5, an order for 180 units is released, and, during week 6, an order for 140 units is released. Let us try to balance carrying costs and ordering, or setup, costs. We assume the carrying cost is $.20 per A1 unit per month. The ordering, or setup, cost is $36.

In Table 12.2, we reproduce the planned order release for part A1 in columns 1 and 2. The summation of the planned order releases is given in column (3). If we produce during the first week a quantity that matches the current week demand only, we should produce 140 units. If we produce during the first week a quantity that matches two weeks' demand, we should produce 320 units. What is the best lot size, Q^*?

The rule we will follow to determine Q^* is to order part A1 for successive periods into the future until the carrying cost is equal to the order cost. We first determine the carrying cost for each lot size. If we produce the first week's demand only, there are no carrying costs. If we produce two weeks' demand (320 units) during the first week, we need to carry 180 units for one week. This involves a carrying cost of

$$180 \text{ units} \times \$.20 \times 1 \text{ week} = \$36$$

If we produce three week's demand during the first week, we need to carry 180 units for one week and 140 units for two weeks. This involves a carrying cost of

$$180 \text{ units} \times \$.20 \times 1 \text{ week } = \$36$$

$$140 \text{ units} \times \$.20 \times 2 \text{ weeks } = \underline{ 56}$$

$$\text{Total } = \$92$$

These are shown in columns (4) and (5) of Table 12.2.

The optimal lot size is, as usual, the one for which the carrying cost equals the order, or setup, cost. Since the setup cost is $36, which is equal to the $36 in column (5) of Table 12.2, we shall produce 320 units, which is equal to two weeks' demand, during the first week.

During other periods, optimal lot size might be different. Thus, the planned order release interval, as well as the planned order release size, will vary. The lot-size method we have just described is called part period balancing.

There are some other ways of calculating the order size. Let us describe them in brief:

1. The *EOQ approach*, which is explained in Chapter 11. The EOQ approach imposes a fixed order size as well as a fixed planned order release interval. Unused parts are carried in inventory for use in subsequent periods.
2. In the *periodic order quantity*, the economic planned order release interval is determined, and an order is placed to satisfy demand for all periods within that interval.
3. While the EOQ approach attempts to use the same order quantity throughout the time horizon, based on an overall average demand, the *moving EOQ approach* takes a shorter time horizon and, thus, reacts faster to changes in demand requirements.[3]

MRP AS AN INFORMATION SYSTEM

MRP is essentially a production and inventory information system. It is not an approach for aggregate planning or for daily shop scheduling, as one is not required to use production time standards in the MRP procedure.

Unless lot sizing is considered, MRP does not consider inventory size economically. It simply states the time in which parts or subassemblies should be available.

MRP is not a capacity planning tool, since it is not related to machine capacities. As a matter of fact, one should reconcile the MRP's planned order release with the individual machines' or work centers' capacities.

However, MRP is an effective production and inventory control information system. It is useful in identifying information that is used to aggregate production planning, scheduling, and inventory control decisions.

[3] See W. A. Ruch, "Economic Lot Sizing in Material Requirements Planning," *American Production and Inventory Control 1976 Conference Proceedings*, pp. 90–93.

MRP has helped management to identify apparent weaknesses in the production planning phase, as the following paragraphs tell us:

MRP systems have made two significant improvements in the management of plant operations. First, they have proven to be an effective tool for production planning. That is, MRP focuses management attention on the critical problem of planning at the end product level, rather than on the multitude of detailed operating problems such as scheduling machines at the shop floor level or controlling the inventory levels of component parts and sub-assemblies. Once the end product production plans have been formalized as master schedules, the MRP system computer programs can be used to translate these schedules into detailed operating plans which show the timing of requirements for purchased and manufactured components.

A second important contribution of MRP systems is in automating many of the routine decisions involved in scheduling the production of component parts and controlling the inventory levels of these items. One example of this contribution is the ability of an MRP system to routinely calculate manufacturing priorities for component parts an sub-assemblies. This enables management to communicate changes in the master schedule directly to the shop floor level in the form of revised scheduling priorities for the production of component parts, thereby keeping shop attention centered on the high priority items. . . .[4]

MRP AS A SCHEDULING SYSTEM

We have defined MRP as an information system that is designed to handle scheduling. We have covered other scheduling systems in preceding chapters. In Chapter 8, we covered the line of balance (LOB) that helps in scheduling high-volume operations. In Chapter 4, we covered the Gantt chart, which helps in scheduling intermittent, low-volume operations in job shops and projects of small scale. How do these scheduling systems compare? What are the strengths and weaknesses of which?

Tables 12.3(a), (b), and (c) summarize the results of our comparison. As one can see, the validity and reliability of the MRP system are higher than for the other techniques, especially when conditions are changing, with a high-volume environment. The technique is flexible and easy to update. However, since a computer system is necessary, the costs are high.

CLOSED-LOOP MRP AND MRP-II

MRP-II has evolved from MRP, which was used primarily as an ordering technique to keep inventories at adequate levels. An advanced MRP system, termed a closed-loop MRP, offered a powerful priority-planning capability by

---

[4] W. L. Berry and D. C. Whybark, "Research Perspectives for Material Requirements Planning Systems," *Production and Inventory Management*, 2nd qtr., 1975, p. 19.

TABLE 12.3(a) LOB TECHNIQUE—STRENGTHS AND WEAKNESSES

CRITERION	STRENGTHS	WEAKNESSES
1. Validity	Uncertainties surrounding times in production operations are minimal; consequently, LOB affords management a sound technique for judging status of operations.	Uncertainties encountered in the development phase impair judgment on actual project status; the techniques for estimation of percent completion can lead to erroneous decisions concerning project development
2. Reliability	Customer oriented. Compares favorably with Gantt technique	Not product oriented.
3. Implementation	Only slightly more difficult to comprehend and to implement than Gantt technique	
4. Universality of Project Coverage	Capable of covering a system life cycle	Does not emphasize resource allocation directly
5. Sensitivity Testing (Simulation)		No significant capability for simulating alternative courses of action
6. Forecasting	Depicts status of project well in production stage and can forecast whether or not schedule will be met	Offers no technique to handle uncertainty in development phase
7. Updating		Considerable clerical effort required to update graphs
8. Flexibility		Inflexible; when major program changes occur, the entire set of graphs must be redrawn.
9. Cost	Data gathering and computations can be handled routinely. Expense is moderate and largely for clerical personnel and chart materials.	Charts require frequent reconstruction, which is time-consuming.

TABLE 12.3(b) GANTT TECHNIQUE—STRENGTHS AND WEAKNESSES

CRITERION	STRENGTHS	WEAKNESSES
1. Validity	Good in production operations. Because of short time duration of each measured operation, only small errors in measurement are likely to occur.	No explicit technique for depicting interrelationships, which are especially important in development
2. Reliability	Simplicity of system affords some reliability.	Frequently unreliable, especially in development stage, because judgment of estimator may change over time. Numerous estimates in a large project, each with some unreliability, may lead to errors in judging status.

TABLE 12.3(b)   (Cont.)

CRITERION	STRENGTHS	WEAKNESSES
3. Implementation	Easiest of all systems in some respects because it is well understood. (System implies existence of time standards.)	Quite difficult to implement for the control of operations in development phase, where time standards do not ordinarily exist and must be developed.
4. Universality of Project Coverage	Can comprehensively cover a given phase of a life cycle. Effective at the resource or input level of control.	Less useful in definition and development phases of life cycle
5. Sensitivity Testing (Simulation)		No significant capability
6. Forecasting	In production operations, good technique to assess ability to meet schedule on a given activity if based on good time standards	Weak in forecasting ability to meet schedule when interrelationships among activities are involved
7. Updating	Easy to update graphs weekly, etc., if not major program changes	
8. Flexibility		If significant program changes occur frequently, numerous charts must be completely reconstructed.
9. Cost	Data gathering and processing relatively inexpensive. Display can be inexpensive if existing charts can be updated and if inexpensive materials are used.	The graph tends to be inflexible. Program changes require new graphs, which are time-consuming and costly. Frequently, expensive display devices are used.

adding two other elements: capacity and execution. Capacity is a plant's rated ability to produce. When the material and capacity requirements for executing a given production plan and master schedule are developed, the question is whether or not these plans are realistic. If the answer to this question is yes, then the execution of the material plan is completed. A daily schedule goes out to each work center on the production line, and a weekly schedule is sent to each vendor. The production plan is executed and monitored to see whether actual output meets the plan.

MRP-II incorporates the elements of closed-loop MRP to generate financial figures. Instead of having one set of numbers for the operations manager and another set for the financial people, every department works with the same set of numbers. That enables operations managers to consider financial trade-offs in which cost and schedule are considered. MRP-II is in essence, therefore, a simulation of a manufacturing business, tying together design, marketing, accounting, and operations.

TABLE 12.3(c) MRP PROCEDURE—STRENGTHS AND WEAKNESSES

CRITERION	STRENGTHS	WEAKNESSES
1. Validity	Expeditious feedback and flexibility keep errors to a minimum. Product oriented	
2. Reliability	Highly reliable	
3. Implementation	Requires to determine the Bill of Materials	Involved. Requires ultimate user's commitment.
4. Universality of Project Coverage	Capable of integrating the whole life cycle from design, through planning and organizing to out-solving; useful in definition and development phases of life cycle	
5. Sensitivity Testing (Simulation)	Significant capability for simulating alternative courses of action	
6. Forecasting	Assess ability to meet schedule on a given activity	
7. Updating	Easy to update daily	
8. Flexibility	Responds to significant program with ease	
9. Cost		High; requires computer system development and user's training

COMPUTERIZED MRP SYSTEMS

The MRP system can be most useful if it is computerized as a conversational program. This way, the operations manager can become familiar with the "behavior" of this planning system. We shall describe a useful conversational program in the context of the VTR top plate case.

BOM Processor

The MRP conversational program includes a bill of materials (BOM) processor. This processor "explodes" a bill of material by computing the quantity of each part and subassembly required. The input of the program is an assembly BOM file (a final assembly finished VTRs). Each assembly may include several parts which themselves have their own separate assembly BOM's. On-hand inventory is also given as input, as shown in Figure 12.8. The output of the program is a BOM that lists the quantity of each part required to make one unit of the final product.

As one can see from Figure 12.9, the operations manager must enter his name and the title MRP. This information is used in descriptive headings for the output that is generated. The computer asks for the following input data:

1. The assembly numbers and description
2. The part numbers, quantity, and description
3. The inventory-on-hand data.

FIGURE 12.8 VTR ASSEMBLY BILL OF MATERIALS (BOM)

ASSEMBLY	PART	QUANTITY REQUIRED FOR ASSEMBLY	DESCRIPTION	QUANTITY ON HAND
00099			VTR	20
	10001	2	Supply/take-up reel	20
	10002	2	Idler	5
	10003	2	Self-aligning post	0
10199			HEAD ASSEMBLY	10
	20003	1	Motor	10
	20004	1	Drum	0
	20005	2	Track head	0
	20006	1	Capstan idler	0

In Figure 12.9, this communication is illustrated. The operations manager first enters all the assembly numbers and then the description of each. If an input error is made, he or she can re-enter the data. Then, for each assembly, the operations manager must enter the parts data. There can be up to 99 parts within each assembly. For each part he or she enters:

1. The part number
2. The quantity on hand
3. The part description.

The program further allows the operations manager to check the input for each assembly and re-enter the data if an error has been made. When the data entries are complete, the program proceeds to the output stage.

The program is also capable of producing net requirements. The question, simply stated: Given that one has some of the required parts and assemblies, what else does one need for a complete batch? The netting is done in Figure 12.10. The operations manager enters the number of inventory items, followed by the part number and quantity for each. The program proceeds to print a table of the input and requests that the operations manager check his or her data for errors. If an error is made, the program begins a correction procedure. This procedure allows for spot changes of the input rather than re-entry of all the data. The program will first print a list of the inventory part numbers with an index. The operations manager enters the index number of the part containing the error and then re-enters the data for that part number. This procedure is repeated until all errors are corrected and the digit "0" is introduced to signal the end of a data input phase.

The first part of the computer output is a printout of the inventory input data. The printout of the input data is intended to facilitate the checking of the input data for validity.

Figure 12.9   Interactive MRP Program (user's entries are underlined)

---

note: all numeric values entered must be separated by a comma and/or a
    space

note: Assembly numbers and Part Numbers must be 5 digit integer
    numbers (include leading zeros)

enter your name and program title or (stop)

(max of 80 characters)

? Dr. E. Menipaz, P.E.

program Material Requirements Planning for Dr. E. Menipaz, P.E.

****

                            BOM INPUT

****

? 00099

? 10199

? 0

enter the description for each assembly
    99 ? VTR

10199 ? Head Assembly

ASSEMBLY NO.   DESCRIPTION
          99   VTR
      10199   Head Assembly
  check input: is it correct (y/n) ? y

****

*For each assembly no. enter the part no., qty and description

*enter (0) when finished

No. (00099) :
    Part No. ? 10001

    Quantity ? 2

    Description ? Supply/Take-up Reel

    Part No. ? 10002

    Quantity ? 2

    Description ? Idler

    Part No. ? 10003

    Quantity ? 2

Figure 12.9   (Cont.)

Description ? <u>Self-Aligning Post</u>

Part No. ? <u>0</u>

correct (y/n) ? <u>y</u>

No. (10199) :
   Part No. ? <u>20003</u>

   Quantity ? <u>1</u>

   Description ? <u>Motor</u>

   Part No. ? <u>20004</u>

   Quantity ? <u>1</u>

   Description ? <u>Drum</u>

   Part No. ? <u>20005</u>

   Quantity ? <u>2</u>

   Description ? <u>Track Head</u>

   Part No. ? <u>20006</u>

   Quantity ? <u>1</u>

   Description ? <u>Capstan Idler</u>

   Part No. ? <u>0</u>

   correct (y/n) ? <u>y</u>

****

Program Material Requirements Planning for Dr. E. Menipaz, P.E.

asm part	qty	description
99		VTR
10001	2	Supply/Take-up Reel
10002	2	Idler
10003	2	Self-Aligning Post
10199		Head Assembly
20003	1	Motor
20004	1	Drum
20005	2	Track Head
20006	1	Capstan Idler

Figure 12.10 MRP's Net Requirements (user's entries are underlined)

---

enter your name and program title or (stop)
(max of 80 characters)
? Dr. E. Menipaz, P.E.
program Material Requirements Planning for Dr. E. Menipaz, P.E.
same Bill of Material data ? y

> TYPE OF ANALYSIS
- - - - - - - - - - - - - - - - - -

   (1) sum
   (2) net
   (3) lead

enter the index number of desired analysis type ? 2

****
> INVENTORY INPUT
****

enter the number of inventory items (max 99) ? 9

Enter the part no. & quantity on hand,
for each inventory item

(1) :
   No. ? 00099

   Qty ? 20

(2) :
   No. ? 10001

   Qty ? 20

(3) :
   No. ? 10199

   Qty ? 10

(4) :
   No. ? 10002

   Qty ? 5

(5) :
   No. ? 10003

   Qty ? 0

(6) :
   No. ? 20003

   Qty ? 10

Figure 12.10 (Cont.)

```
(7) :
    No. ? 20004

    Qty ? 0

(8) :
    No. ? 20005

    Qty ? 0

(9) :
    No. ? 20006

    Qty ? 0
```

****
                              MRP RESULTS
****

program Material Requirements Planning for Dr. E. Menipaz, P.E.

                    Inventory Record Input

program Material Requirements Planning for Dr. E. Menipaz, P.E.

part	on	lt	*qty**wk****on order*****************							
00099	20	1	0	0	0	0	0	0	0	0
10001	20	2	0	0	0	0	0	0	0	0
10199	10	3	0	0	0	0	0	0	0	0
10002	5	1	0	0	0	0	0	0	0	0
10003	0	1	0	0	0	0	0	0	0	0
20003	10	1	0	0	0	0	0	0	0	0
20004	0	1	0	0	0	0	0	0	0	0
20005	0	2	0	0	0	0	0	0	0	0
20006	0	1	0	0	0	0	0	0	0	0

check input: is it correct (y/n) ? y

asm part		description	rqmts	on hand	net
00099		VTR	90	20	70
	10001	Supply/Take-up Reel	140	20	120
	10002	Idler	140	5	135
	10003	Self-Aligning Post	140	0	140
10199		Head Assembly	70	10	60
	20003	Motor	70	10	60
	20004	Drum	70	0	70
	20005	Track Head	70	0	70
	20006	Capstan Idler	70	0	70

The second part of the computer output is the summarized BOM with the required, on-hand, and net requirements shown. The net requirements are the true net, with the parts contained in higher-level assemblies netted out. Once the operations manager has the on-hand quantities and the net requirements shown, he or she can produce a "batch" of VTR.

The third kind of analysis available through programmed MRP is lead time offsetting. A lead time is the difference between the time an order for an item is released and the time it becomes available. The purpose of lead time offsetting is to compute when an order should be placed so that it is available when it is required. Lead time offset is illustrated in Figure 12.11.

After indicating the choice of analysis, (type 3—lead time), the operations manager enters the numbers of inventory items. As has been done earlier, the part number and quantity are entered for each. In addition, the operations manager enters the lead time and firm's order data, if any. Firm order data include the time period (bucket) and quantity of the order receipt, as has been discussed earlier.

The input is printed out in a table and the operations manager must indicate whether the data are correct. If an error is found, the program begins a correction procedure.

The output of this subprogram is a printout of the entire inventory file. The file will be the inventory status for the first four items. The top line is the part description. The main body of the item inventory file contains four entries:

1. Gross requirements (rqmts)
2. Scheduled receipts (receipts)
3. On hand (on hand)
4. Planned order releases (orders).

These are the items that are required in order to summarize an inventory record. In this way, the on-hand inventory is used to represent "net available," ending balance, and beginning balance. A positive "on hand" shows complete coverage of requirements in the specific time bucket. The "on hand" balance might become negative. In this case, the "on hand" now indicates the need to cover some requirements, and an order release is planned, with the proper lead time.

The printout of the item inventory file is rather extensive. This printout may be suppressed for several updates, and may be called for in longer periods of time.

SUMMARY

In this chapter, we have dealt with situations in which the demand for one product determines the demand for its subassemblies and parts.

Figure 12.11 Lead Time Offset in MRP (user's entries are underlined)

---

enter your name and program title or (stop)
(max of 80 characters)
? Dr. E. Menipaz, P.E.
program Material Requirements Planning for Dr. E. Menipaz, P.E.
same Bill of Material data ? y

TYPE OF ANALYSIS

(1) sum
(2) net
(3) lead

enter the index number of desired analysis type ? 3

****

INVENTORY INPUT

****

enter the number of inventory items (max 99) ? 9

Enter the part no. & quantity on hand,
lead time & firm order data
for each inventory item

(1) :

    No. ? 00099

    Qty ? 20

    Lead time ? 1

    Firm orders (y/n) ? n

(2) :

    No. ? 10001

    Qty ? 20

    Lead time ? 2

    Firm orders (y/n) ? n

(3) :

    No. ? 10199

    Qty ? 10

    Lead time ? 3

    Firm orders (y/n) ? n

Figure 12.11 (Cont.)

(4) :

    No. ? <u>10002</u>

    Qty ? <u>5 </u>

    Lead time ? <u>1 </u>

    Firm orders (y/n) ? <u>n </u>

(5) :

    No. ? <u>10003</u>

    Qty ? <u>0 </u>

    Lead time ? <u>1 </u>

    Firm orders (y/n) ? <u>n </u>

(6) :

    No. ? <u>20003</u>

    Qty ? <u>10 </u>

    Lead time ? <u>1 </u>

    Firm orders (y/n) ? <u>n </u>

(7) :

    No. ? <u>20004</u>

    Qty ? <u>0 </u>

    Lead time ? <u>1 </u>

    Firm orders (y/n) ? <u>n </u>

(8) :

    No. ? <u>20005</u>

    Qty ? <u>0 </u>

    Lead time ? <u>2 </u>

    Firm orders (y/n) ? <u>n </u>

(9) :

    No. ? <u>20006</u>

    Qty ? <u>0 </u>

    Lead time ? <u>1 </u>

    Firm orders (y/n) ? <u>n </u>

Figure 12.11 (Cont.)

```
**************************************************************************
                         MRP RESULTS
**************************************************************************
```

program Material Requirements Planning for Dr. E. Menipaz, P.E.

<u>Inventory Record Input</u>

program Material Requirements Planning for Dr. E. Menipaz, P.E.

part	on	lt	*qty**wk****on order******************							
00099	20	1	0	0	0	0	0	0	0	0
10001	20	2	0	0	0	0	0	0	0	0
10199	10	3	0	0	0	0	0	0	0	0
10002	5	1	0	0	0	0	0	0	0	0
10003	0	2	0	0	0	0	0	0	0	0
20003	10	1	0	0	0	0	0	0	0	0
20004	0	1	0	0	0	0	0	0	0	0
20005	0	2	0	0	0	0	0	0	0	0
20006	0	1	0	0	0	0	0	0	0	0

check input: is it correct (y/n) ? <u>y</u>

How many assemblies ? <u>90</u>

In what time period are the assemblies desired ? <u>8</u>

Do you wish to print out your inventory files (y/n) ? <u>y</u>

program Material Requirement Planning for Dr. E. Menipaz, P.E.
VTR

00099 lt = 1	1	2	3	4	5	6	7	8	9
rqmts		0	0	0	0	0	0	0	90	0
receipts		0	0	0	0	0	0	0	0	0
on hand	20	20	20	20	20	20	20	20	−70	−70
orders		0	0	0	0	0	0	70	0	0

Supply/Take-up Reel

10001 lt = 2	1	2	3	4	5	6	7	8	9
rqmts		0	0	0	0	0	0	140	0	0
receipts		0	0	0	0	0	0	0	0	0
on hand	20	20	20	20	20	20	20	−120	−120	−120
orders		0	0	0	0	120	0	0	0	0

Idler

10002 lt = 1	1	2	3	4	5	6	7	8	9
rqmts		0	0	0	0	0	0	140	0	0
receipts		0	0	0	0	0	0	0	0	0
on hand	5	5	5	5	5	5	5	−135	−135	−135
orders		0	0	0	0	0	135	0	0	0

Figure 12.11   (Cont.)

program Material Requirement Planning for Dr. E. Menipaz, P.E.

Self-Aligning Post

10003 lt = 1		1	2	3	4	5	6	7	8	9
rqmts		0	0	0	0	0	0	140	0	0
receipts		0	0	0	0	0	0	0	0	0
on hand	0	0	0	0	0	0	0	−140	−140	−140
orders		0	0	0	0	0	140	0	0	0

Head Assembly

10199 lt = 3		1	2	3	4	5	6	7	8	9
rqmts		0	0	0	0	0	0	70	0	0
receipts		0	0	0	0	0	0	0	0	0
on hand	10	10	10	10	10	10	10	−60	0	0
orders		0	0	0	60	0	0	0	0	0

Motor

20003 lt = 1		1	2	3	4	5	6	7	8	9
rqmts		0	0	0	60	0	0	0	0	0
receipts		0	0	0	0	0	0	0	0	0
on hand	10	10	10	10	−50	0	0	0	0	0
orders		0	0	50	0	0	0	0	0	0

Drum

20004 lt = 1		1	2	3	4	5	6	7	8	9
rqmts		0	0	0	60	0	0	0	0	0
receipts		0	0	0	0	0	0	0	0	0
on hand	0	0	0	0	−60	0	0	0	0	0
orders		0	0	60	0	0	0	0	0	0

Track Head

20005 lt = 2		1	2	3	4	5	6	7	8	9
rqmts		0	0	0	120	0	0	0	0	0
receipts		0	0	0	0	0	0	0	0	0
on hand	0	0	0	0	120	0	0	0	0	0
orders		0	120	0	0	0	0	0	0	0

Capstan Idler

20006 lt = 1		1	2	3	4	5	6	7	8	9
rqmts		0	0	0	60	0	0	0	0	0
receipts		0	0	0	0	0	0	0	0	0
on hand	0	0	0	0	−60	0	0	0	0	0
orders		0	0	60	0	0	0	0	0	0

Material-requirements planning (MRP) is a scheme for the control of a complex manufacturing organization. MRP determines inventory needs and indicates releasing of orders to meet that need. It is further extended to achieve complete control over the flow of materials into the manufacturing plant and to its schedule of handling within the plant.

MRP has been developed to deal with the complexity of assembly operations and with the failure of the economic order quantity methodology to suggest adequate control of these kinds of operations.

MRP usually requires the use of computers, due to large record-keeping and computation requirements.

DISCUSSION PROBLEMS

12.1   Distinguish between and explain dependent demand and independent demand.

12.2   Define material-requirements planning (MRP) and explain how it is used.

12.3   What is the bill of materials (BOM)?

12.4   What is contained in the inventory status file?

12.5   What are the requirements for operating an MRP system?

12.6   List and explain the advantages of an MRP system.

12.7   Comment on the following MRP problems that have been stated recently:

a) "The master schedule used by most companies is not adequate to use for driving an MRP system. The schedules more often reflect what the company wishes it could do, rather than what it is capable of doing. The master schedule must be realistic and balanced with respect to the comany's capabilities in order to allow the MRP system to plan schedules, capacities, and forecasts effectively."

b) "Plant managers do not know how to structure their bills of materials. The objective is to allow the MRP system to pull all the available component parts together to produce the product. A common mistake occurs when bills of materials are written for products that cannot be forecasted, such as specific colors for automobiles. Bills of materials that are meaningful to the plant should be structured, even if this means dropping down to a level below the usual customer description."

c) "Records accuracy is a big problem. I estimate that 50% of all inventory records have a significant error. Records must be kept accurate. This not only allows the MRP system to operate, but it pays real profit dividends on its own."

d) "Most companies don't know how to handle lead times. When actual lead times are longer than planned, many of the companies fall into the trap of simply extending the schedules using their MRP system. This further increases lead times and, eventually, work-in-process inventory increases instead of declines. Then everyone thinks the MRP system is not working. This is one of the more difficult problems to correct."

12.8   List the steps involved in the MRP procedure.

12.9   What is the importance of having a conversational MRP system?

12.10   Material-requirements planning is a straightforward procedure. The logic behind the MRP procedure is very simple. Why, then, did MRP not become widespread until the late 'seventies (that is, following the "MRP crusade" that started during 1971)?

PROBLEMS AND SOLUTIONS

12.1 The High Bike Co., Inc., a manufacturer of bicycles and motorcycles, is planning an order release for bicycle frame #A100. The company is using the MRP procedure. Assume that the company has an inventory of 60 units, and the lead time is one week. Find the net requirements and planned order release to meet the gross requirements for weeks 1 to 5, given the following information:

	Week Number				
Frame #A100	1	2	3	4	5
Gross Requirements	50	60		40	80
On Hand					
Net Requirements					
Scheduled Receipts	0				
Planned Order Release					

Solution

	Week Number				
Frame #A100	1	2	3	4	5
Gross Requirements	50	60	0	40	80
On Hand	60	10	0	0	0
Net Requirements	0	50	0	40	80
Scheduled Receipts	0	50	0	40	80
Planned Order Release	50		40	80	

The action buckets are at weeks 1, 3, and 4. Fifty frames should be ordered in week 1, forty frames should be ordered in week 3, and eighty units should be ordered in week 4.

12.2 MacDonald's Big Mac hamburger is produced in the following fashion. The bottom bun is combined with sauce, lettuce, and cheese, while one beef patty is grilled with onions and spices. Then, the bottom bun and the patty are assembled.

The middle bun is put together with sauce, lettuce, and pickles, while the second beef patty is grilled with onions and spices. Then, the middle bun and the patty are assembled.

The last stage consists of putting together the bottom bun and patty, the middle bun and patty, and the top bun.
a) Construct a product structure tree, and indicate levels.
b) Determine the number of bottom, middle, and top buns, and the number of patties required in order to produce 500 Big Macs.

Solution
a) Assign letters to the various components of the Big Mac:

A: Assembled Big Mac
B: Bottom bun and patty
C: Middle bun and patty
D: Top bun
E: Completed bottom bun
F: Patty
G: Completed middle bun
H: Bottom bun
I: Sauce
J: Lettuce
K: Cheese
L: Onions
M: Spices
N: Patty

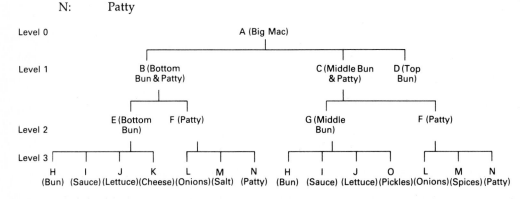

b) We need five hundred top, middle, and bottom buns, as well as (500 × 2 =) 1000 patties.

CHAPTER REVIEW PROBLEMS

12.1   The MRP Workshop manufactures product A. Product A consists of one X part and four Y parts. Part X is made up of two D parts and three E parts. Part Y is made up of one G part and two H parts. Part E is made up of one M part and one J part. All parts to make product A are ordered from an outside vendor. Parts X, D, and G take two weeks to arrive, parts Y and E take three weeks, and H, M, and J take one week. Upon receipt of all of the parts, product A requires one week to make. An order has just been received by the MRP Workshop for 100 units of product A to be completed within 8 weeks.

   a) Draw a products structure tree for product A.
   b) How many of each type of part are needed to make 100 units of product A?
   c) Present in chart form a material-requirements plan for completing 100 units of product A.

12.2 What are the important elements of the MRP system?

12.3 How did the development of high-speed, high-memory, main-frame computers facilitate the development of MRP?

12.4 It is a common practice in industry to run the MRP program once every week or two weeks. Discuss the desirability of a shorter period review—for example, a daily review.

12.5 The bill of material for end item A is shown below.

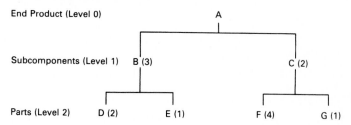

End Product (Level 0)

Subcomponents (Level 1)   B (3)   C (2)

Parts (Level 2)   D (2)   E (1)   F (4)   G (1)

Management wants to determine the material requirements for ordered-part D that will be needed to complete 60 units of A by the start of week 5. Lead times are: one week for level-0 items (end product), one week for level-1 items (subcomponents), and two weeks for level-2 items (parts). There are 60 units of subcomponent B on hand and 100 units of part D. What are the material requirements?

12.6 Given the following list of items, construct a product structure tree, using low-level coding, and determine what quantity of each subassembly and parts is required to make 250 units of end items.

A	B	C	D	E
B(2)	E(2)	G(2)	I	G(4)
C(4)	F		H(2)	F(2)
D(4)				H(4)

READING
The Nuts and Bolts of Japan's Factories*

TOYODA CITY,** JAPAN—Groping to explain "how Japan does it," experts have made much of the close ties between business and government and of the loyalty of Japan's highly skilled workers to their employers. They've noted the fierce competitiveness of Japanese companies in their home market, the nation's high savings rate, even the relative scarcity of lawyers.

Doubtless these are among the pieces needed to solve the puzzle. But some management consultants who've studied how Japan makes such high-quality, competitively priced products say there's another piece often over-

* SOURCE: Reprinted by permission of *The Wall Street Journal*, March 31, © Dow Jones & Co., (1981). All rights reserved.
** Note that almost all Toyota Motor Co. plants are located in Toyoda City in Japan. However, the Japanese assumed that Toyota is easier for North Americans to pronounce than is Toyoda. Thus, the name of this successful car is "Toyota.'"

looked. The Japanese, they say, have proved themselves increasingly adroit at organizing and running manufacturing operations. Japanese managers may lack the MBAs or the ability to plot big-picture business strategy of their American counterparts. But they know how to run factories.

"There's a growing acceptance that Japanese success is based at least in part on the development of manufacturing techniques that often tend to outrun our own," says management consultant Rex Reid, head of A. T. Kearney's Toyota office.

One of the most interesting examples of Japanese production management skills is a concern quite familiar to Americans: Toyota Motor Co., the largest-selling foreign auto maker in the U.S.

Believe in their System

Toyota officials resist claiming that their way of building autos is better than anyone else's. They're somewhat embarrassed by the exuberant projections of Henry Ford's behavior essayed by their former chief production executive, Taiichi Oono, in his 1978 book. But Toyota men clearly remain believers in what Mr. Oono called "the Toyota production system."

For a first-hand look at the system, take a walk through the Tsutsumi plant here in Toyoda City, a town of 280,000 in central Japan that's the site of eight of Toyota's 10 factories. Over here, Muneo Nakahara, 26 years old and an eight-year Toyota veteran, is doing his job. With the help of an overhead crane that Mr. Nakahara controls from a hand-held device, he hoists auto engines onto a conveyor belt that will take them to be matched up with auto bodies.

Mr. Nakahara is lifting the engines onto the conveyor from a small flat-bed truck that has brought them from the engine plant. Only two trucks carrying only 12 engines apiece park at Mr. Nakahara's post at any given time, so every few minutes an empty truck drives back to the engine plant and a new one takes its place.

That's the first feature of the Toyota system: no inventories. Toyota's factories keep on hand only that amount of parts needed for immediate production, from a few minutes' worth up to a few hours' worth depending on the part. When fresh parts are needed—and only when they're needed—they're delivered from other Toyota plants or from outside suppliers directly to the production line.

Outsiders who've seen Toyota in action often call this the "kanban system," kanban being the Japanese word for the piece of paper enclosed in clear plastic that accompanies each bin of parts. (When a worker on the line begins drawing from a new bin, he removes the kanban and routes it back to the supplier, for whom it serves as an order for a new bin of parts.) But Toyota officials say the pieces of paper are just tools. They call this inventory-control aspect of their broader system the "just-in-time" system.

The same philosophy guides the meshing of operations within each plant. An assembly line that is building subcomponents makes just that number of subcomponents immediately needed at the next stage of production. When it's made enough, it's changed over to build some other kind of subcomponent for awhile. Likewise, the final assembly line builds first one kind of car, then another, in small lots—only as much as called for in actual orders from Toyota's sales unit. Toyota engineers "average" and "level" production among the lines to coordinate output without building inventories. They compare auto assembly to rowing a boat: Everybody has to be pulling on the oars at the same rate.

"They concentrate very heavily on avoiding end-item and intermediate-item storage," says a Ford official in Detriot who's seen the system at work. "They throw out the whole concept of mass production."

The benefits are substantial. Toyota doesn't need space for inventory, people to handle and control inventory, or borrowed money to finance inventory. "It cuts costs in a lot of ways," says an official of Nissan Motor Co., Japan's second-largest auto maker, which has adopted an inventory-control system similar to its rival's in some plants.

Then there are the side benefits. Because Toyota is constantly changing over its machines to make new things, its workers have become fast at repair and changeover. In his book, Mr. Oono cites a mold on a press that took two to three hours to change in the 1940s. Today "it takes only three minutes to change the molding," Mr. Oono says.

Aside from its emphasis on holding down inventories, Toyota's system stresses quality controls. Throughout the Tsutsumi plant are boards with electric lights to indicate conditions on each assembly line. A red light means a line has been stopped because of a problem. Every worker has a button or cord with which he can stop the line, and he's told to use it whenever he thinks something's wrong with the operation of the line or when he spots defects in the product.

"We lose production temporarily this way," concedes Fujio Cho, manager of the production control department at Toyota's headquarters. "But in our experience stopping lines helps us detect problems early and avoid bad practices."

Another feature that becomes clear is the company's penchant for training workers to do more than one job. The man who runs one machine switches off every few moments to run another. The man who feeds rear windows to a robot also "tags" car shells with instructions telling workers farther down the line what to install in them. This versatility allows Toyota to realign its work force more efficiently when business is bad.

Indeed, "recession" thinking underlies a big part of Toyota's system. Much of the system originated in the late 1940s and early 1950s, when Toyota was producing exclusively for a domestic market that wasn't very strong. The company had been operating on the conventional assumption that it's most efficient to produce in large lots, "but that kind of thinking had pushed us close to bankruptcy, because the large lots we were producing couldn't be sold," says Mr. Cho. Toyota couldn't lay off workers—Japan's is a "lifetime" employment system—so Toyota executives hit upon the simple yet radical idea that still pervades its operations: Overproduction is waste.

Special Relationship

It is, of course, open to question whether Toyota's is the best way to make cars, and Toyota officials themselves doubt whether other auto makers could adopt it readily. They note among other problems that it takes a special kind of relationship with suppliers to make the system work.

Fully 50 of Toyota's 250 suppliers are headquartered in Toyoda City, and almost all have plants here. They have to be close to make all those deliveries every day. It still shocks Toyota officials to be told that American auto makers buy parts from suppliers all over the U.S. and even from suppliers in Europe and Japan. Toyota's most distant supplier is a five-hour drive away.

Then, too, suppliers must have close working relations with Toyota to adjust to Toyota's peculiar needs. It isn't surprising that many of Toyota's suppliers do all or most of their business with Toyota, and that Toyota owns large blocks of the stock of some of its most important suppliers. Many suppliers, even those Toyota doesn't own, have adopted Toyota's production system for their own operations. It improves coordination with Toyota, and helps them avoid getting stuck with the inventory buildup that Toyota refuses to get stuck with.

The point isn't clear whether Toyota's system is best. The point is that it's very good, and that Toyota is in many ways typical of Japanese manufacturers in its continual striving to improve production techniques. When experts talk about the competitiveness of Japanese products in international market, that's something that shouldn't be forgotten.

Questions

1. Compare the MRP System with the "kanban system."
2. Compare the MRP System with the extension to the "kanban system," the "just-in-time" system.
3. What are the factors that would affect the adoption of the "kanban system" in North America?

BIBLIOGRAPHY

Ammer, D. S., *Purchasing and Materials Management for Health Care Institutions.* Lexington, Mass: D. C. Heath, 1975.

APICS Certification Program Study Guide, "Capacity Planning and Master Production Scheduling," *Journal of the American Production and Inventory Control Society*, 20, 2, 1979.

AMERICAN PRODUCTION AND INVENTORY CONTROL SOCIETY, *APICS Special Report: Materials Requirement Planning by Computer*. Washington, D.C.: American Production and Inventory Control Society, Inc., 1971.

BERRY, W. L., and D. CLAY WHYBARK, "Research Perspectives for Material Requirements Planning Systems," *Production and Inventory Management*, June, 1975, pp. 19–25.

BERRY, W. L., R. A. MOHRAM, and T. CALLARMAN, *Master Scheduling and Capacity Planning: A Case Study*, MAPEC Module, Purdue University, 1977.

BERRY, W. L., T. E. VOLLMAN, and D. C. WHYBARK, *Master Production Scheduling, Principles and Practice*. Washington, D.C.: American Production and Inventory Control Society, Inc., 1979.

BRENIZER, N., "MS to MRP to MSW," *Journal of the American Production and Inventory Control Society*, 19, 5, 1978.

BUFFA, E. S., and WILLIAM H. TAUBERT, eds. *Production-Inventory Systems: Planning and Control* (rev. ed.). Homewood, Ill.: Richard D. Irwin, 1972.

EBNER, M. L., "Master Scheduling the Product-Oriented Job Shop," *AIIE 1977 Systems Engineering Conference Proceedings*. Norcross, Ga.: American Institute of Industrial Engineers, Inc., 1977.

EVERDELL, R., "Master Scheduling: Its New Importance in the Mangement of Materials," *Modern Materials Handling*, October, 1972.

GOODMAN, D. A., "A New Approach to Scheduling Aggregate Production and Work Force," *AIEE Transactions*, 5, 1973, pp. 135–141.

GREEN, J. H., *Production and Inventory Control Systems and Decisions* (rev. ed.). Homewood, Ill.: Richard D. Irwin, 1974.

HANSON, S. R., "The Synergistic Effects of Master Scheduling," *Journal of American Production and Inventory Control Society*, 14, 3, 1973.

IBM, *Materials Requirements Planning Systems*, Publication G320-1970, 1971.

IBM, *Communications Oriented Production Information and Control System*, Publications G320-1974 through G320-1981.

LEACH, S., "A Two-Stage Forecasting Model for Use in Conjunction with a Computerized Master Scheduling System," *AIEE 1977 Systems Engineering Conference Proceedings*. Norcross, Ga.: American Institute of Industrial Engineers, Inc., 1977.

LOVE, STEPHEN, *Inventory Control*. New York: McGraw Hill, 1979.

Master Production Scheduling Reprints. Washington, DC: American Production and Inventory Control Society, Inc., 1977.

"Master Production Schedule Planning," Chapter 4 of *Communications Oriented Production Information and Control System (COPICS)*, 3, G320, 1976, International Business Machines Corporation, 1972.

MATHER, H. F., and G. W. PLOSSL, *The Master Production Schedule, Management's Handle of the Business*. Atlanta, Ga.: Mather and Plossl, 1978.

McCLAIN, JOHN O., and JOSEPH THOMAS, *Operations Management: Production of Goods and Services*. Englewood Cliffs: Prentice-Hall, Inc., 1980.

MILLER, J. G., and L. G. SPRAGUE, "Behind the Growth in Material Requirements Planning," *Harvard Business Review*, Vol. 53, No. 5, Sept.–Oct., 1975, pp. 83–91.

ORLICKY, JOSEPH A., *Material Requirements Planning: The New Way of Life in Production and Inventory Management*. New York: McGraw-Hill Co., 1974.

_____, *Material Requirements Planning*, Chapter 11. New York: McGraw-Hill Company, 1975.

PETERSON, REIN, and EDWARD A. SILVER, *Decision Systems for Inventory Mangement and Production Planning*. Toronto: John Wiley & Sons, 1979.

PLOSSL, G. W., and O. W. WIGHT. *Material Requirements Planning by Computer*. Washington, D.C.: American Production and Inventory Control Society, Inc., 1971.

PLOSSL, G. W., and W. E. WELCH, *The Role of Top Management in the Control of Inventory*, Chapter 6. Reston, Virginia: Reston Publishing Co., 1979.

RUCH, WILLIAM A., "Economic Lot Sizing in MRP: The Marriage of EOQ and MRP," *19th Annual Conference, American Production and Inventory Control Society*, Atlanta, Ga., 1976.

SMOLENS, R. W., "Master Scheduling: Problems and Solutions," *Journal of the American Production and Inventory Control Society*, 18, 3, 1977.

STARR, M. K., and D. W. MILLER, *Inventory Control: Theory and Practice*. Englewood Cliffs, N.J.: Prentice-Hall, Inc., 1962.

STEVENSON, WILLIAM J., *Production/Operations Management*. Homewood, Ill.: Richard D. Irwin, 1982.

SUMMA, W. J., and R. B. DIRKS, *Experiences with the Development of a Master Scheduling Activity*. Society of Manufacturing Engineering, paper MM71-125, 1971.

TERSINE, R. J., *Materials Management and Inventory Systems*. New York: North-Holland, Inc., 1976.

THURSTON, P. H., "Requirements Planning for Inventory Control," *Harvard Business Review*, May–June, 1972, pp. 67–71.

WIGHT, O. W., *Production and Inventory Management in the Computer Age.*, Chapter 4. Boston, Mass.: Cahners Books, 1974.

WIXOM, T. "Plant Scheduling with a Computer," *Journal of the American Production and Inventory Control Society*, 16, 2, 1975.

WOOLSEY, R. E., "A Survey of Quick and Dirty Methods of Production Scheduling," *American Production and Inventory Control Society Annual Conference*, 1972.

Quality Control **13**

INTRODUCTION

In former chapters, we have stressed the fact that any operation, be it manufacturing or service, is judged by three important criteria: cost, timeliness (schedule), and quality. In today's competitive economy, there is an ever-growing need to offer products and services that are of a certain quality level and yet not overpriced. This need imposes many restrictions on an operations manager. There is always a trade-off between quality and cost: higher quality results in higher production costs, and lower quality results in lower production costs and, possibly, higher field service calls.

Every product has "quality." Unfortunately, not every product is of *good* "quality." When the expression "quality product" is used, one usually thinks in terms of a good or excellent product. In operations management, a *quality* product is one that fulfills customers' expectations. These expectations involve:

1. Aesthetic appeal
2. Functionability
3. Reliability.

The first relates to visual appeal of the service or products. The second relates to how well the service is done or how well the product performs its intended use. The third relates to the longevity of the product or the lasting impression or usefulness of a service (e.g., how long a hairdo "holds").

Quality control has been defined as *an effective system for integrating the quality development, quality maintenance, and quality improvement efforts of the various groups in an organization, so as to enable production and service at the most economical levels which allow for full customer satisfaction.*[1] According to this definition the control of quality must occupy the entire organization.

Related to the concept of the quality function, is "fitness for use." The extent to which the product successfully serves the purposes of the user during usage is called its "fitness for use." Fitness for use is determined by the features of the product that the user can recognize as beneficial to his or her requirements—e.g., taste, reception, timeliness, extent of life, beauty, status. The degree of fitness for use is judged as perceived by the user, not by the manufacturer of the product or the provider of the service.

THE SCOPE OF QUALITY CONTROL

Quality control involves control of design of products and services, control of incoming material, control of work in process, and final inspection and testing of completed products and services.

The general public stresses quality, and many manufacturers make it a point to expose their quality-control system in order to impress potential customers. For example, Figure 13.1 shows the final inspection notification for a check order, issued by a printing house. Through this inspection notification, the client is assured that the checks have been passed through an inspection station. (The inspector as well as the inspection date are identified.)

In Figure 13.2, a car manufacturer is presenting in much detail to the general public its car inspection system. An effort is being made to impress the potential customer with the quality of the car through a description of the quality-control system.

INSPECT THIS ORDER BEFORE USING

We have been as careful as possible in preparing your order, however mistakes can occur.

PLEASE EXAMINE THE ACCURACY OF ALL PRINTED DETAILS CAREFULLY.

The account number should be the same as is shown on your monthly statement or account book.

If you find an error, please notify your Branch, make corrections on the card inside your reorder envelope and mail it along with this inspection slip immediately so that your order may be promptly replaced.

INSPECTED BY...*TAMMY*... NOV 2 7 1978

All orders are furnished on the condition that liability is limited to the replacement of the incorrectly printed order.

Figure 13.1   Final Inspection of a Check-Book Notification Issued by a Printing House

---

[1] This definition of quality control was coined by A. V. Feigenbaum, *Total Quality Control* (New York: McGraw-Hill Book Co., 1961), p. 1.

Every Mazda comes equipped with 3 miles.

There's no way you can buy a new Mazda.

Because until we're satisfied that the Mazda you buy meets our standards, it won't leave our assembly plant.

That's why we have 5700 different inspections for every car we produce. And every car is inspected for 3½ hours. On the body shell alone we make 1200 inspections. Every engine is bench tested for 40 minutes. Run without stopping. And there's more we check. And test. And probe. Why?

Because even though Mazda already has a reputation for making some of the finest cars and engines in the world—we want to be even better.

So we've instituted what we think is the most exacting quality control system found anywhere.

1150 specially trained inspectors who have the absolute authority to halt the production of everything from grommets to our emission control components—if they feel there is the slightest flaw in quality.

Every 3 months awards are given to groups of employees who have taken the initiative to improve on our already exacting criteria. Awards for improving the fit of doors. For strengthening welds. For perfecting undercoating and final body painting.

But most important, and most unusual—every employee on the Mazda assembly line considers the man next to him his customer. So the piston processor processes his best to satisfy his customer the piston polisher. And the piston polisher polishes his best to satisfy his customer the engine assembler.

And on and on.

Oh yes, about the 3 miles that come with every Mazda?

Well, after all our assembly line testing is completed—every Mazda is taken out for one last time—and for 3 miles*: driven easy, driven hard, panic-stopped, slalomed, revved to the limit in various gears with easy-clutching, pop-clutching. And only after having passed that final test is it approved for sale.

And you know, those 3 miles might be the most important miles ever put on your car. Mazda. Making tradition. Not following it.

*3 miles equals 4.8 kilometres

Figure 13.2

HISTORICAL PERSPECTIVE

The history of quality control follows the history of industry itself. During the Middle Ages, quality was controlled by the extensive training that was required by the guilds. Until the late 1800's, one worker or a small number of workers were responsible for the manufacture of an entire product.

The concept of division of labor that was introduced in France and England during the Industrial Revolution resulted in the modern factory concept of the foreman. Thus, the foreman became responsible for the quality of output from many workers who performed similar tasks. As products became more complicated and jobs more specialized, it became necessary to inspect products after manufacture.

In 1924, W. A. Shewhart of Bell Telephone Laboratories developed a statistical chart for the control of product variables. This is considered to be the beginning of statistical quality control. Later in the same decade, H. F. Dodge and H. G. Romig, both of Bell Telephone Laboratories, developed acceptance sampling as a substitute for the inspection of each product in a batch. Statistical quality control was not generally implemented by industry until World War II. During World War II, statistical quality control made inspection more efficient by providing statistical tools, such as sampling and control charts, and has proved to be cost effective.

In 1946, the American Society for Quality Control was formed. This organization, through its publications, conferences, and training sessions, has promoted the use of quality control for all types of production and service activities. Recently, a new, all encompassing "assurance science" has evolved. This body of knowledge encompasses quality control, reliability, and maintainability methodology and practices.

PRODUCT LIABILITY AND QUALITY CONTROL

The risk of product liability action is substantial in doing business today. Product liability claims have increased from a few hundreds in the 1970's to millions in the 1980's, not counting out-of-court settlements. The increase in product liability losses has been attributed to changes in the attitude from "let the buyer beware" to "let the supplier beware," and to the development of new legislation that has been supported by consumer advocates. Most lawsuits have involved all parties responsible for the design of the product or service, its manufacture, its distribution, and its sales and aftersale support. Single judgments have been made in excess of several millions of dollars, and recall programs have cost in excess of tens of millions of dollars. A product liability lawsuit might ruin the small manufacturer, and it can also affect members of the company's management on an individual basis. Product liability lawsuits are based on express warranty or implied (by law) warranty.

Quality-control people are the best witnesses and quality-control records and practices are the best evidence in a product liability lawsuit. Tools such as detailed records, design review boards, field-trouble feedback system, liability "arrangements" (distributing of the liability among the manufacturer, wholesaler, and retailer), and detailed interrogatories have been advocated by quality-control personnel. While liability and warranty is not the only reason for the development of quality control, it has certainly been an impetus for its development in recent years.

RESPONSIBILITY FOR QUALITY

Quality should not be the responsibility of any one person or department; it should be the job of every person in the company, including the typist, the purchasing agent, and the president of the company, as well as the assembly-line worker. However, the official responsibility for quality is delegated to the various departments, along with the authority to make quality decisions and the accountability for quality costs and defectives.

The departments responsible for quality are shown in Figure 13.3. They are: marketing, product engineering, purchasing, production engineering, production, inspection and testing, packaging and shipping, and product service. Attention should be given to the fact that the quality-control department itself is not included in the description, since that department has only a support or service function in this regard. The continuous nature of quality effort is indicated by the fact that once the product is with the customer, information having regard to quality requirements is forwarded to the marketing department.

Marketing Department

The marketing department helps to evaluate the level of product quality that the customer wants, requires, and is willing to pay for. In addition, the marketing department provides the customer with product-quality data and help to determine quality specifications. Information concerning customer dissatisfaction is provided by customer complaints, sales representative reports, and product service. This information and its analysis is fed back into product engineering for service design in service organizations, and helps management decide on proper action and improvement.

Product Engineering Department

Product engineering translates the customer's quality requirements into operating characteristics, precise specifications, and appropriate tolerances. As the complexity of the product increases, the difficulty of achieving quality and

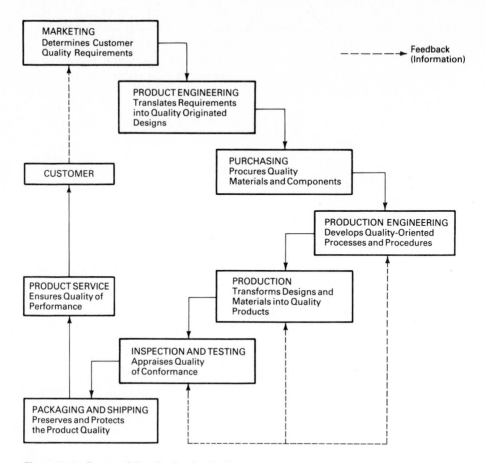

Figure 13.3 Responsibility for Quality by Departments

reliability increases. The function of the product engineering department is to utilize proven designs and standard components in trying to achieve the simplest product operation appropriate.

Tolerance is the permissible variation in the magnitude of the quality characteristics, and the selection of tolerances has a dual effect on quality. As tolerances become smaller, a better product results and the cost of field service is lowered; however, the production and design costs, including quality assurance costs, increase. Ideally, tolerance should be determined scientifically by balancing field service costs with design and production costs. (Consult Figure 13.4.)

Purchasing Department

While using the quality standards established by product engineering, the purchasing department has the responsibility of procuring quality materials and components. Purchases are of four kinds: standard raw materials, standard

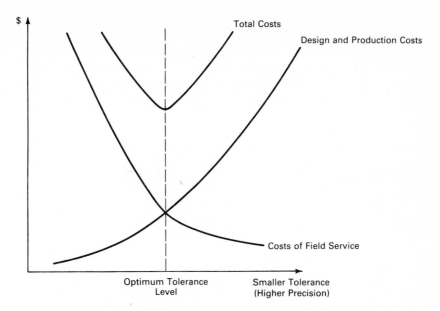

Figure 13.4   Tolerance Trade-Off

machinery, minor parts, and major parts. The type of quality inspection will vary, depending on the category of the purchase.

For standard machinery and minor parts, the purchasing department relies on the vendor's proof of conformance to the quality standards set by the purchasing department. For raw materials and major parts, the purchasing department conducts a vendor quality survey called a vendor's audit. This audit includes the survey of the quality system used by the vendor (account is taken of rejected lots, scrap and rework costs, and complaint information). Inspection of incoming raw material and major parts, either on the vendor's premises (source inspection) or in the plant at the time of arrival (incoming material inspection) is also conducted.

Production Engineering Department

The production engineering department has the responsibility for developing processes and procedures that will produce a quality product. This responsibility is achieved through specific activities, which include product design review and process capability study.

A *product design review* is conducted in order to anticipate quality problems. If product design review indicates severe problems, there are five options: purchase new equipment, revise the tolerance, change the process, revise the system, or sort out the defective product during manufacturing.

Another basic technique of production engineering is the *process capability study*, which determines the ability of the production process to meet specifications. Process capability information provides data for making buying decisions, equipment purchases, and selection of processing sequence.

The sequence of processing operations is developed to minimize the difficulties of quality inspections, such as by eliminating painting operations before visual inspections that are supposed to permit discovery of cracks on a product's surface.

Production Department

The production department has the responsibility of producing quality products. Quality cannot be "inspected into" a product; it must be built into the product. The key to the manufacture of a quality product is the foreman. Since the foreman is considered by operating personnel to represent management, the foreman's ability to convey quality expectations is critical for good employee relations.

In order for the operator to know what is expected of him or her, training sessions on quality should be given periodically. These training sessions reinforce management's commitment to a quality product. The primary objective of the sessions is to develop an attitude of "quality awareness." This approach is further enhanced by introducing "quality circles" that meet regularly to discuss quality problems. In one case, these sessions substantially reduced the percent of failures and resulted in the saving of fourteen hundred dollars per week.[2]

Inspection and Testing Department

The inspection and testing department has the responsibility for appraising the quality of purchased and manufactured items. Its results are used by other departments when corrective action is needed. Although inspection is performed by representatives of the inspection and testing department, this does not relieve the manufacturing department of its responsibility to produce a quality product and to make its own inspections. In fact, with automated production, workers frequently have time to perform complete inspection before and after an operation.

Packaging and Shipping Department

Control of product quality must extend beyond production to the distribution, installation, and use of the product. The packaging and shipping department has the responsibility of preserving and protecting the quality of the product.

[2] D. A. Sprague, B. Zinn, and R. Treitner, "Improved Quality through Behavior Modification," *Quality Progress*, 9, No. 12, December, 1976, pp. 22–24.

Quality specifications are needed for the protection of the product during transit by all types of common carrier: truck, railroad, boat, airplane. These specifications relate to vibration, shock, and environmental conditions.

Product Service Department

Product service has the responsibility of providing the customer with the means for full utilization of the product during its expected life. This responsibility includes installation, maintenance, repair, and replacement-parts service.

Quality-Control Department

The quality control department does not have direct responsibility for quality. It assists or supports the other departments as they carry out the quality-control duties for which they are responsible. The relationship between the other departments and quality control is a line-staff organizational relationship.

The quality-control department appraises the current quality, determines quality problem areas or potential problem areas, assists in the correction or minimization of these problem areas, and executes quality audits. The overall objective is the improvement of the product quality, in cooperation with the departments responsible.

QUALITY-CONTROL PROCEDURES

The quality of operations is controlled through the use of inspection, sampling plans, and process control charts. *Inspection* of raw material, purchased parts, work in process, and completed products involves the observation and measurement of the subject of inspection (a computer program, a typed report to top management, a telephone cord, a desk, a carburetor, etc.).

Sampling involves the selection of representative products from a batch of products in order to make inferences about the whole batch. The basic principle behind sampling is that the inspection cost of the products can be cut down significantly by using a sample, without reducing significantly the level of confidence with which one can determine whether a batch should be rejected or accepted. Based on the number of defective units found in the sample, a decision is made on whether to accept or reject the whole batch.

Process control charts are designed to detect significant changes in product or service specifications while the products and services are being processed or provided. A significant change indicates a necessary change in the process setup, so that no defectives will be turned out.

Sampling Plans

Sampling plans are statistical tools that are used for control of the quality of incoming raw materials and parts and for acceptance sampling of completed products or services. Since sampling plans helps us make judgments about acceptance or rejection of batches, they are sometimes called *acceptance sampling* plans.

When a large batch of parts arrives at the plant or a large number of services are to be provided, a decision should be made on whether to accept or reject the batch. Rather than inspecting all the items in the batch, one can systematically sample a few items. The benefits of using acceptance sampling include the following: First, sampling reduces the amount of monotony that is involved in a job and thus increases the effectiveness of the inspection function itself. (Inspection errors can be as high as 50 percent of the true reading). Second, acceptance sampling decreases the cost of inspection and makes destructive testing feasible. Third, acceptance sampling is often desirable even in those cases in which it is felt that no inspection is necessary, since it provides a positive record that at least a few items were inspected.

Two kinds of errors may result from acceptance sampling. First, a batch of good quality may be mistakenly rejected if a large number of defective items are selected at random from the batch. This type of risk is the producer's risk, denoted by the letter α (alpha). Second, a batch of bad quality may be mistakenly accepted if a large number of good items are selected at random from the batch. This type of risk is the consumer's risk, denoted by the letter β (beta). The sampling plan that we want to adopt is the one that assures that the two risks are no higher than a specified level.

In a sampling plan, one defines the population of interest (the size of the batch) and then randomly selects a sample of n items for inspection. The inspection reveals a number of defectives, x. This x is compared with a critical number of defectives, c. If x is less than or equal to c, the batch is accepted; otherwise the batch is rejected for rework, scrap, or return to the vendor.

The Operating Characteristic Curve (OC Curve)

An operating characteristic curve shows how well the particular sampling plan can discriminate between good and bad lots. The OC curve gives the probability of accepting a lot as a function of the percent defective in the lot for a specific sampling plan.

There are two points on this curve that are of special importance.

1. The *acceptable quality level (AQL)* is the percent defective that can be considered satisfactory as a process average. One is always trying to have a high probability, (1α), of accepting a lot with a fraction defective equal to or less than the AQL. A typical value of α is 0.05.

2. The *lot tolerance percent defective (LTPD)* is the percent defective that can be considered unsatisfactory. One is always trying to have a very low probability, β, of accepting a lot with a percent defective as high as or higher than the LTPD. A typical value of β is 0.10.

Figure 13.5 shows an operating characteristics curve for a specific sampling plan. As stated earlier, sampling plan is consisted of a specific number of products, n, that should be sampled and a maximum number of defectives, c, in the sample that still allows for acceptance of the whole lot. Increasing the sample size, n, while keeping the acceptance number of defectives, c, constant, make the OC curve steeper. Thus, better discrimination between good and bad lots results. The decreasing of c, assuming a constant n, also makes the OC curve become steeper. These points are demonstrated in Figure 13.6.

The Design of A Sampling Plan

The design of a sampling plan is carried out by specifying:

1. AQL and its associated α
2. The LTPD and its associated β.

This will determine singularly the values of n (the sample size) and c (the critical number).

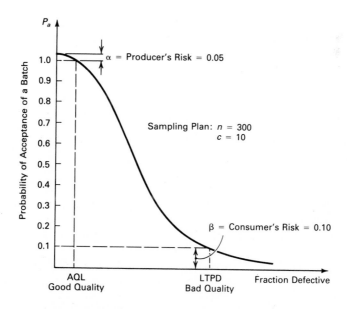

Figure 13.5 Operating Characteristic Curve

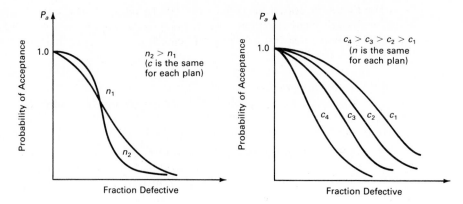

Figure 13.6   Discriminating Power of Various Sampling Plans

The theoretically correct probability distribution to use here is the binomial distribution, but, for simplicity, we shall use the more convenient Poisson distribution as an approximation. The Poisson distribution is given by the following equation:

$$P(x) = \frac{e^{-np}(np)^x}{x!}$$

where:

$n =$ Sample size
$p =$ Fraction defectives in the whole batch (or lot)
$P(x) =$ Probability of finding x defectives in a sample of size n
$x =$ Random variable representing the number of defectives observed

If P_a denotes the probability that the number of defective items in the sample does not exceed the acceptance number, then

$$P_a = \text{Prob } (x \leq c) = \sum_{x=0}^{c} \frac{e^{-np}(np)^x}{x!}$$

The probability of acceptance is computed by using Poisson tables.

The two equations that are needed to describe the OC curve using AQL and LTPD values with the specified values of α and β, respectively, are:

$$\frac{e^{-np_1}(np_1)^x}{x!} = 1 - \alpha, \text{ where } p_1 = \text{AQL}$$

$$\frac{e^{-np_2}(np_2)^x}{x!} = \beta, \text{ where } p_2 = \text{LTPD}$$

The simultaneous solution of the two equations is facilitated by Table 13.1, which is based on the Poisson tables. For increasing values of c, Table 13.1 specifies the values of np_1 and np_2 that yield

$$P_a = 1 - \alpha = 0.95 \quad \text{and} \quad P_a = \beta = 0.10$$

for AQL and LTPD, respectively.

For other values of α and β, similar tables can be developed without much difficulty.

EXAMPLE   A producer of typewriters and a major client decided upon the following inspection sampling parameters. The producer's risk is 0.05 at an AQL of 2 percent ($p_1 = 0.02$), and the client's preferred risk is an LTPD of 8 percent ($p_2 = 0.08$).

The producer now computes $p_2/p_1 = 4.0$. Based on Table 13.1, c should be 4, since there the value of np_2/np_1 is closest to 4.0 (out of the values listed in Table 13.1).

What should the sample size be? To answer this question, one should solve either of the following equations (np_1, and np_2 are given in Table 13.1 on the line corresponding to $c = 4$).

$$n = \frac{np_1}{p_1} = \frac{1.970}{0.02} = 98.500$$

$$n = \frac{np_2}{p_2} = \frac{7.994}{0.08} = 99.925$$

Even though one cannot satisfy exactly the producer's and the consumer's risk requirements, one can get close enough to these requirements by using a sample

TABLE 13.1   VALUES OF ACCEPTANCE NUMBER *(c)* AS A FUNCTION OF AQL (p_1) and LTPD (p_2), for $\alpha = 0.05$ and $\beta = 0.10$

(1) ACCEPTANCE NUMBER c	(2) np_1 (FOR $P_a = 0.95$)	(3) np_2 (FOR $P_a = 0.10$)	(4) $\dfrac{np_2}{np_1} = \dfrac{p_2}{p_1} = \dfrac{\text{LTPD}}{\text{AQL}}$
0	.051	2.303	45.157
1	.355	3.890	10.958
2	.818	5.322	6.506
3	1.366	6.681	4.891
4	1.970	7.994	4.058
5	2.613	9.275	3.550
6	3.286	10.532	3.205
7	3.981	11.771	2.957
8	4.695	12.995	2.768
9	5.426	14.206	2.618
10	6.169	15.407	2.497

size of 99. The producer should select at random 99 typewriters from each lot. If there are no more than four defective typewriters in the lot, the lot is accepted. If more than four typewriters are defective, the lot is rejected.

Average Outgoing Quality

When the same sampling plan is used repeatedly on successive lots, the average outgoing quality (AOQ) of the lots can be calculated if any lot that is rejected is completely screened and all units are removed. If, upon 100 percent inspection of a rejected lot, defective items are removed but not replaced, the average outgoing quality of successive lots is

$$\text{AOQ} = \frac{P_a p(N - n)}{N - pn - p(1 - P_a)(N - n)}$$

where p is the fraction defective, N is the lot size, n is the sample size, and P_a is the probability of acceptance when the fraction of defectives is p.

If defective items are replaced with good ones,

$$\text{AOQ} = \frac{P_a p(N - n)}{N}$$

In both cases, the AOQ will change as a function of p, the true proportion of defectives in the lot, as is shown graphically in Figure 13.7.

Note that even though the items remaining in the rejected lots, after 100 percent inspection and removal of defectives, may be of perfect quality, there are other lots that have been accepted but that do have a certain number of defectives. Thus, the successive lots have, on the average, AOQ proportion of

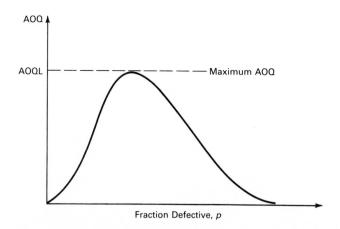

Figure 13.7   Average Outgoing Quality as a Function of Percent Defectives in the Outgoing Lots

defectives. The AOQ peaks at a level called the average outgoing quality limit (AOQL).

There are other kinds of sampling plans for lot-by-lot inspection. In the following section, one such plan is described.

SEQUENTIAL SAMPLING PLAN

Sequential sampling[3] involves observing items from a lot one at a time. After each item is observed and the total number of defective items that have been picked up is compared with calculated standards, a decision is made to accept the lot, reject it, or draw another item.

The importance of this sampling procedure is that, on the average, a sequential plan can reduce the average sample size by as much as 50 percent.

The graphical method of sequential sampling is based on three parameters: s, h_1, and h_2. These three parameters are found in Table 13.2. Based on p_1 (the proportion of defectives corresponding to the AQL) and p_2 (the proportion of defectives corresponding to the LTPD), one determines h_2, h_1, and s.

Once the values of s, h_1, and h_2 are determined, two limit lines are erected.

$$X_1 = sn + h_2$$

$$X_2 = sn + h_1$$

Then a sampling of individual items starts up. The cumulative number of defectives as a function of sample size is graphically presented. If a point falls lower than the two limit lines, the whole lot is accepted. If a point falls between the two lines, the sampling is continued, and if a point falls beyond the two lines, the whole lot is rejected.

EXAMPLE   The Markov Company manufactures swivel-mounted fence seats for politicians and other steady statesmen. The company wants to develop a sequential sampling quality-control procedure for final inspection of completed seats. The producer's risk, as determined by Markov management, is five percent at the point at which p_1 is 0.01. In other words, the company wants a 95 percent probability of accepting any lots of items that are no more than one percent defective. Industry studies show that consumer's risk is 10 percent, and that p_2 is 0.06. That is, the buyer wants only 10 percent chance of accepting any lots that have six percent or more defectives. Using the above data, present a sequential sampling chart. Label the accept and reject regions and the zone of no decision.

---

[3] Described in A. Wald, *Sequential Analysis* (New York: John Wiley and Sons, 1947).

TABLE 13.2 PARAMETER VALUES FOR SEQUENTIAL SAMPLING PLAN FOR VARIOUS COMBINATIONS OF p_1, p_2, $\alpha = 0.05$ AND $\beta = 0.10$

p_1	p_2	h_2	h_1	s
0.005	0.01	4.1398	3.2245	0.007216
	0.02	2.0624	1.6064	0.01084
	0.03	1.5906	1.2389	0.01400
	0.04	1.3664	1.0643	0.01693
	0.05	1.2305	0.9585	0.01970
	0.06	1.1371	0.8857	0.02237
	0.07	1.0679	0.8318	0.02496
0.010	0.03	2.5829	2.0118	0.01824
	0.04	2.0397	1.5887	0.02172
	0.05	1.7510	1.3639	0.02499
	0.06	1.5678	1.2211	0.02811
	0.07	1.4391	1.1209	0.03113
	0.08	1.3426	1.0458	0.03406
0.015	0.03	4.0796	3.1776	0.02166
	0.04	2.8716	2.2367	0.02554
	0.05	2.3307	1.8153	0.02917
	0.06	2.0169	1.5710	0.03263
	0.07	1.8089	1.4089	0.03596
0.020	0.03	6.9527	5.4154	0.02467
	0.04	4.0495	3.1541	0.02889
	0.05	3.0509	2.3763	0.03282
	0.06	2.5348	1.9743	0.03655
	0.07	2.2146	1.7250	0.04012
	0.08	1.9941	1.5532	0.04359
	0.09	1.8315	1.4265	0.04696
	0.10	1.7056	1.3285	0.05025

For the complete table, See Table 2.23 of Statistical Research Group, Columbia University, *Sequential Analysis of Statistical Data: Applications* (New York: Columbia University Press, 1945), pp. 2.39–2.42.

We are given:

$$\alpha = 0.05$$

$$p_1 = 0.01$$

$$\beta = 0.10$$

$$p_2 = 0.06$$

Using Table 13.2 to determine values corresponding to $p_1 = 0.01$ and $p_2 = 0.06$:

$$h_2 = 1.5678$$

$$h_1 = 1.2211$$

$$s = 0.02811$$

Since the control chart is linear, drawing the chart requires the definition of two points for each line; for convenience, the two points chosen are $n = 0$ and $n = 100$.

At n = 0:

$$x_1 = sn + h_2$$
$$= 0 + 1.5678$$
$$= 1.5678$$
$$x_2 = sn - h_1$$
$$= 0 - 1.2211$$
$$= -1.2211$$

At n = 100:

$$x_1 = sn + h_2$$
$$= (0.02811)(100) + 1.5678$$
$$= 2.811 + 1.5678$$
$$= 4.3788$$
$$x_2 = sn - h_2$$
$$= (0.02811)(100) - 1.2211$$
$$= 2.811 - 1.2211$$
$$= 1.5899$$

The control chart is drawn in Figure 13.8.

Now assume that the Markov Company takes a sample of 12 seats and that all of them are found to be acceptable. The company cannot make a decision on whether to accept or reject the lot. Of the following three seats sampled, two of them are found defective. That is, the total sample size now is 15 seats, out of which two are defective. This calls for a rejection of the whole lot. The procedure is marked by intermittent lines in Figure 13.8.

SAMPLING PLANS' MANUALS

Inspection of an item can be by means of *attributes*, where an item is judged as good or bad, "go" or "no-go." Inspection can, alternatively, be by variables, where an actual measurement, such as weight or length, is taken. Two of the most popular acceptance sampling plans are summarized here. They are MIL-

Figure 13.8 A Sequential Sampling Chart

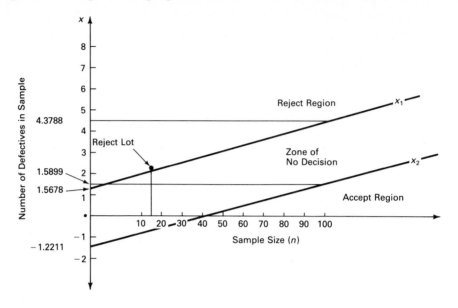

	Accept When Number of
Size of Sample	*Defectives in Sample Is*
0–43	(no decision; continue sampling)
44–80	0
81–114	1
115–150	2

	Reject When Number of
Size of Sample	*Defectives in Sample Is*
2–15	2
16–51	3
52–86	4
87–121	5

STD-105D (attributes)[4] and MIL-STD-414 (variables).[5] Both are widely recognized and accepted for government or commercial work. Both contain a large set of sampling plans usable under a wide range of conditions to accept or reject lots (groups) of items based upon samples taken from each.

---

[4] "Sampling Procedures and Tables for Inspection by Attributes," MIL-STD-105D (Washington, D.C.: U.S. Government Printing Office, 1963).

[5] "Sampling Procedures and Tables for Inspection by Variables for Percent Defective," MIL-STD-414 (Washington, D.C.: U.S. Department of Defense, Military Standard, U.S. Government Printing Office, 1957).

Military Standard 105D (MIL-STD-105D)

The stated purpose of MIL-STD-105D is to put pressure on the producer to turn out material that is as good as some specified (agreed-upon) acceptable quality level (AQL). The AQL is the maximum percent defective that can be considered satisfactory as a process average. MIL-STD-105D is designed to switch from normal to a more rigorous tightened inspection when quality appears to have worsened, and to switch back to normal inspection when quality has again improved.

Instructions and cautions in using MIL-STD-105D are carefully explained in the standard. The basic steps involved are as follows:

1. Decide on the AQL.
2. Decide on the inspection level (usually, level II).
3. Determine the number of items in the lot.
4. Enter the proper table and find the sample-size code letter.
5. Decide on the type of sampling plan to be used (single, double, or multiple sampling).
6. Enter the proper table and find the sampling plan to be used (number of items to sample and maximum allowable number of defectives).
7. Enter a tightened inspection table and find another sampling plan when tightened inspection is required.
8. Perform sampling inspection and make an accept/reject decision.

Tables 13.3, 13.4 and 13.5 are taken from MIL-STD-105D. Table 13.3 is used to determine the sample-size code letter, and Tables 13.4 and 13.5 yield normal and tightened single sample plans, respectively. They can be used to solve the example given below.

EXAMPLE   Shipments of 1000 checkbooks each are received periodically from a printer with whom the High-Rate Central Bank has agreed to use MIL-STD-105D single-sampling inspection, with an acceptable quality level (AQL) of 1 percent. What is the sampling plan to be used?

Using Table 13.3, for a shipment size of 1000 at the general inspection level of II, the sample-size code letter is J. From Table 13.4, for a code letter J, one finds a sample size of 80. For the same code letter and at acceptable quality level (AQL) of 1.0 percent, we find that we should accept (Ac) the shipment when, out of 80 checkbooks, 2 or fewer checkbooks are found to be defective, and reject (Re) the shipment when 3 or more are found to be defective.

According to this sampling plan, if one defective checkbook is found in the sample of 80, one should accept the shipment; if four defectives are found in the sample of 80 checkbooks, one should reject the shipment.

TABLE 13.3 SAMPLE-SIZE CODE LEVELS

LOT OR BATCH SIZE		SPECIAL INSPECTION LEVELS				GENERAL INSPECTION LEVELS		
		S-1	*S-2*	*S-3*	*S-4*	*I*	*II*	*III*
2 to	8	A	A	A	A	A	A	B
9	15	A	A	A	A	A	B	C
16	25	A	A	B	B	B	C	D
26	50	A	B	B	C	C	D	E
51	90	B	B	C	C	C	E	F
91	150	B	B	C	D	D	F	G
151	280	B	C	D	E	E	G	H
281	500	B	C	D	E	F	H	J
301	1200	C	C	E	F	G	J	K
1201	3200	C	D	E	G	H	K	L
3201	10000	C	D	F	G	J	L	M
10001	35000	C	D	F	H	K	M	N
35001	150000	D	E	G	J	L	N	P
150001	500000	D	E	G	J	M	P	Q
500001 and higher		D	E	H	K	N	Q	R

If the quality becomes worse (as judged by the rules given in the standard), a tightened inspection plan should be used. As per Table 13.5, for code letter J and AQL of 1.0 percent, 80 checkbooks should be sampled and the shipment accepted if one or no defectives are found in the sample, and rejected if two or more defectives are found in the sample.

Military Standard 414 (MIL-STD-414)

MIL-STD-414 has the same purpose as does MIL-STD-105D. The lot acceptance or rejection is based on the average and variability (spread) of the measurements, k, taken on a sample from the lot of items in question. The measurements are of a continuous characteristics like: weight, height, etc. The average dimension is calculated easily. However, the variability may be expressed by using either the standard deviation or the range (largest dimension minus smallest dimension). In some cases, variability may be known from past experience and MIL-STD-414 includes plans for these cases as well.

The procedure for using MIL-STD-414 is as follows:

1. Decide on the AQL.
2. Decide on the inspection level (usually, level IV).
3. Determine the number of items in the lot.
4. Enter the proper table and find the sample-size code letter.
5. Decide on the type of sampling plan to be used, based on whether the variability is known or unknown.

TABLE 13.4 NORMAL SINGLE-SAMPLING PLAN

SAMPLE SIZE CODE LETTER	SAMPLE SIZE	ACCEPTABLE QUALITY LEVELS (NORMAL INSPECTION)											
		0.010	0.015	0.025	0.040	0.065	0.10	0.15	0.25	0.40	0.65	1.0	1.5
		Ac Re	Ac Re	Ac Re	Ac Re	Ac Re	Ac Re	Ac Re	Ac Re	Ac Re	Ac Re	Ac Re	Ac Re
A	2	↓	↓	↓	↓	↓	↓	↓	↓	↓	↓	↓	↓
B	3	↓	↓	↓	↓	↓	↓	↓	↓	↓	↓	↓	↓
C	5	↓	↓	↓	↓	↓	↓	↓	↓	↓	↓	↓	↓
D	8	↓	↓	↓	↓	↓	↓	↓	↓	↓	↓	↓	↓
E	13	↓	↓	↓	↓	↓	↓	↓	↓	↓	↓	↓	↓
F	20	↓	↓	↓	↓	↓	↓	↓	↓	↓	↓	↓	0 1
G	32	↓	↓	↓	↓	↓	↓	↓	↓	↓	↓	0 1	1 2
H	50	↓	↓	↓	↓	↓	↓	↓	↓	↓	0 1	1 2	2 3
J	80	↓	↓	↓	↓	↓	↓	↓	↓	0 1	1 2	2 3	3 4
K	125	↓	↓	↓	↓	↓	↓	↓	0 1	1 2	2 3	3 4	5 6
L	200	↓	↓	↓	↓	↓	↓	0 1	1 2	2 3	3 4	5 6	7 8
M	315	↓	↓	↓	↓	↓	0 1	1 2	2 3	3 4	5 6	7 8	10 11
N	500	↓	↓	↓	↓	0 1	1 2	2 3	3 4	5 6	7 8	10 11	14 15
P	800	↓	↓	↓	0 1	1 2	2 3	3 4	5 6	7 8	10 11	14 15	21 22
Q	1250	↓	↓	0 1	1 2	2 3	3 4	5 6	7 8	10 11	14 15	21 22	↑
R	2000	↓	0 1	1 2	2 3	3 4	5 6	7 8	10 11	14 15	21 22	↑	↑

↓ = Use first sampling plan below arrow. ↑ = Use first sampling plan above arrow. Ac = Acceptance number. Re = Rejection number.

TABLE 13.4 (Cont.)

ACCEPTABLE QUALITY LEVELS (NORMAL INSPECTION)

	2.5	4.0	6.5	10	15	25	40	65	100	150	250	400	650	1000
	Ac Re	Ac Re	Ac Re	Ac Re	Ac Re	Ac Re	Ac Re	Ac Re	Ac Re	Ac Re	Ac Re	Ac Re	Ac Re	Ac Re
	0 1	0 1	0 1	↓	↓	1 2	2 3	3 4	5 6	7 8	10 11	14 15	21 22	30 31
	↑	1 2	1 2	1 2	1 2	2 3	3 4	5 6	7 8	10 11	14 15	21 22	30 31	44 45
	2 3	2 3	2 3	2 3	2 3	3 4	5 6	7 8	10 11	14 15	21 22	30 31	44 45	↓
	3 4	3 4	3 4	3 4	3 4	5 6	7 8	10 11	14 15	21 22	30 31	44 45	↑	
	5 6	5 6	5 6	5 6	5 6	7 8	10 11	14 15	21 22	30 31	44 45	↑		
	7 8	7 8	7 8	7 8	7 8	10 11	14 15	21 22	↑	↑	↑			
	10 11	10 11	10 11	10 11	10 11	14 15	21 22	↑						
	14 15	14 15	14 15	14 15	14 15	21 22	↑							
	21 22	21 22	21 22	21 22	21 22	↑								

↓ = Use first sampling plan below arrow. If sample size equals, or exceeds, lot or batch size, do 100 percent inspection.

↑ = Use first sampling plan above arrow.

Ac = Acceptance number.

Re = Rejection number.

TABLE 13.5 TIGHTENED SINGLE-SAMPLING PLAN

Arrows: ↓ = Use first sampling plan below arrow. ↑ = Use first sampling plan above arrow. Each data cell shows *Ac Re* (acceptance number / rejection number).

SAMPLE SIZE CODE LETTER	SAMPLE SIZE	ACCEPTABLE QUALITY LEVELS (TIGHTENED INSPECTION)											
		0.010 Ac Re	**0.015** Ac Re	**0.025** Ac Re	**0.040** Ac Re	**0.065** Ac Re	**0.10** Ac Re	**0.15** Ac Re	**0.25** Ac Re	**0.40** Ac Re	**0.65** Ac Re	**1.0** Ac Re	**1.5** Ac Re
A	2	↓	↓	↓	↓	↓	↓	↓	↓	↓	↓	↓	↓
B	3	↓	↓	↓	↓	↓	↓	↓	↓	↓	↓	↓	↓
C	5	↓	↓	↓	↓	↓	↓	↓	↓	↓	↓	↓	↓
D	8	↓	↓	↓	↓	↓	↓	↓	↓	↓	↓	↓	↓
E	13	↓	↓	↓	↓	↓	↓	↓	↓	↓	↓	↓	↓
F	20	↓	↓	↓	↓	↓	↓	↓	↓	↓	↓	↓	0 1
G	32	↓	↓	↓	↓	↓	↓	↓	↓	↓	↓	0 1	1 2
H	50	↓	↓	↓	↓	↓	↓	↓	↓	↓	0 1	1 2	2 3
J	80	↓	↓	↓	↓	↓	↓	↓	↓	0 1	1 2	2 3	3 4
K	125	↓	↓	↓	↓	↓	↓	↓	0 1	1 2	2 3	3 4	5 6
L	200	↓	↓	↓	↓	↓	↓	0 1	1 2	2 3	3 4	5 6	8 9
M	315	↓	↓	↓	↓	↓	0 1	1 2	2 3	3 4	5 6	8 9	12 13
N	500	↓	↓	↓	↓	0 1	1 2	2 3	3 4	5 6	8 9	12 13	18 19
P	800	↓	↓	↓	0 1	1 2	2 3	3 4	5 6	8 9	12 13	18 19	↑
Q	1250	↓	↓	0 1	1 2	2 3	3 4	5 6	8 9	12 13	18 19	↑	↑
R	2000	↓	0 1	1 2	↑	↑	↑	↑	↑	↑	↑	↑	↑
S	3150	0 1	↑	↑	↑	↑	↑	↑	↑	↑	↑	↑	↑

583

TABLE 13.5 (Cont.)

ACCEPTABLE QUALITY LEVELS (NORMAL INSPECTION)

	2.5	6.0	6.5	10	15	25	60	65	100	150	250	600	650	1000
	Ac Re	Ac Re	Ac Re	Ac Re	Ac Re	Ac Re	Ac Re	Ac Re	Ac Re	Ac Re	Ac Re	Ac Re	Ac Re	Ac Re
	↓	↓	↓	↓	↓	↓	1 2	2 3	3 4	5 6	8 9	12 13	18 19	27 28
	↓	↓	↓	↓	↓	1 2	2 3	3 4	5 6	8 9	12 13	18 19	27 28	61 62
	↓	↓	↓	↓	1 2	2 3	3 4	5 6	8 9	12 13	18 19	27 28	61 62	↑
	↓	↓	0 1	1 2	2 3	3 4	5 6	8 9	12 13	18 19	27 28	41 62	↑	↑
	↓	0 1	1 2	2 3	3 4	5 6	8 9	12 13	18 19	27 28	61 62	↑	↑	↑
	0 1	1 2	2 3	3 4	5 6	8 9	12 13	18 19	↑	↑	↑	↑	↑	↑
	1 2	2 3	3 4	5 6	8 9	12 13	18 19	↑	↑	↑	↑	↑	↑	↑
	2 3	3 4	5 6	8 9	12 13	18 19	↑	↑	↑	↑	↑	↑	↑	↑
	3 4	5 6	8 9	12 13	18 19	↑	↑	↑	↑	↑	↑	↑	↑	↑
	5 6	8 9	12 13	18 19	↑	↑	↑	↑	↑	↑	↑	↑	↑	↑
	8 9	12 13	18 19	↑	↑	↑	↑	↑	↑	↑	↑	↑	↑	↑
	12 13	18 19	↑	↑	↑	↑	↑	↑	↑	↑	↑	↑	↑	↑
	18 19	↑	↑	↑	↑	↑	↑	↑	↑	↑	↑	↑	↑	↑

↓ = Use first sampling plan below arrow. If sample size equals, or exceeds, lot or batch size, do 100 percent inspection.
↑ = Use first sampling plan above arrow.
Ac = Acceptance number.
Re = Rejection number.

6. Enter the proper table and find the sampling plan to be used (the number of items to sample, n, and one other value, k, to be used in the calculation of upper and lower control limit for x.
7. Perform sampling inspection and make accept/reject decisions.

Tables 13.6 and 13.7 are taken from MIL-STD-414. Table 13.6 is used to determine the sample-size code letter, while Table 13.7 determines the sampling plans.

EXAMPLE   Lots of 250 rods each are received periodically from a supplier with whom we have agreed to use MIL-STD-414 sampling inspections, using the range method, at an AQL of 1 percent. Any rod having a tensile strength that is less than the lower specification limit, $L = 20,000$ psi, is considered defective. Determine the sampling plan to be used (that is, sample size n and k).

For lots of 250 and an inspection level of IV, the sample-size code letter is H (see Table 13.6). For the sample-size code letter H and AQL of 1.00 percent, the sample size is $n = 25$ and $k = 0.779$.

The following data have been recorded for a sample taken from a lot:

SubSample	Measurements					Range (R)
1	22030	21800	20980	20750	21480	1280
2	21170	20390	21300	20760	21440	1050
3	20570	21110	20270	18970	22110	3140
4	21780	21800	21580	20990	21740	810
5	22740	21220	21300	21920	21050	1690

Σx = Total measurement = 531,250 Σ R = Total range = 7,970.

We would like to determine an acceptance or rejection decision regarding the lot from which the sample was taken. From the sample:

$$\overline{x} = \frac{\Sigma x}{n} = \frac{531,250}{25} = 21,250 \text{ psi}$$

$$\overline{R} = \frac{\Sigma R}{\text{\# of subsamples of 5}} = \frac{7970}{5} = 1594 \text{ psi}$$

The lower limit is:

$$L + k\overline{R} = 20,000 + (0.779)(1594) = 21,241.73$$

Since $\overline{x} = 21,250$ psi is greater than 21,241.24 psi (the lower limit), one has to accept the lot. If there is an upper limit, then the lot is accepted only if the average, x, is less than or equal to $(L + k\overline{R})$.

TABLE 13.6 CODE TO DETERMINE SAMPLE-SIZE CODE LETTER

LOT SIZE		INSPECTION LEVELS*				
		I	*II*	*III*	*IV*	*V*
3 to	8	B	B	B	B	C
9	15	B	B	B	B	D
16	25	B	B	B	C	E
26	40	B	B	B	D	F
41	65	B	B	C	E	G
66	110	B	B	D	F	H
111	180	B	C	E	G	I
181	300	B	D	F	H	J
301	500	C	E	G	I	K
501	800	D	F	H	J	L
801	1300	E	G	I	K	L
1301	3200	F	H	J	L	M
3201	8000	G	I	L	M	N
8001	22,000	H	J	M	N	O
22,001	110,000	I	K	N	O	P
110,001	550,000	I	K	O	P	Q
550,001 and higher		I	K	P	Q	Q

*Sample-size code letters given in the body of the table are applicable when the indicated inspection levels are to be used.

CONTROL CHARTS FOR PROCESS CONTROL

A control chart is a simple graphical tool used to help bring a process under control and then to help keep it under control. A control chart can pinpoint problems in machines, materials, and processes. It can tell the user when to make adjustments and, equally important, when not to do so.

What do we mean by the words "under control?" The phrase relates to the variability of a process. Just as there is variation among peoples' heights and weights, there is variation among the units of the products that one produces or the quality of services that are provided.

An *average* tells us where a process is centered, and a *range* (largest dimension minus smallest) gives us some measure of variability or spread. Another measure of spread is the *standard deviation*. The process center and spread of dimensions are very predictable if the process is working correctly. These inherent variations are said to be due to *chance (minor) causes*. Introduce a noisy environment, different inputs, untrained workers, or poor measurement equipment, and the pattern of variability will change. This change is said to be due to *assignable causes*. The control chart helps us to keep a process under control by graphically identifying when assignable causes of variability are present. We maintain control by eliminating the assignable causes.

TABLE 13.7 DETERMINATION OF A SAMPLING PLAN

SAMPLE SIZE CODE LETTER	SAMPLE SIZE	ACCEPTABLE QUALITY LEVELS (NORMAL INSPECTION)*													
		0.04	0.065	0.10	0.15	0.25	0.40	0.65	1.00	1.50	2.50	4.00	6.50	10.00	15.00
		k	k	k	k	k	k	k	k	k	k	k	k	k	k
B	3	↓	↓	↓	↓	↓	↓	↓	↓	↓	0.587	0.502	0.401	0.296	0.178
C	4	↓	↓	↓	↓	↓	↓	↓	0.651	0.598	0.525	0.450	0.364	0.276	0.176
D	5	↓	↓	↓	↓	↓	↓	0.663	0.614	0.565	0.498	0.431	0.352	0.272	0.184
E	7	↓	↓	↓	↓	0.702	0.659	0.613	0.569	0.525	0.465	0.405	0.336	0.266	0.189
F	10	↓	↓	↓	0.916	0.863	0.811	0.755	0.703	0.650	0.579	0.507	0.424	0.341	0.252
G	15	1.09	1.04	0.999	0.958	0.903	0.850	0.792	0.738	0.684	0.610	0.536	0.452	0.368	0.276
H	25	1.14	1.10	1.05	1.01	0.951	0.896	0.835	0.779	0.723	0.647	0.571	0.484	0.398	0.305
I	30	1.15	1.10	1.06	1.02	0.959	0.904	0.843	0.787	0.730	0.577	0.577	0.490	0.403	0.310
J	35	1.16	1.11	1.07	1.02	0.964	0.908	0.848	0.791	0.734	0.658	0.581	0.494	0.406	0.313
K	40	1.18	1.13	1.08	1.04	0.978	0.921	0.860	0.803	0.746	0.668	0.591	0.503	0.415	0.321
L	515	1.19	1.14	1.09	1.05	0.988	0.931	0.893	0.812	0.754	0.676	0.598	0.510	0.421	0.327
M	60	1.21	1.16	1.11	1.06	1.00	0.948	0.885	0.826	0.768	0.689	0.610	0.521	0.432	0.336
N	85	1.23	1.17	1.13	1.08	1.02	0.962	0.899	0.839	0.780	0.701	0.621	0.530	0.441	0.345
O	115	1.24	1.19	1.14	1.09	1.03	0.975	0.911	0.851	0.791	0.711	0.631	0.538	0.449	0.351
P	175	1.26	1.21	1.16	1.11	1.05	0.994	0.929	0.868	0.807	0.726	0.644	0.552	0.460	0.363
Q	230	1.27	1.21	1.16	1.12	1.06	0.996	0.931	0.870	0.809	0.728	0.645	0.553	0.462	0.364
		0.065	0.10	0.15	0.25	0.40	0.65	1.00	1.50	2.50	4.00	6.50	10.00	15.00	

Acceptable Quality Levels (Tightened Inspection)

*All AQL values are in percent defective. Use first sampling plan below arrow—that is, sample size as well as k value. When sample size equals or exceeds lot size, every item in the lot must be inspected.

587

Control charts are of two types—those that can be used for *attributes* data (good or bad, go or no-go), and those that can be used for *variables* data (having actual dimension, such as a height or weight). A *p chart* is used to control the fraction of defective products when attributes data are used. The most often used control charts for variables data are: $\bar{x}$ (*x-bar*) and *R charts* (used together), and *dynamic control charts*.

The same basic idea underlies each of these charts. That idea is that one can predict upper and lower limits (called control limits) within which sample numbers will fall if only chance causes are present. If assignable causes are hurting the production process, sample numbers will fall outside the control limits, and the user will know it is time to take action.

p-Chart

This chart is concerned with maintaining the fraction defective (p) within an expected range. As assignable causes are found and eliminated, the central value of p will be reduced. An example of the use of a p chart to control the fraction defective is illustrated in Figure 13.9.

The following steps are used:

1. Take m samples, each of size n. The value of m should be at least 25, and n is often taken to be 50, 100, 200, or higher. The value n is typically large, and thus the time between each of the m samples likely spans an entire shift or day.
2. For each sample, record the number of defectives d, and keep the data separate and in time order for each sample.
3. Calculate the fraction defective for each sample, using

$$p = \frac{d}{n}$$

Then calculate the average value of p ($\bar{p}$) over all m samples, using

$$\bar{p} = \frac{p_1 + p_2 + \cdots + p_m}{m} \quad \text{or} \quad \bar{p} = \frac{d_1 + d_2 + d_3 + d_m}{(m)(n)}$$

Also, calculate the upper and lower control limits, UCLp and LCLp:

$$\text{UCL}p = \bar{p} + 3\sqrt{\frac{\bar{p}(1 - \bar{p})}{n}}$$

where the standard deviation of the fraction of defectives,

$$Sp = \sqrt{\frac{\overline{p}(1 - \overline{p})}{n}}$$

$$LCLp = \overline{p} + 3 \sqrt{\frac{\overline{p}(1 - \overline{p})}{n}}$$

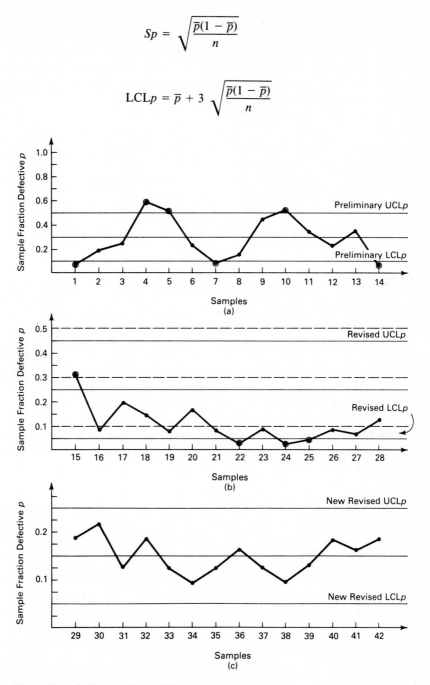

Figure 13.9   *P* Chart to Control Fraction Defective

These limits take into account the natural variation in fraction defective from sample to sample that should be present. Note that instead of 3 standard deviations ($3Sp$), one can choose 1, 2, or any other values to set the UCLp and LCLp.

4. Plot the p control chart, using a central value of p and upper and lower limits of ULCp and LCLp. On the chart, plot the p value for each sample as determined in step 3. If all p values are within limits, assume the fraction defective to be in control, statistically speaking (it may still not be as low as one would like). The p chart is now set up and ready to be continued, as in Figure 13.9(c). If one or more points are outside the limits, as in Figure 13.10(a), go to step 5.

5. Review each of the out-of-control points, attempting to identify what caused the extreme value observed. If a continuing problem is found, it should be corrected. After investigating all out-of-control points, their values should be thrown out of the data. Return to step 3.

$\bar{x}$ and R Charts

These charts are concerned with cases in which the actual measurement of a product's characteristic is possible.

These charts are used together, the $\bar{x}$-chart presents the measurement's average for the process and the R chart presents the difference between the largest and smallest measurement. We always establish control on the R chart first, because use of the $\bar{x}$ chart depends upon an accurate knowledge of the spread or inherent variation (R) attainable.

The following steps are applied to produce the R-Chart:

1. Take m samples, each of size n. The value of m should be at least 25, and n is often taken to be 4 or 5. The sample should consist of n items produced close together. The time between each of the m samples may be, for example, an hour, a half day, or a shift.

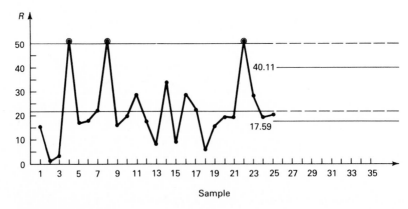

Figure 13.10 R Chart

2. For each sample, record the measurement of each item x, and keep the data separate and in time order for each sample.

3. Calculate the value of the range for each sample using

$$R = x_{largest} - x_{smallest}$$

Then calculate R, the average value of R over all m samples, using

$$\overline{R} = \frac{R_1 + R_2 + R_3 + \cdots + R_m}{m}$$

Also, calculate the upper and lower control limits, UCL_R and LCL_L, using the factors from Table 13.8:

$$UCL_R = D_4\overline{R}$$

$$LCL_R = D_3\overline{R}$$

The factors D_4 and D_3 take into account the natural spread that should be present. The specific reasoning for D_3 and D_4 are beyond the scope of this book. However, the D_3 and D_4 produce three-sigma control limits for the R-charts.

4. Plot the R control chart, using a central value of R and upper and lower limits of UCL_R and LCL_R. On the chart, plot the R value for each sample as determined in step 3. If all R values are within limits, assume the process variability is in control. The R chart is now set up and ready to be continued. Go on to the $\overline{x}$ chart. If one or more points are outside the limits, go to step 5.

5. Review each of the out-of-control points, and attempt to identify what caused the extreme value observed. If a continuing problem is found, it should be corrected. After investigating out-of-control points, their values should be thrown out of the data. Return to step. 3.

TABLE 13.8 FACTORS FOR DETERMINING 3-SIGMA CONTROL LIMITS FOR R CHARTS

n	D_3	D_4
2	0	3.27
3	0	2.57
4	0	2.28
5	0	2.11
6	0	2.00
7	0.08	1.92
8	0.14	1.86
9	0.18	1.82
10	0.22	1.78
11	0.26	1.74
12	0.28	1.72
13	0.31	1.69
14	0.33	1.67
15	0.35	1.65

The following steps are applied to produce the $\bar{x}$-Chart

1. As in Step 1. for R-Chart above.
2. As in Step 2. for R-Chart above.
3. Calculate the average of the values within each sample using

$$x = \frac{x_1 + x_2 + \cdots + x_n}{n}$$

Then calculate x, the average of the averages just calculated.

$$\bar{\bar{x}} = \frac{\bar{x}_1 + \bar{x}_2 + \cdots + \bar{x}m}{m}$$

Also, calculate the upper and lower control limits, $\text{UCL}_{\bar{x}}$ and $\text{LCL}_{\bar{x}}$, using the factor from Table 13.9:

$$\text{UCL}_{\bar{x}} = \bar{\bar{x}} + A_2\bar{R}$$

$$\text{LCL}_{\bar{x}} = \bar{\bar{x}} - A_2\bar{R}$$

The factor A_2 takes into account the natural spread that should be present.

4. Plot the $\bar{x}$ control chart using a central value of $\bar{\bar{x}}$ and upper and lower limits of $\text{UCL}_{\bar{x}}$ and $\text{LCL}_{\bar{x}}$. On the chart, plot the $\bar{x}$ value for each sample as determined in step 3. If all $\bar{x}$ values are within limits, assume the process centering is in control. The $\bar{x}$ chart is now set up and can be continued. If one or more points are outside the limits, go to step 5.
5. Same as step 5 for R chart.

Two additional points should be noted regarding control charts. First, points falling below the lower limits of the p and R charts indicate that something *good* has been happening. We try to find out what it was, and then make it continue happening. Typically, as control charts are used and the

TABLE 13.9 FACTORS FOR DETERMINING 3-SIGMA CONTROLS LIMITS FOR $\bar{X}$ CHART

n	A_2
2	1.88
3	1.02
4	0.73
5	0.58
6	0.48
7	0.42
8	0.37
9	0.34
10	0.31

process is improved over time, the limits will squeeze inward. In the case of the p and R charts, their central values will also decrease.

Second, the rules for the use of control charts are fairly loose, especially those regarding when to eliminate data (step 5 for p, R, and $\bar{x}$ charts). A good rule of thumb is to eliminate data points when it is clear that their values have been affected by an identified and corrected assignable cause.

EXAMPLE A car engine manufacturer had a history of trouble that appeared to be due to a critical cylinder diameter. The company decided to study that diameter using $\bar{x}$ and R charts. To establish the charts, 25 samples of data were collected, with each sample consisting of measurements on 4 engines machined one after the other. One sample was taken per shift. The data were as shown in Table 13.10.

Concentrating first on the R chart,

$$\bar{R} = \frac{R_1 + R_2 + \cdots + R_{25}}{25} = \frac{536}{25} = 21.44$$

$$\text{UCL}_R = D_4\bar{R} = 2.28(21.44) = 48.88$$

$$\text{LCL}_R = D_3\bar{R} = 0(21.44) = 0$$

Plotting the R chart (the observed range values for each sample) as in Figure 13.10, samples 4, 8, and 22 were found to be outside control limits. A thorough check revealed that a substitute operator had been used for that operation on shifts corresponding to samples 4, 8, and 22. All else appeared to be in order.

The out-of-control points were eliminated, and the central value (R) and control limits were recalculated as follows:

$$\bar{R}_{\text{revised}} = \frac{R_1 + R_2 + \cdots + R_{25} \quad (\text{less } R_4, R_8, R_{22})}{22}$$

$$= \frac{536 - 50 - 49}{22} = 17.59$$

$$\text{UCL}_R = D_4R = 2.28(17.59) = 40.11$$

$$\text{LCL}_R = D_3R = 0(17.59) = 0$$

Plotting the new limits on the original R chart showed that no additional points were outside control limits. The revised control chart was considered satisfactory for continued use, and the range was felt to be within control at the level $\bar{R}$ = 17.59.

Attention was now shifted to the $\bar{x}$ chart. It was felt that the data from samples 4, 8, and 22 could not be trusted, and they were eliminated. The central value and control limits were calculated:

TABLE 13.10   DIAMETER MEASUREMENTS

SAMPLE	SURFACE DIAMETER MEASUREMENTS IN SAMPLE				AVERAGE $\overline{X}$	RANGE R
1	47	32	44	35	39.50	15
2	33	33	34	34	33.50	1
3	34	34	31	34	33.25	3
4	3	21	24	53	25.25	50
5	35	23	28	40	34.00	17
6	19	37	31	27	28.50	18
7	23	45	26	37	32.75	22
8	33	2	29	52	29.00	50
9	25	22	37	33	29.25	15
10	29	32	30	13	26.00	19
11	40	18	30	11	24.75	29
12	21	128	36	34	27.25	28
13	26	35	31	29	30.25	9
14	52	29	21	18	30.00	34
15	26	20	30	20	24.00	10
16	19	1	30	30	20.00	29
17	28	34	39	17	29.50	22
18	29	25	24	30	27.00	6
19	21	37	32	25	28.75	16
20	24	22	16	35	24.25	19
21	28	39	23	21	27.75	18
22	41	32	50	1	31.00	49
23	14	23	41	42	30.00	28
24	32	28	46	27	33.25	19
25	42	34	22	34	33.00	20
					731.75	536

$$\overline{\overline{x}} = \frac{\overline{x}_1 + \overline{x}_2 + \cdots + \overline{x}_{25} \quad (\text{less } \overline{x}_4, \overline{x}_8, \overline{x}_{22})}{22}$$

$$= \frac{731.75 - 25.25 - 29.00 - 31.00}{22}$$

$$= \frac{646.50}{22} = 29.39$$

$$\text{UCL}_x = \overline{\overline{x}} + A_2\overline{R} = 29.39 + 0.73 \, (17.59) = 42.23$$

$$\text{LCL}_x = \overline{\overline{x}} - A_2\overline{R} = 29.39 - 0.73 \, (17.59) = 16.55$$

Plotting the $\overline{x}$ chart as in Figure 13.11, it is clear that no points are out of control, and that these limits may continue to be used for future plotting.

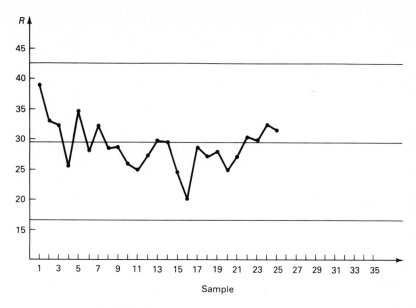

Figure 13.11   Sample $\overline{X}$ Chart

Dynamic Control Chart

These charts are useful when there is a long production run that requires periodic resetting of tools. Frequently, when equipment has been set up and production begun, tool wear and workers' fatigue cause product dimensions to change. A dynamic control chart is constructed to determine the initial setup position that assures the performance of the process as required.

EXAMPLE   If a produced rod has a design diameter limit of 1.000 ± 0.010 inch, and the actual variation of the lathe follows a normal distribution with standard deviation $= \sigma = 0.001$ inch. If one uses 3 standard deviations for the control limits (99.73 percent of rods produced will fall within design limits), the problem is to develop a dynamic control chart that will indicate when to reset the machine.

The lower design limit allows a diameter as small as $(1.000 - 0.010 =) 0.990$ inch. Thus, 3 standard deviations $(= 3\sigma = 0.003$ inch) are added to 0.990, yielding an initial setup of 0.993 inch. The first few rods produced should then vary from 0.990 to 0.996 inch. Subsequent rods produced will be expected to fall within a band of $6\sigma = 0.006$, provided they would not exceed the upper design limit of 1.010 inch. Once they reach this limit, the lathe should be adjusted.

c Chart

There are other control charts that are useful. One such control chart is the c chart. Let us describe it in brief.

The c chart is a control chart for number of defects, and is based upon attributes data. It is used when the number of possible defects in a specific product is relatively large. The measure c_i denotes the number of defects found in a single product.

The distribution underlying the c chart is the Poisson distribution, with mean and variance that are, respectively: $\mu = \lambda$ and $\sigma^2 = \lambda$. Thus, the control chart is established from m subgroups (samples) by using the following equations:

$$\text{Center Line} = \bar{c} = = \frac{\sum_{L=1}^{m} c_i}{m}$$

$$\text{Upper Control Limit} = \text{UCL}_c = \bar{c} + 3\sqrt{\lambda} = \bar{c} + 3\sqrt{\bar{c}}$$

$$\text{Lower Control Limit} = \text{LCL}_c = \bar{c} - 3\sqrt{\lambda} = \bar{c} - 3\sqrt{\bar{c}}$$

DEMONSTRATION   Count the number of raisins in each slice of a presliced loaf of raisin bread. Each count is the c_i for slice i. Calculate UCL_c and LCL_c. Are the mixing practices of the baker under control?

HUMAN FACTORS IN QUALITY CONTROL

Inspection is a very complex procedure. As a matter of fact, absolutely accurate inspection results are impossible to obtain. Many studies have proven that inspector error rates of 10–50 percent are not uncommon.[6]

The schemes discussed under acceptance sampling and process control ignore the fact that an inspector can make a mistake. If the inspection results are not reliable, one loses the entire basis for quantitative measurement of the quality level. Every effort should be made to assure effective inspection. The inspection accuracy is affected by the complexity of the product or service, the defect rate, the number of repeated inspections, and the speed of inspection.

---

[6] See, for example, D. H. Harris and F. B. Chaney, *Human Factors in Quality Assurance* (New York: John Wiley and Sons, Inc., 1969).

The inspection work should be *organized* in a manner that:

1. Minimizes the number of quality characteristics considered (five to six types of defects are approximately the maximum that the human mind can consistently handle well)
2. Minimizes disturbing influences
3. Minimizes time pressure, possibly through sampling rather than 100 percent inspection
4. Requires inspectors to work to only one set of standards, rather than, for example, one set for government work and another for commercial work.

The inspection instructions should be accurate, and the inspection *workplace* should conform to good design practices.[7] In particular, should be uncluttered layout and lighting excellent.

QUALITY CONTROL IN THE SERVICE INDUSTRIES

Service work exists because a service organization can outperform the clients in meeting certain of the client's own needs. For some of these needs—for example, telephone communication—only large, centralized organizations are able to assemble the technology and investment required. Without these organizations, the needs would not be met at all. Other service organizations (such as mass transportation) exist because they offer alternatives that are superior in cost, time, convenience, etc. Still other service organizations exist to meet a wide variety of human psychological and physiological needs: amusement, freedom from disagreeable chores, and opportunity for learning and creativity. There is a long list of service industries: transportation, hospitality, distribution, finance, real estate, news media, personal services (amusements, laundry and cleaning, barber and beauty shops, etc.), professional services (lawyers, doctors), and government.

Some service industries are highly automated, such as the utility industry or the new automated post office plants in Washington, Toronto, and Montreal. However, many are labor intensive. For such industries, wages may represent about 70 percent of total costs, as compared with 30 percent for manufacturing industries. A major consequence is a trend toward increased use of new technology to improve both productivity and quality.[8]

[7] See, for example, R. W. Astley and J. G. Fox, "The Analysis of an Inspection Task in the Rubber Industry," in C. G. Drury and J. G. Fox, *Human Reliability in Quality Control* (New York: Halsted Press, 1975).

[8] See, for example, T. Levitt, "Production Line Approach to Service", *Harvard Business Review*, Sept.–Oct., 1972, pp. 41–52.

Service Quality Design

In establishing the quality of design, the service industries are bound by the same broad considerations as are the manufacturing companies: by the definition of what constitutes fitness for use, choice of a design concept that is responsive to the needs of the user, and translation of these concepts into specifications.

Beyond these basic needs, the service industries must give special emphasis to aspects of design that are inherent in dealing with a clientele of many consumers: "made to order" designs, technical assistance, and simplicity and "fringe" services. An example of a "fringe" service is the cleaning of a client's windshield and checking of his oil, batteries, and tires by a gas station attendant while the gasoline tank is being filled. Hotel chains offer fringe services, such as free long-distance calls to provide reservations for a future night's lodging.

Time and Quality

We have mentioned in earlier chapters the importance of the three criteria of quality, cost, and timeliness in judging an operating system. The important feature of service industries is that the time required to provide service is regarded as an *element* of quality, and not as a separate parameter upon which the service operating system is judged.

Some service industries distinguish sharply between different subdivisions of time:

> *Access Time*   This is the length of time that elapses from the time of the client's first effort to gain the service company's attention until that attention is provided.
>
> *Queueing Time*   The consumer is concerned with the length of a queue and therefore the waiting time, and with the integrity of the queue—that is, the adherence to the principle of "first come, first served." (See Technical Note to Chapter 14.)
>
> *Action Time*   This is commonly defined as the interval between taking the customer's order and providing the service requested.

Due to the critical nature of service time, service industries should establish standards for the various components of service time, and improve their present services by studying enough cases of service to find out exactly where the time is being consumed.[9]

---

[9] L. P. Cornwall, "Quality Control in International Air Freight," "Quality Control in Rail Transportation", August, 1964. Available from Railroad Systems and Management Assoc., Chicago, Ill. This collection of papers deals with the quality aspects of several service industries.

Consumer Well-Being and Quality

Over and above what has been mentioned in earlier paragraphs, a further problem of service quality is that of *consumer well-being*. Consumer well-being is affected by atmosphere, feeling of importance, information, and safety. For example, a serviceman may have repaired a house or an appliance; he may have done so promptly and with competence and his charges may have been fair. However, what the housewife might remember is that he tracked mud into her kitchen and smoked a vile-smelling cigar.

Continuity of Service and Quality

Many designs include provisions for maintaining *continuity of service* despite failures. Telephone companies and airlines, for example, make use of alternative routings in the event of unavailability of standard routes. Professional service groups (such as medical and legal groups) organize their work in a way that permits continuity in the absence of any member.

Internal and External Conformance to Quality Standards

In the service industries, it is necessary to distinguish clearly between two very different problems in control of quality:

1. The conformance of the internal process to the process standards (internal conformance).
2. The conformance to the service design as seen by the client (external conformance).

Internal conformance relates to those aspects of the service company's operations that cannot be observed by the clientele. For example, a power company establishes standards for quality of fuel bought, for energy yield per ton of fuel, and for maintenance of equipment. Many utility companies are heavily involved in processing invoices, cheques, and related paperwork carrying direct financial information to the consumer. Control of quality in these two examples follows closely the methods described for manufacturing quality control.

External conformance is conformance to those features of service quality that can be observed by the consumer. Examples of such features are wholesome restaurant food, clean hotel beds, and correct telephone connections.

Organization for Quality

Service industry organization for quality differs considerably from that used by manufacturing industries. In general, the service industry organization exhibits the following features:

1. The day-to-day regulation of and conformance to quality standards are largely in the hands of the line departments, and take place without the presence of independent inspection and test personnel who have powers to hold up the delivery of nonconforming "product."
2. The concept of a separate staff of specialists in quality control has only minor acceptance.
3. The concept of a high-level executive devoting full time to the quality function is relatively unknown.
4. Organized coordination of the quality function seldom exists in continuing form.

Thus, the organization for quality in service industries is somewhat behind that in manufacturing industries.

EXAMPLE   One of the quality characteristics of a hospital involves the medication of sick people. The medication procedure is quite complex, partly because of sheer numbers and partly because of the nature of the medication procedure itself. The traditional procedure has involved the following basic steps:

1. The physician writes out an order for a medication program (along with other orders) for the patient.
2. The nurse transcribes this order onto a form, a copy of which goes to the pharmacist.
3. The pharmacist dispenses the drugs, which are then delivered to the nurse.
4. The nurse administers the medication to the patient.

In a large hospital, the resulting procedural network becomes formidable. The "pharmacist" becomes a central pharmacy with various branches.

Hospitals define a medication error as "a deviation from the physician's order." In quality-control context, such an error is a nonconformance—that is, a failure to conform to specification. The patient's viewpoint broadens the concept of error to include "quality of design"—that is, the validity of the physician's order. This, in turn, depends on such factors as the adequacy of the diagnostic equipment and the completeness of the research program behind the development of the prescribed drugs.

In the following case,[10] the "medication errors" have been limited to studies of nonconformance—that is, they have followed the hospital's definition. Of 9789 "opportunities for error," a total of 1461 actual errors were detected. This is one error for every 6.7 opportunities, or about one error per patient-day. Table 13.11 shows the error pattern in detail.

[10] K. N. Barker, W. W. Kimbrough, and W. M. Heller, "A Study of Medication Errors in Hospital" (University of Arkansas, 1966).

TABLE 13.11 MEDICATION ERRORS IN A HOSPITAL

ERROR TYPE	NUMBER OF ERRORS	PERCENT OF OPPORTUNITY FOR ERROR	PERCENT OF ALL ERRORS
Dose administered at wrong time	808	8.3	55
Wrong amount administered	253	2.6	17
Dose omitted	188	1.9	13
Extra dose	113	1.2	8
Unordered dose	88	0.9	6
Wrong dosage form	11	0.1	1
Totals	1461	15.0	100

All the comprehensive studies of medication error have made it clear that the root causes of most errors go beyond the simplistic concept of blaming one or another given department. In consequence, there should be a continuous interdepartmental effort to eliminate all opportunities for errors.[11]

COMPUTERS IN QUALITY CONTROL

Quality Control Needs Served by Computer Systems

Computer systems are particularly appropriate in seven key areas of quality control: data accumulation; data reduction, analysis, and reporting; real-time process control; automatic testing and inspection; statistical analysis; information retrieval; and quality management-related techniques. Table 13.12 gives examples pertinent to each of these areas and principal benefits to be expected.

Via computer simulation, it is possible to obtain measures of process dynamics necessary for realtime process control.[12,13,14]

[11] See Dean Conley, "A Management Team Approach to Hospital Systems Analysis," *Hospital Administration*, Vol. 15, No. 1, Winter, 1969–1970, pp. 1–21.

[12] J. R. White, Computer Simulation in Quality Control, *Transactions of the 23rd Annual Technical Conference, ASQC*, Los Angeles, 1969, pp. 139–147. This paper tells how to select a strategy to minimize the percent of batches exceeding specifications and to maximize the production capacity of a batch chemical system. Eleven figures illustrate problem formulation, simulation model building, the computer program, and how to evaluate the experiment.

[13] R. D. Brennan, "Continuous System Simulation for Quality Control Studies," *Transactions of the 24th Annual Technical Conference, ASQC*, Pittsburgh, 1970, pp. 441–448. This paper uses a fabrication facility model to show the effect on scrap losses of sampling control during fabrication.

[14] J. H. Reynolds, "SIMCEL-3: A Quality Control Game," *Transactions of the 23rd Annual Technical Conference Transactions, ASQC*, Los Angeles, 1969, pp. 691–696.

TABLE 13.12 QUALITY-CONTROL COMPUTER APPLICATIONS AND BENEFITS

AREA OF USE	EXAMPLES	PRINCIPAL BENEFITS FROM COMPUTER USE	EXAMPLES OF DIFFERENT INDUSTRIES
1. Data Accumulation	Transmission of data as generated from raw-material receiving areas, production process inspection stations, testing labs, and outgoing quality audit	Faster transmission, fewer errors, reduced delay time from inspection or test to communication of results, lower collection costs	Textiles Automotive—about data input via scanner, teletypes, and data banks Assembly—under data collection and feedback, the use of touch-tone telephones
2. Data Reduction	Screening of data for obvious errors, conversion to common units (errors/1000 units, defects/ton, etc.); scaling or transformation to achieve normality (use of arcsine, lgs, square root, reciprocal, other); time-phasing data collected from different steps in the same process; arithmetic adjustment prior to analysis, (see 5 below); standardized reporting to several different shop and management levels from the same data over different time periods	Consistent, uniform application of selected rules and procedures derived from previous process analysis: Low cost use of advanced techniques not manually possible in time allowed or with limited personnel Automatic reduction and analysis triggered by data as accumulated Exception reporting to pre-planned list according to situation severity	Textiles Electronic Components—computer-aided design Graphic Arts—photo composition computer-assisted Automotive—computer graphics for designing, rough drawings, and preparing NC computer tapes Health services—reports on medication administration
3. Real-Time Process	Control of stock flow rate, head-box air pressure, etc., to paper machine, continuously sensing basis weight and moisture, comparing to standards, calling for automatic valve adjustment of variables according to control equations when action limits exceeded	More uniform process control and product quality with continuous process inspection—combines 1 and 2 above with knowledge of process dynamics to make correct size process changes for upset or shift sensed safer operation with hazardous processes Can build in fail-safe mechanism, greater frequency of inspection and automatic gauge calibration	Chemicals Pulp and Paper Metals Industry Air travel reservations (control of seats sold, rerouting, and blocking of crews) Drugs Product surveillance
4. Automatic Testing and Inspection	Sample taken automatically from process line (line first purged, sample weighed, passed through sensing heads of colorimeters,	Few personnel needed for menial or, alternatively, for highly complex but repetitive tasks; minimizes sampling handling; correc-	Drugs Electronic components

	Description	Benefits	Examples
	hazemeters, particulate counters, spectrophotometers, etc.); comparison of test results may call for additional testing; in electronica, circuit check at different voltages, after temperature cycles; use of diagnostics to advise repair service whether action is to be taken (identified by terminal strip junction, part, etc.)	tive steps can be automatically looked up in a table stored in the computer; frequency of failure logged by defect, related to various measurements, etc.	
5. Statistical Analysis	Use of any and all methods (as needed) described in this book; once data are in retrievable form, analysis can be made via control charts, frequency distribution, correlation with other data, comparison with standards or previous averages, ranges, standard deviations, ratios, etc.; tabulations by defect type, production area, process type, etc, can be checked for unusual occurrence with statistical significance tests	Complete flexibility in processing data through a wide variety of analytical techniques, at low cost, using methods prechosen for specific situations or in specific sequences; can use best numerical methods (recommended by mathematicians, programmed for computers by software specialists, and purchasable)	Chemicals
6. Information Retrieval	Look up specifications, complaint records, production problems by product line for quality planning; search out previous cost experience historically; examine process change record to avoid repetition of previous failures; compile standardized inspection instruction	Assurance that specifications file contains latest changes (i.e., easy maintenance of specifications); Uncover allied (product or customer) complaint histories economically; Programs available for defining files and data bases and for specifying keywords for search	Documentation; Chemicals—data banks; Job shop—memory systems and "job setup cards"; New product quality
7. Quality Management–Related Techniques	Planning for inspection, manpower, new production facilities, process control via discrete and continuous process simulation; project planning via PERT or CPM	Time saving—simulation allows studies of various options prior to installation of inspection schemes, test stations, publication of test frequencies; With CSMP, finding optimum parameter values minimizes process delays and sluggish feedback; Find and eliminate bottlenecks	Chemicals; Accounting firms (auditing)

Computer Programs for Current Control

As has been indicated earlier, the procedures involved in the solution of quality-control problems follow the general trend of modern management techniques. The operations manager consults a terminal that is connected to a central computer, usually a CRT (cathode-ray tube) terminal type. The quality-control program is a "conversational" one, equipped to deal with problems on a "real-time" basis, and is easy to activate.

In Figure 13.12, a printout of such a program is reproduced. The computer directs the manager on how to enter the data, and determines, in this case, the parameters of process-control procedures in less than one minute. It also notifies the manager which samples are out of control.

COMMON PROBLEMS IN APPLYING QUALITY-CONTROL SYSTEMS AND PROCEDURES

In this chapter, we have described the techniques of quality control and have indicated the crucial nature that quality control has in this era of consumerism and increased liability awareness. It is interesting, then, to audit the "popularity" of quality-control procedures in the industry.[15,16,17]

In a study the author conducted, auditing quality control systems of 1000 companies with net worth of between $500,000 and $10 million, the findings (see Table 13.3) indicated that, generally, the quality-control function leaves much to be desired.

Specifically, the study indicated that:

1. Food, chemical, and electrical industries lead in quality-control practices. This is due to government standards in these industries.
2. The majority of companies did not use statistical quality-control procedures. The predominant quality-control method is 100 percent inspection. This is especially interesting in view of the wide discussion of statistical techniques in the literature. (Consult Tables 13.14 and 13.15 for more information.)
3. The problems associated with the application of quality-control techniques are:

[15] E. Menipaz, "Maintaining Proper Quality Standards in an Era of High Economic Uncertainty", *Fourth International Conference on Production Research Proceedings*, Tokyo, Japan, August 1977, pp. 1179–85.

[16] E. Menipaz, "A Taxonomy of Economically Based Quality Control Procedures", *International Journal of Production Research*, Vol. 16, No. 2, 1978, pp. 153–67.

[17] E. M. Saniga and L. E. Shirland, "Quality Control in Practice: A Survey", *Quality Progress*, May 1977, pp. 30–31.

Figure 13.12 Quality Control Program—Conversational Mode Printout (data entered by the operations manager is underlined)

EXECUTION BEGINS   1.29 SECONDS.

NOTE: ALL NUMERIC VALUES ENTERED ARE SEPARATED BY A COMMA AND/OR SPACES

ENTER YOUR NAME AND RUN TITLE (MAX OF 40 CHARACTERS) OR STOP

?

John Run 1

PROGRAM QUALITY CONTROL FOR JOHN RUN 1

ENTER # OF SAMPLES, # OF ITEMS PER SAMPLE

?

25,4

SPECIFY TYPE OF INPUT:

0 FOR RAW SAMP. READINGS OR 1 FOR SAMP. AVERAGE AND RANGE VALUES

?

0

READ IN 25 SAMPLES OF 4

ENTER SAMP. #, SAMP. READING ITEM1,SAMP. READING ITEM2, . . .FOR EACH SAMPLE

?

1,45,51,50,44

   1   45. 51. 50. 44.

?

2,49,55,53,54

   2   49. 55. 53. 54.

?

3,44,43,52,50

   3   44. 43. 52. 50.

?

4,50,50,50,44

   4   50. 50. 50. 44.

?

5,48,48,52,48

   5   48. 48. 52. 48.

Figure 13.12 (Cont.)

?

6,53,50,48,46

  6   53. 50. 48. 46.

?

7,47,53,56,50

  7   47. 53. 56. 50.

?

8,51,45,44,51

  8   51. 45. 44. 51.

?

9,53,58,60,57

  9   53. 58. 60. 57.

?

10,50,47,44,45

10   50. 47. 44. 45.

?

11,51,52,45,47

11   51. 47. 44. 45.

?

12,56,52,44,50

12   56. 52. 44. 50.

?

13,45,55,55,50

13   45. 55. 55. 50.

?

14,57,52,51,44

14   57. 52. 51. 44.

?

15,46,50,51,50

15   46. 50. 51. 50.

?

16,51,52,48,48

16   51. 52. 48. 48.

Figure 13.12 (Cont.)

```
?
 17,50,51,49,44
 17      50.  51.  49.  44.
?
 18,56,52,51,47
 18      56.  52.  51.  47.
?
 19,48,49,52,51
 19      48.  49.  52.  51.
?
 20,50,52,50,49
 20      50.  52.  50.  49.
?
 21,48,50,44,55
 21      48.  50.  44.  55.
?
 22,46,45,60,55
 22      46.  45.  60.  55.
?
 23,49,50,49,52
 23      49.  50.  49.  52.
?
 24,47,47,50,51
 24      47.  47.  50.  51.
?
 25,48,49,45,45
 25      48.  49.  45.  45.
QUALITY CONTROL RESULTS FOR JOHN RUN 1
ENTER # OF STANDARD DEVIATIONS (1,2 OR 3)
?
 3
KNOWN PROCESS CHARACTERISTICS? SPECIFY 1 FOR NO, 2 FOR
YES
?
 1
```

Figure 13.12   (Cont.)

```
ANALYSIS CONTROL REQUESTS
CODE   SIGMA     UCLX    LCLX      UCLR      LCLR
  1      3        0.0     0.0       0.0       0.0
FOR 3 STANDARD DEVIATIONS
COMPUTED CONTROL LIMITS ARE
XBAR =     49.76   RBAR =      7.16
UCLX =     54.98   UCLR =     16.34
LCLX =     44.54   LCLR =      0.0
THE SAMPLE VALUES WERE
SAMPLE NO.     MEAN      RANGE
    1          47.50      7.00
    2          52.75      6.00
    3          47.25      9.00
    4          48.50      6.00
    5          49.00      4.00
    6          49.25      7.00
    7          51.50      9.00
    8          47.75      7.00
    9          57.00      7.00       OUT OF CONTROL
   10          46.50      6.00
   11          48.75      7.00
   12          50.50     12.00
   13          51.25     10.00
   14          51.00     13.00
   15          49.25      5.00
   16          49.75      4.00
   17          48.50      7.00
   18          51.50      9.00
   19          50.00      4.00
   20          50.25      3.00
   21          49.25     11.00
   22          51.50     15.00
   23          50.00      3.00
   24          48.75      4.00
   25          46.75      4.00
THE PROCESS IS OUT OF CONTROL
SPECIFY:  1 FOR ANOTHER ANALYSIS OF SAME SAMPLES, OR 2
FOR A NEW RUN
```

TABLE 13.13 BASIC INFORMATION ON QUALITY-CONTROL STATUS IN NORTH AMERICA

VARIABLE	PERCENT OF COMPANIES
Have quality standards	75
Have 100 percent inspection	92
Employ inspectors and Q.C. experts	30
Have quality standards that are set by customers	50
Quality control is not an issue	20
Plan improvements in the quality-control system	50
Seek assistance for Q.C. improvements (e.g., training courses, seminars, consulting services, audits of quality-control programs)	25

First, a lack of knowledge about the techniques on the part of personnel not directly involved in quality control (e.g., operations managers, top management)

Second, short runs that could not be subjected to control charts and acceptance sampling plans

Third, difficulty in collecting data

Fourth, a general feeling that the techniques are time-consuming and costly, and indications of customer resistance to acceptance sample.

SUMMARY

Quality control is an effective system for integrating the quality development, quality maintenance, and quality improvement efforts of the various groups in an organization so as to enable production and service at the most economical levels that allow for full customer satisfaction.

A most important facet of quality control is a clear definition of what constitutes desired quality. In this chapter, the essentials of quality control and methods of improving quality have been discussed.

Attributes and variable acceptance sampling procedures and the standard manuals that are commonly used in the industry have also been described.

Statistical procedures and manuals are highly desirable in that they save inspection costs and increase accuracy.

The issue of service industries quality control, including problems in applying quality-control principles in the service industry, has been covered. This coverage reflects the growing interest in quality control by service organizations.

It is our belief that the modern organization, whether manufacturing or service, should create a viable program of quality control, as the consumer has

TABLE 13.14   PERCENTAGE OF FIRMS USING THE LISTED CONTROL-CHART TECHNIQUES

TECHNIQUE	FIRM SIZE (NUMBER OF EMPLOYEES) 0 to 100	101 to 500	501 to 1000	1001 to 5000	Over 5000	All Firm Sizes
$\bar{x}$ Chart (Mean/Average)	69	66	77	78	70	71
$\bar{R}$ Chart (Range)	57	61	67	71	67	64
σ Chart (Standard Deviation)	35	40	67	53	70	51
p Chart (Proportion)	13	47	43	61	67	48
c Chart (Number of Defects)	35	53	39	43	59	45
d Chart (Defects per Unit)	17	24	20	18	44	22
Test for Runs	13	21	7	18	19	16
Median Chart	9	13	10	6	26	12
Midrange Chart	4	13	0	2	4	5
Lot Plot Method	0	16	2	12	11	9

TABLE 13.15   PERCENTAGE OF FIRMS USING THE LISTED ACCEPTANCE SAMPLING TECHNIQUES

TECHNIQUE	FIRM SIZE NUMBER OF EMPLOYEES 0 to 100	101 to 500	501 to 1000	1001 to 5000	Over 5000	All Firm Sizes
Single-Sample Fraction Defective with Specified AQL and LTPD	43	76	77	70	89	72
Double-Sample Fraction Defective with Specified AQL and LTPD	26	29	23	37	22	28
Multiple-Sample Fraction Defective with Specified AQL and LTPD	22	16	7	25	19	18
Dodge/Romig AOQL	4	10	10	20	22	16
Dodge/Romig LTPD	9	8	7	14	15	10
Item-by-Item Sequential Sampling	9	16	20	10	15	13
Defects per Unit Sampling	30	24	17	23	15	19
Continuous Sampling Plans	30	53	47	47	55	48
Military Standards:						
MIL-STD-105D	65	87	73	71	82	76
MIL-STD-414	4	13	3	22	26	15

become more demanding and aware of the quality of products and services he or she is acquiring.

DISCUSSION QUESTIONS

13.1 Define the term "quality control."

13.2 How has the concept of a modern factory affected the development of the quality-control function?

13.3 How has the concept of product liability affected the development of the quality-control function?

13.4 Describe briefly the responsibility for quality of each of the departments in a company.

13.5 Explain the following terms: inspection, acceptance sampling, and process-control charts.

13.6 What are the benefits of acceptance sampling?

13.7 Can one always meet exactly the desired producer's risk and consumer's risk at the desired AQL and LTPD?

13.8 Differentiate between attribute acceptance sampling and variable acceptance sampling.

13.9 How does one determine at what organizational level the manager of quality control should be placed?

13.10 When is the cost of inspection justified, and when is it not worthwhile to perform inspection?

13.11 How would quality-control procedures be used in the following services: airline, drug store, law office, car dealership?

13.12 Ideally, what is the optimal quality level that should be followed by an organization?

13.13 Discuss and explain p chart, $\bar{x}$ and R charts, and c chart.

13.14 "All incentive programs designed to increase productivity should include a quality component as well." Discuss this statement and give an example of such an incentive program.

13.15 Identify key quality characteristics of: a ball-point pen and a McDonald's hamburger. How could these characteristics be qualified?

PROBLEMS AND SOLUTIONS

13.1 The Zig Zag Company manufactures sewing machines. One of the components of these machines is made by a subsidiary in Singerville. The subsidiary producing the components works to an acceptable quality level of three percent defectives, and allows a five percent risk of having lots of this level rejected. The president of the Zig Zag Company, Dan Zig, considers lots of 10 percent or more defectives to be unacceptable, and wants to assure that they will accept such poor quality lots no more than 10 percent of the time. A lot of size N has just arrived. Using Table 13.1, for $\alpha = 0.05$ and $\beta = 0.10$, what values of n and c should be selected to determine the quality of this lot:

Solution

We are given:
$$AQL = 0.03$$
$$\alpha = 0.05$$
$$LTPD = 0.10$$
$$\beta = 0.10$$

To determine values of n and c:
$$LTPD \div AQL$$
$$0.10 \div .03 = 3.33$$

Refer to sampling inspection Table 13.1, column (4):
$$3.33 \sim 3.205, c = 6$$

Refer to column (2) in Table 13.1:
$$(n)(AQL) = 3.286$$

$$n = \frac{3.286}{AQL} = \frac{3.286}{0.03} = 109.53$$

$$c = 6, n = 110$$

13.2 Refer to Problem 13.1. The Zig Zag Company wants to modify its acceptance sampling plan. The company wants its risk levels and AQL to remain unchanged, but believes that poor quality should be defined as eight percent defective rather than 10 percent. What will be the acceptance sampling plan if this change is made:

Solution

$$AQL = 0.03$$
$$\alpha = 0.05$$
$$LTPD = 0.08$$
$$\beta = 0.10$$
$$LTPD \div AQL = 0.08 \div 0.03 = 2.667$$

Refer to Table 13.1, column (4):
$$2.667 \sim 2.618, c = 9$$

Refer to column (2) in Table 13.1:
$$(n)(AQL) = 5.426$$

$$n = \frac{5.426}{AQL} = \frac{5.426}{0.03} = 180.867$$

Thus, $c = 9$, $n = 181$

13.3 Refer to Figure 13.9. Would you recommend: rejection, acceptance, or no decision, based on the following data:
a) After checking five items that were acceptable, the sixth item was defective. Would you reject the lot?
b) Another 21 items were checked and were found to be acceptable. The 22nd item was found to be defective. Would you reject the lot?
c) The next five units were acceptable, the sixth item was defective. Would you reject the lot?

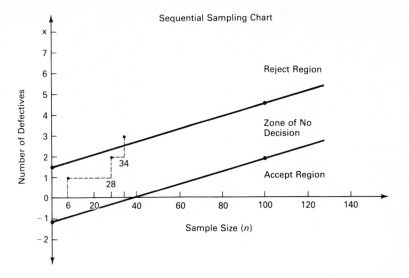

Solution

a) No decision

b) No decision

c) Reject

13.4 The quality-control manager of the Parker Company took six samples, 1200 units per sample, and found the following number of defectives:

Sample Number	Number of Defectives (d)
1	8
2	11
3	8
4	8
5	8
6	11

Construct a p chart for 95 percent confidence (1.96 Sp) and plot each of the samples.

Solution

Sample Number	Number of Defectives (d)	Sample Size	Fraction Defective
1	8	1200	0.00667
2	11	1200	0.009167
3	8	1200	0.00667
4	8	1200	0.00667
5	8	1200	0.00667
6	11	1200	0.009167

$$\overline{p} = \frac{\text{Total number of defectives from all samples}}{\text{Number of samples} \times \text{Sample size}}$$

$$= \frac{54}{6 \times 1200} = 0.0075$$

$$Sp = \sqrt{\frac{\overline{p}\,(1 - \overline{p})}{n}}$$

$$= \sqrt{\frac{0.0075\,(0.9925)}{1200}} = 0.00249$$

For a 95 percent confidence interval, limits are placed at $\overline{p} \pm 1.96Sp$:

$$\text{UCL}_p = \overline{p} + 1.96Sp = 0.0075 + (1.96 \times 0.00249) = 0.0124$$

$$\text{LCL}_p = \overline{p} - 1.96Sp = 0.0075 - (1.96 \times 0.00249) = 0.0026$$

13.5 The Standby Manufacturing Company produces a special bolt that is used later in the production assembly process. In order to fit correctly, the diameter of the bolt must be 1.000 inch plus or minus 0.0075 inch. The special tool required to produce this bolt has a natural variation in output of $S = 0.00075$ inch (normally distributed), and the diameter of the bolt becomes smaller as the tool wears. Construct a dynamic control chart for accepting 95 percent of the output $(1.96S)$ for the longest period of time before the tool must be replaced.

Solution

Part Specification:	1.000 inch $\pm$ 0.0075 inch
Machine Output:	$S = 0.00075$
Control Limits:	$1.96S$ (95 percent)

Boundary limits for dynamic control chart:
Upper design limit:

$$1.000 + 0.0075 = 1.0075 \text{ inches}$$

For a 95 percent confidence, the initial setup should be at UCL less $1.96S$ or:

$$\overline{x} = 1.0075 - (1.96 \times 0.00075) = 1.00603$$

The upper control limit is then at the design limit of 1.0075, and the lower control limit is:

$$\text{LCL} = \overline{x} - 1.96S$$
$$= 1.00603 - (1.96 \times 0.00075)$$
$$= 1.00456$$

The lower design limit is $1.000 - 0.0075 = 0.9925$.

The point of stopping the process occurs where the lower control limit reaches the lower design limit of 0.9925. The process mean is:

$$\overline{x} = 0.9925 + (1.96 \times 0.00075) = 0.99397$$

The upper control limit at the point of stopping the process is:

$$0.99397 + (1.96 \times 0.00075) = 0.99544$$

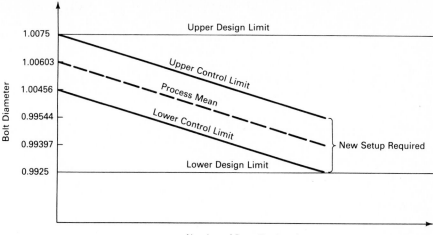

Number of Parts Produced

CHAPTER REVIEW PROBLEMS

13.1   In your new position as assistant manager of quality control for the Mimba Corporation, you are asked to prepare a list of attributes of the following company-made products: light bulbs, ohm meters, stereo systems, switches, radios, electric motors, and electric heaters.

      Your problem is to duplicate the work of the new assistant manager.

13.2   The fire department in a given city controls the 911 emergency telephone system, and routes incoming calls to the police, fire, and ambulance services, as required. The number of operators required must meet 99 percent (± 3 standard deviations) of the calls placed to 911 on the first ring. From the following data, construct a c chart of the calls per 8-hour shift that require the services of an emergency operator:

Shift	Calls (c_i)	Shift	Calls (c_i)
1	78	11	93
2	86	12	94
3	115	13	82
4	103	14	81
5	119	15	88
6	81	16	87
7	91	17	106
8	102	18	84
9	74	19	96
10	63	20	104
			1827

13.3   Martin O'Grady is a life insurance salesman who wants to compare his success rate with that of the company for which he works. Over the last six months, he sold insurance to a number of individuals, couples, and families, but not all of these were accepted by the life insurance company because of health factors, according to the schedule below.

Month	Policies Sold (n)	Rejected Policies (d)	Fraction Defective (d/n)
1	25	1	0.040
2	25	2	0.080
3	25	3	0.120
4	25	1	0.040
5	25	0	0.000
6	25	2	0.080
	150	9	

a) Develop a $\bar{p}$ chart for these data, using two standard deviations. Is the process in control?

b) Develop a $\bar{p}$ chart for these data, using one standard deviation. Is the process in control?

13.4 Using the data from problem 13.3 above, what would be the result if there were seven rejected policies in month number 5, and one uses two standard deviations?

13.5 A cable manufacturing company makes several types of wire rope used in "critical" situations in which deviation from the standard could have a high cost in terms of liability and human lives. These cables are used in elevators, helicopter winches, and similar devices. Construct $\bar{x}$ and R charts based on the following data:

Hour	Breaking Point (000's PSI)				
1	47	49	47	43	44
2	44	48	51	46	43
3	44	41	50	46	40
4	42	46	48	48	40
5	50	46	42	46	46
6	45	45	50	46	48
7	47	45	49	47	44
8	51	47	45	48	49
9	48	47	49	46	50
10	46	46	48	45	46
11	50	44	44	48	47
12	51	46	44	52	46
13	49	50	44	49	46
14	42	47	47	49	48
15	43	48	48	46	50
16	47	44	43	40	45

Using factors from Tables 13.8 and 13.9:

$$\bar{x} \text{ chart: } UCL_{\bar{x}} = \bar{\bar{x}} + A_2 R = 46.3875 + (0.577)(6.4375)$$
$$= 50.1019375$$
$$LCL_{\bar{x}} = \bar{\bar{x}} - A_2 \bar{R} = 42.6730625$$

R chart:

$$UCL_R = D_4\bar{R} \quad = (2.115)(6.4375) = 13.6153125$$
$$LCL_R = D_3\bar{R} \quad = (0)(6.4375) = 0$$

13.6 A university medical research lab has developed a new electronic tool for internal surgery. A manufacturer says he can make 5 of the tools at a time, and, from this lot, one is selected for testing. Only one is tested because the testing process is extremely expensive and the medical research staff has suggested that hypergeometric sampling be used. If a defect is found, the remaining tools are all tested. The process average for defectives is $\bar{p} = 0.18$. What is the average number of tools inspected?

13.7 Ajax Crystals is a manufacturer of radio frequency crystals for use in two-way radio systems. The company manufactures the various frequencies in lots of 5000 because they are used world-wide, and the company uses acceptance sampling. Through an agreement with a radio manufacturer, the producer's risk, α, is set at 2 percent and the consumer's risk, β, at 3 percent. If $c = 0$, what should be the sample size and the lot tolerance percent defective, if the process average is 0.003?

13.8 a) Which of the following commodities are candidates for acceptance sampling in the manufacturing process: calculators, ammunition, matches, staplers, sport coats, suitcases, watches, stamps (gummed)?

b) If reliability of a product is a measure of quality, how does it apply in the case of the following items: tires, calculators, batteries, matches, radios?

13.9 Several samples of size $n = 8$ were taken from a continuous process over a period of time. The estimated process average was $\bar{x} = 0.031$ mm, and the estimated process range was $R = 0.0030$ mm. From this data, determine the control limits for an $\bar{x}$ chart and an R chart.

13.10 The search and rescue authorities have become increasingly concerned about the possibility of serious accidents or fatalities occurring when recreational fishermen take to the sea in their small boats. As a precaution, they have for the past seven years had the Coast Guard check these fishermen on a random basis along the coast to determine whether their boats were seaworthy and whether they were equipped with the required safety equipment. Serious violators were charged and then taken to court. Each year the Coast Guard checks about 25 percent of the boating population.

The following statistics were collected over the seven-year period.

Year	Convictions	Sample Size	Conviction Rate
1980	35	4000	0.00875
1979	42	3900	0.01077
1978	58	3900	0.01487
1977	26	3800	0.00684
1976	37	3700	0.01000
1975	38	3850	0.00987
1974	33	3500	0.00943

Construct a p chart for 99 percent (2.58S) confidence level, and plot the results.

13.11 A bearing manufacturer has set up special machinery to manufacture a line of special high-pressure bearings for use in the aviation and space exploration fields. These bearings are all pressure-fit, meaning that the outside tolerances are as critical as the inside diameter. One size has an outside diameter specified at 2.6500 cm plus or minus 0.0040 cm. Construct a dynamic control chart to encompass ±3 standard deviations before retooling. (*Hint:* The lathe used has variation of 0.0002 cm *(S)*, and the outside diameter of the bearing is reduced in size as the machine wears.)

13.12   Refer to problem 13.11. If the process mean shifts 0.0001 cm for every 120 bearings turned out, how many are made before the process is stopped for retooling?

BIBLIOGRAPHY

ADAM, E. E., "Behaviour Modification in Quality Control," *The Academy of Management Journal*, 18, No. 4, December, 1975, pp. 662–79.

AMERICAN SOCIETY FOR QUALITY CONTROL, *Quality Motivation Workbook*. Milwaukee, Wisconsin: ASQC, 1967.

DODGE, H. F., AND H. G. ROMIG, *Sampling Inspection Tables*. New York: John Wiley & Sons, Inc., 1959.

FETTER, ROBERT B., *The Quality Control System*. Homewood, Illinois: Richard D. Irwin, Inc., 1967.

GAVETT, J. W., *Production and Operations Management*. New York: Harcourt Brace Jovanovich, Inc., 1968.

JURAN, J. M. (ed.), *Quality Control Handbook* (2nd ed.), McGraw-Hill Book Company, New York, 1962.

LARSON, HARRY R., "A Nomograph of the Cumulative Binomial Distribution," *Industrial Quality Control*, December, 1966.

MENIPAZ, E., "A Taxonomy of Economically Based Quality Control Procedures," *International Journal of Production Research*, 1978, Vol. 16, No. 2, pp. 153–167.

——— "On Economically Based Quality Control Decisions," *European Journal of Operations Research*, Vol. 2, No. 4, July, 1978, pp. 246–256.

——— "Maintaining Proper Quality Standards in an Era of High Economic Uncertainty," in Muramatsu, R., and N. A. Dudley, (ed.), *Production and Industrial Systems*. London: Taylor and Francis, 1978, pp. 1179–1185.

——— *Automated Production: Decision Support Systems Approach*, Ottawa: Randcomp, 1984.

SHAININ, DORIAN, "How to Calculate the Risk of a Decision," *Quality Progress*, August, 1968.

14

Maintenance

INTRODUCTION

The operations manager employs, in the course of one day, machinery and other equipment valued at hundreds of thousands or millions of dollars. A breakdown in a machine or a transfer line or the injury of a worker causes a significant expense in the form of downtime, idle labor, schedule interruption, and rushed-in spare parts. Thus, the operations manager should hedge against a downtime by ensuring that the equipment is maintained in operating condition and is as safe as possible to operate.

For example, in automotive assembly plants, a major effort is made to cut downtime. This is done through regularly scheduled preventive maintenance, including overhaul of the machinery; stocking back-up spares for critical equipment; and maintaining nearly total flexibility, so that most of the products can be made on any line.

Industrial enterprises exist to make a profit, and maintenance departments must contribute to that objective. Maintenance, with its high cost and low efficiency, is one of the last cost-saving frontiers of management because productivity in manufacturing processes seems to be progressively approaching its limit. Maintenance costs are rising at about 15 to 30 percent per year.

The scope and importance of the maintenance function is further under-lined by the fact that an estimated 35 billion dollars are spent on maintenance in American industry. The Working Party of Maintenance Engineering, set up by the British Ministry of Technology, estimated that over two billion dollars are spent annually on maintenance in manufacturing industry alone, excluding nationalized industries and services. These maintenance expenses exceed the annual budget of the whole British National Health Service. If one holds to the notion that health services "maintain" people, that means that in Great Britain more expense is involved in maintaining machinery than in maintaining people. In the USSR, more than 2.5 million workers and 20 billion dollars are occupied in maintenance.

Maintenance management (planning, control, scheduling, administering) is at times more complex than the management of the production function itself. Thus, it is important to include the maintenance function in a text on operating systems.

MAINTENANCE FUNCTION OBJECTIVES

The objectives of the maintenance function are:

1. To maximize availability of machinery
2. To preserve the value of the plant
3. To accomplish 1. and 2. at minimum cost.

In order to attain these objectives, the operations manager has to make a series of short- and long-term decisions. The short-term decisions involve: planning and scheduling maintenance work; arranging for downtime; maintaining and overhauling machinery, grounds, utilities, furniture, cafeteria equipment, etc.; installing and rearranging machinery; lubricating periodically; arranging for a conservation program in regard to lubricants, cutting compounds, hydraulic oils, and energy; cleaning spray booths, oil tanks, ducts, dust collectors, etc.; overseeing sweeping and sanitary services; disposing of waste and scrap metal; controlling inventory of spare parts; and controlling the safety of ovens, furnaces, etc.

The long-term decisions involve: analyzing equipment replacement; selecting and training personnel; reviewing procurement specifications; developing maintenance procedures; preparing and controlling spare-parts requirements; and purchasing maintenance supplies.

As the concern over the cost of energy and the effort to reduce energy consumption grow, the maintenance department becomes involved in energy management—in particular: peak-demand monitoring and projection; equipment and lighting on/off control via time of day/week; fan speed control and selection; equipment scheduling; temperature/humidity monitoring and control; boiler monitoring; and pump monitoring and control.

As one can see, the range of decisions and activities in regard to the maintenance function is wide. Furthermore, as production equipment becomes more complex and expensive, maintenance decisions have a greater impact on the overall operation of the organization. A major manufacturer that produces

15,000 small electric appliances every day has decided to limit the variety of items that a maintenance worker has to deal with in order to shorten the time needed to bring a failed piece of equipment back to the operating state. Consequently, it has cut the number of different types of drives used on the 20 final assembly lines from three to two and has limited procurement of replacement assembly-line conveyors to a single source.

Furthermore, in order to keep downtime on the assembly line to a minimum, the manufacturer has instituted:

1. Regularly scheduled preventive maintenance, including periodic overhaul of the drives
2. Stocking of backup spares for critical equipment
3. Maintaining of nearly total design flexibility, so that most of the products can be made on any line.[1]

THE PLACE OF THE MAINTENANCE FUNCTION IN THE ORGANIZATION STRUCTURE

Organization charts can be of great help in that they:

1. Establish reasonably clear lines of authority with little or no overlap
2. Keep vertical lines of authority and responsibility as short as possible
3. Maintain an optimum number of people reporting to one individual
4. Fit the organization to the personalities involved
5. Assure continuity of operations, such as by executing preventive maintenance activities during the night shift.

Several times in this text, we have stressed trade-offs regarding cost, quality, and schedule. These trade-offs are paramount in the context of the maintenance function. The production manager or foreman is interested in pushing production to meet schedule, while the plant engineer who is responsible for maintenance is interested in setting a downtime during which machines can be maintained. The experience of this author has been that the production manager and the plant engineer should both report directly to the plant manager. In this way, the plant manager is in a position to decide when and how often to maintain downtime, as well as to help in other decisions regarding production and maintenance. An organization chart like the one in Figure 14.1 is optimal for a maintenance department. The electrical and mechanical general foremen report to the maintenance supervisor. The maintenance supervisor, in

---

[1] D. E. Hegland, "Tactics for Boosting Your Uptime," *Production Engineering*, April, 1978, pp. 73–82.

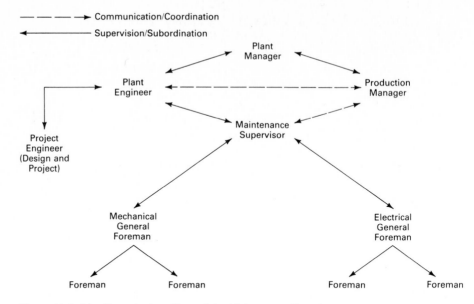

Figure 14.1   The Organization Chart of the Maintenance Function

turn, reports to the plant engineer and maintains communication with the production manager. Both the production manager and the plant engineer report directly to the plant manager.

In the following section, we shall cover a most important decision that affects the maintenance function.

EQUIPMENT REPLACEMENT ANALYSIS

An important decision is when to replace a piece of equipment. Over time, the machine ages and more maintenance expenses are incurred due to breakdowns. Operating expenses such as those for fuel and oil increase due to a decrease in equipment operating efficiency. However, keeping the machine longer would eliminate the need for a capital outlay. This trade-off should help the operations manager determine the best time to replace a piece of equipment. In order to make this trade-off, one uses the monthly equipment record and the replacement analysis form.

In Table 14.1, the monthly equipment record of a forklift truck is presented. Each month, a record is made of the use of the machine (column 2), idle labor cost due to breakdowns (column 3), labor cost due to outside repairs (column 4), labor cost due to in-house repairs (column 5), parts (column 6), lubrication and oil (column 7), fuel or electricity consumption (column 8), and total operating maintenance expenses (column (9).

TABLE 14.1 MONTHLY EQUIPMENT RECORD

Make and model: *1980 Crane*
Serial number: *CR 80/9245*
Description: *Electrical Forklift Truck*
Department: *Warehouse*

In-Plant number: *MEN-102.80*
Date of purchase: *July, 1980*
Purchase price: *$10,000*
Hours in use this year (or miles driven): *1800 hours*

(1) MONTH	(2) METER READING	(3) IDLE LABOR DUE TO BREAKDOWNS	(4) OUTSIDE REPAIRS (LABOR)	(5) IN-HOUSE REPAIRS (LABOR)	(6) PARTS	(7) LUBE AND OIL	(8) ELECTRICITY/ FUEL	(9) TOTAL OPERATING AND MAINTENANCE
June								
July	30	$25.00	$0.00	$0.00	$0.00	$0.00	$30.00	$55.00
August	300	0.00	0.00	0.00	0.00	0.00	33.00	33.00
September	500	0.00	0.00	0.00	5.00	3.00	40.00	48.00
October	620	15.00	0.00	0.00	10.00	0.00	31.00	56.00
November	790	0.00	0.00	0.00	15.00	3.00	26.00	44.00
December	900	0.00	0.00	0.00	0.00	0.00	29.00	29.00
January	1090	0.00	0.00	0.00	0.00	0.00	38.00	38.00
February	1300	0.00	0.00	0.00	5.00	7.00	45.00	57.00
March	1500	0.00	0.00	0.00	5.00	3.00	50.00	58.00
April	1680	10.00	0.00	0.00	3.00	4.00	55.00	72.00
May	1800	0.00	10.00	5.00	0.00	4.00	69.00	98.00
							Total	$588.00

A record like Table 14.1 is kept for each year in which the forklift truck is in operation. The accumulated information is used for the replacement analysis in Table 14.2.

The replacement time is determined in the following way:

1. From the replacement analysis form, obtain the difference between the last entry of column (7) and that entry of column (7) corresponding to the minimum value of column (9).
2. Multiply the value obtained in (1) by the number of years the equipment has been in service.
3. Add this value to the initial purchase price of the equipment. This is the maximum amount one should pay for new equipment.

In this way, one compares the expected annual increase in operating and maintenance costs of the existing unit with the observed increase in the initial cost for the replacement unit.

From Table 14.2, the calculations are as follows:

$$\$1453.88 - \$1145.51 = \$308.37$$

$$(\$308.37) \times (7) = \$2158.59$$

$$\$2158.59 + \$10,000 = \$12,158.59$$

If the purchase price of a new unit is lower than $12,158.59, then the unit should be replaced. Otherwise, the unit should be kept for another year.

This analysis is done every year, based on the information accumulated on the Monthly Equipment Record. One should note that the replacement analysis is very easy to use. However, it does not take into account the time value of money. In order to account for the time value of money, one should use any of the techniques treated in the Technical Note to Chapter 2.

MAINTENANCE COSTS AND LOSSES

The maintenance budget differs from one company to another and from one industry to another. The maintenance budget depends on the machinery maintained, the skills required, the number of shifts, the utilization of machinery, the use of subcontractors, and the environmental conditions. However, some interesting conclusions can be made, based on Table 14.3.

In continuous processing industries, such as the chemical industry and the steel industry, where the equipment is very expensive and downtime is very costly, the average maintenance budget is high. Relatively high budgets are evident in assembly-line operations, such as in the automotive industry. However, there is a wide range between the minimum and the maximum maintenance budgets for every industry.

TABLE 14.2 REPLACEMENT ANALYSIS FORM

In-Plant number: *MEN-102.80*

Purchase price: *$10,000*

Standard use for first 12 months' operation (hours or miles driven): *2000 hours*

(1) END OF YEAR	(2) TOTAL OPERATING AND MAIN-TENANCE EXPENSES*	(3) HOURS OPERATING (OR MILES DRIVEN)	(4) MULTIPLI-CATION FACTOR 2,000 HOURS ÷ (3)	(5) ADJ. OPTG. AND MAINT. (4) × (2)	(6) CUM. OF COLUMN (5)	(7) AVG. ANNUAL OPTG. AND MAINT. (6) ÷ (1)	(8) AVG. ANNUAL CAPITAL COST $10,000 ÷ (1)	(9) AVG. ANNUAL TOTAL COST (7) + (8)
1	$588.00	1800	1.11	653.33	653.33	653.33	10000.00	10653.33
2	702.00	2105	0.95	666.98	1320.31	660.16	5000.00	5660.16
3	790.00	1910	1.05	827.22	2147.53	715.84	3333.34	4049.18
4	990.00	2080	0.96	951.92	3099.45	774.86	2500.00	3274.86
5	1230.20	1500	1.33	1640.27	4739.72	947.94	2000.00	2947.94
6	1600.00	1500	1.33	2133.33	6873.05	1145.51	1666.67	2812.19
7	1982.48	1200	1.67	3304.13	10177.18	1453.88	1428.57	2882.45

*From Table 14.1.

TABLE 14.3   MAINTENANCE BUDGET AS PERCENT OF SALES

INDUSTRY	NUMBER OF COMPANIES	6-YEAR AVERAGE (PERCENT) (1976–82)	RANGE	
			High	*Low*
Radio/TV	5	.9	1.2	0.2
Shoe	3	1.4	2.8	0.7
Metal	7	1.2	1.5	0.7
Aircraft	6	1.6	2.7	0.3
Foods	4	1.9	2.8	0.9
Automotive	4	6.2	9.2	2.1
Drugs	5	1.8	3.5	0.5
Electrical	4	2.2	2.9	1.4
Rubber	6	3.3	4.2	2.5
Petroleum	6	3.2	5.7	2.6
Chemical	5	6.9	10.6	2.5
Glass	4	7.3	10.6	4.3
Steel	4	13.1	17.0	8.9

The maintenance budget includes all the maintenance expenses involved in the maintenance function: labor and material for installation of new equipment and other capital projects, labor and material for lubrication, repairs, and sanitation, and inventory of parts and tools. All these expenses are called *maintenance costs*.

Maintenance losses are the expenses accrued because of an unplanned stoppage of production—that is, forced downtime. These expenses include: idle labor, extra overtime, subcontracting, and cost of rushed-in spare parts (see Figure 14.2).

The objective is to strike the right balance between maintenance costs and losses. A reduction in maintenance losses is effected by using preventive maintenance, which is described in the next section.

CALL MAINTENANCE AND PREVENTIVE MAINTENANCE

When a piece of machinery fails this triggers a *call (breakdown) maintenance* activity. This activity involves workers, parts, supplies, specialized tools, and machines. All these resources are used and coordinated to repair the failed piece as quickly as possible. If the maintenance call is an emergency call, overtime is scheduled, subcontractors are called in, and missing spare parts are rushed in. The goal is to minimize the downtime resulting from breakdowns. If the failing piece of machinery can be replaced expeditiously with a good piece, the failed piece is repaired in facilities that are managed as production departments.

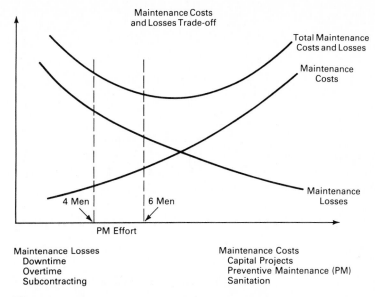

Figure 14.2   Maintenance Costs and Losses Trade-off

The major problems that should be resolved in the context of call maintenance activities are:

1. What is the optimal crew size?
2. What is the best way to schedule maintenance workers and activities?
3. What should be the number of standby units to support an operating unit?

Preventive maintenance is the planned maintenance of equipment through periodic inspections that disclose faulty conditions and describe maintenance necessary to alleviate such conditions.

A preventive maintenance program aims at minimizing breakdowns and excessive depreciation.

Preventive maintenance reduces costs through: reduced production downtime due to fewer breakdowns and better-planned maintenance operations; decreased replacement rates; reduced emergency maintenance expenses; fewer major repairs; reduced repairs cost; reduced product rework and reject rate; identification of obsolete equipment; and improved safety.

An increase in the number of workers devoted to preventive maintenance activities causes a reduction in the maintenance losses. Figure 14.2 shows that an increase in the preventive maintenance work force from four to six men causes a reduction in maintenance losses that is greater than the increase in maintenance costs. Eventually, one should strive to reach a minimum in the total expenses of costs and losses.

PREVENTIVE MAINTENANCE

In every plant, there are numerous components and pieces of machinery. Belts, drives, wheel bearings, shafts, electric motors, gears, electrical and hydraulic controls, and hoses all fail and call for repair. Which components should be inspected by the preventive maintenance team? Preventive maintenance should inspect: process equipment, safety equipment, utility equipment, buildings, tanks, and fire protection equipment.

In choosing the items for preventive maintenance, one may look at the equipment records and identify the 10 machines that have had the most frequent breakdowns, the 10 machines that have had the most costly breakdowns, and the 10 machines with the longest downtimes. This identification process is called the "three top ten" principle.

The preventive maintenance function includes inspections of various kinds:

1. *Routine upkeep*   In regular short intervals, one adjusts, lubricates, cleans, and, for example, checks lighting, heating fixtures, and filters.
2. *Periodic inspections*   As work at prescribed intervals on equipment goes on, visual inspections are performed.
3. *Contingent work inspections*   These are done at indefinite intervals when equipment is down for other reasons—e.g., inspection of gas burners when relining a furnace.

Figure 14.3 describes the process of establishing a preventive maintenance (PM) program. Usually, the process starts when most of the maintenance calls are due to breakdowns. An analysis of past troubles reveals whether or not preventive maintenance is needed. This trouble history data may come from:

1. Review of the maintenance work orders for the past several years
2. Analysis of the equipment records, if such records exist (see Figure 14.4).

There should be personnel assigned to precondition the machinery so that preventive maintenance can start. Check sheets, similar to the one presented in Figure 14.5, are developed. They serve as a record for corrective maintenance, ensure commonality, indicate degree of deterioration, and provide maintenance control. These check-sheets may be of the daily, weekly, semiannual, or annual variety, and may refer to a machine, work area, or the whole plant.

Inspection frequencies are developed for all equipment. The same piece of equipment may require radically different inspection frequencies, depending on the type of plant in which it is installed and on the condition of use.

Initial inspection frequencies are available through the original equipment manufacturer, the National Electric Manufacturers Association in New York, the Factory Insurance Association in Hartford, Connecticut, the Factory Mutual

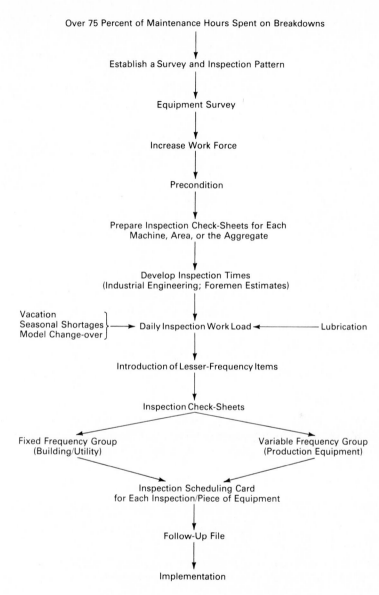

Over 75 Percent of Maintenance Hours Spent on Breakdowns

Establish a Survey and Inspection Pattern

Equipment Survey

Increase Work Force

Precondition

Prepare Inspection Check-Sheets for Each
Machine, Area, or the Aggregate

Develop Inspection Times
(Industrial Engineering; Foremen Estimates)

Vacation
Seasonal Shortages   ⟶   Daily Inspection Work Load ◂——————— Lubrication
Model Change-over

Introduction of Lesser-Frequency Items

Inspection Check-Sheets

Fixed Frequency Group   Variable Frequency Group
(Building/Utility)   (Production Equipment)

Inspection Scheduling Card
for Each Inspection/Piece of Equipment

Follow-Up File

Implementation

Figure 14.3   Getting Into a Preventive Maintenance (PM) Program

Engineering Division in Norwood, Massachusetts, or the National Security Council in Chicago, Illinois. All these different sources are used to establish general inspection frequencies, as well as specialized inspection frequencies. *General inspection frequencies* are developed and used by small to medium-sized plants because of their simplicity. The entire plant's equipment or a portion of

214-010			G407	
Dept.	Mach. Name & No.		Bldg. No.	Card No.
Coating	41 Coater		24	
Time	Number of Men		Frequency	When Done
2 hrs.	1 Electrician 1 Pipefitter		4 months	Down Time

Work to be done: Inspect ovens fire boxes, check burners and flame rods. Check all valves for free operation. If needed, lubricate—check for paper and lint.

Date	Foreman	Total Man Hrs.	No. of Men	Remarks
5/27/82	Paulsen	2 hrs.	Larrimore Toeppe Cook	Need lub for eclipse burners valve. Lub— use DTE 26 Lubricant
9/18/82	Ruckman	1 hrs.	Cook	
1/9/82	McNealy	3 hrs.	Warrington Sarabia	
4/21/83	McNealy	2 hrs.	Cook	
8/19/83	Paulsen	2 hrs.	Lacy Larrimore	
1/13/84	McNealy	1 hrs.	Estes Jar	

Figure 14.4 Equipment Record—An Example

the equipment is inspected at one time. The basic equipment, plus all motors, gears, drives, controls, etc., is inspected at the same time, following an inspection check-sheet, like the one presented in Figure 14.5. It is accomplished by one inspector, possibly assisted by several specialists. The inspection cycle of an entire machine must be determined by its most frequently failing part. For example, if an electric motor is the most frequently failing part of a transfer line, and if its trouble-free life expectancy is seven months, the entire transfer line should be inspected every five or six months, to minimize downtime, provided that the life of the motor cannot be extended.

Specialized inspection carries a higher degree of sophistication than does general inspection. It is used in larger plants, and allows for an inspection economy. Parts of the equipment that are longer-lasting need not be inspected as often as parts that fail more frequently. Where there are a large number of machines under a preventive maintenance program, considerable savings in inspection time can be effected if the frequencies employed take advantage of the full trouble-free operational period of each part of the equipment. For example, a drive may require inspection every three months, whereas an electric motor for the same equipment might be inspected annually.

Daily: Machine Maintenance Check	
Machine Sr. No. _____ Date: _____ Time: _____	
Required Machine Inspection Items	**Signature**

1. Safety Check:
    a) Check front safety door switch operation LS-2.*
    b) Check door operated safety pawl operation.
    c) Clean safety door window.
    d) Check all other machine safety guards in place and secure.
Note: Correct all discrepancies before further machine operation
*Switch is LA-1 on 50 and 100 TD-TE.	

2. Oil System:
    a) Check oil level.
    b) Check oil temp. (normal 100# to 120#)
    c) With pumps operating, check condition of suction filters.
        If in "bypass" or "dirty," clean before further machine operation.	

3. Lubrication System:
    a) Check grease reservoir if 2″ from empty fill with proper grease.
    b) Check control panel lube fault light if "on" trouble shoot and repair
        before further machine operation.
    c) Operate hand lubrication pump on 50 and 100 TD-TE.	

4. Machine General:
    a) Check entire machine for evidence of oil leaks and repair as required.
    b) Brush-clean all material from top and base under screw unit.	

5. Note: Mark Below any additional dicrepancies and/or parts that may be required for repairs during scheduled machine downtime.	

Please Note All Repairs on Back of This Form.

Figure 14.5 Daily Check-Sheet—An Example

Periodically, the inspection frequencies should be reviewed. The amount of inspection can sometimes be reduced when the downtime frequency is minimal. Otherwise, an increased frequency of inspection is called for.

Lubrication is an integral part of preventive maintenance. It is necessary to survey the equipment to determine the proper lubricants and the lubrication frequency. Major oil companies cooperate in making such surveys and provide a lubrication manual for the plant. A daily, weekly, and monthly lubrication check-sheet should be developed. An effective lubrication plan gives substantial results by cutting down replacement frequencies.

JUSTIFYING A PREVENTIVE REPLACEMENT

As has been mentioned earlier, preventive maintenance is performed on machines and buildings in order to avoid costly breakdowns. However, one should consider carefully the economics involved in shutdown, as well as the failure data of the equipment.

Replacing a yet-operating part at predetermined intervals is a recommended practice when:

1. The total cost of a failure replacement is greater than the total cost of a preventive replacement, and
2. The instantaneous failure rate, $r(t)$, (sometimes called hazard rate) is increasing. $r(t)$ is defined as follows:

$$r(t) = \frac{f(t)}{1 - F(t)}$$

where $f(t)$ is the failure probability density function and $F(t) = \int_0^t f(x)(dx)$ is the cumulative probability function.

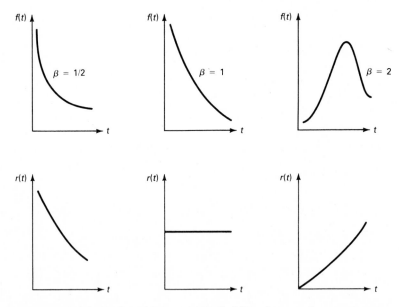

Figure 14.6 Relationships Between the Weibull Distribution's Shape Parameter and the Failure Rate

In many cases, the failure data presents a special distribution called the Weibull distribution. The value of a certain parameter of that distribution, β (beta), is the key to the decision on whether or not the failure rate is increasing. As one can see from Figure 14.6, when β is greater than a unit, the failure rate is increasing.

Figure 14.7 is a Weibull probability paper that is used to plot the failure data. If the failure data come from a Weibull distribution, then the plotted points fall on a straight line.[2] From the Weibull probability paper one can determine the β coefficient value as well as the mean time between Failures (MTBF).

Beta Coefficient Determination Procedure

1. Plot the failure data points on the paper (Figure 14.7).
2. Fit a straight line through the data points.
3. Extend a vertical line to the straight line of 2. that passes through the estimation point at the upper-left-most corner of the paper.
4. Read the beta value off the scale marked β.

If β is greater than a unit, a preventive replacement can be justified (provided the cost of failure replacement is greater than the cost of preventive replacement).

Mean Time Between Failure (MTBF) Determination Procedure

1. Read the value of Pμ off the appropriate scale.
2. Mark this value on the y-axis.
3. Extend a horizontal line at the level of Pμ, until it crosses the fitted straight line.
4. Determine the projection of the intersection point found in 2. onto the x-axis. The reading on the x-axis is the mean time between failures (MTBF). (MTBF is μ, the average life of the equipment).

EXAMPLE   The High Marble Manufacturing Company has 20 air-conditioning units in its offices. The dust collectors are clogged every once in a while and cause a sharp reduction in the efficiency level of the units. The problem is whether to replace the dust collectors on a preventive basis.

The information regarding the failure of the dust collectors is as follows:

---

[2] The problems are: whether or not the plotted points indicate a straight line, and what is the most appropriate straight line.

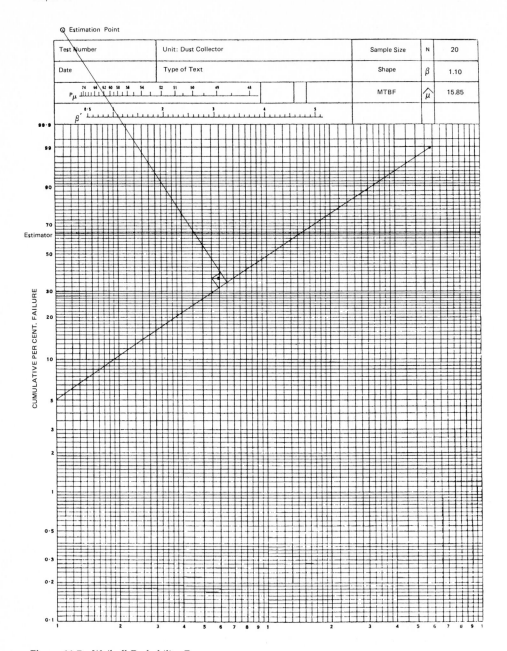

Figure 14.7 Weibull Probability Paper

Weeks to Failure X_i	Number Failed N_i	Relative Frequency f_i	Cumulative Frequency Σf_i
2	2	0.10	0.10
3	1	0.05	0.15
5	2	0.10	0.25
10	5	0.25	0.50
20	5	0.25	0.75
30	5	0.25	1.00
	$\Sigma N_i = 20$	$\Sigma f_i = 1.00$	

From Figure 14.7, the β value is 1.10, which is greater than 1.00. If, as well, the emergency replacement cost is greater than the preventive replacement cost, planned replacement is a preferred policy. The MTBF is 15.85 weeks, which indicates that preventive replacement is to be done at intervals that are shorter than 15.85 weeks.

How much shorter? The answer to this question is found through the use of the following procedure and a set of curves.

DETERMINING THE FREQUENCY OF PREVENTIVE REPLACEMENT

Basically, there are two alternatives in the administration of a preventive replacement program:

1. The preventive replacement is done at fixed intervals of time, irrespective of the age of a component, and failure replacements occur when necessary. This procedure is termed *block replacement*.
2. The preventive replacement occurs only when a component has reached a specified age, and failed replacements occur when necessary. This procedure is termed *age replacement*.

The first program is an easier program to administer since it does not require the knowledge of a specific component's age.

Figure 14.8 and Figure 14.9 present the relationships necessary to determine the best replacement frequencies and potential savings from using a block replacement program and an age replacement program, respectively, for a Weibull failure distribution.

Replacement Interval Determination Procedure

1. Determine the mean time between failures (MTBF) by using the Weibull probability paper or by using the following formula:

$$\text{MTBF} = \mu = \frac{\sum\limits_{i=1}^{n} f_i x_i}{\sum\limits_{i=1}^{n} f_i}$$

2. Determine the variance of the time to failure by using the following formula:

$$\text{Variance} = \sigma^2 = \frac{\sum\limits_{i=1}^{n} f_i(x_i - \mu)^2}{\sum\limits_{i=1}^{n} f_i}$$

3. Find the ratio of MTBF to the standard deviation,

$$\frac{\text{MTBF}}{\text{Standard deviation}} = \frac{\mu}{\text{Standard division}} = \frac{\mu}{\sigma}$$

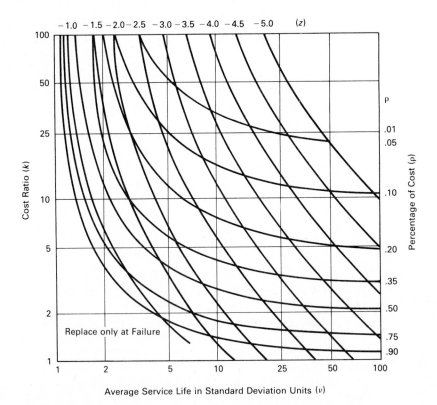

Figure 14.8 Best Replacement Intervals for a Block Replacement Program

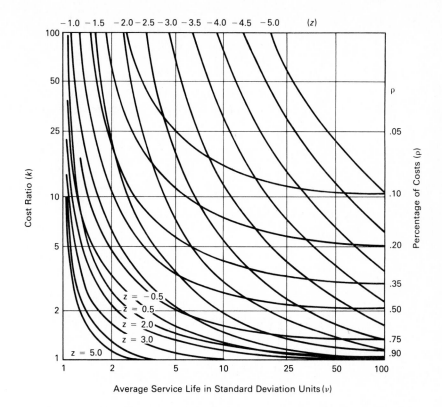

Figure 14.9   Best Replacement Intervals for an Age Replacement Program

4. Determine the ratio of the emergency replacement cost, C_e, to the preventive replacement cost, C_p. That is, find:

$$K = \frac{C_e}{C_p}$$

5. Read off Figure 14.8 or Figure 14.9, the value of z corresponding to the values of v (nu) and K found in steps 3. and 4.
6. The best preventive replacement interval, t_p, is obtained from:

$$t_p = \mu + z\sigma$$

7. Read off Figure 14.8 or Figure 14.9, the standardized cost ratio, ρ (rho). The value of ρ at the intersection of the appropriate K and v gives the cost per unit of time of the best preventive replacement program as a decimal fraction of the cost of a "replace only at failure" program.

EXAMPLE   The High Marble Manufacturing Company of the preceding example has determined that the failure data indicate an increasing failure rate and that the MTBF is 15.85. Through its records the company has established an emergency replacement cost, C_e, of $50 (labor and parts) and a preventive replacement cost C_p, of $10 (labor and parts). What should be the preventive replacement interval for an *age replacement* program? How much money is saved by following a preventive replacement program?

Since the emergency replacement cost is greater than the preventive replacement cost, and since the failure data indicate an increasing failure rate, preventive replacement is justified. Let us find the replacement interval that minimizes the cost of the program per unit of time.

1. The MTBF is 15.85 weeks.
2. The variance is:

$$\text{Variance} = \sigma^2 = \frac{\Sigma f_i (X_i - \mu)^2}{\Sigma f_i} = \frac{2(2 - 15.85)^2 + (3 - 15.85)^2}{20}$$

$$+ \frac{2(5 - 15.85)^2 + 5(10 - 15.85)^2 + 5(20 - 15.85)^2 + 5(30 - 15.85)^2}{20}$$

$$= 102.00$$

The standard deviation

$$\sigma = \sqrt{102.00} \cong 10 \text{ weeks}$$

3. The ratio of MTBF to the variance is

$$v = \frac{15.85}{10} = 1.585$$

4. The ratio of the emergency replacement cost to the preventive replacement cost

$$K = \frac{50}{10} = 5$$

5. The High Marble Manufacturing Company is interested in an age replacement program. Let us read off Figure 14.9 the appropriate z.

$$z = -0.5$$

6. The best preventive replacement interval is

$$t_p = 15.85 + (-0.5)(10) = 10.85 \text{ weeks.}$$

7. From Figure 14.9, one reads from the vertical axis on the right hand side the standardized cost ratio $\rho = 0.80$. That is, the cost of an age preventive replacement program is 80 percent of the cost of replacement only at failure program.

The High Marble Manufacturing Company should employ an age preventive replacement program. Each dust collector installed should be replaced when it fails, as well as when it reaches the age of approximately 11 weeks. This program is 20 percent cheaper than simply replacing the dust collectors as they fail.

The same procedure can be followed for a block replacement program. More examples are given in the problems at the end of the chapter.

There are various other maintenance programs that have been presented to help the manager with his decisions.[3] All these programs calculate the trade-offs between a planned downtime and a forced downtime, and between a preventive replacement and an emergency replacement. Formerly, decisions in regard to downtime have been based on qualitative judgment. Now, decisions of this kind are made by using historical data that are stored in a manual or computerized file.

COMPUTERIZED MAINTENANCE INFORMATION SYSTEM

There is a large amount of data that can support an integrated maintenance program. The data are to be converted into useful information that may be used for long- and short-range maintenance decisions. In order to help transform the data into information and to reduce the time required in processing the information into decisions, the computer is used extensively.

The input to a computerized system by plant engineering is identical to the input to the manual records of the activity. These data are translated from the original input document to an intermediary document, such as a punched card or paper tape. Even better, the original document itself, designed on a tabulating card, can be used as the input document.

The output of the system becomes the timely, accurate reports that will enable the plant engineer to analyze operations quickly and easily and then take action at an appropriate time. Between the input and the output is the programming of the computer by a trained employee or by a computer service organization. It is not necessary that all personnel become expert programmers, but all should be sufficiently familar with the EDP system to know that the accuracy and usefulness of the system depends on the accuracy of the input data fed to the computer.

Since the goal of any accounting system is to permit a detailed analysis of costs, the input to the computer must be reduced to a set of basic units of information that will not have to be subdivided during later analysis. As a

[3] See, for example, E. Menipaz, "Optimization of Stochastic Maintenance Policies," *European Journal of Operations Research*, Vol. 2, No. 2, March, 1978, pp. 97–106; or E. Menipaz, "Cost Optimization of Some Stochastic Maintenance Policies," *IEEE Transactions on Reliability*, R-28, No. 2, June, 1979, pp. 123–126.

consequence, a code number is assigned to describe each relevant characteristic of the unit of information that may be needed later.

Each piece of machinery or equipment is given an identification number or asset number; each department is numbered; repair codes are established to indicate the type of repair work done, and codes are established to indicate either scheduled preventive repair or breakdown (or call) repair. In addition, codes are assigned to indicate lubrication, cleaning and sanitation, overtime, rearrangements and improvements, overhauls, and other input codes are designated to give the plant engineer the output he or she desires from the system.

Under certain circumstances, some of the procedures in maintenance work can be performed better manually than they can by data processing; however, the speed and accuracy of computations would argue for data processing rather than for manual operations. Other factors to be considered are the size of the organization, the volume of paper work, the timing of maintenance reports, and the savings potential in better coordination. In large and complex plants, the importance of relevant information in a problematic situation is significant. There is also the factor of cost to be considered. The cost of processing data at a computer service center or the cost of installing and maintaining purchased or leased data-processing equipment must be weighed against the benefits.

There are no hard and fast rules about minimum plant size that would make the installation of computerized maintenance systems worthwhile. Each application must be examined on its own merits, considering the type and size of the plant and the amount and importance of accurate, timely information required, as well as the cost of the system. There are no particular prerequisites for installation of EDP beyond well-organized activity. The better the organization is, the more advantages EDP will show. The EDP information system will be no better than the data that go into it.

Figure 14.10 presents the general structure of a computer maintenance system. The system includes routines for: acceptance of new records, update of inventory status, update of completed work orders, update of Weibull coefficient for preventive replacement, issue of purchase orders, issue maintenance work orders, and printing and deleting records.

One of the important outputs of a computerized system is the preventive maintenance schedule. This includes the identification of the number of preventive maintenance operations required, their suggested frequency, and specific instructions for performing these operations. Manual systems are based on a formalized tickler file or list.[4] The computerized system quickly creates weekly schedules. An example of such an output is presented in Figure 14.11.

The weekly machine maintenance schedule includes a code of the maintenance activity, a description of the machine or equipment maintained, and of the

---

[4] An example of a manual system is the VISIrecord system, available from VISIrecord, 71 Wingold Ave., Toronto, Ontario, Canada.

specific part for lubrication. It also includes the lubrication method to be used (lubrication gun, for example), the lubricant used, the maintenance and inspection frequency, and an indication of a program starting week. This schedule is the basis for planned shutdowns, and initiates notes like the one appearing in Figure 14.12.

There are various other computerized systems that have been constructed. FAME (Facilities Maintenance Engineering) has been conceived and constructed by General Electric Company. It provides a preventive data base that is used to develop schedules of preventive maintenance. It can handle 10,000 equipment records and 72,000 maintenance records, reports craft man-hour requirements schedules, and generates preventive maintenance schedules. FAME is an interactive program, and generates maintenance schedules in response to the user's keyboard request.

AMOS (aircraft maintenance operation simulation), conceived and constructed by Air Canada, is another interactive computer system. As a simulation system, it is used both for generating maintenance activities schedules and for planning and budgeting.

It gives the user the ability to generate plans or work programs of up to five years in an online (interactive) environment. The simulation is continuous and deterministic and utilizes a heuristic (a formalized "rule of thumb") specifically designed for the unique problem area. It considers resources, operational requirements, reliability and time between checks.

Figure 14.13 presents the reports and decision-making aspects of AMOS.

The computer needs of the maintenance department can be met in various ways. If the amount of maintenance work orders and equipment records is relatively small, it is common to share the company's computer or to rent computer time from outside service centers. Buying a minicomputer may be considered when the volume of maintenance activities increases.

SYSTEMS APPROACH IN MAINTENANCE MANAGEMENT— TEROTECHNOLOGY

Terotechnology is a system approach toward maintenance management. Terotechnology consists of various activities, including the maintenance function. It is a combination of management, financial, engineering, and other practices applied to physical assets in pursuit of economic lifecycle costs. It is concerned with the specification and design for reliability and maintainability of plant, machinery, equipment, buildings and structures, with their installation, commissioning, maintenance, modification and replacement, and with feedback of information on design, performance, and costs.

The word terotechnology itself stems from the Greek word *terein*, which means "to look after," "to guard over," or "to take care of." The terotechnology process is summarized in Figure 14.14.

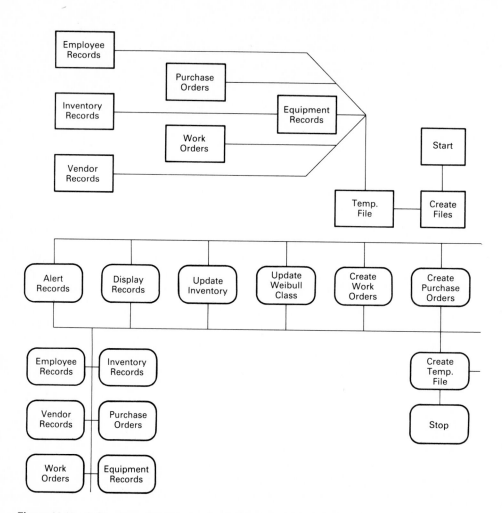

Figure 14.10   A Structure of a Computerized Maintenance System

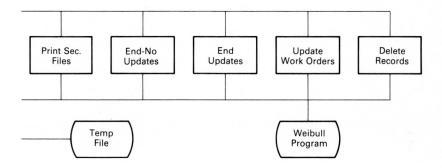

Figure 14.10 (Cont.)

Figure 14.11   A Computerized Weekly Machine Maintenance Schedule

GTR COATED FABRICS COMPANY
TOLEDO DIVISION

RN-M00001   THE WEEKLY MACHINE MAINTENANCE LISTING   3/05/79   PAGE 2

CODE	DESCRIPTION	METHOD	LUBRI-CANT	MAINT FREQ	INSP FREQ	START-ING WEEK
00910 02	GREASE BEARING	GUN	LUX EP2	W		01
00910 03	COUPLING	GUN	LUX EP2	W		01
00992 00	TANK 112					
00992 01	GEAR REDUCER	RES	DTE BB	W		01
00992 02	COUPLING	GUN	LUX EP2	W		01
00992 03	SHAFT BEARING	GUN	LUX EP2	W		01
00993 00	TANK 113					
00992 01	GEAR REDUCER	RES	DTE BB	W		01
00992 02	COUPLING	GUN	LUX EP2	W		01
00992 03	SHAFT BEARING	GUN	LUX EP2	W		01
00994 00	TANK 114					
00992 01	GEAR REDUCER	RES	DTE BB	W		01
00992 02	COUPLING	GUN	LUX EP2	W		01
00992 03	SHAFT BEARING	GUN	LUX EP2	W		01
01010 00	THOR AIR HOIST					
01010 01	GEAR CASE	RES	DTE BB	M		05
01010 02	MISC. OILED PARTS	H.O.	DTE 26	M		05
01010 03	GREASE TROLLEY	GUN	LUX EP2	M		05
01010 04	CRANKCASE	RES	DTE BB	M		05
01020 00	LAB SAMPLE COATING MACHINE					
01020 01	BEARINGS	H.O.	DTE BB	M		05
01030 00	THOR AIR HOIST—2					
01030 01	GEAR CASE	RES	DTE BB	M		05
01030 02	TROLLEY BEARINGS	GUN	LUX EP2	M		05
01040 00	CEILING FAN—2					
01040 01	OILED BEARING	H.O.	DTE BB	M		05
01041 00	CEILING FAN—2					
01041 01	OILED BEARING	H.O.	DTE BB	M		05
01050 00	HOBART MIXER					
01050 01	GEAR CASE	RES	DTE BB	M		05
01050 02	SHAFT BEARING	GUN	LUX EP2	M		05
01050 03	PULLEY BEARINGS	GUN	LUX EP2	M		05
01070 00	THOR AIR HOIST					
01070 01	GEAR CASE	RES	DTE BB	M		05
01070 02	CRANKCASE	RES	DTE BB	M		05
01070 03	MISC. OILED PARTS	H.O.	DTE BB	M		05
01070 04	TROLLEY	GUN	LUX EP2	M		05
01080 00	ARO AIR HOIST IN WASH ROOM					
01080 01	AIR CONTROLS	RES	DTE 26	M		05

Figure 14.12   A Shutdown Notice Generated According to Schedule

---

TO: All Faculty and Staff   Inter-Office

FROM: Becky Wilson   DATE: 1981-04-08

Maintenance Operations Building Check

We have been advised by the Maintenance Department that the main air distribution systems serving Math Science building will be off on the following dates and times. (Please note in your calendar in case you have meetings scheduled for these days, since the offices and conference rooms may become extremely warm.)

Thank you.

Air System Down for Math Science

1. Apr. 14th/82   8:30–4:00 p.m.
2. July 14th/82   "   "
3. Oct. 13th/82   "   "
4. Jan. 12th/83   "   "

If there are any problems with these dates and times, please give me a call at 5689.

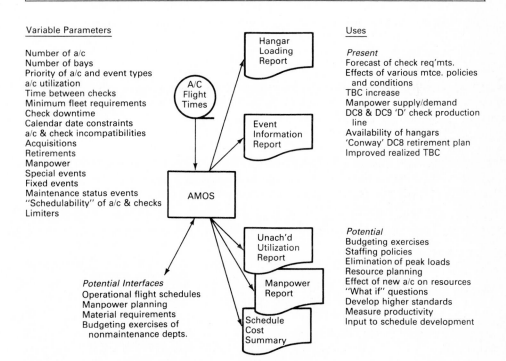

Variable Parameters		Uses

Variable Parameters

Number of a/c
Number of bays
Priority of a/c and event types
a/c utilization
Time between checks
Minimum fleet requirements
Check downtime
Calendar date constraints
a/c & check incompatibilities
Acquisitions
Retirements
Manpower
Special events
Fixed events
Maintenance status events
"Schedulability" of a/c & checks
Limiters

A/C Flight Times

Hangar Loading Report

Event Information Report

AMOS

Unach'd Utilization Report

Manpower Report

Schedule Cost Summary

Potential Interfaces
Operational flight schedules
Manpower planning
Material requirements
Budgeting exercises of
  nonmaintenance depts.

Uses

Present
Forecast of check req'mts.
Effects of various mtce. policies
  and conditions
TBC increase
Manpower supply/demand
DC8 & DC9 'D' check production
  line
Availability of hangars
'Conway' DC8 retirement plan
Improved realized TBC

Potential
Budgeting exercises
Staffing policies
Elimination of peak loads
Resource planning
Effect of new a/c on resources
"What if" questions
Develop higher standards
Measure productivity
Input to schedule development

Figure 14.13   Reports and Decision-Making Aspects of AMOS

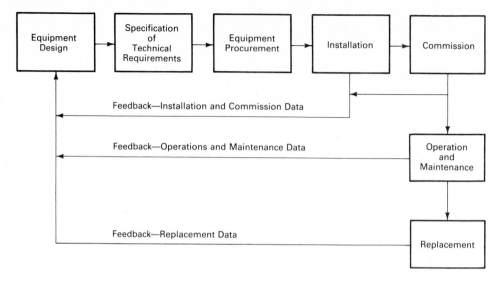

Figure 14.14 The Terotechnology System

Terotechnology, which is concerned with the total life cost of equipment, is based on trade-off notions. For instance, lower equipment investment cost can be offset by higher operating maintenance costs, and vice versa. The main idea in terotechnology is that there should be communication between various stages of the equipment life cycle, providing a formal and consistent flow of information around the system. As seen from Figure 14.14, feedback information about equipment comes to the design stage from all five phases: installation, commissioning, operation, maintenance, and replacement. Under the terotechnology concept, maintenance is perceived as a part of an overall resource management and not as a simple repair function. It is also expected that maintenance managers will be involved in the various phases of the life cycle of machinery and especially in the design phase.

Several successful applications of the terotechnology approach in the British Steel Corporation, British Rails, and Italian and German steel companies are reported in the literature.[5]

SUMMARY

During the last 20 years, operations managers have become increasingly aware of the impact of maintenance operations and production costs. This is due to high equipment and labor costs and extraordinary technical requirements

---

[5] T. M. Husband, *Maintenance Management and Terotechnology*, London, England: Saxon House, 1976.

presented by modern equipment (airplanes, military systems, computers, and other electronic equipment).

The objectives of the maintenance function are to maximize availability of machinery and to preserve the value of the plant at minimum cost. The objectives are translated to specific long- and short-term decisions.

The decisions can be arrived at by using a "rule of thumb" or more sophisticated approaches. The decisions presented in detail in this chapter relate to preventive maintenance and replacement consideration. In this chapter, the importance of the systems approach to maintenance management was indicated, and computerized maintenance concepts were presented.

DISCUSSION QUESTIONS

14.1 What are the objectives of the maintenance function?

14.2 What are the short- and long-term decisions the operations manager has to make in order to achieve these objectives?

14.3 What are the objectives of the organization charts of enterprise and maintenance department?

14.4 Explain why the equipment replacement analysis described in this chapter does not necessarily call for the use of NPV calculations. (NPV has been described in the Technical Note to Chapter 2.)

14.5 Compare and contrast maintenance costs and losses.

14.6 What are the items that lend themselves to preventive maintenance?

14.7 Under what circumstances can preventive maintenance be justified?

14.8 What are the steps involved in justifying a computer for maintenance?

14.9 Describe the basics of terotechnology.

14.10 According to the text, management can be of great help in reducing downtime and increasing equipment performance efficiency. How?

PROBLEMS AND SOLUTIONS

14.1 Mill-Right, Incorporated, has decided to replace the gear of a milling machine without regard to its age. Thus, preventive replacement occur at fixed intervals of time, and failure replacements occur whenever the component fails. Labor and material cost of a preventive or failure replacement is $50. The value of production losses associated with preventive replacement is $100. There is no production loss associated with a preventive replacement. The gear of a milling machine presents a Weibull failure distribution with mean = 200 hours and standard deviation = 10 hours. Determine the optimal preventive replacement interval to minimize total cost per unit of time.

Solution

$$C_p = \$50$$
$$C_e = \$150$$
$$\text{MTBF} = 200$$
$$\sigma = 10$$

$$\frac{C_e}{C_p} = \frac{150}{50} = 30$$

$$\frac{\text{MTBF}}{\sigma} = \frac{200}{10} = 20$$

From Figure 14.8, $z = -2.5$, $t_p = 200 + (-2.5)(10) = 175.00$ hours. Preventive replacement should be done every 175.00 hours.

14.2   Eastern Airlines is operating a terminal system for ticketing. The terminals are considered to be candidates for preventive replacement. Determine the best "block replacement" policy. At constant intervals, t_p, the terminals are to be replaced. The labor and material cost associated with a preventive or failure replacement is $200. The service loss due to preventive replacement is $100, while, for a failure distribution, it is $700. The failure distribution of a terminal can be described adequately by a Weibull distribution with shaping parameter.

$$\beta = 1.5, \text{MTBF} = 150 \text{ hrs.}, \sigma = 15 \text{ hrs.}$$

a) Determine the optimal preventive replacement interval for a terminal.
b) What is the approximate cost of the optimal policy as a percentage of a failure replacement policy?

Solution

$$C_p = 200 + 100 = \$300$$
$$C_e = \$700$$
$$\text{MTBF} = 150 \text{ hours}$$
$$\sigma = 15$$

$$\frac{C_e}{C_p} = \frac{700}{300} = 2.3 \qquad \frac{\text{MTBF}}{\sigma} = \frac{150}{15} = 10$$

a) From Figure 14.8, $z = -2$
   $t_p = \text{MTBF} + (-2)\sigma = 150 + (-2)(15) = 120$ hours
   Preventive replacement should be done every 120 hours.
b) From Figure 14.8, preventive replacement policy costs 55 percent of the replacement-only-at-failure policy.

CHAPTER REVIEW PROBLEMS

14.1   a) What are the objectives of the maintenance function?
        b) What are the factors affecting equipment replacements?
        c) What is the difference between call maintenance and preventive maintenance?

14.2   A word-processor rental company has kept records on the printing element of the system. A goodness-of-fit text on the data revealed a Weibull failure distribution with a mean = 2000 hours, standard deviation of 100 hours, and shape parameter β = 2.5.

    The cost of a preventive replacement of the printing element is $100. The failure replacement cost is $200. An age-based preventive replacement policy is being considered.

a) Determine the optimal preventive replacement interval for an element.

b) What is the approximate percentage cost savings that the policy gives over the replace-only-at-failure policy?

BIBLIOGRAPHY

CHANIN, M. N., *Maintenance Management: Major Problems and Models,* unpublished position paper. New York: The City University of New York, 1978.

CORDER, A. S., *Maintenance Management Techniques.* New York: McGraw-Hill Book Co., 1976.

GLASSER, G. J., "The Age Replacement Problem," *Technometrics,* Vol. 9, No. 1, February, 1967, pp. 83–91.

HOVEY, R. W., and M. M. WAGNER, "A Sample Survey of Industrial Operations Research Activities," *Operations Research,* Vol. VI, No. 6, pp. 876–881.

HUSBAND, T. M., *Maintenance Management and Terotechnology.* London, England: Saxon House, 1976.

JARDIN, A. K. S., "The Use of Mathematical Models in Industrial Maintenance," *The Institute of Mathematics and Its Applications,* August–September, 1976, pp. 232–235.

———, *Maintenance Replacement and Reliability.* New York: John Wiley and Sons, 1973.

JORGENSON, D. W., J. J. McCALL, and R. RADNER, *Optimal Replacement Policy.* Chicago: Rand McNally & Company, 1967.

JUUL, P. T., "The Sad State of Maintenance Management," *Plant Engineering,* February 7, 1977, pp. 125–128.

McCALL, J. J., "Maintenance Policies for Stochastically Failing Equipment: A Survey," *Management Science,* Vol. 11, No. 5, 1965, pp. 493–524.

MENIPAZ, E., "Cost Optimization of Some Stochastic Maintenance Policies," *IEEE Transactions on Reliability,* R28, No. 2, June, 1979, pp. 123–126.

———, "Optimization of Stochastic Maintenance Policies," *European Journal of Operations Research,* Vol. 2, March, 1978, pp. 97–106.

Ministry of Technology, *Study of Engineering Maintenance in Manufacturing Industry.* London, England, 1969.

PIERSKALLA, W., and J. VOELKER, "A Survey of Maintenance Models: The Control and Surveillance of Deteriorating Systems," *Naval Research Logistics Quarterly,* Vol. 23, 1976, pp. 353–388.

RADNER, R., and D. W. Jorgenson, "Optimal Replacement and Inspection of Stochastically Failing Equipment," in *Studies in Applied Probability and Management Science.* Stanford, California: Stanford University Press, 1962, pp. 184–206.

STUART, S. W., "Managing Maintenance: The State of Art," *Plant Engineering,* July, 1974, pp. 27–29.

TURBAN, E., "The Use of Mathematical Models in Plant Maintenance Decision-Making," *Management Science,* Vol. 13, No. 6, 1967, pp. B342–B358.

TECHNICAL NOTE: Waiting Lines

INTRODUCTION

Waiting lines can be termed the most common "social disease" afflicting all of us. How many lines are you part of when you go to a movie theatre? You wait at several stoplights on the way, wait for a parking spot, wait at the ticket office, wait at the popcorn counter, wait at the theatre-hall door, etc. Waiting lines are confronted at the dentist's, the barber shop, the bank, the washroom. Virtually every service one uses forces one to join a line of some sort.

Waiting-lines techniques (sometimes termed queuing theory) are now well established techniques used for many operations-management-related topics. Waiting-lines techniques were first used during the early 1900's for problems encountered by the Copenhagen Telephone Company. Since then waiting-lines techniques have been applied to manufacturing, communications, transportation, and service industries. In service industries, waiting-line theory is used in hospitals, criminal justice systems, banks, and computer operations. In manufacturing industries, waiting-line theory is used to solve problems of machine manning, maintenance operations, parts dispensing in tool cribs, assembly-line balancing (ALB), job-shop scheduling, and inventory control.

Though a number of formulas for solving waiting-line problems will be provided here, the emphasis will be on the structure of waiting-line problems and on practical approaches for the solution of some common waiting-line problems.

THE STRUCTURE OF WAITING LINES

A queuing system (see Figure TN14.1) is composed of the following parts:

The Customers. Customers are defined as those in need of service. Customers can be people, airplanes, machines, or raw materials. The customers are generated from a population or a source. For example, a hospital's "population" consists of the sick requiring hospitalization.

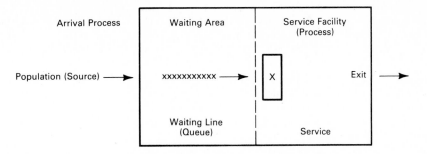

Figure TN14.1 The Major Components of a Queuing System

The Arrival Process.   The frequency with which customers show up at the service facility is called the arrival process.

The Service Facility and the Service Process.   The service is provided by a service facility (e.g., a bank teller, a barber, an airport runway).

The Waiting Line.   Whenever an arriving customer finds that the service facility is busy, a queue, or waiting line, is formed.

In general, the basic problem of the management of waiting lines is: How large should the service facility be? In answering this question, management must consider both the cost of maintaining the service facility and the cost of customers' waiting (lost time, ill will, lost sales, etc.). Unfortunately, these costs are in direct opposition to each other, as is shown in Figure TN14.2. That is, the cost of the facility increases with the size of the facility. The waiting time (and its cost) declines as the size of the facility increases. The problem is to find the size of the service facility that will minimize the total cost.

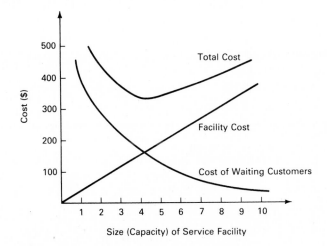

Figure TN14.2 Queuing Systems Costs

COSTS

There are several costs involved in a queuing situation. Let us discuss them.

The Facility Cost.   The cost of operating a service facility includes: cost of construction (capital investment), as expressed by interest and amortization; cost of operation, or labor and materials required for operation; cost of maintenance and repair; and insurance, taxes, rental of space, and other fixed costs.

The Cost of Customers' Waiting.   The cost of waiting time is more difficult to assess. It involves several components. For example a waiting customer may become impatient and leave, resulting in a loss of revenue and possible loss of repeat business due to his or her dissatisfaction. There may also be an "ill-will" cost incurred. A more extreme situation is that of a patient waiting for surgery. If the patient waits too long, he or she may die.

Arrival Process

Arrivals may be either expected or unexpected. In both cases, the arrival process can be described by either the arrival rate (the number of arrivals per unit of time) or by the interarrival times. The difference is that in scheduled arrivals (such as at a dentist's or a hairdresser's) the arrival rates and the interarrival times are constant, whereas in unscheduled arrivals, one talks in terms of averages and frequency distributions.

"Random arrival" is used to describe situations in which, even if the mean number of arrivals in a time period is known, the exact moment of arrival cannot be predicted. Thus, each moment in the time span has the same chance of having an arrival. Such behavior is observed when arrivals are independent of each other—namely, when the arrival time is unaffected by preceding or future arrivals (such as in the case of arrivals to gas stations and toll gates). These random arrivals can be described by the *Poisson distribution.* If the arrival rate follows the Poisson distribution, then the interarrival times are distributed according to the negative exponential distribution.

Arrangements of Service Facilities

Several basic arrangements of service facilities exist:

1. Single facility (such as a dentist's chair)
2. Multiple, parallel, identical facilities (such as a set of pumps in a gasoline station)
3. Multiple, parallel, but not identical facilities (such as express and regular check-out counters in a supermarket)

4. Service facilities that are arranged in a series, the customer entering the first facility and receiving a portion of the service, then moving on to the second facility, and so on, as though he or she were on an assembly line; examples of such an arrangement is a university registration process and a restaurant procedure in which you may wait first for a table, then for food, and finally for the cashier

5. Combinations of the above.

Figure TN14.3 illustrates some of these possible service arrangements. The arrows into the boxes describe arriving and waiting customers, the boxes describe arriving and waiting customers, the boxes describe the service facilities, and the arrows out describe served customers.

Service Process

The service given in a facility consumes time. The length of time of the service may be constant (e.g., exactly five minutes for each service) or it may fluctuate. There are two ways of describing fluctuating service times. One is to describe the

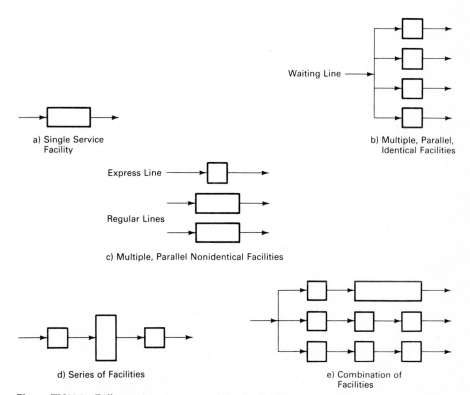

a) Single Service
   Facility

b) Multiple, Parallel,
   Identical Facilities

Waiting Line

Express Line

Regular Lines

c) Multiple, Parallel Nonidentical Facilities

d) Series of Facilities

e) Combination of
   Facilities

Figure TN14.3   Different Arrangements of Service Facilities

average length of the service (e.g., 20 minutes, on the average); the other is to describe the average service rate, or how many customers can be served, on the average, each hour (e.g., four per hour).

A fluctuating service time may follow one of several statistical distributions. Most common is the *negative exponential distribution*. For example, the length of telephone calls is distributed in this fashion. A less common distribution is the normal distribution, such as might be used in describing the time required for repairing a car.

The mean service rate is the inverse of the mean service time. For example, if the average service time is one half of an hour, then the mean service rate is 1 ÷ 1/2 = 2 customers per hour. If the service time is exponentially distributed, then the service rate can be proven to be random and is thus Poisson-distributed.

Waiting Line Formation

A waiting line is formed whenever customers arrive and the facility is busy. The characteristics of the line depend on the arrival process and the service process.

Most of the lines we deal with here have Poisson arrival and negative exponential service. A Poisson-exponential system exhibits the following characteristics:

1. *Arrival rate.*   The arrival rate is assumed to be random and is described by the Poisson distribution. The average arrival rate is designated by A (in many texts the Greek letter lambda, λ, is used).
2. *Service time.*   The service time is assumed to follow the negative exponential distribution. The average service time is designated by $1/S$, where S is the average service rate (in many texts the Greek letter mu, μ, is used instead of S).

The major assumptions for the operation of such a single-server system are:

1. Infinite source or population size
2. First-come, first-served treatment
3. The system is in a steady state (equilibrium) condition
4. The ratio A/S is smaller than 1. This ratio is labeled U (in some texts, the Greek letter rho, ρ, is used). The ratio is a measure of the utilization of the system. If the utilization factor, U, is equal to or larger than 1, the waiting line will increase without bound (will be explosive), a situation that is unacceptable to management.

MATHEMATICAL REPRESENTATION

Let us develop the basic formula for the Poisson arrivals, exponential service, single-facility case when there are infinite waiting-line spaces, infinite population, and a first-come, first-served (FCFS) priority rule.

Each circle in the figure below indicates a state of the waiting-line system. *State* is the number of customers in the system (both waiting and in service).

The system has specific probabilities to be in each state: $P_0, P_1, \ldots, P_n$, $\ldots$. The system moves to a lower state—let us say, state 3 to 2—when service is completed (with intensity S), and moves to a higher state with each arrival (with intensity A). For the system to be in a steady state, one has to make sure that the probability of moving higher equals the probability of moving lower, between each of the states. Thus:

Balance equation at state 0: $AP_0 = SP_1$

Balance equation at state 1: $AP_1 = SP_2$

Balance equation at state 2: $AP_2 = SP_3$

Balance equation at state $n - 1$: $AP_{n-1} = SP_n$

These balance equations are used to calculate the steady-state probabilities of the system in the following manner. The first balance equation can be used to define probability P_1 as a function of A, S, and P_0 (P_0 is the probability that no customers are in the system).

$$SP_1 = AP_0$$

or

$$P_1 = \left(\frac{A}{S}\right) P_0$$

Similarly, the second balance equation can be used to define probability P_2 as a function of A, S, and P_0:

$$P_2 = \left(\frac{A}{S}\right) P_1$$

or

$$P_2 = \left(\frac{A}{S}\right) \left(\frac{A}{S}\right) P_0 = \left(\frac{A}{S}\right)^2 P_0$$

By the same procedures, P_3 is defined as a function of A, S, and P_0:

$$P_3 = \left(\frac{A}{S}\right)^3 P_0$$

In general, it can be shown that probability P_n is

$$P_n = \left(\frac{A}{S}\right)^n P_0$$

The value of P_0 can be defined based on the fundamental probability law that

$$\sum_{n=0}^{\infty} P_n = P_0 + P_1 + P_2 + P_3 + \ldots + P_n + \ldots = 1$$

$$P_1 + \ldots + P_n = 1 - P_0$$

$$\left(\frac{A}{S}\right) P_0 + \ldots + \left(\frac{A}{S}\right)^n P_0 = 1 - P_0$$

$$(P_0) \frac{A/S}{(1 - A/S)} = 1 - P_0$$

$$(1 - A/S)(1 - P_0) = \left(\frac{A}{S}\right) P_0$$

The derivation of P_0 yields

$$P_0 = \left(1 - \frac{A}{S}\right)$$

$$= 1 - U$$

where

$$U = \text{Utilization factor}$$

Now we can substitute into the general expression of P_n:

$$P_n = \left(\frac{A}{S}\right)^n \left(1 - \frac{A}{S}\right) = U^n (1 - U) \text{ for } n = 0, 1, 2, \ldots$$

THE SINGLE-FACILITY WAITING LINE

The single-facility waiting-line system is usually evaluated by one or more of the following measures of performance (given with their respective formulas).[1]

1. The average waiting time, W, is the average time a customer spends in the system—waiting for the service and being served.

$$W = \frac{1}{S - A} \tag{TN14.1}$$

[1] For a complete discussion, consult E. Turban and J. R. Meredith, *Fundamentals of Management Science* (Plano, Texas: Business Publications, Inc., 1981).

2. The average waiting time in the line, W_q, is the average time a customer will wait in the queue before the service starts.

$$W_q = \frac{A}{S(S - A)}$$ (TN14.2)

3. The average number of customers in the system, L, including those in the queue and those being served, is:

$$L = \frac{A}{S - A}$$ (TN14.3)

4. The average number of customers in the queue, L_q, measures the average length of the waiting line.

$$L_q = \frac{A^2}{S(S - A)}$$ (TN14.4)

5. The probability of an empty facility, P_0 is the probability that there are no customers in the system (that the facility is idle)

$$P_0 = 1 - \frac{A}{S}$$ (TN14.5)

6. The probability of having a waiting line, P_w, is the same as the probability of not finding an empty system, i.e.:

$$P_w = 1 - P_0 = \frac{A}{S}$$ (TN14.6)

7. The probability of being in the system (waiting and being served) longer than time t is:

$$P(T > t) = e^{(A - S)t}$$ (TN14.7)

where:

e = 2.718 (the base of the natural logarithm)
t = specified time.
T = time in the system.

8. The probability of finding exactly n customers in the system, P_n, is:

$$P_n = \left(\frac{A}{S}\right)^n \left(1 - \frac{A}{S}\right)$$ (TN14.8)

9. The probability that the number of customers in the system, N, will be larger than a desired number of customers, n: $P(N > n)$, is:

$$P(N > n) = \left(\frac{A}{S}\right)^{n+1}$$ (TN14.9)

Some or all of these measures of performance are computed for the alternative systems under consideration. Then, an evaluation of the overall performance is conducted, as will be shown next.

The following relationships hold for other waiting systems as well:

$$L = AW$$

$$L_q = AW_q$$ (TN14.10)

$$W = W_q + \frac{1}{S}$$

They enable us to find L, L_q, W and W_q if one of these has been found analytically. These relationships hold for other queuing systems as well.

EXAMPLE   The United Bank's deposit counter is staffed by one teller who can serve 24 customers, on the average, each hour. The service times follow a negative exponential distribution. The customers arrive at the counter, at random, one every three minutes, on the average. What are the measures of performance expressed in equations (TN14.1–TN14.10)?

It is necessary first to make the time dimensions of A and S identical, as A was given in minutes, S in hours. We shall use hours as the common denominator.

The problem states that $S = 24$ per hour. The arrival of one customer every three minutes means one customer every 1/20 of an hour. Therefore, the arrival rate, A, is twenty customers per hour. Since $A = 20$ is less than $S = 24$ we are able to proceed.

In all the following formulas we shall use: $A = 20$, $S = 24$.

$$W = \frac{1}{S - A} = \frac{1}{24 - 20} = 0.25 \text{ hours per customer}$$

$$W_q = \frac{A}{S(S - A)} = \frac{20}{24(24 - 20)} = 0.208 \text{ hours per customer}$$

$$L = \frac{A}{S - A} = \frac{20}{24 - 20} = 5 \text{ customers}$$

$$L_q = \frac{A^2}{S(S - A)} = \frac{400}{24(24 - 20)} = 4.17 \text{ customers}$$

$$P_0 = 1 - \frac{A}{S} = 1 - \frac{20}{24} = 0.167$$

$$P_w = \left(\frac{A}{S}\right) = \frac{20}{24} = 0.833$$

If $t = 1/2$,

$$P(T > t) = e^{(20 - 24)1/2} = \frac{1}{e^2} = 0.135$$

The probability of finding four customers in the system, $n = 4$, is:

$$P_4 = \left(\frac{A}{S}\right)^n \left(1 - \frac{A}{S}\right) = \left(\frac{20}{24}\right)^4 \left(1 - \frac{20}{24}\right) = 0.0804$$

The probability of finding more than three customers in the system is:

$$P(N > 3) = \left(\frac{A}{S}\right)^{n+1} = \left(\frac{20}{24}\right)^4 = 0.482$$

In the following example, it will be shown how to use such measures of effectiveness in a comparative analysis.

MULTICHANNEL WAITING LINES

A multichannel (or multiserver) waiting-line system is composed of several identical and parallel service facilities. Such a situation is depicted in Figure TN14.4. Note that only one waiting line, which feeds the multiple service facilities, exists. Whenever a server is free, the first customer in the queue goes to that service facility. An example of such a situation is in the bakery, where arrivals receive a number as they arrive, and then the numbers are called sequentially as servers become free.

There are several managerial problems in a multichannel system. For example, management is concerned with determining the proper number of servers, with whether to use identical or nonidentical servers (e.g., whether or not to open a "residents only" counter in the passport control at an international airport), and with the organization of the waiting line (one line for all servers, one line per server). Such decisions are based on the computation of the measures of effectiveness.

In this section, the simplest multiserver system is analyzed. The assumptions are made that there exist:

1. A Poisson-exponential system, as described earlier
2. Identical service facilities
3. One waiting line.

Let:

K = Number of servers (service facilities)
U = Utilization factor of one server. $U = A/S$, as in the single facility system.
$\bar{U}$ = Utilization factor of the entire system.

$$\bar{U} = \frac{U}{K} = \frac{A}{KS} \tag{TN14.11}$$

Assuming that $A < KS$, then some of the most common measures of effectiveness are:

The probability of finding no customers in the system (an "idle" system):

$$P_0 = \frac{1}{\dfrac{U^K}{K!(1 - \bar{U})} + \displaystyle\sum_{i=0}^{K-1} \dfrac{U^i}{i!}} \tag{TN14.12}$$

where i = index of summation.

The probability of finding exactly n customers in the system is:

$$P_n = P_0 \frac{U^n}{n!} \qquad\qquad \text{when } n \leq k$$

and

$$P_n = \frac{P_0 \bar{U}^n K^K}{K!} \qquad\qquad \text{when } n \geq k \tag{TN14.13}$$

The average number of customers in the waiting line:

$$L_q = \frac{P_0 U^K \bar{U}}{K!(1 - \bar{U})^2} \text{ or } P_0 = \frac{L_q K!(1 - \bar{U})^2}{U^K \bar{U}} \tag{TN14.14}$$

The average number of customers in the system is:

$$L = L_q + U \tag{TN14.15}$$

The average waiting time per customer, before service is:

$$W_q = \frac{L_q}{A} \tag{TN14.16}$$

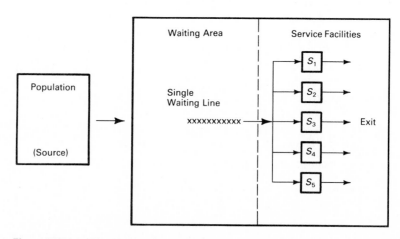

Figure TN14.4 The Multichannel Waiting Line System

The average time a customer spends in the system (waiting and service) is:

$$W = \frac{L}{A} = W_q + \frac{1}{S} \qquad \text{(TN14.17)}$$

The average number of working service facilities (or customers being served) is:

$$\bar{K} = \begin{cases} U & U < K \\ \text{if} & \\ K & U \ge K \end{cases} \qquad \text{(TN14.18)}$$

In order to save computational time in applying equations (TN14.11) to (TN14.18), a graphical equivalent can be used. Figure TN14.5 is a graph of Equation (TN14.14) in terms of various values of K, A, and S. For example, given: $K = 5$, $A = 36$, and $S = 10$, then $A/S = 36/10 = 3.6$, and L_q is found to be about 1.0 at the intersection of the curve $K = 5$ with $A/S = 3.6$ (point Y in Figure TN14.5). Once the value of L_q is found, related variables, such as L, W, and W_q can be derived using equations (TN14.15), (TN14.16), and (TN14.17).

FINITE POPULATION WAITING LINES

In all waiting-line situations discussed thus far, an infinite population source was assumed. However, in some real-life situations, the number of customers is

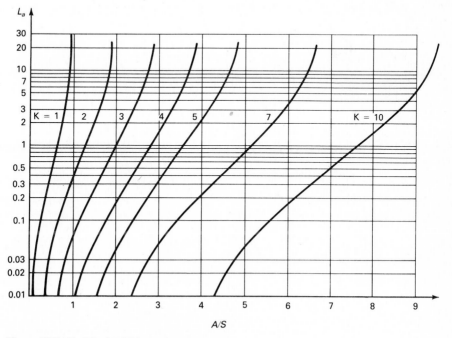

Figure TN14.5   The Multichannel Waiting Line

small and cannot be considered infinite. For example, there may be only nine production employees who come to a tool crib; or there may be only 15 airplanes arriving at a small airport each day. Another very common situation is the so-called machine repair problem:

Companies often have maintenance teams whose primary function is to repair certain machines used for production when these break down. For instance, there may be one service person and five bottling machines. Another example is that of a production employee who supervises 15 textile machines. In such cases, the machines are viewed as the "customers" that require service.

Finite Population with a Single Server

Let M denote the finite number of customers in the source, and A denote each (identical) customer's individual arrival rate (not the arrival rate for the group of all M customers). The basic formulas, assuming a Poisson-exponential system, are:

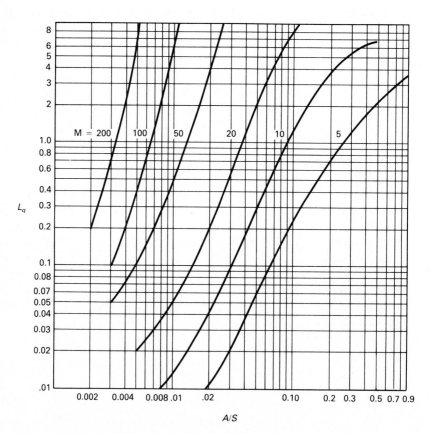

Figure TN14.6   The Single-Server Finite Population Waiting Line

$$P_0 = 1 \bigg/ \sum_{i=0}^{M} \left[\frac{M!}{(M-i)!} \left(\frac{A}{S} \right)^i \right] \qquad \text{(TN14.19)}$$

where i = summation index.

$$P_n = P_0 \left(\frac{A}{S} \right)^n \frac{M!}{(M-n)!} \qquad \text{(TN14.20)}$$

$$L_q = M - \frac{A+S}{A}(1-P_0) \qquad \text{or} \qquad P_0 = \frac{A(L_q - M) + A + S}{A+S} \qquad \text{(TN14.21)}$$

$$L = L_q + (1 - P_0) \qquad \text{(TN14.22)}$$

$$W_q = \frac{L_q}{S(1-P_0)} \qquad \text{(TN14.23)}$$

$$W = W_q + \frac{1}{S} \qquad \text{(TN14.24)}$$

Figure TN14.6 may be used to identify L_q; then, equation TN14.21 may be used to find P_0.

Finite Population with Multiple Servers

Figures TN14.7 and TN14.8 give the results for five servers, $K = 5$, and ten servers, $K = 10$. Equations (TN14.22) to (TN14.24) are applicable here, as well.

WAITING LINE WITH A MAXIMUM LINE LENGTH

In all the previous situations, no limits were set on the size of the waiting line. In the real world, however, there are many situations in which the storage capacity of the waiting line is limited. For example, at gas stations there is only so much room for cars to wait. Another example is a parking lot, which has limited capacity. Any customers who arrive while the waiting area is full must leave the system permanently without being served.

Let the maximum capacity of the system (including both the waiting line and the customers who are being served) be designated by T. Again, a Poisson-exponential system is assumed.

The relevant equations for the single-server ($K = 1$) case are:

$$P_0 = \frac{1-U}{1-U^{T+1}} \qquad \text{(TN14.25)}$$

$$P_n = P_0 U^n \qquad \text{(TN14.26)}$$

$$L_q = \frac{U}{1-U} \frac{TU^{T+1} + U}{1 - U^{T+1}} \qquad \text{(TN14.27)}$$

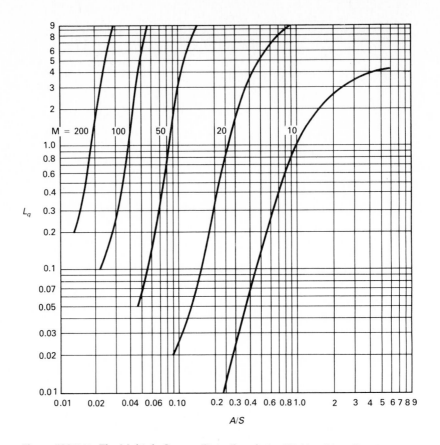

Figure TN14.7 The Multiple-Servers Finite Population Waiting Line: $K = 5$

The values of L, W_q, and W are the same as those given by equations (TN14.22) to (TN14.24). Figure TN14.9 is the graph of equation (TN14.27), for various values of T. The figure can also be used to find L_q for multiple servers ($K = 5$ and $K = 10$).

WAITING LINES WITH A CONSTANT SERVICE TIME AND POISSON ARRIVALS

In some situations, the service time can be considered constant. For example, automated servers, such as vending machines, perform service at essentially a constant rate. Also, human beings servicing nonhuman customers (example: an "oil change" on a car) frequently perform at an approximately constant rate.

The measures of performance for a single-server system with Poisson (random) arrivals and a constant service time, assuming all the other assumptions of a Poisson-exponential system, are given below.

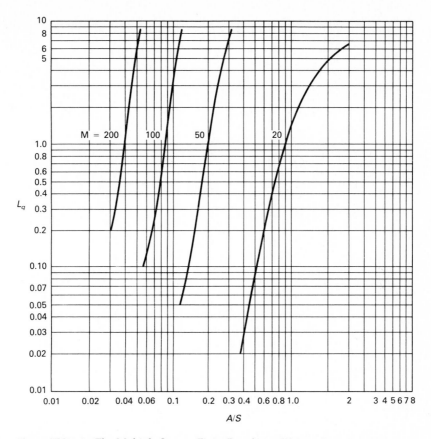

Figure TN14.8   The Multiple-Servers Finite Population Waiting Line: $K = 10$

The Single-Server Case

$$L_q = \frac{A^2}{2S(S - A)} \tag{TN14.28}$$

Note that this value is exactly one half of the value of L_q for a negative exponential service time, as expressed in equation (TN14.4). The equations for P_0, L, W_q, and W are:

$$P_0 = 1 - \frac{A}{S} \tag{TN14.29}$$

$$L = L_q + U = \frac{2AS - A^2}{2S(S-A)} \tag{TN14.30}$$

$$W_q = L_q/A = \frac{A}{2S(S - A)} \tag{TN14.31}$$

$$W = L/A = \frac{2S - A}{2S(S - A)} \tag{TN14.32}$$

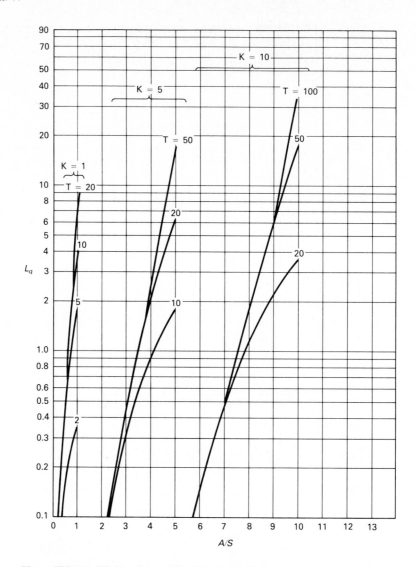

Figure TN14.9 Waiting Line with a Maximum Line

Figure TN14.10 presents the values of L_q corresponding to equation (TN14.28) (use the value $K = 1$).

The Multiple-Servers Case

This situation is considerably more complex than the negative exponential case; therefore, formulas are not given here. Figure TN14.10 depicts the values of L_q for both single and multiple servers (K = number of servers).

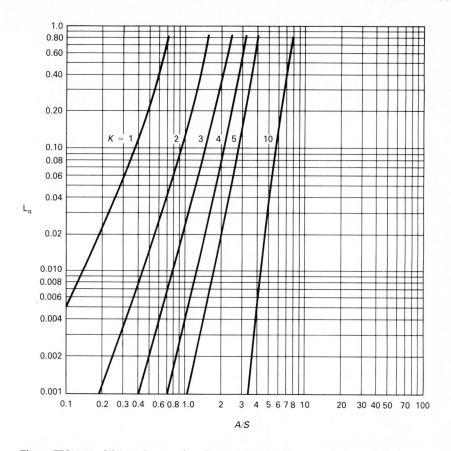

Figure TN14.10   Waiting Line with a Constant Service Time and Poisson Arrival

SERIAL WAITING LINES

In certain service situations, a customer or a product receives service at a number of stations. The customer (product) moves from station to station and possibly from queue to queue. Under certain assumptions, such a process may be analyzed rather easily. Multiple servers may even be included in the process.

The necessary assumptions are as follows. First, the source is infinite and the queues in each station are not limited in length. Second, in case of multiple servers within each station, all servers must have the same exponential service time distribution. Third, the customers at the first station arrive randomly (Poisson assumed). Finally, $A < KS$ at every station (where $K =$ number of servers), so that an explosive queue is not formed somewhere in the system. Under the above assumptions, the output from each station will also be Poisson, with the average rate A. Since each station has Poisson arrivals, it may be treated independently of the others and Figure TN14.5 can be used for computing the measures of performance throughout the entire process. (See problem TN14.7).

SUMMARY

The waiting line is a very important component in operations. Some waiting lines are planned for and actually help smooth out operations by being used as a buffer (for example, in process inventory between successive production stages). Other waiting lines are imposed on the customer and should be kept to a minimum if possible (for example, a waiting line of depositors in the bank). This technical note has suggested several cases of waiting lines and a method to determine the waiting time as a function of the operationsl characteristics of an operating system. The manager has to choose the system that balances the cost of the operating system design and the cost involved in waiting.

TECHNICAL NOTE PROBLEMS

14.1 What are the components of a queuing system?

14.2 Give three examples of waiting lines. Identify the components of the queuing system in each example.

14.3 What are the costs involved in a queuing situation?

14.4 What are the basic arrangements of service facilities?

14.5 What are the characteristics of a Poisson-exponential system?

14.6 What is the physical meaning of the utilization factor?

14.7 A university registration system consists of a three station process with Poisson arrival A = 5/hour, and exponential service in each station, where the first station has one server and S_1 = 6. The second station has three servers and S_2 = 2. The third station has two servers and S_3 = 4. What is the waiting time before entering the stations?

Solution
For station 1, A = 5/hour, S_1 = 6/hour, and K = 1. Thus, A/S_1 = 5/6 = 0.833. According to Figure TN14.5, L_{q_1} = 4.5. According to equation (TN14.10),

$$W_{q_1} \frac{L_{q_1}}{A} = \frac{4.5}{5} = 0.90 \text{ hours}$$

For station 2, A = 5/hour, S_2 = 2/hour, and K = 3. Thus, A/S_2 = 5/2 = 2.5. According to Figure TN14.5, L_{q_2} = 3.6. According to equation (TN14.10),

$$W_{q_2} \frac{L_{q_2}}{A} = \frac{3.6}{5} = 0.72 \text{ hours}$$

For station 3, A = 5/hour, S_3 = 4/hour, and K = 2. Thus, A/S_3 = 5/4 = 1.25. According to Figure TN14.5, L_{q_3} = 0.8. According to equation (TN14.10),

$$W_{q_3} \frac{L_{q_3}}{A} = \frac{8}{5} = 0.16 \text{ hours}$$

The total waiting time in the process is:
$$0.90 + 0.72 + 0.16 = 1.78 \text{ hours}$$

14.8 Each of the lawyers Mr. Honest and Mr. Straight has a Xerox machine that can produce copies at the average rate of four per hour. Each uses a machine at the rate of three per hour. Should they pool the use of the two Xerox machines?

Solution
Since the objective is to get the Xeroxed material as fast as possible, let us compare W. If each uses his own machine:
$$A = 3/\text{hour}, \ S = 4/\text{hour}$$

$$W = \frac{1}{S - A} = \frac{1}{4 - 3} = 1 \text{ hour}$$

If they pool the use of the machines:
$A = 6/\text{hour}$, $S = 4/\text{hour}$, $K = 2$, $A/S = 6/4 = 1.5$. According to Figure TN14.5, for $A/S = 1.5$, $L_q = 2$. According to equation (TN14.10)

$$W_q = \frac{L_q}{A} = \frac{2}{6} = 1/3 \text{ hour}$$

As well,

$$W = W_q + \frac{1}{S} = \frac{1}{3} + \frac{1}{4} = \frac{7}{12} \text{ hour}$$

Since 7/12 hour is less than 1 hour, they should pool the use of the Xerox machines.

14.9 Southern Seas Company has a forklift truck that loads trucks at a rate of four per hour. An hour of forklift truck operation costs $100. The trucks arrive at an average rate of three per hour. An hour of waiting time for the truck costs $160. Determine the number of forklifts that should be used.

14.10 A gas station has one attendant. The attendant can serve 30 customers/hour. Only five cars can be in the station. Cars arrival rate is 20/hour. Determine:
a) The probability of finding the station empty
b) The average number of cars in the line
c) The average waiting time in line
d) The probability of finding three cars in the station.

14.11 An assembly line consists of four work stations. Arrival rate of units that should be assembled is 1.5/hour during an eight-hour day. The first work station has 2 workers; each can work on 7 units during an eight-hour day. The second work station has one worker who can work on 15 units during an eight-hour day. The third work station has 5 workers; each can work on 3 units during an eight-hour day. The fourth work station has 3 workers; each can work on 4.5 units during an eight-hour day.
a) Determine the average time for assembly of a unit from arrival until completion.
b) Determine the average waiting time throughout the whole assembly line.
c) If the cost of a worker is $12/hour, and unit working time costs $2/hour, where would you recommend adding another worker?

BIBLIOGRAPHY

BOLLING, W. B., "Queueing Model of a Hospital Emergency Room," *Industrial Engineering*, Vol. 4, September, 1972, p. 26.

COOPER, J. K., AND T. M. CORCORAN, "Estimating Bed Needs by Means of Queueing Theory," *New England Journal of Medicine*, Vol. 291, 1974, pp. 404–405.

DRISCOLL, M. F., AND N. A. WEISS, "An Application of Queueing Theory to Reservation Networks," *Management Science*, Vol. 22, Jan., 1976, pp. 540–46.

FOOTE, B. L., "A Queueing Case Study of Drive-In Banking," *Interfaces*, Vol. 6, August, 1976, pp. 31–37.

GUPTA, J., J. ZAREDA, AND N. KRAMER, "Hospital Manpower Planning by Use of Queueing Theory," *Health Services Research*, Vol. 6, 1971.

HARRIS, C. M., AND T. R. THIAGARAJAN, "Queueing Models of Community Correctional Centers in the District of Columbia," *Management Science*, Vol. 22, October, 1975, pp. 167–71.

HILLIER, F. S., AND G. J. LIEBERMAN, *Introduction to Operations Research* (2nd ed.), San Francisco: Holden Day, 1974.

KELLER, T. F., AND D. J. LAUGHHUNN, "An Application of Queueing Theory to a Congestion Problem in an Outpatient Clinic," *Decision Sciences*, Vol. 4, July, 1973, pp. 379–93.

KLEINROCK, L., *Queueing Systems, Volume 2: Computer Applications*, New York: John Wiley & Sons, 1976.

KOLESAR, P. J., ET AL, "A Queueing-Linear Programming Approach to Scheduling Police Patrol Cars," *Operations Research*, Vol. 23, Nov., 1975, pp. 1045–62.

PECK, L. G., AND R. N. HAZELWOOD, *Finite Queuing Tables*. New York: John Wiley & Sons, 1958.

ROSENSHINE, M., "Queueing Theory: The State of the Art," *AIIE Transactions*, Vol. 7, September, 1975.

TURBAN, E., AND J. R. MEREDITH, *Fundamentals of Management Science* (revised edition). Dallas, Texas: Business Publications, Inc., 1981.

15

Enhancing Productivity: Putting the Essentials to Work

INTRODUCTION

This book presents the essentials of operations management. As such, it touches upon the various elements, or subsystems, of operating organizations.

The operations manager brings together and employs various resources and skills. He or she designs and plans the system, organizes it, and controls it, using the various techniques that are treated in this book.

The systems approach is an important part of production/operations management. While earlier in the 20th century, detailed *analysis* of elements and subsystems is a necessary part of production/operations management today. Only when the operations manager understands the overall functioning of the organization is it possible to attain the total organization's goals and objectives.

PRODUCTIVITY AND PRODUCTION/OPERATIONS MANAGEMENT

By definition, *productivity is the ratio of the quantity of goods or services produced or turned out, to the quantity of resources employed in turning out these goods or services.* The Western world is facing a severe problem of productivity. There are numerous indications that this problem is being recognized by government, the business sector, and the unions. The U.S. Government recently passed a bill recommending the establishment of a Productivity

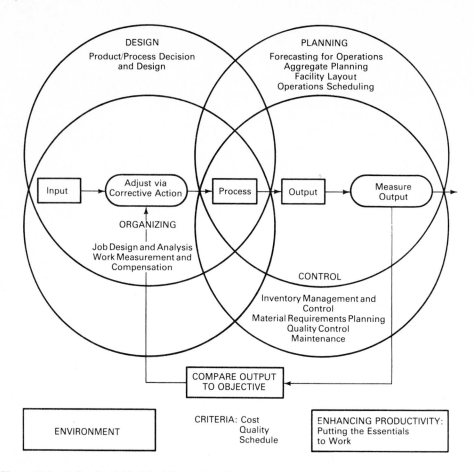

Figure 15.1   A Graphical Model of Operations Management

Center, reflecting the growing concern over the topic. Meanwhile, the government is sponsoring research into the various aspects of productivity and how to enhance it. Numerous companies are undertaking productivity improvement programs. The American Institute of Industrial Engineers, as well as other institutions, is sponsoring productivity programs and conferences. The World Confederation of Productivity Science, an international organization, has evolved out of a desire among businessmen and colleagues of various societies in many countries to share their knowledge and experience. Other productivity institutes, such as the American Productivity Center, based in Houston, Texas, have been sponsored by various businesses.

The following quotation[1] deals with some of the causes for falling productivity in the U.S. coal and steel industries:

[1] *Newsweek*, September 8, 1980, p. 55.

FIGURE 15.2 LONG-TERM RATE OF
GROWTH IN PRODUCTIVITY IS
FALLING IN INDUSTRIALIZED
NATIONS

	1963–66	1967–73	1973–82
Canada	4.3	4.9	2.8
Japan	8.5	10.0	4.2
Italy	7.3	6.6	3.3
W. Germany	5.8	5.0	5.0
U.K.	4.1	3.8	0.8
U.S.	4.2	2.9	2.1

Productivity: Percent change annually.

One was the energy source that fueled America's industrial revolution, the other the basic product that seemed to give it physical shape. Now, both coal and steel are in deep trouble—victims of slow or declining productivity. Over the past decade, productivity in the nation's coal mines has plunged at an average rate of 3.6 percent a year as the average miner's daily output dropped from 19.9 tons to 13.5 tons. The steel business has done only slightly better: production in recession-scarred 1980 will be no more than it was in 1963. President Thomas C. Graham of Jones & Lauglin Steel Corp. is hardly sanguine about the prospects. "It's an open question," he says candidly, "whether this industry will survive."

The causes for the decrease in productivity can be listed as follows:

1. Higher wages, relative to other industries
2. Old technologies (e.g. open-hearth steel-making, a batch process, as opposed to the continuous-casting process)
3. Higher expenses for pollution-control equipment
4. More service and staff personnel employed by the industry in order to comply with health and safety legislation
5. Higher costs of energy
6. Federal and state laws governing landscaping
7. High strike rate.

In part, the steel industry's problems are rooted in its historic importance to the U.S. economy. Over the years, several administrations have feared that long steel strikes would have disastrous rippling effects through the rest of the industrial base, and political jawboning often undercut management efforts to resist wage increases demanded by the United Steelworkers of America. "For three consecutive settlements, the steel contract was literally reached at the White House," recalls U.S. Steel Corp. chairman David M. Roderick.

The result is that steelworkers are among the nation's industrial elite: their wages and benefits average $18.90 an hour, compared with $7.28 for the average factory worker. Japanese steelworkers, in contrast, cost their companies an average of $9.20 an hour—and the gap helps explain why Tokyo's steel giants can produce their product $70 a ton cheaper than can American firms. But high wage costs in the U.S. mills are only part of the story. Perhaps more important is the inattention of Pittsburgh to state-of-the-art technology. Open-hearth steel-making—a turn-of-the-century process—still accounts for 15 percent of U.S. output; the Japanese have no open hearths at all. Similarly, the Japanese use the "continuous-casting" process to convert 50 percent of their steel production directly into semifinished forms, bypassing the intermediate step of making ingots; American companies use continuous casters on less than 20 percent of output. U.S. Steel executives defend their workers, saying they produce just as much metal in an hour as do their counterparts overseas. "I do not believe the Japanese steelworker is a superman," says Roderick. "[But] you can't win a race if the opponent's in a Mercedes SL and you put your guy in a Model T Ford."

Steelmen argue that huge outlays for pollution-control equipment mandated by Washington have cut sharply into capital available for new technology. To catch up, they estimate, the industry must spend $5 billion a year over the next decade on new plants and equipment. Even with all their problems, the U.S. steel companies maintain that they could compete at home with imported steel if the Japanese and other foreign producers did not "dump" output at prices below their actual production costs. Foreign producers deny that they do engage in such dumping, and the issue probably will not be resolved until a formal legal action—pressed by U.S. Steel and now in the courts—is adjudicated.

Productivity in the nation's coal mines began to fall after Congress passed the landmark Coal Mine Health and Safety Act in 1969. "Disasters in the mines now are rare," says vice president Morris Feibusch of the Bituminous Coal Operators' Association. However, productivity has suffered. State and federal laws requiring strip miners to return stripped areas to nearly their original shape have had the same effect. And a series of wildcat strikes in the Eastern mines in the mid-1970's also reduced efficiency. In the meantime, there have been few offsetting breakthroughs in mining technology: the last major improvement, the "continuous miner," was introduced 20 years ago.

Both coal and steel executives have a hunch that the worst may be over. Steel officials are optimistic that the government will prohibit dumping and help finance equipment purchases by writing faster depreciation schedules into the tax code—and the steelworker's union has been sympathetic to the industry's efforts to promote efficiency, even if it means the loss of jobs. Productivity in the older Eastern and Midwestern coal mines actually went up by 10 percent in the first four months of this year, and should improve countrywide in the long term as companies increase exports and open new Western strip mines with seams of coal ten to twenty times as thick as those east of the Mississippi River. If both basic industries turn around, the entire U.S. productivity picture will suddenly look a lot better.

Obviously there are reasons for falling productivity other than those we have already suggested: one is *inflation,* which has had a profound impact on investment, and, thus, on productivity. Inflation has hurt investment by constantly increasing the rates of return that the operating organization must receive in order to stay even with rising prices. With the recent low percentage of GNP for investment (3% for 1982), businesses are not able to upgrade equipment, and are working with outdated technology. This has hurt productivity.

During the last several years every one of the factors affecting productivity has gone through major changes: more militant unions, erratic energy costs, higher price of raw materials, decreased amounts of capital due to extremely high interest rates followed by a recession, etc. It seems that all these factors are beyond our control. They are part of the *environment,* and include the uncontrollable variables we dealt with in Chapter 1.

This book suggests yet another way of affecting productivity: through *planning the best interaction of the factors of production,* otherwise termed the systematic industrial development approach (SIDA). Even though each factor by itself is uncontrollable, the interaction of factors can still be planned in an optimal fashion. This is one of the essential messages of this book. The essence of the production and operations management approach is the control of the interaction of factors in order to assure high productivity.

MEASURING PRODUCTIVITY

Productivity can be measured in different ways. For example, a hospital may use the following measure of productivity:

$$\text{Productivity} = \frac{\text{Patients} \times \text{Beds} \times \text{Days}}{\text{Staff hours}}$$

This measure of productivity is good, provided that management does not consider prolonging the length of stay of the patients in the hospital or putting two patients in one bed to increase productivity (by 100 percent!).

An oil company might use the following productivity measure:

$$\text{Productivity} = \frac{\text{Total sales of barrels of oil}}{\text{Sales expense}}$$

While the term efficiency for physical systems pertains to a value which is less than one, the ratio for economic organizations *should* be greater than one in order that the organization be able to survive. This ratio, termed productivity, can be measured in terms of ratio of output to input of labor, capital, materials, energy, or a combination of these.

The *productivity index* is the ratio of the current productivity to the productivity during a base period. This index describes productivity growth or decrease.

Throughout the book we have stressed the common characteristics of manufacturing and service organizations. The comparable productivity measures are as follows. For a manufacturing organization, the productivity measure is expressed as:

$$\text{Productivity} = \frac{\text{Net annual sales}}{\text{Number of employees} + \dfrac{\text{Capital outlay}}{\text{Average annual earnings per employee}}}$$

EXAMPLE   A company invested $5 million in a new machine with 5 year straight-line depreciation. By the end of the year, net sales were up to $50,000. Fifty employees were employed and they earned, on the average, $15,000.

$$\text{Productivity} = \frac{50,000}{\dfrac{50 + (5,000,000/5)}{15,000}} = 428.56$$

Obviously, this productivity number does not mean much unless it is compared to that of some base year or the preceding period.

Service organizations may use the value-added approach. Value added is the increase in net worth of the object of production due to the service performed.

$$\text{Productivity} = \frac{\text{Annual value added}}{\text{Number of employees}}$$

EXAMPLE   A company that specializes in coating petroleum and gas pipelines prior to installation is charging $100 per pipeline coated. The pipes are shipped in, coated, and shipped out. The company processed 10,000 pipes last year, using 50 employees.

$$\text{Productivity} = \frac{100 \times 10,000}{50} = 20,000$$

The productivity measure is usually related to the base year value, in order to cancel the effect of inflation on the comparison of two consecutive periods. The base year productivity measure is assigned the value of 100, and all other productivity measure periods are related to the base year.

As can be seen from the examples above, high productivity measures are affected by the functions performed by operations management. There are other measures of a project's productivity that have been covered in this book. These measures include quality consideration, and are described in detail in Chapter 4.

PRODUCTIVITY IMPROVEMENT AND SYSTEMATIC INDUSTRIAL DEVELOPMENT APPROACH

Each of the chapters of this book provides an insight into some function of the operations manager. Specifically, the methods of analysis provided in each chapter help P/OM to understand the functional area and, thus, to improve its productivity.

Generally speaking, the evaluation of the operating system should follow the functions covered in this book. The order of functions studies can follow the steps of the operations, from receiving to shipping. A service operation, such as a hospital, should be analyzed from patient admission to patient release stages.

The following is a representative list of the order in which productivity analysis and improvement should be conducted:

Manufacturing Organization

Receiving
Storage/inventory
Product/process planning
Job design and methods
Job standards
Layout
Production control
Finished goods storage
Shipping
Equipment maintenance

Service Organization

Admission
Waiting arrangement
Service/process
Planning
Work design and methods
Job standards
Layout
Operation control
(Completed service
cannot be stored)
Process maintenance

The productivity analysis and improvement of equipment, personnel, and processes should involve the following steps:

1. Problem identification through a plant tour, employee suggestions, or earlier observation of data
2. Problem-scope determination
3. Objectives establishment, which includes the basis for the evaluation and solution (e.g. if a reduction in the percentage of late job releases is required, the magnitude of the percentage reduction should be specified)
4. Problem definition
5. Data determination
6. Work plan and schedule determination for data collection; it is important to have a definite schedule that will facilitate consultation and delegation
7. Data collection
8. Data reduction, which results in information that could serve as a basis for changes and improvement; various tools that may be used are: bills of materials, assembly charts, operation charts, process charts, flow diagrams, activity charts, man-machine charts, and linear programming, waiting lines, and other quantitative tools
9. Improvement recommendations
10. Justification preparation; use economic measures similar to the ones covered in the Technical Note of Chapter 3; the examination should be followed by an approval implementation and follow-up steps
11. Approval granting
12. Preparation of a procedure for implementation
13. Installation
14. Follow-up evaluation.

Many problems can be recognized through well-evidenced symptoms, such as: idle or overworked personnel and equipment, high in-process inventories, frequent breakdowns, poor quality, congested areas, high accident rate, and unpleasant working conditions. One should remember that most problems are not necessarily equipment related *or* personnel related. The systems approach should be used, as all factors (labor, raw material, capital, energy) should be coordinated to facilitate productivity improvement.

THE SYSTEM APPROACH TO OPERATIONS MANAGEMENT

This book presents a cybernetic overview of operations management systems. That is to say, the system is viewed as a feedback mechanism (as in Figure 15.1). Resources are brought together and employed by the operations manager. The operations manager is responsible for designing and planning the system, organizing it, and controlling it. The more effort invested in design, planning, and organizing, the less effort is needed to control the operations.

It should be noted, however, that the systems approach is still at an early stage of development. Thus, synthesis should be preceded by analysis—that is, the operations manager should first be familiar with the procedures of layout, scheduling, and quality control, etc. Once these problems have been solved, the interrelationships between subsystems (functions) are to be accounted for.

PEOPLE AND PRODUCTIVITY

As was stated earlier, many factors contribute to productivity: producible designs, superior tools, clever processes, minimal regulations, etc. Heading the list is *people*. Most of us are aware of the impressive productivity improvements Japanese companies have realized with their people by using teams of cooperating workers, called quality circles. Hundreds of American companies now are duplicating these efforts in their factories.

For example, over a decade ago Motorola initiated a plan, called the participative management program (PMP), that reaches beyond the factory floor. This program has helped achieve the same (and often better) quality and productivity results as those for which Japanese companies receive credit.

PMP is an effective way to get the individual worker more involved, and make him or her more responsible, informed, and, therefore, more productive. Any individual worker can suggest things about any job he or she does that a supervisor may not know as well. As management listens and acts, quality and output rise. In PMP, teams of employees meet frequently, sometimes daily, among themselves and with support groups, to tackle the basics. Everyone is encouraged to define problems and suggest solutions. The management listens, contributes, and acts. Each team operates to high, published standards that it participates in setting. The teams measure their improving performance relative to these standards daily, weekly, and monthly.

Employees who want to can communicate additionally by submitting written recommendations. These are posted prominently on bulletin boards and must be answered within 72 hours, and not merely with words, but with changes in tools, procedures, or policies, when possible. The results have been dramatic. Quality, output, and customer service are much higher. Costs are down, and jobs have become more satisfying.

One third of Motorola's U.S. employees were operating under PMP in 1980. Building on years of experience, the balance of Motorola's U.S. operations are now fully managed through employee participation.

SERVICES AND OPERATIONS MANAGEMENT

As Western civilization develops, more and more people are employed in service industries, and the larger share of the gross national product is generated by these industries. Insurance companies, research laboratories, social services, restaurants, governments, universities, motels, transportation, communication—all are expanding. The field of operations management extends to service

"Well, I, for one, do not think you are a bunch of dumb clucks. I find you exceptional Rhode Island Reds, excellent layers, doing an outstanding job in a highly competitive field."

Figure 15.3 Producible Designs, Superior Tools, Clever Processes, and Minimal Regulations Are Necessary But Not Sufficient Conditions for High Productivity *Source: Datamation,* September, 1980, p. 208.

operations, as well as to manufacturing operations. Involved in the production of goals services is the use of techniques (that traditionally have been used by manufacturing managers) to solve problems in the context of the service industry.

It should be understood that what sets the service industry apart from the manufacturing industry, with respect to operations managers, is *the extent to which the ultimate customer of the service or product is in direct contact with the operating system.* If a service can be provided in the absence of a customer, the service operating system can operate according to traditional manufacturing management concepts.

We can develop three categories of service systems. The first category is the "high-contact service." In this kind of service, the customer is in continuous and intensive contact with the service organization (e.g., movie theatres, hospitals, hotels, shoe-polish stands, jails, schools, restaurants). Such services only seldom resemble traditional manufacturing systems, and thus do not lend themselves easily to assembly-line techniques.

The second category is the "medium-contact service." In this kind of service, the customer is in contact with the service organization for some time (e.g., bank branches, legal-aid offices, real-estate companies, emergency services). These services can be subjected on a limited basis to traditional manufacturing practices.

The third category is the "low contact service." In this kind of service, the customer has no contact or almost no contact with the service system (e.g., head offices, central government agencies, wholesale institutions, mail order services). These services are quasi-manufacturing, and all techniques presented in this book can be applied to the analysis, design, planning, organizing, and control of such services.

RESOURCE MANAGEMENT APPROACH

As employment in service industries and wholesale-retail has increased, employment in the manufacturing industry has decreased. More and more attention has also been given to resources—their deployment, their conservation, and their efficient and effective use.

This suggests a major change of philosophy with regard to operations management. Whereas organizations are extensively different with regard to resources, all use space and equipment, tools, materials, people, information, and energy. Furthermore, traditional manufacturing practices were concerned with production, or *output*. Resources, people, tools, space, and equipment, were readily available at relatively low cost. However, now, resources are becoming extremely expensive. Energy costs soar, blue-collar employees earn $15,000 or more, and a numerically controlled machine costs several million dollars. Thus, the operations manager should focus his attention on resources. For example, production scheduling should be retitled "resource scheduling," and the major effort of such scheduling should be on scheduling machines and people for maximum utilization, rather than on scheduling machines to maximize output.[2]

COMPUTERS AND OPERATIONS MANAGEMENT

In the 1950's, only a few organizations in North America, Europe, and Japan used digital computers in and for operations management. The major applications of digital computers were in the area of accounting, such as payroll and billing, and the use of computers in operations scheduling, planning, maintenance, quality control, and the like remained slow until the late 1970's.

Several factors have helped to effect the increased use of computers in operations. First, minicomputers with smaller core capacity that are less expensive than the main-frame computers were developed. Second, microprocessors for controlling operations were developed (assuming that one may define this form of control as computing). Third, outside computer shops began to offer computer time on their main-frame computers. Companies may justify computerization of operations, since they are not forced to buy their own computers.

---

[2] I. Asplund, *Management Control*, (Lund, Sweden: Student-literature, 1969); R. J. Schonberger, "The Resource Management Movement," *Academy of Management Journal*, September, 1972, pp. 382–5.

Fourth, computer companies now sell their software and hardware separately, and both of these components have become more standardized. This has caused an increase in software applications in areas such as production and operations management. Fifth, more and more organizations accept the idea of computer use in various areas of operations. The old saying, that we are "in the age of third-generation computer hardware, second-generation computer software and zero-generation management enlightenment," is no longer true. Sixth, the "explosion" in various output/input mediums, such as cathode-ray tubes (CRT) and hard-copy mobile terminals, make it simpler to converse with the computer on a real-time, conversational basis when solving operational problems.

From all indicators, it seems that the use of computers for operations management will continue, especially in service operations such as communications, transportation, and government agency operations. The major effort will be on large-scale data bases, smaller main-frame and more sophisticated terminals with increased memory that can stand-by for each other. One should also include the use of computers in manufacturing and design: Computer Integrated Manufacturing (CIM), computer aided design (CAD), computer aided manufacturing (CAM) systems, as well as the use of automated control systems that are activated by voice-synthesizers.

INDUSTRIAL AND OPERATIONS MANAGEMENT: THE FUTURE

As has been described in Chapter 2, many environmental elements will have an impact on industrial and operations management in the future. These elements include energy, inflation, work force, international business, and government regulation.

Energy

Energy costs will be on the increase, as most industries depend largely on oil and gas for their energy resources. The trend is to find alternative sources of energy, such as coal, gasification of coal, nuclear energy, and solar energy. Efforts are also being made to use tar sands and shale. However, any change in the form of energy for industry requires a major adjustment in processes and products. The industrial and operations manager will have to cope with these changes, while keeping the operation productive and effective.

Inflation

The late 'seventies' double-digit inflation rate in North American and Europe, as well as three-digit inflation in South America and other continents, has been followed by a recession in the early 'eighties. This has affected the productivity and effectiveness of operating organizations.

Equipment costs have been soaring, wages are in constant need of cost-of-living adjustments, and raw materials' costs are changing at a pace that defies planning. Whatever course future inflation takes, the net present calculation of productivity and effectiveness should, first and foremost, involve the exclusion of the inflation impact on various measures of sales, raw materials' costs, and the like.

Work Force

The changing profile of work force greatly affects the operations manager. More women and more college-degreed workers are joining the work force. Jobs should be designed to reflect the needs of the profile of this new work force. Enriched jobs, assignments of qualified workers to jobs that call for dexterity and endurance, and other changes should be affected. The high rate of unemployment characteristic of the early 1980's will, most probably, decrease, indicating a possible return of union demands for constant adjustments of cost of living.

International Business

Operation managers are becoming more and more involved in international operations. Extensive export programs, faster communication channels, managers better informed on procedures used in various parts of the world all mean that faster changes in processes, products, and operation practices are being imposed on operation managers.

IBM, for example, does not produce Selectric II typewriters from scratch, but rather subcontracts the components to plants in various countries, and is engaged only in final assembly in Amsterdam, the Netherlands. This procedure requires an overall standardization of the production processes.

Government Regulation

During the last decade, government has become involved in price controls, transportation, and communications industry regulations. Also, the U.S. government has established the Equal Employment Opportunity Commission (EEOC) and has passed the Occupational Safety and Health Act (OSHA). Other regulations regarding pollution and health care have been instituted. The production/operations manager has to be aware of the various regulations and acts, and must follow them. The regulatory role of governments will continue into the future.

SUMMARY

The effect of environmental elements has played and will play a major role in production/operations management practices. The most critical elements are: energy, inflation, work force, international business, and government regulation. The production/operations manager should be aware of these elements and learn how to adjust processes and change products and services accordingly.

There are basically four functions in any organization: production/operations, finance, marketing and personnel. Each of them is essential to the long-term viability of the organizations. However, the last three types of functions support the fundamental function of creating goods and services.

The importance of production/operations management is expected to increase further in future years, as many factors of production will become uncontrollable due to changes in the environment (energy cost, raw-material availability, etc.). The planning of the best interaction of these factors by the production/operations manager will become the most critical function of the organization.

DISCUSSION QUESTIONS

15.1 Explain and contrast the analysis and synthesis approach in production/operations management.

15.2 Categorize service organizations, and give examples for each category.

15.3 Consider the environmental elements that affect production/operations management practices. Give an example from your locality that shows the impact of a change in any one of these elements.

15.4 The Secretary of Commerce of the U.S. recently announced the establishment of the Office of Productivity, Technology, and Innovation, whose purpose will be to fight U.S. "economic anemia." This office will work with both business and labor to develop precise, strategically significant targets for productivity assistance and to provide such assistance. The office will include a Center for the Utilization of Federal Technology that will "actively market Federal technology to the private sector." Comment.

15.5 Define and contrast productivity, efficiency, and effectiveness.

15.6 What are the causes of falling productivity?

15.7 What is a productivity index?

15.8 What are the steps involved in a critical examination of an operating system?

15.9 Describe the resource management approach.

15.10 What are the factors affecting the increased use of computers in operations?

READING
Training Bosses—No more shouting

> When a man becomes a foreman, he has to forget about even being human, as far as feelings are concerned.
> —A factory hand in Studs Terkel's *Working*

In their drive to *improve productivity*, a growing number of U.S. companies have begun to appreciate the crucial importance of shop-floor supervisors. For better or worse, that hard-pressed first level of bosses often sets the working tone for an entire plant. The style has traditionally been management by shouting: bark out orders like a Marine drill instructor until they get results.

Some companies, though, are beginning to challenge that old approach because it no longer works, especially with younger workers. One of the hottest new fields of management training involves teaching shop-floor bosses how to be better supervisors.

Zenger-Miller, a Menlo Park, Calif., consulting firm, has sold shop-floor training programs to 250 companies since 1977, including such firms as American Can Co., Honeywell and FMC Corp. Its 15-week courses include role playing and studying videotapes of typical contacts between bosses and workers. Fairchild Republic Co., division of Fairchild Industries (1982 revenues: $1.4 billion), is an enthusiastic new user of shop-floor training. Morale in its Farmingdale, N.Y., plant that builds U.S. Air Force jets collapsed early this year when the company laid off almost 1,000 workers—about 15% of its labor force. Absenteeism averaged 5.3% of scheduled working time. Disputes sometimes led to shouting matches on the plant floor that were settled by fistfights in the parking lot. Some Fairchild Republic officials believed that the supervisors were a key to the company's problems. Workers were being made shop-floor bosses with little or no preparation, and some tended to bully those below them.

Fairchild Republic is now sending 93 supervisors from the plant through the Zenger-Mills course, which meets for one three-hour session every other week. Participants memorize guidelines like "Calmly describe the employee's behaviour which concerns you," and "Express support and reassurance."

The company is already benefiting from the program, which began in March. Morale of supervisors in the course is improving, despite continued layoffs. The *training sessions have contributed to the completion of more jobs on schedule and* the company this spring won an Air Force productivity award for its work on the A-10 Thunderbolt II jet fighter.

Source: *Time*, June 7, 1982, p. 70. Copyright 1982 Time, Inc. All rights reserved. Reprinted by permission from Time, Inc.

Fairchild Republic had tried several management programs before, but had been unhappy with all of them. The new method of role playing and teaching by example seems to produce the best results. Says Linda Dwyer, supervisor of training and development: "The other programs were too abstract. They were entertaining like the Dallas Cowboys cheerleaders, but they didn't get the ball downfield."

Management consultants that use similar methods include Development Dimensions, International in Pittsburgh and the Forum Corp. of North America in Boston. They and Zenger-Miller have now sold their courses for supervisors to about 750 corporations. Says Thomas Bedocs, Fairchild Republic director of employee relations: "You pay for personnel training programs in one way or another. They either cost you in money up front, or in lost productivity in the end."

READING
Now Hear This: Full Ahead

The *Kinokawa Maru,* a 92,207-ton ore carrier, pulled out of Tokyo harbor last week on its maiden voyage to Australia. When Captain Yukio Imai wanted to change speed, he did not order a crew member to yank the traditional brass-handled lever. Instead, he spoke through a microphone to the ship's computerized engine control, which has a voice synthesizer and recognition device developed by Japan's Sodensha Electronics Ltd. The control device can comprehend eleven verbal commands, from "Full ahead" to "Full astern," given by the captain or two or more officers. To show that an order has been received, the machines repeats it in a flat voice reminiscent of Hal, the talking computer in the movie *2001.*

This voice-controlled engine is one of the new applications in the rapidly emerging technology that allows machines, in a primitive fashion, to use human language. Dallas-based Texas Instruments, which pioneered low-cost talking computers with its Speak & Spell learning aid, last week unveiled Magic Wand, a machine that can read to children. It is disc-shaped like an LP record album. A youngster passes a wand attached to the disc over books that contain not only pictures and words but also bar codes on pages similar to those that now appear on grocery items, magazines and other goods. The wand reads the codes, and the unit makes the appropriate sounds. The machine can also sing, bark or even say "supercalifragilisticexpialidocious." Texas Instruments this year will publish at least eight coded books, including *Stranded E.T.'s Adventure,* a spin-off from the new Steven Spielberg movie. The Magic Wand costs $120 and each book $12.

Source: *Time,* June 7, 1982, p. 70. Copyright 1982 Time, Inc. All rights reserved. Reprinted by permission from Time, Inc.

Job hunters who phoned the Softwork Voyce employment service in Cambridge, Mass., last week heard the greeting: "Hello, I am the Voyce. I am a robot helping employers and job seekers meet each other." The Voyce, which is a computer at Softwork headquarters, explains that it will compile a resume for the caller if he answers the robot's questions by pushing the proper buttons on a touch-tone phone. If the caller is using a dial phone, the Voyce tells him that it cannot hear his answers. A sample question: "Are you presently a student or a worker? Enter one if student, two if worker." The machine uses the answers to produce a resume which Softwork sends to employers. Softwork President Joel Manion thinks that his new service will be appealing to job hunters. Says he: "They don't have to worry about somebody intimidating or embarrassing them." That is just as long as they like talking to a machine.

BIBLIOGRAPHY

BRITNEY, R. R., "Continuing Education in Production/Operations Management," presented at the 34th Annual Meeting, Academy of Management, Seattle, Washington, 1974.

Bureau of National Affairs, *The Consumer Product Safety Act*, Washington, D.C., 1973.

Bureau of National Affairs, *The Job Safety and Health Act of 1970*, Washington, D.C., 1971.

CHASE, R. B., and N. J. AQUILANO, *Production and Operations Management: A Life Cycle Approach*. Homewood, Ill: Richard D. Irwin, Inc., 1973.

DAVIS, K., and R. L. BLOMSTROM, *Business, Society and Environment: Social Power and Social Responses* (2nd ed.). New York: McGraw-Hill Book Co., 1971.

FUCHS, V., *The Service Economy*. New York: Columbia University Press, 1968.

GAITHER, N., "The Adoption of Operations Research Techniques by Manufacturing Organizations," *Decision Sciences* 6, No. 3, October, 1975, pp. 797–813.

GREEN, T. B., W. B. NEWSOM, and S. R. JONES, "A Survey of the Application of Quantitative Techniques to Production/Operations Management in Large Corporations," Proceedings of the 1976 Academy of Management 36th Annual Meeting, Kansas City, Missouri, August, 1976.

HINRICHS, J. R., *Practical Management for Productivity*. New York: Van Nostrand Reinhold, 1983.

HOOGENBOOM, A., and O. HOOGENBOOM, *A History of the ICC*. New York: Norton, 1976.

JONES, C. O., *Clean Air: The Policies and Politics of Pollution Control*. Pittsburgh: University of Pittsburgh Press, 1975.

KATZELL, R. A., P. BIENSTOCK, and P. H. FAENSTEIN, *A Guide to Worker Productivity Experiments in the United States 1971–75*. New York: New York University Press, 1977.

KNESSE, A. V., and C. L. SCHULTZE, *Pollution, Prices, and Public Policy.* Washington, D.C.: Bookings Institution, 1975.

MENIPAZ, E., *Automated Production: Decision Support Systems Approach.* Ottawa: Randcomp, 1984.

MOCERI, D. J., "Energy Management Systems", Proceedings of American Institute of Industrial Engineers' 1980 Fall Industrial Engineering Conference, Minneapolis/St. Paul, Minnesota, December 7–10, 1980.

MUNDEL, M. E., *Measuring and Enhancing the Productivity of Service and Government Organizations.* Asian Productivity Organization, Tokyo, 1975.

REDFORD, E. S., *The Regulatory Process.* Austin: University of Texas Press, 1969.

REDMOND, J. C., J. C. COOK, and A. A. J. HOFFMAN, eds., *Clearing the Air: The Impact of the Clean Air Act on Technology.* New York: Institute of Electrical and Electronics Engineers, 1971.

ROSEN, S. J., *Manual for Environmental Impact Evaluation.* Englewood Cliffs, N.J.: Prentice-Hall, Inc., 1976.

RUCH, W. A., ed. *Proceedings of the Grantees Conference on Research on Productivity Measurement Systems for Administrative Services,* sponsored by the National Science Foundation, Tempe, Arizona, November, 1976.

SAMUELSON, P. A., *Economics* (10th ed.), Chap. 38. New York: McGraw-Hill Book Co., 1976.

"Zeroing in on Dumping," *Time,* November 7, 1977.

Appendix

TABLE A CUMULATIVE PROBABILITIES FOR THE NORMAL PROBABILITY DISTRIBUTION

The table on the following page presents cumulative probability values of the variable z. As an example, to find the area under the normal distribution curve between $z = 0.0$ and $z = 1.42$, find the entry in row $z = 1.4$ that intersects with column 0.02. The reading is 0.9222. Therefore, there is a 92.22 percent chance that z will have the value 1.42 or lower.

z^*	0.00	0.01	0.02	0.03	0.04	0.05	0.06	0.07	0.08	0.09
0.0	0.5000	0.5040	0.5080	0.5120	0.5160	0.5199	0.5239	0.5279	0.5319	0.5359
0.1	0.5398	0.5438	0.5478	0.5517	0.5557	0.5596	0.5636	0.5675	0.5714	0.5753
0.2	0.5793	0.5832	0.5871	0.5910	0.5948	0.5987	0.6026	0.6064	0.6103	0.6141
0.3	0.6179	0.6217	0.6255	0.6293	0.6331	0.6368	0.6406	0.6443	0.6480	0.6517
0.4	0.6554	0.6591	0.6628	0.6664	0.6700	0.6736	0.6772	0.6808	0.6844	0.6879
0.5	0.6915	0.6950	0.6985	0.7019	0.7054	0.7088	0.7123	0.7157	0.7190	0.7224
0.6	0.7257	0.7291	0.7324	0.7357	0.7389	0.7422	0.7454	0.7486	0.7517	0.7549
0.7	0.7580	0.7611	0.7642	0.7673	0.7704	0.7734	0.7764	0.7794	0.7823	0.7852
0.8	0.7881	0.7910	0.7939	0.7967	0.7995	0.8023	0.8051	0.8078	0.8106	0.8133
0.9	0.8195	0.8186	0.8212	0.8238	0.8264	0.8289	0.8315	0.8340	0.8365	0.8389
1.0	0.8413	0.8438	0.8461	0.8485	0.8508	0.8531	0.8554	0.8577	0.8599	0.8621
1.1	0.8643	0.8665	0.8686	0.8708	0.8729	0.8749	0.8770	0.8790	0.8810	0.8830
1.2	0.8894	0.8869	0.8888	0.8907	0.8925	0.8944	0.8962	0.8980	0.8997	0.9015
1.3	0.9032	0.9049	0.9066	0.9082	0.9099	0.9115	0.9131	0.9147	0.9162	0.9177
1.4	0.9192	0.9207	0.9222	0.9236	0.9251	0.9265	0.9279	0.9292	0.9306	0.9319
1.5	0.9332	0.9345	0.9357	0.9370	0.9382	0.9394	0.9406	0.9418	0.9429	0.9441
1.6	0.9452	0.9463	0.9474	0.9484	0.9495	0.9505	0.9515	0.9525	0.9535	0.9545
1.7	0.9554	0.9564	0.9573	0.9582	0.9591	0.9599	0.9608	0.9616	0.9625	0.9633
1.8	0.9641	0.9649	0.9656	0.9664	0.9671	0.9678	0.9686	0.9693	0.9699	0.9706
1.9	0.9713	0.9719	0.9726	0.9732	0.9738	0.9744	0.9750	0.9756	0.9761	0.9767
2.0	0.9772	0.9778	0.9783	0.9788	0.9793	0.9798	0.9803	0.9808	0.9812	0.9817
2.1	0.9821	0.9826	0.9830	0.9834	0.9838	0.9842	0.9846	0.9850	0.9854	0.9857
2.2	0.9861	0.9864	0.9868	0.9871	0.9875	0.9878	0.9881	0.9884	0.9887	0.9890
2.3	0.9893	0.9896	0.9898	0.9901	0.9904	0.9906	0.9909	0.9911	0.9913	0.9916
2.4	0.9918	0.9920	0.9922	0.9925	0.9927	0.9929	0.9931	0.9932	0.9934	0.9936
2.5	0.9938	0.9940	0.9941	0.9943	0.9945	0.9946	0.9948	0.9949	0.9951	0.9952
2.6	0.9953	0.9955	0.9956	0.9957	0.9959	0.9960	0.9961	0.9962	0.9963	0.9964
2.7	0.9965	0.9966	0.9967	0.9968	0.9969	0.9970	0.9971	0.9972	0.9973	0.9974
2.8	0.9974	0.9975	0.9976	0.9977	0.9977	0.9978	0.9979	0.9979	0.9980	0.9981
2.9	0.9981	0.9982	0.9982	0.9983	0.9984	0.9984	0.9985	0.9985	0.9986	0.9986
3.0	0.9987	0.9987	0.9987	0.9988	0.9988	0.9989	0.9989	0.9989	0.9990	0.9990
3.1	0.9990	0.9991	0.9991	0.9991	0.9992	0.9992	0.9992	0.9992	0.9993	0.9993
3.2	0.9993	0.9993	0.9994	0.9994	0.9994	0.9994	0.9994	0.9995	0.9995	0.9995
3.3	0.9995	0.9995	0.9995	0.9996	0.9996	0.9996	0.9996	0.9996	0.9996	0.9997
3.4	0.9997	0.9997	0.9997	0.9997	0.9997	0.9997	0.9997	0.9997	0.9997	0.9998

*Areas under the normal curve from $-\infty$ to z.

TABLE B PRESENT VALUE OF A SINGLE PAYMENT

YEARS HENCE	1%	2%	4%	6%	8%	10%	12%	14%	15%	16%	18%
1	0.990	0.980	0.962	0.943	0.926	0.909	0.893	0.877	0.870	0.862	0.847
2	0.980	0.961	0.925	0.890	0.857	0.826	0.797	0.769	0.756	0.743	0.718
3	0.971	0.942	0.889	0.840	0.794	0.751	0.712	0.675	0.658	0.641	0.609
4	0.961	0.924	0.855	0.792	0.735	0.683	0.636	0.592	0.572	0.552	0.516
5	0.951	0.906	0.822	0.747	0.681	0.621	0.567	0.519	0.497	0.476	0.437
6	0.942	0.888	0.790	0.705	0.630	0.564	0.507	0.456	0.432	0.410	0.370
7	0.933	0.871	0.760	0.665	0.583	0.513	0.452	0.400	0.376	0.354	0.314
8	0.923	0.853	0.731	0.627	0.540	0.467	0.404	0.351	0.327	0.305	0.266
9	0.914	0.837	0.703	0.592	0.500	0.424	0.361	0.308	0.284	0.263	0.225
10	0.905	0.820	0.676	0.558	0.463	0.386	0.322	0.270	0.247	0.227	0.191
11	0.896	0.804	0.650	0.527	0.429	0.350	0.287	0.237	0.215	0.195	0.162
12	0.887	0.788	0.625	0.497	0.397	0.319	0.257	0.208	0.187	0.168	0.137
13	0.879	0.773	0.601	0.469	0.368	0.290	0.229	0.182	0.163	0.145	0.116
14	0.870	0.758	0.577	0.442	0.340	0.263	0.205	0.160	0.141	0.125	0.099
15	0.861	0.743	0.555	0.417	0.315	0.239	0.183	0.140	0.123	0.108	0.084
16	0.853	0.728	0.534	0.394	0.292	0.218	0.163	0.123	0.107	0.093	0.071
17	0.844	0.714	0.513	0.371	0.270	0.198	0.146	0.108	0.093	0.080	0.060
18	0.836	0.700	0.494	0.350	0.250	0.180	0.130	0.095	0.081	0.069	0.051
19	0.828	0.686	0.475	0.331	0.232	0.164	0.116	0.083	0.070	0.060	0.043
20	0.820	0.673	0.456	0.312	0.215	0.149	0.104	0.073	0.061	0.051	0.037
21	0.811	0.660	0.439	0.294	0.199	0.135	0.093	0.064	0.053	0.044	0.031
22	0.803	0.647	0.422	0.278	0.184	0.123	0.083	0.056	0.046	0.038	0.026
23	0.795	0.634	0.406	0.262	0.170	0.112	0.074	0.049	0.040	0.033	0.022
24	0.788	0.622	0.390	0.247	0.158	0.102	0.066	0.043	0.035	0.028	0.019
25	0.780	0.610	0.375	0.233	0.146	0.092	0.059	0.038	0.030	0.024	0.016
26	0.772	0.598	0.361	0.220	0.135	0.084	0.053	0.033	0.026	0.021	0.014
27	0.764	0.586	0.347	0.207	0.125	0.076	0.047	0.029	0.023	0.018	0.011
28	0.757	0.574	0.335	0.196	0.116	0.069	0.042	0.026	0.020	0.016	0.010
29	0.749	0.563	0.321	0.185	0.107	0.063	0.037	0.022	0.017	0.014	0.008
30	0.742	0.552	0.308	0.174	0.099	0.057	0.033	0.020	0.015	0.012	0.007
40	0.672	0.453	0.208	0.097	0.046	0.022	0.011	0.005	0.004	0.003	0.001
50	0.608	0.372	0.141	0.054	0.021	0.009	0.003	0.001	0.001	0.001	0.001

TABLE B (Cont.)

20%	22%	24%	25%	26%	28%	30%	35%	40%	45%	50%
0.833	0.820	0.806	0.800	0.794	0.781	0.769	0.741	0.714	0.690	0.667
0.694	0.672	0.650	0.640	0.630	0.592	0.592	0.549	0.510	0.476	0.444
0.579	0.551	0.524	0.512	0.500	0.477	0.455	0.406	0.364	0.328	0.296
0.482	0.451	0.423	0.410	0.397	0.373	0.350	0.301	0.260	0.226	0.198
0.402	0.370	0.341	0.328	0.315	0.291	0.269	0.223	0.186	0.156	0.132
0.335	0.303	0.275	0.262	0.250	0.227	0.207	0.165	0.133	0.108	0.088
0.279	0.249	0.222	0.210	0.198	0.178	0.159	0.122	0.095	0.074	0.059
0.233	0.204	0.179	0.168	0.157	0.139	0.123	0.091	0.068	0.051	0.039
0.194	0.167	0.144	0.134	0.125	0.108	0.094	0.067	0.048	0.035	0.026
0.162	0.137	0.116	0.107	0.099	0.085	0.073	0.050	0.035	0.024	0.017
0.135	0.112	0.094	0.086	0.079	0.066	0.056	0.037	0.025	0.017	0.012
0.112	0.092	0.076	0.069	0.062	0.052	0.043	0.027	0.018	0.012	0.008
0.093	0.075	0.061	0.055	0.050	0.040	0.033	0.020	0.013	0.008	0.005
0.078	0.062	0.049	0.044	0.039	0.032	0.025	0.015	0.009	0.006	0.002
0.065	0.051	0.040	0.035	0.031	0.025	0.020	0.011	0.006	0.004	0.002
0.054	0.042	0.032	0.028	0.025	0.019	0.015	0.008	0.005	0.003	0.002
0.045	0.034	0.026	0.023	0.020	0.015	0.012	0.006	0.003	0.002	0.001
0.038	0.028	0.021	0.018	0.016	0.012	0.009	0.005	0.002	0.001	0.001
0.031	0.023	0.017	0.014	0.012	0.009	0.007	0.003	0.002	0.001	
0.026	0.019	0.014	0.012	0.010	0.007	0.005	0.002	0.001	0.001	
0.022	0.015	0.011	0.009	0.008	0.006	0.004	0.002	0.001		
0.018	0.013	0.009	0.007	0.006	0.004	0.002	0.001	0.001		
0.015	0.010	0.007	0.006	0.004	0.003	0.002	0.001			
0.013	0.008	0.006	0.005	0.004	0.003	0.002	0.001			
0.010	0.007	0.005	0.004	0.003	0.002	0.001	0.001			
0.009	0.006	0.004	0.003	0.002	0.002	0.001				
0.007	0.005	0.003	0.002	0.002	0.001	0.001				
0.006	0.004	0.002	0.002	0.002	0.001	0.001				
0.005	0.003	0.002	0.002	0.001	0.001	0.001				
0.004	0.003	0.002	0.001	0.001	0.001					
0.001										

TABLE C PRESENT VALUE OF AN ANNUITY

YEARS HENCE	1%	2%	4%	6%	8%	10%	12%	14%	15%	16%	18%
1	0.990	0.980	0.962	0.943	0.926	0.909	0.893	0.877	0.870	0.862	0.847
2	1.970	1.942	1.886	1.833	1.783	1.736	1.690	1.647	1.626	1.605	1.566
3	2.941	2.884	2.775	2.673	2.577	2.487	2.402	2.322	2.283	2.246	2.174
4	3.902	3.808	3.630	3.465	3.312	3.170	3.037	2.914	2.855	2.798	2.690
5	4.853	4.713	4.452	4.212	3.993	3.791	3.605	3.433	3.352	3.274	3.127
6	5.795	5.601	5.242	4.917	4.623	4.355	4.111	3.889	3.784	3.685	3.498
7	6.728	6.472	6.002	5.582	5.206	4.868	4.564	4.288	4.160	4.039	3.812
8	7.632	7.325	6.733	6.210	5.747	5.335	4.968	4.639	4.487	4.344	4.078
9	8.566	8.162	7.435	6.802	6.247	5.759	5.328	4.946	4.772	4.607	4.303
10	9.471	8.983	8.111	7.360	6.710	6.145	5.650	5.216	5.019	4.833	4.494
11	10.368	9.787	8.760	7.887	7.139	6.495	5.937	5.453	5.234	5.029	4.656
12	11.255	10.575	9.385	8.384	7.536	6.814	6.194	5.660	5.421	5.197	4.793
13	12.134	11.343	9.986	8.853	7.904	7.103	6.424	5.842	5.583	5.342	4.910
14	13.004	12.106	10.563	9.295	8.244	7.367	6.628	6.002	5.724	5.468	5.008
15	13.865	12.849	10.118	9.712	8.559	7.606	6.811	6.142	5.847	5.575	5.092
16	14.718	13.578	11.652	10.106	8.851	7.824	6.974	6.265	5.954	5.669	5.162
17	15.562	14.292	12.166	10.477	9.122	8.022	7.120	6.373	6.047	5.749	5.222
18	16.398	14.992	12.659	10.828	9.372	8.201	7.250	6.467	6.128	5.818	5.273
19	17.226	15.678	13.134	11.158	9.604	8.365	7.366	6.550	6.198	5.877	5.316
20	18.046	16.351	13.590	11.470	9.818	8.514	7.469	6.623	6.259	5.929	5.353
21	18.857	17.011	14.029	11.764	10.017	8.649	7.562	6.687	6.312	5.973	5.384
22	19.660	17.658	14.451	12.042	10.201	8.772	7.645	6.743	6.359	6.011	5.410
23	20.456	18.292	14.857	12.303	10.371	8.883	7.718	6.792	6.399	6.044	5.432
24	21.243	18.914	15.247	12.550	10.529	8.985	7.784	6.835	6.434	6.073	5.451
25	22.023	19.523	15.622	12.783	10.675	9.077	7.843	6.873	6.464	6.097	5.467
26	22.795	20.121	15.983	13.003	10.810	9.161	7.896	6.906	6.491	6.118	5.480
27	23.560	20.707	16.330	13.211	10.935	9.237	7.943	6.935	6.514	6.136	5.492
28	24.316	21.281	16.663	13.406	11.051	9.307	7.984	6.961	6.534	6.152	5.502
29	25.066	21.844	16.984	13.591	11.158	9.370	8.022	6.983	6.551	6.166	5.510
30	25.808	22.396	17.292	13.765	11.258	9.427	8.055	7.003	6.566	6.177	5.517
40	32.835	27.355	19.793	15.046	11.925	9.779	8.244	7.105	6.642	6.234	5.548
50	39.196	31.424	21.482	15.762	12.234	9.915	8.304	7.133	6.661	6.246	5.554

TABLE C (Cont.)

20%	22%	24%	25%	26%	28%	30%	35%	40%	45%	50%
0.833	0.820	0.806	0.800	0.794	0.781	0.769	0.741	0.714	0.690	0.667
1.528	1.492	1.457	1.440	1.424	1.392	1.361	1.289	1.224	1.165	1.111
2.106	2.042	1.981	1.952	1.923	1.868	1.816	1.696	1.589	1.493	1.407
2.589	2.494	2.404	2.362	2.320	2.241	2.166	1.997	1.849	1.720	1.605
2.991	2.864	2.745	2.689	2.635	2.532	2.436	2.220	2.035	1.876	1.737
3.326	3.167	3.020	2.951	2.885	2.759	2.643	2.385	2.168	1.983	1.824
3.605	3.416	3.242	3.161	3.083	2.937	2.802	2.508	2.263	2.057	1.883
3.837	3.619	3.421	3.329	3.241	3.076	2.925	2.598	2.331	2.108	1.922
4.031	3.786	3.566	3.463	3.366	3.184	3.019	2.665	2.379	2.144	1.948
4.192	3.923	3.682	3.571	3.465	3.269	3.092	2.715	2.414	2.168	1.965
4.327	4.035	3.776	3.656	3.544	3.335	3.147	2.752	2.438	2.185	1.977
4.439	4.127	3.851	3.725	3.606	3.387	3.190	2.779	2.456	2.196	1.985
4.533	4.203	3.912	3.780	3.656	3.427	3.223	2.799	2.468	2.204	1.990
4.611	4.265	3.962	3.824	3.695	3.459	3.249	2.814	2.477	2.210	1.993
4.675	4.315	4.001	3.859	3.726	3.483	3.268	2.825	2.484	2.214	1.995
4.730	4.357	4.033	3.887	3.751	3.503	3.283	2.834	2.489	2.216	1.997
4.775	4.391	4.059	3.910	3.771	3.518	3.295	2.840	2.492	2.218	1.998
4.812	4.419	4.080	3.928	3.786	3.529	3.304	2.844	2.494	2.219	1.999
4.844	4.442	4.007	3.942	3.799	3.539	3.311	2.848	2.496	2.220	1.999
4.870	4.460	4.110	3.954	3.808	3.546	3.316	2.850	2.497	2.221	1.999
4.891	4.476	4.121	3.963	3.816	3.551	3.320	2.852	2.498	2.221	2.000
4.909	4.488	4.130	3.970	3.822	3.556	3.323	2.853	2.498	2.222	2.000
4.925	4.499	4.137	3.976	3.827	3.559	3.325	2.854	2.499	2.222	2.000
4.937	4.507	4.143	3.981	3.831	3.562	3.327	2.855	2.499	2.222	2.000
4.948	4.514	4.147	3.985	3.834	3.564	3.329	2.856	2.499	2.222	2.000
4.956	4.520	4.151	3.988	3.837	3.566	3.330	2.856	2.500	2.222	2.000
4.964	4.524	4.154	3.990	3.839	3.567	3.331	2.856	2.500	2.222	2.000
4.970	4.528	4.157	3.992	3.840	3.568	3.331	2.857	2.500	2.222	2.000
4.975	4.531	4.159	3.994	3.841	3.569	3.332	2.857	2.500	2.222	2.000
4.979	4.534	4.160	3.995	3.842	3.569	3.332	2.857	2.500	2.222	2.000
4.997	4.544	4.166	3.999	3.846	3.571	3.333	2.857	2.500	2.222	2.000
4.999	4.545	4.167	4.000	3.846	3.571	3.333	2.857	2.500	2.222	2.000

TABLE D   LEARNING CURVE COEFFICIENTS

φ	70%		75%		80%		85%		90%	
UNIT NUMBER	Unit Time	Total Time	Unit Time	Total Time	Unit Time	Total Time	Unit Time	Total Time	Unit Time	Total Time
1	1.000	1.000	1.000	1.000	1.000	1.000	1.000	1.000	1.000	1.000
2	0.700	1.700	0.750	1.750	0.800	1.800	0.850	1.850	0.900	1.900
3	0.568	2.268	0.634	2.384	0.702	2.502	0.773	2.623	0.846	2.746
4	0.490	2.758	0.562	2.946	0.640	3.142	0.723	3.345	0.810	3.556
5	0.437	3.195	0.513	3.459	0.596	3.738	0.686	4.031	0.783	4.339
6	0.398	3.593	0.475	3.934	0.562	4.299	0.657	4.688	0.762	5.101
7	0.367	3.960	0.446	4.380	0.534	4.834	0.634	5.322	0.744	5.845
8	0.343	4.303	0.422	4.802	0.512	5.346	0.614	5.936	0.729	6.574
9	0.323	4.626	0.402	5.204	0.493	5.839	0.597	6.533	0.716	7.290
10	0.306	4.932	0.385	5.589	0.477	6.315	0.583	7.116	0.705	7.994
11	0.291	5.223	0.370	5.958	0.462	6.777	0.570	7.686	0.695	8.689
12	0.278	5.501	0.357	6.315	0.449	7.227	0.558	8.244	0.685	9.374
13	0.267	5.769	0.345	6.660	0.438	7.665	0.548	8.792	0.677	10.052
14	0.257	6.026	0.334	6.994	0.428	8.092	0.539	9.331	0.670	10.721
15	0.248	6.274	0.325	7.319	0.418	8.511	0.530	9.861	0.663	11.384
16	0.240	6.514	0.316	7.635	0.410	8.920	0.522	10.383	0.656	12.040
17	0.233	6.747	0.309	7.944	0.402	9.322	0.515	10.898	0.650	12.690
18	0.226	6.973	0.301	8.245	0.394	9.716	0.508	11.405	0.644	13.334
19	0.220	7.192	0.295	8.540	0.338	10.104	0.501	11.907	0.639	13.974
20	0.214	7.407	0.288	8.828	0.381	10.485	0.495	12.402	0.634	14.608
21	0.209	7.615	0.283	9.111	0.375	10.860	0.490	12.892	0.630	15.237
22	0.204	7.819	0.277	9.388	0.370	11.230	0.484	13.376	0.625	15.862
23	0.199	8.018	0.272	9.660	0.364	11.594	0.479	13.856	0.621	16.483
24	0.195	8.213	0.267	9.928	0.359	11.954	0.475	14.331	0.617	17.100
25	0.191	8.404	0.263	10.191	0.355	12.309	0.470	14.801	0.613	17.713
26	0.187	8.591	0.259	10.449	0.350	12.659	0.466	15.267	0.609	18.323
27	0.183	8.774	0.255	10.704	0.346	13.005	0.462	15.728	0.606	18.929
28	0.180	8.954	0.251	10.955	0.342	13.347	0.458	16.186	0.603	19.531
29	0.177	9.131	0.247	11.202	0.338	13.685	0.454	16.640	0.599	20.131
30	0.174	9.305	0.244	11.446	0.335	14.020	0.450	17.091	0.596	20.727
31	0.171	9.476	0.240	11.686	0.331	14.351	0.447	17.538	0.593	21.320
32	0.168	9.644	0.237	11.924	0.328	14.679	0.444	17.981	0.590	21.911
33	0.165	9.809	0.234	12.158	0.324	15.003	0.441	18.422	0.588	22.498
34	0.163	9.972	0.231	12.389	0.321	15.324	0.437	18.859	0.585	23.084
35	0.160	10.133	0.229	12.618	0.318	15.643	0.434	19.294	0.583	23.666
36	0.158	10.291	0.226	12.844	0.315	15.958	0.432	19.725	0.580	24.246
37	0.156	10.447	0.223	13.067	0.313	16.271	0.429	20.154	0.578	24.824
38	0.154	10.601	0.221	13.288	0.310	16.581	0.426	20.580	0.575	25.399
39	0.152	10.753	0.219	13.507	0.307	16.888	0.424	21.004	0.573	25.972
40	0.150	10.902	0.216	13.723	0.305	17.193	0.421	21.425	0.571	26.543
41	0.148	11.050	0.214	13.937	0.303	17.496	0.419	21.844	0.569	27.111
42	0.146	11.196	0.212	14.149	0.300	17.796	0.416	22.260	0.567	27.678
43	0.144	11.341	0.210	14.359	0.298	18.094	0.414	22.674	0.565	28.243
44	0.143	11.484	0.208	14.567	0.296	18.390	0.412	23.086	0.563	28.805
45	0.141	11.625	0.206	14.773	0.294	18.684	0.408	23.496	0.561	29.366

TABLE D (Cont.)

φ	70%		75%		80%		85%		90%	
UNIT NUMBER	Unit Time	Total Time	Unit Time	Total Time	Unit Time	Total Time	Unit Time	Total Time	Unit Time	Total Time
46	0.139	11.764	0.204	14.977	0.292	18.975	0.405	23.903	0.559	29.925
47	0.138	11.902	0.202	15.180	0.290	19.265	0.403	24.309	0.557	30.482
48	0.136	12.038	0.201	15.380	0.288	19.552	0.402	24.712	0.555	31.037
49	0.135	12.173	0.199	15.579	0.286	19.838	0.400	25.113	0.553	31.590
50	0.134	12.307	0.197	15.776	0.284	20.122	0.410	25.513	0.552	32.142
51	0.132	12.439	0.196	15.972	0.282	20.404	0.398	25.911	0.550	32.692
52	0.131	12.570	0.194	16.166	0.280	20.684	0.396	26.307	0.548	33.241
53	0.130	12.700	0.192	16.358	0.279	20.963	0.394	26.701	0.547	33.787
54	0.128	12.828	0.191	16.549	0.277	21.239	0.392	27.094	0.545	34.333
55	0.127	12.955	0.190	16.739	0.275	21.515	0.391	27.484	0.544	34.877
56	0.126	13.081	0.188	16.927	0.274	21.788	0.389	27.873	0.542	35.419
57	0.125	13.206	0.187	17.144	0.272	22.060	0.388	28.261	0.541	35.960
58	0.124	13.330	0.185	17.299	0.271	22.331	0.386	28.647	0.539	36.499
59	0.123	13.453	0.184	17.483	0.269	22.600	0.384	29.031	0.538	37.037
60	0.122	13.574	0.183	17.666	0.268	22.868	0.383	29.414	0.537	37.574

TABLE E   TABLE OF RANDOM NUMBERS

21787	69620	29751	96379	46324	53186	67538	32312	28608	83230
76774	82939	18166	15945	06525	67492	73394	81794	50768	99804
79319	64491	92720	89465	97486	02003	65024	18261	73199	83797
80436	99245	68784	61977	73156	15793	18066	75202	48821	34054
88711	66271	42414	72402	57496	91266	58999	64614	52121	66469
28248	15570	61113	23767	70662	07821	98669	43387	25469	72436
87973	18610	52015	86233	49087	50791	09856	33290	71106	94178
42377	22678	74206	67697	94393	35325	05726	21897	04035	68616
08911	23294	10075	17071	83118	76833	16076	39361	74342	98730
90991	04468	25982	06412	01066	20112	07977	51175	14807	59473
21539	09100	97403	05535	47522	82320	49906	34919	67451	33496
15513	98470	27074	56623	12916	64713	94393	49772	83403	99633
04005	74597	72136	11386	31080	61844	83268	48117	94026	11616
31221	85053	15392	05677	03357	66672	47750	55871	94885	14789
96440	46472	36899	88410	11832	41777	67488	61557	62539	97648
52150	40256	84851	58305	89049	62374	76346	04316	65136	23931
28667	96683	10455	29306	13518	38886	01964	27511	00278	43202
54989	99505	57973	10202	65445	67101	51443	39165	45167	94613
28811	71492	65191	64950	86785	51721	82368	12269	46056	90887
81695	30636	93762	58278	46886	27535	06882	97777	73255	39805
95587	80548	39973	77523	89349	52938	88665	00791	46688	50716
38826	86860	73110	69897	78800	61920	40596	99627	39381	62711
64383	62460	08724	65660	37494	87285	50343	01302	03307	86912
32358	87525	30044	99954	41082	89725	64013	90592	37256	91027

Index